CAT WORLD

A FELINE ENCYCLOPEDIA

DESMOND MORRIS

EBURY PRESS

First published 1996

1 3 5 7 9 10 8 6 4 2

Designer: David Fordham
Picture research: Nadine Bazar
Project editor: Alison Wormleighton

First published in Great Britain in 1996 by Ebury Press
Random House, 20 Vauxhall Bridge Road, London SW1V 2SA

Random House Australia Pty Limited
20 Alfred Street, Milsons Point, Sydney, New South Wales 2061, Australia

Random House New Zealand Limited
18 Poland Road, Glenfield, Auckland 10, New Zealand

Random House South Africa (Pty) Limited
PO Box 2263, Rosebank 2121, South Africa

Random House UK Limited Reg. No. 954009

A CIP catalogue record for this book is available from the British Library

ISBN 0 09 182030 8

Typeset by M.A.T.S.
Printed in Italy by Amilcare Pizzi, Milan

Time spent with cats is never wasted

(Colette)

Introduction

Catworld is a feline reference work, arranged alphabetically, with nearly a thousand entries, covering all the 80 breeds of domestic cats, all the 36 species of wild cats, and all the most famous pet cats, fictional cats, legendary cats and cat owners. It also includes entries for feline anatomy, behaviour, biology, folklore, history, literature and art. With a text of nearly a quarter of a million words, it is the most extensive treatment of the subject ever attempted.

The emphasis is on the domestic cat, with as much detail as possible being given on the origins of the various pedigree cat breeds. With many breeds there are often several conflicting ideas concerning how and where they began. In such instances, all the rival theories are presented, from the most outlandish to the most acceptable, to provide as complete a picture as possible of the history of the breed and the myths and legends that surround it, as well as the more modern, factual interpretations of its development.

Under each entry, where appropriate, bibliographies are included, but these have been limited almost entirely to general books on the subjects in question. As a useful guide to factual feline writings there is a special entry listing a personal selection of 'The 100 Best Cat Books'. And there are other sections listing cat anthologies, cat collections, cat films, cat publications, cat societies, and cat welfare organizations.

The one deliberate omission in this general encyclopedia is the subject of feline veterinary care. The ailments, diseases and injuries of cats are best dealt with by a qualified vet or an animal clinic.

Although the book is arranged alphabetically, an index is included for quick scanning and for easy comparison of the various entries.

QUADRUPEDS

Linn Syst. *CLASS* I.[st] MAMMALIA *ORDER* III.[d] FERÆ *GENUS* FELIS. *PLATE III of Order F.*[w]

J. Edwards del.[t] *J. Scott sc.*[t]

Fig. 1. Felis Pardalis, Ocelot _ 2. Felis Tigrina, Margay _ 3. Felis Serval, Serval _ 4. Felis Catus, Wild Cat _ 5. var. Domestic Cat _ 6. var. Spanish or Tortoise-shell Cat
7. var. Angora Cat _ 8. var. Slate Coloured Cat, or Chartreux.

A Personal Note

Cats entered my life early and stayed late. I have known working cats, pet cats, wild cats and pedigree cats and have fallen under the spell of each in turn. As a boy I watched the serious world of farm cats busy earning a living as pest-controllers. At home I enjoyed the company of an ever-breeding female cat of mixed parentage and her conveyor-belt production of an endless stream of sturdy, alley-conceived kittens.

As a young man I had the unbelievable luck of finding myself in charge of the largest collection of wild felines in the world – at London Zoo. There I was able to study the breeding of Lions, Tigers and Pumas. I was able to gaze in awe at the power and the beauty of Leopards and Jaguars, Snow Leopards and Clouded Leopards, Cheetahs and Caracals, Bobcats and Lynx, Ocelots and Servals, Leopard Cats and Tiger Cats, and was able to observe at close quarters such rarities as the Jaguarundi, Pallas's Cat, Geoffroy's Cat, Temminck's Cat, the Fishing Cat and the Margay. And through a series of over 500 television programmes transmitted from the Zoo I was able to present these graceful animals to a wide public.

Then, later in life, when I returned to television to make over 100 programmes on the subject of companion animals, I had the unique opportunity of meeting most kinds of pedigree cats and interviewing the dedicated experts who breed them.

Over the years I have often wanted to consult a really detailed feline reference work, but have not been able to find one. True, there are nearly 500 different cat books in my library, and many of them are excellent, but none was detailed enough to satisfy me. This left me with no alternative but to write one myself, and so that is what I have done.

Desmond Morris

CAT WORLD

DESMOND MORRIS

Order 3. Genus 13. Species 6. Catus, Variety 2. Angorensis or Cat of Angora.

Abnormal Breeds

Domestic Breeds. There is a great deal of argument about what constitutes an abnormality in the world of pedigree cats. A new colour form creates no problems, but when a mutation occurs that alters the anatomy of the cat in some way, there is often a heated debate as to whether the new variant should be encouraged or allowed to die out. If it puts the cat at a major disadvantage then the answer is obvious, but if it is only a minor disadvantage then cat breeders split into two warring camps. The result is that one official feline organization will recognize the new mutation as an additional breed, while another official body outlaws it and refuses to allow it to enter its cat shows.

At the present time there are several unusual breeds that fall into this category – accepted by some, rejected by others – and they include the Scottish Fold Cat, the Canadian Sphynx Cat, the Californian Ragdoll Cat, the American Peke-faced Cat and the American Munchkin.

The Peke-faced Cat was known back in the 1930s, but the other three breeds were all discovered in the 1960s and were quickly established by enthusiastic local breeders, delighted to be founding new lines of pedigree cats. As there is not a huge number of anatomically distinctive breeds, the discovery of new types was extremely exciting, and the intense interest aroused by them is easy to understand. But some authorities argue that, in the euphoria of the moment, the local breeders were blinding themselves to the fact that what they were really doing was preserving freaks.

In the case of the Scottish Fold, where the ears are permanently folded downwards and forwards, opponents of the breed have suggested that it might suffer from ear mites or deafness. Supporters of the breed have replied that there is no evidence for this. Critics have pointed out that if a Scottish Fold Cat is mated with another Scottish Fold Cat this may lead to skeletal abnormalities. Supporters counter that they always avoid this by mating Scottish Folds with normal Shorthairs.

The Scottish Fold Cat *(opposite)*, discovered in the early 1960s, has a strange ear formation. Because of this, some authorities have described it as an abnormal breed, but its many loyal supporters strongly oppose this view.

From the cat's point of view, the folded ears have the slight disadvantage that they do not communicate the usual mood signals seen when a cat, becoming angry or scared, starts to flatten its ears ready for fighting. It is the shift from fully erect to fully flattened ones that transmits the all-important social signal. The Scottish Fold appears as though it is permanently in the act of lowering its ears. This should make it look like a cat that is about to fight, but strangely it does not. The reason is that the folding of the ears brings them forward and this places them in a posture that is not part of the usual ear-lowering signal. In a normal cat, ears flattened to this degree would already be twisted round to the rear. So the Scottish Fold has a unique 'squashed' ear, as distinct from a 'flattened' posture. Whether the cats themselves make this distinction is not clear. If they do, then there is no reason why this breed should not take its place among other pedigree types.

In the case of the Sphynx Cat, where the skin is naked, opponents of the breed have pointed out that the breed could suffer considerably in cold weather, without adequate protection. Supporters of the breed point out that these rare, valuable cats are always going to be looked after with extreme care by their owners and that because of this there is no problem.

A truly abnormal cat, with two extra feet sprouting from its hind legs. A freak mutant illustrated by Aldrovandus in his monumental 17th century *Natural History*.

Apart from its lack of fur, the Sphynx is a normal cat with a charming personality. If its owners can afford central heating, or live in a hot climate, there is little serious risk for the animal. The fact that the Sphinx appears ugly to many cat enthusiasts is irrelevant as far as the cat itself is concerned.

The Ragdoll Cat is reputed to lack sensitivity to pain and to go limp when held. Opponents argue that this means it can be abused and hurt by children who might think of it as a toy rather than as a living animal. Supporters of the breed argue that it is simply an unusually relaxed cat that, in the right hands, is ideal for an indoor environment.

The Peke-faced Cat, a flat-faced version of the Persian, is a different matter. This breed has been shown to suffer from difficulties with its eyes, its teeth and its breathing. To some owners, it may have the most appealing face in the feline world, but it also happens to suffer frequently from blocked tear-ducts, a poor bite when its mouth is closed, and problems with its respiration as it grows older, due to its reduced nasal cavities. Because of its facial appeal, the Peke-faced Cat has survived as a popular breed for over half a century, but whether it should be encouraged is another matter.

Another very new breed, the Munchkin, a cat with short legs like a dachshund, also has strong opponents, but largely on aesthetic grounds rather than medical ones. Its supporters claim that, like the Ragdoll, it is ideally suited to a life indoors.

These 'abnormal' breeds are all comparatively recent and still have an uphill struggle to gain worldwide recognition. The long-established Manx Cat is as abnormal as any of them, with its strangely abbreviated backbone, but its presence at cat shows is taken for granted. The breed is hallowed by tradition as part of feline history. The new breeds lack this historical advantage.

Of the five new breeds mentioned, four are in no trouble providing they are well looked after. If the Scottish Fold is out-crossed and has its ears cleaned, the Canadian Sphynx is kept warm, the Californian Ragdoll is kept away from juvenile tormentors, and the American Munchkin is protected from any situation in which it would have to leap high to protect itself, then they can all lead contented and fulfilled lives. Only the Peke-faced Cat seems inevitably doomed to difficulties. No matter how much love and attention is lavished upon it, there will always be a danger that its respiration will suffer. A slight reduction in the extreme flattening of its face is probably all that is necessary to solve its problem.

Abuherrira's Cat

Legendary Cat. A pet belonging to one of the companions of the prophet Mohammed, Abu Huraira. Such was his love of cats that he was known as 'the father of the little cat'. In Goethe's poem 'The Favoured Beasts', his favourite cat was one of the four animals admitted to the Moslem paradise: 'Abuherrira's Cat, too, here purrs around his master blest, for holy must the beast appear the Prophet has caressed.'

Abyssinian Cat

Domestic Breed. At the turn of the century sometimes called the 'Ticked', 'British Tick', 'Bunny Cat', 'Rabbit Cat', 'Hare Cat' or 'Cunny'. Often referred to today as the 'Aby'. In France it is known as the *Abyssin;* in Germany as the *Abessinier;* and in Holland the *Abessijn.*

Appearance: Medium-sized, muscular, slender-bodied, short-haired cat with characteristically ticked coat. Each of the orange-brown hairs is marked with two or three dark bands; the darkest of the bands is the one nearest the tip of the hair. Head slightly wedge-shaped, with large ears and almond-shaped eyes. Soft, dense fur. Long, tapering tail. There is a long-haired variant of this breed, recently developed from it, called the Somali.

History: We probably owe the existence of the modern Abyssinian breed to a bizarre historical incident. In the 1860s, the Emperor of Abyssinia (now Ethiopia) wrote a letter to Queen Victoria in which, among other things, he asked for her hand in marriage. Not surprisingly, the letter was ignored. Her failure to respond so incensed the Emperor that he proceeded to arrest a number of Europeans, including the British Consul.

Overreacting in a spectacular fashion, the British government sent a force of 32,000 to ensure their release. This so panicked the Emperor that, as the troops approached, he blew his brains out with a pistol that had, ironically, been an earlier gift from Queen Victoria.

The British troops, having no need to fight, offered gifts to a local chief and set off for home. Along the way, some of the soldiers appear to have acquired pet kittens from the now friendly locals, and brought these back with them to Britain.

Gordon Stables, writing in 1874, reports that the first Abyssinian Cat to be identified as an individual was called 'Zula' (not 'Zulu' as some books say) and was brought to England by the wife of Captain Barrett-Lennard in 1868. This date coincides with the end of the Abyssinian confrontation and it seems likely that she obtained the animal from one of the returning soldiers. This idea is reinforced by the fact that Zula is the name of the northern Abyssinian port at which the British military force established its first base, in 1867.

Early writers on this breed, noting the proximity of Abyssinia to Egypt, suggested that it might be the direct descendant of the sacred cat of the ancient Egyptians. Although the Abyssinian Cat

The Abyssinian Cat *(below),* a breed famous for its ticked coat. Known affectionately as the 'Aby', it may owe its existence as a pedigree show-cat to a bizarre incident involving Queen Victoria and a pistol.

does, indeed, have the correct body proportions when compared with the many small bronze statuettes of the cat goddess Bastet, there is no hard evidence to support this theory.

A less romantic version of the Abyssinian's origin sees it as a cat 'more at home on the Thames than the Nile' – created by careful selective breeding in England at the end of the 19th century. This view holds that individual cats with ticked coats were brought together repeatedly to fix the 'ticked' quality and create the breed out of existing British shorthairs.

The truth about the origin of the breed probably lies in a combination of these theories. It seems quite likely that a few unusual cats with ticked coats, distantly related to those of nearby Egypt, were brought back to England after the brief 'war' with Abyssinia. These cats were probably then mated with carefully chosen British shorthairs in order to develop the new breed of 'ticked' cats.

According to several authors, the Abyssinian was first listed as a distinct breed in 1882, but its status was strongly contested by certain authorities of the day. The first Standard of Points for the breed was published in 1889, by Harrison Weir, and the first Abyssinians to be registered in the National Cat Club Stud Book had their names entered there in 1896. In 1907 the first specimens were sent to the United States.

In the inter-war period, in 1929, the Abyssinian Cat Club was formed in England by Major E.S. Woodiwiss. After a dormant period during World War II, it was reactivated in 1947. Barely a dozen pure-bred Abyssinians had survived the austerity and destruction of the war years, but serious breeding was soon started again and the Club went from strength to strength until it was eventually able to celebrate 60 years of existence with a special Jubilee Show in 1989.

Personality: Terms that have been used to describe this breed include: intelligent, affectionate, gentle, graceful, sinuous, energetic, companionable, friendly, fearless, quiet, active, playful, alert, fast, sun-worshipping. Lithe and pantherine in its movements. Requires considerable freedom and dislikes close confinement.

A critic of the breed has commented that it is difficult to handle, undisciplined, introverted, shy and cautious, but against this, an eminent cat judge has declared: 'The quiet unassuming Abyssinian combines all the good points and none of the failings of his more widely advertised relations.'

Colour Forms: The original colour form of this species was described as 'ruddy'. It stood alone as the sole acceptable colour until, in 1963, it was joined by a 'sorrel' or 'red'. Blue was not added as a championship colour until 1984. Today a number of further colours have been added, and the recognized lists read as follows:

GCCF: Usual (=Ruddy/ Ruddy Brown/ Burnt Sienna); Sorrel (= Red/ Cinnamon/ Russet); Chocolate; Blue; Lilac (Chocolate Dilute); Fawn (Sorrel Dilute); Red (Sex-linked Red); Cream (Sex-linked Cream); Tortie; Sorrel Tortie; Chocolate Tortie; Blue Tortie; Lilac Tortie; Fawn Tortie; Silver; Sorrel Silver; Chocolate Silver; Blue Silver; Lilac Silver; Fawn Silver; Red Silver; Cream Silver; Tortie Silver; Sorrel Tortie Silver; Chocolate Tortie Silver; Blue Tortie Silver; Lilac Tortie Silver; Fawn Tortie Silver.

CFA: Ruddy (= Usual/ Ruddy Brown/ Burnt Sienna); Red (= Sorrel/ Cinnamon/ Russet); Blue; Fawn.

The heraldic emblem of the long-established Abyssinian Cat Club, founded in 1929 by Major Sydney Woodiwiss.

Bibliography:

1929. Brooke, H.C. *The Abyssinian Cat.* (Pamphlet)

1951. Denham, H. and Denham, S. *Child of the Gods; Notes on the Abyssinian Cat Today and Yesterday.* Denham, London.

1963. Zanetti, A.B. *Journey from the Blue Nile. A History of the Abyssinian Cat.* The United Abyssinian Club, New York.

1973. Ashford, A.E. and Pond, G. *Rex, Abyssinian and Turkish Cats.* Gifford, London.

1973. Peltz, R. *The Abyssinian Cat.* TEX-ABY Club, Houston, Texas.

1983. Faler, K. *This is the Abyssinian Cat.* TFH, New Jersey.

1991. Cooke-Zimmermann, R. *Abyssinians.* TFH, New Jersey.

1995. Helgren, J.A. *Abyssinian Cats.* Barron's Educational Services. Hauppauge, New York.

Breed Clubs:
Abyssinian Cat Association. Address: Danum, Fields Road, Chedworth, Glos., GL54 4NQ, England.
Abyssinian Cat Club. Publishes a twice-yearly journal, *Papyrus*. Address: Alwyne, 15 Cramhurst Lane, Whitley, Surrey, GU8 5RA, England.
Abyssinian Cat Club of America. Address: 4060 Croaker Lane, Woodbridge, VA 22193, USA.

Acinonyx

Wild Feline. The generic name for the Cheetah *(Acinonyx jubatus)*. Because of its anatomical peculiarities, the Cheetah is always placed alone in a separate genus, and sometimes even in a separate sub-family (Acinonychinae) of the Felidae. There is no specific record as to why the Cheetah was given this name in 1828, but it has been assumed that the word was derived from the Greek *akaina* and *onux*, meaning 'thorn-claw', referring to the fact that its feet have visible, unsheathed claws. Alternatively, it may have been derived from the Greek *a* and *kineo*, meaning 'without movement' again referring to the unsheathed claws. (In reality, the claws do have some movement and can be retracted, like the claws of other cat species, but when this happens they remain visible because the Cheetah uniquely lacks the claw-sheaths of the other cats.)

Advertising

Feline History. Cats have figured prominently in advertising campaigns for over a century. From the brilliant posters of Toulouse-Lautrec and Steinlen in Paris in the late 19th century, right through to the highly professional TV performances of the famous feline pet-food purveyors, Morris I & II (in the USA) and Arthur I & II (In Britain) in the late 20th century, cats have been featured time and again by advertisers wishing to trap the attention of a preoccupied public.

Two Chicago-based Americans have collected together, in three volumes, a wide range of colourful examples of these illustrative uses of the cat. Alice Muncaster is an advertising and promotion manager for one of America's largest financial institutions. Her co-author, Ellen Yanow (later to become Ellen Yanow Sawyer), is the executive director of a national humane organization. Their collection of 'cats in advertising art' is the most extensive in the world, as their 1980s trilogy has ably demonstrated.

Cats have been used to advertise many products. Here a jet black cat, looming over a cigarette advertisement, sends a protective offer of 'good luck' to those who purchase this particular brand.

Bibliography:
1984. Muncaster, A. & Yanow, E. *The Cat Made Me Buy It!* Crown, New York.
1986. Muncaster, A. & Sawyer, E. *The Cat Sold It!* Crown, New York.
1988. Muncaster, A. & Sawyer, E. *The Black Cat Made Me Buy It!* Crown, New York.

Aelwaer's Cat

Legendary Cat. Saint Aelwaer was a satirical image meant to display attributes that were the exact opposite of the qualities of the Virgin Mary. She was described as a 'demonic anti-saint, patroness of all tribulation . . . an intemperate cavalier, mother of all vices . . . a sort of Virgin Mary in reverse'. In a Dutch woodcut of 1550 she is portrayed riding a donkey, with a magpie on her head symbolizing immorality, a pig under her left arm symbolizing gluttony, and a cat held aloft on her right hand symbolizing the forces of evil. The cat is raised high like an emblem or ensign and is clearly meant to advertise the fact that this figure is in league with the devil, for this was the period when Europe was brutally persecuting all felines as familiars of witches and creatures of wickedness.

African Golden Cat

Wild Feline. *(Felis aurata)* In Africa it is known simply as the Golden Cat, but internationally this can lead to confusion with the Asiatic Golden Cat, which in Asia is often called simply the Golden Cat. Today, confusion is avoided by calling the Asiatic species by its other name, Temminck's Cat, and giving the African species its full name. It is referred to locally as 'the leopard's brother'. German: *Goldkatze*; French: *Le Chat Doré*.

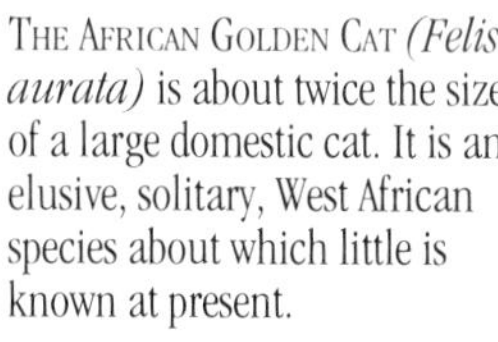

The African Golden Cat *(Felis aurata)* is about twice the size of a large domestic cat. It is an elusive, solitary, West African species about which little is known at present.

This is the rain-forest cat of West Africa, adapted to the hot humid forests that other cats tend to avoid. Its coat is variable, but is most commonly a rich golden colour.

Grey and black individuals have also been recorded. There is a slight spotting of the coat on the paler underside and, in some cases, these marks may spread to other parts of the body. The medium-length tail tapers to the pointed tip.

They are stealthy, solitary hunters, operating at dawn and at dusk, stalking their prey both on the ground and in the trees. Their main diet consists of monkeys, tree-hyraxes, birds and, down on the ground, rodents, duikers and small antelopes.

This species is so elusive that little is known about its social behaviour.

Size: Length of Head + Body: 65–90 cm (25½–35½ in). Tail: 20–35 cm (8–13¾ in). Weight: 5–12 kg (11–26½ lb).

Distribution: Tropical West Africa.

African Lynx

Wild Feline. An earlier name for the Caracal *(Felis caracal),* given to this species because it is the only lynx-like animal in Africa. However, because the animal's range also spreads into the Middle East and western Asia, the term African Lynx has been abandoned in favour of Caracal. (For details see Caracal.)

African Wild Cat

Wild Feline. *(Felis sylvestris lybica)* Also known as the Grey Wild Cat, or the Caffer, Caffre, or Kaffir Cat. German: *Falbkatze,* or *Afrikanische Wildkatze;* French: *Le Chat Sauvage d'Afrique,* or *Le Chat Ganté;* Swahili: *Kimburu* or *Paka Pori;* Afrikaans: *Vaalboskat.*

This, the African race of the Wild Cat, is slightly larger than the average domestic cat and with slightly longer legs. The backs of its ears are a rich brownish-red colour. Otherwise it is remarkably similar to a pet tabby cat. It is a nocturnal rodent-hunter that inhabits a wide range of habitats, so long as they provide it with some cover and safe retreats. It avoids climatic

extremes, such as arid desert and rain forests. It tends to hunt mostly at ground level, but is an excellent climber when the need arises. Rats and mice account for over 70 per cent of its food intake, with birds, reptiles, amphibians and insects together making up the other 30 per cent.

Its hunting techniques, social life, sexual activities and parental care all follow the same pattern as the European Wild Cat or the domestic cat. In areas of human habitation, the African Wild Cat interbreeds so freely with domestic cats that the pure form of the wild species is almost extinct. It only survives in the most remote areas.

This African race is generally accepted as the true, original ancestor of the modern domestic cat. Because the process of domestication began in ancient Egypt and because this is the local race of Wild Cat found in that region, it is logical to assume that there can be no other ancestral form. Also, this cat's markings, its general build, and its personality all support this view.

The markings are very close to those seen on a Mackerel Tabby, although not quite as distinct. Sometimes they can be very faint indeed. The body proportions are similar to those of a modern moggie, and the tail is less bushy than that seen in more northerly Wild Cats. Above all, the personality is right. It is well known that European Wild Cats are shy, secretive and extremely angry when brought into captivity. African Wild Cats appear to be far more amenable and much easier to tame, which helps to explain how they came to graduate from pest-controlling working cats to purring house-pets. An early explorer wrote of them: 'the natives . . . catch them separately when they are quite young and find no difficulties in reconciling them to a life about their huts and enclosures, where they grow up and . . . adapt themselves to an indoor existence so as to approach in many ways to the habits of the common cat.'

After centuries of progressive domestication by the Egyptians, the African Wild Cat had virtually become the 'modern' cat as we know it and it only needed the intervention of international traders, like the Phoenicians, to carry it far and wide. As it spread through the ancient world, via Greece and Rome, to the rest of Europe, and then beyond, it would, from time to time, have encountered its fiercer, less tractable European counterpart and undoubtedly would then have interbred with it. The results of such matings must originally have been rather varied. Some kittens would have grown up with the bodies of the more slender African Wild

A wild cat, as depicted in the 17th century *Natural History* of Aldrovandus.

The African Wild Cat *(Felis sylvestris libyca)*, is generally accepted to be the true wild ancestor of all modern domestic cats. Originally domesticated by the ancient Egyptians, it was later taken by sea to all parts of the globe.

Cat combined with the savage, spitting personalities of the European. Others would have retained the sweeter disposition of the African, but kept the stockier build of the European. It is the latter type that would have proved to be excellent domestic cats for their European owners, having a friendly nature, but being well furred to withstand the colder climate, and it is from such individuals that the new strains of 'moggie' would have developed into what we now call the sturdy, sociable European Shorthair Cat.

Size: Length of Head + Body: 55–65 cm (21½–25½ in). Tail: 30–35 cm (12–14 in). Weight: 5–6 kg (11–13 lb).

Distribution: Most of Africa except the Sahara and the tropical rain-forest region of West Africa. It is said that the wild cats inhabiting the larger Mediterranean islands such as Corsica and Sardinia are closer to the African than the European race. Wild cats from the Middle East are intermediate between the two, creating a 'cline' or graded series of races. Their existence explains why it is impossible to separate the African and the European into two distinct, separate species.

ANOTHER WILD CAT depicted in the 17th century *Natural History* of Aldrovandus.

AGOUTI

COAT PATTERN. Agouti is the name given to a coat in which each individual hair is marked with bands of black, brown and yellow. The typical agouti pattern is seen most clearly on the ticked coat of the Abyssinian Cat. This is an 'all-agouti' cat, unlike the tabby, in which the agouti areas are interspersed with darker markings. Genetically, these dark patches are superimposed on the agouti hairs, the yellow bands on each hair being overlaid with darker pigment, creating what looks to the naked eye like an all-dark hair.

The name 'agouti' is borrowed from a large South American rodent which has a coat with a similar textural appearance to that of the Abyssinian Cat.

AIDS

FELINE BIOLOGY. A recent scare concerning 'Feline Aids' led to the needless slaughter of a large number of healthy household pets. When newspapers in California reported that a number of domestic cats had been identified as carrying the Aids virus, many owners panicked and had their pet cats put to sleep, in case a simple scratch from a feline claw gave them the dreaded disease. Within hours of the reports appearing in the press, vets and cat sanctuaries were flooded with requests to have cats destroyed or to find them new homes.

Fears of infection were quite unfounded, because the so-called Feline Aids is caused by a different virus from the one that attacks humans. True, it belongs to the same group of viruses, but within that group it is only distantly related. So, even if bitten or scratched by a cat that had somehow smeared its teeth or claws with infected blood from its sores, the human victim would still not be able to pick up the disease. There is no evidence from any source that Feline Aids can infect the human body. (Similarly, human Aids cannot be transmitted to cats.)

The technical term for Feline Aids is *feline-T-lymphotrophic lentivirus* (FTLV).

AILUROPHILIA

FELINE TERM. The love of cats. Many famous people, especially authors, can be classified as genuine ailurophiles. Some famous figures become cat-lovers only by association, but most of the celebrated names listed here have a genuine history of devotion to felines. The more interesting examples, where details are known, are also given separate entries; they are indicated below by an asterisk (*).

AUTHORS

BRIAN ALDISS (1925–): Cats – *Macramé; Yum-Yum; Foxie; Jackson; Nickie.* ('At many human faults a cat will never take offence;/ Two things though they cannot stand:/ The wretched Door, the horrid Fence.')

KINGSLEY AMIS* (1922–1995): Cat – *Sarah Snow.* ('There is no doubt that it is very flattering when a cat jumps on to your lap.')

HONORÉ DE BALZAC (1799–1850); Works include *The Heartbreaks of an English Cat.*
JORGE LUIS BORGES (1899–1986): Cat – *Beppo*
CHARLOTTE BRONTË (1816–1855): Cat – *Tiger**
EMILY BRONTË (1818–1848): Cat – *Tiger** (which played at her feet while she wrote *Wuthering Heights*)
SAMUEL BUTLER (1835–1902): Cat – *Purdoe;* + strays in trouble ('I must have a cat whom I find homeless . . . ')
LORD BYRON (1788–1824): Had five cats, which travelled with him, including one called *Beppo.*
KAREL CAPEK (1890–1938): Cats – *Pudlenka I, II* and *III**
THOMAS CARLYLE (1795–1881): Cat – *Columbine*
RAYMOND CHANDLER (1888–1959): Cat – Black Persian female: *Taki* (his 'feline secretary', to whom he always read the first drafts of his murder mysteries)
JEAN COCTEAU (1889–1963): Cat – *Karoun**. ('I love cats because I love my home, and after a while they become its visible soul.')
COLETTE* (1873–1854): Cats – *Kiki-la-Doucette*; Saha; Mini-mini; Kro; Kapok; Muscat; La Touteu; Petiteu; Franchette; Zwerg; Pinichette; Ba-tou*, Minionne; Toune; La Chatte; One and Only; La Chatte Dernière.* ('There are no ordinary cats . . . ')
CHARLES DICKENS (1812–1870): Cats – *William/Williamina*; the Master's Cat**
ALEXANDRE DUMAS (1824–1895): Cats – *Mysouff I* and *II**; *Le Docteur.* ('The cat, aristocrat both in type and origin, which has been so greatly maligned, deserves our respect at least.')
ANATOLE FRANCE (1844–1924): Cats – *Hamilcar; Pascal* ('silent guardians of my city of books')
ANNE FRANK* (1929–1945): Cats – *Boche; Tommy; Mouschi*
PAUL GALLICO (1897–1976): His book, *The Silent Miaow,* translated from the feline, was a tract explaining to cats how to exploit humans.
THÉOPHILE GAUTIER* (1811–1872): Cats – *Childebrand; Madame Théophile*; Don Perrot de Navarre; Séraphita; Eponine*; Gavroche; Enjolras; Zizi; Cléopatre.* ('Pashas love tigers and I love cats because cats are the tigers of us poor devils'.)
THOMAS HARDY* (1840–1928): Cat – *Cobby* (a Blue Persian)
ERNEST HEMINGWAY* (1899–1961): Had 30 cats, including *F. Puss; Dillinger, Thruster; Furhouse; Fats; Willy; Crazy Christian; Friendless Brother; Ecstasy.* ('The cat has complete emotional honesty – an attribute not often found in humans.')
VICTOR HUGO* (1802–1885): Cats – *Mouche; Gavroche = Chanoine*
ALDOUS HUXLEY (1894–1963): 'If you want to write, keep cats.'
HENRY JAMES (1843–1916): Sometimes wrote with a cat on his shoulder.
JEROME K. JEROME (1859–1927): His 'over-motherly' cat fostered a puppy and a squirrel.
SAMUEL JOHNSON (1709–1784): Cats – *Lilly* (a white kitling); *Hodge** ('a very fine cat, a very fine cat indeed')
MICHAEL JOSEPH (1897–1958): Cats – *Charles; Minna Minna Mowbray**. ('The surest way to forfeit the esteem of a cat is to treat him as an inferior being.')
RUDYARD KIPLING (1865–1936): 'He will kill mice and he will be kind to babies . . . but when the moon gets up and the night comes, he is the Cat that Walks by Himself . . . '
DORIS LESSING (1919–): 'If a fish is the movement of water embodied, given shape, cat is a diagram and pattern of subtle air.'
BERNARD LEVIN (1928–) 'I have loved cats from infancy; I am certain that I have been one in an earlier existence, perhaps several times . . . '
COMPTON MACKENZIE* (1883–1972): Cats – *Tootoose; Sylvia; Pippo* and many others. ('Nobody who is not prepared to spoil cats will get from them the reward they are able to give . . . ')
GUY DE MAUPASSANT (1850–1893): A founder-member of Alexandre Dumas's 'Feline Defence League'.
MICHEL DE MONTAIGNE (1533–1592): Cat – *Madame Vanity**
IRIS MURDOCH (1919–): Cat – *General Butchkin*

THE FRENCH AUTHOR and film-maker Jean Cocteau, at home with his Siamese cat in 1955. He used one of his pet cats as the model for 'The Beast' in his classic film version of *Beauty and the Beast.*

BEVERLEY NICHOLS* (1898–1983): Cat – *Oscar*

EDGAR ALLEN POE (1811–1849) Cat – *Catarina**

AGNES REPPLIER* (1855–1945): Cats – *Agrippina; Banquo; Banshee; Nero; Carl.* ('The vanity of man revolts from the serene indifference of the cat.')

GEORGE SAND (1804–1876): Cat – *Minou.* (George Sand ate her breakfast from the same bowl as her cat.)

DOROTHY L. SAYERS (1893–1958): Cat – *Timothy**

SIR WALTER SCOTT (1771–1832): Cat – Hinse*

EDITH SITWELL (1887–1964): Owned 'the most beautiful cat in the world'.

HARRIET BEECHER STOWE (1811–1896): Cat – *Calvin*

SIR ROY STRONG (1935–): Cat – black tomcat called *The Reverend Wenceslas Muff*

WILLIAM MAKEPEACE THACKERAY (1811–1863): Cat – *Louisa*

MARK TWAIN* (1835–1910): Cats – *Sour Mash; Apollinaris; Zoroaster; Blatherskite.* ('If man could be crossed with the cat it would improve man, but it would deteriorate the cat.')

HORACE WALPOLE (1717–1797): Cats – *Selima*; Fatima; Harold; Patapan; Zara*

H.G. WELLS (1866–1946): Cat – *Mr Peter Wells*

SIR ANGUS WILSON (1913–1991): Last of many cats: stray cat – *Cookie*

EMILE ZOLA (1840–1902) In his *Paradise of Cats*, an Angora Cat relates the story.

AN ELDERLY MARK TWAIN with one of his favourite kittens, photographed in 1908. When playing billiards, he introduced special rules to allow for feline interference with the moving ball.

Poets

MATTHEW ARNOLD (1822–1888): Cats – *Atossa*;* (three-legged) *Blacky*

CHARLES BAUDELAIRE* (1821–1867): 'It is easy to see why the rabble dislike cats. A cat is beautiful; it suggests ideas of luxury, cleanliness, voluptuous pleasures . . . '

WILLIAM COWPER (1731–1800): 'I have a kitten . . . the drollest of all creatures that ever wore a cat's skin.'

CECIL DAY-LEWIS (1904–1972): Cat – *Simpkin*

T.S. ELIOT (1888–1965): Cats – *Wiscus; Pattipaws; George Pushdragon; Noilly Prat; Tantomile.* ('With Cats, some say, one rule is true:/ Don't speak till you are spoken to./ Myself, I do not hold with that – / I say, you should ad-dress a Cat.')

JOHN KEATS (1795–1821): 'Gaze with those bright, languid segments green, and prick those velvet ears . . . '

LOUIS MACNIECE (1907–1963): 'A pharaoh's profile, a Krishna's grace, tail like a question-mark.'

DON MARQUIS (1878–1937): Created the defiantly optimistic alley cat mehitabel*: 'I would fear greatly for the morals of mehitabel the cat if she had any.'

PETRARCH* (1304–1374) Had his cat embalmed.

GABRIEL ROSSETTI (1783–1954): Cat – black and white female called *Zoë*

PERCY BYSSHE SHELLEY (1792–1822): ' . . . beautiful and swift! Sweet lover of pale night . . . '

ROBERT SOUTHEY (1774–1843): Cats – *Bona Marietta; The Zombi; Pulcheria; Sir Thomas Dido; Rumpel**. ('A kitten is in the animal world what a rosebud is in a garden.')

PAUL VERLAINE (1844–1896): 'She played with her cat and it was a wonder to watch the white hand and the white paw frolic in the shade of night.'

ELLA WHEELER WILCOX (1850–1919): Cats – *Ajax; Banjo; Goody Two Eyes; Madame Ref*

WILLIAM WORDSWORTH (1770–1850): 'See the kitten on the wall/ Sporting with the leaves that fall . . . But the kitten, how she starts/ Crouches, stretches, paws and darts!'

WILLIAM BUTLER YEATS (1865–1939): Cat – *Minnaloushe** in poem 'The Cat and the Moon'

Artists

JEAN AUGUSTE DOMINIQUE INGRES (1780–1867): Cats – *Procope; Patrocle*

PAUL KLEE* (1879–1940): Cats – *Myz, Nuggi, Fritzi, Bimbo*

EDWARD LEAR (1812–1888): Cat – *Foss**

LEONARDO DA VINCI (1452–1519): 'Even the smallest feline is a work of art.'

EDOUARD MANET (1832–1883): Designed a poster for Gautier's book *Les Chats.*

HENRI MATISSE* (1869–1954): Black cat
PABLO PICASSO* (1881–1973): Cat – Siamese
RUSKIN SPEAR (1911–1990): Cats – *Manny; Trixie; Leo*
ANDY WARHOL* (1928–1987): Cats – *Hester* and *Sam*
JAMES MCNEILL WHISTLER (1834–1903): Cats – A brown, gold and white female and her kittens

HEADS OF STATE AND CULTURAL LEADERS

US PRESIDENT JIMMY CARTER (1924–): Cat – Siamese: *Misty Malarky Yin Yang**
KING CHARLES I (1600–1649): Cat – a lucky black cat that died the day before the King was arrested, later to be beheaded
EMPEROR CHU HOU-TSUNG*, Ruler of China (1507–1566): Cat – *Frost Eyebrows*
SIR WINSTON CHURCHILL* (1874–1965): Cats – ginger toms: *Jock* and *Tango* (also known as *Mr Cat*); black and white: Bob; black: *Nelson* and *Margate**
FRENCH PRESIDENT GEORGES CLEMENCEAU (1841–1929): Cat – Blue Persian: *Prudence*
US PRESIDENT BILL CLINTON (1946–): Cat – Black and white: *Socks**
US PRESIDENT CALVIN COOLIDGE (1872–1933): Cats – *Smokey; Blackie; Tiger**, and *Timmy*, who would allow the President's pet canary to sleep between his paws
KING EDWARD VII (1841–1910): Several Manx Cats
US PRESIDENT GERALD FORD (1913–): Cat – Siamese: *Shan*
POPE GREGORY I* (540–604): Monastery cat (probably apocryphal)
US PRESIDENT RUTHERFORD B. HAYES (1822–1893): Cat – *Siam*
GERMAN PRESIDENT PAUL VON HINDENBERG (1847–1934): 'I cannot imagine a pleasant retired life of peace and meditation without a cat in the house.'
EMPEROR ICHIJO, RULER OF JAPAN (986–1011): Cat – *Myobu No Omoto**
US PRESIDENT JOHN F. KENNEDY (1917–1963): Cat – *Tom Kitten**
POPE LEO XII (1760–1829): Cat – *Micetto** – small, greyish-red with black stripes
US PRESIDENT ABRAHAM LINCOLN (1809–1865): Cat – *Tabby** ('No matter how much cats fight, there always seem to be plenty of kittens.')
LOUIS XIII OF FRANCE (1601–1643): Called a halt to Christian cat-burning.
LOUIS XV OF FRANCE (1710–1774): His white cat came to his bedroom every morning, and was allowed to play on the table at Royal Councils.
MOHAMMED (570–632): Cat – *Muezza**; in the Koran, cats are 'pure', dogs 'impure'.
POPE PIUS IX (1792–1878): Vatican cat, dined at the papal table
US PRESIDENT RONALD REAGAN (1911–): Cats – Two tortoiseshell strays: *Cleo* and *Sara*
CARDINAL RICHELIEU* (1585–1642): Cats – many, including the following 14 when he died: *Mounard le Fougueux, Soumise, Serpolet, Gazette, Ludovic le Cruel, Mimie Paillon, Félimare, Lucifer, Lodoviska, Rubis sur l'Ongle, Pyrame, Thisbe, Racan*, and *Perruque*.
US PRESIDENT THEODORE ROOSEVELT (1859–1919): Cats – Grey cat: *Slippers*; Tom Quartz**
QUEEN VICTORIA (1819–1901): Cat – Persian: *White Heather**
PRIME MINISTER HAROLD WILSON (1916–1995): Cat – Siamese: *Nemo**
CARDINAL THOMAS WOLSEY* (1471–1530): Large tabby cat (probably apocryphal)

DETAIL OF ONE OF THE CATS from a page of feline sketches by Leonardo da Vinci, revealing his close understanding of his subject. The page of sketches in question belongs to H.M. The Queen and is in the Royal Library at Windsor.

COMPOSERS AND MUSICIANS

ALEXANDER BORODIN* (1833–1887): Cats – *Fisherman; Longy; Tommy*
FRÉDÉRIC CHOPIN (1810–1849): His 'Cat Waltz' (*Valse brilliante* in A minor, opus 34. no.3) was partially inspired by his pet cat, which jumped on to his keyboard while he was composing it.
JEAN MICHEL JARRE (1948–): Cats – *Woody* and *Allen*
MAURICE RAVEL (1875–1937): Had 30–40 cats, and included a cat duet in his *L'Enfant et les Sortilèges*, for which Colette wrote the libretto.
DOMENICO SCARLATTI (1685–1757): His work 'The Cat's Fugue' was inspired by his pet cat, called *Pulcinella**

Sir Andrew Lloyd Webber (1948–): His long-running musical *Cats*, first staged in 1981, has been performed in 13 countries and ten languages.

Philosophers

Jeremy Bentham (1748–1832): Cat – *Sir John Langbourne**

Scientists

Erasmus Darwin (1731–1802): Cat – *Persian Snow*

Albert Einstein (1879–1955): 'Contemporary physics is based on concepts somewhat analogous to the smile of the absent cat.'

Thomas Huxley (1825–1895): Cat – tabby called *Oliver*

Isaac Newton (1642–1727): Invented the cat-flap for his female cat and her kittens.

Humanitarians

Florence Nightingale* (1820–1910): Cats – Persian: *Disraeli, Gladstone, Bismarck*

Albert Schweitzer (1875–1965): Cat – *Sizi* ('There are two ways to escape human misery, playing the organ and watching cats play.')

Sport

Frank Bruno (1961–): Cats – Siamese: *Samson; Del Boy.* ('They influence the way I move in the ring – they're so flexible.')

Sally Gunnell (1966–): Cats – Black cat: *Demi*; tabby: *Chloe*; tabby-and-white cat: *Poppy*

O.J. Simpson (1947–): Cat – *Sheena*

Stage and Screen

Ann-Margret (1941–): Cats – *Big Red* and *Tuffy*

Fred Astaire (1899–1987): Black cat

Tallulah Bankhead (1903–1968): Lion cub

Brigitte Bardot* (1934–): 60 cats

Kim Basinger (1953–): Demanded custody of her cats in divorce case

Warren Beatty (1937–): Cat – *Cake*

Doris Day (1924–): Cats: 10 + (rescued); *Punky*. ('You haven't lived until you have lived with a cat.')

Melanie Griffith (1957–): Cat – tabby-and-white

Van Heflin (1910–1971): Cats – *Mousetrap* and *Silkhat*

Charles Laughton (1889–1962): Stray cats

Janet Leigh (1927–): Cat – *Turkey*

Vivien Leigh (1913–1967): Cats – Sealpoint Siamese: *Boy; New* (after New Theatre)

James Mason* (1909–1984): Cats – Siamese

Max Ophüls (1902–1957): Cat – White Persian

Robert de Niro (1943–): Has seven cats.

Beryl Reid (1920–): Cats: *Lulu, Jenny, Dimly, Cleopatra* and many others

Edward G. Robinson (1893–1973): Cat – Siamese

Elizabeth Taylor (1932–): Three cats

Franco Zeffirelli (1923–): Cat – Persian

Ailurophobia

Feline Term. The fear of cats. Some ailurophobes cannot bear to be in the same room as a cat. Others can tolerate their presence, but cannot bear to be touched by them. Still others have a specific fear of a cat jumping up on them unexpectedly. Apart from these intense phobic responses, there survives in some regions a more general fear of felines because of their supposed mystical powers and their close relationship with witchcraft and the Devil.

Those with an acute phobic response include Alexander the Great (356–323 BC), who is said to have swooned at the sight of a cat. Julius Caesar (100–44 BC), the mighty Emperor, is also said to have held cats in horror. Henri III (1551–1589), the French King, lost consciousness if he set eyes on a cat (and it is said that during his reign he executed 30,000 cats). Napoleon Bonaparte (1769–1821) became frantic in the presence of a cat. One night after the Emperor had retired to his bedroom, he was heard screaming for help. When one of his aides rushed in, he found the great man in a state of panic, sweating profusely, and thrashing around wildly with his sword, because a cat was hiding behind a tapestry. Abdul Hamid (1725–1789), the Ottoman Sultan, who flourished at the end of the 18th century, also felt a real terror of cats.

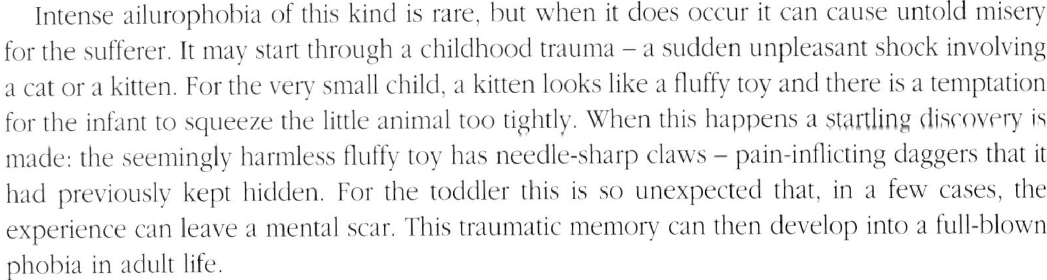

Intense ailurophobia of this kind is rare, but when it does occur it can cause untold misery for the sufferer. It may start through a childhood trauma – a sudden unpleasant shock involving a cat or a kitten. For the very small child, a kitten looks like a fluffy toy and there is a temptation for the infant to squeeze the little animal too tightly. When this happens a startling discovery is made: the seemingly harmless fluffy toy has needle-sharp claws – pain-inflicting daggers that it had previously kept hidden. For the toddler this is so unexpected that, in a few cases, the experience can leave a mental scar. This traumatic memory can then develop into a full-blown phobia in adult life.

A second way in which cat phobia can arise stems from an irrational fear on the part of parents that the family cat may try to smother the newly arrived baby, by sitting on top of its face when the child lies sleeping in its crib. This old wives' tale is amazingly persistent, despite the fact that no cat could possibly relax and sleep on top of a squirming, suffocating baby. As a result, many an infant may experience a shrieking mother rushing into the nursery and yelling at the cat to leave the room. These early associations between cats and panic may leave their mark and resurface later in the life of the child.

Strangely, studies of phobic reactions have revealed that women are far more likely to suffer from the affliction than men. This requires some additional explanation and it has been suggested by psychoanalysts that there may also be a sexual element involved. The cat has often been seen as a symbol of sexuality and it is possible that, in some instances, an intense fear of cats may reflect a suppressed sexuality on the part of the woman concerned.

The cure for cat phobia is straightforward enough, but distressing for the patient. It requires a series of step-by-step familiarization lessons, in which, at first, things only remotely feline are presented to the victim. These may be simply photographs of cats or kittens, or toy animals. After a while, a kitten is placed in a small, secure cage and left on the far side of a room, while the phobic person is gently reassured that it cannot get near. Gradually the animal is moved closer and day by day the phobia can be reduced in intensity until eventually the victim can actually hold a kitten. After this, the longer the sufferer spends in the company of cats the better, but always with the careful avoidance of any sudden, unanticipated move. After a few months of therapy, it is usual for even the most intense forms of cat phobia to disappear.

Many sufferers wrongly believe that there is no cure and can never be one. For them there is a needless, lifelong fear of encountering a strange cat, a fear that sometimes ends with their refusing to go out of doors at all. Their condition is beyond reason, but it is certainly not, as they believe, beyond cure.

AILURUS

FELINE TERM. The ancient Greek name for the domestic cat. Also spelled 'ailouros'. It is said to have been coined by Herodotus, the Greek historian, when he first encountered cats during a visit to Egypt in the fifth century BC and referred to them as 'ailuroi', meaning 'tail-wavers'.

ALLERGIES

FELINE HISTORY. There is a long history of certain individuals suffering from severe allergic responses to cats. There are two schools of thought as to how this reaction originates. One sees it as a genetic weakness – a specific, inborn sensitivity to certain proteins which, when inhaled

or ingested, even in minute quantities, create unpleasant physiological reactions. The other views it more as a psychological disturbance that begins in childhood and involves some kind of emotional trauma, unconsciously associated with a particular object. If that object happens to be a cat, then a serious allergic response may develop later in life. Whichever of these explanations is the relevant one, the result can be all too real and extremely unpleasant, involving itchy eyes, a runny nose, a sore throat, a headache, breathing difficulties and asthmatic attacks.

Tests have shown that, in the case of a cat allergy, these symptoms are essentially a reaction to the animal's fur. To be more precise, it is a reaction to a mixture of shed hairs, cat's saliva and tiny particles of shed skin. This almost invisible 'dander' or 'dandruff', when it floats in the air, triggers the response in individuals who have this particular over-sensitivity.

Today there are two breeds which may avoid this problem, should an allergy-sufferer wish to become a cat-owner:

The first is the Cornish Rex Cat (see separate entry). The coat of this breed is short, sparse and curly and lacking in the usual long guard hairs. These guard hairs appear to cause the allergic response in human sufferers, so when the Cornish Rex was first discovered it was hailed as the new answer to allergy problems. Several sufferers who tried keeping these cats reported delightedly that this was indeed the case, but it remains to be seen whether it works in every instance. Some sufferers are much more sensitive than others.

For extreme cases there is always the Sphynx Cat from Canada (see separate entry). This is an almost naked cat and even the most sensitive allergy sufferers would be unable to generate much of a reaction to this remarkable animal. All it shows on its body surface is a short, soft down in place of the usual fur. As the cat grows to adulthood, this down persists only on the animal's extremities. It is therefore covered with what looks like a suede or velvet coat and which, to the touch, feels like warm, soft moss. Providing that the ultra-sensitive allergy sufferer or asthmatic would-be cat-owner owns a house with central heating, this bizarre new breed of cat is clearly the best answer at present.

Before long a new solution may be available. Research is being carried out by a pharmaceutical corporation in Cambridge, Massachusetts, on a cat-allergy vaccine called Catvax. Tests are in progress with human volunteers at the Johns Hopkins University in Maryland to establish its efficiency. Unlike other allergy vaccines in the past, Catvax promises to be permanently effective after only a few injections and to have no side effects. If this is confirmed, it should be on the market by 1997 and will then put an end to the frustrations faced by allergy-sensitive individuals who long to own a cat.

Alley Cat

Domestic Cat. In America, in the earlier part of the 20th century, it was common to refer to the non-pedigree household pet cat as an 'alley cat'. When good examples of these cats were later developed as show cats they were given the more dignified name of 'Domestic Shorthair Cats'. Those who favoured them were always ready to leap to their defence. Marguerite Norton, commenting in 1949, says: 'Some people call the Domestic Short Hair cats "alley cats" and try to give the impression that they are not a distinct breed. To the contrary, these cats . . . have a definite place in the home, in cat shows, and many can be registered like the Persians and the Siamese.'

Those who did not favour them preferred to remind people of their humble origins. One authority, Milan Greer, writing in 1961, commented sourly: 'Many cat-fancier associations now recognize a breed of cat known as the Domestic Shorthair. This is merely an alley cat dressed up in show terms. I do not believe that the alley cat should be a show competitor.'

Allogrooming

Feline Behaviour. When a cat grooms itself, this is referred to as 'autogrooming'. When one cat grooms another, this is called 'allogrooming'. A kitten experiences this almost from the

ALLOGROOMING is the name given to the action when one cat grooms another. (When it grooms itself, it is called Autogrooming.) Allogrooming is most commonly seen when a mother cat is fussing over her kittens.

moment of birth, when it is vigorously licked and cleaned by its mother. Later, allogrooming may also occur between adult cats, especially if they have grown up together and have developed a close social bond. Its primary function is not mutual hygiene but rather a cementing of the friendly relations that exist between the two animals. However, licking in a region that is hard for the cat itself to reach does have a special appeal, and cats are partial to attention behind the ears. This is why tickling and rubbing behind the ears is such a popular form of contact between cat-owners and their cats.

ALPACA CAT

DOMESTIC BREED. An alternative name for the La Perm Cat, a very recent discovery being developed as a new breed, from The Dalles area of Oregon in the United States. It is a mutation with an unusual hair texture, having 'a distinctive coat that falls in loose ringlets, reminiscent of the Komondor or Puli Dog'. (For details see La Perm Cat.)

AMERICAN BLUE CAT

DOMESTIC BREED. According to Rush Shippen Huidekoper, writing in 1895, this was an early name for the Russian Blue Cat. He points out that this cat had been given many names, including 'Blue Cat', 'Maltese Cat', 'Archangel Cat', 'Russian Cat', 'Spanish Blue', and 'Chartreuse Blue'. He explains that the name 'American Blue' is 'probably due to the fact that the Maltese for some years has been a very favourite cat in America, and has probably been bred more carefully than any other breed of cat, so that its representatives formed a distinctive type of good quality'. (For details see Russian Blue Cat.)

American Bobtail Cat

Domestic Breed. A short-tailed cat, similar to a Stumpy Manx. It should not be confused with the wild species, the American Bobcat *(Lynx rufus).*

Appearance: A stocky, long-haired cat with an abbreviated tail. The double coat appears in two lengths: long and medium. The head is broad and rounded with wide ears and large eyes. The tail may be straight or slightly curled and is always well-haired. (This description is for Type 2 below.)

History: There appear to be several distinct origins for this breed. To put it another way, there seem to be at least three different breeds using this same name. They are as follows:

1 Writing in 1940, American zoologist Ida Mellen comments: 'The American domestic Bobtail Cat of the New England and Middle Atlantic States (called the Rabbit Cat) traces its ancestry to the Manx Cat, but the distribution of tailless cats is wide, covering the Crimea and other Parts of Russia, Japan, China, the Bismarck Archipelago, the Malayan Archipelago, Burma and Siam . . . ' Nothing more seems to be known about this version of the American Bobtail.

2 A completely different source is given for the cat that is now widely recognized in pedigree circles as the true American Bobtail. The 'founding father' of this breed was a homeless male tabby kitten seen near an Indian Reservation in Arizona in the 1960s. A holidaying couple, John and Brenda Sanders, adopted him, christened him Yodie and took him home with them to Iowa. There, he eventually mated with their Siamese Cat, Mishi, producing a litter, some of which were short-tailed. One of these kittens grew up to mate with a 'cream point and white cat'. The kittens in this new litter were all short-tailed and they attracted the attention of Mindy Schultz, a friend of the Sanders family, who, in the 1970s, designated them as a new breed which she called the American Bobtail.

At first, these Bobtails had short coats, but when crossed with Himalayans, they produced thick-coated kittens. These kittens were to become the foundation stock of the breed.

Certain other crossing experiments resulted in completely tailless kittens, suggesting that the American Bobtail gene is similar to the Manx gene, which also gives rise to tails of varying length, from the Rumpy (no-tail) to the Stumpy (short-tail) to the long-tail.

3 One author has recently claimed that there is another distinct form of American Bobtail in existence. This one is supposed to be the result of crosses between domestic cats and wild Bobcats that occurred in the late 1970s. Writing in 1992, Amy Shojai comments that 'Rose Estes has been breeding Bobtails for fourteen years . . . According to Rose, wild Bobcats interbreed most often with Siamese because the scent of the Siamese in season closely resembles the smell of the female Bobcat.'

Bearing in mind that the wild Bobcat belongs to a different genus *(Lynx)* from the domestic cat *(Felis),* and is nearly twice as big, the idea that the two species would interbreed seems far-fetched, to say the least. However, before rejecting it out of hand, it is worth noting that Stanley Young, in his detailed study of the wild Bobtail published in 1958, had this to say about hybridization:

'There is evidence of a successful mating between a male Bobcat and a domestic cat at Sandy Creek, Texas during 1949. The offspring were observed by several persons in the area.' He also mentions a similar incident that occurred in 1954 in South Dakota. There, a black female domestic cat mated with a wild male Bobcat and in early June produced seven kittens. Three of the litter 'had bobtails, large feet, tufted ears, and were light grey in color with a speckling of black dots on the stomach, legs and sides. The ears were larger and hard and stiff. The tufts on them . . . were up to approximately a quarter of an inch [6mm] in length. This litter of kittens lived until 27th June 1954, when they were killed by a domestic tomcat.' It is impossible to tell whether these hybrid kittens would have been fertile or sterile when they became mature, but this report certainly makes the Rose Estes American Bobtails that were reported by Amy Shojai seem a little less unlikely.

The American Bobtail Cat, a recent domestic breed with an abbreviated tail. It is generally accepted that it was first discovered near an Indian reservation in Arizona in the 1960s, but there are rival theories concerning its origin.

It would seem from this that both the abbreviated tail and the name to go with it have cropped up more than once in the United States during the 20th century. Lisa Black, writing about the Bobtail in 1994, confirms this, commenting: 'Many other reports exist of this type of cat being produced.' For the time being, however, we must accept Type 2 above as the 'official' American Bobtail for show purposes.

Personality: Terms used to describe this breed (Type 2) include: friendly, patient, calm, watchful, intelligent, mischievous and good-natured. Inevitably, because of their lack of a balancing tail, they are not particularly fond of climbing. Vocally, they are described as having 'a scratchy little rambling voice which makes some people ask "When will they learn how to meow?"'. They are said to be more doglike than other cat breeds.

Colour Forms: All colours are acceptable in this breed.

American Coon Cat

Domestic Breed. An early name for the Maine Coon Cat.

American Curl Cat

Domestic Breed. A recently discovered American breed which has strongly curved ears.

Appearance: This breed is identified by the shape of its ears, which are curled back on themselves, exposing hairy ear-tufts. The ears feel rigid and stiff to the touch. This was a chance mutation, discovered accidentally. It involves a simple dominant gene which will give 50 per cent curly-eared kittens in litters resulting from crosses between curled cats and plain ones. It is quite different from the ear-curling that occurs with the Scottish Fold Cat. The American Curl's ears curl up, while the Scottish Fold's ears fold down.

The kittens are born with straight ears, which then curl up tightly within 24–72 hours. During the next four months, the tight curling starts to relax until finally the ears settle into their typical adult, semi-curled condition.

There are both long-haired (the original cats) and (later) short-haired forms of this breed.

AMERICAN CURL CAT

History: This breed first appeared as recently as 1981, in Lakewood, California. In June 1981 John and Grace Ruga found two stray kittens on their doorstep. One of them, a silky, long-haired, black female, stayed with them and they called her 'Shulamith' (not 'Shulasmith', as is sometimes reported). The name means 'black but comely'. The Rugas noticed that she had strangely shaped ears, and they decided to keep her. Later that year, on December 12th, she gave birth to a litter of four kittens. Two of these kittens showed the same curled ears as their mother and it was clear that there was a possibility of using these cats as the foundation stock of a new breed.

An acquaintance of the Rugas, Nancy Kestrel, encouraged them to exhibit Shulamith and her two curly-eared kittens in a cat show being held at Palm Springs in California in October 1983. This was the first time this new breed had been shown in public. The reaction was favourable and in a matter of only a few years it became an officially registered breed with certain of the

THE AMERICAN CURL, with its uniquely curved ears, is a new breed, not discovered until 1981. It first appeared in the form of a stray kitten on a doorstep in Lakewood, California, and was soon developed into a popular pedigree show-cat.

American Cat Societies. In 1985, TICA (The International Cat Association) formally recognized it as 'The American Curl' and in 1986 the CFA (Cat Fanciers' Association) followed suit.

Although the unusual shape of the ears of this cat does not appear to cause the animal any problems, some critics nevertheless see the curl mutation as a 'deformity' and the breed is not yet universally accepted. It remains a comparatively rare breed. In 1993 it was estimated that, even after 12 years of breeding, there were fewer than 1,000 American Curls in existence.

Personality: Terms used to describe this breed include: mischievous, curious, placid, playful, even-tempered, amusing, lively, whimsical, adaptable, friendly, sturdy, affectionate, intelligent and thieving. They are said to 'think like kittens all their lives'.

Colour Forms: All colours are acceptable in this breed. The foundation stock was black. The CFA in America lists the following colours for this breed. To simplify the list, the colours are grouped into convenient categories.

CFA: SOLID: White; Black; Blue; Red; Cream; Chocolate; Lilac.

SHADED, SILVER AND GOLDEN: Chinchilla Silver; Shaded Silver; Chinchilla Golden; Shaded Golden; Shell Cameo; Shaded Cameo (Red Shaded); Shell Tortie; Shaded Tortie.

Smoke: Black Smoke; Blue Smoke; Cameo Smoke (Red Smoke); Chocolate Smoke; Lavender Smoke; Cream Smoke; Smoke Tortie; Chocolate Tortie Smoke; Blue-Cream Smoke.
Tabby: (Classic, Mackerel, Patched, Spotted and Ticked Tabby Patterns) Brown Patched Tabby; Blue Patched Tabby; Silver Patched Tabby; Silver Tabby; Red Tabby; Brown Tabby; Blue Tabby; Cream Tabby; Blue Silver and Cream Silver Tabbies; Chocolate Silver Tabby; Lavender Silver Tabby; Cameo Tabby.
Parti-color: Tortie; Blue-Cream.
Bicolor: Bicolor; Van Bicolor, Calico; Dilute Calico; Van Calico; Van Dilute Calico.
Tabby and White: Seal Point; Chocolate Point; Blue Point; Lilac-Lynx Point; Lilac-Cream Point; Lilac-Cream Lynx Point; Flame (Red) Point; Cream Point; Cream Lynx Point; Tortie Point; Chocolate-Tortie Point; Chocolate-Tortie Lynx Point; Blue-Cream Point; Blue-Cream Point; Chocolate Lynx Point; Seal Lynx Point; Blue Lynx Point; Tortie-Lynx Point; Blue-Cream Lynx Point.
Breed Clubs:
American Curl Cat Club. Address: 100 Westmont Road, Syracuse, NY 13219, USA.
United Society of American Curls. Address: 11691 Kagel Canyon, Lake View Terrace, CA 91342-7422, USA.

The American Lion The puma has attracted many different names, more possibly than any other cat in the world. Apart from the Lion, it is the only large unspotted cat, and it is easy to see how it acquired the name of 'American Lion'.

American Lion

Wild Feline. An alternative name for the Puma *(Felis concolor)*. This species has been known by many names, including, commonly, Cougar or Mountain Lion and, less commonly, Deer Tiger, Painter, Mexican Lion, Catamount or American Panther. (For details see Puma.)

American Lynx

Domestic Breed. A new breed of stump-tailed cat that has recently appeared in the United States. In Germany it is known as the *Amerikanische Luchskatze*. It was developed in the 1980s by American breeders Joe Childers of North Carolina and Robert Mock of Seattle. There are both short-haired and long-haired versions. Coat patterns include two tabby variants known as Leopard and Tawny.

American Panther

Wild Feline. An alternative name for the Puma *(Felis concolor)*. This species has been known by many names (see American Lion).

American Shorthair Cat

Domestic Breed: An American pedigree cat, originally called the 'Domestic Shorthair'. It was officially renamed the American Shorthair in 1966 (known as ASH, for short). This was done to raise its status and to distinguish it from the common, non-pedigree, domestic house-pets.

Appearance: A muscular, compact, heavy-bodied cat with a short, rounded face. American Shorthairs have slightly longer legs than their British counterparts. They also tend to have a denser, thicker coat.

History: According to tradition, the first American Shorthairs were ship's cats employed as pest-controllers on the *Mayflower*, arriving in America in 1620. Many more ship's cats must have followed and, before long, they were spreading out across the New World, some living wild but most continuing to act as domestic rodent-destroyers. During the great California Gold Rush these cats were so highly valued as mousers that they were selling at $50 each, a huge price to pay back in the middle of the 19th century.

By the end of the 19th century, some of the best examples of the descendants of these working cats were starting to appear at cat shows. Classified as 'Domestic Shorthairs', they included some exceptional individuals. Despite this, however, they were often relegated to a minor role, because of strong competition from the more glamorous foreign breeds that were being imported from Europe. As Ingeborg Urcia reports: 'Those who raised the new exotic breeds looked down upon the American cats. Rumours circulated that the breeders of the Domestic got their breeding stock from the animal shelter, and their cats were disdained and neglected. At some cat shows they were not even benched . . . Domestic breeders found no cages available for them at shows, and no rosettes or trophies were provided for the Domestic Shorthair class.'

In the early years of the 20th century, the breed was enhanced by the arrival in the United States of a British pedigree Shorthair named Champion Belle of Bradford. An orange tabby imported by Jane Cathcart, it was the first Domestic Shorthair to be registered as a pedigree cat in the United States. In 1904, the first home-bred, truly American, Domestic Shorthair to be registered was a male smoke called Buster Brown, which also belonged to Miss Cathcart.

After World War II, Domestic Shorthairs started winning prizes at American cat shows and it was this that eventually led to their being honoured with the new title of American Shorthairs. A group of enthusiasts met in the early 1960s and decided on this new name because they felt that the word 'Domestic' was an obstacle to the success of these cats. The strategy proved a success and by the 1970s the American Shorthairs were fully established as a major force to be reckoned with at pedigree shows all over America.

Personality: Terms used to describe this breed include: hearty, healthy, versatile, friendly, intelligent, robust, strong, good-natured and independent.

Colour Forms: The CFA in America lists the following colours for this breed. To simplify the list, the colours are grouped into convenient categories.

CFA: Solid: White; Black; Blue; Red; Cream.

Shaded and Silver: Chinchilla Silver; Shaded Silver; Shell Cameo; Shaded Cameo; Blue Chinchilla Silver; Blue Shaded Silver; Cream Shell Cameo; Cream Shaded Cameo.

Smoke: Black Smoke; Blue Smoke; Cameo Smoke (Red Smoke); Tortoiseshell Smoke; Blue Cream Smoke.

Tabby: (Classic, Mackerel and Patched Tabby Patterns) Blue Silver Tabby (Pewter Tabby); Blue Silver Patched Tabby (Pewter Patched Tabby); Cream Cameo Tabby (Dilute Cameo); Brown Patched Tabby; Blue Patched Tabby; Silver Patched Tabby; Silver Tabby; Red Tabby; Brown Tabby; Blue Tabby; Cream Tabby; Cameo Tabby.

Smoke and White (including Vans): Black Smoke and White; Blue Smoke and White;

The American Shorthair was originally known at cat shows simply as the Domestic Shorthair, and was then little more than a common house-pet. But as the quality of the show cat improved, year by year, it was given a formal name, to set it apart.

Tortoiseshell Smoke and White; Shell Cameo and White; Shaded Cameo and White; Smoke Cameo and White.

Tabby and White: Silver Tabby and White; Silver Patched Tabby and White; Cameo Tabby and White; Brown Tabby and White; Brown Patched Tabby and White; Blue Tabby and White; Blue Patched Tabby and White; Red Tabby and White; Cream Tabby and White; Van Blue-Cream and White.

Parti-color: Tortie; Chinchilla Shaded Tortie; Shaded Tortie; Dilute Chinchilla Shaded Tortie; Dilute Shaded Tortie; Blue-Cream.

Bi-color: Bi-color; Van Bi-color; Calico; Dilute Calico; Van Calico.

Bibliography:

1981. Lauder, P. *The British, European and American Shorthair Cat.* Batsford, London.

1992. Urcia, I. *American Shorthair Cat.* Elias Holl Press, Cheney, WA.

Breed Club:

National American Shorthair Club. Address: P.O. Box 280831, San Francisco, CA 94128-0831, USA, or 1331 N. Wingra Drive, Madison, WI 53715, USA.

Note: There is a breed publication, *American Connection.* Address: P.O. Box 280831, San Francisco, CA 94128-0831, USA.

American Wirehair Cat

Domestic Breed. Appeared in 1966 on a farm near New York.

Appearance: The fur of this breed is unique among cats. Each hair is bent or hooked, giving the animal a harsh, dense, springy coat. Apart from this special feature, the cat is similar to the American Shorthair, with its typically strong, muscular body. In some individuals the whiskers are curly – a similarity to the Rex Cats.

History: This breed began as a single, spontaneous mutation in a litter born to a pair of farm cats called Bootsie and Fluffy, in a barn near Vernon (not Verona, Vermont or Utica, as quoted by various authors) in upper New York State. Among the litter of six, a red and white male kitten

The American Wirehair is a recent American breed, first discovered on a farm in New York State in 1966. It is characterized by its uniquely harsh, wiry coat.

was seen to have a strange, wiry coat, unlike its litter-mates. The farmer contacted Mrs William O'Shea, a cat breeder living nearby, who kept Rex Cats and was familiar with strange feline hair patterns. She immediately recognized the importance of this kitten and acquired it (for $50) to start a serious breeding programme. With a view to in-breeding, she also purchased a normal-coated female from the same litter. The male was called Adam and the female Tip-Toe (full names: Council Rock Farm Adam of Hi-Fi and Tip-Toe of Hi-Fi).

Subsequent breeding successfully produced a number of Wirehair kittens. Some of these were acquired by other breeders in the United States and word soon began to spread about this remarkable new type of feline. Before long kittens were being exported to breeders in Canada and Germany. As early as 1969, a true-breeding American Wirehair had been developed and the breed was secure for the future. It was officially recognized by the CFA in 1977, and by the 1990s it had achieved championship status throughout the United States. It has also appeared at cat shows in Canada, Germany and Japan. Worldwide, however, it remains a rare breed.

Whereas the Rex gene proved to be recessive, the Wirehair gene is dominant to normal coat. It has been given the gene symbol 'Wh'.

Unlike the Cornish Rex gene, the Wirehair gene has not been preserved from more than one source, and this means that every American Wirehair Cat in existence today can be traced directly back to the aptly named Adam. There were rumours of harsh-haired cats being seen on derelict bomb sites in London at the end of World War II, but these cats were never used for breeding purposes. Two of them were apparently exhibited at the National Cat Club Show in England, some years before Adam's discovery in America, but they were treated as a mere curiosity and not developed.

Personality: Terms that have been used to describe this new breed include: friendly, intelligent, adaptable, sweet-tempered, affectionate. There is some contradiction – one authority describes this cat as quiet and reserved, while others say it is playful, zany, independent and inquisitive. Because its hair stands on end, it has been described as 'the punk of the feline world'. It has also been said to 'rule its home and other cats with an iron paw'.

Colour Forms: Almost any colour is acceptable in this breed. The Cat Fanciers' Association in America lists the following colours:
CFA: White; Black; Blue; Red; Cream; Chinchilla Silver; Shaded Silver; Shell Cameo (Red Chinchilla); Shaded Cameo (Red Shaded); Black Smoke; Blue Smoke; Cameo Smoke (Red Smoke); Classic Tabby Pattern; Mackerel Tabby Pattern; Silver Tabby; Red Tabby; Brown Tabby; Blue Tabby; Cream Tabby; Cameo Tabby; Tortie; Calico; Dilute Calico; Blue-Cream; Bi-color.

Amis, Kingsley

Cat Owner. Like many authors who must spend long hours at their keyboard, Kingsley Amis (1922–1995) enjoyed the company of a cat. In his case it was a magnificent long-haired, green-eyed, pure white cat called Sarah Snow. He referred to her as a 'Hertfordshire White', but she looked remarkably like an old-fashioned Angora.

Like many cat owners, he had strong reservations about people who do not have house-pets: 'I am enough of a cat-lover to be suspicious of a household that doesn't have a cat . . . I associate a person having a cat with them being gentler than other people.' He admitted to talking to his cat. 'People are silly about their cats . . . There is no point in having a cat and being prosaic about it. Cats stimulate the fancy; we weave fantasies about them.' His own fantasy about Sarah Snow was that she was trying to learn English.

In his 1987 poem 'Cat-English', he commented: 'If you've a sympathetic ear, Cat-English comes through loud and clear,/ Of course, the words are short and few, the accent strange and strident, too,/ And our side never gets a crack, at any sort of answer back.'

Bibliography:

1988. Surges, M. *The English Cat at Home.* Chatto & Windus, London.

Amsterdam Cats

Feral Cats. One of the best known cat sanctuaries in the world is to be found in the heart of Amsterdam. De Poezenboot (The Pussycat-boat) is a barge permanently moored alongside the Singel Canal, one of the famous waterways in the centre of the city. The barge was bought in 1969 by cat-lover Henriette van Weelde to provide a home for the orphaned, stray, sick and rejected cats of Amsterdam, and quickly became a tourist attraction. Originally she offered her own house as a sanctuary for the strays, but soon there were far too many of them. The barge provided the answer and also enabled visitors to see the animals and provide much needed funds to support her work. By 1971 she was forced to expand again and bought a second barge.

The original boat now holds about 60 elderly and sickly cats who will live out the remainder of their lives on board. The second boat houses the younger and healthier cats, which are awaiting adoption. Since no stray cats are ever turned away (and it has been estimated that altogether there are about 50,000 stray cats in Amsterdam), it is not surprising that a third barge is already being sought, as the city's feline problem continues to escalate. Henriette, who is no longer young, is helped by five volunteers, but receives no financial aid from the city authorities. Her feline Noah's Ark is open to the public every day between 1 pm and 3 pm. The address is: De Poezenboot, Singel T/O nr 40, NL 1012 VL Amsterdam, Netherlands.

Andean Cat

Wild Feline. An alternative name for the Mountain Cat *(Felis jacobita)*, a rare, small cat that inhabits the Andes Mountains in South America, above the 3,000 metre (10,000 foot) level. It is also called the Andean Mountain Cat and the Andean Highland Cat, and is known locally as the Gato Andino. (For details see Mountain Cat.)

Andy

Pet Cat. Owned by Florida Senator Ken Myer in the 1970s, he fell from the 16th floor of an apartment building in Florida and survived, making him the record-holder for the longest non-lethal fall in feline history.

Angola Cat

Domestic Breed. Incorrect name for the Angora Cat, sometimes used in the 19th century.

Angora Cat

Domestic Breed. An ancient Turkish breed of long-haired cat. (Angora means Ankara. The capital city of Turkey changed its spelling in 1930, but the animals named for it, such as the Angora Cat and the Angora Goat, have retained their original forms.) According to Turkish legend, their great national hero, Kemel Ataturk, will one day be reincarnated as a pure white Angora Cat.

Appearance: Traditionally a blue-eyed, white-coated cat with long, soft fur. The hairs are especially long on the neck, underside and tail, but less so on the rest of the body. This, and the absence of a woolly undercoat, gives the Angora a slender, bushy-tailed look that clearly distinguishes it from the heavier-coated Persian with its more rounded silhouette. The Angora kittens are slow to develop the typical adult coat, it not being fully displayed until the age of two years. Perhaps because of their hot-country homeland, the summer moult is extreme and leaves them looking almost like a short-haired breed.

History: There are three rival ideas concerning the origin of the Angora Cat. The first theory suggests that it was originally developed from the wild Pallas's Cat *(Felis manul)* by the ancient Chinese and the Tartars, and only later taken to Turkey. There is no scientific evidence to support this.

A more acceptable theory envisages an old-established Russian domestic cat developing an unusually long-haired coat as a protection against the intense winter cold. This breed, taken south to Asia Minor on board trading ships, eventually arrived in Turkey and Iran, giving rise in these two warmer regions to the Angora and Persian Cats respectively. This theory would explain the apparent anomaly of long-haired cats being named after hot countries.

An alternative theory suggests that the Angora was taken from the cold mountains of eastern Persia by Islamic invaders in the 15th century. Once in Turkey, its coat changed slightly, becoming less thick and fluffy than that of its Persian ancestors. (For details see Persian Cat.)

Whichever is true, in Turkey there were soon several colour forms of Angora Cat, each with its own title. There was, for example, a red tabby called the *sarmen* and a silver tabby called the *teku*. There was also an odd-eyed white cat with one blue eye and one amber eye, called the *Angora kedi*. In some circles, the white form became the favoured one and purists usually insist on this as the 'only true Angora colour'.

The Angora Cat is recorded as a distinct breed in Turkey as early as the 1400s, and was the first long-haired cat to be brought to Western Europe. The earliest specimens arrived in the 16th century as special gifts from the Turkish Sultans to noble families in England and France. In addition, at about the same time, it is reported that the French naturalist Nicholas Claude Fabri de Pereise brought some of these cats back to France from Turkey as novelties. It was only later, in the 17th century and especially towards the end of the 18th century, that this lithely elegant breed was joined by the even longer-coated Persian Cat.

By the 19th century, the more luxurious Persian had come to dominate the scene and the true Angora was becoming something of a rarity. Eventually, by the turn of the century, the traditional Angora Cat had been completely eclipsed by the glamorous Persian and pure Angora specimens eventually vanished from the West.

However, in the 1960s some British breeders set about recreating the delicately beautiful Angora and achieved this goal by the careful selection of Angora types from long-haired Oriental cats. The soft-coated, bushy-tailed look was soon regained, but the typical Angora head was less easily perfected. The angular, pointed face of the typical Oriental cat persisted, setting these new, 'pseudo-Angoras' apart from the true originals. The new Angoras also retained the more vocal personality of their Oriental ancestors.

Happily, although the original breed had long ago vanished from the show rings, it was not entirely extinct. A few pure lines remained in the Ankara region of Turkey and, thanks to the

One of the many early illustrations of the Angora Cat, an exquisite breed which made a tremendous impact when it first appeared in Western Europe. It was lovingly depicted as a creature of luxury by many Continental artists.

intervention of the Ankara Zoo, the true Angora was eventually rescued from oblivion. The zoo collected together a number of the surviving Turkish specimens and began a serious breeding programme with them, keeping only white cats with blue, amber or odd eyes. Some of the progeny of this programme were exported and two unrelated pairs reached North America in the 1960s to form a new breeding nucleus there. These cats and their descendants are now referred to as Turkish Angoras, to distinguish them from the reconstituted British Angoras.

The re-introduction of the true Turkish Angoras in the 1960s was due to the efforts of Walter and Leisa Grant. In 1962 they visited Ankara and, with the blessing of the Governor of the city, purchased a pair of cats from the zoo there. The male was an odd-eyed white called Yildiz and the female an amber-eyed white called Yildizcik. They were joined by a second pair, also white, but this time with the male amber-eyed and the female odd-eyed, called Yaman and Marvis, in 1966. Together, these four animals became the foundation stock for the re-introduction of the ancient breed, and in 1970 the Turkish Angora was finally accepted back into the show ring as a distinct category by the CFA in America. At about the same time, American breeders formed the Original Turkish Angora Society to consolidate the revival of this distinguished cat. In the 1970s additional cats were imported from Ankara Zoo, this time to Britain and Sweden, and the breed has since become re-established in many parts of Europe.

Personality: Terms that have been used to describe this breed include: polite, courteous, responsive, fastidious, gentle, kind, sweet, affectionate, alert, loyal and intelligent; sometimes shy and aloof, sometimes outgoing and gregarious. Graceful in movement, but unusually immobile – the ideal indoor house cat.

One of the earliest descriptions of this breed, by Sir William Jardine in 1834, reads as follows: '[Angora Cats] are frequently kept in this country as drawing-room pets, and are said to be more mild and gentle in their tempers than the common cat . . . We have not heard much in praise of their utility.'

Charles Ross, writing in 1868, provides another early evaluation of the character of this breed: 'The Cat of Angora is a very beautiful variety, with silvery hair of fine silken texture . . . they are all delicate creatures, and of gentle dispositions. Mr Wood, while staying in Paris, made the

Another early drawing of the Angora Cat, this one from a French work by J.B. Huet, *Collection des mammifères du Muséum d'Histoire Naturelle* (Paris, 1808).

The Angora Cat, one of the most ancient of all domestic breeds, having been known since at least the 15th century in Turkey. It was the first glamorous long-haired cat to reach Western Europe.

acquaintance of an Angora, which ate two plates of almond biscuits at a sitting. This breed of Cats has singular tastes; I knew one that took very kindly to gin and water, and was rather partial to curry. He also ate peas, greens and broad beans (in moderation).'

Colour Forms: The traditional Angora is the blue-eyed white. Many other colours are now acceptable. Because there are two 'Angoras' – the British and the Turkish – it is important to consider their colour forms separately. The GCCF lists the British Angora simply as the 'Angora', and ignores the Turkish Angora. The CFA ignores the British Angora and lists only the Turkish Angora.

GCCF: (British) Angora: White; Black; Chocolate; Lilac; Red Self; Cinnamon; Caramel; Fawn; Blue; Cream; Silver Tabby; Red Tabby; Brown Tabby; Tortie; Chocolate Tortie; Lilac Tortie; Cinnamon Tortie; Caramel Tortie; Fawn Tortie; Blue Tortie; Brown Spotted; Black Smoke; Colourpointed; Black Shaded; Brown Ticked Tabby.

CFA: (Turkish) Angora: White; Black; Blue; Cream; Red; Black Smoke; Blue Smoke; Classic Tabby Pattern; Mackerel Tabby Pattern; Patched Tabby Pattern; Silver Tabby; Red Tabby; Brown Tabby; Blue Tabby; Cream Tabby; Tortie; Calico; Dilute Calico; Blue-Cream; Bi-color.

Bibliography:

1898. James, R.K. *The Angora Cat: How to Breed, Train and Keep it.* James Brothers, Boston.
1911. Benavente y Martinez, J. *The Angora Cat.*

Breed Club:

The Angora Breed Club. Address: 26 Essex Road, Enfield, Middlesex, EN2 6UA, England.

Ankara Cat

Domestic Breed. An alternative name for the Angora Cat. It was most commonly used in the middle of the 19th century, but occurs occasionally in later writings. For example, Laura Lushington, who brought the first Turkish Van Cats to the West in 1955, wrote as follows in 1962: 'The Turkish people do not as a rule make a great fuss about animals, unless they serve some useful purpose. But there are two exceptions, the Ankara Cat and the Van Cat, both of which have been kept as domestic pets for hundreds of years.'

Annamese Cat

Domestic Breed. The ancient state of Annam is today part of Vietnam. The Annamese Cat has been cited as a possible ancestor of the Siamese Cat. According to one theory, mentioned by Rose Tenent in 1950, 'the Siamese cat is the result of a cross-mating between the sacred cat of Burma and the Annamese cat, the latter being imported into Siam about three centuries ago at the time of the great victory of the Siamese and Annamese peoples over the Cambodian Empire of the Kymers.' She concludes, 'I am of the opinion that this . . . theory may be the correct one.'

Apple-head Siamese Cat

Domestic Breed. The recent development of the Apple-head Siamese is an attempt by American breeders to revive the original form of the Siamese Cat. During the past century the body shape of the Siamese has become increasingly exaggerated – more and more elongated, angular and slender, with a wedge-shaped head. In recent years this process has been taken to such lengths, and the Siamese show cats have become so extreme in type, that a number of breeders have felt the time was ripe for a return to something closer to the original Siamese, known so well from early, turn-of-the-century photographs. A group was formed to promote this plan and careful breeding programmes have now achieved what has been called the 'Apple-head', or Opal Cat. A statement made by this group in 1994 reads as follows:

'The Apple-head Siamese is now being recognized as a unique national cat breed named the Opal Cat. In short, the Opal Cat is a short-haired, American-style colorpoint as beautiful as the gem that inspired its name. Its sweet face is the setting for brilliant blue eyes that blaze with the stunning iridescent glow of precious blue opals. And, like the opal gem, the Opal Cat has a

creamy lustrous coat that may be pointed in a wide range of delightful colors. Its body type is not Oriental. Rather, the Opal Cat has a body that uniquely reflects its American heritage.'

Other efforts to promote the old-style Siamese have given us cats known today by a variety of names, such as Classic Siamese, Old-fashioned Siamese, Traditional Siamese and Thai Cat. In France this type of Siamese is called the *Thaï*, and in Germany the *Thaikatze*. (For further details see Thai Cat and Traditional Siamese Cat.)

Breed Clubs:

Fanciers of the Opal Cat of the United States (FOCUS). Publishes a quarterly magazine, *The Point of Focus*. Address: 1385 Hooper Avenue, Suite 280, Toms River, NJ 08753, USA.

Traditional Cat Association. Address: 1000 Pegasus Farms Lane, Alpharetta, GA 30201, USA.

Traditional Siamese. Address: 8752 Woodsman Court, Washington, MI 48094, USA.

Archangel Cat

Domestic Breed. An early, alternative name for the Russian Blue Cat. Also referred to (in 1889) as the Archangel Blue Cat. It was given this name because it was believed that the Russian Blue Cats originally travelled west, as ships' cats, from the port of Archangel on the White Sea. (For further details see Russian Blue Cat.)

Arching the back

Feline Behaviour. If a cat feels threatened by a large dog, it pulls itself up on fully stretched legs and at the same time arches its back in the shape of an inverted 'U'. The function of this display is clearly to make the cat look as big as possible, in an attempt to convince the dog that it is confronting a daunting opponent. To understand the origin of this display it is necessary to look at what happens when cats are threatening one another.

If one cat is intensely hostile to another and feels little fear, it approaches on stiffly stretched legs with a straight back. If its rival is extremely frightened and feels no hostility, it arches its back and crouches low on the ground. In the case of the cat approached by a dog, there is both intense aggression *and* intense fear. It is this conflicting, double mood that gives rise to the special display. The cat borrows the most conspicuous element of its anger reaction – the stiff legs – and the most conspicuous element of its fear reaction – the arched back – and combines them to produce the 'enlarged cat' display. If it had borrowed the other, less conspicuous elements – the straight back of anger and the low crouch of fear – the result would have been far from impressive.

Aiding its 'transformation display' is the fact that the animal, while stretching its legs and arching its back, also erects its fur and stands broadside on to the dog. Together these four elements make up a compound display of maximum size increase. Even if the cat retreats a little, or advances towards the dog, it carefully keeps its broadside-on position, spreading its body in front of the dog like a bullfighter's cloak.

During the arched-back display the cat hisses ominously, like a snake, but this hissing turns to growling if it risks an attack. Then, when it actually lashes out at the dog, it adds an explosive 'spit' to its display. Experienced cats soon learn that the best policy when faced with a hostile dog is to go into the attack rather than run away, but it takes some nerve to do this when the dog is several times the cat's weight. The alternative of 'running for it' is much riskier, however, because once the cat is fleeing it triggers off the dog's hunting urges. To a dog, a 'fleeing object' means only one thing – food – and it is hard to shift the canine hunting mood once it has been aroused. Even if the fleeing cat halts and makes a brave stand, it has little hope, because the dog's blood is up and it goes straight for the kill, arched back or no arched back. But if the cat makes a stand right from the first moment of the encounter with the dog, it has a good chance of defeating the larger animal, simply because, by attacking it, the cat gives off none of the usual 'prey signals'. The dog, with sharp feline claws slashing at its sensitive nose, is much more likely then to beat a dignified retreat, and leave the hissing fury to its own devices. So, where dogs are concerned, the bolder the cat, the safer it is.

The action of arching the back, when in defiant mood, makes the cat look suddenly much bigger, as shown in this copper engraving of 1760, depicting a mother cat defending her kittens against attack.

Ariel

Pet Cat. An 'orange Persian' cat owned by author Carl Van Vetchen is discussed in his classic work *The Tiger in the House* (1938), where he describes its unusual love of water. Ariel would 'leap voluntarily into my warm morning tub and she particularly liked to sit in the wash-hand-bowl under the open faucet'. This cat would retrieve a catnip mouse 'as often as I would throw it' and 'used to hide spools, keys, pens, pencils and scissors under the rug'.

Arthur

Arthur, the British television star, demonstrating the paw-scooping action that made him famous. This publicity photograph was taken during a book-signing tour undertaken by Arthur in 1975 to publicize his biography.

Television Cat. Arthur was hired by Spillers, the British pet-food company in the 1960s because he could scoop his food out of a tin with his paw. Between 1966 and 1975 he appeared in 309 TV commercials. Such was Arthur's fame that, according to one report, Spillers bought him outright for £700. Contradicting this, a young actor claimed that Arthur was still his, and a bitter custody battle began in the High Court. On the first day of the court case, Arthur was missing and the young actor insisted that the animal had sought asylum in the Russian Embassy. A Russian spokesman denied this, rather angrily pointing out that the Soviets had better things to do than worry about high-earning, capitalist felines.

With Arthur still invisible, the actor was jailed for two weeks for contempt of court. The day after he went to jail, Arthur mysteriously resurfaced and was handed back to Spillers. The case dragged on for two years, with the actor claiming damages from Spillers, to the tune of £150,000. He failed in this attempt, and at last Arthur was the secure property of the pet-food company.

The cat's professional life blossomed. He moved into T-shirts and towels and other advertising campaigns. He even had his autobiography ghosted for him by author John Montgomery. After a long and successful professional career, he finally died in February 1976, just before his 17th birthday.

Ten years later, animal trainer Ann Head found a replacement for Arthur. She was inspecting the animals at the Wood Green Animal Shelter when she spotted a skinny, bedraggled white cat called Snowy. The vet had given him 48 hours to live, but Ann took him home and, nursing him day and night, carefully brought him back to full health.

It is surprising that he survived, as he was found to be suffering from malnutrition, various parasites including worms, an eye infection, ear mites, eczema and a cold. But she persevered and, two months later, fully recovered and renamed, he was making his first TV commercial. His first public appearance was in January 1987 at the Savoy Hotel in London, where he was launched as Spiller's second Arthur. Like the original Arthur, Arthur II was able to scoop food out of a tin with his paw, and also use it in other ways. In response to the command 'paw', he would place his left foot on anything near to him. Ann Head is at pains to point out that she used rewards rather than punishments in the training of Arthur II, and that he was never starved before the filming of a commercial, as some people seem to think.

Nine years after Ann Head discovered Arthur II, feeling that his long and successful career was coming to an end, she commented: 'Now the time has come for him to "put his paws up" and take it easy. There is a youngster waiting in the wings to take over the role and, by an incredible coincidence he is yet another "Snowy" from the Wood Green Animal Shelter. The dynasty lives on.'

The long saga of Arthur I and Arthur II has a remarkably close parallel in the United States, in the story of Morris I and Morris II. (See separate entry.)

Bibliography:

1970. Dudley, E. *Arthur.* London.

1975. Montgomery, J. *Arthur the Television Cat.* W.H. Allen, London.

1995. Head, A. *Arthur's World of Cats.* Lennard Publishing, Harpenden, Herts.

Asian Cats

Domestic Breeds. The term 'Asian' has been introduced to cover the group of breeds that can best be described as 'unusually coloured Burmese'. During recent years a number of specialists have created new breeds that are based on the traditional Burmese type, but which have new colouring or coat-type. Some cat societies refuse to recognize these new forms as distinct breeds and call them all 'Burmese'. Others only accept the traditional, dark brown Burmese as 'Burmese' and call the modern colour-variants by other, separate breed names. This causes some confusion for the non-specialist.

In the broadest sense, the category 'Asian Cats' includes breeds such as the Burmilla, the Burmoiré (or Asian Smoke), the Asian Tabby, the Bombay, the Tiffanie (or Asian Longhair) and the Singapura. In the narrow sense it includes only Burmese types which are Smokes or Tabbies.

Breed Clubs:

Asian Cat Club. Address: 54 Norfolk Road, Rickmansworth, Hertfordshire WD3 1LA, England.

Burmilla-Asian Association. Formed in London in 1986 to develop the Asian Cat Group. Address: The Old Post Office, Cottam, Retford, Notts., DN22 0EZ, England.

Asian Longhair Cat

Domestic Breed. The original name for the Tiffanie, or Longhair Burmese. (For details see entry for Tiffanie.)

Asian Smoke Cat

Domestic Breed. An alternative name for the Burmoiré, a British-developed member of the Asian Group of cats. It was developed from crosses between Burmillas and Burmese. The ghost tabby markings on its coat give the impression of rippling or watered silk.

Asian Tabby Cat

Domestic Breed. A member of the Asian Group. Essentially this is a Burmese with tabby markings. The pattern may be mackerel, classic (= blotched), spotted or ticked.

Asiatic Cats

Domestic Breeds. An early name for Long-haired Cats. Writing in 1876, Gorton Stables divided all domestic cats neatly into two groups: 'There are, first, the European or Western cat, a short-haired animal; and secondly, the Asiatic or Eastern cat called also Persian or Angora, according to the difference in the texture of the coat.' Two decades later, the same term was still being used: 'The Long-haired Cats, otherwise known as the Asiatic or Eastern Cats . . . ' (Huidekoper, 1895), but by the time Frances Simpson came to write the first major cat book, in 1903, it had vanished. The Simpson chapter on the subject is headed simply 'Long-haired or Persian Cats', with no reference to Asia.

Asiatic Golden Cat

Wild Feline. *(Felis temminckii)* This is an alternative name for Temminck's Cat (see separate entry). It is also sometimes referred to as the Asian Golden Cat, or simply the Golden Cat. A medium-sized cat from tropical Asia, it has a plain golden coat with markings only on the face and under the tail.

Asiatic Lion

Wild Feline. *(Panthera leo persica)* Known locally in India as Sherbabba, Singh, or Unthia-bagh. The Asiatic Lion is now a rare sub-species of *Panthera leo*. It differs only slightly from the more familiar African Lion, having a longer tail tassel, a more conspicuous elbow tuft, a longer belly-fringe, a generally thicker coat and, in the adult male, a slightly smaller mane. Recent studies indicate that the two sub-species of lion probably separated between 55,000 and 200,000 years ago.

The lion was once common throughout Asia, from the Middle East to India. It has since been exterminated by man everywhere except for one small, protected area in the south-west region

of the Kathiawar peninsula, in north-west India. There, in the Gir Forest, there is a small remnant population of about 300 animals. They have survived thanks, originally, to the efforts of the Nawab of Junagadh who, at the beginning of the 20th century, insisted that they should be properly protected. There were about 100 Asiatic Lions surviving at Gir in 1900 and further losses occurred until, in 1913, the number had shrunk to no more than 20. At this point extinction seemed certain, but the decline was reversed just in time and the population slowly began to grow. Eventually, in 1965, a Gir Wildlife Sanctuary was established in the forest, covering an area of 1,265 sq km (488 sq mi). Carefully administered, it gave the animals better protection than before, but this in turn created a new problem. With several hundred lions now living in the sanctuary, certain adult individuals started to stray into the surrounding areas and slaughter the domestic livestock there. Even the human population has been attacked and 15 people have been killed, some of them even eaten. This has naturally caused local anger and resentment and there is an ever-present risk of retaliation. The more the lions breed, the more this problem will grow, so even now the situation is unstable and the future of the Asiatic Lion remains uncertain.

The Asiatic Lion *(Panthera leo persica),* a rare and vanishing race that may soon become extinct. There are only about 500 of them left alive in the entire world today – 300 in a game reserve in India and 200 in zoos.

Fortunately there is a back-up, captive population of about 200 Asiatic Lions (to be precise, in 1988 there were 196), which could one day be used to repopulate the wild, if all else fails.

The human population explosion throughout Asia has eliminated the Asiatic Lion in the following sequence: In Israel it was exterminated in the 13th century; in Pakistan the last known lion was killed in 1842; the last wild Lion seen in India outside the Gir Forest reserve was killed in 1884; in Arabia it survived in remote corners until the early part of the 20th century; in Iraq the last two lions were captured just before 1914; and the last wild lion observed in Iran was seen in 1941.

Asiatic Steppe Cat

Wild Feline. *(Felis sylvestris ornata)* Also called the Desert Cat or the Asiatic Wild Cat. It is known locally in India as the Jhang Meno.

The common Wild Cat has three main sub-species: the European, the African and the Asiatic. They are connected by an intermediate form in the Middle East. The differences between them are very slight. The African form has a more slender body with a thinner, more pointed tail, and a lightly striped coat. The European Wild Cat has a heavier, stockier body with a thickly furred, blunt-ended tail. The Asiatic form, which is usually given the name of Asiatic Steppe Cat, tends to resort to more open, sandy plains than its cousins, seeking what shelter it can find in the scrubland and bushes near bodies of water. Perhaps connected with this different habitat, its coat pattern is different. The striping that is typical of the European and African forms is here usually broken up into brown or grey dots. The thin, tapering tail is spotted near the base and dark-ringed near the tip. In the long-haired Mongolian race, the pale coat lacks any markings at all.

In its behaviour, the Asiatic Steppe Cat differs little from its close relatives in Africa and Europe, or from the domestic cat. It is a solitary, nocturnal hunter, with small mammals – mostly rats, mice, gerbils and jerboas – making up 81 per cent of its food intake.

Size: Length of Head + Body: 50–65 cm (20–25½ in). Tail: 25–30 cm (10–12 in). Weight: 3-4 kg (6½ lb).

Distribution: Turkey, Iran, southern Russia, Afghanistan and northern India, through to Mongolia and N.W. China.

Atabi

Feline Term. Believed to be the origin of the name 'Tabby', 'Atabi' is the local name for a particular kind of silken material manufactured in Baghdad. The wavy markings of the watered silks resembled the hair pattern seen on the body of the striped tabby cat. The word 'Atabi' was itself derived from 'Atab', which was the name of the street in Baghdad inhabited by the manufacturers of these silken fabrics.

Atossa

Pet Cat. A Persian Cat immortalized by the English poet Matthew Arnold (1822–1888). In his 1882 poem about his canary, 'Matthias', he recalls the way his old cat Atossa would sit for hours, immobile, beside the bird's cage, never attempting to attack it, but never giving up hope: 'Cruel, but composed and bland, Dumb, inscrutable and grand, So Tiberius might have sat, had Tiberius been a cat.'

Auburn

Coat Colour. As a cat colour, this is rarely encountered, except in the case of the Turkish Van Cat, where it is used to describe the colour of the darker extremities.

Australian Cat

Domestic Breed. Said to 'have arisen as a mutation from the Siamese breed'. In 1946 it was already said to be 'very rare'. Its body was shaped like that of the Siamese, but its coat varied in colour. The ears were large, the nose long, the whiskers short – sometimes completely absent.' Little more appears to be known about it.

Autogrooming is the name given to the action when a cat grooms its own body (as distinct from allogrooming, when one cat grooms another). There are ten stages to the autogrooming sequence, of which this, from Howey, 1885, is No. 7.

Autogrooming

Feline Behaviour. Autogrooming, or self-grooming, is first seen in kittens when they are three weeks old. Prior to that, all grooming of their fur is done by the mother. When fully developed, the grooming sequence is as follows: (1) Lick the lips. (2) Lick the side of one paw until it is wet. (3) Rub the wet paw over the head, including ear, eye, cheek and chin. (4) Wet the other paw in the same way. (5) Rub the wet paw over that side of the head. (6) Lick front legs and shoulders. (7) Lick flanks. (8) Lick genitals. (9) Lick hind legs. (10) Lick tail from base to tip.

If at any stage during this process an obstruction is encountered – a tangled bit of fur, for example – the licking is momentarily abandoned in favour of a localized nibble with the teeth.

Then, when all is clear, the grooming sequence is resumed. Foot and claw nibbling are particularly common, removing dirt and improving the condition of the claws.

This complicated cleaning sequence differs from that seen in many other mammals. Rats and mice, for example, use the whole of their front paws for grooming their heads, whereas the cat uses only the side of the paw and part of the forearm. Also, rodents sit up on their back legs and groom with both front feet at the same time, while the feline technique is to employ each front leg alternately, resting its body on the one not in use.

Grooming is important to the cat in seven different ways:

1 It helps to keep the fur free of dirt and disease by removing foreign particles.
2 It helps to improve the insulating properties of the coat by smoothing its surface. A ruffled coat is a poor insulator, which can be a serious hazard for a cat in freezing weather.
3 It helps to protect the cat from overheating. Felines can easily suffer from high temperatures in the summer months and grooming actions become more frequent then, for a special reason. Cats do not have sweat glands all over their bodies as we do, so they cannot use sweating as a rapid method of cooling. Panting is useful, but it is not enough. The solution is to lick repeatedly at the fur and deposit on it as much saliva as possible. The evaporation of this saliva then acts in the same way as the evaporation of sweat on our skin.
4 It helps to improve vitamin intake. If a cat has been exposed to sunlight it increases its grooming even more. This is not simply because it has become hotter, but because the action of the sun on its fur produces essential vitamin D. The animal acquires this crucial additive to its diet by the licking movements of its tongue over the sun-warmed fur.
5 It helps to reinforce the cat's personal odour. If a cat has been handled by its owner, it frequently starts to groom as soon as it has been released. It wanders off, sits down and then, nearly always, begins to lick its fur. This is only partly because it needs to smooth its ruffled coat. In addition, it is weakening the human scent left on its hairs and strengthening its own odour on its body surface. Because odours are so important in the world of the cat, an overdose of human scent on its fur is disturbing and has to be rapidly corrected.
6 It helps the cat to read the scent signals of its human companions. The grooming that occurs after the animal has been handled also acts as a way of 'tasting' its owners, and gaining information about them in this way. We ourselves may not be able to smell the odour of our hands, but the cat can.
7 Finally, it helps to improve the waterproofing of the coat. The vigorous tugging of the fur so typical of a cat's self-grooming actions plays a special role in stimulating the skin glands at the base of the individual hairs. The secretions of these glands are vital to keep the fur weather-proofed, and the tugging of the cat's busy tongue steps up the waterproofing as a protection against the rain.

A black cat washing itself (1896), by the British artist Sir William Nicholson. This animal is in the act of wetting its paw, immediately prior to rubbing it over its face and head.

There is one danger inherent in this activity, especially for certain breeds of domestic cats. Moulting cats and cats with very long fur quickly accumulate a large number of hairs inside their alimentary tracts and these form hairballs which can cause obstructions. In the usual course of events, hairballs are vomited up naturally without causing any trouble, but if they grow too large they may become a serious hazard. For long-haired breeds, regular grooming by the cat's owner is particularly important to avoid this.

Balance

Feline Behaviour. Thanks to their sharp claws, cats are good climbers, and their agility is greatly enhanced by their remarkable sense of balance. This is achieved partly because of the flexibility of their bodies and partly because of sensitive movements of their long, rudder-like tails. Their refined sense of balance also explains their amazing ability to land on their feet when accidentally falling to the ground. Without this 'righting reflex' they could easily suffer from a broken back.

Careful studies have revealed how a cat manages to achieve a perfect landing. As it starts to fall, with its body upside-down, an automatic twisting reaction begins at the head end of the body. The head rotates first, until it is upright, then the front legs are brought up close to the face, ready to protect it from impact. (A blow to the cat's chin from underneath can be particularly serious.) Next, the upper part of the spine is twisted, bringing the front half of the body round in line with the head. Finally, the hind legs are bent up, so that all four limbs are now ready for touchdown and, as this happens, the cat twists the rear half of its body round to catch up with the front. Finally, as it is about to make contact, it stretches all four legs out towards the ground and arches its back, as a way of reducing the force of the impact.

While this body-twisting is taking place, the stiffened tail is rotating rapidly, acting as a counterbalancing device. All this occurs in a fraction of a second and it requires slow-motion film to analyse these rapid stages of the righting response.

In feline folklore there is a charming legend as to how the cat first acquired this ability to land on its feet. The prophet Mohammed was called to prayer at a moment when his favourite cat, Muezza, was sleeping on the sleeve of his robe. Rather than disturb the animal, he cut off the sleeve and left. When he returned, the cat bowed to him in appreciation of his act of kindness and as a reward for this politeness, Mohammed bestowed on the cat the gift of always being able to fall on its feet.

B

Bald Cat

Domestic Breed. A name given to hairless cats in the 1960s, before the arrival of the Sphynx Cat. Professor Étienne Letard of the French National Veterinary College at Alfort became interested in the biology of these cats at one stage, but they never became popular with pedigree cat breeders in France and soon disappeared. It was not until the Sphynx Cat appeared in Canada in 1966 that a breed of naked cat was taken seriously.

Balinese Cat

Domestic Breed. The long-haired version of the Siamese Cat. In the United States some colour forms (see below) are called Javanese Cats. When the breed first appeared it was given the name 'Long-haired Siamese' but this was unpopular with Siamese breeders and a new name was sought. 'Balinese' was selected for two reasons. First, Bali is close to Siam (Thailand) and secondly the elegant movements of the cats were thought to be reminiscent of Balinese dancers. In Australia it is also known as the Oriental Longhair. In France it is the *Balinais;* in Germany the *Balinesen*.

Appearance: Described as 'slim and dainty', it has been called 'the fashion model of the cat world'. The elongated, angular body of this breed, its colourpointed coat pattern and its vivid blue eyes are identical to those of the Siamese, the only difference being that the Balinese has a soft, silky, medium-long coat with a plumed tail.

History: The Balinese began as an accident. Siamese kittens started to appear with much longer fur than usual. At first they were looked upon as unfortunate oddities and were discarded from breeding programmes, until a Californian breeder decided to turn a negative into a positive and develop them as a distinct new breed. Marion Dorset is said to have first taken an interest in them as early as the 1940s and by the mid-1950s she had developed a planned breeding programme with them. In the early 1960s she was joined in this venture by a New York breeder, Helen Smith, and it was she who suggested changing the name to Balinese. Other breeders were soon attracted and in 1968 they formed a club called 'The Balinese Breeders and Fans International'. They also launched a magazine, *Speaking Balinese.* By the end of the decade the

A Lilac Point Balinese Cat. When this elegant breed first appeared, it was referred to simply as the 'Long-haired Siamese', but there were strong objections to this from Siamese breeders and it was eventually renamed.

new breed had achieved championship status with all the American cat societies. In the 1970s it had spread to Europe and had also gained championship status there by the 1980s.

There are two theories as to how the long coat came to appear in pure-bred Siamese stock. One sees it as a spontaneous mutation, while the other regards it as the delayed result of the occasional introduction of Angoras into Siamese lines, which apparently happened in England back in the 1920s.

Note: The Balinese should not be confused with the Himalayan. Both could loosely be described as 'Long-haired Siamese', but this is misleading. They are very different animals. The Himalayan is essentially a modified Persian, with Siamese colourpoints, whereas the Balinese is a modified Siamese, with a long coat.

Personality: The following terms have been used to describe this breed: extrovert and lively throughout life. Intelligent, eager, enthusiastic, active, athletic, acrobatic, expressive, regal, graceful, loyal, friendly, warm, curious and affectionate. Like their Siamese ancestors, they are vocally noisy.

Colour Forms: In the United States, Seal, Chocolate, Blue and Lilac Point are the only colours permitted. Other colours, such as Red, Tortie and Lynx (Tabby) Point, are referred to as Javanese. In the UK this separation is not made, all the colours being included in the breed.

GCCF: Seal Point; Blue Point; Chocolate Point; Lilac Point; Red Point; Seal Tortie Point; Cream Point; Blue Tortie Point; Chocolate Tortie Point; Lilac Tortie Point; Seal Tabby Point; Blue Tabby Point; Chocolate Tabby Point; Lilac Tabby Point; Red Tabby Point; Seal Tortie Tabby Point; Cream Tabby Point; Blue Tortie Tabby Point; Chocolate Tortie Tabby Point; Lilac Tortie Tabby Point.

CFA: Seal Point; Chocolate Point; Blue Point; Lilac Point.

Breed Clubs:

American Balinese Association. Address: 29 Harvest Lane, West Hartford, CT 06117, USA.

Balinese and Siamese Cat Club. Address: Holly Tree Cottage, Clacton Road, Horsley Cross, Manningtree, Essex, CO11 2NR, England.

Balinese and Siamese Cat Society. Address: Lapislazuli, 10 Osborne Road, Westcliff-on-Sea, Essex, SS0 7DW, England.

Balinese Cat Society. Issues a magazine. Address: 5, Lamaleach Drive, Freckleton, Preston, Lancs., PR4 1AJ, England.

Banned Breeds

Domestic Breeds. Controversial bureaucratic interference in the affairs of the pedigree cat world has recently surfaced in new recommendations made by the Council of Europe. As part of their Multi-Lateral Convention for the Protection of Pet Animals, they are suggesting the future banning of breeds such as: (1) the Manx; (2) the Scottish Fold; (3) the Sphynx; (4) blue-eyed white cats.

Britain has rejected these suggestions, but in January 1995 the German government did respond positively and introduced laws banning these breeds. It is also considering adding the most extreme forms of Persian and Siamese Cats to the prohibited list. It remains to be seen whether any of the other 34 European member states will follow suit.

Whatever one may feel about the appearance of some of the more extreme and unusual breeds, there is no justification for this type of government intervention unless it can be proved beyond doubt that the animals concerned are suffering undue pain or health risks. To ban a breed simply because, to bureaucrats, it looks 'odd' is unjustified. (See Abnormal Breeds.)

Barbary Lion

Wild Feline. The Barbary Lion was a sub-species *(Panthera leo leo)* in which the male possessed an unusually large, dark mane, extending from the head, neck and chest, right down to the belly. It was once common across the whole of North Africa, from Egypt to Morocco. Thanks to human intervention, it is now extinct.

As the Arab communities north of the Sahara began to increase, the indigenous lion population became a nuisance. Livestock was attacked and eaten and eventually a reward was offered for every lion destroyed. This officially encouraged killing continued for many years until the great Barbary Lion was becoming rare everywhere in its wide range.

In Libya, the last lion was exterminated as early as 1700. In Egypt, a few managed to cling on in the most remote areas until near the end of the 18th century. In Tunisia the last one was despatched in 1891. In Algeria it was reported to be nearing extinction by the beginning of the 20th century. The last Algerian lion was killed in 1912.

The last one to be seen alive anywhere in the world was shot by a hunter in Morocco in 1920. Since then, there has been no trace.

BARDOT, BRIGITTE

CAT OWNER. When she retired from film-making, the French actress Brigitte Bardot devoted herself to animal welfare. In 1986 she established the Bardot Foundation in St Tropez. The following year she sold her jewellery and other personal possessions to raise the funds necessary for her welfare work. In her own home she gives shelter to 60 neutered stray cats that are allowed to sleep with her at night.

BASTET

LEGENDARY CAT. Bastet was a sacred cat goddess of ancient Egypt. Her name means literally 'She of the City of Bast'.

Cats had played several roles in the ancient civilization of Egypt (see Egyptian Cats), and had been domesticated for many centuries before the cult of the friendly, protective goddess Bastet started to grow and flourish. An earlier feline goddess had been far from friendly. She was a fierce, lion-headed, war-goddess called Sekhmet. Blood-thirsty and terrifying, she bore no relation to the increasingly important, small domesticated cat that was ridding Egypt of its detested rodent pests. With the rise of this valued companion cat, something had to change. A new, more helpful goddess was needed. Around 1500 BC, this began to happen. Sekhmet was joined by the new goddess Bastet and they were seen as a contrasting pair. Together they represented the two faces of the sun: Sekhmet was the cruel, searing heat of the destructive sun, while Bastet was the warming, life-giving aspect of the sun.

As the domestic cat became more and more respected (and the threat of attack from wild lions became less and less likely), Bastet gradually began to dominate as the major feline deity. The Egyptians cleverly explained away this shift of emphasis in a legendary tale, recorded on an ancient papyrus: '[The goddess] had fled in a temper to the Nubian desert where she hid in the shape of a lioness. Her father, who needed her presence to protect him against his enemies, sent Onuris and Thoth to bring her back to Egypt. The messengers of the Sun managed to persuade her to return. On the way home she drowned her anger by bathing in the sacred waters of Philae on the southern border of Egypt, calmly adopting the form of a cat. She sailed down the Nile acclaimed by the people on the banks, until she came to Bubastis, which became a holy place where periodic feasts were held in her honour.'

THE ANCIENT EGYPTIANS sought to gain favour with the cat goddess Bastet by offering her bronze effigies of herself and also mummified cats.

This story neatly converted the angry old lion-goddess into a friendly new cat-goddess, and the Cult of the Cat was under way. Bubastis, a town about 60 km (37 miles) north-east of Cairo, became the headquarters of this cult and a huge temple was built there to honour Bastet. (Sadly, little of this red granite temple survives today.)

At first, Bastet was only a local deity, but her fame spread until she was known and revered far and wide. Each year vast crowds descended on the town for the annual celebrations. These became the most popular, the bawdiest and the most drunken in all of Egypt. Writing in the fifth century BC, Herodotus reported that, as the crowds converged on Bubastis, 'men and women embark together, and great numbers of both sexes in every barge'. They made music, playing castanets and flutes and clapping their hands to the sound. Whenever they came near to a town, on their way to the festival, they would stop the barge and 'shout and scoff at the

The two most popular images of Bastet show either a cat sitting up on its haunches (*left*) or a standing cat-headed woman (*right*).

women of the place; some dance, others stand up and pull up their clothes; this they do at every town by the riverside.' This hint at ribald sexual exposure reflects the fecundity aspect of the cat goddess.

It is thought that the main attraction of Bastet's religious festivals was that they were essentially an excuse for drunken, mass orgies. According to Herodotus, 'more wine is consumed at this festival than in all the rest of the year' and this appealing form of religious ceremony attracted men and women 'to the number of seven hundred thousand'. Although this figure is undoubtedly a wild exaggeration, it is clear that Bastet was by far the most popular deity ever known in ancient Egypt, and it is not surprising that literally thousands of small bronze images of her, in the shape of a sitting cat, were found among the rubble of the temple ruins.

The cult of Bastet lasted for over a thousand years, during which time she offered an impressive range of protections to her followers, including protection in childbirth, against illness, against infertility, and against all bodily dangers especially from poisonous animals. She protected children, especially the newborn, and she was also the goddess of pleasure, music and dance. With these valuable qualities it is hardly surprising that her popularity was so great.

Apart from offering Bastet small bronze effigies of herself, people also took mummified cats to the festivals to gain favour with the goddess by showing their reverence for their dead feline pets. At first this appears to have been a genuine reverence, but as time passed it became more cynical. Dead pet cats were not always conveniently available, so they had to be supplied. What is more, they had to be supplied in huge numbers to satisfy the growing demand. To answer this demand, the priesthood began a lucrative trade in ready-made cat mummies. The extent of this trade is known from the vast scale of the cat cemeteries that have been unearthed in Egypt. Literally millions of cats were mummified and buried in praise of the cat goddess, Bastet. Careful X-ray examination of some of these has revealed that their deaths had often been 'encouraged'. Many were very young adult cats and had had their necks neatly broken. This clearly illustrates one of the dangers of becoming a symbolic animal – you end up as more of a revered abstract generality than as a much loved individual pet. (See also Mummified Cats and Egyptian Cats.)

Ba-tou

Pet Cat. An African wildcat adopted by the French novelist Colette. She wrote about the animal in her 1922 story *La Maison de Claudine*, where she commented that, although domestic cats are by nature secretive, 'Ba-tou hid nothing'. Eventually, after she found the cat caressing a puppy in a suggestively predatory manner, she accepted the inevitable and had Ba-tou despatched to the zoo. (See also entry for Colette.)

Baudelaire, Charles

Cat Owner. The French poet's obsession with cats was so great that he frequently caused minor scandals on occasions when he paid more attention to the animals than to his human companions. Even his friends referred to his reactions to cats as 'startling and excessive', and he was ridiculed in the press. One journalist complained:

'It has become the fashion in the society formed by Baudelaire and his companions to make too much of cats . . . Baudelaire, going for the first time to a house, and on business, is uneasy and restless until he has seen the household cat. But when he sees it he takes it up, kisses and strokes it, and is so completely occupied with it that he makes no answer to anything that is said to him. People stare at this breach of good manners, but he is a man of letters, an oddity, and the lady of the house henceforth regards him with curiosity.'

So great was the poet's affinity for cats that he himself was once described as being 'a voluptuous wheedling cat, with velvety manners'.

Bay Cat (1)

Wild Feline. *(Felis badia)* Also known as the Bornean Bay Cat or the Bornean Red Cat. A rare species, which gains its name from its reddish-brown, chestnut colour. It is confined entirely to Borneo. The coat is uniformly coloured, although slightly paler on the underside. There are only a few weak markings on the legs and lower parts. There are also a few streaks and dark lines on the face, and the backs of the rounded ears are dark brown. It has a short, rounded head and is in most respects a miniature form of the closely related Temminck's Cat.

The Bay Cat *(Felis badia)* from Borneo is the least-known feline in the world and is the only wild species that has never been photographed. This artist's impression, based on a few skins, is as close as we can get to guessing its appearance.

Little is known of this species, with the result that it is usually recorded as being extremely rare. The alternative, of course, is that it is extremely wary and highly efficient at avoiding human investigation. According to one report, it lives only in dense jungle. According to another, it prefers rocky outcrops on the edges of forest. It appears to be a ground-dwelling cat, hunting small mammals, including monkeys, and various birds. Known only from a few museum specimens and the occasional sighting, it has apparently never been filmed, photographed, or captured alive. Of all the species of wild cats, this one remains the most elusive.

Size: Length of Head + Body: 50–60 cm (20–23½ in). Tail: 35–40 cm (14–16 in). Weight: 2–3 kg (4½–6½ lb).

Distribution: Borneo.

Bay Cat (2)

Wild Feline. An early, alternative name for the Asiatic Golden Cat, or Temminck's Cat *(Felis temminckii)*. It is no longer used for this cat because of confusion with the exclusively Bornean species of Bay Cat *(Felis badia)* (see above).

Bay Lynx

Wild Feline. An alternative name, now little used, for the American Bobcat *(Lynx rufa)*. (For details see Bobcat.)

Beckoning Cat

Talismanic Cat. The image of a cat with one paw raised in a beckoning movement is a popular Japanese talisman or lucky charm. It is known as the *maneki-neko*. If worn on the body it brings good luck and also wards off bad luck. Images of Beckoning Cats tied around the waist are said to protect the wearer from pain and ill-health. If placed at the entrance of a building, a Beckoning Cat made of clay, wood, or papier-mâché protects the occupants in a similar way. In the absence of an image, even the written symbol for the cat is alone considered to have protective value.

The famous Japanese Beckoning Cat, or maneki-neko, is thought to bring good luck and is often encountered today in Japanese shops. As a protective talisman it appears in many forms, but always with one paw raised.

The legend of the origin of the Beckoning Cat is as follows: The temple at *Gotoku-ji* was a very poor one. Although the monks were starving, they shared their food with their pet cat. One day the cat was sitting by the side of the road outside the temple, when a group of rich Samurai rode up. The cat beckoned to them and they followed it into the temple. Once inside, heavy rain forced them to shelter there and they passed the time learning about the Buddhist philosophy. Later, one of the Samurai returned to take religious instruction and eventually endowed the temple with a large estate. His family were buried there and near their tombs a small cat-shrine was built to the memory of the Beckoning Cat.

Today the temple has been swallowed up by the western suburbs of Tokyo, but it remains a popular centre for those who wish to pray for their cats, and the cat-shrine is regularly festooned with offerings.

The cat breed known as the Japanese Bobtail is now closely identified with the legendary Beckoning Cat, and it is thought that to own one will bring good luck.

A popular embellishment of the legend adds a more dramatic moment to the Samurai incident. When the terrible rainstorm arrived it brought lightning with it. A bolt of lightning struck the ground exactly where the Samurai had been standing, just before they followed the cat into the temple. The cat therefore saved their lives, for which they were immensely grateful.

Some authors record a completely different legend to explain the popularity of the Beckoning Cat. According to this tale, a famous woman in Yoshiwara was about to be attacked by a dangerous snake. Her favourite cat saw the danger and tried to warn her, but was killed in the attempt. The woman had an effigy of this cat carved in wood, to commemorate its brave deed, and copies of this carving then became popular as lucky charms, to protect their owners from danger.

BEERBOHM

PET CAT. Beerbohm was London's longest-serving theatre cat. For 20 years he was the resident mouser at the Globe Theatre (now renamed the Gielgud) in London's West End and became a favourite with many of the stars who appeared there. Occasionally he would wander on stage during a play, to the delight of the audience and the dismay of the performers, who were always upstaged by his entrance.

A well-built tabby cat, he was named after Herbert Beerbohm Tree, the famous actor–manager at Her Majesty's Theatre. It was there that he was born and reared before being transferred to mousing duties at the Globe in the mid-1970s. He survived a near-fatal road accident to become famous enough to have his picture hung in the theatre's lobby. He had a close relationship with Fleur, an elegant theatrical mouser who worked at the nearby Lyric Theatre. Their vocalizations often filled the night air. He died in March 1995, after retiring to Kent with the theatre's carpenter.

BEHAVIOUR

FELINE BEHAVIOUR. The pioneer studies of cat behaviour were carried out after World War II by the German ethologist Paul Leyhausen. The results of his researches were first published in Germany in 1956 and, after a long delay, were eventually translated into English in 1979. Since then there have been many academic investigations into the behaviour of both wild and domestic cats and reports of these are to be found in the various scientific journals. There have also been a number of general books published on the subject in recent years, including those listed in the following bibliography.

Bibliography:

1956. Leyhausen, P. *Verhaltensstudien an Katzen.* Paul Parey, Berlin.

1977. Beadle, M. *The Cat: History, Biology and Behaviour.* Collins Harvill, London.

1974. Fox, M.W. *Understanding Your Cat.* Coward, McCann, New York.

1977. Corey, P. *Do Cats Think?* Castle, New Jersey.

1977. Manolson, F. *The Language of Your Cat.* Quarto, London.

1978. Moyes, P. *How to Talk to Your Cat.* Arthur Barker, London.

1978. Sautter, J & Glover, J.A. *Behavior, Development and Training of the Cat.* Arco, New York.

1979. Baerends, J.M. & Baernends-Van Roon, G.P. *The Morphogenesis of the Behaviour of the Domestic Cat.* North-Holland Publishing, Amsterdam.

1979. Leyhausen, P. *Cat Behavior: The Predatory and Social Behavior of Domestic and Wild Cats.* Garland STPM Press, New York.

1982. Allaby, M. & Crawford, P. *Curious Cats.* Michael Joseph, London.

1983. Tabor, R. *The Wildlife of the Domestic Cat.* Arrow Books, London.

1985. Allaby. M. & Burton, J. *Nine Lives: A Year in the Life of a Cat Family.* Ebury Press, London.

1986. Morris, D. *Catwatching.* Jonathan Cape, London.

1987. Milani, M. M. *The Body Language and Emotion of Cats.* William Morrow, New York.

1987. Morris, D. *Catlore.* Jonathan Cape, London.

1988. Turner, D.C. & Bateson, P. (Editors). *The Domestic Cat: the Biology of its Behaviour.* Cambridge University Press, Cambridge.

1990. Neville, P.F. *Cat Behaviour Explained.* Parragon, London.

1990. Neville, P.F. *Do Cats Need Shrinks?* Sidgwick & Jackson, London. (Despite different titles, this and the previous book have the same text.)

1991. Fogle, B. *The Cat's Mind: Understanding Your Cat's Behaviour.* Pelham Books, London.

1992. Bradshaw, J.W.S. *The Behaviour of the Domestic Cat.* CAB International, Wallingford, Oxon.

1993. MacDonald, M. *The Cat Psychologist.* Robson Books, London.

1994. Morris, D. *Illustrated Catwatching.* Ebury Press, London.

1994. Pirinçci, A. & Degen, R. *Cat Sense: Inside the Feline Mind*. Fourth Estate, London.
1994. Thomas, E.M. *The Tribe of Tiger*. Simon & Schuster, London.
1995. Tabor, R. *Understanding Cats*. David & Charles, Newton Abbot.

See also separate entries for the following behaviour topics: allogrooming, arching the back, autogrooming, balance, birth, claw-stropping, climbing, drinking, ear signals, earthquakes, ESP, eye signals, faeces, fighting, flehmen, food preparation, food rejection, grass-eating, greeting, grooming, hissing, homing, hunting, maternal care, mating, milk-treading, music, nest-moving, paternal care, play, purring, repellents, sleep, sociability, spraying, staring, stroking, suckling, tail signals, teeth-chattering, territory, voice, walks, weaning, and wool-sucking.

Belling the Cat

Folk-tale. The mice meet to discuss how to rid themselves of the cat. After a long debate they decide to tie a bell around the cat's neck, so that they can hear it approaching. The only difficulty is how to put the bell in place. This ancient folk-tale is known from regions as widely separated as Estonia, Italy, Finland and the United States. The phrase 'belling the cat' is widely used to imply that an offered solution is impossible.

An engraving depicting the ancient folk-tale about the mice who wish to 'bell the cat'.

Bengal Cat (1)

Domestic Breed. Originally christened the 'Leopardette' and referred to by some authors as the 'Bengali'. It originated from a cross between a wild Asian Leopard Cat *(Felis bengalensis)* and a domestic cat. It is therefore a hybrid cat, and one would expect all the offspring to be infertile. Surprisingly, although the first male offspring did prove to be infertile, the females did not, and it was possible to use them in a planned breeding programme to develop the new breed.

Appearance: A large cat for a domestic breed, with the females weighing 4.5-5.5 kg (10-12 lb) and the males as much as 10 kg (22 lb). It has a powerful, muscular body with high hindquarters, large feet and a characteristically spotted coat. Even the belly is spotted. The black spots are usually solid, but occasionally they appear as dark rosettes. The tail-tip is black. The main difference between the coat of the wild cat and this new domestic hybrid is found on the ear and the tail. The ear of the domestic animal lacks the vivid white patch ringed with black that is seen in the wild ancestor, and the domestic tail lacks the wild cat spotting.

History: It is believed that, over the centuries, there have been many matings between wild Leopard Cats in tropical Asia and the domestic cats taken to that region. But none of these hybrids were ever kept and developed as a special breed. Then, in 1963 an American geneticist, Mrs Jean Sugden of Yuma, Arizona, crossed a female Leopard Cat, which she had obtained from a pet shop in the late 1950s, with a black short-haired domestic male. A female offspring from this mating, called Kinkin, was then bred back to its wild father and this resulted in some plain and some spotted offspring. This could have been the start of a new, spotted breed, but the project was abandoned when Mrs Sugden was widowed.

Then, in the late 1970s, Dr Willard Centerwall, a geneticist working at the University of California, began a breeding programme that involved crossing Leopard Cats with short-haired domestic cats as part of a study of feline leukemia. Jean Sugden, now Mrs Jean Mill following her remarriage, and living in Covina, near Los Angeles, acquired eight female hybrids from Dr Centerwall in 1981 and used these as the foundation stock for a new Bengal Cat project. As before, it was her aim to combine the markings of a wild Leopard Cat with the friendly temperament of a tame domestic cat. The female hybrids were mated with a red feral domestic cat that had been found living rough in the rhinoceros enclosure of Delhi Zoo, and a brown spotted tabby found in a Los Angeles cat shelter. From these unlikely beginnings, the new breed of domesticated Bengal Cats was developed.

Several other American breeders were also active, and one in particular, Dr Gregg Kent, was successful in producing crosses between a male Leopard Cat and a female Egyptian Mau. Other domestic breeds used from time to time include the Ocicat, the Abyssinian, the Bombay and the British Shorthair.

B

BENGAL CAT (1)

THE NEW BREED called the Bengal Cat is claimed to have originated as a cross between a wild Asian Leopard Cat *(Felis bengalensis)* and a domestic cat. It is a remarkably active cat with a wonderfully spotted coat.

In 1983 TICA accepted the domesticated Bengal Cat for registration as a new breed and it was first exhibited at cat shows in 1984–1985. It achieved National Championship status in 1990–1991.

By 1989 there were estimated to be about 200 Bengal Cats in existence. In the early 1990s some were imported into Britain, where their value was put at £2,500 (about $3,750) each, making them the most expensive domestic cats in the country at that time. (One British owner, who spent £100,000 [about $150,000] assembling his family of Bengals, claimed to have refused an offer of £12,000 [about $18,000] for one particular animal). Since then, with increased interest and further breeding, the numbers have risen dramatically and the initial high values have fallen. There are now thought to be as many as 500 in Britain and, according to a TICA estimate in 1995, there are at least 9,000 domestic Bengal Cats registered with cat clubs worldwide today.

Personality: Terms used to describe this breed include: intelligent, agile, alert, active, athletic, cunning, curious, busy, powerful, determined, outgoing, social, loving, affectionate, confident and independent. They are fond of water and have been known to jump into bathtubs to join their owners. They also love climbing and indulge in endless bouts of play-hunting. Their vocalizations differ from the ordinary domestic cat, containing several 'wild' elements.

Colour Forms: Leopard; Marble; Snow Leopard; Snow Marble; Sorrel (= Golden); Mink.

Bibliography:

1991. Johnson, G. *Getting to Know the Bengal Cat.* Gogees Cattery, Greenwell Springs, Los Angeles.

1995. Rice, D. *Bengal Cats. A Complete Pet Owner's Guide.* Barron's, Hauppauge, New York.

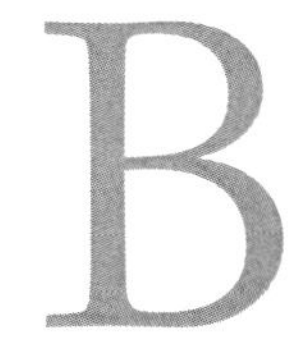

1995. Edwards, A. 'The Bengal Cat'. in: *All About Cats.* December 1995, p.17-23.
Mill, J. *History of the Bengal Cat.* Wildom Quarterly.
Maggitti, P. *The Bengal.* Cats Magazine.

Breed Clubs:

Several breed clubs already exist for the Bengal Cat, including:

Authentic Bengal Cat Club (ABC). Publishes a bi-monthly newsletter. Address: P.O. Box 1653, Roseburg, OR 97470, USA.

Bengal Breeders Alliance. Address: P.O. Box 6028, Great Falls, MT 59406, USA; or P.O. Box 2387, Park City, UT 84060, USA.

Bengal Cat Club. Address: Dovecote House, 1 Thornton Avenue, Warsash, Southampton, Hampshire, SO31 9FL, England.

Bengal Cat Club of Great Britain. Address: 15 Princes Road, Dartford, Kent, DAB 3HJ, England.

Ocicat and Bengal Cat Cub. Address: The Braes, 160 Hermitage Road, Woking, Surrey, England.

The International Bengal Cat Society (TIBCS). Publishes a bi-monthly newsletter, the *Bengal Bulletin.* Address: P.O. Box 403, Powell, OH, 43065-0403, USA; or 19726 E. Colimar Rd., Box 123, Rowlands Height, CA 91748, USA.

Bengal Cat (2)

Wild Feline. This is an alternative name for the Leopard Cat *(Felis bengalensis).* The name was given to this species of small, spotted cat because the very first specimen to be examined scientifically was found swimming in the Bay of Bengal, but when it was later discovered that its geographical range extends from Siberia to the Philippines, the Bengal title was dropped. Now, today, with a new domestic breed going by the same name, the term Bengal Cat for this species is even more unsuitable. (See Leopard Cat for details.)

Berkshire Brown Cat

Domestic Breed. An alternative name for the Havana, derived from the geographical location of the 1952 foundation stock, which first appeared in England at Reading in Berkshire. It was rejected at an early date.

Bi-colour

Coat Pattern. In a general sense, any cat with a boldly patched coat of two colours is a Bi-colour Cat, but in practice the term is restricted to those that show a pattern of white plus another colour; for example: white and black, white and blue, white and orange, or white and cream. Most of the white colouring appears on the lower surfaces of the cat and there is typically a 'two-tone' face.

Such patterns are most common in non-pedigree cats such as household pets or ferals, but they are also accepted in some pedigree breeds. In earlier days, this acceptance was limited because it was felt that a bi-colour coat made a pure-bred animal look like a 'moggie'. The prejudice was overcome only if the coat pattern was attractively balanced in a special way. This might involve symmetry of markings, distribution of colour, or ratio of white to colour. For example, the American Cat Fanciers' Association requires that the white areas of the coat must amount to between one-third and one-half of the overall surface, and the coloured portion from two-thirds to one-half.

In earlier days any cat exhibiting a bold black and white coat pattern was referred to as a 'Magpie Cat'. In the United States, Bi-colour (spelt Bi-color) Cats are sometimes called 'Parti-colored Cats'. The terms 'Piebald' and 'Pied', commonly used with other animals, are rarely employed when referring to the coat patterns of cats.

Championship status for Bi-colour Cats was not gained until 1966. After a few years it was felt that the official standards set for the bi-colour pattern were too strict (they demanded perfect symmetry of markings, for example) and, in 1971, they were relaxed.

This coat pattern occurs in both short and long-haired versions, and in the following breeds: American Shorthair, British Shorthair, Cornish Rex, Cymric, Devon Rex, European Shorthair, Exotic Shorthair, Japanese Bobtail, Maine Coon, Manx, Persian and Scottish Fold.

Birman Cat

Domestic Breed. An ancient Burmese breed looking rather like a heavily built, long-haired Siamese, but with a unique paw-colouring. Also known as 'The Sacred Cat of Burma'. In France, where it has its strongest following, it is known as the 'Burman', or the *Chat Sacré de Birmanie.* In Germany it is called the *Birmakatze;* in Holland the *Heilige Birmann.* This breed has no connection with the Burmese Cat.

Appearance: The diagnostic feature of this breed is its pure white paws, giving the impression that it is wearing white gloves. The rest of the long, silky coat is essentially golden-fawn in colour, with the addition of the dark points typical of a Siamese. It is the combination of this dark-pointed pattern with the white paw colour that gives the breed its extraordinary, kid-gloved appearance. The gene that causes the white markings obviously clashes with the typical 'Siamese' colouring and overrides it, so that the darkening of the legs has to stop short of the paws, creating a sharp margin. The eyes are a vivid blue, again like the Siamese. The body, however, is long and stocky, with short, powerful legs and a large rounded head.

In the cat show world, the white front paws are referred to as 'gloves' and the back paws as 'socks'. The white markings underneath the back paws are called 'gauntlets'.

Legendary History: The legend of the Birman tells the story of the hundred pure white cats with yellow eyes who were the guardians of the sacred Khmer temple at Lao-Tsun on the side of Mount Lugh in Burma, many centuries ago, before the time of Buddha. The temple housed a golden image of the blue-eyed goddess called Tsun-Kyan-Kse, who was able to order the reincarnation of priests in the bodies of holy animals. Once the soul of a priest had been transferred to the body of one of the sacred cats it was then possible for it to pass on from the innocent feline to a heavenly state in the afterlife. In other words, for the priests, the cats were seen as the spiritual pathway to paradise, which explains why they were so carefully protected.

The Birman Cat, also known as the Sacred Cat of Burma, has a mysterious, controversial origin, but nobody can deny that it is one of the most beautifully marked of all domestic cats.

The high priest, Mun-Ha, had a favourite cat known as Sinh. One day they were sitting together in front of the idol when the temple was attacked by raiders from Siam. Elderly Mun-Ha suffered a heart attack as he prayed. Sinh reacted by placing his paws on the body of the dying priest. As he did so, he was facing the golden, blue-eyed idol and in the moment of his master's death he was transformed, his eyes turning blue and his fur golden. Then the extremities of his body darkened to the colour of the earth, except for his paws which, where they were in contact with his master's snowy white hair, retained their original, pure white colouring. As these changes occurred, the soul of the dead priest passed into Sinh's body.

Witnessing this amazing metamorphosis, the other priests sprung into action and drove their attackers from the temple. Sinh never ate again and died a few days later, dutifully taking his master's soul to paradise. The other cats then reappeared in the temple, and it was soon obvious that every one of them had changed into the new, sacred colours – golden fur with dark points, white paws and blue eyes. They encircled a young priest called Lioa, indicating that he was chosen to become the new high priest. From that day onward the Sacred Cats of Burma retained their colouring and the Birman breed was fixed for all time.

Factual History: The truth about the origin of this breed is difficult to ascertain. If a colony of long-haired white cats really did exist in the ancient temple, the chances are that it was the sudden arrival of a virile Siamese Cat that caused the transformation rather than any supernatural occurrence.

Whatever their ancient origin, it remains to explain their recent history – how they came to be in the hands of French breeders just after the end of World War I. There are four different versions of this story:

1 In 1898 there was a large colony of these cats living in the Burmese temple of Lao-Tsun, where they were revered and cared for by the priests. There was a Brahmin invasion in the region and an English Officer by the name of The Hon. Russell Gordon, who had been active locally in the Third Burmese War in 1885, came to the rescue of the priests and saved them from certain massacre. He was received at the temple, situated east of Lake Incaougji, between Magaoung and Sembo, where the Lama-kittah (the head priest) showed him the sacred cats and presented him with a plaque depicting one of them at the feet of a bizarre deity, whose eyes were made of two long sapphires. As a result of his actions, he was later to be presented with a pair of the sacred cats, which were sent to France.

2 There is a variation of this tale, as follows: There was a rebellion in the region of the Lao-Tsun temple in 1916. Two Europeans, a British officer, Major Gordon Russell, and a Frenchman called Auguste Pavie, came to the aid of the priests during this crisis and helped some of them to flee to the mountains of Tibet. They took some of their sacred cats with them to perpetuate the breed and established a new temple of Lao-Tsun. The holy men were later to show their gratitude. In 1919 they sent a pair of their precious cats to France as a special gift.

On the surface, either of these stories sounds plausible enough, but on close examination they have many flaws and appear to be as fictitious as the original, legendary tale.

First, the Hon. Russell Gordon did not exist. According to Brian Vesey-Fitzgerald, Vice-president of the National Cat Club, writing in 1969, neither of the noble families to which he could have belonged had ever heard of him. Nor does he appear in any of the appropriate works of reference listing 'Honourables'. But supposing his name was, in reality, 'Russell, Gordon'? Could he have been the Hon. Gordon Russell? Apparently not. Once again, the noble families of that surname knew nothing of him. Supposing, then, that he was not an 'Hon.', but simply a Major? Unfortunately, neither a Major Russell Gordon, nor a Major Gordon Russell appears in any Army List for the period.

Not only is the Birman's saviour a mystery figure, but the Brahmin invasion is also in doubt. Vesey-Fitzgerald will have none of it: 'There could not . . . have been a Brahmin invasion of Burma. A Brahmin is a member of a Hindu priestly caste: and Burma and India were united under British rule. It would be better if the "Hon. Russell Gordon" and his fairy tales were forgotten.' In addition, the large discrepancies in the dates in the two versions of the 'attacked temple' story do not exactly enhance their reliability.

3 An alternative version of how these cats came to the West suggests that, in reality, an American millionaire travelling in the Far East – the name of Vanderbilt is mentioned – managed to purchase two Birmans in 1918, by bribing a disloyal temple servant to release them against the wishes of the priests. If the sacred temple cats were thought to harbour the souls of departed brethren, a reluctance to disposing of them as gifts would not be surprising.

A slight weakness in this story is that, if an American millionaire was involved, one would have expected the first exported Birman cats to end up in the United States, when in reality they arrived in France. According to one rumour, Mr Vanderbilt sent them to a Mme Thadde Hadisch in Nice.

Once we reach the stage in these three stories where the pair of sacred cats is on the high seas, heading for France, all three versions begin to agree with one another. In each case, the pair of 'founding cats' is recorded as consisting of a male called Madalpour and a female called Sita. The male is said to have died during the long journey, but the female was more resilient and managed to survive. By a stroke of luck, she was pregnant and, on arrival, produced a litter in which there was one perfectly marked female kitten that was given the name of Poupée. Poupée was then bred either to a Persian or a Siamese, and the modern history of the Birman Cat began.

4 All three of the foregoing 'histories' of the Birman Cat have been questioned by certain authorities. They suspect that, not only the fanciful legend of Mun-Ha, but the whole Burma story is a complete fiction. It is their contention that the breed was artificially created by French breeders who carefully cross-bred a variety of Siamese and Long-haired Cats. Once they had created a delightful hybrid they then invented an exotic background for it, to make it more appealing and to add to its pedigree status. There may, of course, have been a real cat that was given to a real Monsieur Pavie, or a real Mr Vanderbilt, but it may not have looked anything like the present day Birman. It could have been a rather ordinary feline, which, with a little judicious help in French catteries was converted into the enchanting cat that the Birman undoubtedly is today.

One fact of which we can be certain is that, in France, the Birman became a great favourite and was quickly established as a pedigree breed. It was recognized as such as early as 1925 by the French Feline Federation and remained popular in that country in the decades that followed. As late as 1946, two American authors were labelling this cat, rather confusingly, as the 'French Burmese', confirming at least that France was the centre of the breed's development.

Despite its growing popularity there, however, it is said that during World War II, the population of Birmans in France was decimated and that eventually, at the end of the war, there were only a few left. In Germany only two breeders managed to keep their Birmans alive. Although it was hanging by such a slender thread, the breed was saved and after the war the numbers were soon increasing again. The first of the Continental Birmans to be exported were sent to the United States in 1959. The breed first arrived in Britain in 1964.

In 1966 the Birman was recognized as a pedigree cat for competition purposes in the UK and in 1967 the United States followed suit.

There is an intriguing footnote to the confusing history of the Birman Cat. It is reported that in 1960 an American breeder, Mrs G. Griswold, acquired a pair of 'Tibetan Temple Cats' which, on inspection, turned out to be Birmans. To some, the conclusion was obvious: these cats must be descended from the few that were rescued from the temple and taken into exile with the priests.

Just at the point when many people were beginning to believe the criticisms of the Burmese origin of the breed, the importation of these Tibetan Temple Cats created a dilemma. If they are genuine, the Birman must, after all, have an ancient temple history, and the whole story of its historical beginnings must be re-examined.

A YOUNG BIRMAN CAT *(opposite)*, showing its elegantly marked, white feet. According to the famous legend, this special colouring was magically acquired as the ancestral Birman placed his paws on the white hair of his dying master.

Personality. Terms that have been used to describe this breed include the following: gentle, faithful, even-tempered, civilized, amenable, affectionate, intelligent, outgoing, robust and hardy. One Birman judge has referred to the breed as 'puppy-dogs in cats' bodies', because they are so responsive to their owners. Another commented: 'Birmans are really very polite cats . . . They speak in very soft, sweet voices, if at all.'

Colour Forms:

GCCF: Seal Point; Blue Point; Chocolate Point; Lilac Point; Red Point; Cream Point; Seal Tortie Point; Blue Tortie Point; Chocolate Tortie Point; Lilac Tortie Point; Seal Tabby Point; Blue Tabby Point; Chocolate Tabby Point; Lilac Tabby Point; Red Tabby Point; Cream Tabby Point; Seal Tortie Tabby Point; Blue Tortie Tabby Point; Chocolate Tortie Tabby Point; Lilac Tortie Tabby Point.

CFA: Seal Point; Blue Point; Chocolate Point; Lilac Point.

Breed Clubs:

Birman Cat Club. Address: 20 Hillside Drive, Little Haywood, Stafford, ST18 0NN, England. There is an annual publication, *The Birman Year*. Address: Gate Cottage, Church Hill, Sedlescombe, E. Sussex TN33 0QP, England.

National Birman Fanciers (NBF). Publishes a magazine, *NBF News*. Address: P.O. Box 1830, Stephenville, Texas 76401, USA. or 14007 Campaign St., Fredricksburg, VA 22407, USA.

Nine Silver Bells (Birmans). Address: 115 S. Springvalley Road, McMurray, PA 15317, USA.

Sacred Cat of Burma (Birman) Fanciers (SCBF). Address: 5542 Cleveland Road, Wooster, OH 44691, USA. (Through this club it is possible to obtain a copy of *The Birman Book* by Vivienne Smith.)

Birth

Feline Behaviour. As the nine-week gestation period comes to an end the pregnant cat becomes restless, searching around for a suitable den or nest in which to deliver her kittens. She looks for somewhere quiet, private and dry. In a house, strange noises emanate from cupboards and other nooks and crannies as the cat tests out a variety of suitable sites.

Suddenly, from being increasingly ravenous, the cat's hunger vanishes and she refuses food, which means that the moment of birth is imminent – perhaps only a few hours away. At this point she disappears and settles down to the serious business of bringing a litter of kittens into the world.

Some cats hate interference at this stage and become upset by too much attention. Others – usually those that have never been given much privacy in the house – do not seem to care one way or the other. The happy-go-lucky ones will co-operatively move into a specially prepared birth-box, with soft, warm bedding provided and easy accessibility for a human midwife, should one be needed. Other cats stubbornly refuse the perfect nest-bed offered them and perversely disappear into the shoe-cupboard or some such dark, private place,

Giving birth is a lengthy process for the average cat. With a typical litter of, say, five kittens, and with a typical delay of, say, 30 minutes between the arrival of each one, the whole process lasts for two hours, after which both cat and kittens are quite exhausted. Some cats give birth much more quickly – even as rapidly as one kitten per minute, though this is rare. Others may take as long as an hour between kittens – but this is also uncommon. The typical time delay of about half an hour is not an accident. It gives the mother long enough to attend to one kitten before the next arrives.

The attention she gives the newborn baby consists of three main phases. First, she breaks away the birth sac (the amniotic sac) which encases the kitten as it emerges into the world. She then pays special care to the cleaning of the nose and mouth of the newborn, enabling it to take its first breath. Once this crucial stage is over, she starts to clean up, biting through the umbilical cord and eating it, up to about one inch from the kitten's belly. The little stump she leaves alone, and this eventually dries out and finally drops off of its own accord. She then eats the afterbirth – the placenta – which provides her with valuable nourishment to see her through the long hours of total kitten-caring that now face her, during their first day of life. After this, she licks the kitten all over, helping to dry its fur, and then she rests. Soon the next kitten will appear and the whole process will have to be repeated. If she grows tired, towards the end of an unusually large litter, the last one or two kittens may be ignored and left to die, but most female cats are amazingly good midwives and need no help from their human owners.

Black

Coat Colour. The ideal black coat is so intensely black that it completely masks any other pigment or pattern. Inferior black coats may reveal, in bright light, a brown tinge or a faint tabby pattern.

An alternative name for black, sometimes used by American breeders in certain cases, is Ebony.

Variants of this colour include the following: (1) Black Smoke; (2) Black and White; (3) Van Black and White; (4) Black, Red and White (= Tricolour).

Black Cat

Feline History. In folklore, the all-black cat plays a special role. In earlier centuries, when cats were being severely persecuted by the Christian Church, it was always black cats that were singled out for the most savage treatment. All cats were considered to be wicked, but *they* were considered to be especially fiendish. This was because they were strongly associated with the Devil – the Prince of Darkness – who was believed to borrow the coat of a black cat when he wanted to torment his victims. So, when the Church organized annual burning-cats-alive ceremonies on the day of the Feast of St John, the most depraved of 'Satan's Felines' were strongly preferred and all-black cats were eagerly sought out for the flames.

Writing in 1727, Moncrif comments: 'It is true that the colour black does much harm to Cats among vulgar minds; it augments the fire of their eyes: this is enough for them to be thought sorcerers at the least.'

These victimized cats had to be totally black to be really evil in the minds of the pious worshippers. Any touch of white on their black coats might be taken as a sign that they were

In many countries black cats are thought to bring good luck, and are often used as signs and emblems.

The sign of a black cat acts as a protective talisman for this restaurant at Angoulême in France. It also offers a hint of nocturnal sexuality, stemming from the cat's noisy love-life.

THE REASON a jet black cat crossing your path was said to bring you good luck was that, since this animal was thought to embody evil forces, to see such a cat and live meant that the devil had spared you.

not, after all, cats consecrated to the Devil. As a result of this distinction, cats that were totally black became less and less common, while those that were black with a touch of white survived. Religion acted as a powerful selection pressure on feline coloration. This is the reason why today so many black moggies (as distinct from pedigree 'Black Shorthairs') have a small patch of white hairs somewhere on their body – often on the chest or around the whiskers. This patch, thought to be a sign of innocence, was given the name of 'Angel's mark' or 'God's finger'.

The fear of all-black cats as agents of the Devil also led to a common superstition that has survived to the present day. In Britain it is said that if a black cat crosses your path this will bring you good luck. This is based upon the idea that evil has passed you by – it has come close but has not harmed you, hence you have enjoyed a moment of good luck. In North America a different superstition exists. There, a black cat signifies bad luck, on the principle that it is an evil spirit and therefore dangerous merely by its presence.

BLACK-FOOTED CAT

WILD FELINE. *(Felis nigripes)* Remarkably well supplied with alternative names, this species is also known as the African Black-footed Cat, the Small Spotted Cat, the Sebala Cat, the *Sebula-bulakwana,* the *Swartpoot-wildekat,* the *Swartvoetkat,* the *Klein Gevlekte Kat,* or the *Klein Gekolde Kat.* Sometimes referred to locally as the Ant-hill Tiger (or, in Afrikaans, the *Miershooptier*) because it often makes its den in an abandoned termite mound. German: *Schwarzfusskatze*; French: *Le Chat à Pieds Noir.*

This little African wild cat has a tawny coat covered in black spots which, on the legs and tail, tend to fuse to form dark rings. There is a black tip to the short tail. The undersides of its paws, as its name indicates, are also black. It has large ears and extremely acute hearing. They are solitary, nocturnal hunters that do not venture out of their hiding places until two hours after sunset. They prey on gerbils, mice, other small rodents, small birds, small reptiles and even large spiders and insects. Unusually for cats, they have been seen digging for prey. On the other hand, they have not been seen to climb, being strictly earthbound predators. In captivity they demand grass to eat as a regular diet supplement. Without it, they go off their food altogether.

Smaller than a domestic cat, this is the tiniest of all the wild felines, and stands little chance if physically attacked by any other kind of animal. It has adapted to this problem in several ways. It is extremely shy and secretive and retreats to its hiding places at the slightest sign of any disturbance. It makes use of the abandoned burrow systems of other small animals, such as the Springhaas or the Aardvark. It also takes over cavities under termite hills.

The breeding system has been modified, with the male and female developing a very loud cry that enables them to keep in touch even when widely separated. This alarmingly loud noise has been described as the 'very high-pitched roar of a tiny tiger'. Apparently, if it is recorded and played at half speed it sounds remarkably like a tiger's roar.

THE BLACK-FOOTED CAT *(Felis nigripes)*, a small, spotted African wild cat which, unusually for a feline, is reluctant to climb. It apparently makes up for this by being particularly good at digging.

There is a shorter than usual mating period (only five to ten hours instead of several days) followed by a 67-day gestation (which is longer than that of the larger domestic cat), after which the young are born in an advanced state. The litter is small, usually only two kittens, and this enables the mother to move her offspring from nest-site to nest-site with greater ease. She makes these moves more often than might be expected, again as a defence against predation. She also modifies the den to make it more secure. This is known because a captive female was observed to scoop up sand around the entrance to her artificial den, making the access hole much smaller. If offered no covered hiding place in which to give birth and rear her young, a captive female simply abandons them.

One rather specialized defence mechanism the kittens possess is the scatter reaction to a maternal alarm call. When the mother senses danger, she gives a special cry and her young ones dart off in different directions and hide. In this way, if a predator finds and kills one, the other one (or more) will escape detection and survive.

When the danger has passed, the mother has yet another special signal, this time an 'all-clear' signal. It is a unique, barely audible staccato call, accompanied by ear-twitching, in which the half-flattened ears are raised and lowered in synchrony. Her kittens respond to this by emerging from hiding and rejoining her.

There are reports that this species will hybridize easily with domestic cats 'with little, if any, loss of fertility in the progeny'. If this is the case, it raises the intriguing possibility – with carefully controlled breeding programmes – of creating some fascinating new domestic breeds.

Size: Length of Head + Body: 40–50 cm (16–20 in). Tail: 16–25 cm (6–10 in). Weight: 1.5–2.5 kg (3½–5½).

Distribution: This species has a restricted range, being confined to the more arid regions of southern Africa. It is found on the dry savannah grasslands and in the semi-desert regions of Botswana, Namibia and South Africa. In most regions it is now said to be extremely rare, but is still managing to hold its own in the more remote regions of the Kalahari Desert.

Folklore: According to Bushman legend, this little cat is so fierce that it will fasten its jaws onto the neck of a giraffe, just as it does when killing its more usual small prey.

A Black-footed Cat *(Felis nigripes)* at bay, showing its fierce reaction to being cornered. The smallest of all the wild cat species, it typically avoids all such confrontations, preferring to retreat and hide at the slightest sign of trouble.

B

A Black Panther in the Amazon rain forest. The term 'Black Panther' is confusing because it may refer to a Leopard, a Puma or, as here, a Jaguar. Melanistic wild felines are usually found in the hotter, more humid environments.

Black Panther

Wild Feline. This term is occasionally used today when referring to a melanistic specimen of one of the large cats, but it is confusing because it is never clear which particular species is involved. Usually it is a black Leopard, this being the species most prone to melanism, but in the Americas it is just as likely to be a black Jaguar or a black Puma. For this reason, the term 'panther' has largely been abandoned.

Black Tiger

Mystery Cat. Although black mutants of several species of wild felines have been observed and in some species are quite common (see Black Panther), no Black Tigers have ever been officially recorded. However, evidence that some melanistic specimens may have existed has been found dating back as early as 1772. In that year a watercolour of a Black Tiger was painted from a specimen that had been shot in south-west India. Although black in colour it was still just possible to discern the normal striping. It was described by the artist as having a coat like 'a black cloth variegated with shades of rich velvet'.

Blotched Tabby

Coat Pattern. This pattern is often referred to as the 'Classic Tabby', or 'Marbled Tabby'. In place of the dark, narrow streaks typical of the Mackerel Tabby, there are broader bands arranged in whorls and spirals on the sides of the body. At the centre of this pattern there is usually an oyster-shaped patch surrounded by one or more lines. This region of the Blotched Tabby pattern is sometimes referred to as the 'bull's-eye'.

The blotched markings of this type of tabby vary from cat to cat and sometimes become so extensive and fused with one another that the cat appears to be generally very dark-coated.

The Blotched Tabby pattern is more recent that the ancient Mackerel Tabby pattern, arising in medieval Europe in the 13th century and spreading outwards around the globe. Roger Tabor has christened this cat 'The British Imperial Cat', because 'it spread around the world in the

wake of British colonialization . . . The initial waves of British settlers sailing to America in the 17th century, Canada in the 18th and Australia in the 19th took with them the cats that reflected the proportion of blotched tabbies in Britain at the time . . . In countries without British settlement, such as Egypt and Thailand, the numbers of blotched tabbies are minimal.'

Blue

Coat Colour. Essentially, this is a dilution of a black coat. The so-called 'blue' in reality varies between pale grey and slate grey. There are many pattern variants of this colour among modern pedigree cats, including the following: (1) Blue Chinchilla Silver; (2) Blue Cream Smoke; (3) Blue, Cream and White (Dilute Tricolour); (4) Blue Silver Tabby; (5) Blue Silver Patched Tabby; (6) Blue Silver Tabby and White; (7) Blue Smoke; (8) Blue Tabby; (9) Blue Tabby and White; (10) Blue Patched Tabby; (11) Blue Patched Tabby and White; (12) Blue Tortie; (13) Blue and White (Bi-colour); (14) Van Blue and White.

Four breeds of blue cat are officially recognized today: the Chartreux, Korat, Russian Blue and British Blue. Although these breeds are all treated separately today, in earlier times there was confusion between the Chartreux, the Russian Blue and the British Blue. It was believed by some authorities that the distinctions between them were not at all clear. Early authors often refer to a blue breed known as the Maltese Cat, which was said to be the ancestor of both the Russian Blue and the Chartreux. Other authors claim that, at one stage, there was no difference between the Chartreux and the British Blue. Whether these beliefs are valid or not, the four 'blues' have certainly diverged since then, and are now distinct breeds in their own right.

Bibliography:

1993. Martyn, E. and Taylor, D. *The Little Grey Cat Book.* Dorling Kindersley, London.

Blue Cat

Domestic Breed. An early, alternative name for the Russian Blue Cat, used towards the end of the 19th century.

Blue-Cream

Coat Pattern. This is the dilute form of the tortoiseshell pattern, with blue replacing the black, and cream replacing the red. According to geneticist Roy Robinson, European and American ideals for this coat pattern differ slightly: 'In Britain, the colours of the blue-cream should be softly intermingled whereas in the USA preference is given to those cats with segregated patches of blue and cream.'

Variants include the following: (1) Blue-Cream Shaded; (2) Blue-Cream Smoke; (3) Blue-Cream and White; (4) Blue-Cream Point; (5) Blue-Cream Lynx Point; (6) Parti-colour Blue-Cream; (7) Van Blue-Cream and White.

Blue Lynx

Feline Mutation. In 1938 the skin of a Canadian Lynx, obtained from Alaska and donated to the US National Museum, proved to be of a bluish-grey colour instead of the usual fawn. Enquiries with fur traders in the region where it originated revealed that such mutants, with dilutant coat-colour genes, occurred once or twice in every thousand pelts. Clearly, the 'blue' gene that lies behind the various colour forms of domestic cats is also expressing itself, in a small way, among wild felines.

Blue Russian Shorthair Cat

Domestic Breed. An alternative name for the Russian Blue Cat.

Blue Tiger

Mystery Cat. In 1910 a Methodist missionary was hunting in the Fujian Province of south-east China, when he encountered a Blue Tiger. It was normally striped, but with a deep blue

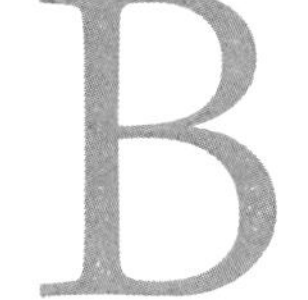

background colour in place of the usual red. It vanished before he could shoot it, but in 1925 he published a book entitled *Blue Tiger*, in which he recorded that there had also been other similar sightings in the region. There is no scientific evidence to support his claim.

Boar-Cat

Feline Term. An early name for a male cat. An alternative name was 'ram-cat', but both were replaced by 'tom-cat' in the 18th century.

Bobcat

Wild Feline. *(Lynx rufus)* Originally called the Red Lynx, because of the reddish tinge to its fur. It has also been called the Barred Bobcat (because of its tail markings), the Bay Lynx (which confuses it with the Old World Caracal) and the Wild Cat (which confuses it with the Old World Wild Cat). To the French Canadians, it is the *Lynx Bai;* to the Mexicans, the *Gato Monte.*

The Bobcat takes over from the Canadian Lynx in the less northerly regions of North America. It does not extend into the snowier landscape of northern Canada, but until recently was common everywhere else on the continent before the coming of man – its greatest enemy. It accepts a wide range of habitats from forest to semi-desert, although it prefers wooded country.

The Bobcat is about twice the size of a domestic cat and is slightly smaller than the Canadian Lynx. It also has shorter legs and smaller feet than its northern cousin and a more distinctly spotted coat. Its ear-tufts are much shorter. There is also a small, but significant difference in the tail markings. The tail of the Canadian Lynx is plain except for its extreme tip which is black. The tail of the Bobcat has several black bands above and a black tip, but underneath it is white, and this white just shows at the extreme end of the tip.

A solitary hunter with large territories of up to 170 sq km (66 sq mi), the Bobcat preys largely on rabbits and hares (up to 90 per cent of the diet). It will also occasionally take rats, mice, opossums, snakes, ground birds and small deer. It has two techniques – the ambush and the stalk-and-pounce. Occasionally it has been known to bury excess food for later use, but more often it will simply leave the surplus to the local scavengers.

The North American Bobcat *(Lynx rufus)*, a medium-sized cat that has been exterminated over large stretches of its extensive range. The background colour of its coat is rather variable – anything from pale grey to reddish brown.

Breeding usually takes place in the spring, but has been known to occur at almost any time of year. The female retreats to give birth in a thicket, cave or hollow tree, where she will prepare a snug nest for her kittens, lining it with leaves and soft mosses. The male, as well as the female, will bring food to the young. The offspring become independent at about seven months of age.
Size: Length of Head + Body: 65–72 cm (25½–28¼ in). Tail: 14–15 cm (5½–6 in). Weight: 7–10 kg (15½–22 lb).
Distribution: From southern Canada in the north of its range, down through the United States to northern Mexico in the south. It has however been exterminated in many areas.
Bibliography:

1958. Young, S.P. *The Bobcat of North America.* Stackpole, Harrisburg, Pennsylvania.
1981. Ryden, H. *Bobcat Year.* Viking, New York.

Bombay Cat

Domestic Breed. A recent American breed, it was called the Bombay because its intensely black coat was reminiscent of that of an Indian Black Leopard. It has been described as a 'Black Burmese', a 'mini-panther' or 'the patent-leather kid with new-penny eyes'.
Appearance: A compact, muscular black cat with a sheen to its very short, satin-like coat. It has large, golden eyes and wide-set ears on its rounded head.
History: The breed was deliberately created in Kentucky in 1958 by Nikki Horner, who crossed sable Burmese with black American Shorthairs. Her aim was create 'a copper-eyed mini-panther with patent-leather fur' by combining the black colour of the Shorthair with the coat sheen of the Burmese.

The Bombay achieved championship status in the United States in 1976, but is still fairly rare outside America. Some breeding had occurred in Britain, using British-type Burmese and black British Shorthair Cats. Because of slight differences between the American and British parental stock, the resultant Bombays are also slightly different from one another.
Personality: Terms used to describe this breed include: assertive, confident, gentle, vocal but soft-voiced, intelligent, sensitive, active, inquisitive, playful, patient and unusually friendly.

The Bombay Cat, a domestic breed developed in America in the late 1950s, is essentially a jet black Burmese. The aim of its creator was to produce a sleek, mini-panther.

Colour Forms: Black is the only colour permitted in this breed.
Breed Clubs:
The Bombay Connection. Address: 200 Raintree Trail, Lafayette, LA 70507, USA.
International Bombay Society. Address: 5782 Dalton Drive, Farmington, NY 14425, USA.

BOOTH'S CATS

CARTOON CATS. George Booth, cartoonist for *The New Yorker* and other American magazines, specializes in cat cartoons, inspired by his own feline pets, Amberson and Tata (who started out as Ambrosia and James Taylor, until it emerged that they were male and female respectively). His cat cartoons have appeared in book form with titles such as *Think Good Thoughts about a Pussy-Cat*.

BORNEAN BAY CAT

WILD FELINE. *(Felis badia)* Alternative name for the Bay Cat. Also called the Bornean Red Cat. (See Bay Cat (1) for further details.)

BORODIN, ALEXANDER

CAT OWNER. The Russian composer Borodin (1833–1887) and his wife passed their days surrounded by cats. Rimsky-Korsakoff's bemused account of their tolerance of their feline companions includes the following observations:

'[The cats] paraded across the dinner-table, sticking their noses into plates, unceremoniously leaping to the diner's back . . . You might sit at their tea-table – and behold! Tommy marches along the board and makes for your plate. You shoo him off, but [Mrs Borodin] invariably takes his part . . . Meanwhile, zip! another cat has bounded at [Borodin's] neck and, twining himself about it, has fallen to warming that neck without pity.'

One of their tabby cats was called Rybolov, meaning Fisherman, because he managed to catch small fish through the ice-holes. Another tabby was named Dlinyenki, meaning 'Longy'. According to Rimsky-Korsakoff, he was in the habit of bringing home kittens by the scruff of the neck. If he was indeed a 'he', this is remarkable behaviour, but the chances are that the great composer was mistaken and that 'he' was really a 'she' who was simply bringing her kittens home to the security of the house.

BOUHAKI

PET CAT. Certain authors have given this particular feline the distinction of being 'the first cat known to have had a name'. It appears on an ancient Egyptian limestone wall-carving dating from the XI Dynasty (1950 BC). The animal is shown beneath the chair of a seated husband and wife. It is a rather strange-looking creature with a short, curled tail, a fat body with swollen teats and a rather pointed face.

According to the famous Egyptologist Flinders Petrie, who first examined the carving, the tomb where it was placed belonged to a King An.āa and the animal depicted is not a cat, but a pet dog. He states that 'on the tablet is the image of the king, standing, having between his feet his dog named Behukaa'.

Early cat authors have a different interpretation. Champfleury, writing in 1869, says, 'One of the most ancient representations of the cat is to be found in the necropolis of Thebes, which contains the tomb of Hana. On the stela is the statue of the King, standing erect, with his cat, Bouhaki, between his feet.' This version was repeated time and again in later cat books, until more scholarly authors turned again to the original source and rejected the feline interpretation, insisting, with Petrie, that the animal must have been a dog.

The confusion was partly caused by the fact that the stone block on which the carving was made has a picture on both sides. On one side is a standing man with his pet dog, while on the other side is the depiction of the man and his wife, seated, with the 'cat-figure' beneath their chair. Clearly the two scenes have been confused over the years, but this is only part of the

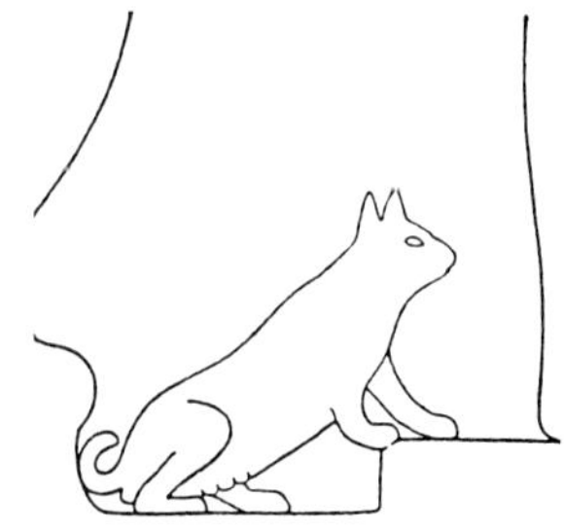

BOUHAKI, traditionally the first cat known to have been given a pet name, appears on a relief-decorated wall-fragment from Koptos, in ancient Egypt. Egyptologists are still arguing over the true identity of this strangely shaped animal.

problem. Egyptologists themselves are still arguing over the identity of the cat-like animal itself, and some believe that this too is a dog. To a zoologist, however, there seems little doubt that it is, in fact, meant to be a female cat in the late stages of pregnancy. There are no dog portrayals in the art of ancient Egypt that look remotely like this animal. Also, all the later examples of 'pet animal under woman's chair' are undeniably feline.

The only difficulty with this interpretation is the figure's short, curled tail, but even this is less of an obstacle than might be imagined, as this particular mutation is now known to have been rather widespread in the history of domestic cats. (For further details see Curly-tailed Cat.) Alternatively, the end of its tail could have been amputated accidentally or removed for some superstitious reason.

If this view is accepted, there remains the question of the cat's name. Unfortunately, the title of Bouhaki belongs to the pet dog on the opposite side of the stone tablet. The cat-figure has no name. So, although this may well be the earliest representation of a pet house-cat anywhere in the world, it cannot sustain its popular reputation of being 'the first cat known to have had a name'. That accolade must go to a pet cat called Nedjem (meaning 'Sweet' or 'Pleasant') that dates from the reign of Thutmose III (1479 BC–1425 BC).

Breed Popularity

Feline History. The most popular cats have always been the moggies, the non-pedigrees, the ordinary house pets. They are the rough, tough survivors whose parents have somehow managed to avoid being neutered by kindly feline welfare workers. Despite endless trips to the vet for 'altering' sessions, moggies are still the most common and the most widespread of all

Gizmo, a prize-winning moggie, displaying the kind of exciting colour pattern that can be found among non-pedigree cats today. 'Mongrel' house-pets are still by far the most popular of all cats.

kinds of cats today, right across the globe. Their tenacity and their ability to infiltrate their way into the homes and the hearts of the public is second to none. Pedigree cats are everywhere rare by comparison.

But among those pure-bred individuals, which are the most popular breeds? In the very beginning, in the cat shows of the Victorian era, it was the short-haired cats (the aristocratic cousins of the moggies) that were originally the most favoured. Then, the long-haired cats, the Angoras and the Persians, arrived, and they quickly rose to dominate the exhibition scene. The Angoras were soon swamped out by the Persians, who were then joined by the exotic Siamese. As the years passed, more and more breeds were introduced, each finding followers and fanatical supporters.

Today a pedigree cat show is fascinatingly complex, with new breeds appearing each year and with new colours of old breeds being developed. But which, today, are the 'top cats'? After all the changes that have occurred in over a century of pedigree cat exhibitions, which are the breeds that have finally won through to become the most popular pedigree breeds at the end of the 20th century?

The best way of finding out is to check the number of registrations for each breed at one of the major cat societies. One of the biggest registration organizations in the world is the CFA (The Cat Fanciers' Association), and here are the 'top ten' breeds, as reflected by their registration records at the start of the 1990s. Although the dominance of the Persian was to be expected, its extent is perhaps surprising:

CFA 'Top Ten' Breeds

RANK	BREED	REGISTRATIONS	RANK	BREED	REGISTRATIONS
1	Persian	79.4%	6	Oriental Shorthair	1.6%
2	Siamese	5.5%	7	American Shorthair	1.6%
3	Abyssinian	3.6%	8	Exotic Shorthair	1.3%
4	Maine Coon	2.8%	9	Scottish Fold	1.2%
5	Burmese	1.9%	10	Colourpoint Shorthair	1.1%

Brindled Cat

Domestic Cat. An early, alternative name for a tabby cat. Frances Simpson, writing in 1903, comments: '[The tabby] was also called the brindled cat, or the tiger cat, and with some the grey cat – "graymalkin". We are told also . . . that tabby cats in Norfolk and Suffolk were called cyprus cats, cyprus being a reddish-yellow colour, so that the term may have applied to orange as well as brown tabbies. The term "tiger cat" is, I believe, often used in America, and it well describes the true type of a brown tabby.'

Bristol Cat

Domestic Breed. A new experimental breed.

British Angora Cat

Domestic Breed. In the 1960s some British breeders decided to re-create the elegant Angora Cat. It had been immensely popular in Victorian times, but was soon to be eclipsed by the even more exotic Persian. By the early part of the 20th century the original Angora had virtually vanished in the West. A nostalgic desire for its return prompted certain breeders to reconstitute it by careful selective breeding from suitable long-haired Oriental cats. The soft coat and the bushy tail were successfully obtained, but the bone structure proved more difficult. The angular head typical of the Oriental remained as a reminder that this new British Angora was a copy of the true Angora and not the original.

Since then, the original breed has been rediscovered in its Turkish homeland and once again brought to the West for development as a pedigree cat. This has led to some confusion, because

The British Angora Cat is the product of a 1960s breeding programme that set out to reconstitute the traditional Angora Cat. Careful selection re-created the elegant Angora coat, but the body-shape is more angular and elongated than the original.

there are now two Angoras, with very different origins. Misunderstandings are avoided by calling the new imports 'Turkish Angoras' and the re-created ones 'British Angoras'. (For further details see Angora Cat.)

British Big Cat

Mystery Cat. Modern folklore has created its own legends, from flying saucers to crop circles, to replace the obsolete angels and ghouls of the past. Fairies have become aliens, as the supernatural has kept pace with modern technology. In animal folklore there has been a similar shift. The dragons and unicorns of yesterday required a modern, believable equivalent and it was found in the form of the 'mystery cat'. As recently as 1983 it was claimed that, even in overpopulated and over-explored Britain, 'a large, unidentified carnivore is quietly living in our countryside, a living fossil, waiting to be discovered and classified'.

Given the name of 'The British Big Cat', from the 1960s onwards it became the subject of countless newspaper articles and several books. The phenomenon embraced the following dramatic sightings: The Shooter's Hill Cheetah (1963); The Surrey Puma (362 sitings between 1964 and 1966); The Nottingham Lioness (1976); The Glenfarg Lynx (1976); The Cannich Puma (1979); The Powys Beast (1980); The Beast of Exmoor (1983); The Kellas Cat (1984).

There are three plausible explanations for these sitings:

1 In the boom period of the 1960s many small zoos opened in Britain. Some were well run, but many were amateurish. Captive-bred pumas were a glut on the market at the time, thanks to repeated breeding successes at London Zoo and elsewhere. As a result, quite a large number of pumas found their way into these new and often imperfectly secured menageries. Some even found their way into private hands as exotic pets. It is highly likely that some of these escaped from their flimsy enclosures. Wishing to avoid criticism, the zoo owners simply kept quiet about these incidents. This would certainly explain the Surrey Puma sightings. Other exotic-cat escapes could also explain most of the other sightings listed above.

2 In 1976, the Dangerous Wild Animals Act was passed in the UK, which meant that anyone owning a large cat, whether in a zoo or as a pet, required a licence. The licenses in question were extremely expensive and difficult to obtain, with the result that many desperate owners of large cats probably reacted by simply turning them loose in the British countryside. This would account for the sudden increase in sightings in the late 1970s and the 1980s.
3 The Kellas Cat, and other similar sightings of a more modest feline, little bigger than a British Wild Cat, were originally thought to be evidence of another 'mystery cat' species, but the animals involved are now believed to be hybrids between feral black domestic cats and Scottish Wild Cats. (See Kellas Cat.)

Cases where the 'British Big Cat' is supposed to have savaged farm animals are in most cases probably due to attacks by dogs. The killing methods of cats and dogs are quite different and the wounds inflicted in these instances seldom match with feline predatory techniques.

Bibliography:

1974. Dent, A. *Lost Beasts of Britain.* Harrap, London.
1983. Francis, D. *Cat Country: The Quest for the British Big Cat.* David & Charles, Newton Abbot, Devon.
1984. Beer, T. *The Beast of Exmoor.* Countryside Productions, Barnstaple.
1986. McEwan, G. *Mystery Animals of Britain and Ireland.* Robert Hale, London.
1989. Shuker, K. *Mystery Cats of the World.* Robert Hale, London.
1993. Francis, D. *The Beast of Exmoor.* Jonathan Cape, London.
1993. Francis, D. *My Highland Kellas Cats.* Jonathan Cape, London.

British Blue Cat

Domestic Breed. The bluish-grey version of the British Shorthair. Because it has always been the most popular colour for that breed, some authorities have in the past raised it to the level of a separate breed. Writing in 1955, Rose Tenent comments: 'The British Blue has been called the "aristocrat" of short-hairs.' She continues: 'In the United States the British Blue is known as the Maltese cat, and recently has enjoyed much popularity there as a household pet. On the Continent, too, this cat is becoming increasingly popular, and there its name is the Chartreuse.' This is confusing, since the name 'Maltese' has also in the past been given to the Russian Blue Cat. Furthermore, there is disagreement about the relationship between the British Blue and the French cat called the 'Chartreuse' or 'Chartreux'. Some authorities consider them to be so similar as to be the same breed. Others see them as distinct breeds and classify them separately.

The British Blue is said to have the plushest coat of any shorthair. In recent times the preferred colour of this breed has shown slight changes, the dark slate-blue of the early days becoming much paler.

British Shorthair Cat

Domestic Breed. The modern pedigree British Shorthair has been developed from the ancient British working cats whose ancestors arrived with the Romans somewhere between the first and fourth century AD.

Appearance: A sturdy, muscular cat with a massive, broad head, rather short neck and legs and thick tail. The coat, although short, is dense and plush. The pedigree version of this cat is an altogether stockier, heavier animal than the typical domestic pet shorthair.

History: It is difficult to be certain of the precise date that domestic cats arrived in Britain. During the Roman period there were many wild cats in the country, and it is not always easy to tell from skeletal remains whether a particular animal was wild or domesticated. There are some feline footprints impressed into tiles in the foundation of a third century temple in Roman Chelmsford. It has been argued that these are unlikely to have been made by wild cats, but we cannot be certain.

B

British Shorthair Cat

One of the earliest known examples of an undeniably domestic British cat was discovered during excavations at Lullingstone in Kent. There, in the basement of a rich man's house dating from the second half of the fourth century, was a skeleton of a cat that had perished in a fire. Its bones and teeth showed that it was a domesticated specimen and not a trapped wild cat.

During the 1,600 years that followed, the domestic cat survived as a pest-controller, despite repeated, systematic persecution and torture by pious Christians, who believed that the feline body housed the spirit of the devil. Eventually, in the Victorian era, cats were at last treated as appealing household pets.

With the advent of competitive cat shows, starting in 1871, the best examples of the British working cats were selected and developed as pedigree animals. A large number of colour forms was soon available. These short-haired animals dominated the earliest cats shows because the long-haired breeds were so new and were outnumbered by about ten to one. By 1896, however, the longhairs has become the favoured breeds and were given the place of honour at all shows.

By the turn of the century it was reported that the short-haired cats were 'in a very small minority'. So popular were the new longhairs that there was at one point a danger that the old, original shorthairs might have been completely eclipsed. However, dedicated supporters came to their rescue and in 1901 the Short-haired Cat Society was formed to promote them. Since then they have always had a significant part to play in competitive cat showing.

In Continental Europe there used to be no difference between the British Shorthair and what was referred to as the 'European Shorthair'. The British breed clubs had been the first to develop shorthairs as pedigree cats, so they had precedence over the Continentals, and many of the first pedigree 'European Shorthairs' were imported British Shorthairs. But then the Continentals began to develop and improve their own shorthair cats and, in 1982, a distinction was made between the two breeds. After that, inevitably, they began to diverge. Today, the main differences are that the British Shorthair has a cobbier, sturdier body and a heavier, wider head.

Personality: Terms used to describe this breed include: hardy, good-natured, calm, affable, loyal, intelligent, reserved, prosaic, stolid, loving, untemperamental, tranquil, dignified, independent and affectionate.

Colour Forms: The traditional and most popular colour for the British Shorthair is Blue. Black is also one of the earliest colours. Today, however, almost every colour is accepted and the list has grown longer and longer, year by year. To simplify the list, the colours are grouped into convenient categories.

GCCF: Self Colours: White; Black; Chocolate; Lilac; Red Self; Blue; Cream.

Tabby (both Classic and Mackerel): Red Tabby; Brown Tabby; Blue Tabby; Chocolate Tabby; Lilac Tabby; Cream Tabby.

Silver Tabby: Silver Tabby; Blue Silver Tabby; Chocolate Silver Tabby; Lilac Silver Tabby; Red Silver Tabby; Cream Silver Tabby.

Tabby and White: Brown Tabby and White; Blue Tabby and White; Chocolate Tabby and White; Lilac Tabby and White; Red Tabby and White; Cream Tabby and White.

Silver Tabby and White: Silver Tabby and White; Blue Silver Tabby and White; Chocolate Silver Tabby and White; Lilac Silver Tabby and White; Red Silver Tabby and White; Cream Silver Tabby and White.

Spotted: Brown Spotted; Blue Spotted; Chocolate Spotted; Lilac Spotted; Red Spotted; Cream Spotted;

Silver Spotted: Silver Spotted; Blue Silver Spotted; Chocolate Silver Spotted; Lilac Silver Spotted; Red Silver Spotted; Cream Silver Spotted;

Tortie Tabby: Tortie Tabby; Tortie Silver Tabby; Tortie Spotted; Tortie Silver Spotted.

Tortie: Tortie; Blue-Cream; Chocolate Tortie; Lilac Tortie.

Tortie and White: Tortie and White; Blue Tortie and White; Chocolate Tortie and White; Lilac Tortie and White.

Bi-colour: Black and White Bi-colour; Blue and White Bi-colour; Chocolate and White Bi-colour; Lilac and White Bi-colour; Red and White Bi-colour; Cream and White Bi-colour.

The British Blue, the most popular colour form of the British Shorthair Cat, is sometimes referred to as the 'aristocrat of shorthairs'. In appearance it is similar to the French Charteux.

Smoke: Black Smoke; Blue Smoke; Chocolate Smoke; Lilac Smoke; Red Smoke; Cream Smoke; Tortie Smoke; Blue Tortie Smoke; Chocolate Tortie Smoke; Lilac Tortie Smoke.

Smoke and White: Black Smoke and White; Blue Smoke and White; Chocolate Smoke and White; Lilac Smoke and White; Red Smoke and White; Cream Smoke and White.

Tipped: Black Tipped; Blue Tipped; Chocolate Tipped; Lilac Tipped; Red Tipped; Cream Tipped; Black Tortie Tipped; Blue Tortie Tipped; Chocolate Tortie Tipped; Lilac Tortie Tipped; Golden Tipped.

Self Pointed: Seal Colourpointed; Blue Colourpointed; Chocolate Colourpointed; Lilac Colourpointed; Red Colourpointed; Cream Colourpointed;

Tortie Pointed: Seal Tortie Colourpointed; Blue-Cream Colourpointed; Chocolate Tortie Colourpointed; Lilac Tortie Colourpointed;

Tabby Pointed: Seal Tabby Colourpointed; Blue Tabby Colourpointed; Chocolate Tabby Colour Pointed; Lilac Tabby Colourpointed; Red Tabby Colourpointed; Cream Tabby Colourpointed;

Tortie Tabby Pointed: Seal Tortie Tabby Colourpointed; Blue-Cream Tabby Colourpointed; Chocolate Tortie Tabby Colourpointed; Lilac Tortie Tabby Colourpointed.

CFA: White; Black; Blue; Cream; Black Smoke; Blue Smoke; Classic Tabby Pattern; Mackerel Tabby Pattern; Spotted Tabby; Silver Tabby; Red Tabby; Brown Tabby; Blue Tabby; Cream Tabby; Tortie; Calico; Dilute Calico; Blue-Cream; Bi-color.

Bibliography:

1981. Lauder, P. *The British, European and American Shorthair Cat.* Batsford, London.

Breed Clubs:

British Shorthair and Tipped Club. Address: Rowan, Shas Lane, Uppermill, Oldham, Lancs OL3 6HP, England.

Short Haired Cat Society. Address: Highridge, Parsonage Hill, Somerton, Somerset TA11 7PF, England.

Note: In America there is a breed publication, *The British Shorthair Newsletter*. Address: 17275 Hammock Lane, Fort Pierce, FL 34988, USA.

British Tick Cat

Domestic Breed. An early, alternative name for the Abyssinian Cat that refers to its ticked coat.

Brobdingnagian Cat

Fictional Cat. A gigantic domestic cat, 'three times larger than an ox', encountered by Lemuel Gulliver in Part II of Jonathan Swift's *Gulliver's Travels* (1726).

Bronze

Coat Colour. A warm, coppery brown ground colour, lightening to tawny buff. The term 'bronze' is applied to one of the coat colours of the spotted Egyptian Mau.

Brown

Coat Colour. There are two kinds of brown colour in the coats of domestic cats. First, there is the natural brown that exists as part of the pattern of the wild tabby. Second, there is a domestic brown resulting from a mutated brown gene that reduces the strength of black pigment and increases the strength of brown pigment. Breeders have been able to vary the quality of this domestic brown – from dark red-browns to light golden-browns – by manipulating other genes that modify the darkness and lightness of colours.

Brownie

Pet Cat. Became one of the richest cats in the world in 1963 when, along with its companion, 'Hellcat', it inherited $415,000 on the death of its owner, a Dr William Grier of San Diego.

Bunny Cat

Domestic Breed. An early, alternative name for the Abyssinian Cat: 'The colour of an Abyssinian should be a sort of reddish-fawn, each individual hair being "ticked" like that of a wild rabbit – hence the popular name of "bunny cat".' (Frances Simpson, 1903)

Burmese Cat

Domestic Breed. A short-haired breed named after the country of origin of the founder cat. In reality, its ancestors may have been found over a wider range of the Far East, including Thailand (where it is known locally as 'The Copper'). Because of recent breeding variations, some owners refer to their cats as 'Traditional Burmese'. In Germany the breed is known as the *Burma;* in Holland as the *Burmee*. Among English-speaking breeders it is usually nicknamed 'The Burm'.

Appearance: A muscular, athletic, compact, short-haired cat with a glossy, rich, dark brown coat. The underparts are slightly lighter in colour than the rest of the body, but the change from light areas to dark is gradual. The rounded, domed head, with ears set wide apart, has a short face with golden-yellow eyes.

History: It is claimed that this breed is mentioned as the Su-pa-lak, or Thong Daeng, in one of the poems of the ancient Thai Cat Book, written during the Ayudhya Period, which stretched from 1350 to 1767. It is recorded there as a courageous, protective cat and described in the following words: 'Of magnificent appearance with shape the best/ Coloured like copper, this cat is beautiful:/ The light of her eyes is as a shining ray.'

According to local folklore, these beautiful brown, golden-eyed cats – presumably the ancestors of what we now know as the Burmese Cat – were kept as sacred animals in the temples, monasteries and palaces of Burma. Pampered by the rich and holy, these revered felines were provided with personal servants in the form of student-priests. These servants acted as guardians to ensure the safety of their charges and were severely punished if they failed in their duties. The purity of the breed was maintained by the strict control over the movements of the cats that prevented them from mating with the highly varied felines that roamed the rest of the country. Occasionally, a single cat was presented as a special gift to a visiting dignitary, but apart from that they seldom left their Burmese strongholds.

The story goes that a certain Major Finch, stationed in the East during World War II, who made good use of his spare time there by visiting Buddhist temples, saw many beautiful examples of these sacred brown cats. He called them 'Rajah Cats', but it is clear from his description that what he was calling Rajah Cats and what we today know as Burmese Cats were one and the same. He claimed that they were the true 'Royal Cats' and were held in high esteem in the Royal courts long before the pale-bodied Siamese Cats put in an appearance. In fact, in his opinion, the Rajah Cat was the parent form of the Siamese Cat, which in ancient times was viewed merely as a poorly coloured, semi-albino version of this sacred, rich brown cat.

Whether this is all true, or merely a romantic legend, by the 1930s a key event occurred in the history of the breed. It was then that the 'founding female' of the modern Burmese Cat arrived in the United States and was used as the starting point for a carefully developed breeding programme. Even at this more recent date, however, there is some confusion as to precisely how she came to be on American soil. There are four contradictory versions:

1 She was brought from Rangoon to the United States in 1933, where she was sold as a 'Brown Siamese'.
2 She was brought from India to the United States in the early 1930s.
3 A sailor brought her to New Orleans in 1934, where he sold her to a local pet shop, saying he had obtained her in Burma and that she was a 'Burmese Cat'. She was eventually purchased by a retired ship's doctor (ex-US Navy) by the name of Joseph C. Thompson.
4 She was purchased from a native carnival in Rangoon by the famous wild-animal dealer Frank ('Bring 'Em Back Alive') Buck, who sold her, in Burma, to Dr Joseph Thompson, who then took her back with him to his home in San Francisco in 1930.

We may never be certain which of these four 'arrival' stories is the true one, but we do know for sure that, one way or another, a remarkable brown female cat did come into Dr Thompson's possession in the early 1930s. It is instructive to read Dr Thompson's own words, from an article he wrote with three of his colleagues in 1943 (the year of his death) on *The Genetics of the Burmese Cat*: 'The First "Burmese" cat was a female imported into the United States from Burma by the senior author [Dr Thompson himself] in the year 1930.' This statement firmly fixes the date, but is ambiguous concerning the mode of acquisition of the cat. 'Importing a cat from Burma' leaves open the question of whether Dr Thompson himself brought the animal in, or whether it was brought into the country for him. The original source of the animal therefore remains something of a mystery.

Once Dr Thompson had acquired the cat, however, the picture becomes much clearer. A brown female cat, she was named Wong Mau. At the time of her arrival, Dr Thompson was working as a psychiatrist in San Francisco and was employing a rather unusual type of treatment. His enlightened form of therapy consisted of giving each of his rich patients a pregnant Siamese Cat to look after. The problems these patients faced – and the rewards they gained – from raising a litter of kittens were so successful in taking them out of themselves, that they soon forgot their neuroses, started to look outward instead of inward, and rapidly regained their mental balance.

Thompson had been fascinated by the Far East for many years, at one time becoming a monk in a Tibetan monastery, and became especially attached to this new arrival from Burma. Wong Mau was allowed to sit at his side during his consultations, and soon became the most important cat in the doctor's feline collection. At first, she was looked upon as simply a brown Siamese, but careful breeding experiments revealed that she was in fact a cross between a Siamese and a dark-coated breed that was new to the West. Enlisting the aid of some geneticist friends, Dr Thompson was able to segregate this brown breed, which was given the name of Burmese Cat. By crossing Wong Mau with a Siamese male (the first mating took place in 1932 with a Siamese stud called Tai Mau) and then back-crossing the male offspring with her, it was possible to create three types of kittens: those that had Siamese markings, those that were brown but with darker points (like Wong Mau herself) and those with all-over brown colouring. This last type became the foundation stock for the Burmese Cat breed.

These first true Burmese Cats were used in further breeding programmes in a deliberate attempt to establish a new pedigree cat. In the early 1940s, three more individuals were imported into America from Burma, to strengthen the stock. These were a male and two females. They left Rangoon in 1941 on the S.S. *Chart* and had to endure a wartime sea voyage lasting five months, during which they had to survive attacks by bombers. At last, they arrived in New York in 1942 and became the property of Guy Fisher. Only one of the three, a female called Tangyi of Forbidden City, appears on any of the pedigree lists of the period, but she was able to provide a valuable addition of new blood to the breeding programmes. Unfortunately, once again we do not appear to have any information about Tangyi's original source in Burma. The arrival of these three additional cats from Rangoon does, however, suggest that the brown Burmese Cat was a true breed in its original homeland, and that Wong Mau was not an isolated oddity, as has been suggested by some critics.

After some initial setbacks, the success of the breeding programme was recognized in the United States when the CFA officially accepted the Burmese breed. In the late 1940s three Burmese Cats (a male and two females) were imported from America into Britain by breeders Sydney and Lillian France of Derby, and in 1952 the breed was also recognized there by the GCCF. In 1955, the Burmese Cat Club was formed in Britain and now has 1,500 members.

Finally, although it is generally accepted today that Wong Mau was the founding cat of the modern breed it has been pointed out that, back in the 19th century, dark brown 'Siamese' cats were being exhibited at cat shows in Britain, and that these were probably of the same type. Writing in 1889, Harrison Weir explains that there are two types of 'Royal Cat of Siam', one pale-bodied and one dark: 'light rich dun is the preferable colour, but a light fawn, light silver-grey or light orange is permissible; deeper and richer browns, almost chocolate, are admissible . . . the last merely a variety of much beauty and excellence; but the dun and light tints take precedence.' He also refers to an exhibitor who 'possesses a chocolate variety of this Royal Siamese cat . . . Although this peculiar colour is very beautiful and scarce, I am of the opinion that the light grey or fawn colour with black and well-marked muzzle, ears, and legs is the typical variety . . . I take that to be the correct form and colour, and the darker colour to be an accidental deviation.'

The owner of the 'Chocolate Siamese' is then quoted as saying, 'The dun invariably beats the chocolate at shows.' This situation obviously led to a favouring of the pale-bodied Siamese with dark extremities, and the rapid disappearance of the overall dark-bodied form. As far as can be

The Burmese Cat *(opposite)*, believed to be an ancient breed from South-east Asia where it was once revered as a sacred animal. Modern Burmese are descended from an individual imported into the United States in 1930.

told, the chocolate specimens were never specially bred from or developed and soon vanished without trace. However, their brief appearance at these early shows indicates that a Burmese-type of cat has been around for a very long time and supports the view that Wong Mau had an ancient Eastern lineage.

Personality: Terms that have been used to describe this breed include the following: affectionate, alert, active, agile, sociable, inquisitive, athletic, ingenious, intelligent, curious, zestful, adaptable, lively, energetic, smart, playful, devoted, vocal, highly strung, rumbustious, boisterous, bold, bossy, stubborn and demanding. In general, its character is felt to be close to that of the Siamese.

Colour Forms: In some countries many different colour forms are recognized (see below); elsewhere, only a few colour forms are accepted, the others being given different breed names, such as Malayan.

The traditional colour for this breed is Brown. Other colours were added later: Blue in 1955; Cream in 1971; Chocolate, Lilac and Red in 1972; Brown Tortie, Chocolate Tortie, Lilac Tortie, Blue Tortie in 1973.

GCCF: Brown; Blue; Chocolate; Lilac; Red; Cream; Brown Tortie; Blue Tortie; Chocolate Tortie; Lilac Tortie.

CFA: Sable (= Brown); Champagne (= Chocolate); Blue; Platinum (= Lilac).

The CFA also lists 'European Burmese' colours, as follows: Brown; Blue; Chocolate; Lilac; Red; Cream; Seal Tortie; Blue Tortie; Chocolate Tortie; Lilac Tortie.

Bibliography:

1943. Thompson, J.C., Cobb, V.C., Keeler, C.E. & Dmytryk, M. 'Genetics of the Burmese Cat'. In: *Journal of Heredity*. Vol. 34, No. 4, April 1943.

1966. Smyth, J. *Ming*. London. (Anecdotal)

1976. Burgess, G. *Burmese Cats*. Price Milburn, Wellington, New Zealand.

1979. Pocock, R. et al. *The Burmese Cat*. Batsford, London.

1983. Swift, M.K. *Burmese Cats*. Batsford, London.

1989. Swift, M.K. et al. *Burmese Cats in Camera*. Panther Photographic, Norfolk.

A dilute colour form of the Burmese Cat. From the 1950s onwards, new colour varieties were developed and the traditional brown colour of this breed was joined by several delicate, paler hues.

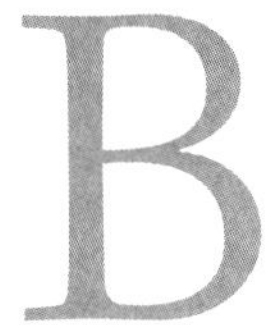

1991. Pocock, R. (Editor) *The Burmese Cat*. The Burmese Cat Club.
Kelsey-Wood, D. *The Proper Care of Burmese Cats*. TFH, New Jersey.

Breed Clubs:

Burmese Breeders Society. Address: 11 Hawksworth Avenue, Guiseley, Leeds, LS20 8EJ, England.

Burmese Cat Club (with a membership of 1,250). Issues a quarterly magazine, *The Burmese Cat Club News*. Address: Southview, Landmere Lane, Edwalton, Nottingham, NG12 4DG, England.

Burmese Cat Society. Address: 11 Hawksworth Avenue, Guiseley, Leeds, LS20 8EJ, England.

Burmese Limited. Address: 168 Delavan Avenue, Newark, NJ 04104, USA.

Burmese Please. Address: 2184 Oneida Crescent, Mississauga, Ontario, Canada.

National Alliance of Burmese Breeders. Address: 11057 Saffold Way, Reston, VA 22090, USA.

National Burmese Cat Club. Address: Normandy Heights Road, Morristown, NJ 07960, USA.

Top Burmese Academe. Address: Route 1, Box 344A, Florence, SC 29051, USA.

United Burmese Cat Fanciers. Address: 2395 N.E. 185th Street, North Miami Beach, FL 33180, USA. (Originally there were two pioneer Burmese clubs in the United States, The Burmese Cat Society and Burmese Breeders of America, but they amalgamated in 1960 to form the United Burmese Cat Fanciers.)

Burmilla Cat

Domestic Breed. A recent British breed resulting from an accidental mating between a male Silver Chinchilla and a female Lilac Burmese.

Appearance: In appearance, this cat is essentially a silver Burmese. The combination of the Burmese body-type with a soft, dense, delicately tipped-silver, short-haired coat, gives it a special appeal. In addition it has dark pencilling around the eyes, as though wearing eyeliner.

History: The Burmilla was accidentally created by the Baroness Miranda von Kirchberg in 1981. A male Silver Chinchilla called Sanquist and a female Burmese called Fabergé were awaiting mates of their own respective breeds, but began to demonstrate an unusual degree of interest in one another. When Fabergé came into season she was immediately isolated in preparation for a journey to a Burmese stud male. Before this could happen, however, Sanquist was accidentally given brief access to her by a cleaner who did not realize the consequence of her actions. In the Baroness's own words: 'A kind lady, passing the door and seeing the dejected Sanquist, took pity on him and let him into Fabergé's room, just to say a last farewell.' Fabergé was then sent away for her official mating with another pedigree Burmese. When she returned, her litter was not Burmese as expected, but from their appearance had clearly been fathered by Sanquist, who now took a strong paternal interest in them, grooming them and protecting them.

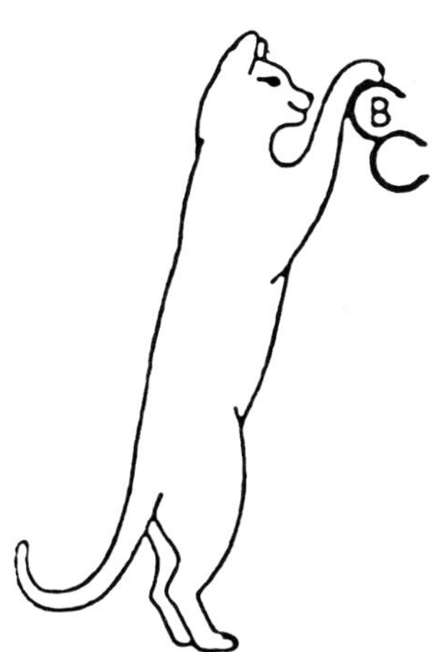

The BCC emblem of the Burmilla Cat Club, founded in 1984 by Therese Clarke.

The litter consisted of four female kittens and they were named Galatea, Gemma, Gabriella and Gisella. They were so attractive that, instead of neutering them and disposing of them as pets, as usually happens with 'accidents', the Baroness decided to keep them and develop them as the foundation stock of a new breed. They were back-crossed to Burmese and it was found that their appealing characteristics were maintained in the next generation. Further breeding helped to fix the Burmilla as a distinct new type of pedigree cat and the Baroness was soon to form the Burmilla Association, with a view to promoting the breed.

Another breeder, Therese Clarke, who acquired Gemma from the original litter, launched the Burmilla Cat Club in 1984, with a regular publication called the 'BCC Mews'. Within four years the club had 50 active members and more recently this figure has risen to 70.

With the two groups of breeders both actively developing the Burmilla, it was soon safely established as an important new breed. The first (Kirchberg) group made efforts to improve the body shape, while the second (Clarke) group concentrated on improving the tipped coat.

The Burmilla was granted preliminary championship status in Britain in 1990.

Personality: Terms used to describe this breed include: playful, outgoing, sociable, friendly, affectionate, sweet-tempered and gentle.

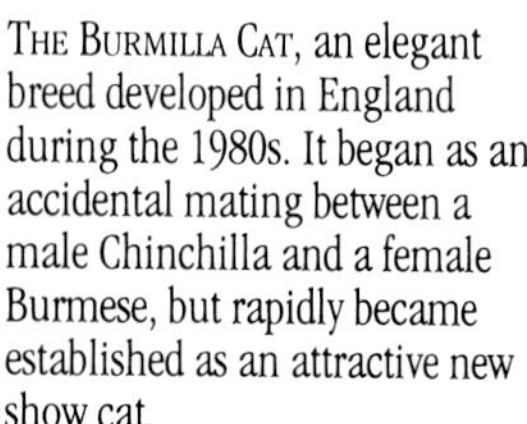

The Burmilla Cat, an elegant breed developed in England during the 1980s. It began as an accidental mating between a male Chinchilla and a female Burmese, but rapidly became established as an attractive new show cat.

Colour Forms:
GCCF: The agouti coat, which appears in both standard and silver versions, may either be tipped or shaded, in the following colours: Black; Blue; Chocolate; Lilac; Red; Caramel; Apricot; Cream; Black Tortie; Blue Tortie; Chocolate Tortie; Lilac Tortie; Caramel Tortie.
Breed Clubs:
Burmilla-Asian Association. Address: 1 Thistlecroft Rd, Hersham, Surrey, KT12 5QT, England.
Burmilla Cat Club. Address: Mill House, Letcombe Regis, Oxon, OX12 9JD, England.

Burmoiré Cat

Domestic Breed. A recent British breed created by mating Burmilla with Burmese. Ghost tabby markings on the body give the fur the look of rippling, or the moiré pattern of watered silk. In its anatomy and the texture of its fur it resembles the Burmese Cat, but its colour and markings are like those of the Oriental Smoke. A member of the Asian Group, it has now been renamed the Asian Smoke.

Bustopher Jones

Fictional Cat. 'The Cat About Town' from T. S. Eliot's 1939 *Old Possum's Book of Practical Cats.* An immaculate, night-clubbing cat whose story begins: 'Bustopher Jones is *not* skin and bones – /In fact, he's remarkably fat. /He doesn't haunt pubs – he has eight or nine clubs, /For he's the St. James's Street Cat!'

Butter Cat

Legendary Cat. In Scandinavia there was a mythical cat known over a wide range as the 'Butter Cat'. Unlike most legendary cats, this one was not evil, but a protector and a provider. Because it was noticed that cats loved their bowls of cream, it became a superstitious belief that they were 'bringers-of-gifts', especially milk and butter. In Finland this benign cat was known as 'Para'. Further north, in Lapland, she became 'Smieragatto'.

Cactus Cat

Legendary Cat. The Cactus Cat was one of the 'Fearsome Critters' invented in the 19th century by the frontiersmen of the American West. It was an amusement of theirs to pass the time telling tall tales and these developed into a whole cycle of bizarre animals. The Cactus Cat had thorny hair, especially exaggerated on the ears. Its tail was branched. On its front legs there were savage, sharp blades of bone, with which it slashed the giant cacti to get at the sap within. The sap fermented and the cat then drank it, quickly becoming intoxicated, after which it ran off uttering horrible screams.

Caffer Cat

Wild Feline. *(Felis sylvestris lybica)* The Caffer Cat used to be thought of as a full species *(Felis caffra,* or *Felis ocreata)* but it is now considered to be no more than a subspecies of the common Wild Cat. Today it is usually known as the African Wild Cat (see entry). Also referred to as Caffre Cat, Kaffir Cat or Egyptian Cat. It is the original ancestor of the domestic cat.

The Caffer Cat was the name given by earlier authors to what is now generally known as the African Wild Cat, the ancestor of modern domestic cats. This illustration of it appeared in Edward Hamilton's 1896 *The Wild Cat of Europe.*

Cait Sith

Legendary Cat. According to the folklore of the Scottish Highlands, there exists a fairy cat called the *Cait Sith*. It is larger than a domestic cat, black in colour and with a white spot on its breast. It has an arched back and erect bristles in its fur. Unlike other fairy-creatures, this one is believed to have a solid physical presence. It is thought to be a transformed witch.

In reality, the *Cait Sith* is almost certainly what is now known as the Kellas Cat – a large black hybrid between feral domestic cats and Scottish Wildcats. Specimens of these impressive hybrids were examined scientifically in the 1980s. (See Kellas Cat.)

Bibliography:

1989. Shuker, K. *Mystery Cats of the World.* Robert Hale, London.

Calamanco Cat

Domestic Breed. A local name for a tortoiseshell cat. Sometimes spelled Calimanco. The term was in use in the 19th century in several regions of England including Cheshire, Lancashire and East Anglia. Calamanco was a material defined as 'a woollen stuff of Flanders, glossy on the surface, and woven with a satin twill and chequered in the warp, so that the checks are seen on one side only'.

Calico

Coat Pattern. An American name for a Tortoiseshell and White Cat. Like the Tortoiseshell Cat, this colour form is sex-linked and nearly always female. Males do occur occasionally but are extremely rare.

For most Americans, the Calico Cat and the Tortie and White are one and the same, but for some there are subtle distinctions between the two. Writing in 1989, Dennis Kelsey-Wood describes the Calico Cat coat as 'white with unbrindled patches of black and red. As a preferred minimum, the cat should have white feet, legs, underside, chest and muzzle . . . Once a cat has more than half of its body total in white, then it is a calico.' He explains that, with less white, a cat may be classified as either tortie and white or as calico, depending on how the white patches are distributed. In the calico, the lower parts of the cat should be predominantly white, as if the animal had stepped in a pail of milk.

Calico Cats were first taken seriously in the world of pedigree cat shows in the late 1950s. Since then, a number of variant forms have been developed including the following: (1) Cinnamon-Cream Calico; (2) Dilute Calico (= white with unbrindled blue and cream); (3) Fawn-Cream Calico; (4) Lavender-Cream Calico; (5) Van Calico (white with black and red confined to the extremities); (6) Cinnamon-Cream Van Calico; (7) Dilute Van Calico (white with blue and cream confined to the extremities); (8) Fawn-Cream Van Calico; (9) Lavender-Cream Van Calico.

Specialist Club:

Calico Cat Registry International. Address: P.O. Box 944, Morongo Valley, CA 92256, USA.

California Rex Cat

Domestic Breed. First discovered in California in 1959. Better known as the Marcel Cat.

History: Mrs F. Blancheri discovered two wavy-haired cats in a San Bernadino animal shelter, a female called 'Mystery Lady of Rodell', who was an odd-eyed tortoiseshell, and her son, who was a red tabby. They were acquired by Bob and Dell Smith who, on seeing that their curly coats were longer and silkier than those of typical Rex Cats, decided to give them a distinctive name – 'The Marcel Cat'. When they mated Mystery Lady with her son, the result was an even longer-coated offspring, a red tabby female.

These Marcel Cats were found to be genetically compatible with the Cornish Rex.

California Spangled Cat

Domestic Breed. A new American spotted breed deliberately created by a carefully planned breeding programme. Sometimes called the 'California Spangle'.

Appearance: The special feature of this short-haired cat is that its coat is covered in distinct, conspicuous, round, black spots. Its long, well-muscled body is carried low, as if the animal is permanently on the hunt. In a strange way, this low-slung walk makes the cat reminiscent of a much larger feline species. The blunt tail always has a black tip.

History: When American screen writer Paul Casey of Burbank, California, was on an assignment to the Olduvai Gorge in Africa in 1971, he was horrified at the wanton destruction of African leopards that was still taking place. He commented later: 'While I was there, we received word that a poacher had just killed and skinned the last remaining breeding leopard in the area. This, to me, seemed a sad signal of things to come.'

He resolved to create a domestic breed of cat to serve as a reminder of the beauty of all spotted felines. On returning home, he drew up an elaborate and ambitious eleven-generation

blueprint for a breeding programme that would, in theory, give him the new breed he wanted. The idea was to create a wild-looking cat by using a combination of purely domestic stock. The foundation stock was chosen personally by him from four continents. Eight different lines were involved, including an Abyssinian/domestic cross-breed, an American Shorthair, an Angora-type silver spotted tabby, a British Shorthair, a feral Egyptian cat (a Cairo street cat), a domestic shorthair from Malaysia (a house-cat), a spotted Manx and a traditional Seal Point Siamese. The project was a success. With the 11th generation, the first true Spangled Cats arrived on cue. By 1991, the breed had been accepted by two American associations (TICA and the ACA). A California Spangled Cat Association has been formed, with Paul Casey as its president.

A unique feature of this breed, and one that has caused severe criticism in some quarters, is that it was introduced to the world, not at a major cat show, but on the pages of the Neiman Marcus department store's 1986 Christmas mail-order catalogue. Spangled kittens were offered for sale at $1,400 in a 'his and hers Xmas surprise present package'. This unusual debut saw it branded by many as a purely commercial cat – a designer cat for the rich. The catalogue made it clear that kittens could be bought 'in any color clients may desire to match their clothes or their house decorations'.

A humane society called for a boycott of Neiman Marcus, and it is reported that there was protest picketing. One author described the new breed as 'an exclusive West Coast feline starlet'. Another commented sternly: 'Living things are not appropriate catalogue items to be bred for a luxury market and sold as high-priced toys.'

Defenders of the breed retort that it was 'an environmental symbol for the protection of endangered species of spotted wild cat', and it would seem that they eventually won the day because, by 1992, the price of California Spangled kittens had risen to $3,600 and there was a long waiting-list of would-be owners. In a 1994 interview, Paul Casey stated that he had originally intended 'to provide only five cats. Instead they took in orders for over 350 in the first month alone. We never even came close to filling all the orders.' He saw the value of the publicity surrounding the launch of the Spangled Cats as giving him a launching platform to further his original aims, namely 'to draw attention to the plight of the wild cats'. And he has

THE CALIFORNIAN SPANGLED CAT, a recently created spotted breed which has caused considerable controversy because it was launched, not at a major cat show, but in a mail-order catalogue.

since been active in trying to stamp out the illegal hunting and slaughter of Central and South American wild cats.

Personality: The following terms have been used to describe this breed: expressive, good-tempered, active, athletic and unusually intelligent.

Colour Forms: Nine colours have been recorded: Black; Blue; Bronze; Brown; Charcoal; Gold; Red; Silver; White.

Breed Club:

The California Spangled Cat Association (CSCA). Address: P.O. Box 386, Sun Valley, CA 91352, USA.

Call Name

Feline Term. Each pedigree cat has two names – a short 'Call Name', used at home when calling the cat, and a long 'Registered Name', used for competitions and registrations. The Registered Names are often amazingly lengthy, flowery and complicated, and owners of ordinary pet cats sometimes ridicule them, but they are essential for precise identification in competitive showing, and are also useful in telling experts something about the breeding source and relationships of an individual cat. In some breeds it is even possible to tell a cat's age by its name since the breeders will give all their kittens born in one year names starting with one letter.

Calvin

Calvin, an unusually intelligent stray cat that American author Harriet Beecher Stowe shared with her literary friend Charles Dudley Warner. When Calvin died in 1882, Warner wrote a moving essay in his honour.

Pet Cat. Calvin was a Maltese Cat who arrived one day at the home of Harriet Beecher Stowe, the American author who wrote *Uncle Tom's Cabin*. He was an assertive, gastronomic cat who, having taken over the house, never left, and frequently sat on the author's shoulder as she worked on her manuscripts. He was a dignified animal with a serene air, who 'radiated calm during the hours of frenzied writing', who was intelligent enough to learn to open door-handles, and who was never late for meals in the dining room. A literary friend of Stowe's, who looked after the cat when she was away, wrote of him that 'he is a reasonable cat and understands pretty much everything except binomial theorem'.

Cameo

Coat Colour. An American name for a cat with a coat that is made up of hairs which are white with red tips. There are three types: Smoke, Shaded and Shell, according to the extent of the tipping. The Smoke variety is deeply tipped, the Shaded is moderately tipped and the Shell is lightly tipped. When the cat is still, its coat appears to be the colour of the tips of the hairs, but when it moves, the white bases of the hairs are revealed, so that its coat colour seems to change.

Modern variants include the following: (1) Shaded Cameo (= Red Shaded); (2) Cream Shaded Cameo; (3) Shell Cameo (= Red Chinchilla); (4) Cream Shell Cameo; (5) Smoke Cameo (= Red Smoke); (6) Dilute Smoke Cameo (= Cream Smoke); (7) Red Smoke Cameo; (8) Tabby Cameo; (9) Dilute Tabby Cameo; (10) Tabby and White Cameo.

Specialist Club:

Cameo Cat Club of America. Address: 1800 West Ardel, Kuna, ID 83634, USA.

Canadian Lynx

Wild Feline. *(Lynx canadensis)* Also known as the North American Lynx, because, in addition to most of northern Canada, it also occurs in Alaska.

The Canadian Lynx is a medium-sized, cold-country cat with a stocky body, very thick, dense fur, long legs with enormous, 'snow-shoe' paws, black-tufted ears, and a very short, black-tipped tail. Its coat is usually plain, but sometimes a faint spotting is visible. There is a black and white throat ruff that fans outwards when the cat hisses.

A solitary hunter, with individual territories of up to 250 sq km (100 sq mi), the Canadian Lynx feeds almost entirely on Snowshoe Hares, but will occasionally eat mice, voles, squirrels and some ground birds.

C

THE CANADIAN LYNX *(Lynx canadensis),* a cold-country feline from the frozen north of the American continent. Because of its exceptionally long hind legs, its back slopes upwards towards its stumpy, black-tipped tail.

It is very similar to the Northern Lynx of Europe and Asia, but is only about half the size and has a shorter tail and a plainer coat. Some authorities feel that these two lynxes belong to the same species, but the general feeling today is that they should be recognized as separate. (See entry for Northern Lynx.)

Size: Length of Head + Body: 80–100 cm (31½–39½ in). Tail: 5–13 cm (2–5 in). Weight: 8–10 kg (17½–22 lb).

Distribution: Northern Canada and Alaska.

CARACAL

WILD FELINE. *(Felis caracal)* The name comes from the Turkish word *karacal* or *karakulak,* meaning 'black ear'. It used to be known as the Desert Lynx, Red Lynx, Persian Lynx, or African Lynx. German: *Karacal,* or *Wüstenluchs;* French: *Le Caracal.* Swahili: *Simbamangu;* Afrikaans: *Rooikat;* Thai: *Siagosh* (or *Siya-gush*) also meaning 'black ear'.

The Caracal is a lynx-like animal of dry woodlands, grasslands and scrub, where it hunts birds, rodents and small antelopes. A medium-sized cat, it is very fast in its movements, employing a stalk-and-spring technique with a high-speed climax. They are particularly efficient at striking down birds as they take flight, leaping high in the air to deliver a powerful blow with an outstretched paw.

The short, dense fur is a uniform pale reddish-brown with hardly any markings. It has a slender, supple body, long legs and a short tail, but its most characteristic feature is the unusual design of its ears. Several other species have small ear-tufts, but in the Caracal they are elongated and highly conspicuous. The ears themselves are already very tall and, with the black tufts of hairs protruding at their tips, they become a dominant feature. Whenever the Caracal is agitated, it rapidly twitches its ears – far more than any other feline species – and this frequent mood signal gives it a communication system that is lacking in other cats.

Like the Cheetah, the Caracal has in the past been trained as a hunting companion by sportsmen. It has never seriously rivalled the Cheetah in this respect, but in India some local

The Caracal *(Felis caracal)* gets its name from its 'black ears', from which sprout enormous tufts of hair. These tufts are conspicuously twitched whenever the animal becomes agitated.

rulers have kept packs to hunt peafowl and in Iran they used to be set against pigeons. Like Cheetahs, they become remarkably tame and co-operative, compared with other wild cat species.

Size: Length of Head + Body: 60–90 cm ($23\frac{1}{2}$–$35\frac{1}{2}$ in). Tail: 23–31 cm (9–12 in). Weight: 14–19 kg (31–42 lb).

Distribution: Africa, the Middle East and S.W. Asia. In Africa it is found everywhere except in the Sahara and the rain-forest zone in the west. In the Middle East it is found almost everywhere except in the Arabian Desert. In Asia it reaches Turkey, Afghanistan, southernmost Russia, Pakistan and N.W. India. Despite its earlier name of 'Desert Lynx' and its pale, uniform camouflage colouring, it avoids the bleakness of the true deserts.

Caramel

Coat Colour. This term is employed differently by different cat organizations. It can refer either to a cat with a reddish-brown coat, in which case it is the same as a Cinnamon Cat, or it can apply to a cat with a bluish-fawn coat.

Carousel Cats

Cat Art. A Carousel Cat is a painted, wood-carved figure large enough to carry a human rider.

Fairground carousels or roundabouts have used a number of different animal models in the past. The original and most common was, of course, the horse, but riders were eventually offered a choice of other wooden steeds, including several felines. Lions and tigers were the most popular, but two wood-carvers working in the United States did produce a number of gigantic domestic cats. These were fashioned by craftsmen at the Hershell-Spillman Company and the Dentzel Carousel Works.

According to American author Staci Layne Wilson, it was the Dentzel carver Salvatore 'Cherni' Cerniglario who created the best cats – playful animals, usually with a fish, frog, bird or squid held in their jaws. Sadly, from the 1920s onwards these original wood-carved figures were

The Caracal is a medium-sized, Lynx-like African cat with a plain reddish-brown coat that blends well with its savannah habitat.

gradually phased out and today all carousel animals are made of fibreglass. (Only 300 of the 9,000 early wooden carousels are still operating.)

The antique wooden cats, some of which were saved when the old carousels were broken up, are now recognized as a major form of folk art, and have become collectors' items. One was sold at auction in 1992 for $27,500.

(Further information is available from the American Carousel Society, Dept. CF, 470 S. Pleasant Avenue, Ridgewood, NJ 07450, USA.)

Carthusian Cat

Domestic Breed. This is an early name for the Chartreux Cat. It is described by Richard Lydekker in 1876 as follows: 'The Carthusian or "Blue" Cat is a very beautiful long and soft-haired breed with fur of a dark greyish-blue colour, the lips and the soles of the feet retaining, however, the normal black hue.'

Castle Cats

Working Cats. Many British castles still house resident cats whose official duties include reducing the rodent populations. However, now that most of these great buildings have become tourist attractions, complete with restaurants, snack-bars and picnic areas, their feline occupants have enjoyed an unexpected softening of their lifestyle. For example, Sumo, the huge ginger-and-white tom cat who patrols the castle grounds and 35 acres of gardens at Hever Castle, where Henry VIII so ardently courted the ill-fated Ann Boleyn, has become so well fed that the water-fowl around the castle moat completely ignore his approach.

Bibliography:

1995. Surman, R. *Castle Cats of Britain and Ireland.* HarperCollins, London.

Note: There are two similar, previous books on working cats by the same author, called *Cathedral Cats* (1993) and *College Cats* (1994).

Cat

Feline Term. The English name for a member of the feline family. The name is similar in other languages:

Names Similar to English 'Cat'

The Domestic Cat. A 17th century illustration from the *Historiae Naturalis* of Johannes Jonstonus (1657).

LANGUAGE	WORD FOR 'CAT'
Anglo-Saxon	*cat / catt*
Armenian	*gatz / gadoo*
Arabic	*quttah / kittah / kitte / qitt / qutt*
Basque	*catua / catus*
Bohemian	*kot / kocour (m)/ kote / kotka* (f)
Breton	*kaz*
Bulgarian	*kotka / kotki*
Catalan	*gat / cat* (m)/ *cata* (f)
Celtic	*cat*
Cornish	*cath / kath / katt*
Czechoslovakian	*kocka*
Danish	*kat*
Dutch	*kat*
Egyptian	*kut*
Finnish	*katti*
French	*chat* (m)/ *chatte* (f)
Gaelic	*cat*

LANGUAGE	WORD FOR 'CAT'
German	*katze / katti / ket*
Greek	*gata / catta / kata*
Hebrew (Sephardic)	*chatool* (m) / *chatoola* (f)
Hebrew (Ashkenazi)	*chasul*
Hindustani	*katas*
Hungarian	*kaczer*
Icelandic	*köttr / kottur* (m)/ *ketta* (f)
Irish	*cat / cait*
Italian	*gatto* (m)/ *gatta* (f)
Latin	*catus / cattus.*
Lithuanian	*kate*
Maltese	*qattus*
Manx	*cayt*
Middle English	*cat / catt / kat / katt*
Middle German	*kattaro*
Modern Egyptian	*kut* (m) / *kutta* (f)
Norwegian	*katt* (m)/ *katta* (f)

LANGUAGE	WORD FOR 'CAT'
Nubian	*kadis*
Old English	*gattus*
Old French	*hater*
Old High German	*chazza / chataro / cazza / caza*
Old Norse	*kött-r*
Old Slavonic	*kot'ka*
Polish	*kot/ koczor* (m)
Portuguese	*gato* (m)/ *gata* (f)
Provençal	*cat* (m)/ *cate* (f)
Prussian	*catto*
Russian	*kot* (m) / *kotchka / koshka* (f)
Scottish	*catti*
Slovenish	*kot*
Sorabian	*kotka*
Spanish	*gato* (m)/ *gata* (f)
Swedish	*katt* (m)/ *katta* (f)
Swiss	*chaz*
Turkish	*keti / kedi / qadi*
Ukranian	*kotuk*
Welsh	*cath/ kath / cetti*
Yiddish	*kats / gattus / chatul*

Clearly, this is an ancient word that has spread across the world from a single source. The source appears to be Arabic, because the oldest use of it is found in North Africa. This fits with the idea that all domestic cats are descended from the North African Wild Cat, *Felis sylvestris lybica,* via domestication by the early Egyptians.

Languages that use a completely different word for cat include the following:

NAMES VERY DIFFERENT FROM ENGLISH 'CAT'

LANGUAGE	WORD FOR 'CAT'
Arabic	*biss* (m)/ *bissie* (f)
Chinese	*miu / mio / mao*
Dutch	*poes*
Modern Egyptian	*mau / mait*
Filipino	*pusa*
Finnish	*kissa*
Hawaiian	*owan / popoki*
Hindi	*billy*
Hungarian	*macska*
India	*billy*
Indochinese	*puss*
Indonesian	*kutjing*
Japanese	*neko*
Latin	*felis*
Malay	*kuching*
Mohawk	*tako's*
Rumanian	*pisica*
Sanskrit	*mârgâras*
Swahili	*paka*
Thai	*meo*
Vietnamese	*meo*
Yugoslavian	*macka*

THE CHINESE symbol for the cat.

CATAMOUNT

WILD FELINE. An abbreviation of Cat-a-Mountain (see entry), in the past this was frequently used to refer to any wild feline, but is most commonly used today as an alternative name for the American Puma. It was probably favoured for the Puma because that species was also known as the Mountain Lion.

CAT-A-MOUNTAIN

LEGENDARY CAT. Marco Polo reported the existence of a predatory cat in the Far East with the body of a leopard but with a strange skin that stretches out when it hunts, enabling it to fly in pursuit of its prey. The Cat-a-Mountain appears to be an imaginative amalgam of a big cat and a large bat, but later authors frequently used it simply as a name for a wild cat. By the 17th century some authors had abbreviated it to Catamount (see entry).

CAT ANTHOLOGIES

CAT LITERATURE. In recent years it has become popular to publish cat anthologies, bringing together many short pieces of feline literature in single volumes. Although these is a great deal of repetition, with favourite writings appearing time after time, these books do provide a valuable first introduction to the subject. In the post-war period, since 1945, the publication of a cat anthology has become almost an annual event. Examples of anthologies are as follows:

1900. Gielgud, V. H. (Compiler) *Cats, a Personal Anthology.* Newnes, London.
1903. Miller, R. (Editor) *Just Cats.* Doubleday, New York.
1912. Repplier, A. (Editor) *The Cat.* Sturgis & Walton, New York.
1921. Van Vetchen, K. (Editor) *Lords of the Housetops.* Knopf, New York.
1932. Anon. *The Genius of the Hearth.* Methuen, London.
1932. Drew, E. & Joseph, M. (Editors) *Puss in Books.* Geoffrey Bles, London.
1937. Clarke, F.E. (Editor) *Cats – and Cats.* Macmillan, New York. (second edition in 1949).
1944. Zistel, E. (Editor) *A Treasury of Cat Stories.* Greenberg, New York.
1946. Scott, W.S. (Editor) *A Clowder of Cats.* Westhouse, London.
1946. Zistel, E. (Editor) *Golden Book of Cat Stories.* Ziff Davis, Chicago.
1947. Crawford, N.A. (Editor) *Cats in Prose and Verse.* Coward McCann, New York.
1949. Hilditch, G. (Editor) *In Praise of Cats.* Muller, London.
1952. Joseph, M. (Editor) *Best Cat Stories.* Faber & Faber, London.
1956. Mason, P. & Mason, J. *Favourite Cat Stories.* Messmer, New York.
1957. Clarke, F.E. (Editor) *Of Cats and Men.* Macmillan, New York.
1958. Aymar, B. (Editor) *The Personality of the Cat.* Bonanza Books, New York.
1958. Beecroft, J. (Editor) *Plain and Fancy Cats.* Rinehart, New York.
1960. Brown, B. (Compiler) *All Cats Go to Heaven.* Grosset & Dunlap, New York.
1961. Brown, B. (Compiler) *The Wonderful World of Cats.* Harper, New York.
1963. Lee, E. & Kneebone, P. (Editors) *A Quorum of Cats.* Elek Books, London.
1964. Beecroft, J. (Editor) *Cat Magic.* Little, Brown, Boston.
1966. Sillar, F. C. & Meyler, R.M.(Editors) *Cats Ancient and Modern.* Studio Vista, London.
1968. Montgomery, J. (Editor) *The Best Cat Stories.* London.
1969. Currah, A. (Editor) *The Cat Compendium.* Meredith, New York (and in UK in 1972, Kimber, London).
1969. Necker, C. (Compiler) *Cats and Dogs.* Barnes, New York.
1969. Silverberg, B. (Editor) *Kitten Caboodle.* Holt, Rinehart & Winston, New York.
1972. Necker, C. (Editor) *Supernatural Cats.* Doubleday, New York (and in paperback in 1973 by Warner Books, New York).
1974. Pond, G. (Editor) *The Cat-lover's Bedside Book.* Batsford, London.
1976. MacBeth, G. & Booth, M. (Editors) *The Book of Cats.* Secker & Warburg, London.
1977. Suares, J.C. & Chwast, S. (Editors) *The Literary Cat.* Berkley, New York.
1981. Mander, R. (Editor) *CATegories.* Weidenfeld & Nicolson, London.
1987. Caras, R. (Editor) *Treasury of Great Cat Stories.* Robson Books, London
1990. Stephens, J. R. (Editor) *The Enchanted Cat.* Prima, Rocklin, CA.
1992. Oates, J. C. & Halpern, D. (Editors) *The Sophisticated Cat.* Dutton, New York (and in UK in 1993 by Macmillan, London).
1993. Wheen, F. (Editor) *The Chatto Book of Cats.* Chatto & Windus, London.

Catarina

Pet Cat. Edgar Allen Poe's pet cat was the inspiration for his story *The Black Cat.* When Poe's wife was dying of tuberculosis in the winter of 1846, the couple were destitute. A visitor found the stricken woman lying on a bed of straw 'wrapped in her husband's great coat with a large tortoiseshell cat in her bosom. The wonderful cat seemed conscious of her great usefulness. The coat and the cat were the sufferer's only means of warmth.'

Drawing of a cat by Michelangelo (1475–1564).

Cat Art

Feline History. Many great artists have included cats in their work, and some have made them the main subject of drawings, paintings or sculptures. They include Leonardo da Vinci, Michelangelo, Boucher, Watteau, Delacroix, Géricault, Rubens, Manet, Gainsborough, Reynolds, Courbet, Renoir, Vuillard, Bonnard, Gauguin, Franz Marc, Marie Laurencin, Klee, Picasso, Giacometti, Balthus, Leonor Fini, Lucien Freud, Andy Warhol and David Hockney.

GIRL WITH A KITTEN, 1947,
by Lucien Freud.
(Private Collection)

Less famous artists who have become well known especially for their cat studies include Gottfried Mind (1768–1814), an eccentric hunchback from Berne, Switzerland, over-enthusiastically called 'the Raphael of Cats'; Japanese artist Tsugouharu Foujita (1886–1968); Dutch-born Henrietta Ronner (1821–1909), the epitome of the sentimental Victorian artist; Frenchman Théophile Steinlen (1859–1923) whose Parisian cat posters became collectors' items; and British illustrator Louis Wain (1860–1939), whose anthropomorphic felines are loved by some and detested by others.

A number of books have been devoted to the subject of cat art. They include those listed in the following bibliography.

Bibliography:

1892. Spielmann, M.H. *Henrietta Ronner. Painter of Cats and Cat Life*. Cassell, London.
1970. Fish, E. *The Cat in Art*. Lerner, Minneapolis.

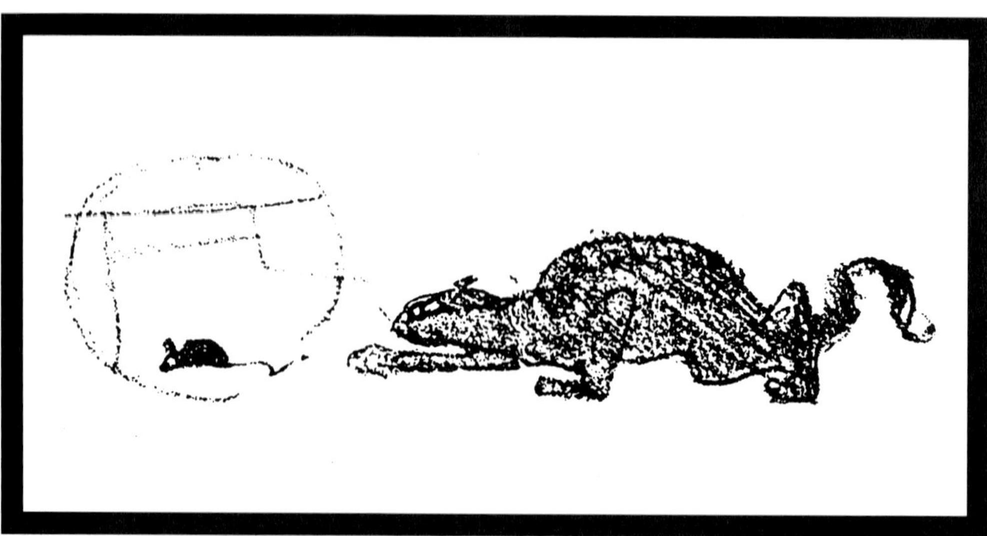

Cat Stalking a Mouse,
by Henri de Toulouse-Lautrec
(1864–1901).

1974. McClinton, K.M. *Antique Cats for Collectors.* Lutterworth Press, London.
1976. Suares, J-C. and Chwast, S. *The Illustrated Cat.* Harmony Books, New York.
1976. Johnson, B. *American Cat-alogue. The Cat in American Folk Art.* Avon Books, New York.
1981. O'Neill, J.P. *Metropolitan Cats.* Abrams, New York.
1981. Steinlen. *Des Chats. Images sans Parole.* Flammarion, Paris. (Libro reprint)
1984. Fournier, K. and Lehmann, J. *Chats Naïfs.* Galerie Naïfs et Primitifs, Paris.
1984. Muncaster, A.L. and Sawyer, E.Y. *The Cat Made Me Buy It!* Crown, New York.
1985. Fournier, K. and Lehmann, J. *All Our Cats.* Dutton, New York (Revised edition of *Chats Naïfs*).
1986. Muncaster, A.L. and Sawyer, E.Y. *The Cat Sold It!* Crown, New York.
1987. Foucart-Walter, E. and Rosenberg, P. *Le Chat et la Palette.* Adam Biro, Paris.
1988. Foucart-Walter, E. and Rosenberg, P. *The Painted Cat.* Rizzoli, New York (English version of *Le Chat et la Palette*).
1989. Leman, M. *Martin Leman's Cats.* Pelham Books, London.
1991. Bryant, M. *The Artful Cat.* Quarto, London.
1991. Silvester, J. and Mobbs, A. *A Catland Companion.* Michael O'Mara, London.
1992. Martins, P. *A Brush With Cats.* Souvenir Press, London.
1994. Busch, H. and Silver, B. *Why Cats Paint.* Ten Speed Press, Berkeley, California.(An amusing spoof book about paintings by cats.)
1994. Howard, T. *The Illustrated Cat.* Grange Books, London.

There has also been an excellent series of *Cats in Art* diaries, published by Alan Hutchison, London (annually from 1986 to 1992) and Four Seasons Publishing, London (1995), as well as a number of *Cats in Art* address books, also by Alan Hutchison, London. All are heavily illustrated with colour plates of paintings featuring cats.

Catasauqua

Fictional Cat. A female Manx Cat invented by Mark Twain in a bedtime story for his daughters. She first appeared in print in *Letters from the Earth*.

Cat Authorities

Feline History. Over the years, many feline experts have devoted themselves to increasing our knowledge of the world of cats. Some have studied their natural history, others have laboured in the archives of cat literature, and still others have helped to develop the many exciting pedigree breeds we have today. Among them a few stand out as true authorities, individuals who have in one way or another made a major, original contribution to the subject. They include the following (for further details see separate entries):

François-Augustin Paradis de Moncrif (1687–1770): Author of the first serious book on cats.
Champfleury (1821–1889): Author of the first scholarly book on the cat.
Harrison Weir (1824–1906): Father of the modern cat show.
George Mivart (1827–1900): Author of the first major volume on the anatomy of the cat.
Frances Simpson: Author of the first major book about cats in the 20th century.
Grace Pond (1910–): The most prolific author of cat books.
Paul Leyhausen: Zoologist who made the most detailed studies of the behaviour of cats.
Claire Necker: The major bibliographer of cat literature.
Angela Sayer: The most wide-ranging of modern authorities on pedigree cats, being breeder, innovator, photographer, editor, author and President of the CA.
George Schaller: The first field-worker to make detailed studies of big cats in the wild.
Roger Tabor (1948–): The field-worker who pioneered studies of feral urban cats.

Cat Books

Cat Literature. In her invaluable cat bibliography, *Four Centuries of Cat Books,* published in 1972, Claire Necker lists 2,293 books on the subject of domestic cats. Since then, hundreds more have appeared, so that there are now probably more than 3,000 in the English language. Of these, many are either fictional or anecdotal, or are factual books of minor importance. Some, however, stand out as factual landmarks, for either their originality or their comprehensivity. The most significant ones are listed below, in chronological order.
Note: A few important works in foreign languages are included, but only when they have been made available later in English translations. Books on single breeds, specific topics, wild species or anthologies are excluded here, but can be found elsewhere under the relevant headings.)

The 100 Best Cat Books
A personal selection of general, factual works

1727. Moncrif, Francois Augustin Paradis de. *Les Chats.*
Gabriel-Francois Quillau, Paris. 204p. + 16p.
This is the earliest 'classic' cat book, and one of the first books ever written solely about cats. An English version appeared in 1961, translated from the French by Reginald Bretnor. Published in a luxury edition by the Golden Cockerel Press in London, it was limited to 400 copies. A facsimile of this English edition was published in 1965 by A.S. Barnes in New York and Thomas Yoseloff in London.

Illustration from the earliest of all cat books, Moncrif's *Les Chats* of 1727.

1834. Jardine, William. *The Natural History of the Felinae.*
W.H. Lizars, Edinburgh. 276p.
One of the earliest popular books on the wild cat species of the world, illustrated with 38 colour plates. Part of the series called The Naturalists' Library (Mammalia. Vol. II).
1868. Ross, Charles H. *The Book of Cats.*
Griffin & Farran, London. 296p.
A feline chronicle referred to by the author as cat 'facts and fancies, legendary, lyrical, medical, mirthful and miscellaneous'.
1869. Fleury-Husson, Jules (Under the name M. Champfleury) *Les Chats; Histoire, Meours, Observations, Anecdotes.*
Paris. 214p.
Considered to be one of the cat classics. Translated into English in 1885 by Mrs Cashel Hoey, under the title of *The Cat Past and Present.*
1874. Stables, William Gordon. *Cats: their Points and Characteristics.*
Dean & Son, London. 484p.
A detailed, wide-ranging study of cats with some of the earliest colour plates of the domestic breeds. The author was a naval surgeon who retired early due to ill-health, after which he wrote over 120 books, including five on cats, of which this is the most important.

1881. Mivart, St George Jackson. *The Cat.*
John Murray, London. 557p.
Includes a detailed study of the cat's anatomy and physiology.

1883. Elliot, Daniel Giraud. *A Monograph of the Felidae.*
London. 108p.
The most coveted of all cat books. A copy was recently offered for sale at £25,000 ($40,000). There are 43 large (imperial folio) hand-coloured plates by Wolf and Smit, considered to be their finest animal illustrations.

The title page from one of the first books to be written on the subject of domestic cats by an English author: *The Book of Cats* by Charles Ross (1868).

1887. Rule, Philip M. *The Cat: its Natural History; Domestic Varieties, Management and Treatment.*
Swan Sonnenschein, Lowrey & Co, London. 176p.
One of the earliest examples of serious advice on the subject of cat care.

1889. Weir, Harrison. *Our Cats and all about them.*
R. Clements, Tunbridge Wells. 248p.
A classic volume on all aspects of domestic cats by the President of the National Cat Club and the father of competitive cat showing.

1893. Jennings, John. *Domestic or Fancy Cats.*
L. Upcott Gill, London. 123p.
A practical guide to cat-keeping, with the emphasis on exhibiting and cat-show judging.

1895. Huidekoper, Rush Shippen. *The Cat.*
D. Appleton & Co, New York. 148p.
An American veterinarian's treatise on cat breeds and their diseases.

1896. Lydekker, Richard. *Cats, Civets and Mungooses.*
Edward Lloyd, London. 312p.
One of the volumes in the Lloyd's Natural History series *(A Hand-book of the Carnivora. Part I)*, this includes a species-by-species survey of wild cats. With 23 colour plates of cats.

1900. Winslow, Helen W. *Concerning Cats.*
David Nutt, London. 284p.
A collection of feline miscellanea made interesting by its turn-of-the-century date.

1901. Repplier, Agnes. *The Fireside Sphinx.*
Gay & Bird, London. 305p.
A scholarly history of cats, by a leading American essayist.

1903. Simpson, Frances. *The Book of the Cat.*
Cassell, London. 380p.
The first truly encyclopedic breed-by-breed survey of domestic cats. Far more ambitious and comprehensive than anything that had gone before it, and remarkably advanced for its period. There are 362 illustrations, including 12 coloured plates.

1909. Marks, Anne. *The Cat in History, Legend and Art.*
Elliot Stock, London. 98p.
An informative history of the cat from early Egyptian times, with rather more detail on ancient cats, including translations from relevant inscriptions and texts.

1920. Van Vechten, Carl. *The Tiger in the House.*
Knopf, New York. 367p.
An important early study of the history, folklore and literature of cats.

1930. Howey, M. Oldfield. *The Cat in the Mysteries of Religion and Magic.*
Rider, London. 254p.
A major study of feline mythology and symbolism.

1940. Langton, N. and Langton, B. *The Cat in Ancient Egypt.*
Cambridge University Press, Cambridge. 92p.
Although little more than an illustrated catalogue of the authors' collection of Egyptian cat figures, this book is important because it is the first attempt to present the subject of ancient Egyptian cats in any detail.

1940. Mellen, Ida. *The Science and the Mystery of the Cat.*
Scribner's, New York. 275p. (London edition in 1946)
The author, both a zoologist and a Vice-president of the Allied Cat Lovers organization in America, provided a painstakingly researched text that was largely overlooked during the crisis days of World War II.

1946. Hickey, John and Beach, Priscilla. *Know Your Cat.*
Harper, New York. 251p.
Despite being a poorly produced austerity volume dating from the end of World War II, this book contains some unusual information not available elsewhere and provides the only reprint of the rare *Murthy's Cattage*, a collection of 'cats of the famous' originally published as a pamphlet by Howard Chapin in 1911.

1948. Soderberg, P.M. *Cat Breeding and General Management.*
Cassell, London. 343p.
A useful if somewhat stolid treatise on the breeding and care of pedigree cats, with the topics arranged alphabetically.

1949. Aberconway, Christabel. *A Dictionary of Cat Lovers: XV Century B.C. to XX Century A.D.*
Michael Joseph, London. 466p.
Packed with an amazing amount of original research into the lives of important cat-lovers from many epochs, this unique cat book is a mine of historical information.

1950. Lockridge, Frances and Lockridge, Richard. *Cats and People.*
Lippincott, New York. 286p.
Two well-known mystery writers took time off to write this study of the relationship between cats and people, which has recently been reprinted in a new edition nearly half a century after it first appeared.

1954. Simms, Jill. *They Walked Beside Me.*
Hutchinson, London. 252p.
A miscellany of feline facts and anecdotes by a well-travelled author, with interesting chapters on domestic cats in India, Africa and Ireland.

1958. Soderberg, P.M. *Pedigree Cats, their Varieties, Breeding and Exhibition.*
Cassell, London. 309p.
A sober, reliable survey of the breeding and exhibiting of pedigree cats by a former Vice-President of the GCCF.

1960. Dechambre, E. *The Pocket Encyclopedia of Cats.*
Elek Books, London. 166p.
This little book hardly justifies the name of encyclopedia, but is nevertheless a useful small dictionary of cats by a French authority.

1963. Conger, Jean. *The Velvet Paw.*
Ivan Obolensky, New York. 182p.
This diverting, extended essay on a variety of feline subjects is described as a history of cats in life, mythology and art, 'from the Sahara to the sandbox'.

1963. Dale-Green, Patricia. *Cult of the Cat.*
Heinemann, London. 189p.
An unusual study of feline folklore, symbolism and superstition.

1965. Manolson, Frank. *C is for Cat.*
Studio Vista, London. 227p.
A guide to cats by a vet with a sense of humour. Although a wide range of topics is covered, the emphasis is on health problems. Disarmingly, the author begins by saying: 'If you really think you can treat your own cat out of a book I pity you a little and your cat a lot.'

1967. Eustace, May and Towe, Elizabeth. *Fifty Years of Pedigree Cats.*
Pelham Books, London. 212p.
Two connoisseurs of pedigree cats trace the history of cat shows and discuss the various breeds.

The jacket design for M. Oldfield Howey's remarkable study of feline symbolism, *The Cat in the Mysteries of Religion and Magic* (1930). The strange picture depicts the 'Sacrifice of an Intruder in the Shrine of Bast'.

1967. Mery, Fernand. *The Life, History and Magic of the Cat.*
Paul Hamlyn, London. 237p.
A rewarding, copiously illustrated history of the cat, translated from the French.

1969. Vesey-Fitzgerald, Brian. *The Domestic Cat.*
Pelham Books, London. 199p.
A stimulating book by the Vice-chairman of the National Cat Club in which he seems to enjoy debunking a great deal of the accepted wisdom of the world of pedigree cats.

1970. Eustace, May. *The World of Show Cats.*
Pelham Books, London. 229p.
A history of cat shows and show cats. The author acknowledges the assistance of over 30 specialist experts, who assisted her with the latest information on particular breeds, or geographical regions.

1970. Necker, Claire. *The Natural History of Cats.*
Delta, New York. 350p.
Perhaps the best-read authority on cats in the world, the author provides a wealth of information on both the biology and the history of the domestic cat.

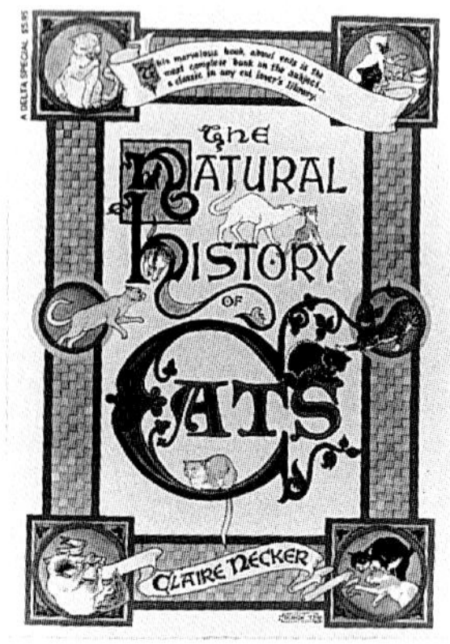

The cover design *(above)* for Claire Necker's invaluable 1970 volume *The Natural History of Cats*.

1972. Ing, Catherine and Pond, Grace. *Champion Cats of the World.*
Harrap, London. 128p.
A scholarly text by an Oxford University lecturer in English Literature, combined with useful texts on the various breeds by an international cat judge, make this a valuable work. In particular, the section detailing the history of the Cat Fancy in 11 major countries provides information that is not available elsewhere.

1972. Pond, Grace (Editor). *The Complete Cat Encyclopedia.*
Heinemann, London. 384p.
At the time of its publication, this was the most ambitious feline encyclopedia attempted. Edited by the organizer of the annual National Cat Club Show in Britain, it has contributions from a wide range of specialists.

1973. Henderson, G.N. and Coffey, D.J. (Editors) *The International Encyclopedia of Cats.*
McGraw-Hill, New York. 256p.
A highly informative, if rather dryly written compilation of feline facts, by a team of sixteen expert contributors. The illustrations are largely in black-and-white.

1974. Grilhé, Gillette. *The Cat and Man.*
Putnam's, New York. 254p.
A splendidly illustrated history of mankind's relationship with cats, originally published in Switzerland.

1976. Fireman, Judy (Editor). *The Cat Catalog. The Ultimate Cat Book.*
Workman Publishing, New York. 352p.
A fascinating miscellany of articles on every possible aspect of domestic cats, including many offbeat topics. The text is far superior to the production quality of the book.

The jacket design for Gillette Grilhé's superbly illustrated book, *The Cat and Man* (1974). The painting, *La Chatte blanche sous un Parasol*, is by Fernand Desnos.

1977. Beadle, Muriel. *The Cat: History, Biology and Behaviour.*
Collins & Harvill Press, London. 251p.
A carefully researched, highly intelligent history of cats ranging over a wide variety of topics. There are no photographs and it wastes little space on illustrations, allowing the scholarly text to dominate, in a way that is all too rare in modern cat books.

1977. Kirk, Mildred. *The Everlasting Cat.*
The Overlook Press, Woodstock, New York. 207p.
A valuable survey of the cat's role in religion, mysticism, folklore and literature, throughout history.

1977. Manolson, Frank. *The Language of your Cat.*
Quarto, London. 159p.
A book by a vet who really understands cats, well illustrated with some unusual action photographs.

1978. Steech, Judith. *The Complete Book of Cats.*

Bison Books, Greenwich, Connecticut. 255p.

A good general reference work covering most aspects of the cat's life including a long section detailing the various domestic breeds.

1978. Wilson, Meredith. *Encyclopedia of American Cat Breeds.*

TFH, New Jersey. 352p.

The highly informative texts on the various breeds compensate for the rather poor quality of the photographs.

1979. Gebhardt, Richard H., Pond, Grace and Raleigh, Ivor. (Editors). *A Standard Guide to Cat Breeds.*

Macmillan, London. 319p.

A complete guide to the Official Standards of cat breeds, for those interested in pedigree cat showing.

1979. Hamilton, E. *In Celebration of Cats.*

David & Charles, Newton Abbot, Devon. 160p.

A delightfully literate commentary in praise of cats.

1979. Leyhausen, Paul. *Cat Behaviour: The Predatory and Social Behaviour of Domestic and Wild Cats.*

Garland STPM Press, New York. 340p.

Translated from the German, this is the most original study ever made of feline behaviour and has been used as a source book by countless authors since it first appeared.

1979. Sayer, Angela. *The Encyclopedia of the Cat.*

Octopus Books, London. 224p.

A useful, well illustrated, general reference work covering feline biology, cat care, wild cats and pedigree breeds.

1980. Briggs, Katharine. *Nine Lives: Cats in Folklore.*

Routledge and Kegan Paul. 222p.

Of special interest because this is the only book to have been written solely about feline folklore.

1980. Burger, Manfred. *Cats: The Complete Book.*

Exeter Books, New York. 253p.

Translated from the original German, this wide-ranging text, illustrated mostly by black-and-white photographs, covers most aspects of cat life, with an emphasis on cat care and ailments.

1980. Hart, Ernest and Hart, Allan. *The Complete Guide to All Cats.*

Scribner's, New York. 318p.

The title of this work by a father and son team is misleading, because the sections which cover feline history and breeds play only a minor role, while the main value of the book lies in its treatment of cat health, breeding and care, reflecting the fact that the second author is a vet.

1980. Henderson, Nick. *The Book of Cats.*

Albany Books, London. 189p.

A leading vet's general introduction to the world of cats, including sections on choosing a kitten, housing a cat, feline communication, ailments, breeding and showing.

1980. Pond, Grace. *Rand McNally Pictorial Encyclopedia of Cats.*

Rand McNally, Chicago. 160p.

A well-illustrated and reliable general encyclopedia of cats covering a wide range of topics, by a major authority on the subject.

1980. Wright, Michael and Walters, Sally. (Editors) *The Book of the Cat.*

Pan Books, London. 256p.

Another impressive feline encyclopedia, with an extensive list of consultants and contributors.

1981. Wasserman, Rosanne (Editor). *Metropolitan Cats.*
Metropolitan Museum, New York. 112p.
A visual feast of domestic felines of all kinds from the Museum's vast collection, accompanied by extended captions.

1982. Allaby, Michael and Crawford, Peter. *The Curious Cat.*
Michael Joseph, London. 160p.
A report on an original field study of a group of Devon farm cats carried out by zoologist Peter Apps, which was filmed by the BBC.

1982. Pond, Grace. et al. *The Cat: The Breeds, the Care and the Training.*
Exeter Books, New York. 144p.
The main value of this book is that it sets out to describe, both verbally and visually, all the breeds recognized by the GCCF.

1983. Alderton, D. *The Cat.*
Macdonald, London. 208p.
Although the claim of the book's sub-title – 'The most complete, illustrated practical guide to cats and their world.' – is slightly exaggerated, this is nevertheless a well designed and wide-ranging general introduction to the subject by a leading vet.

The cover design for the New York Metropolitan Museum's book of works from their collections: *Metropolitan Cats.* The cover picture is a detail from a silk painting, *Cat and Spider,* by the Japanese artist Toko.

1983. Pugnetti, Gino. *The Macdonald Encyclopedia of Cats.*
Macdonald, London. 256p.
The best of the smaller handbooks, with concise, well-illustrated information available at a glance.

1983. Tabor, Roger. *The Wildlife of the Domestic Cat.*
Arrow Books, London. 223p.
An original, pioneering study of urban feral cats and their social organization.

1984. Sayer, Angela. *The Complete Book of the Cat.*
Octopus Books, London. 208p.
A wide-ranging, heavily illustrated, reliable, general reference work by the Chairman of the Cat Association of Great Britain.

1984. Suarès, J.C. *The Indispensable Cat.*
Webb & Bower, Exeter. 192p.
A beautifully designed and lavishly illustrated study of the cat's relationship with mankind – from great art and advertising to cartoons and comic strips.

1985. Angel, Jeremy. *Cats' Kingdom.*
Souvenir Press, London. 176p.
A meticulously observed study of a large colony of 120 cats living together at a Japanese animal sanctuary.

1985. Burton, Jane and Allaby, M. *Nine Lives: A Year in the Life of a Cat Family.*
Ebury Press, London. 128p.
An original approach to the subject of cat life, this carefully photographed study traces the development of a family of kittens from birth to maturity.

1985. Pond, Grace and Dunhill, Mary. *Cat Shows and Successful Showing.*
Blandford Press, Poole, Dorset. 144p.
A valuable guide to the history of cat shows by the organizer of the National Cat Show, who specializes in long-haired cats, and a leading expert on short-haired cats.

1985. Sproule, Michael and Sproule, Anna. *Complete Cat Book.*
Admiral Books, London. 192p.
A lavishly illustrated general reference work that is genuinely comprehensive, covering all aspects of feline life.

1986. Caras, Roger. *A Celebration of Cats.*
Simon & Schuster, New York. 238p.
A personal celebration of the special qualities of cats written by one of America's foremost animal authors.

1986. SACASE, CHRISTIANE. *THE CAT.*
HAMLYN, LONDON. 192P.
The English translation of a modestly-sized, modern French cat encyclopedia. A useful general reference work that is well planned and illustrated.

1987. ANDERSON, JANICE. *THE CAT-A-LOGUE.*
GUINNESS BOOKS, ENFIELD, MIDDLESEX. 128P.
A small book, but containing a compact assembly of carefully collected feline facts and figures.

1987. WOOD, PHILIP (EDITOR). *A PASSION FOR CATS.*
DAVID & CHARLES, NEWTON ABBOT, DEVON. 208P.
An interesting miscellany of articles written to celebrate the jubilee of the Cats Protection League.

1988. CLUTTON-BROCK, JULIET. *THE BRITISH MUSEUM BOOK OF CATS.*
BRITISH MUSEUM PUBLICATIONS, LONDON. 96P.
A brief but brilliant study of the history of the cat by the world's greatest expert on the history of domestic animals.

1988. FOUCART-WALTER, ELISABETH AND ROSENBERG, PIERRE. *THE PAINTED CAT.*
RIZZOLI, NEW YORK. 224P.
There are a number of books on the subject of painted felines, but this heavily illustrated study of the cat in the history of art by two curators from the department of Painting at the Louvre has no equal.

1988. NATOLI, EUGENIA. *CATS.*
W.H. ALLEN, LONDON. 168P.
A general treatment, beautifully illustrated, by the leading Italian authority on feline biology and behaviour.

1988. TURNER, DENNIS AND BATESON, PATRICK (EDITORS). *THE DOMESTIC CAT: THE BIOLOGY OF ITS BEHAVIOUR.*
CAMBRIDGE UNIVERSITY PRESS, CAMBRIDGE. 222P.
An important collection of recent academic papers on various aspects of feline behaviour, including kitten development, territorial organization, sexual and social life, predation and domestication.

1989. GETTINGS, FRED. *THE SECRET LORE OF THE CAT.*
GRAFTON BOOKS, LONDON. 207P.
A guide to the mysteries and mythology of sacred, demonic and magical cats by an expert on the occult.

1989. TAYLOR, DAVID. *THE ULTIMATE CAT BOOK.*
DORLING KINDERSLEY, LONDON. 192P.
A general guide, with superb colour photographs which are so lovingly presented that they often reduce the text to a secondary role.

1989. KELSEY-WOOD, DENNIS. *THE ATLAS OF CATS OF THE WORLD.*
TFH, NEW JERSEY. 384P.
A heavy volume with over 350 illustrations that boldly claims to illustrate 'every cat in the world'. Although it fails to fulfil this promise, it is nevertheless a major addition to works of feline reference.

1990. LOXTON, HOWARD. *THE NOBLE CAT.*
MEREHURST, LONDON. 335P.
Another general, encyclopedic treatment of the feline world, but on a grand scale and lavishly illustrated.

1990. SCHNECK, MARCUS AND CARAVAN, JILL. *CAT FACTS.*
STANLEY PAUL, LONDON. 160P.
A modest but clearly designed guide to cat breeds, which is particularly useful for quick reference.

1990. Stephens, Gloria. *Legacy of the Cat.*
Chronicle Books, San Francisco. 137p.

The text is brief, but the strength of the book lies in the superb colour photographs of the various cat breeds by the Japanese photographer Tetsu Yamazaki.

1991. De Prisco, Andrew and Johnson, James. *The Mini-Atlas of Cats.*
TFH, New Jersey. 448p.

Despite its unfortunate title, this is not a pocket edition of Kelsey-Wood's *Atlas*. It is, in fact, an unusual combination – a solid reference work laced with eccentrically amusing comments. In their foreword, the authors set the tone for the book when they acknowledge that they are 'indebted to the cats we have known, the cat lovers we have pestered, the cat haters we have lynched and the fellow authors we have pinched'.

1991. Saunders, Nicholas. *The Cult of the Cat.*
Thames & Hudson, London. 96p.

A brief but exciting study of feline symbolism, with unusually interesting illustrations.

1991. Tabor, Roger. Cats: *The Rise of the Cat.*
BBC Books, London. 192p.

The illustrated book of the BBC television series in which the author travelled the world to study the rise of the domestic cat from ancient Egypt to the present day.

1991. Warner, Peter. *Perfect Cats.*
Sidgwick & Jackson, London. 128p.

The author is described as one of the finest feline artists of modern times and this volume is essentially a platform for his brilliant portraits of pedigree cats. This should not, however, be allowed to overshadow the fact that the accompanying texts are carefully researched and highly informative.

1992. Alderton, David. *Eyewitness Handbooks: Cats.*
Dorling Kindersley, London. 256p.

A heavily illustrated handbook of domestic cat breeds. The text is brief, but the range of breeds covered is impressive.

1992. Bradshaw, John. *The Behaviour of the Domestic Cat.*
C.A.B. International, Wallingford, Oxfordshire. 219p.

An excellent, highly informative report on our present knowledge of the behaviour of the cat, but a little too academic for most general readers. The tone of the volume can be judged by the summary which calls it 'a readable overview . . . adopting both a mechanistic and functional approach'.

1992. Cutts, Paddy. *The Complete Cat Book.*
Acropolis Books, Enderby, Leicestershire. 256p.

A large-format, all-encompassing study of the domestic cat, unusual in that the author is responsible for both the text and the excellent photographs.

1992. Gebhardt, Richard. H. and Bannon, John. *The Allure of the Cat.*
TFH, New Jersey. 304p.

An unashamedly luxurious coffee-table volume, with almost life-sized colour photographs of the various cat breeds. The text is scanty, but the illustrations are magnificent.

1992. Rutherford, Alice. (Editor) *The Reader's Digest Illustrated Book of Cats.*
Reader's Digest Association, New York. 256p.

A highly efficient, reliable and well-organized reference work.

1992. Shojai, Amy. *The Cat Companion.*
Friedman, New York. 128p.

An elegant illustrated volume covering a broad range of feline topics.

1993. Cutts, Paddy. *Cats.*
Sunburst Books, London. 256p.

The text is virtually non-existent, but the large colour photographs of a variety of breeds (mostly by the author), which make up the bulk of this impressive volume, are outstanding.

1993. De Laroche, Robert and Labat, Jean-Michel. *The Secret Life of Cats.*
Aurum Press, London. 116p.
An intelligent text dealing with the history of domestic cats, by the first author, combined with the brilliant photographs by his co-author, make this a fascinating, elegant volume. Translated from the French original.
1993. Malek, Jaromir. *The Cat in Ancient Egypt.*
British Museum Press, London. 144p.
An extremely useful survey of the role of felines in early Egyptian civilization.
1994. Altman, Roberta. *The Quintessential Cat.*
Blandford, London. 289p.
A delightful assembly of feline information, taken from a rich variety of sources.
1994. Howard, Tom. The Illustrated Cat.
Grange Books, London. 80p.
A copiously illustrated history of the cat, as seen through works of art.
1994. Thomas, Elizabeth Marshall. *The Tribe of Tiger.*
Simon & Schuster, New York. 240p.
Despite its errors and exaggerations, the stylish text is provocative and absorbing.
1995. Rixon, Angela. *The Illustrated Encyclopedia of Cat Breeds.*
Blandford, London. 256p.
Written by the President of the Cat Association of Great Britain, this is one of the best of the general illustrated encyclopedias of cat breeds, with excellent colour illustrations.
1995. Tabor, Roger. *Understanding Cats.*
David & Charles, Newton Abbot, Devon.
A book full of insights into the ways of cats, written to accompany a BBC TV series.
1995. Thompson, Will. (Editor) *The Cat Fanciers' Association Cat Encyclopedia.*
Simon & Schuster, New York. 220p.
Although the text is brief, this well-illustrated volume is especially valuable for its full presentation of the CFA's show standards, including detailed descriptions of every colour form of each recognized breed.

The jacket design from Roberta Altman's delightful reference work, *The Quintessential Cat.* The cover picture is from a painting by Martin Leman.

Specialist Cat Booksellers:
Maxine Aston, 19 Styvechale Avenue, Earlsdon, Coventry, West Midlands, CV5 6DW, England. (Issues regular catalogues)
The Cat Book Center, P.O. Box 112, Wykagyl Station, New Rochelle, NY 10804, USA. (Issues book-lists)
Direct Book Service, P.O. Box 2778, Wenatchee, WA 98807-2778, USA.
Tarman's Cat Books, P.O. Box E, Hummelstown, PA 17036, USA.

Cat Breed Classes

Feline History. For convenience, at competitive cat shows, the various breeds are grouped together into major categories. These categories have a long and complex history which makes them seem odd when viewed objectively today.

In Britain, at the two major cat shows, the (November) Supreme Show in Birmingham and the (December) National Cat Club Championship Show in London, there are seven classes:

1 Longhair (= Persian)
2 Semi-longhair (= Non-Persian Longhair Cats)
3 British Shorthair (The UK equivalent of American or European Shorthairs)
4 Foreign (Breeds intermediate between the stocky Persian and elongated Siamese)
5 Oriental (Siamese Breeds without the Siamese coat pattern)
6 Burmese
7 Siamese

C

Cat Breeds

CAT BREEDS

Feline History. Although there are large numbers of colour forms, there are fewer than a hundred recorded cat breeds. Some of them appeared briefly and then vanished before they could become established. Others developed into major exhibition breeds with histories covering many years. They are listed here in approximate historical order, with the date of their creation indicated where this is known. With the early breeds the dates are, inevitably, somewhat speculative. With the later breeds greater accuracy is often possible.

1 Birman (Burma: early)
2 Manx (Isle of Man: early)
3 Norwegian Forest (Norway: early)
4 Persian (Iran: early)
5 Russian Blue (Russia: early)
6 Siberian Forest (Russia: early)
7 Turkish Van (Turkey: early)
8 Japanese Bobtail (Japan: 6th–10th century)
9 Chartreux (France: 1300s)
10 Siamese (Siam: 1350–1767)
11 Korat (Siam: 1350–1767)
12 Burmese (Siam: 1350–1767)
13 Angora (Turkey: 1400s)
14 Maine Coon (USA: 1860s)
15 Abyssinian (Ethiopia: 1868)
16 British Shorthair (Britain: 1870s)
17 Mexican Hairless (USA: 1902)
18 Himalayan (USA: 1930s)
19 Karakul (USA: 1930s)
20 Peke-faced (USA: 1930s)
21 Prussian Rex (East Prussia: 1930s)
22 Balinese (USA: 1940s)
23 Ohio Rex (USA: 1944)
24 Australian (Australia: 1946)
25 German Rex (East Germany: 1946)
26 Colourpoint Shorthair (Britain: 1947)
27 Kashmir (USA: 1950s)
28 Oriental Shorthair (Britain: 1950s)
29 Tonkinese (USA: 1950s)
30 Cornish Rex (Britain: 1950)
31 Italian Rex (Italy: 1950)
32 Havana Brown (Britain: 1952)
33 Egyptian Mau (Egypt: 1953)
34 Japanese Bobtail Longhair (Japan: 1954)
35 Bombay (USA: 1958)
36 California Rex (Marcel) (USA: 1959)
37 Oregon Rex (USA: 1959)
38 American Bobtail (USA: 1960s)
39 British Angora (Britain: 1960s)
40 Cymric (Canada: 1960s)
41 Javanese (Britain & USA: 1960s)
42 Ragdoll (USA: 1960s)
43 Snowshoe (USA: 1960s)
44 Devon Rex (Britain: 1960)
45 Scottish Fold (Scotland: 1961)
46 Bengal (USA: 1963)
47 Ocicat (USA: 1964)
48 American Shorthair (USA: 1966)
49 American Wirehair (USA: 1966)
50 Exotic Shorthair (USA: 1966)
51 Sphynx (Canada: 1966)
52 Somali (USA: 1967)
53 Tiffany (USA: 1967)
54 California Spangled (USA: 1971)
55 Singapura (Singapore: 1971)
56 Spotted Mist (Australia: 1976)
57 Sokoke Forest (Kenya: 1977)
58 American Lynx (USA: 1980s)
59 Colourpoint British Shorthair (Britain: 1980s)
60 Coupari (Britain 1980s)
61 Tiffanie (Britain: 1980s)
62 Wild Abyssinian (Singapore: 1980s)
63 Malayan (USA: 1980)
64 American Curl (USA: 1981)
65 Burmilla (Britain: 1981)
66 Colourpoint European Shorthair (Italy: 1982)
67 European Shorthair (Italy: 1982)
68 York Chocolate (USA: 1983)
69 Ojos Azules (USA: 1984)
70 Seychellois (Britain: 1984)
71 Dutch Rex (Holland: 1985)
72 La Perm (USA: 1986)
73 Si-rex (USA:1986)
74 Selkirk Rex (USA: 1987)
75 Rexed Maine Coon (Britain: 1988)
76 Nebelung (USA: 1990s)
77 Suqutranese (Britain: 1990)
78 Munchkin (USA: 1991)
79 Urals Rex (Russia: 1991)
80 Ragamuffin (USA: 1994)

Although there are fewer than a hundred distinct breeds of domestic cats, there are countless colour forms. The one shown opposite is a fawn Abyssinian.

In addition there are a number of obscure, unrecognized or experimental breeds, including the following: Bristol, Cherubim, Chinese Harlequin, Cornelian, Himbur, Honeybear, Karelian Bobtail, Khmer, Longhair Rex, Mandarin (= Oriental Longhair), Palomino, Poodle Cat, Safari and Sterling. Altogether this makes a total of 95 domestic cat breeds without taking into account all the colour variations of each breed.

Cat Collections

Feline History. Cat collectibles have recently become a growing area of interest for ailurophiles. Sought-after items include paintings, drawings, prints, lithographs, posters, antique advertisements, early cat books, sculpture, ceramics, bronzes, wood carvings, glass cats, needlework cats, coins, spoons, postage stamps, T-shirts, games, jewellery, antique toys and curios.

A number of enthusiasts in this field have established major collections that are now open to the public, in one form or another. They include:

Cataware. A shop selling a wide variety of feline artefacts. Address: Hebden Court, Matlock Street, Bakewell, Derbyshire, DE45 1EE, England.

The Cat Box. A shop selling feline antiques of all kinds, from ceramics to jewellery. Address: York Arcade, Camden Passage, 80 Islington High Street, London N1, England.

The Cat Company. A shop selling feline items including knitwear, artefacts, gifts and collectibles. Address: 10 Piccadilly Arcade, New Street, Birmingham, England.

Cat House in Key West. A shop in the old city dealing exclusively in cat items. The joke is that the building was originally another kind of cathouse – a brothel. Address: 411 Green Street, Key West, FL 33040, USA.

Cathouse Restaurant. A Florida restaurant decorated with over four thousand cat artefacts. Opened in 1972, it is located inland, in the town of Sebring, in the very centre of Florida.

Cat Pottery. A small family business specializing in the making of ceramic cats. Address: 1 Grammar School Road, North Walsham, Norfolk, England.

The Cat Shop. A Brighton shop dealing exclusively in feline artefacts, including jewellery, ornaments, cards, prints and paintings. Address: 21 Prince Albert Street, Brighton, East Sussex, England.

The Cat's Meow. An American cat gallery specializing in watercolour paintings, jewellery, and other art work, cat toys, books and gifts. Address: 2234 Paradise Road, Las Vegas, NV 89104, USA.

Cosy Cat Cottage. A small hotel in Whitianga, New Zealand, packed full of cat artefacts by the owners, not to mention live cats. Address: 41 South Highway, Whitianga, New Zealand.

The Cotswold Cat Company. A company set up by a ceramicist to produce works exclusively devoted to cats. Ceramics, woodwork, mirrors, stained glass, fabrics and other feline arts and crafts are mostly commissioned to order. Address: 6 Salt Boxes, Pinvin, Pershore, Worcestershire, WR10 2LB, England.

The Dozy Cat Company. A company selling modern cat ceramics. Address: 32 Magna Close, Great Abington, Cambridge, CB1 6AF. England.

Durango Cat Company. An American company specializing in cat collectibles, including prints, T-shirts, earrings, clocks, dishes and other cat gifts. Address: 115 West 11th Street, Durango, CO 81301, USA.

Felix Gallery. A small feline gallery containing literally hundreds of cat artefacts. Address: 2 Sun Street, Lewes, Sussex, BN7 2QB, England.

Galerie Européenne du Chat. A Paris gallery and shop devoted to feline subjects, showing paintings, drawings, posters, cards and objects. Address: 73 Rue du Cherche, 75006 Paris, France.

Glendale Cat Library. An American library specializing in cat publications, of which they have the largest collection in the world, from rare books to greeting cards and posters. (In the Glendale Central Library).

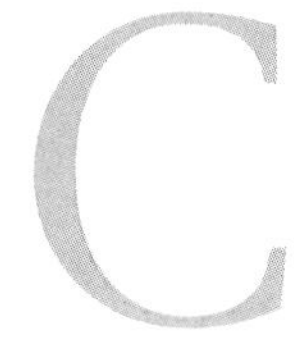

EARLY FELINE artefacts are now much sought after by collectors. Paintings by the Victorian artist Louis Wain, like this sentimental *Cat's Tea Party*, fetch surprisingly high prices.

James Russell Webster Mansion Inn. In New York State, this inn houses a huge collection of cat artefacts collected together by the antique dealer owners. Address: 115 East Main Street, Waterloo, NY 13165, USA.

Just Cats. A feline boutique exclusively concerned with cats, cat artefacts, and cat accessories. In addition to a huge range of cat collectibles and equipment, they also supply live cats, including most of the rarer breeds. Address: 244 East 60th Street, New York, NY 10022, USA.

Just Cats & Co. A company specializing in ceramic cats. Address: The Cat Factory, Booth Street, Stoke-on-Trent, Staffs., ST4 4AL, England.

Kattenkabinet. A Dutch cat museum, full of cat artefacts, founded by businessman Bod Meijer and dedicated to his pet cat called J.P. Morgan. Located in an old house in the centre of Amsterdam, it was opened in 1990. Address: Herengracht 497, Amsterdam, Netherlands.

Katzen Museum. A Swiss cat museum, in the small town of Riehen, near Basel. Containing over ten thousand cat artefacts, it was a private collection that grew so large it was opened to the public in 1982. Address: Baselstrasse 101, 4125 Riehen, Basel, Switzerland.

Musée du Chat. A recently established cat museum housed in an old, converted barn in north-west France. Containing over two thousand feline artefacts, it was opened in 1992 in the town of Ainvelle. Address: Rue de l'Eglise, 70880 Ainvelle, France.

Ponckles Cat Gallery. Address: Island Square, Back Road East, St. Ives, Cornwall, TR26 1NX, England.

There is also reported to be a cat museum in Kuching, on the island of Borneo. A large feline exhibition opened at the Sarawak Museum in 1989 and was due to be moved into its own museum building in 1991.

In addition, there is now a Cat Collectors' Club, with over 1,000 members internationally. It was started by Marilyn Dipboye in the United States in 1982, and issues a *Cat Collectors' Catalog* and its own fortnightly newsletter called *Cat Talk*. Address: 33161 Wendy Drive, Sterling Heights, MI 48310, USA; or 31311 Blair Drive Warren, Michigan 48092, USA.

Bibliography:

1973. McClinton, K.M. *Antique Cats for Collectors.* Lutterworth, London.
1977. Artley, A. (Editor) *The Great All-Picture Cat Show.* Astragal, London.
1980. Hoffmann, P. *Katzen.* (German text)
1982. Sylvester, J. & Mobbs, A. *The Cat Fancier.* Longman, London.
1985. Bruce, E. *The Great Cat Game Book.* Michael Joseph, London.
1987. Streitenfeld, R & Streinenfeld, D. *Katzenkultur.* (German text)
1988. Johnson, P. *Cats and Dogs. Phillips Collectors' Guide.* Boxtree, London.
1992. Ivory, L. *Collectable Cats.* London.
1994. Altman, R. *The Quintessential Cat.* Blandford, London.
1995. Flick, P. *Cat Collectibles.* Grange Books, London.
1996. Fyke, M. *Collectible Cats.* Collector Books, Paducah, Kentucky.

Cat Cures

Folklore. In early centuries, cats were used in the making of certain potions and medicines. Perhaps because of their association with witches, it was thought that different parts of their bodies would have dramatic curative effects. In the 17th-century works of Edward Topsel, there are the following suggestions for the afflicted:

For Gout: This can be cured by taking the fat of a cat 'and anointing therewith the sick part, and then wetting Wool or Tow in the same, and binding it to the offending place'.

For Blindness: 'Take the head of a black Cat, which has not the spot of another colour in it and burn it to powder in an earthen pot leaded or glazed within, then take this powder and through a quill blow it thrice a day into thy eye . . . '

For Gallstones: 'The liver of a Cat dryed and beat to powder is good against the stone.'

For Fever: 'The dung of a female Cat with the claw of an Owl hanged about the neck of a man that hath had seven fits of Quartain Ague, cureth the same.'

For Convulsion: 'A powder made of the gall of a black Cat . . . helpeth the convulsion and wryness of the mouth.'

For Inducing the Birth of a Stillborn: 'If the gall of a Cat with the black dung of the same Cat, be burned in perfume under a woman travelling with a dead childe, it will cause it presently to come forth.'

Illustration of a domestic cat from Edward Topsel's early *Natural History*, in which he offers some remarkable 'Cat Cures'.

In the Revd. James Woodforde's *Diary of a Country Parson*, published in the 18th century, there is an additional feline cure:

For a Sty on the Eyelid: 'It is commonly said that the eyelid being rubbed by the tail of a black Cat, would do much good, if not entirely cure it.' (Having tried this himself with the tail of his own black tom-cat, he reported that 'very soon after dinner I found my Eyelid much abated of the swelling and almost free from pain.')

Bibliography:

1658. Topsel, E. *The History of Four-footed Beasts and Serpents.* London.

Caterwaul

Feline Term. Since Chaucer's day, the noise made by courting cats has been referred to as 'caterwrawling' or 'caterwauling'. (It means, literally, 'cat-wailing'.) The *Oxford English Dictionary* defines this word as 'the cry of the cat at rutting time'. Another dictionary calls it the cry of 'cats under the influence of the sexual instinct'.

Although it is true that the sound is most likely to be heard when cats are gathered for mating, it is misleading to assume that, because of this, its primary function is sexual. It is essentially an aggressive, threatening sound made by sexual or territorial rivals. Indeed, it may be heard at any time when two or more cats are fighting and may, on occasion, have nothing to do with sexual encounters. Even two spayed females disputing a territorial boundary can caterwaul as dramatically as any 'rutting toms'.

C

NOCTURNAL FELINE caterwauling, from a 19th century German print in the Swiss Katzen Museum at Riehen, near Basel.

To human ears this is a disturbing sound and has been described as 'a discordant, hideous noise'. It consists of a series of rising and falling cries that vary from deep growls and gurgles to high-pitched wails and howls, as the intensities of the hostile interactions fluctuate.

CAT-FLAP

FELINE TERM. Cats hate doors. When a cat is indoors it always wants to be outdoors, and when it is outdoors it always wants to be in. To feel at ease, it needs to be able to patrol its entire domain at frequent intervals. Human doors are a hideous invention that robs it of this natural, territorial freedom.

It required a genius to solve this problem and fortunately one was at hand. No less a person than Sir Isaac Newton, the greatest natural philosopher of all time, considered the dilemma that faced his pet cats and, mindful of their comfort, promptly came up with the answer – a small cat-door set within the larger, human one. It is somehow apt that the great man whose laws of motion and gravity made him world-famous should also have invented the cat-flap.

Newton has, however, been ridiculed for also inventing the kitten-flap. When his cat had kittens, he had a smaller hole made for them. Critics, who have pointed out that the kittens could easily have passed through the main cat-door, are overlooking the fact that the tiny creatures may not have been strong enough to push up the larger flap.

Today, he would have been impressed to see the latest, high-tech cat-flaps that are available. These include electronically operated cat-doors which allow only the cat of the house to enter and exit. A small, battery operated 'key' is attached to the cat's collar. As it approaches the cat-door, the flap automatically opens. After the cat has passed through, the flap closes and the door automatically locks itself shut. There are four settings: in only, out only, in and out, and fully locked. This system gives the owner complete control of feline movements and eliminates the shock of discovering a kitchen full of strays.

The cat-door appears to have been independently invented in Spain. It is reported that, in old Spanish houses, there was a small hole, or *gatera,* to provide free passage for the domestic cats. These holes became well-known as aids to human courtship. If the señorita's balcony was too high off the ground, the young lovers would lie down on the ground, one on the inside and one on the outside of the gatera, to whisper their secret words of love, when their parents refused to let them be together.

Catgut

Feline Term. Despite its name, catgut is not part of the guts of a cat. It comes instead from the entrails of sheep. Their intestines are prepared in a special way to make them into strong, flexible cords that have been used for centuries in making strings for musical instruments and for bowstrings. There are three alternative explanations as to how sheepgut came to be known as catgut:

1 In Japan there is a traditional, three-stringed musical instrument, the *Samisen,* which is shaped rather like a banjo. It is played by Geishas to accompany their songs. Unlike all other musical instruments, its strings are actually made from the intestines of cats. On one occasion the Geishas, presumably saddened by the slaughter of cats for this purpose, held a ceremonial service for the souls of the felines that had met their end in the service of Japanese music.

There was also a bronze statue dedicated to these cats. It was erected in front of the great Buddhist temple to Nichiren in the Yamanashi Prefecture on the orders of the *Samisen* manufacturers. One of the figures on the statue was designed to show a human form with a cat's head. Prayers were said there to appease the wrath of the departed felines and to ensure that they did not return to haunt those who killed them.

It is possible that knowledge of this unusual musical instrument filtered through to the West to give rise to the name 'catgut', but historically this seems unlikely.

2 In the 17th century, Italian violin-makers were using sheepgut to make their strings, but wished to keep their manufacturing techniques to themselves. To ensure that the source of their wonderful violin strings remained a trade secret, they gave out the false information that they were made, not of sheepgut, but of catgut.

3 The most popular explanation is that the sheepgut became known as catgut because of the noises made when it is plucked or scraped. At the beginning of the 17th century, one author wrote of fiddlers 'tickling the dryed gutts of a mewing cat'. Later we read of a man upset 'at every twang of the cat-gut, as if he heard at the moment the wailings of the helpless animal that had been sacrificed to harmony'. These references come from a period when domestic cats were all too often the victims of persecution or torture, and the sound of squealing cats was not unfamiliar to human ears. These, and the typical caterwauling of mating cats, provided the obvious basis for a comparison with the din that was inevitably created by inexpert musicians scraping on their stringed instruments. In the imaginations of the tormented listeners, the inappropriate sheepgut became transformed into the appropriate catgut – a vivid fiction to replace a dull fact.

Cat-haters

Feline History. It is important to make a distinction between ailurophobes and cat-haters. True ailurophobes, such as Napoleon, had a cat phobia – a deep-seated *fear* of cats. If this did lead them to become cat-haters, the hatred was secondary. Their primary response was panic in the presence of a feline. But many other historical figures, who have lacked this terror, have nevertheless detested cats. Famous cat-haters include the following:

Wu-Chao, Empress of China (624–705): The Empress hated cats and had them banished from her palace for a special reason. A lady-in-waiting whom she had condemned to death took her revenge, before she died, by issuing a threat that, in the after-life, she would turn the Empress into a rat. Then she, the lady-in-waiting, transformed into a spectre cat, would hunt her down and torment her.

Pope Gregory IX (1147–1241): He initiated the feline holocaust in Europe that was to continue right through the Middle Ages and beyond. In a Papal Bull of 1233 he denounced the black cat as diabolical, thereby giving his official blessing to the widespread persecution of cats – already occurring locally in Europe – and set the course for five centuries of cat hatred, torture and burning. (See also Witchcraft.)

Pope Innocent VII (1336–1415): In the early 15th century, this Pope added his voice to the persecution of cats, stepping up the onslaught, resulting in millions more feline deaths.

Pope Innocent VIII (1432–1492): Another pious Pope who failed to live up to his name. In his Bull of 1484 he condemned witchcraft and despatched inquisitors to try witches and destroy them. He made a particular point that the witches' cats were to be burned with them. He was persuaded to issue his Bull by two Dominican friars from Germany called Kraemer and Sprenger, names that should go down in history as the cat's worst enemies.

Elizabeth I (1533–1603): A feature of the Queen's coronation procession was a huge wicker Pope filled with live cats which was wheeled through the streets and then set on fire, so that they 'squalled in a most hideous fashion' as they burned to death. In origin this was, of course, symbolic cat hatred. It does not imply that the Queen personally hated the cats as animals. She was simply following the custom of the day of persecuting cats as agents of the devil. But for the cats concerned, this was of little comfort.

William Shakespeare (1564–1616): Unhappily for those who respect both cats and Shakespeare, the majority of the bard's references to felines are vilifications. For example, in *All's Well that Ends Well:* 'I could endure anything but a cat, And now he's a cat to me . . . A pox upon him! For he is more and more a cat.'; in *Cymbeline:* 'Creatures vile as cats . . . '; in *The Merchant of Venice:* 'Some that are mad if they behold a cat'; in *Much Ado about Nothing:* 'What though care killed a cat.'

Johannes Brahms (1833–1897): The composer disliked cats so much that he used to shoot them with arrows. His assaults began after the Czech composer Antonín Dvořák gave him a Bohemian sparrow-slaying bow. Brahms used to take aim from his apartment window in Vienna and, if we are to believe an account by Wagner: 'After spearing the poor brutes, he reeled them into his room after the manner of a trout fisher. Then he eagerly listened to the expiring groans of his victims and carefully jotted down in his notebook their antemortem remarks.' According to Wagner, who disliked Brahms, he worked these sounds into his chamber music.

King Louis XIV (1638–1715): In 1648, the French Monarch, crowned with a wreath of roses, ignited the fires and then danced around the pyres of cats being burned alive at the Midsummer Gala in the Place de Grève in Paris. He was a callous ten-year-old boy-king when this happened, and later reformed.

Buffon, George Louis Leclerc, Comte de (1707–1788): In his 1767 *Natural History* he described cats as follows: 'The cat is an unfaithful domestic, and kept only from the necessity we find of opposing him to other domestics still more incommodious, and which cannot be hunted; for we value not those people, who, being fond of all brutes, foolishly keep cats for their amusement.' He adds that cats 'possess . . . an innate malice and perverse disposition, which increase as they grow up, and which education teaches them to conceal but not to subdue. From determined robbers, the best education can only convert them into flattering thieves . . . they have only the appearance of attachment or friendship.'

Hilaire Belloc (1870–1953): The Anglo–French author, writing about cats in 1908, said: 'I do not like Them . . . when one hears Them praised, it goads one to expressing one's hatred and fear of Them . . . so utterly lacking are They in simplicity and humility, and so abominably well filled with cunning by whatever demon first brought Their race into existence. All that They do is venomous, and all that They think is evil.'

Isadora Duncan (1878–1927): At Neuilly in France, Isadora Duncan, the revolutionary American choreographer and dancer, lived next door to a countess who ran a cat sanctuary. The cats were constantly invading her garden and since, surprisingly, she detested felines, this drove her to extreme measures. The great dancer ordered her staff to hunt them down and drown them. At the height of this persecution the distraught Countess found the corpse of one of her rescued strays hanging by a cord from the wall that divided the two properties.

Dwight Eisenhower (1890–1969): During his occupancy of the White House, the American President banished all cats. He hated cats so much that he instructed his staff to shoot on sight any they spotted in the grounds.

Apart from these famous names, Ida Mellen, writing in 1946, reports that one of the world's greatest cat-haters was a Chicago banker by the name of Rockwell Sayre. In the early 1920s, he started a campaign to rid the entire world of cats by the year 1925. Using the slogan 'A Catless World Quick' and distributing a verse that began, 'Who kills a cat gains a year, who kills a hundred never dies', he offered financial incentives to cat killers (ten cents each for the first hundred and $100 for the person who killed the last cat on Earth).

He said that cats were 'filthy and useless' and that it was 'toadying to depravity to keep a cat around the house'. He claimed to have inspired the killing of seven million cats during the first three months of his campaign, but was dismayed to discover that, when 1925 eventually arrived, there were still some left. He then decided to extend his purge for another ten years but, happily for the cat population, he himself was soon dead.

Note: In order to make cat-haters seem as loathsome as possible, some authors have added the tyrants Hitler and Mussolini to the list, but there seems to be little evidence for this. Mussolini was, in fact, a cat-lover who owned a splendid Persian Cat, and his daughter always took breakfast with her pet cat sitting on the table, even though it had long since died and been stuffed.

Bibliography:

1940. Mellen, I. *The Science and Mystery of the Cat.* Scribner's. New York.

1963. Cole, W. and Ungerer, T. *A Cat-Hater's Handbook.* W.H. Allen, London.

Cathouse

Feline Term. The slang term 'cathouse' has been used to describe a brothel for several centuries. Prostitutes have been called cats since the 15th century, for the simple reason that the urban female cat attracts many toms when she is on heat and mates with them one after the other. As early as 1401, men were warned of the risks of chasing the *cattis tailis,* or cat's tail. This also explains why the word 'tail' is sometimes used today as slang for female genitals. A similar use for the word 'pussy' dates from the 17th century.

Cat-in-hell's Chance

Feline Saying. The meaning of this phrase (he doesn't have a cat-in-hell's chance – in other words, he has no chance at all) is well known, but its origin is not. It is an abbreviation of the phrase 'no more chance than a cat in hell without claws'. It was originally a reference to being in a fight without adequate weapons.

Cat in the Hat

Fictional Cat. The Cat in the Hat is the alarming feline at the core of Dr Seuss's children's story of the same name. The cat decides to keep two bored children entertained while their mother is away. Chaos is caused by the cat's antics, but the magical feline manages to return everything to normal before the mother returns. Dr Seuss is the pen-name of Theodor Seuss Geisel.

Bibliography:

1957. Geisel, T.S. *The Cat in the Hat.* Random House, New York.

1958. Geisel, T.S. *The Cat in the Hat* Comes Back. Random House, New York.

1969. Geisel, T.S. *I can Lick 30 Tigers Today.* Random House, New York.

Cat Litter

Feline History. For many years, indoor feline hygiene was based on the dirt-box, a tray filled with earth or other crude substances. As recently as 1969, cat care books were recommending the use of sand or torn paper. This was a poor solution for the ever-growing population of urban cats. Then an American, Edward Lowe from Michigan, applied himself to the problem and invented modern, absorbent cat litter.

As so often happens, the invention happened by accident. He was working in his father's sawdust business in 1947 when a woman asked him if she could have a bag of sawdust to put in her cat's sand tray, which had frozen over in the cold weather. Knowing that, at work, they used kiln-dried, granulated clay to soak up grease spills, it occurred to him that this might be a better substance to put in a cat's dirt box. So, instead of sawdust, he gave the woman a bag of this granulated clay. It worked so well that she soon came back for more. Lowe was bright enough to realize that he was onto something big and, testing the material himself, found that it was indeed a vast improvement on everything that had gone before it.

In no time at all he was selling bags of Kitty Litter by the hundred, then by the thousand, then by the tens of thousands, until marketing the granulated clay had taken over his life as a massive business concern. Before long this new type of cat litter had made him a multi-millionaire and when he finally sold up the business in 1990, it was worth over 150 million dollars. By the time of his death, in 1995, it had developed into a business empire with an annual turnover of half a billion dollars.

It has been argued that Edward Lowe helped make it possible for cats to overtake dogs as the most popular domestic pet of modern times, because, with ever-growing urban populations, his invention made a significant difference to the ease with which it was possible to keep an 'indoor cat'.

Catmint

Feline Term. An alternative name for Catnip.

Catnip

Feline Term. Catnip is the popular name given to a plant *(Nepeta cataria)* of Asiatic origin that has a powerful attraction for cats. Its appeal lies in a chemical called *nepetalactone* which is present in its stems and leaves.

When a cat finds this plant in a garden it may indulge in what has been described as a ten-minute drug 'trip'. It rubs and rolls on it, but does not attempt to eat it. So intense is the response that the animal appears to be in a state of ecstasy.

Wild members of the cat family, including even the lion, react in the same way, but not every individual cat does so. There are some non-reactors and the difference is known to be genetic. A cat is either born a catnip-junkie, or it is not. Conditioning and experience have nothing to do with it.

Young kittens do not show the response. For the first two months of life all kittens avoid catnip, and the positive response does not appear until they are three months old. Then they split into two groups – those that no longer actively avoid catnip, but simply ignore it and treat it like any other plant in the garden, and those that go wild as soon as they contact it. The split is roughly 50/50, with slightly more in the positive group.

The positive reaction takes the following form: the cat approaches the catnip plant and sniffs it; then, with growing frenzy, it starts to lick it, bite it, chew it, rub against it repeatedly with its cheek and its chin, head-shake, rub it with its body, purr loudly, growl, miaow, roll over and even leap in the air. Washing and clawing are sometimes observed. Even the most reserved of cats seems to be totally disinhibited by the catnip chemical.

Because the rolling behaviour seen during the trancelike state is similar to the body actions of female cats in oestrus, it has been suggested that catnip is a kind of feline aphrodisiac. This is not particularly convincing, because the 50 per cent of the cats that show the full reaction include both male and females, and both entire animals and those that have been castrated or spayed. So it does not seem to be a 'sex trip', but rather a drug trip which produces similar states of ecstasy to those experienced during the peak of sexual activity.

Feline catnip addicts are lucky. Unlike so many human drugs, catnip does no lasting damage, and after the ten-minute experience is over the cat is back to normal with no ill-effects.

Catnip is not the only plant to produce these strange reactions in cats. Valerian *(Valeriana officinalis)* is another one, and there are several more that have strong cat-appeal. The substance *actinidine* in the plant *Actinidia polygama* acts in the same way. The strangest

discovery, which seems to make no sense at all, is that if catnip or valerian is administered to cats internally, it acts as a tranquillizer. How either of these can be an 'upper' externally and a 'downer' internally remains a mystery.

Cat-o'-nine-tails

Feline Term. An implement of torture whose design was influenced by the idea that a cat has nine lives. It was a whip with nine cords, each cord having nine knots tied in it. As a result, every stroke inflicted a large number of small marks, giving the overall impression of a body that has been clawed and scratched repeatedly by a savage cat. This type of whip was used as an authorized instrument of punishment in the British Navy and Army from the 17th century until it was finally outlawed in 1881. Its use was particularly brutal in the 18th century, when victims were given as many as 300 lashes, virtually flaying them alive.

The 'cat', as this whip was known in the Navy, has given us the popular expression 'no room to swing a cat', meaning 'cramped quarters'. Some people imagine that this saying alludes to swinging a live cat around by its tail, but this is not so. It refers to the fact that the cat-o'-nine-tails was too long to swing below decks. As a result, sailors condemned to be punished with a whipping had to be taken up above, where there *was* room to swing a cat.

A 17th century print *(above)* showing a 'Cat-Showman' with his musical cats. The sign above his head reads 'Boarding pupils taken here and the master comes to perform in town'.

Cat Organ

Feline History. In the days when cruelty to cats was an accepted form of public entertainment, there were several loathsome inventions to facilitate this callous pastime. One of these was the cat organ. This consisted of an instrument designed to make music from the terrified cries of a group of captive cats.

A cat organ was paraded through the streets of Brussels in a procession that took place in the year 1549 in honour of Philip II. It involved a live bear, 20 cats and some monkeys: 'In the middle sat a great bear playing on a kind of organ, not composed of pipes, as usual, but of twenty cats, separately confined in narrow cases, in which they could not stir; their tails protruded from the top and were tied to cords attached to the keyboard of the organ; according as the bear pressed upon the keys, the cords were raised, and the tails of the cats were pulled to make them mew in bass or treble tones, as required by the nature of the airs. Live monkeys . . . danced to the music . . . Although Philip II was the most serious and the gravest of men, he could not refrain from laughter at the oddity of this spectacle.'

Sadly for the animals concerned, the cat organ became a popular spectacle and improvements were made. The cords attached to their tails were replaced by 'spikes fixed at

The infamous 'cat organ', in which the tormented felines uttered supposedly musical notes as they cried out in pain. The playing of the instrument caused spikes to prod the cats, or to pull on their tails.

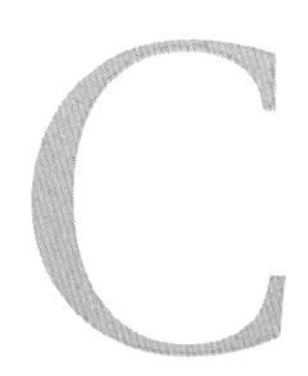

the ends of the keys, which prodded the poor animals, and made them mew piteously'. This form of feline torture remained in vogue for at least a hundred years, but eventually disappeared and was replaced by strange feline musical performances. A poster from the late 17th century depicts a French cat-showman with his performing cats, some reading music, others playing musical instruments. It is not clear how he managed to make them sing or play, but it seems likely that he used some kind of pain to provoke the sounds. The difference now was that the pain was hidden rather than obvious, so that the onlookers could enjoy the strange 'concert' without being confronted by the obvious animal torture of the infamous cat organ.

Cat Photography

Cat Art. Many famous photographers have sought to catch the moods and actions of cats and a few of them have become feline specialists. Among them are the following:

England: Jane Burton, Paddy Cutts, Toby Glanville, Marc Henrie

France: Yann Arthus-Bertrand, Jean-Michel Labat

Italy: Adriano Bacchella, Bob Schwartz

Japan: Tetsu Yamazaki

United States: Chanan, Bill Hayward ('If you really want to know people, ask them about their cats'), Larry Johnson and Terry Gruber ('I was up to my ears in cats – my camera began to develop hairballs')

Bibliography:

1958. Spies, J. *Cats and How I Photograph Them*. New York.
1978. Hayward, B. *Cat People*. Doubleday, New York.
1979. Gruber, T. *Working Cats*. Lippincott, New York.
1987. Suarès, J.C. *The Photographed Cat*. Doubleday, New York.
1988. Sturgis, M. and Glanville, T. *The English Cat at Home*. Chatto & Windus, London.
1990. Eauclaire, S. *The Cat in Photography*. Little, Brown, Boston.
1992. Coppé, P. *1001 Images of Cats*. Tiger Books International, London.
1992. Gebhardt, R.H., Bannon, J. and Yamazaki, T. *The Allure of the Cat*. TFH, New Jersey.
1992. Suarès, J.C. (Editor) *Black and White Cats*. Collins, San Francisco.
1993. Henrie, M. *Captivating Cats*. Salamander Books, London.
1993. Laruelle, D. *Les Chats de Yann Arthus-Bertrand*. Éditions du Chêne, Paris.

Cats Protection League (CPL)

Cat Welfare. The Cats Protection League is the oldest and largest charity devoted solely to the care of cats. It was founded in 1927 with the aim of rescuing, rehabilitating and re-homing stray and unwanted cats. With 140 local groups and seven large rescue centres, it finds homes for as many as 70,000 cats a year. It also undertakes a public information service on the care of cats. (See Cat Welfare.)

The emblem of the Cats Protection League, one of the largest feline charities in the world.

Cat Publications

Cat Literature. Many cat magazines have been published during the past century. They include the following:

All About Cats. 'The Magazine for Cat Lovers'; published monthly. Address: 40 Gray's Inn Road, London, WC1X 8LR, England. Tel: 0171-404 2604; fax: 0171-831 5426.

All Cats. Published monthly. Address: Pacific Palisades, California, USA.

Atout Chat: Address: B.P. 205-78003 Versailles Cedex, France. Tel: (1) 39-49-95-95).

Bulletin of the Feline Advisory Bureau (Has now changed its name to FAB, see page 113).

Cat Companion. Published bi-monthly. Address: The Quarton Group, 2701 Troy Center Drive, Suite 430, Troy, MI 48084, USA.

Cat Fanciers' Almanac. Official journal of the Cat Fanciers' Association; published monthly. Primarily for cat breeders and exhibitors. Address: 1805 Atlantic Avenue, P.O. Box 1005, Manasqan, NJ 08736-1005, USA.Tel: 908-528 9797.

CAT MAGAZINES are becoming increasingly popular worldwide and have now started to appear in Russia, something unthinkable during the Communist regime. This 1995 cover shows the third issue of a Cat Fancy publication from Moscow.

Cat Fancy. 'Cat Care for the Responsible Owner'; published monthly since 1965. Circulation: 320,000. Address: P.O. Box 52864, Boulder, Colorado 80322-2864, USA. Tel: 303-786 7306.

Cat News. Newsletter; published twice-yearly. Address: Cat Specialist Group, IUCN Species Survival Commission, World Conservation Centre, 1196 Gland, Switzerland.

Cats (UK). Official journal of the Governing Council of the Cat Fancy; published weekly – 'The World's Only Weekly Cat Magazine'. Address: 5 James Leigh Street, Manchester, M1 6EX, England. Tel: 0161-236 0577.

Cats (USA). Address: 2750-A South Ridgewood Avenue, South Daytona, FL 32119, USA.

Cats U.S.A. Address: P.O. Box 55811, Boulder, CO 80322-5811, USA. Tel: 303-786 7652.

Cats Magazine. Published monthly since 1951. Circulation 165,000. Address: P.O. Box 420240, Palm Coast, FL 32142-0240, USA or P.O. Box 290037, Port Orange, FL 32129-0037, USA. Tel: 904-788 2770; e-mail: Cats@pwr.com.

Cat World. 'The Monthly Magazine for Cat Lovers'. 10 Western Road, Shoreham-by-Sea, West Sussex, BN43 5WD, England. Tel: 01273-462000.

Cat World International. Published bi-monthly since 1973. Circulation 8,000. P.O. Box 35635, Phoenix, AZ 85069-5635, USA.Tel: 602-995 1822.

Fab. Official journal of the Feline Advisory Bureau; published quarterly. Address: 235 Upper Richmond Road, Putney, London, SW15 6SN, England. Tel: 0181-789 9553.

Feline Practice. Address: Veterinary Practice Publishing Co., Santa Barbara, CA, USA.

I Love Cats. Address: Grass Roots Publishing Co. 950 Third Avenue, New York, NY 10022, USA.

Locate-a-Cat. 'The Essential Guide for Cat and Kitten Buyers'. Address: 10 Western Road, Shoreham-by-Sea, West Sussex, BN43 5WD, England.

Maine Coon International Information Network'. The World's First Single Breed Colour Magazine'; published quarterly, from Winter 1994. Address: MCI Group, P.O. Box 59, Uckfield, East Sussex, TN22 4ZY, England. Tel. 01025-733761.

National Cat. 'All-breed Magazine for the Cat Fancier, Breeder and Exhibitor'; published monthly. Address: Sterling Media Pty Ltd., P.O. Box 670, Seven Hills, New South Wales 2147, Australia.

Paws. 10 Western Road, Shoreham-by-Sea, West Sussex, BN43 5WD, England. Tel: 01273-462000.

Show World. 'The Magazine for all Cat Breeders and Exhibitors'. Address: 10 Western Road, Shoreham-by-Sea, West Sussex, BN43 5WD, England. Tel: 01273-462000.

The Cat. Official journal of the Cats Protection League; published every two months. Address: 17 Kings Road, Horsham, West Sussex, RH13 5PN, England. Tel: 01403-261947.

Tica Trend. Official journal of The International Cat Association; published bi-monthly. Address: P.O. Box 2684, Harlingen, TX 78551, USA.

Wild Cat. Official journal of the Cat Survival Trust. Address: The Cat Survival Trust, Marlind Centre, Codicote Road, Welwyn, Hertfordshire, AL6 9TU, England. Tel: 01438-716873.

Your Cat. Address: Bretton Court, Bretton, Peterborough, PE3 8DZ, England. Tel: 01733-264666; fax: 01733-261984.

Cat-racing

Feline History. Competitive cat-racing seems highly improbable as a serious sport, but in the 19th century it did take place annually in Belgium. The manner in which it was organized does not reflect well on the Belgian attitude towards their feline friends at the time. In the first major cat book ever published (in 1889), Harrison Weir quotes a publication called *The Pictorial Times* of 16th June 1860: 'Cat-racing is a sport which stands high in popular favour. In one of the suburbs of Liège it is an affair of annual observance during carnival time . . . The cats are tied up in sacks, and as soon as the clock strikes the solemn hour of midnight the sacks are unfastened, the cats let loose, and the race begins. The winner is the cat which first reaches home, and the prize awarded to its owner is sometimes a ham, sometimes a silver spoon. On the occasion of the last competition the prize was won by a blind cat.'

Cat-racing resurfaced briefly in England in the 1930s. In a brave bid to imitate greyhound racing, a cat racetrack was opened in 1936 at Portisham in Dorset. The competing cats were set to chase an electric mouse, which they pursued down a 202 metre (220 yard) course. Another display of organized cat-racing was apparently staged in Kent in 1949. Not surprisingly, both enterprises were dismal failures and serious cat-racing has never been attempted again.

Cat's Cradle

Feline Term. Cat's Cradle is a game played by children in which a loop of string is wound back and forth over the fingers of both hands to create a pattern. Once the first child has created a pattern, the loop is transferred to the hands of a second child, creating a new pattern in the process. The loop is then handed back and forth repeatedly, making a different pattern each time. There are three rival explanations for the name 'Cat's Cradle' being given to this game:

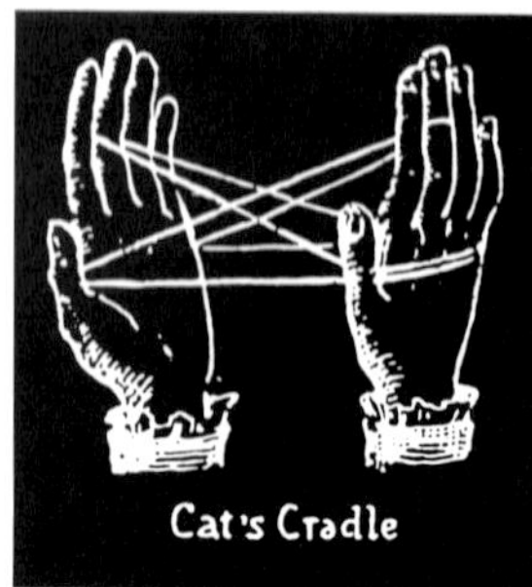

1 The cradle formed by the string is the right size for a cat.
2 In Eastern Europe an old folk custom involved a live cat (as a symbol of fecundity) being secured in a cradle one month before a wedding took place. This cradle was then ceremonially carried to the newlyweds' house, where it was rocked back and forth in their presence. This, it was claimed, would ensure an early pregnancy for the young bride. A child's game could easily have developed from this ceremony, with its origins eventually forgotten.
3 Similar string games are played by peoples as far apart as Congo tribesmen and the Inuit, and these games have a magical significance. The string patterns are formed, altered and re-formed in the belief that these actions will influence the path of the sun. In the Congo this is done to persuade the sun to rest; in the frozen north it is just the opposite – the Inuit try to trap the sun in their strings to shorten its winter absence. The sun in these cases is envisaged as a 'solar cat', to be symbolically ensnared in the twisting string patterns. This 'solar cat' is reminiscent of the ancient Egyptian legend of the sun god Ra who, in his battle with the power of darkness, took the form of a cat (see entry for Ra). This equation between the cat and the sun is thought by some to have spread across the globe from culture to culture and to provide the true origin of the magical game of Cat's Cradle.

Cat Shows

Feline History. The first cat show took place in Winchester, in southern England, in the year 1598. It was no more than a side-show at the annual St. Giles Fair, but it was nevertheless a competitive event, since it is recorded that prizes were given for the best ratter and the best mouser.

Similar small shows were staged at similar fairs, but these were of little significance and had no official status. The breeding of pedigreed cats had little meaning at this time.

In was not until the second half of the 19th century that serious, competitive cat showing was staged. The earliest example was at a London house in 1861, but this was still not a true public exhibition.

In the 1860s minor cat shows were held in both England and the United States. In America there had already been annual livestock shows for many years. In New England, these started in earnest in 1832, and by the 1860s it is thought they must have included cat competitions because, by the 1870s, the Maine Coon, for example, was already considered as a separate and established breed for competition.

The first major cat show in the world took place on Thursday, 13th July 1871 at the Crystal Palace in London. It was organized by a well-known animal artist of the day, Harrison Weir. There were so many visitors that the cats themselves were barely visible in the dense throng. Weir was amazed by the public response. On the journey to the Crystal Palace he had had serious doubts about the wisdom of his plan, fearing the animals would 'sulk or cry for liberty'. But when he arrived he found them lying peacefully on crimson cushions. There was no noise except for widespread purring and gentle lapping of fresh milk.

A total of 170 cats were entered, although the prize money amounted to less than £10 for the whole competition. One of the prize-winners was Harrison Weir's own 14-year-old tabby called The Old Lady – which is not surprising when one discovers that two of the three judges were Weir's brother and Weir himself.

If this system of judging left something to be desired, it must be recorded that, thanks to Harrison Weir, cats were, for the very first time, given specific standards and classes. These form the basis of the system still employed at modern cat shows all over the world.

This first cat major cat show was so successful that a second one was staged later in the same year and, although it was only open for one day, it attracted 19,310 visitors. Two more shows were held in the following year, after which it became an annual event. The enormous popularity of these cat shows saw the idea spread rapidly to other cities in the British Isles and eventually around the world.

In 1887 the National Cat Club was formed to rule this new competitive world. The president

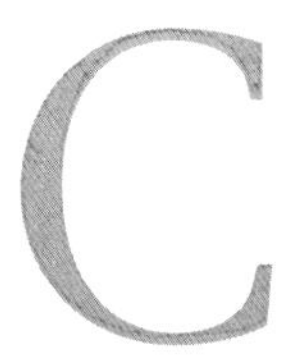

was, needless to say, Harrison Weir. By 1893 the first official cat stud book had been started, and pedigree cat breeding had begun in earnest.

The first major American cat shows also took place in the 1870s. As early as 1878, for instance, there was a six-day National Cat Show in Boston. During that decade there were others in most of the Eastern cities, and as far west as Chicago. Later, in 1895, the biggest of all these early American shows was held at Madison Square Garden in New York. It was organized by an Englishman, Mr J. Hyde, and attracted 176 entries. Due to its success, other shows quickly followed and were soon established as annual fixtures.

Today there are no fewer than 65 annual shows in Britain and 400 in the United States. Unfortunately, the world of cat-show organizers has become increasingly competitive within its ranks, and there have been splits and divisions since the earliest days. The result is that there is no single authority in either Great Britain or the United States, and each club or society has its own slightly different rules and classes. All of this can be confusing to the outsider, but for the cats it does not make a great deal of difference. The survival of pedigree competition is the important thing, maintaining the serious attitude towards pure-bred felines and preventing cats from losing status in 20th-century society. With more than 94 per cent of cats today being non-pedigree, the cats of the show world constitute only a tiny minority of the general feline population, but this does not matter. As long as the elite pedigrees exist to be photographed and exhibited, they will lend an aura of importance to domestic cats in general. They are the ambassadors of the feline world, and when over 2,000 of them gather each December for the biggest cat show in the world – the National Cat Show in London – the interest they arouse is an admirable advertisement for the value we place on our feline companions.

Cat Societies

Feline History. Early cat societies were formed in the wake of the first cat shows, as organizing bodies, complete with official stud books, registries, disciplinary rules and 'black lists'.

Early Cat Societies

Some of those very early ones, established in the 19th century, include (in chronological order):

National Cat Club (1887). Formed in 1887 in London as a result of the interest aroused by the first official cat shows. The club's official motto was 'Beauty Lives by Kindness'. It was the first registering body for pedigree cats in the world, and issued its first stud book in 1893. Its first President was Harrison Weir. Its second was Louis Wain. It still holds an annual show each December at Olympia in London, the largest cat show in the world. (Address: The Laurels, Rocky Lane, Wendover, Bucks, England.)

Cruft's Cat Show (1894). Most people think of Cruft's as an exclusively canine organization, but this is not the case. The early organization of a 'Cruft's Great International Cat Show' proved immensely popular (although in reality it was no more international than the American Baseball 'World Series'). It was held on March 7th and 8th (three years after the first Cruft's Dog Show) at the Royal Aquarium in London. There were 567 exhibits in 74 classes. A second Cruft's Cat Show was held in March 1895, but both events lost money and cats were abandoned in favour of dogs.

Scottish Cat Club (1894). This became the central organizing body for cat shows in Scotland. It held major shows in both Glasgow and Edinburgh.

American Cat Club (1896). Formed in 1896 in New York, with veterinarian Rush Huidekoper as President. He had just published his 'Guide to the Classification and Varieties of Cats', following the success of the National Cat Show in New York, and was keen to bring some order and control to the competitive showing of breeds.

The Cat Club (1898). Founded by Lady Marcus Beresford as a breakaway group from the National Cat Club. One of its aims was to use the proceeds of its cat shows to help worthy charities. At first it did successfully make profits for various charities, but when, in 1904, it started to lose money, it was disbanded.

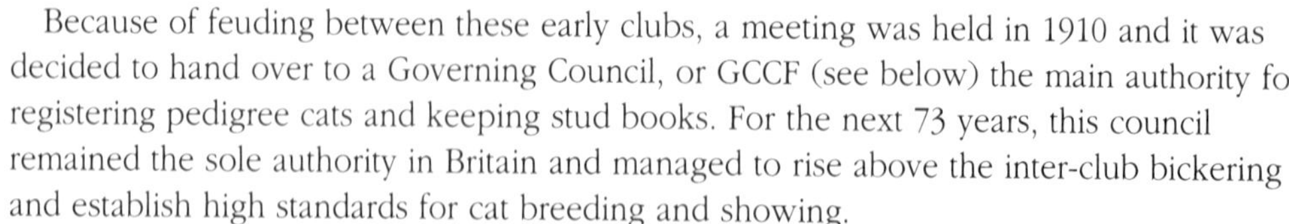

Because of feuding between these early clubs, a meeting was held in 1910 and it was decided to hand over to a Governing Council, or GCCF (see below) the main authority for registering pedigree cats and keeping stud books. For the next 73 years, this council remained the sole authority in Britain and managed to rise above the inter-club bickering and establish high standards for cat breeding and showing.

Chicago Cat Club (1899). The first major feline organization in Chicago, this club not only ran cat shows, but in addition established a home for stray cats and a boarding cattery.

Beresford Cat Club (1899). Also formed in Chicago, a few months after the Chicago Cat Club, with cat breeder Mrs Clinton Locke as President. It held its first major show in 1900. This club had strong ties to England and its President was already a member of the early English Cat Clubs. It proved to be the most successful club of its day in organizing large cat shows.

American cat breeder and show organizer, Mrs Clinton Locke *(above)*, with her Siamese cats, Calif and Bangkok.

Modern Cat Societies

More modern cat societies include the following, in alphabetical order. (Only national societies are listed here. For specific breed clubs, see the breeds in question.)

Allied Cat Lovers (ACL) Founded by Truman Pierson (President) of Minneapolis and Charles Johnson of Philadelphia, with headquarters in Goshen, Indiana, in 1939. This was the first cat protection society formed in the United States. It provided shelters for homeless cats, dissemination of cat care information, encouragement for improvements in cat breeding and the promotion of cat cemeteries.

The American Association of Cat Enthusiasts (AACE). Organizes shows at which exhibitors can compete with breeds that are not accepted by the large organizations. Address: P.O. Box 213, Pine Brook, NJ 07058, USA. Tel: 201-335 6717.

The American Cat Association (ACA). 8101 Katherine Avenue, Panorama City, CA 91402, USA. Tel: 818-782 6080 or 818-781 5656. The ACA is the oldest feline registry in the United States, having been active since 1899.

American Cat Council (ACC). Address: P.O. Box 662, Pasadena, CA 91102, USA. A small organization based on the West Coast of the United States which follows exhibition rules similar to those of the GCCF in Britain (with exhibitors vacating the hall during judging).

American Cat Fanciers' Association (ACFA). Address: P.O. Box 203, Point Lookout, MO 65726, USA. Tel: 417-334 5430. An international organization with affiliations in Canada and Japan. It publishes a monthly news bulletin.

Association Internationale Féline (AIF). Address: 38 Avenue du Président-Wilson, 75116 Paris, France. Tel: 45 53 71 48.

Association Nationale des Cercles Félins Français (ANCFF). Address: 7 Rue Chaptal, 75009 Paris, France. Tel: 48 78 43 54.

Association Nationale Féline (ANF). Address: Km 1 – Route de Montner, 66310 Estagel, France. Tel: 68 29 15 91.

Australian Cat Federation (ACF) Address: P.O. Box 40752, Casuarina, NT 0811, Australia.

Austrian Feline Fanciers Alliance (AFFA). Address: Postfach 75, 1172 Wien, Austria. Tel: 02 22/4 57 00 43.

Canadian Cat Association (CCA). The only national cat organization in Canada. It publishes a bilingual (French and English) quarterly newsletter: *Chats Canada*. Address: 83 Kennedy Road, South Unit 1805, Brampton, Ontario, L6W 3P3, Canada. Tel: 905-459 1481

Cat Action Trust (CAT). Address: The Crippets, Jordans, Beaconsfield, Bucks, England.

The Cat Association of Britain (CA). Formed in 1983 as an alternative to the GCCF, it became a member of FIFe in 1990. Address: Mill House, Letcombe Regis, Oxfordshire, OX12 9JD, England. Tel: 01235-766543.

The emblem of the Cat Association of Britain, formed as an alternative to the GCCF in 1983.

Cat Club de Belgique (CCB). Address: 33 Rue Duquesnoy, B-1000, Brussels, Belgium.

Cat Club de Espagne (CCE). Address: 60 Olivido, Barcelona, 26, Spain.

The Cat Fanciers' Association (CFA). The biggest of the American organizations. With its

affiliates, it produces more than 360 cat shows each year. It claims to be 'the largest cat registry in the world'. Like the ACFA it has affiliations in Canada and Japan. It publishes a yearbook and a bi-monthly newsletter called *Trend*. It has also produced a *CFA Cat Encyclopedia* giving details of the show Standards of all the 43 'official' breeds which it recognizes for competition. Address: P.O. Box 1005, Manasquan, NJ 08738-1005, USA. Tel: 908-528 9797. OR 1309 Allare Avenue, Ocean, New NJ, USA. Tel: 201-531 2390.

The Cat Fanciers Federation (CFF). Tel: 513-787 9009. A registering body that centres its activities in the North-east of the USA. It publishes a *CFF Newsletter* and a *CFF Yearbook*. Address: 9509 Montgomery Road, Cincinnati, OH 45242, USA. Tel: 513-984 1841. OR P.O. Box 661, Gratis OH 45330.

Cat Lovers of America (CLA). Issues a quarterly *Cat Lovers* magazine and a monthly *Bulletin*. Address: P.O. Box 5050, El Toro, CA 92630-9982, USA.

Cats Protection League (CPL). Address: 17 Kings Road, Horsham, West Sussex, RH13 5PN, England. Tel: 01403-61947.

Cat Survival Trust (CST). Address: Marlind Centre, Codicote Road, Welwyn, Herts., AL6 9TV, England. Tel: 01438-716873 or 01438-716478.

Chovatelu Drobneho Zvirectva. Address: Hermanova 6, 170 000 Prague 7, Czechoslovakia.

Club Félin Français (CFF). Address: 15 bis, Avenue du Parc, 78150 Le Chesnay, France. Tel: 39 54 37 85.

Co-ordinating Cat Council of Australia (CCCA). Address: P.O. Box 404, Dickson, ACT 2602, Australia.

Crown Cat Fanciers' Federation (CROWN or CCFF). Organized cat shows in eastern USA and western Canada. (Now disbanded.) Address: P.O. Box 34, Nazareth, KY 40048, USA.

Deutscher Edelkatzenzuchter - Verband (DEKZV). Address: 48 Friedrichstrasse, D-6200, Wiesbaden, Germany.

Fauna Cat Lovers' Association. Address: 129041, Moscow 68, Prospect Mira, USSR.

Fédération Féline Française (FFF). Address: 75 Rue Decaen, 75012 Paris, France. Tel: 46 28 26 09.

Federation Feline Helvetique (FFH). Address: Via Quiete 15, CH-6962, Viganello, Switzerland.

Federation Feline Italienne (FFI) Address: 20 Via Principi d'Acaja, 1-10138, Torino, Italy.

Fédération Internationale Féline (FIFe). Established in 1949, this has become the largest feline organization in the world, with affiliated societies throughout Europe and beyond. It has been estimated that it now unites over 150,000 pedigree-cat breeders. Address: Boerhaavelaan 23, NL-5644 BB, Eindhoven, Holland or 33 Rue Duquesnoy, B-1000, Brussels, Belgium or Friedrichstrasse 48, 6200 Wiesbaden, Germany.

Felikat Mundikat. Address: Rotterdamse Rijweg 94, NL-3042, AR Rotterdam, Holland.

Feline Advisory Bureau (FAB). Address: 350 Upper Richmond Road, Putney, London, SW15 6TL, England. Tel: 0181-789 9553.

Friends of the Cat (FOTC). Address: P.O. Box 52429, Saxonwold 2132, South Africa.

Governing Council of Associated Cat Clubs of South Africa (GCACC). Address: P.O. Box 532, Florida, Transvaal, South Africa.

The Governing Council of the Cat Fancy (GCCF). Founded in 1910, this major cat organization now has over 100 affiliated clubs. It was the sole feline authority in Great Britain until 1983, when the Cat Association of Britain was formed as a breakaway group. Address: 4-6, Penel Orlieu, Bridgwater, Somerset, TA6 3PG, England. Tel: 01278-427575.

The Independent Cat Association (ICA). Address: 211 East Oliver (Suite 201), Burbank, CA 91502, USA.

The Independent Pet Cat Society (IPCS). Formed in 1985. Address: 109 Locksway Road, Milton, Southsea, Hants, PO4 8JW, England.

Independent Feline Alliance (IFA). Formed in 1994 as an 'alternative show system' with the motto 'Equal Opportunities for all Cats', it includes special classes for household pets and even disabled cats. Address: Gremora, Shepeau Stow, Whaplode Drove, Spalding, Lincs., PE12 0TU, England.

The International Cat Association (TICA). Formed in 1979, TICA organizes cat shows throughout the USA, with affiliates in Canada and Japan, and claims to have created the largest genetically based cat registry in the world. It produces a TICA Yearbook and a twice-monthly newsletter called TICA Trend. Address: P.O. Box 2684, Harlingen, TX 78551, USA. and 134 Avenue de Paris, 78740 Vaux-sur-Seine, France. Tel: 210-428 8046.

Landsforeningen Felis Danica. Address: Tranehusene 44, DK-2620, Albertslund, Denmark.

Loisirs Félins Français (LFF). Address: 8, Rue du Parc, 78980 Paris, France Tel: 34 78 05 51.

Lukz. Address: Csetneki v 13, 11-1113, Budapest, Hungary.

National Cat Club. Address: The Laurels, Chesham Lane, Wendover, Bucks, England.

National Cat Fanciers' Association (NCFA). Now disbanded. Address: 20305 W. Burt Road, Brant, MI 48164, USA.

New Zealand Cat Fancy (NZCFa). Address: P.O. Box 3167, Richmond, Nelson, New Zealand.

New Zealand Cat Federation (NZCFe). Address: 20 Warren Kelly Street, Richmond, Nelson, New Zealand. Tel: 054-46721.

The Domestic Cat, from a woodcut by Thomas Bewick (1807).

Norske Rasekattklubbers Riksforbund (NNR). Address: Nordane Valkyriegate 9, N-Olso 3, Norway.

Oevek. K.K.O. Address: Spaunstrasse 40, A-4020 Linz, Austria.

Royal Austrian Cat Club. Address: Postfach 75, 1172 Wien, Austria. Tel: 02 22/4 09-48 69.

Société Centrale Féline de France (SCFF). Address: 24 Rue de Nantes, 75019 Paris, France. Tel: 40 35 18 04.

South African Cat Register (SACR). Address: P.O. Box 4382, Randberg, Transvaal 2125, South Africa.

Suomen Rotukisshayhdistysten Keskusliitto r.v. (SRK). Address: Raappavuorenrinne 1 D 59, SF-01620 Vantaa 62, Finland.

Sveriges Raskattklubbars Riksforbund (SVERAK). Address: PL 4094 A, S-524 00, Herrljunga, Sweden.

United Cat Federation (UCF). A medium-sized organization centred on the West Coast of the USA. Address: 6621 Thornwood Street, San Diego, CA 92111, USA.

United Feline Organization (UFO). Address: P.O. Box 770578, Coral Springs, FL 33077, USA.Tel: 305-726-9556.

World Cat Federation. Address: Hubertstr. 280, D-45307, Essen, Germany. Tel: 02 01-55 07 55.

Cat's Only Trick

Folk-tale. The 'cat's only trick' is to climb a tree when in trouble. An early fable about the cat and the fox tells the story of how, one day, the fox was explaining to the cat that it had a hundred different tricks with which it could survive. The cat replied that it had only one trick. Just then a pack of hounds appeared and the cat quickly climbed a tree, where it was safe. The fox went though its repertoire of a hundred tricks, one by one, but in the end was caught and killed by the hounds. The story is well-known all over Europe from Greece to Lapland.

Cat's Paw

Folk-tale. A 16th-century fable in which a cunning monkey, wishing to take some roasted chestnuts out of a hot fire, does so by using the paw of a friendly cat. As a result, the term 'cat's paw' was applied to anyone who was a tool of another.

Cat Survival Trust

Cat Conservation. The trust was founded in 1976 by Terry Moore with the aim of providing the means 'by which all species of wild cat are preserved, preferably in their own habitat, such that none of them become extinct'. In addition to working towards the establishment of reserves in the wild, the trust also has a captive breeding programme. To date they have successfully bred over 160 cats from five wild species. The trust occupies a four-hectare (ten-acre) site at Welwyn in Hertfordshire, England, with large breeding enclosures, offices, a meeting room and a library. Membership is invited. Members receive the Trust's journal *Wild Cat,* and are permitted to visit the cats at the centre and use the library. (Tel: 01438-716873 or 01438-716478.)

Catta

Feline Term. A female cat. In 1950, the American veterinary surgeon Leon Whitney prefaced his book on cat care with a plea for the introduction of a new name for a female cat. In his considered opinion, although 'tom' was suitable for a male cat, 'queen' was a 'silly word' for a female.

He commented: 'I should like to propose a new word for our language . . . I propose the word *catta* for the female cat . . . *catta* is the Latin word for the female of an unknown species of animal. Why not apply it to the cat? Why has some word not been used in our language long ago? I propose to use it throughout this book.'

He employed it in sentences such as: 'Breeders usually allow a catta to call for two or three days and then put her with the male.' For some reason the word sounded uncomfortably strange and, presumably to his great disappointment, was not taken up by other authors, or the cat world in general.

Bibliography:
1950. Whitney, L.F. *The Complete Book of Cat Care.* Doubleday, New York.

Cat that Walked by Himself

Fictional Cat. *The Cat that Walked by Himself* is the title of a tale by Rudyard Kipling (1865–1936) in his *Just So Stories* (1902) in which he creates a fable to epitomize the personality of the domestic cat – part tame companion and part independent spirit. After the dog, the horse and the cow have agreed to become domesticated, the cat holds out for the wild life. But then it finally appears at the human den and says, 'I am not a friend, and I am not a servant, I am the cat who walks by himself and I wish to come into your cave.' Some hard bargaining follows in which the cat promises to catch mice 'for always and always and always; but *still* I am the cat that walks by himself.'

Catwalk

Feline Term. A catwalk is defined as a narrow footway or platform. It was originally used to describe a narrow footway along a bridge. Later it became a common term for a high walkway above a theatre stage, inside an aeroplane, or in various military contexts. Today it has become more associated with the narrow display area on which fashion models parade up and down. The question arises: why catwalk rather than a dogwalk, or some other name? The answer, according to Jean Conger in *The Velvet Paw,* is that 'this name began at the bridge, and with the idea that puss would be very careful to make any bit of dry land hold his footsteps, because of his dislike of the water'.

Cat Welfare

Feline History. Ever since the domestication of the cat in ancient Egypt, urban cats have multiplied at an astounding rate. As a result, there have all too often been populations of starving strays in cities and towns all over the world. For every well-fed pet cat and every protected working cat, there has been another feline, wary and furtive, that has moved outside the sphere of human protection to fend for itself. In the back alleys and the parks, the side streets and rubbish tips, these often pathetic, starving animals have done their best to eke out a living, barely surviving on the garbage of urban humanity.

In recent years their plight has become the focus of a great deal of well-organized human charity, but contrary to popular opinion, this kind of feline welfare work is far from new. Ever since the Prophet Mohammed let it be known that cats held a special place in his heart, there have been reports of Moslem kindness to needy felines. The most notable example of this dates from the 13th century, when the great Moslem warrior El-Daher-Beybars, the Sultan of Egypt

and Syria, who was described as being 'brave as Caesar and cruel as Nero' in his dealings with fellow humans, proved to be gentle and kind when in the company of cats. Writing at the end of the 19th century, Agnes Repplier describes how he 'had so true an affection for cats that he bequeathed a fertile garden called Gheyt-el-Quottah (the cat's orchard) for the support of homeless and necessitous pussies. This garden lay close to his own mosque, and but a short distance from Cairo. With the revenue it yielded, food was brought and distributed every noon in the outer court of the Mehkémeh to all cats who, wishing to live in freedom, were yet driven by hunger or neglect to accept generous alms.'

Although the mosque eventually crumbled into ruins and the site of the orchard was lost for ever, the tradition that had been established so long ago was kept alive for centuries and the stray cats of Cairo continued to benefit from Moslem generosity. Repplier reports that 'as late as 1870 the cats of Cairo received their daily dole, no longer in memory of their benefactor, but in unconscious perpetuation of his bounty.'

A 19th-century French Egyptologist witnessed the scene: 'As feeding time approaches, every terrace is covered with cats; you see them all around the Mehkémeh – jumping from roofs across the narrow Cairo streets fearful of missing their pittance; they come from every side . . . spreading out into the courtyard, miaowing with desperate eagerness and fighting over the pitifully small quantity allowed for so many. The old hands gulp it down in an instant; the young cats and new arrivals dare not join in the fight and are reduced to licking the spot where the meat lay. Anyone who wants to get rid of a cat goes and loses it among the throng of this strange banquet.'

Moving to more recent times, the plight of abandoned, abused and feral cats has disturbed many people in the West during the past century and some have cared deeply enough to take active steps to help these often desperate animals. Often, private individuals have set up feeding posts for starving city strays, taking on a heavy personal burden of daily feeding sessions. Others have organized societies for feline protection and have founded sanctuaries where cats can be temporarily housed and then placed in new homes. Around the world there are countless groups and organizations of this kind. Many have remained local organizations dealing with a small area, while others have grown to become major institutions. The details of a few that are devoted exclusively to cats are as follows:

Alley Cat Allies. Address: P.O. Box 397, Mount Ranier, MD 20712, USA.

American Feline Society. Address: 204 West 20th Street, New York, NY 10011, USA.

Association pour la Sauvegarde des Chats Sauvages. Address: 130 Boulevard Murat, 75016, Paris, France.

Cat Action Trust. Address: The Crippets, Jordans, Beaconsfield, Bucks, England.

Cat Rescue and Welfare. Address: 6, Conway Avenue, Carlton, Nottingham, England.

Cats and Kittens Rescue Service. Address: CKRS Head Office, Maen Cottage, Meifod, Powys, SY22 6BW, Wales.

Cats in Care. Address: 11 Lower Barn Road, Purley, Surrey, CR2 1HY, England.

Cat Specialist Group. Address: IUCN, World Conservation Centre, 1196 Gland, Switzerland.

Cats Protection League. Address: 17 Kings Road, Horsham, West Sussex, RH13 5PN, England.

Cat Survival Trust. Address: Marlind Centre, Codicote Road, Welwyn, Herts., AL6 9TV, England.

Catwatch Rescue. Address: 81 Green End Road, Sawtry, Huntingdon, Cambs., PE17 5UZ, England.

Cat Welfare Liason Group (GCCF). Address: 79 Pilgrims Way, Kemsing, Sevenoaks, Kent, TN15 6TD, England.

Cat Welfare Trust. Address: 58 Mandeville, Stevenage, Herts., SG2 8JN, England.

CHAT (Celia Hammond Animal Trust). Address: High Street, Wadhurst, East Sussex, TN15 6AG, England.

Feline Advisory Bureau. Address: 350 Upper Richmond Road, Putney, London, SW15 6TL, England.

Feline Centre. Address: University of Bristol, Department of Clinical Veterinary Science, Division of Companion Animals (Medicine), Langford House, Langford, Bristol, BS18 7DU, England.

Feline Conservation Centre. Address: Box 84, Rosamond, CA 93560-9750, USA.

National Cat Protection Society. Address: 1528 West 17th Street, Long Beach, CA 90813, USA.

Ridgeway Trust for Endangered Cats. Address: P.O. Box 29, Hastings, East Sussex, TN34 2SD, England.

Ccoa

Legendary Cat. Ccoa is an evil cat demon, greatly feared by the South American Indians of the Quechua tribe in Peru. He is about a metre (three feet) long, with dark stripes down the length of his body. He has a large head with glowing eyes. He controls hail and lightning, with which he sets out to ruin crops and destroy people. He has to be appeased by regular offerings, to prevent him from causing havoc.

Three rare Wemyss Cats. Late 19th century, Scottish. Antique ceramic cats such as these are now highly valued by collectors.

Ceramic Cats

Feline History. From the 17th century onwards, small ceramic figurines of cats have been popular ornaments in both the West and the Orient. The peak period, however, was the 18th century and the most dedicated collectors of feline artefacts focus on that epoch.

The favourite pose for these decorative cat figures is squatting with the front legs straight, and with the face of the animal turned towards the spectator. In heraldic terms this would be called 'sejant guardant' – sitting and watching. Among the major types of ceramic cat are the following:

Chelsea Cats. English, 18th century. These, the earliest of the English porcelain cats, were imitations of the expensive Meissen Cats. Most were made between 1750 and 1760.

Ch'ing Cats. Chinese, 17th to 19th century. Many porcelain cats were made in the K'ang-Hsi period of Ch'ing, between 1662 and 1722. They were followed later by the Chinese Export Porcelain Cats. These were 18th and 19th century figures from the Ch'ien-Lung period, 1736–1795, and the Chia-Ch'ing period, 1796–1821. Further examples were made in the late 19th century.

Delft Cats. Dutch, 17th century and onwards. Several English centres made Delftware pottery cats, but the finest ones were made in Holland in the 18th century.

Derby Cats. English, Late 18th to early 19th century (up to 1848). Derby and Rockingham (see below), between them, made most of the English ceramic cats.

Gallé Cats. French, late 19th century. Gaily painted pottery cats made at Nancy in the 1890s. (One of Emile Gallé's cats was recently sold at auction for £4,000.)

Jackfield Cats. English, 18th century. Pottery cats made in Shropshire between 1740 and 1780, with later imitations produced elsewhere.

Meissen Cats. German, 18th century. Generally considered to be the most important of all the ceramic cats, most of their porcelain feline figurines were made between 1740 and 1765.

Rockingham Cats. English, early 19th century. Their brown-glazed cat figures were made mostly between 1810 and 1830, although some date from as early as 1780.

Royal Copenhagen Cats. Danish, 19th century.

Staffordshire Cats. English, 18th and 19th century. Pottery cats made from about 1715 until 1750.

Wemyss Cats. Scottish, late 19th century. Originally made at the Fife of Gallatown pottery from about 1895. Also made later, in England in the 1930s, at the Bovey Tracy pottery in Devon.

Whieldon Cats. English, 18th century. Mottled, tortoiseshell pottery cats made between 1740 and 1780.

Bibliography:

1974. McClinton, K.M. *Antique Cats for Collectors.* Lutterworth, London.

1996. Tenent, R. 'Cats for Collectors'. In: *Cat World Annual,* 1996. p.42-43.

Ceylon Cat

Domestic Breed. A cat developed by the Cat Club of Ceylon (now Sri Lanka), which looks like an early form of the Abyssinian. Also known as the 'Ceylonese Cat' or 'Celonese Cat'.

Appearance: It has the typical ticked coat of the modern Abyssinian, but with the addition of the barred leg-markings common in that breed at the turn of the century. It is very similar to the so-called 'Wild Abyssinian' developed in the 1980s from feral stock found in Singapore.

History: In recent years it has found favour among Italian breeders. In January 1984, Dr Paolo Pellegatta, a Milanese veterinary surgeon, was exploring some of the smaller villages in Sri Lanka, when he came across an unusual and delightful form of local cat. Although feral, the animals in question were remarkably friendly and Dr Pellegata decided to take a small group of them back to Italy. There were two males, Tisa and Serendib, and two females, Taranga and Aralyia. They were later to be joined by a few more, and together formed the European nucleus of the breed. They made their first public appearance in the West a few months later, in May 1984, at the Como Cat Show in Italy, and were an immediate success. There followed four years of carefully planned breeding and then, in May 1988, the Ceylon Cat was submitted to FIFe, and started on the first phase of its official recognition as a new form of pedigree cat.

Colour Forms: The traditional colouring is a sandy-golden background with black markings. This is known as the Manila. There are also Blue, Red, Cream and Tortoiseshell variations.

Bibliography:

1992. Capra, F. 'The Cat from the Shining Isle'. In: *Cat World,* September 1992. p.18-20.

Breed Club:

Club Amatori Gatto di Ceylon (The Ceylon Cat Lovers Club) was formed by Dr Pellegatta at Verigate and is based at Corgeno, near Milan, Italy.

Champagne

Coat Colour. An American name for a buff-cream coat. It is used to denote one of the dilute version of the sable brown Burmese Cat, whose coat is described as 'warm honey beige, shading to a pale gold tan underside'. Its nearest British equivalent is chocolate.

Champfleury

Cat Authority. Champfleury was the pseudonym of the French author Jules Fleury-Husson (1821–1889), who wrote one of the most important cat books of the 19th century: *Les Chats; histoire – meours – observations – anecdotes*. It was translated into English by Frances Cashel Hoey and published by George Bell as *The Cat Past and Present*. A feline classic, it is one of the very first attempts to produce a factual, scholarly account of the domestic cat.

Bibliography:

1869. Champfleury. *Les Chats; histoires – meours – observations – anecdotes*.

1885. Champfleury. Translated (with supplementary notes) by Mrs Cashel Hoey, *The Cat Past and Present*. Bell, London.

Chantilly Cat

Domestic Breed. An alternative name for the Tiffany Cat. The double-naming appears to have arisen because some cat societies felt that confusion could arise between the North American 'Tiffany Cat' and the British 'Tiffanie Cat'. This does already appear to have occurred and it may well be that eventually the little-used Chantilly will replace the better known 'Tiffany', to avoid further misunderstandings.

Danette Babyn, writing in 1995, comments: 'The former "Foreign-Longhair" is registered in North America as "Chantilly", "Tiffany", or "Chantilly/Tiffany", depending on the association; some registries felt the breed was entitled to use the original "Tiffany" name, so the breed has a dual designation.' (For further details see Tiffany Cat.)

Charcoal

Coat Colour. A dark grey coat, caused by a slight dilution of black.

Chartreuse Blue Cat

Domestic breed. According to Rush Shippen Huidekoper, writing in 1895, this was an early name for the Russian Blue Cat.

Chartreux Cat

Domestic Breed. An old French breed, dating from the 1300s or even earlier. The name of 'Chartreux Cat' was first used for this breed in 1750. It is sometimes referred to as the 'Chartreuse cat', the 'Carthusian Cat', the 'Monastery Cat', or the 'Blue Cat of France'. Sometimes known as the 'smiling cat'. In France it is called the *Chat des Chartreux;* in Germany it is the *Kartäuser;* in Holland it is the *Karthuizer;* and in Italy the *Certosino*.

Appearance: A strong, heavily built, broad-headed, short-haired, blue-coated, orange-eyed cat with rather finely boned legs. Affectionately described by one American breeder as 'a potato on toothpicks'.

History: A cat of obscure origin. As with several other ancient breeds, there are a number of conflicting stories as to how it began.

1 It originated as a cross between an Egyptian Cat and a Manul Cat. There is no scientific evidence whatever to support this fanciful idea.

2 It was originally imported into France, in the 17th century, from the Cape of Good Hope in South Africa by Monks of the Carthusian Order. La Grande Chartreuse, just north of Grenoble, in south-east France near the Italian border, was the principal monastery of the Carthusians, a Roman Catholic order established in the year 1084. Renowned for their yellow and green liqueurs, the Carthusian monks have also become famous for their own special breed of monastic cat. The oldest reference to link the monks with this breed is found in Bruslon's 1723 *Universal Dictionary,* in which he says it 'is called Chartreux because of the monks of this name who owned the breed first'. Thirty years later, a little doubt has crept in: 'Chartreux cats, perhaps named because it was the monks of this name that were the first to have this breed.' (Chevalier

An early French illustration of a Chartreux Cat, from Demarest's *Mammalogy* of 1820.

de Jancourt in the *Grand Encyclopédie* of 1753). Unfortunately there is no archival evidence that they ever possessed such a breed. Replying to a query about the Chartreux Cat in 1972, the Prior of the Grand Chartreuse had this to say: 'We have never had the Chartreuse order . . . at the Cape of Good Hope. As for the subject of a breed of cat which had been of use by the Grand Chartreuse, our archives stand silent. Nothing lets us assume that a breed of this type of cat had been utilized in any epoch of our long history.'

3 It originated in the Middle East and was given to the Carthusian Monks by the knights returning from the Crusades. The fact that blue-grey cats were recorded from Syria, Cyprus and Malta, all places where the crusaders were active, has been offered in support of this theory. But again, there is no archival evidence that the monks ever received this type of cat.

4 It originated in the Middle East and arrived in Europe about 450 years ago, where it was exploited by the fur trade, its woolly pelts being highly prized for their fine, dense texture.

5 It began in Northern Europe and Siberia, where its thick, woolly coat protected it from the intense cold, and later developed into both the Russian Blue and the Chartreux. If this is true, then the famous Blue Cat of France may simply have been a non-pedigree European domestic, wandering the fields and alleyways until it was taken up as a special breed. An early encyclopedia published in London in the 1780s suggests that blue cats were, at that time, the dominant form of domestic feline in France. The author of the encyclopedia, George Howard, states categorically: 'In France the cats are all of a bluish-lead colour.'

If either of the last two stories is correct, it begs an obvious question. How did this cat become associated with the Chartreuse Monastery? A possible answer may lie in a reference to the word 'Chartreux', in Bruslon's 1723 *Universal Dictionary*. There, mention is made of a fine wool imported into France from Spain, which was called the 'Pile de Chartreux'. Bearing in mind the very fine, woolly coat of this breed of cat, it may well have been that the animal was named after the wool and that the monks of La Grande Chartreuse had nothing to do with it. Later, their connection may have been assumed, simply because they had the same name. In this way, legends can easily be born and then repeated time and again until they are part of a widely accepted tradition.

Whichever of these stories is true, we do know for certain that the breed is recorded, named and illustrated by Buffon in his 18th-century *Natural History*. And 19th-century British authors were also aware of the breed, although by then it seems to have become less common: 'Bluish-grey is not a common colour; this species are styled "Chartreux Cats", and are esteemed rarities.' (Charles Ross, 1868).

By the 1920s, French cat breeders had started to take a serious interest in the Chartreux. In 1928, two spinsters, the Leger sisters of the Guerveur Cattery, began a selective breeding programme on the small island known as the Belle-Ile-sur-Mère. Their foundation pair were a male called Coquito and a female called Marquire. They made good progress and, by 1931, were able to exhibit the breed in Paris. Sadly, however, their efforts were interrupted by the chaos of World War II.

After the war the breed was barely surviving and the decision was taken to reconstruct it using non-pedigree French cats that had blue-grey coats. This was done until the original shape and style of the Chartreux had been achieved. These reconstituted cats comprise the foundation stock of the modern Chartreux. (This also explains why some authorities now refuse to distinguish between the British Blue, the European Blue and the modern Chartreux.)

In 1970 ten of these new Chartreux were imported into the United States by the California breeder Helen Gamon. There, an enthusiastic group of breeders continued to develop them until they had gained championship status.

Personality: Terms used to describe this breed include: friendly, good-natured, accommodating, playful, self-assured, hardy, uncomplaining, quiet, devoted, gentle and placid. The cat is said to like children and dogs. It is characteristically lazy until a rodent appears, when it becomes a savage hunter.

THE CHARTREUX CAT, an early French breed with a long history and an obscure origin. It is sometimes referred to as the Monastery Cat, because of its close association with the Carthusian Order.

Related Breeds: There are several breeds of blue-grey cat and the relationship between them has been hotly disputed for many years. They are: the Russian Blue; the British Blue; the Maltese; the Chartreuse Blue; the Blue European Shorthair; the Exotic Shorthair Blue.

Other blue breeds, not confused with the above, include: the Blue Burmese; the Korat; the Foreign Blue; the Blue Longhair.

Colour Form: Only one colour is recognized: Blue-Grey. (Genetically, this is a 'diluted black'.)

Bibliography:

1990. Simonnet, J. *The Chartreux Cat.* Synchro Co., Paris. (Translation of *Le Chat des Chartreux,* 1989)

CHATI

WILD FELINE. An early name for a race of Ocelot *(Felis pardalis)* which, in the 19th century, was thought to be a distinct species and was then called *Felis mitis.*

CHAUS CAT

WILD FELINE. An alternative name for the Jungle Cat *(Felis chaus).* The word *chaus* is an ancient African name for a wildcat.

CHEETAH

WILD FELINE. *(Acinonyx jubatus)* One of the most unusual of all cats, the Cheetah has also been known as the Chita or the Hunting Leopard. The name Cheetah comes from the Hindu word *cital* which in turn comes from the Sanskrit *chitraka,* meaning 'Spotted One'. German: *Gepard;* French: *Le Guépard;* Swahili: *Msongo* or *Duma;* Afrikaans: *Jagluiperd.* The scientific name *jubatus* comes from the Latin *iubatus,* meaning 'maned', and refers to the crest-like mane that is present on the cubs.

Two variant forms, the Woolly Cheetah and the King Cheetah, which have been considered as separate species in the past, are now looked upon as no more than isolated mutants or, at best, local sub-species.

The Cheetah has two unique features. It is the fastest land mammal in the world and is the only member of the cat family with claws that cannot be sheathed. Its whole body is designed for speed, with a slender trunk, long neck, very long legs, and a lengthy tail used as a rudder and balancing aid. Its head is unusually small and its ears are short and rounded. Its strong, dog-like claws help to give it extra grip as it sprints across the ground. Its tawny coat is covered in small black spots and its tail is black-ringed with a white tip.

When Cheetahs were speed-tested against racing greyhounds (the fastest dogs in the world) on an oval track, the dogs only managed to average 59 km (37 miles) an hour, while the Cheetahs clocked up 69 km (43 miles) an hour. On the open plains Cheetahs do even better, reaching amazing speeds of 80–96 km (50–60 miles) an hour. The record is said to be 109 km (68 miles) an hour. They use a different hunting technique from other cats. Instead of hiding, stalking, ambushing and then making a short dash, the Cheetahs lie in wait, their spotted coats camouflaging them well, and then, when they break cover, will engage in a sustained pursuit of the prey. A Cheetah's average sprint-chase will cover as much as 200 metres (220 yards) and ends with a swipe from the cat's front leg that sends the prey – usually a gazelle or small antelope – sprawling head over heels. The Cheetah then skids to a halt and grabs the stunned prey by the throat. It pauses and keeps a firm grip, killing by suffocation. In a matter of seconds from the start of the hunt, the prey is dead.

If the hunting Cheetah happens to be a mother with cubs, she will then drag the kill to a suitable place for her offspring to join her in the feast. When they are born, these cubs, usually three to a litter, have a silver mane or crest of long hairs, which runs right down their backs. At this age they can sheath their claws like any other cat species. They lose their manes and the ability to sheath their claws at about the same time, when they are roughly ten weeks old. They are weaned at three months and will start to breed at two years.

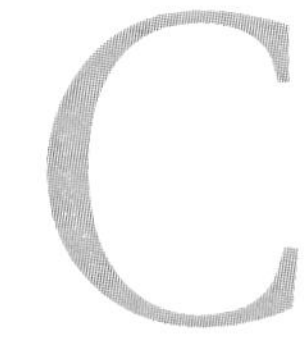

Female cheetahs are always solitary and have huge home ranges – up to 780 sq km (300 sq mi). The majority of males live in small coalitions of two or three together, although some are solitary like the females. Certain males are strictly territorial, with defended ranges of less than 50 sq km (20 sq mi), while others lack a 'home base' and roam over wide areas. When a female is on heat, she may visit males, or they may find her. If she encounters a male coalition, she may mate with more than one male there, although details of this behaviour are still uncertain.

Unlike other large cats, Cheetahs do not roar. Strangely, they bark rather like dogs and chirrup like birds.

The world population of Cheetahs has declined rapidly in the last few centuries. This was originally due to the taking of these animals for hunting purposes. They were kept in stables and hooded like birds of prey. Once on the hunting field, the hoods would be removed and they would be sent after game as a royal sport. Since nobody bred them in captivity, this meant that huge numbers were taken from the wild to fill the great stables throughout Asia. One ruler boasted that he had more than one thousand Cheetahs at his command. Another, Akbar, the Mogul Emperor, outshone everyone with a stable of 3,000. The Cheetah had become a high status animal and this was its undoing.

Later, when tourist safaris became popular, especially in East Africa, a new hazard faced the beleaguered Cheetahs. Being daytime hunters, they provided a spectacle for the visitors to the game parks. Unfortunately, so many gathered to watch them hunt that they were often unable to do so and had to become increasingly nocturnal, which did not suit their style of pursuit. Today, the numbers of Cheetahs in game parks throughout Africa have fallen lower and lower, until the species is seriously endangered everywhere.

THE CHEETAH *(Acinonyx jubatus)*, with its elegant, athletic build, is the fastest land mammal in the world. The young cub has a conspicuous mane or crest of long, pale fur down its back.

Size: The extremely thin, elongated body-design of the Cheetah means that its dimensions are much greater than its body weight would suggest:

Length of Head + Body: 120–150 cm (47–59 in). Tail: 65–85 cm (25½–33½ in). Weight: 30–60 kg (66–132 lb).

Distribution: The range of the Cheetah has been drastically reduced in the 20th century, entirely as a result of human intervention. It is estimated that in 1900 the world population stood at about 100,000. It was then a common sight on the open plains of Africa, the Middle East and parts of Asia, but since then the numbers have dwindled dramatically. A survey made in the 1970s showed that there were only 14,000 left in the whole of the vast continent of Africa. This revealed a halving of the total Cheetah population in less than two decades. Today that figure has fallen again, to between 9,000 and 12,000. Outside Africa there is only a relic population of a mere 200 in a remote area of Iran.

The Middle Eastern stronghold of Arabia saw its last Cheetah in 1950. And the last ones seen in India were three adults caught in the headlights of a car as it drove down a country road one night in 1952. The driver, a local ruler, stopped his car, got out, and calmly shot them. That was the end of the Indian Cheetah. The species has never been seen on that continent again.

In addition to the surviving wild population, there are approximately 1,100 Cheetahs in captivity. All their details are recorded in stud books and their breeding successes are carefully monitored. There are also specialist Cheetah protection groups in operation: the CCF (The Cheetah Conservation Fund), a registered Namibian Trust and, in England, the Cheetalert project, centred at the Lifeline Survival Trust in Woodcombe, Somerset.

Bibliography:

1961. Mercier, A. *Our Friend Yambo.* Souvenir Press, London.
1964. Varaday, D. *Gara-Yaka. The Story of a Cheetah.* Collins, London.
1966. Varaday, D. *Gara-Yaka's Domain.* Collins, London.
1969. Adamson, J. *The Spotted Sphinx.* Collins, London.
1974. Eaton, R.L. *The Cheetah.* Van Nostrand Reinhold, New York.
1975. Wrogemann, N. *Cheetah Under the Sun.* McGraw-Hill, Johannesburg.
1984. Ammann, K & Ammann, K. *Cheetah.* Bodley Head, London.
1987. Bottriell, L.G. *King Cheetah: The Story of a Quest.* Brill, Leiden.
1994. Caro, T.M. *Cheetahs of the Serengeti Plains.* University of Chicago Press.

CHERRY-COLOURED CAT

MYSTERY CAT. The search for a genuine, bright red cat has always fascinated cat lovers, so when the famous American showman Phineas Barnum proudly announced that he had acquired such an animal and was about to put it on display, excited crowds flocked to see it. After paying their money, they found themselves staring at an ordinary black cat. Angry at being deceived they demanded their money back, but were bluntly refused by Barnum who reminded them, truthfully, that some cherries are indeed black.

CHERUBIM CAT

DOMESTIC BREED. This is a new, experimental breed developed as a variant of the Ragdoll Cat. It has not, as yet, been accepted by any official cat organization.

THE FAMOUS, grinning Cheshire Cat from Lewis Carroll's *Alice in Wonderland* (1865).

CHESHIRE CAT

FICTIONAL CAT. In chapter six of Lewis Carroll's *Alice in Wonderland* (1865) a large cat is encountered, lying on a hearth and grinning from ear to ear. Alice asks, 'Please would you tell me why your cat grins like that?' The only answer she gets is, 'It's a Cheshire cat and that's why.' There is no explanation as to why cats from that particular English county should be prone to smiling. A clue comes with the final disappearance of the cat, when it slowly vanishes, starting with the end of its tail and ending with the broad grin, which remains some time after the rest of the animal has gone. It is this disembodied grin that some authorities claim explains the

source of Lewis Carroll's image, for there used to be a special kind of Cheshire cheese which had a grinning feline face marked on one end of it. The rest of the cat was omitted by the cheesemaker, giving the impression that all but the grin had vanished.

Lewis Carroll may well have seen these cheeses. But he may have taken his reference from an even earlier source. The reason the Cheshire cheesemakers saw fit to add a grinning cat to their product was that the expression 'grin like a Cheshire cat' was already in use for another reason altogether. It was an abbreviation of 'grin like a Cheshire Caterling', which was current about five centuries ago. Caterling was a lethal swordsman in the time of Richard III, a protector of the Royal Forests who was renowned for his evil grin, a grin that became even broader when he was despatching a poacher with his trusty sword. Caterling soon became shortened to 'Cat' and anyone adopting a particularly wicked smile was said to be 'grinning like a Cheshire Cat'. Lewis Carroll possibly knew of this phrase but, because he refers to the grin outlasting the rest of the body, it is more likely that his real influence was the cheese rather than the swordsman.

A third, but less favoured explanation has been offered, namely that one of the leading families in Cheshire had the face of a lion as part of its coat of arms. In the hands of local sign painters, the lion's image gradually got to look like a grinning cat.

Whichever is the true origin, the fact remains that the saying does not start with Carroll, as most people assume, but was in reality much older and was merely borrowed and made famous by him.

Chestnut

Coat Colour. A rich chestnut brown coat, similar to chocolate. It is used today in the United States in connection with the Oriental Shorthair.

The following variants have been recorded: (1) Chestnut Silver; (2) Chestnut Silver Tabby; (3) Chestnut Smoke; (4) Chestnut Tabby; (5) Chestnut Tortie.

Chestnut Brown Foreign Shorthair Cat

Domestic Breed. In the late 1950s it was decided to rename the newly developed, brown-coloured Siamese, then known as the Havana. Only a committee could have devised a title as cumbersome as 'The Chestnut Brown Foreign Shorthair'. Breeders hated it, and by 1970 had managed to persuade feline officialdom to reinstate the original name of Havana. In America, where it has a slightly less Oriental shape, it is known as the Havana Brown. (For details, see Havana Brown.)

Chinchilla

Coat Pattern. A Chinchilla Cat has a translucent silvery coat of a special kind. Each individual hair is white with a black tip. To put it another way, a Chinchilla Cat is a white cat ticked with black. The correct eye-colour to accompany this coat pattern is green or blue-green.

Some silver-coloured cats have a mixture of all-white and all-black hairs, but those are not true Chinchillas.

The name was borrowed from the silvery-grey South American rodent called the Chinchilla. The first Chinchilla class at a major cat show appeared in 1894 at the Crystal Palace Show. The earliest Chinchilla Cat Club was formed in 1901 in a London suburb. In those days the typical Chinchilla Cat was much darker than its modern equivalent. As breeders moved more and more towards a paler version, the original form had to be given a new name: Shaded Silver.

Pedigree breeds that appear in the Chinchilla colour include American Curl, American Shorthair, American Wirehair, Cornish Rex, Devon Rex, Exotic, Maine Coon, Manx, Norwegian Forest Cat, Persian and Scottish Fold.

The first recorded Chinchilla Cat was a female called Chinnie, born at a vicarage near Wakefield in England in 1882. She was sold to a breeder for a guinea (21 shillings, or £1.05) and became what Frances Simpson called ' The Mother of Chinchillas'.

The Chinchilla Persian is arguably the most glamorous of all cats. It appeared in 1882, was first exhibited at a cat show in 1894, and had its first breed club in 1901. In the 1960s it became famous as the pampered pet of a James Bond villain.

Perhaps the most internationally famous of all Chinchillas was Solomon, the Persian Cat that was lovingly caressed by the fiendish master-criminal Blofeld in the James Bond films *You Only Live Twice* (1967), *On Her Majesty's Secret Service* (1969) and *Diamonds are Forever* (1971).

Several colour variants of the Chinchilla Cat's silver coat have been developed in recent years, including the following: Blue Chinchilla Silver; Chinchilla Golden (for details, see entry); Chinchilla Shaded Tortoiseshell (= Shell Tortoiseshell); Dilute Chinchilla Shaded Tortoiseshell; Red Chinchilla.

Bibliography:

1993. Single, D.J. *Silver and Golden Persians.* TFH, New Jersey.

Breed Clubs:

The Chinchilla, Silver Tabby and Smoke Cat Society, established in 1908. Issues a glossy quarterly Journal. Address: Lucky-Lite Farm, 219 Catherington Lane, Catherington, Waterlooville, Hants, PO8 0TB, England.

The United Chinchilla Association. Address: 35 Colebrook Avenue, West Ealing, London, W13 8JZ, England.

Chinchilla Golden

Coat Colour. There appear to be two ways in which the golden sheen is created. One authority describes the coat as differing from the typical Chinchilla in having the tips of the white hairs dark brown instead of black. A second authority describes the coat as having an undercoat of rich, warm, cream-coloured hairs with black tips. Either way, the overall effect is that of a luxurious, shimmering golden fur. When they first appeared in Chinchilla Persian litters, these golden cats were called 'Brownies' and were discarded as unwanted variants. Eventually some breeders decided to retain them and develop them as a separate colour form. They were officially recognized as such by the CFA in America in 1977.

Pedigree breeds that appear in the Chinchilla Golden colour include American Curl, Exotic, Norwegian Forest and Persian.

Chinese Cat

Domestic Breed. A lost breed that remains something of a mystery. In 1796 the *Universal Magazine of Knowledge and Pleasure* asserted that in China, 'which is an empire very anciently policed, and where the climate is very mild, domestic cats may be seen with hanging ears'.

Several Victorian authors referred to the 'Chinese Cat' as a distinctive long-eared breed. Charles Ross, in his *Book of Cats* of 1868, comments: 'The Chinese Cat has the fur beautifully glossed . . . It is variegated with black and yellow, and, unlike most of the race, has the ears pendulous.' Bosman, writing about the ears, says, 'It is worthy of observation, that there is in animals evident signs of ancestry of their slavery. Long ears are produced by time and civilization and all wild animals have straight round ears.'

The clear implication is that the Chinese Cat had been domesticated since ancient times and was a well-established oddity in the Orient. Bosman was a serious naturalist and Ross would have had no reason to doubt him. The idea of such a strange breed of cats clearly excited the experts of the day, but despite their efforts, supporting evidence was hard to obtain

Frances Simpson, writing in 1903, reports: 'There is said to be a variety of Chinese cat which is remarkable for its pendent ears. We have never been able to ascertain anything definite with regard to this variety. Some years back a class was provided for them at a certain Continental cat show, and we went across in the hope of seeing and, if possible, acquiring some specimens; but, alas, the class was empty! We have seen a stuffed specimen in a Continental museum, which was a half-long-haired cat, the ears being pendent down the sides of the head instead of erect; but do not attach much value to this.'

The idea of a rabbit-like, lop-eared cat is so extraordinary that it seems certain such an animal would have been obtained by travellers and developed as a curiosity, had it really existed. The stuffed specimen was probably no more than a taxidermist's joke, with rabbit's ears attached to the body of a stuffed cat. Perhaps the reality was an Oriental mutation giving rise to a cat with downturned ears rather like the modern Scottish Fold, or American Curl. By word of mouth, this modest condition could easily have become exaggerated into the full lop-eared state. Unless early Chinese records are discovered one day, we may never know the truth.

Exotic ancient breeds from the Far East fuelled the Victorians' imaginations, as in this chromolithograph of 1880 depicting two Chinese Cats and, beneath them, the Malay Cat (see page 277).

Bibliography:

1926. Torrance, T. *The Chinese Cat.* Journal of the North-China Branch of the Royal Asiatic Society, Vol. 57, p.113.

Chinese Desert Cat

Wild Feline. *(Felis bieti)* Also known as the Pale Desert Cat or, in earlier works, simply as the Pale Cat.

Slightly larger than a domestic house-pet, this is a wild cat without the usual feline spots or stripes. Instead, it has an overall yellowish-grey colour and is paler underneath. It has a black-tipped tail with a few dark rings on it and pointed, almost lynx-like ears with small tufts of dark hairs at the tips. This is a cold-country cat with a suitably thick coat of fur that includes many long guard hairs. There are tufts of hair sprouting between the pads of its paws that no doubt help to keep its feet warm on icy cold surfaces.

The extremely elusive and rarely photographed Chinese Desert Cat *(Felis bieti)*. It lives in the same region as the Giant Panda.

It is not really a desert cat at all, and has been badly named. In reality, it inhabits barren steppe country and mountain brush terrain, so a better name for it might be the Chinese Steppe Cat. It lives in the same general area as the Giant Panda.

Less is known about this species than any other wild feline. Most of our knowledge comes from skins that have been offered for sale by fur-trappers in the local markets. We have no idea whether it is rare or common, but given its restricted range, the world population cannot be all that large.

Size: Length of Head + Body: 70–85 cm (27½–33½ in). Tail: 29–35 cm (11½–14 in). Weight: 5–6 kg (11–13 lb).

Distribution: Limited to the border region between eastern Tibet and western China, the Chinese Desert Cat is most commonly found in the provinces of Szechwan and Kansu. Its range may reach as far as Inner Mongolia.

Chinese Harlequin Cat

Domestic Breed. A new type of short-haired black and white cat. A predominantly white cat, but with a black tail and black patches on the head and body. It is now recognized by TICA. It is said to have been an attempt to re-create an ancient Chinese cat.

Chintz

Coat Pattern. According to Frances Simpson in her classic, turn-of-the-century study of cats, *The Book of the Cat* (1903), 'Chintz Cat' was the 'old-fashioned', northern name for the Tortoiseshell-and-White Persian. The modern American equivalent is 'Calico Cat'.

Chocolate

Coat Colour. A medium to pale brown coat, this is a milk-chocolate colour that is paler than seal. In the United States, in the Burmese and Tonkinese breeds, the chocolate colour is given the special name of 'champagne'.

The following variants have been listed: (1) Chocolate Shaded; (2) Chocolate Silver; (3) Chocolate Smoke; (4) Chocolate Tortie; (5) Chocolate Tortie Shaded; (6) Chocolate Tortie Smoke; (7) Chocolate Point; (8) Chocolate Lynx Point; (9) Chocolate Tortie Point; (10) Chocolate Tortie Lynx Point.

Chu Hou-Tsung

Cat Owner. The Emperor of China, Chu Hou-Tsung (1507–1566), the 11th Emperor of the Ming Dynasty, had a favourite cat called Shuang-mei, which translates as 'Frost-eyebrows'. According to a contemporary report: 'She was of faintly blue colour but her two eyebrows were clearly jade-white . . . wherever her Imperial master went, she always led. She waited upon the Emperor until he slept and then she lay still like a stump.'

When she died she was given a special honour, being buried in a grave with a stone tablet inscribed with the words 'Ch'iu-lung Chung'. This means 'The Grave of a Dragon with Two Horns', which was a term of special praise when applied to a human being and therefore even more flattering when applied to a cat.

Churchill, Winston

Cat Owner. The wartime Prime Minister adored cats and never failed to react to their presence, even at the height of the war. Both in the Cabinet Room and at Churchill's dining table, a chair next to him was reserved for his favourite cat. The main occupant of these chairs was a black cat from Admiralty House appropriately named Nelson. This cat, which, from 1940, also shared the great man's bed, was helping the war effort, said Churchill, by acting as a hot water bottle and therefore saving fuel.

Among his various cats were Bob, a black and white cat who waited for the PM at the steps of No. 10 Downing Street and was usually rewarded with a friendly stroking; Mr Cat (also known as Mr Kat or Tango), with whom he discussed political issues; the autocratic Nelson; an adopted stray called Margate; and Jock, a ginger tom given to him on his 88th birthday in 1962 by Sir John Colville. Jock was mentioned in Churchill's will, being guaranteed permanent 'comfortable residence' in his country house for life. (See also entry for Margate.)

One of a series of drawings of Sir Winston Churchill's ginger tom, Jock, by Sir William Nicholson.

Cinnamon

Coat Colour. A reddish brown coat. An alternative name for this colour is Sorrel. Variants recorded include the following: (1) Cinnamon Shaded; (2) Cinnamon Silver; (3) Cinnamon Silver Tabby; (4) Cinnamon Smoke; (5) Cinnamon Tabby; (6) Cinnamon Tortie; (7) Cinnamon Tortie Shaded; (8) Cinnamon Tortie Smoke; (9) Cinnamon-Cream Calico; (10) Cinnamon-Cream Van Calico.

Clarence

Film Cat. Clarence was a cross-eyed lion who starred in a feature film and a television series in the 1960s. Two animal trainers, Ralph Helfer and Ivan Tors, had set up a centre called 'Africa, USA' just outside Los Angeles. One day a small lion cub with a squint arrived and the idea for a gentle, lovable, leonine star was born. Clarence grew to be one of the most amenable of all tame lions and starred in a feature film called *Clarence the Cross-eyed Lion* in 1965. Then, from

1966 to 1969, he went on to feature in the popular TV series *Daktari* which, although it was set in East Africa, was filmed entirely at their compound in California.

Classic Tabby

Coat Pattern. This is another name for the 'Blotched Tabby', and is sometimes also referred to as the Marbled Tabby. On the flanks of the cat, the dark markings of this tabby pattern are arranged in whorls and spirals, with a central, oyster-shaped patch. This contrasts with the thinner lines of the Mackerel Tabby. (For further details see Blotched Tabby.)

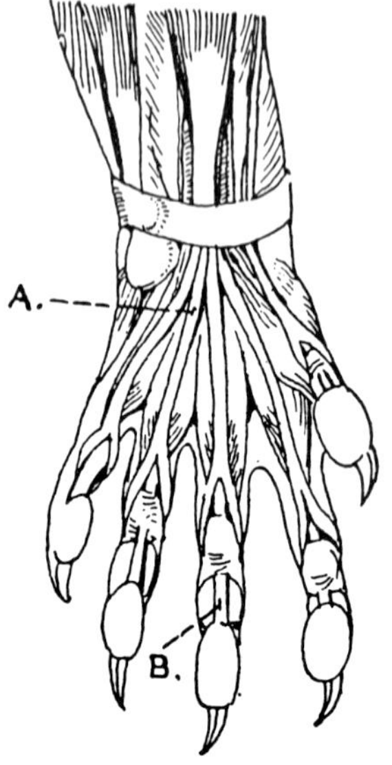

The claws of the cat, showing the superficial flexor tendons of the left front foot.

Claws

Feline Anatomy. The powerful, curved claws of cats are valuable when the animals are climbing, digging, defending themselves, fighting rivals or attacking prey. Each of the claws is attached to a final toe-bone and is movable. The advantage of this system is that the cat can keep its claws pin-prick sharp at all times. Many other kinds of animals, with fixed claws, have them worn down and blunted by constant wear and tear. The claws of the cat are as fresh and sharp as sheathed daggers.

Feline claws are usually referred to as retractile, but this gives a false impression of the way they operate. It is when they are relaxed that they are retracted. To bring them into operation they must be extended. In other words, they are normally sheathed and are only displayed when the cat tightens special muscles by a voluntary action. To put it another way, the claws of a cat are *protractile*, rather than retractile. This may be a small, anatomical quibble, but it is important for the cat. If the claws had to be actively retracted every time the animal wished to hide them, it would have to keep the muscles tensed for hour after hour, because the condition of 'hidden claws' is the usual one. The 'claws out' condition only occurs briefly, when there is some kind of emergency.

Claw-stropping

Feline Behaviour. Most cat owners have experienced the unpleasant discovery of a favourite fabric torn by a pet feline. It is usually stated that the cat was 'sharpening its claws'. This is true, but not in precisely the way that is imagined. The claws are not being sharpened like knives, with the blunt ends being stropped until they are finer and more pointed. What the cat really achieves by its tearing actions is the removal of its old, worn-out claw-sheaths, to reveal glistening new claws underneath. The action is more like the shedding of a snake's skin than the sharpening of a kitchen knife.

Sometimes, when people run their hands over the place where the cat has been tearing at the furniture, they find what they think is a ripped-out claw and they then fear that their animal has accidentally caught its claw in some stubborn threads of the fabric and damaged its foot. But the 'ripped-out claw' is nothing more than the old outer layer that was ready to be discarded.

Cats do not employ these powerful stropping actions with their hind feet. Instead they use their teeth to chew off the old outer-casings from their hind claws.

A second important function of stropping with the front feet is the exercising and strengthening of the retraction and protrusion apparatus of the claws, so vital to catching prey, fighting rivals and climbing.

A third function, not suspected by most people, is that of scent-marking. There are scent-glands on the underside of the cat's front paws and these are rubbed vigorously against the fabric of the furniture being clawed. The rhythmic stropping, right paw, left paw, squeezes scent on to the surface of the cloth and rubs it in, depositing the cat's personal signature on the furniture. This is why it is always the owner's favourite chair which seems to suffer most attention, because the cat is responding to the owner's personal fragrance and adding to it. Some people buy an expensive scratching-post from a pet shop, carefully impregnated with catnip to make it appealing, and are bitterly disappointed when the cat quickly ignores it and

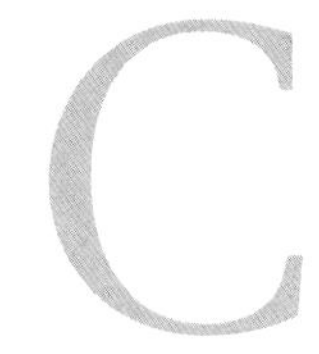

returns to stropping the furniture. Hanging an old sweatshirt over the scratching post might help to solve the problem, but if a cat has already established a particular chair or a special part of the house as its 'stropping-spot', it is extremely hard to alter the habit.

In desperation some cat-owners resort to the cruel practice of having their pets de-clawed. Apart from the physical pain this inflicts, it is also psychologically damaging to the cat and puts it at a serious disadvantage in all climbing pursuits, hunting activities and feline social relationships. A cat with claws is not a true cat. (See separate entry for 'de-clawing'.)

Climbing

Feline Behaviour. The sharp claws, strong legs, flexible body and balancing tail of the cat enable it to climb with great efficiency. This ability provides it with advantages both in relation to predation and self-protection. Some wild species employ climbing as part of an ambush strategy, leaping down on prey from above. Some, such as the Leopard, also use it when storing food beyond the grasp of land-bound rival predators. Others, such as lions, use climbing as a way of avoiding over-heating, their elevated position among the branches of trees providing them with cooling breezes not available at ground level.

Among domestic felines, climbing is most often seen in cases where cats are being persecuted by rival cats, aggressive dogs or hostile humans. In such instances they can be seen to clamber up trees with great speed and athleticism, sometimes with such vigour that they find themselves trapped, high up, and unable to descend.

Perhaps the most remarkable instance of domestic feline climbing ability concerns a female cat in Bradford, Yorkshire in 1980. Attacked by a dog, it climbed 21 metres (70 feet) up a sheer, vertical, pebbledash wall of a five-storey apartment block.

A climbing record of a completely different kind has been reported from Switzerland, where, in August 1950, a four-month old kitten followed mountaineers to the top of the Matterhorn in the Alps, a climb of over 4,000 metres (14,000 feet). The kitten in question belonged to Josephine Aufdenblatten of Geneva. At dawn each day, it watched the climbers depart for the mountain and then, one morning, decided to emulate them. To the amazement of a climbing party led by Edmund Biner, it reached a hut at 3,736 metres (12,556 feet) and the next day went even higher. It did its best to keep up with the climbers and eventually managed to reach the Swiss summit and then finally even the Italian summit. It started to fall several times, but always managed to cling on, and never lost sight of the mountaineers. Finally, miaowing and with tail proudly erect at the summit, the remarkable kitten was rewarded with a share of the climbers' meal, and was then given a free ride back down to its home, in the rucksack of one of the mountain guides.

Clouded Leopard

Wild Feline. *(Neofelis nebulosa)* Also known in Malaya as the Rimau-Dahan, the Tree-tiger (or, more correctly, the 'Fork-of-a-branch-tiger', because the animals like to rest spread out across a fork in a branch). Sometimes also called the Rimauda-han. In China it is referred to as the Mint Leopard. In earlier days it was sometimes called the Snow Panther, or Diard's Cat. The scientific name *nebulosa* comes from the Latin word *nebula* meaning a cloud.

This is the largest of the 'Small Cats' in Asia. Although it is called a 'Leopard', it is not closely related to the true Big Cats. It does not roar like them, but purrs like a small cat. It is, however, a very well-built animal, the size of a small Leopard, with a heavy, leopard-like skull. The canines in its upper jaw are so huge that they are reminiscent of those of the extinct Sabre-tooth Tiger. The Clouded Leopard also lies down like a Big Cat, with its front feet out forwards, instead of tucked up underneath it, and its tail out straight behind it.

It gains its name from the fact that the spots on its back are so extensive that they look like clouds with dark trailing edges. Its legs are rather short, with big paws, and its body and tail are both very long, reflecting the fact that it is an arboreal species. It is claimed that it can run down trees head-first, can hang and swing from a single hind-paw, can pounce on prey directly from

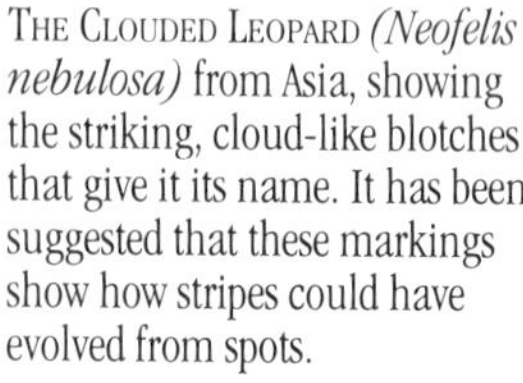

The Clouded Leopard *(Neofelis nebulosa)* from Asia, showing the striking, cloud-like blotches that give it its name. It has been suggested that these markings show how stripes could have evolved from spots.

above, and can even climb along the underside of large branches upside-down. The only other cat that is arboreal to this degree is the Margay from South America.

The Clouded Leopard sleeps high in the trees and is reported to break up branches to build itself a bed. If this is true, it is a most unusual activity for a feline. It does seem certain, however, that it frequently lies hidden among the branches as it waits to ambush a prey animal moving about on the ground below. Its food consists of birds, snakes, squirrels, monkeys, pigs, small deer, and other medium-sized mammals. The prey is usually killed by a blow from a heavy paw, followed by a stabbing bite with the massive canine teeth. Clouded Leopards are fastidious feeders, carefully removing as much fur and feather from their prey as they can before eating. According to some reports, the Clouded Leopard is as much at home on the ground as in the trees, but it is so secretive and elusive that careful field-studies have never been made to record its daily life in any detail.

It has a long, moaning call which can be heard over great distances through the forest. These calls are made from the vantage point of a special 'tiger hill' – some kind of elevated landmark in its home range.

On several occasions sightings have been made of Clouded Leopards which have been hunting or moving about in pairs, but it is not known whether such pairs stay together for long periods of time.

This species has been ruthlessly hunted for its beautiful pelt and has lost many of its forest strongholds to advancing agriculture. As with so many wild cats, its numbers are therefore on the decline. In earlier days, an unusual extra problem for this particular cat was that, in Borneo, its canine teeth were highly sought after by the local people as ear-ornaments, and its pelt was used as a war-coat.

Size: Length of Head + Body: 75–95 cm (29½–37½ in). Tail: 55–80 cm (21½–31½ in). Weight: 16–23 kg (35–50½ lb).

Distribution: Its range extends from Nepal and Sikkim in the north, down through Burma, Thailand and China, and south to Taiwan, Malaya, Borneo and Sumatra.

Coat Colours and Patterns

Feline Anatomy. Many of the breeds of domestic cat have appeared in a large variety of colour forms and patterns. These increase in number, year by year, as breeders strive to develop new tones and variants. Each of the main colours and patterns may be subdivided; for these, see the separate entries for each. Unfortunately, some confusion has been caused because different cat societies use slightly different names. Where this has occurred, the alternatives are given. For simplicity, all the terms that have been used in the past to describe the visual quality of the coats are listed here, without any attempt to separate colours from patterns:

1 Agouti (Banded hairs. Agouti coat = Ticked coat.)
2 Auburn (Golden brown – especially on extremities of Van Cat)
3 Bi-colour (White coat with dark patches. White: 33–50%; Colour: 66–50%.)
4 Black (Jet black = ebony. Often fails to reach ideal and shows a brown tinge.)
5 Blotched (The Blotched Tabby = The Classic Tabby.)
6 Blue (Dilution of black coat. Blue = pale grey to slate grey.)
7 Bronze (Warm coppery brown ground colour, lightening to tawny buff.)
8 Brown (Reduction of black pigment so that it appears brown.)
9 Calico (American name for tortoiseshell and white.)
10 Cameo (Coat of white hairs with red tips.)
11 Caramel (Reddish-brown coat = Cinnamon; alternatively called a bluish fawn.)
12 Champagne (American name for a buff-cream coat.)
13 Charcoal (Dark grey coat, caused by slight dilution of black.)
14 Chestnut (Rich chestnut brown coat, similar to chocolate.)
15 Chinchilla (Coat of white hairs with coloured tips.)
16 Chintz (Chintz = tortoiseshell and white = calico)
17 Chocolate (Medium to pale brown coat. Paler than seal.)
18 Cinnamon (Reddish-brown coat = sorrel.)
19 Classic (The Classic Tabby = The Blotched Tabby.)
20 Colourpoint (Pale coat with darker extremities.)
21 Cream (Dilution of red coat.)
22 Dilute (Paler version of coat colour.)
23 Ebony (Alternative name for black coat.)
24 Fawn (Light, pinkish cream coat.)
25 Flame (Flame-point = red point.)
26 Frost (Frost-point is an American name for Lilac-point.)
27 Ginger (Ginger = marmalade = orange = red.)
28 Golden (Warm apricot coloured hairs with darker tips.)
29 Grey (Dilution of black coat. Usually called 'blue'.)
30 Harlequin (A bi-colour coat with: white 50–75%; colour 50–25%.)
31 Lavender (American name. Dilution of chocolate. A pinkish-grey coat.)
32 Lilac (Warm pinkish grey coat.)
33 Lynx (Lynx-pointed coat = Tabby-pointed coat.)
34 Mackerel (Mackerel Tabby = Striped Tabby.)
35 Maculate (Maculate coat = Spotted coat)
36 Magpie (Black and white coat)
37 Mink (Brown coat)
38 Orange (Orange = marmalade = red = ginger.)
39 Parti-colour (General term to include bi-colours, tortoiseshells, etc.)
40 Patched (Two-tone tabby coat with darker and lighter patches = Torbie.)
41 Peach (Australian name. Pinkish-salmon markings on pinkish-cream ground.)
42 Pewter (Blue-silver tabby coat. Shaded silver.)
43 Platinum (Pale, silvery-grey with pale fawn undertones.)

44 **Piebald** (Black and white coat.)
45 **Red** (Red = orange = marmalade = ginger.)
46 **Ruddy** (Ruddy-brown coat. Burnt sienna.)
47 **Sable** (American name. Dark brown coat = Seal.)
48 **Seal** (Dark brown coat = Sable.)
49 **Self** (Uniform coat of one colour = Solid.)
50 **Sepia** (Dark brown coat.)
51 **Shaded** (Coat of pale hairs becoming gradually darker towards tips.)
52 **Shell** (Coat of pale hairs with dark colouring only on extreme ends of tips.)
53 **Silver** (Coat of pale grey hair with dark tips.)
54 **Smoke** (Coat of pale hairs with extensive dark tips. In France = Fumé)
55 **Solid** (American name. Uniform coat of one colour = Self-coloured)
56 **Sorrel** (Brownish-orange to light brown coat = Cinnamon.)
57 **Spotted** (Tabby coat in which dark patches form distinct spots = Maculate coat.)
58 **Striped** (Coat with dark lines.)
59 **Tabby** (Coat pattern with dark patches in the form of blotches, stripes or spots.)
60 **Ticked** (Banded hairs. Ticked coat = Agouti coat.)
61 **Torbie** (Two-tone tabby coat with darker and lighter patches = Patched Tabby.)
62 **Tortoiseshell** (Tortoiseshell = Red Tabby + Black Marks.)
63 **Tricolour** (Coat with three colours.)
64 **Usual** (The original colour of a breed, before colour variants were developed.)
65 **Van** (White cat with colour only on head and tail.)
66 **White** (Pure white coat, masking all other colours.)

Critics have occasionally complained that, when naming the various tones and shades of their animals, pedigree cat breeders have sometimes fallen prey to what might be termed optimistic exaggeration. One plaintive cat owner was heard to remark: 'I often think that I might be colour-blind when I am among breeders discussing colours of their cats.' Despite this, it cannot be overlooked that, through careful and lengthy breeding programmes, the world of pedigree cats has managed during the past century to develop many stunningly beautiful feline coats.

Colette

Cat Owner. French novelist (1873–1954) with a lifelong passion for cats, who wrote a number of books about her pets. She is quoted as saying: 'Making friends with a cat can only be a profitable experience.'

French author Colette (1873–1954) in her Paris apartment with one of her much-loved cats, a Chartreux, in the late 1920s. In the 1930s she wrote a book, *La Chatte*, about a cat called Saha, who also happened to be a blue-grey Chartreux.

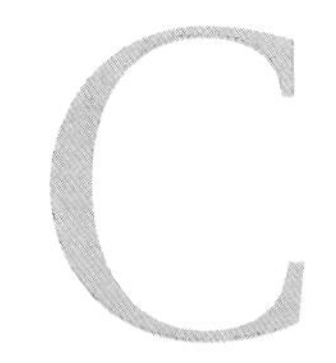

Bibliography:
1913. *Barks and Purrs.* Fitzgerald, New York. *(Sept dialogues de bêtes:* about her grey Angora Cat, Kiki-la-Doucette, and its companion a French bulldog called Toby)
1924. *Cats, Dogs and I.* Holt, New York. (stories from *La paix chez les bêtes*)
1936. *The Cat.* Farrar & Rinehart, New York. *(La Chatte:* about a cat called Saha, a blue-grey Chartreux, whose owner left his wife because she was cruel to the animal)
1951. *Creatures Great and Small.* Secker & Warburg, London. *(Dialogues des bêtes; Sept dialogues des bêtes; Douze dialogues des bêtes; La paix chez les bêtes)*
1953. *Gigi and the Cat.* Secker & Warburg, London. (New translation of *La Chatte*)
(See also entries for Kiki-la-Doucette and Ba-tou.)

Colocolo

Wild Feline. *(Felis colocolo)* This South American cat is better known today as the Pampas Cat. It was given the local name of Colocolo after a famous local warrior chief in Chile, by the 18th century explorer, Molina. (For details see Pampas Cat.)

Colourpoint

Coat Pattern. The typical Siamese coat pattern, namely a pale ground colour with dark extremities. This pattern is temperature-dependent, the extremities, which are colder, growing darker as the animal matures, while the warmer regions remain pale. If an extremity is injured or infected and that part of the cat's body becomes abnormally hot, pale hair will grow there as a consequence.

In the course of cross-breeding, this Siamese coat pattern has been injected into other breeds. Today, colourpoint breeds include the following:

1 **Siamese** (and Somali)
2 **Colourpoint Shorthair** (= New Colour Siamese)
3 **Colourpoint British Shorthair** (British Shorthair with Siamese points)
4 **Colourpoint European Shorthair** (European Shorthair with Siamese points)
5 **Himalayan** (= Colourpoint Longhair; Colourpoint Persian; Pointed Persian)
6 **Balinese** (= Longhair Siamese; Oriental Longhair)
7 **Javanese** (Longhair Siamese with unusual points-colours, in some countries)
8 **Tonkinese** (= Golden Siamese)
9 **Birman** (Longhair Siamese markings, but with white feet)
10 **Ragdoll** (Longhair Siamese markings, plus variable amounts of white)
11 **Ragamuffin** (as for Ragdoll, but with unusual points-colours)
12 **Snowshoe** (Siamese with the addition of white spotting on the feet and face)

In recent years many minor colour variants of the colourpoint coat pattern have been developed, including the following: (1) Blue Point; (2) Blue Lynx Point; (3) Blue-Cream Point; (4) Blue-Cream Lynx Point, (5) Chocolate Point; (6) Chocolate Lynx Point; (7) Chocolate Tortoiseshell Point; (8) Chocolate Tortoiseshell Lynx Point; (9) Cream Point; (10) Cream Lynx Point; (11) Flame Point; (12) Lilac Point; (13) Lilac Lynx Point; (14) Lilac-Cream Point; (15) Lilac-Cream Lynx Point; (16) Red Point; (17) Red Lynx Point; (18) Seal Point; (19) Seal Lynx Point; (20) Seal Tortoiseshell Point; (21) Seal Tortoiseshell Lynx Point; (22) Tortoiseshell Point; (23) Tortoiseshell Lynx Point.

Colourpoint British Shorthair Cat

Domestic Breed. A recently created breed in which a typical British Shorthair Cat has been enhanced by the addition of a typical Siamese coat pattern. It should not be confused with the American cat referred to as the 'Colorpoint Shorthair'. The latter is essentially a Siamese Cat with unusual colouring on its points.

The Colourpoint British Shorthair Cat, a 1980s breed in which Siamese markings have been added to a typically British Shorthair body. Although it has acquired the Siamese coat-pattern, it has retained the personality of the Shorthair.

Because of this confusion and because the Colourpoint British Shorthair Cat has such a cumbersome name, a new title will no doubt be forthcoming for this attractive breed.

Appearance: The same as for the British Shorthair Cat, except for the coat pattern. The dark extremities – the Siamese points – may be present in any of the usual colours. The short body has a stocky, cobby shape, with strong, thick legs, rounded head, large feet and heavy tail.

History: This breed was artificially developed by careful crossing experiments. The programme was started in England in the 1980s but the breed was not formally recognized until 1991. The aim was to 'borrow' the pointed coat pattern of the Siamese without any of the other Oriental qualities, such as angular body shape.

Personality: This cat remains essentially a typical British Shorthair, with a personality to match. Despite gaining the Siamese colouring, it has not acquired the Siamese character.

Colour Forms: All the various Siamese point colours are acceptable, and many have already appeared, including the following: Blue-Cream Point; Blue Point; Chocolate Point; Cream Point; Red Point; Seal Point; Seal Tortie Point.

Breed Club:

The Colourpoint British Shorthair Cat Club. Address: 77 Hallsfield Road, Bridgewood, Chatham, Kent, ME5 9RT, England.

Colourpoint European Shorthair Cat

Domestic Breed. A similar development to the Colourpoint British Shorthair (see entry). Created in Italy in 1982, the typical European Shorthair was successfully given a Siamese pointed coat-pattern, without altering its character or anatomy in any other way. Despite its Oriental colouring, the breed remains a stocky, quiet Shorthair Cat.

Colourpoint Longhair Cat

Domestic Breed. The British name for a Persian Cat with Siamese colourpoint markings. Elsewhere it is known as the Himalayan, the Colourpoint Persian or the Pointed Persian. (For details see Himalayan Cat.)

Colour Forms: To simplify the list, the colours are grouped into convenient categories.

GCCF: Solid Point Colours: Seal Point; Blue Point; Chocolate Point; Lilac Point; Red Point; Cream Point.

Tortie Point Colours: Seal Tortie Point; Blue-Cream Point; Chocolate Tortie Point; Lilac-Cream Point.

Non-tortie Tabby Point Colours: Seal Tabby Point; Blue Tabby Point; Chocolate Tabby Point; Lilac Tabby Point; Red Tabby Point; Cream Tabby Point.

Tortie Tabby Point Colours: Seal Tortie Tabby Point; Blue-Cream Tabby Point; Chocolate Tortie Tabby Point; Lilac-Cream Tabby Point.

Breed Clubs:

Colourpoint Cat Club. Publishes a twice-yearly magazine. Address: 1 Chestnut Avenue, Ravenshead, Notts., England; Tel: 01623-793980.

Colourpoint Society of Great Britain. Address: 77 Nursery Hill, Shamley Green, Guildford, Surrey, GU5 OUL, England.

Colourpoint Shorthair Cat

Domestic Breed. This is essentially a Siamese Cat with newly developed colouring to the points. In some cat societies it is referred to simply as 'New Colour Siamese'. In others, it is grouped separately under its own name.

Appearance: The body has the slender, angular shape of the typical Siamese, with the same close coat, and the same wedge-shaped head with huge ears and blue eyes.

History: For many years, breeders have been experimenting with new colours for the extremities of their Siamese Cats. Extreme traditionalists insist on the original Seal Point (a pale fawn coat with seal-brown extremities) and nothing else. Less extreme traditionalists accept both the seal-point and the Chocolate Point. Others also allow the two dilutants, Blue and Lilac. Any further colours are frowned upon and placed outside the strict 'Siamese' category, hence the introduction of the name 'Colourpoint Shorthair' for these other variants.

For non-traditionalists, they are all Siamese, regardless of the colour of their points, because they have the same body shape and personality and are truly Siamese in all but colour. The argument against this is that, in order to introduce these new colours, it was necessary to cross the Siamese foundation stock with other breeds, and this, therefore, makes them 'non-Siamese' to the purist.

The first seriously planned attempts to create new Siamese colours began in England in the 1940s, just after the end of World War II. In 1947 and 1948, red tabby cats and Abyssinians were mated with traditional Siamese Cats. When the offspring of these matings were back-crossed to Siamese Cats, the results were, as predicted, Red, Cream and Tortie Points. Some individuals were solid or full-coloured and these, too, were developed as a new breed: the Oriental Shorthair.

In the 1960s there was another special breeding programme that was designed to add further colours to the points, this time concentrating on 'tabby points'. (Tabby is called Lynx in America.)

Perhaps surprisingly, it is certain American cat societies that have adopted the more traditional stance and refused to allowed these new colour types to be called 'Siamese', while the British officials lump them all together in one class. Although breeding logic seems to be on the side of the Americans, an awkward fact has come to light that tends to support the British approach. Studying the feline population of Thailand recently, feline scholar Roger Tabor unexpectedly 'found tabby and tortie point Siamese among Thai temple cats'. Clearly, with true, home-bred Siamese, 'purity' is a matter of degree.

Personality: Terms used to describe this breed include: unpredictable, audacious, demanding, inquisitive, active, vocal, jealous, extroverted and arrogant, but also very loving and exceptionally intelligent. Their character was summed up by one owner with the phrase 'they are always on stage'.

Colour Forms: All Colourpoint Shorthairs have the typical Siamese points pattern, but *not* in the four traditional Siamese colours (Seal, Chocolate, Blue and Lilac). All other colours are permitted, and those already listed by the Cat Fanciers' Association in America are:

CFA: Red Point; Cream Point; Seal-Lynx Point; Chocolate Lynx Point; Blue-Lynx Point; Lilac-Lynx Point; Red-Lynx Point; Cream-Lynx Point; Seal-Tortie Point; Chocolate-Tortie Point; Blue-Cream Point; Lilac-Cream Point; Seal-Tortie-Lynx Point; Chocolate-Tortie-Lynx Point; Blue-Cream-Lynx Point; Lilac-Cream-Lynx Point.

Breed Club:

Colourpoint, Rex-coated and AOV Club. Address: 17 Rackenford, Shoeburyness, Essex, SS3 8BE, England.

The Colourpoint Shorthair Cat, an American breed not to be confused with the Colourpoint British Shorthair, is a Siamese Cat with newly developed colouring to the points. This one is a Seal-Lynx Point.

Contraception

Feline Reproduction. Serious attempts have been made to employ oral contraceptives to control cat populations. This has been done on a large scale in Israel, where it has been claimed that 20,000 kittens a year have been prevented by this method.

There are several kinds of contraceptive pills available, and they act in slightly different ways. The *progestogens* have the same effect on the cat's body as the natural pregnancy hormone, progesterone. They give the female cat a false pregnancy, complete with all the usual accompanying symptoms, such as increased appetite and increased weight. They can be administered either as simple tablets or as a special long-acting injection. But in both instances there are dangers of infection and for this reason other methods have since been tried.

A modified version of this treatment employing weaker progestogens has been tested recently and there is now a much safer pill of this type available, called *proligesterone,* for which the side-effects appear to be much less damaging.

A different approach is to inhibit the hormone which starts off the female sexual cycle. This hormone, called gonadotrophin, can be suppressed by certain drugs that stop the oestrus cycle without causing serious side-effects. This is a new method and is being developed further with some optimism.

A non-chemical method is also possible, but requires skilful, expert handling. This involves stimulating a female cat that is on heat with a glass rod, so that her body is fooled into reacting as if she has been mated by a tom-cat. Because it is the mating act in cats that induces ovulation, it is possible in this way to start the female cat's ovulation as if she is carrying male sperm. Because she is not, the eggs she sheds will be wasted and contraception will have been achieved. Her sexual appetite will pass and she will be quiet again until her next heat. As before, however, she will have to go through a phantom pregnancy as a result of this treatment.

All these methods require veterinary assistance and should not be attempted without professional help or approved prescriptions. There is no doubt, though, that within the next half-century we will see this type of biological control of feline populations perfected.

Convent Cats

Working Cats. In Cyprus, the Byzantine convent of St. Nicholas of the Cats today houses only five nuns but has a feline population of over 200 cats. Although the animals are traditionally tended by the nuns, most of them live semi-wild. The convent is situated near the British military base at Akrotiri, on the south coast of Cyprus, not far from Limassol. The feline community there is an ancient one, dating back to the fourth century. At the beginning of that century there had been a disastrous drought on the island, which had decimated the human population. The long years of drought had also resulted in an infestation of dangerous local snakes. When St. Helena of the Cross, the mother of King Constantine the Great, visited the island in AD 328, she became aware of this problem and persuaded her son to take action. He appointed Calocaerus, the chief of his camel corps, as Governor of the island and Calocaerus arranged for a special group of serpent-killing cats to be brought there from Egypt. The cats were taken to the Akrotiri peninsula, which is still known today as the Cape of Cats (Cape Gata). There they were cared for by the monks of the then active monastery of St. Nicholas. According to legend there were soon over a thousand of these snake-hunting felines.

The cats apparently carried out their duties efficiently, and survived well over the centuries. A Venetian monk, who visited the island in 1484, reported that, between Limassol and the Cape, 'the soil produces so many snakes that men cannot till it, or work without hurt thereon . . . At this place there is a Greek monastery which rears an infinite number of cats, which wage unceasing war with these snakes . . . Nearly all are maimed by the snakes: one has lost a nose, another an ear; the skin of one is torn, another is lame; one is blind of one eye, another of both.' He records that the monks summoned the cats to eat by tolling a bell. After their meal, they then trooped back outside again to continue their ceaseless battle with the venomous serpents.

Writing a century later, in 1580, Father Stephen Lusignan mentions that the Basilian monks who originally occupied St. Nicholas of the Cats were presented with all the surrounding land, 'on one condition, namely that they should be under obligation to maintain always at least a hundred cats and to provide some food for them every day in the morning and evening at the ringing of a small bell, to the intent that they should not eat nothing but venom and that for the rest of the day and night they should go a-hunting for those serpents'.

Eventually, with the Turkish conquest of Cyprus in the 16th century, the monastery fell into ruins and many of the cats died of starvation. After a period of abandonment, the present Greek Orthodox convent was established to give new life to St. Nicholas of the Cats, with nuns replacing the monks in the role of cat-protectors, and providing a continuing sanctuary for the descendants of the feline survivors of the ancient monastery.

Despite the best efforts of the nuns, however, by 1994 the cat population was in poor condition. Many of the animals were diseased and others were emaciated and suffering from malnutrition. The colony was breeding so fast that it was impossible for the sisters to keep up

an adequate food supply. Tourists visiting the convent were horrified by the condition of the cats and the WSPA (the World Society for the Protection of Animals) was called in to help. They caught up the cats, medicated them, treated their wounds, neutered 63 females and then released them all again. Regular food supplies were also arranged and at last the famous Convent Cats of Cyprus were healthy and secure for the future.

Copper Cat

Domestic Breed. A lesser-known, alternative name for the Burmese Cat. Thai cat expert Pichai-Ramadi Vasnasong comments that of the eight types of 'Siamese cats' (using the term in a broad sense), number eight is 'the Copper – which is better known to foreigners as the Burmese'. (For details see Burmese Cat.)

Cornelian Cat

Domestic Breed. An experimental breed referred to as: 'a self red short-haired cat of Burmese type; it can be regarded as the red equivalent of the Bombay. The name was adopted because it perfectly describes the beautiful rich russet red coat, just the colour of the cornelian gemstone.' It arose more or less accidentally during breeding programmes intended to improve the colouring of certain types of Burmese Cat, but now looks as though it may end up being officially recognized in its own right.

Cornish Rex Cat

Domestic Breed. Appeared in 1950 in the county of Cornwall, England. Originally called the 'English Rex', until a second form of Rex Cat was discovered in nearby Devon. Sometimes referred to in the popular press as the 'Poodle Cat' or 'Coodle'.

Appearance. A short-coated, wavy-furred cat with curly whiskers and eyebrows. Slim-bodied, with long, slender legs, the hind legs being taller than the front ones. The head is wedge-shaped and the ears large and pointed. The tail is long, fine and tapering.

In a typical feline coat there are three main kinds of hairs: guard hairs, awn hairs and down hairs; the guard hairs and awn hairs are together called the 'top-coat', and the down hairs are referred to as the 'undercoat'. It is generally stated that in the Cornish Rex Cat there are no guard hairs and that the coat is almost entirely made up of down hairs. This is not strictly true. Microscopic analysis of Rex hairs reveals that the awn hairs are present but greatly reduced, so that they are almost like down hairs. In fact, all the hairs, even the down hairs, are reduced in length by the Cornish Rex gene, giving the Rex Cat a coat that is about half the thickness of that on a typical cat. The fur is also much finer, each hair being about 60 per cent the typical thickness. This delicate coat falls into ripples or waves that give the animal its unique appearance.

Unusual Features: Because the thin coat lacks guard hairs, this breed suffers from exposure to extreme cold or heat. A feral Rex Cat would therefore be at a disadvantage in many climates. As with most thinly protected or naked species, the Rex Cat has a slightly higher body temperature than normal – one degree higher than typical breeds of domestic cat. Its metabolism is also higher, giving it a much bigger appetite. If its coat is brushed too vigorously, bald patches may appear. Generally speaking, this is a delicate cat that requires more careful attention than a typical breed. As a breed, it has one special advantage – namely, that it is less likely to cause allergic responses in people who are sensitive to normal cat hair.

This breed typically has a strange body posture, with the back arched and the underside 'tucked up'. Associated with this is a remarkable leaping ability, even from a stationary starting position.

History: The first Cornish Rex Cat was born in an old farmhouse on Bodmin Moor in Cornwall on 21st July 1950. A red tabby male in a litter of five kittens, born to an ordinary farm cat called 'Serena', was observed to have an unusual, curly coat. The owner, a Mrs Nina Ennismore, kept this kitten and, on the advice of a geneticist, mated it back to its mother, a tortoiseshell.

The Cornish Rex Cat *(opposite)*, first discovered in England in 1950. This Red Smoke example clearly shows the typical wavy coat and the elongated body of this unusual breed.

The new litter contained two curly-coated kittens and one plain-coated one. A second back-cross produced further curly-coated kittens, and the new breed was established.

Mrs Ennismore had, in the past, bred Rex Rabbits and decided to name this new feline mutation after the rabbit breed. The comparison is not particularly accurate. The first Rex Rabbit appeared as a mutation in France in 1919. It was given the name of Castorrex, meaning 'King of the Beavers', but this was eventually abbreviated simply to 'Rex'. The special quality of its coat was that it was 'heavily plushed and velvety' and lacking in guard hairs. If the dense, even coat showed any signs of being wavy or curly it was considered faulty. This is where the comparison with Rex Cats falls down, since for them a closely curled coat is an essential characteristic. A more correct term would have been 'Astrex' – the name given to another breed of rabbit, introduced in 1932, in which the fur is tightly waved. Despite this, the name Rex has survived and become generally accepted.

The first male Cornish Rex Cat, the founding father of the breed, was named 'Kallibunker'. He sired two litters, and then his son 'Poldhu' continued to act as a stud and produced several more litters by being mated to his female relatives.

Rather surprisingly, Kallibunker was put to sleep by his owner as part of an economy drive to reduce her growing cat population which, by 1956, had grown to 40 individuals. Mrs Ennismore, disillusioned at the lack of appreciation for her new breed, and short of funds to support her large feline family, had most of them destroyed, including both Serena and Kallibunker, a sad end for these historic felines. She did however, keep enough of the Rex cats to enable the breed to continue.

One of 'Poldhu's' daughters, called 'Lamorna Cove' was exported to America. She was already pregnant, having been back-crossed to her father, 'Poldhu', before leaving Cornwall. Arriving at San Diego in 1957, she produced a litter of four Rex kittens and established the breed in the United States.

Because the very first Cornish Rex Cats reputedly lacked stamina, careful outbreeding with a variety of non-Rex queens was undertaken to strengthen the breed. This was done using one of Kallibunker's sons, 'Champagne Charlie', and Burmese, Siamese, Russian Blue and British

The Lilac colour form of the Cornish Rex Cat. All colours and patterns are acceptable in this breed.

Shorthairs. This out-breeding reduced the number of Rex kittens in litters to one in four, but considerably improved the stock. It also added the possibility of a wider variety of colour forms.

The Cornish Rex Cat was eventually given official recognition, by the CFA in America in 1964, and by the GCCF in Britain in 1967.

The question has been asked as to why such a slender, elongated breed should be found living on a farm in southern England. Because of the climate, with its long, cold, wet winters, British feral cats tend to be of the stockier, heavy-bodied type. The Cornish Rex looks much more suited to a hot, dry climate, and it has been suggested that Kallibunker's ancestors may have arrived in Cornwall from North Africa or the Middle East, brought there in ancient times by Phoenician traders visiting the famous local tin mines. There is no proof of this, but it would certainly explain the rangy, skinny body of this remarkable breed.

Personality: Terms that have been used to describe this breed include: individualistic, playful, extrovert, intelligent, inquisitive, affectionate, spirited, sweet tempered, gentle and friendly. It has been called 'the greyhound of the cat fancy'.

Related Breeds: The Cornish Rex is closely related to the German Rex. They share the same gene for curly-coat. The Devon Rex, despite its close geographical proximity to the Cornish Rex, has a different curly-coat gene.

Colour Forms:

GCCF: All colours, patterns and combinations of colours and patterns are acceptable in this breed.

CFA: Also accepts all colour and patterns, but specifies the following: White; Black; Blue; Red; Cream; Chinchilla Silver; Shaded Silver; Black Smoke; Blue Smoke; Classic Tabby Pattern; Mackerel Tabby Pattern; Patched Tabby Pattern; Brown Patched Tabby; Blue Patched Tabby; Silver Patched Tabby; Silver Tabby; Red Tabby; Brown Tabby; Blue Tabby; Cream Tabby; Tortoiseshell; Calico; Van Calico; Dilute Calico; Blue-Cream; Van Blue-Cream and White; Bi-color; Van Bi-color.

Bibliography:

1973. Ashford, A.E. and Pond, G. *Rex, Abyssinian and Turkish Cats.* Gifford, London.

1974. Lauder, P. *The Rex Cat.* David & Charles, Newton Abbot.

1982. Urcia, I. *All About Rex Cats.* TFH, New Jersey.

Breed Clubs:

Cornish Rex Society. Address: 720 Fisherville Road, Fisherville, KY 40023, USA.

Rex Breeders United. 446 Itasca Ct. N.W., Rochester, MN 55901, USA.

Cougar

Wild Feline. An alternative name for the Puma *(Felis concolor)*. Also known in the Rocky Mountains as the Mountain Lion. The name Cougar originated in the Pacific Northwest, and is still popular with some people, although the title of Puma is nowadays generally preferred. (For details see entry for Puma.)

Coupari

Domestic Breed. The name given to the long-haired version of the Scottish Fold Cat by British breeders. One American cat society introduced the name Highland Fold for this breed, but British breeders, knowing that it originated in the Lowlands of Scotland, preferred a more appropriate name based on its true home – the village of Coupar Angus, 21 km (13 miles) north-east of Perth. (See also Longhair Fold Cat.)

There were long-haired individuals in the Scottish Fold stock from the very beginning of the breed in 1961, but when the official standard was written it referred only to the short-haired version. That became the dominant form, but no attempt was made to eliminate the long-haired gene.

The short-haired version was preferred because the long-haired individuals 'looked earless'. But then, in the early 1980s, an American exhibitor by the name of Hazel Swadberg started showing the Longhair Fold Cat for the first time. It was confined to the household-pet classes, but its presence began to make an impact and, in 1986, it was at last taken seriously when TICA officials voted by 39 to 1 to accept it as a separate breed in its own right.

Although the breed quickly became established, its name did not. TICA called it the Scottish Fold Longhair. Then in 1991 the CFF gave it the name of Longhair Fold, while the ACFA preferred the more colourful title of Highland Fold. British breeders chose Coupari. It remains to be seen which of these four names will eventually win through to become the internationally accepted form.

Breed Club:

The Longhair Clan - Longhair Scottish Fold Breed Club. Address: 49 Hancock Street, Salem, MA 01920, USA.

Courageous Cat

Cartoon Cat. A feline skit on *Batman,* with Courageous Cat and his assistant Minute Mouse emerging from the Cat Cave in the Cat Mobile to administer justice to a variety of villains such as The Frog and Harry the Gorilla. The animated cartoon created by Bob Kane in 1961 was seen in a long series of 130 television programmes.

Cowardly Lion

American actor Bert Lahr (1895–1967) in his remarkable make-up as the Cowardly Lion in *The Wizard of Oz,* 1939. His biography, *Notes on a Cowardly Lion,* appeared in 1975.

Fictional Cat. In Frank Baum's fantasy *The Wonderful Wizard of Oz* (1900), the Cowardly Lion joins the expedition to find the Wizard in order to gain some courage. At the end of the quest, the Wizard pours it from a green bottle into a dish. The lion laps it up until he is 'full of courage' and then retires to the jungle to become King of the Forest. In the 1939 MGM film version of the story, the lion was played by Bert Lahr.

Cream

Coat Colour. A cream coat is a dilution of red. Its precise tone varies slightly from breed to breed – from buff cream to pale pink cream to cool cream. It is known in both long-haired and short-haired forms. The palest of the creams is usually preferred because it decreases the chances of any tabby markings showing through the cream ground.

This is one of the older colour forms, one of the first 'exotic' colours of the early pedigree Persian Cats. Writing in 1903, Frances Simpson comments: 'This may be said to be the very latest of Persian breeds, and one which bids fair to become very fashionable.'

In more recent times, a number of variants have been recorded, including the following: (1) Cream Point; (2) Cream Shaded Cameo; (3) Cream Shell Cameo; (4) Cream Silver; (5) Cream Silver Tabby; (6) Cream Smoke; (7) Cream Tabby; (8) Cream Tabby and White; (9) Cream and White (= Bi-colour); (10) Dilute Blue, Cream and White (= Dilute Tricolour); (11) Fawn Cream; (12) Lavender Cream; (13) Van Cream and Tabby and White.

Crested Cat

Extinct Feline. According to Frances Simpson, writing in 1903, the Crested Cat was an ancient feline *(Felis crestata),* the size of a tiger, known only from the fossil record.

Cuckoo Cat

Domestic Breed. Cuckoo was the pet name given to one of the original cats involved in the re-creation of the Angora breed in Britain in the 1970s. He had been referred to as the 'cuckoo in the nest' because he was a long-haired cat of Oriental type at a cattery full of shorthaired cats. He was about to be neutered when he was spotted by American visitors who remarked on his similarity to the Turkish Angoras that were now being seen in the United States. As a result it was decided to use him in an attempt to re-create the Angora artificially in Britain. This was done, but eventually, in 1989, the British Angora breed was renamed the Javanese to distinguish it from the true Turkish Angora. (This has caused another confusion. See Javanese Cat.)

Because Cuckoo became so well known for his part in this programme, it often happened that breeders would refer to any longhaired cats that appeared in their Oriental breeding programmes as 'Cuckoo Cats'. A club was even formed, called 'The Cuckoo Cat Club'.

Curly-legged Cat

Legendary Cat. Within the pages of the vast, 13-volume, 17th-century *Natural History* of Aldrovandus, there lurks a bizarre feline, the Curly-legged Cat. It appears to be a striped tabby cat with both its right front and right rear legs curled around in a spiral. The author's only comment is that it was so afflicted from birth. It was either a freak mutation (that must have kept falling on its side) or, more likely, a garbled interpretation of a crippled cat.

Bibliography:

1638–1668. Aldrovandus. *Opera Omnia.*

1890. Ashton, J. *Curious Creatures in Zoology.* Nimmo, London.

The strange Curly-legged Cat from the 17th century *Natural History* of Aldrovandus, a freak to which he gave the expressive name of *Felis pedibus horrendis.*

Curly-tailed Cat

Feline Mutation. Writing in 1940, American zoologist Ida Mellen comments: 'Oddities in cats' tails, such as truncated tails, double tails and curly tails, seen world over, furnish excellent examples of the manner in which mutations arise throughout the animal kingdom. Curly-tailed cats were found in China in the 12th century, and like bobtailed and double-tailed cats they have been found in the United States.' She includes a photograph of a remarkable ginger and white cat from Jenkintown, Pennsylvania, which clearly displays a long tail curled round in a tight spiral, but it is not clear how common this mutation has been.

Cymric Cat

Domestic Breed. The long-haired version of the Manx Cat. The name (pronounced kim-rick) is taken from the Celtic word for Wales (Cymru) and was given to the breed because Wales is close to the Isle of Man, just as the Cymric Cat is close to the Manx Cat. Some cat societies do not use the breed's Welsh name, however, preferring to call it simply the Longhair Manx.

The Cymric Cat – the long-haired version of the short-haired, tailless Manx Cat. This form was first developed seriously in Canada in the 1960s, although long-haired examples of the Manx had appeared occasionally before.

Appearance: Exactly like the Manx Cat in every way except for the coat, which is long and thick. The woolly undercoat is even thicker than the outer coat. The texture of the fur has been compared with that of the Norwegian Forest Cat.

History: Long-haired kittens had been born to Manx Cat mothers on the Isle of Man on many occasions, but had always been discarded as unwanted variants. Then, in the mid-1960s, similar kittens born in Canada were treated with greater respect. They were carefully kept and developed as a separate breed. The driving force behind this project was Canadian cat breeder Althea Frahm, who first exhibited the cats as 'Manx Mutants', before they were given their own breed name. In 1976 a special group was formed to promote the breed, called the 'United Cymric Association'.

The earliest records that can be found for the showing of this breed are those from the American Cat Association (ACA), dating from late 1963.

Critics of the Cymric have suggested that it resulted from crosses between Manx Cats and Persians or Maine Coons, but there is no evidence to support this. Indeed, had these longhairs been involved in the cat's ancestry they would undoubtedly have altered its Manx conformation.

Personality: Similar to the Manx Cat. Confident, playful, intelligent, docile, friendly, alert, observant and relaxed. A good indoor cat.

Colour Forms: All colours are acceptable, although some authorities reject colour-point patterns.

Bibliography:

1984. Swantek, M. *The Manx Cat*. TFH, New Jersey. (See Chapter 14.)

Cyprian Cat

Fictional Cat. *The Cyprian Cat* (1940) is the title of a short horror story by mystery writer Dorothy L. Sayers. A man who is terrified of cats stays at an inn owned by a friend of his. Outside the inn, every night, a circle of cats gathers, dominated by the Cyprian Cat. Later, this cat climbs up to the man's closed window, but cannot get in. When there is a thunderstorm, he opens his window and the Cyprian Cat enters his bedroom. He hits it and at that very moment, his friend's wife falls sick. The next night, when the cat enters his room again, he shoots it and his friend's wife falls dead.

Cyprus Cat

Domestic Cat. A local, East Anglian name for a tabby cat. Frances Simpson, in 1903, comments: 'We are told . . . that tabby cats in Norfolk and Suffolk were called Cyprus Cats, cyprus being a reddish-yellow colour, so that the term may have applied to orange as well as brown tabbies.' The 'cyprus' referred to here is a kind of material, sometimes called 'cypress', which Edward Phillip's *Dictionary*, published in 1720, describes as 'a sort of fine curled Stuff, partly Silk and partly Hair, of which Hoods etc. for women are usually made'. (Unfortunately some authors refer to the Cyprus Cat as the Cyprian Cat, thus creating confusion with the fictional feline mentioned above.)

Deafness

Feline Biology. It is well known among cat-breeders that some white cats are genetically prone to deafness. Those with blue eyes are the most at risk. In a recent investigation it was discovered that, of 125 blue-eyed white cats tested, 54 per cent were deaf. When 60 golden-eyed white cats were examined, it was found that only 22 per cent of those had hearing difficulties.

Because many people have been unaware of this problem, they have sometimes wrongly imagined that their white cats were bad mothers. This is because, when their kittens call to them, they do not hear them and ignore their vocal pleas for help.

Simple tests can be carried out by any owner of a white cat to see if it reacts to a sharp noise made immediately behind it. If the cat proves to be deaf there is sadly nothing that can be done for it medically. Its cochlea, the vital snail-shaped organ in the inner ear, will have started to degenerate a few days after birth, and the deterioration is completely irreversible. It is a genetically linked defect and will be passed on to the white offspring of the deaf mother. If breeding from such cats is restricted, there will be a gradual increase in the proportion of white cats that *can* hear, until the deaf factor is eliminated altogether. With careful, selective breeding programmes, it should be possible to wipe it out in a few generations.

Sometimes white cats are born with one blue eye and one golden one. In such cases, tests show that the ear on the blue side is more likely to lack hearing than the one on the golden side, confirming the link between blue eyes and deafness.

Owners of deaf white cats report that their pets are brilliant at compensating for their genetic disability. They become extra sensitive to tiny vibrations made by sounds, and can almost 'hear through their feet'. Their watchfulness is also dramatically increased, enabling them to make maximum use of their excellent sense of vision. Like the cats themselves, the owners of deaf animals can learn to become more visual in their feline exchanges, using gestures and movements where otherwise they might have used the human voice.

DEATH

FELINE BIOLOGY. One of the most common causes of death for domestic cats (that are not totally confined to an indoor life) is road accident. If they manage to avoid this hazard, then they are most likely to succumb to kidney failure or leukaemia when they reach old age.

When death is approaching, the cat behaves in a special way – it hides itself away to die alone. Cat-owners are sometimes distressed by this. Knowing that their much loved cat is unwell, they wish to be able to offer it all the help they can. But suddenly it is not there. Uncharacteristically, it is not in its favourite places. Then, a few days later its corpse is found in a corner of the garden shed next door, or in some even more secret place. The owners feel spurned, wondering why their cat has not come to them for help when it feels so seriously ill. To abandon them at such a moment implies that they did not, after all, mean so much to the animal – they were not a 'safe haven' in quite the way they had pictured themselves. But they do themselves an injustice.

This 'dying alone' is not a new phenomenon. An Oriental author, writing as long ago as 1708, records that one of the cat's unique features is that 'it perishes in a place quite out of human sight, as if it wills not to let man see its dying look, which is usually ugly'. Much later, a mere half century ago, the author Alan Devoe makes a similar comment: 'One day, often with no forewarning whatever, he is gone from the house and never returns. He has felt the presaging shadow of death, and he goes to meet it in the old unchanging way of the wild – alone. A cat does not want to die with the smell of humanity in his nostrils and the noise of humanity in his delicate peaked ears. Unless death strikes very quickly and suddenly, he creeps away to where it is proper that a proud wild beast should die – not on one of man's rags or cushions, but in a lonely quiet place, with his muzzle pressed against the cold earth.'

The motives described by these authors are little more than romantic inventions, but the fact that the dying cat's actions have been recorded in this way by very different writers is of some interest. It suggests that 'dying alone' is a feline phenomenon that is not isolated and accidental, but more a regular, typical feature of cat behaviour. To understand why this should be, it is essential to consider the question of how the cat faces death. Human beings know they are going to die one day and act accordingly. A cat has no concept of its own death and so it cannot anticipate it, no matter how ill it feels. What falling ill means to a cat, or any other non-human animal, is that something unpleasant is threatening it. If it feels pain, it considers itself to be under attack. It is difficult for it to distinguish between one kind of pain and another, when trying to work out what is going wrong. If the pain becomes acute, the cat knows that it is in great danger. If it cannot see the source of the danger, it cannot turn to face it and lash out in defence – there is nothing there at which to lash out. This leaves only two alternative strategies: to flee or to hide. If the pain comes on when the cat is out patrolling its territory, its natural reaction will be to attempt to hide from the 'attacker'. If the cat sees a shed nearby, or some other hiding place, it will make for this and then stay concealed, alone, waiting for the threat to pass, for the pain to cease. It dare not come out, in case the source of the pain is waiting for it, and so it remains there, dying alone and in private. Despite the earlier authors' comments on the matter, at the moment of death the cat is not thinking of its human owners' feelings, but simply about how it can protect itself from the terrifying, unseen danger that is causing so much pain.

MANY CAT-OWNERS wish to honour their pets with some kind of memorial. This particular feline tomb in Paris, illustrated in Moncrif's 1727 *Cats,* commemorates the cat that belonged to a Madame de Lesdiguières.

If cat owners feel sorry for the dying cat that cannot understand what is happening to it, they should remember that it has one enormous advantage over them: it has no fear of death, which is something human beings must carry with them throughout their long lives.

DE-CLAWING

FELINE ANATOMY. Some house-proud cat-owners today have the claws of their pets surgically removed by a veterinary surgeon. This is usually done to prevent the animals from scratching valuable furnishings. It is not a major operation, but it robs the cat of a vital part of its anatomy. A de-clawed cat is a maimed cat.

To remove a cat's claws is far worse than to deprive cat owners of their finger-nails. This is because the claws have so many important functions in the life of a cat:

Cleaning: It is important that every cat should keep itself well groomed. A smooth, clean coat of fur is essential for a cat's well-being. It is vital for temperature control, for cleanliness, for waterproofing and for controlling the scent-signalling of the feline body. As a result, cats spend a great deal of time every day dealing with their toilet and, in addition to the typical licking movements, they perform repeated scratchings. These scratching actions are a crucial part of the cleaning routine, getting rid of skin irritations, dislodging dead hairs and combing out tangles in the fur. Without claws it is impossible for any cat to scratch itself efficiently and the whole grooming pattern suffers as a result. Even if human owners help out with brush and comb, there is no way they can replace the sensitivity of the natural scratching response of their pet. Any people who have ever suffered from itches that they cannot scratch will sympathize with the dilemma of the de-clawed cat.

Climbing: A second problem faces a de-clawed cat when it tries to climb. Climbing is second nature to all small felines and it is virtually impossible for a cat to switch off its urge to climb, even if it is punished for doing so. And punished it certainly will be if it attempts to climb after having its claws removed, for it will no longer have any grip with its feet. Out of doors, if it is being chased by a rival cat, a dog, or some human enemy, it will try, as always, to scamper up a wall or a tree, using its non-existent claws to cling to the surfaces as it leaps upwards. To its horror, it will find itself slipping and sliding, tumbling down at the mercy of its foes.

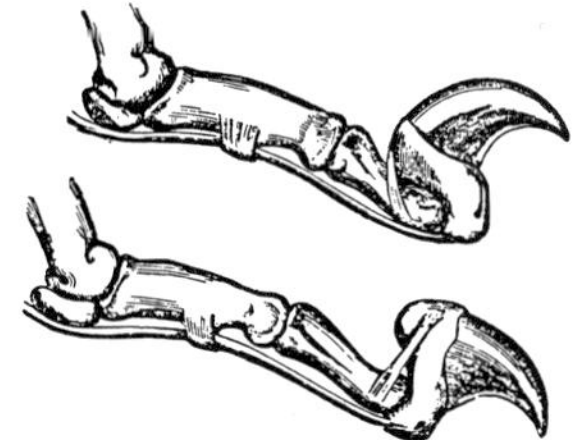

One of the claws of a cat, showing the mechanism for moving it. To amputate these claws can only be described as maiming a cat for human convenience.

Defending: If it is faced with the need to protect itself, when confronted with an enemy, it will be at an even greater disadvantage because, when it strikes out with its paws, it will find itself robbed of its defensive weapons. Often, it is only the sharpness of the pain caused by the stiletto-pointed claws that stands between life and death for the cornered cat.

Hunting: In addition to destroying the animal's ability to groom, climb, defend itself against rivals and protect itself against enemies, the operation of de-clawing also eliminates the cat's ability to hunt. This may not be important for a well-fed family pet, but if ever such a cat were to find itself lost or homeless it would rapidly die of starvation. The vital grab at a mouse with sharp claws extended would become a useless gesture.

In short, a de-clawed cat is a crippled, mutilated cat and no excuse can justify the operation. In some countries 'convenience surgery' of this kind on healthy animals is routinely refused by qualified vets. In others it has become commonplace, and is referred to as *onychectomy* (which is Greek for 'nail-cutting-out').

The reason for the popularity of the operation in recent years is that more and more pet felines in urban areas are being kept as 'indoor cats'. They never have the opportunity to wander out of doors where there are plenty of natural scratching surfaces for them to use. They must therefore carry out their essential claw-servicing routines in one of their owner's carefully furnished rooms. There are four precautions that can be taken to lessen the damage this can cause to soft furnishings:

1 The cat can be provided with a commercially designed scratching-post, or (a far less expensive) log of wood.

2 The favourite zones on furniture, such as the vertical parts of the arms of chairs or sofas, can be provided with a thick, removable, protective cover that can be taken off when the cat's owners are entertaining visitors.

3 The cat can be trained not to scratch the furniture. This is not as easy as it sounds and usually fails if the owner resorts to shouting at the cat or swatting at it with a newspaper. Some authorities suggest the judicious use of a water-pistol. Perhaps the best solution is to mimic the behaviour of exasperated mother cats. There is a feline signal, employed by mothers towards their over-active kittens, which has the effect of stopping them from doing whatever it is that is annoying her. This signal consists of a low growl, and imitating it may be more effective than any other form of deterrent.

4 The cat can be provided with blunt 'nail-caps' that can be fitted over the top of the claws. These temporary, vinyl claw-covers are now commercially available, take only a few minutes to fix in place, and last from four to six weeks. They are completely safe, even if the cat manages to dislodge one and eat it. For those who can stomach the idea of owning a cat that appears to be wearing nail-varnish, these nail-caps are available in bright colours: 'discriminating feline owners can chose from four bright new nail cap shades – red, pink, purple and blue, in addition to natural, in three adult sizes. Kitten size in natural only.' Some cat-lovers may scoff at the artificiality of this device, but as a solution for a desperate owner, nail-caps are a thousand times better than de-clawing. ('Soft Paws' nail caps for cats are manufactured by SmartPractice, 3400 East McDowell Road, Phoenix, AZ 85018, USA.)

If all this fails, then the distressed owner can either give up keeping a cat altogether, or follow the advice of Frank Manolson in his 1965 *C is for Cat*: 'The thing is you must train a cat from kittenhood to scratch only those furnishings that your mother-in-law loves and you hate.'

Desert Cat

Wild Feline. *(Felis sylvestris ornata)* Originally considered to be a separate, distinct species *(Felis ornata)*, this is now looked upon as only an Asiatic sub-species of the common Wild Cat that is also found in Europe and Africa. The Desert Cat (which should not be confused with the Chinese Desert Cat) is also sometimes called the Asiatic Wild Cat, or the Asiatic Steppe Cat. (See separate entries for Wild Cat and Asiatic Steppe Cat.)

Desert Lynx

Wild Feline. An alternative name for the Caracal *(Felis caracal)*. This name is no longer used because it is not certain whether the Caracal is a true lynx, closely related to the other lynx species, or merely looks rather like them. Its similarities (such as its ear-tufts, short tail and long legs) may be superficial. Therefore a name that does not use the word 'lynx' is preferred.

Devon Rex Cat

Domestic Breed. Appeared in 1960 in the county of Devon, England. This was the second form of Rex Cat to be discovered in the West Country, the Cornish Rex having been found in the neighbouring county of Cornwall ten years earlier. The Devon Rex is sometimes referred to as the 'Pixie Cat' because of its strange head shape.

Appearance: A thin-coated, wavy-furred cat with curly whiskers and eyebrows. The hind legs are long, but the front legs are bowed and shorter. The chest is broad. The wedge-shaped head has wide cheeks and huge, low-set ears with small lynx-like tufts at their tips. There is a distinct 'stop' to the nose – giving a dip, or break in the profile of the cat's face.

Unusual Features: Despite their frail appearance, these cats are remarkably healthy and hardy animals. They cannot tolerate cold sleeping conditions because of their thin coat, but when active they will even play in the snow. As a result of their body heat-losses, they have a huge appetite with a high fat requirement.

The coat of this cat is made up largely of down hairs, with a only a few guard hairs, so that what is visible is essentially the cat's undercoat. Some individuals suffer from bare patches.

The Devon Rex coat has two advantages: there are few moulted hairs; and people with cat-hair allergies are far less likely to suffer when they come into close contact with this breed.

History: The first Devon Rex Cat was a stray tom living wild in a disused tin mine near Buckfastleigh in Devon. It was hoped to breed from him, but despite many attempts to catch him, he always eluded capture. However, in 1960 he mated with a stray tortie-and-white female and she produced a litter of kittens. This female had been befriended by a Miss Beryl Cox, who lived near the tin mine, and who had been observing the strange-looking tom for some time. The litter was born in a field at the end of her garden and, taking a close look at them, she was able to see that one of the kittens, a male, had the same curly coat as the wild tom. She took

The wavy-coated Devon Rex Cat. It first appeared in south-west England in 1960, not far from the site of the previously discovered Cornish Rex. Despite their proximity they were not, however, related.

this kitten and reared it carefully in her home. Named 'Kirlee', it was to become the founding father of the Devon Rex breed.

Miss Cox had seen photographs of the Cornish Rex Cat 'Kallibunker', who had been discovered nearby ten years earlier, and contacted the group who were developing that breed, with a view to a mating. They took Kirlee and mated him with several of the female descendants of Kallibunker, but to their astonishment found that all the kittens born from these pairings were straight-haired. Despite repeated attempts, the Cornish X Devon Rex cross did not produce a single curly-haired Rex Cat.

They were therefore forced to the surprising conclusion that, despite the geographical closeness, the wavy-haired gene in the Devon Rex was not the same as the one which was causing wavy hair in the Cornish Rex breed. The two recessive genes were therefore named: Gene 1 (Cornish) Rex, and Gene 2 (Devon) Rex. (They have been given the gene symbols 'r' and 're' respectively.)

Because of this difference, the only way to establish the Devon Rex as a distinct breed was to in-breed from Kirlee. A similar in-breeding programme had been successfully employed with Kallibunker. Kirlee was mated with his daughters and before long the Devon Rex Cat was safely established. Kirlee lived a long and productive life, until he was eventually killed in a road accident in 1970.

Personality: Terms that have been used to describe this breed include: friendly, lively, affectionate, playful, intelligent, mischievous, impish, enterprising, active, inquisitive, extrovert.

It has been called 'a feline comedian' and 'a monkey in cat's clothing'. Its climbing abilities are exceptional. One authority referred to it as 'an animal suited to gentle owners'.

Some authors suggest that this breed has several dog-like qualities: it retrieves; it follows its owner; it wags its tail when pleased. The dog-like tail-wagging action would be highly unusual for a cat, but closer examination reveals that it occurred in special circumstances: 'One of his [Kirlee's] favourite tricks was to walk a tight-rope, wagging his tail for approval as he did so.' On another occasion, involving a Devon Rex kitten, 'loud purring and a wagging tail were the

prelude to another amorous leap'. Clearly, these were cases of tail-wagging employed for its primary function of keeping the body balanced, rather than as a social signal.

Related Breeds: The Devon Rex is superficially similar to other Rex cats, such as the Cornish and German, and was at first thought to be just another example of the same breed. But once it had been shown that its wavy coat was caused by a different gene, it was clear that it would have to be granted separate breed status.

The Devon Rex was accepted as a separate show breed from 1967, except in the United States where the CFA only accepted one 'Rex' breed, based on the Cornish Rex standard, until 1979. The fur of the Devon Rex is slightly different from that of the other Rex breeds. It contains a few guard hairs among the numerous down hairs, and is slightly harsher to the touch.

Colour Forms:

GCCF: All colours, patterns and combinations are acceptable in this breed.

CFA: All colours and patterns accepted, but specifically lists the following. (To simplify the list, the colours are grouped into convenient categories.)

Self: White; Black, Blue; Red; Cream; Chocolate; Lavender; Cinnamon; Fawn.

Shaded: Shaded Silver; Blue Shaded; Chocolate Shaded; Lavender Shaded; Cameo Shaded; Cinnamon Shaded; Fawn Shaded; Tortie Shaded; Blue-Cream Shaded; Chocolate Tortie Shaded; Cinnamon Tortie Shaded; Lavender-Cream Shaded; Fawn-Cream Shaded; Chinchilla.

Smoke: Black Smoke; Blue Smoke; Red Smoke Cameo (Cameo); Chocolate Smoke; Lavender Smoke; Cinnamon Smoke; Cream Smoke; Fawn Smoke; Tortie Smoke; Blue-Cream Smoke; Chocolate Tortie Smoke; Lavender-Cream Smoke; Cinnamon Tortie Smoke; Fawn-Cream Smoke.

Tabby: (Classic, Mackerel, Spotted and Patched Tabby Patterns) Silver Tabby; Brown Tabby; Blue Tabby; Red Tabby; Cream Tabby; Chocolate (Chestnut) Tabby; Chocolate Silver Tabby; Cinnamon Tabby; Cinnamon Silver Tabby; Lavender Tabby; Lavender Silver Tabby; Fawn Tabby; Cameo Tabby; Blue Silver Tabby; Cream Silver Tabby; Fawn Silver Tabby.

Tortie: Tortie; Blue-Cream; Chocolate (Chestnut) Tortie; Cinnamon Tortie; Lavender-Cream; Fawn-Cream.

Calico: Calico; Fawn-Cream Calico; Lavender-Cream Calico; Cinnamon-Cream Calico; Van Calico; Fawn-Cream Van Calico; Lavender-Cream Van Calico; Cinnamon-Cream Van Calico; Dilute Calico; Dilute Van Calico.

Bi-color: Bi-color; Van Bi-color.

Bibliography:

1973. Ashford, A.E. and Pond, G. *Rex, Abyssinian and Turkish Cats.* Gifford, London.

1974. Lauder, P. *The Rex Cat.* David & Charles, Newton Abbot.

1982. Urcia, I. *All About Rex Cats.* TFH, New Jersey.

Breed Clubs:

Devon Rex Breed Club. Publishes a newsletter. Address: 6251 North Sheridan, No. 18, Chicago, IL 60660, USA.

Rex Breeders United. Address: 446 Itasca Ct. N.W., Rochester, MN 55901, USA.

Note: There is an additional breed publication, *Devon Rex Newsletter.* Address: 32 Myer Drive, Ft. Gordon, GA 30905, USA.

Diard's Cat

Wild Feline. An early name for the Clouded Leopard *(Neofelis nebulosa)* from Asia. Widely used in the 19th century, when there was considerable confusion concerning the various species of wild cats. Its scientific name *(Felis diardi)* has also become obsolete. (See Clouded Leopard.)

Dick Whittington's Cat

Fictional Cat. There are those who feel that Dick Whittington's famous cat was a factual feline, but the evidence is against this. The popular legend of the cat, which was based on a much earlier fable, runs as follows:

The remarkable head-shape of the Devon Rex Cat that has given it the nickname of 'Pixie Cat'. The gene that produces its wavy coat also endows it with characteristic curly whiskers.

A poor orphan boy called Dick Whittington sets out for London where he hopes to make his fortune. He had been told that the streets of the city are paved with gold, but instead he finds only hardship and nearly starves to death. He is saved by a rich merchant called Hugh Fitzwarren who puts him to work in his kitchen. The boy's room is infested with rats and mice and to get rid of them he buys a cat for a penny from a little girl he meets in the street. The cat succeeds at its task and Dick becomes extremely fond of his feline companion. But then his employer asks him to let his cat travel on one of his trading ships, the *Unicorn,* to control the vermin on board. Dick is unhappy about losing the company of his cat, but finally, with great reluctance, he agrees.

At this point in the story, Dick is treated badly by the cook in the kitchen where he works and decides to run away. Just as he is leaving the city, on Highgate Hill (where today there is a bronze statue of his cat), he hears the pealing of Bow bells and they seem to say to him, 'Turn again, Whittington, Lord Mayor of London.' This strange experience persuades him to return to the city.

When the ship on which his much loved cat is sailing reaches its destination on the Barbary coast, the animal is sold for a huge sum to a Moorish ruler. The Moorish court is overrun with rodents and the cat's destructive impact is so impressive that the price paid for it is ten times that offered for the whole of the rest of the cargo.

With this money, young Dick's fortune is made and he is able to marry Alice, his employer's daughter. He continues to improve his position in society until he eventually becomes Lord Mayor of London.

This story has been told and retold, and has even become enshrined as the theme of a popular British pantomime. Although it is widely believed to have been based on the truth, it is in reality a romantic invention. Significantly, it does not appear until 1605, over 200 years after the events it describes, and is a completely garbled version of the events that led up to the installation of Whittington as Lord Mayor.

Far from being a poor orphan boy, young Dick was in fact the son of a Gloucestershire knight, Sir William Whittington. In London, Dick became an important mercer, a dealer in expensive textile fabrics. He supplied velvets and damasks to the nobility, including his future king. His success relied heavily on the purchase of favours, a form of bribery which in those

An 18th century ballad-sheet retelling the tale of Dick Whittington and his Cat. On the left, Dick holds his cat ready to place it on *The Unicorn,* for the voyage that will make his fortune. On the right the bells ring out to persuade him to 'turn again'.

days was called 'achat' (pronounced 'a-cat'). (The wording of a popular ballad refers to his meteoric rise to fame and 'how his rise was by a cat'.)

So it would seem that Dick Whittington and his 'cat' had nothing to do with the feline world, but instead referred to his somewhat dubious business methods. These were so successful that he soon became immensely rich. Indeed, his wealth was such that he was able to make large loans to both King Henry IV and Henry V. On his death he bequeathed his enormous fortune to charity. He rose to become Lord Mayor of London three times: 1397–1399; 1406–1407; 1419–1420. In 1416 he also became Member of Parliament for London. He married Alice, daughter of Sir Ivo Fitzwaryn, and he died in 1423.

Those are the facts of his life, as far as they can be ascertained, and it would seem that the popular feline element was added at a much later date as a satirical comment. In the process, his 'cat', or bribery, became transformed into a real feline, giving us a delightful but entirely fictitious folktale.

A portrait of Whittington by Reginald Elstrock, dating from roughly 1590, showing him with his cat, was doctored to pander to public opinion. In the original version, his right hand rested upon a skull. In the modified version, the skull was replaced by a cat.

(An alternative theory proposes that Whittington's cat was an abbreviation of 'cat-boat'. A cat-boat, often spoken of simply as a 'cat' was a ketch employed to bring coal up the Thames to London. It is suggested that this enterprise was the true source of Whittington's wealth and that the boat was therefore 'the cat that made his fortune'. This is highly unlikely, as the business on which his fortune was based was concerned with fine materials rather than fuel.)

Dick Whittington, as Lord Mayor of London, with his (unusually ugly) cat, from the title page of an Aldermary Church Yard chap-book. It appears that the cat was no more than a romantic invention.

Diet

Feline Biology. To understand the diet of domestic cats, it helps to look at the natural food of their wild relatives. The European Wild Cat *(Felis sylvestris)* feeds largely on rodents, especially voles. This may be because it prefers the taste of voles, but is more probably because it finds them easier to catch. Wood mice are also popular. In the spring, young rabbits are taken and an occasional hare. Surprisingly, birds were never found to be high on the wild cat menu, despite popular belief to the contrary. The persecution of wild cats as imagined predators of game birds is therefore unjustified, although it has been going on for centuries.

The African Wild Cat *(Felis sylvestis libyca,* the original ancestor of domestic cats) has much the same diet as the European Wild Cat, with various kinds of African mice making up 70 per cent of the diet. Again, birds (10–20 per cent) were a minority interest and little more popular than reptiles (10–13 per cent).

Translated into domestic terms, this means that as one feline expert put it, 'the ideal diet for a modern cat would be canned vole or mouse – mostly meat, with some roughage, and with a little vegetable supplement, all in one neat package.'

Marketing such a product would give the cats the food natural to their species and at the same time would help to rid the environment of rodent pests. As this is not readily available on supermarket shelves at the present time, cat-owners must make do with other forms of meat. There is a huge array of tinned and packaged cat foods from which to choose, most of which provide a balanced diet based on the cat's high need for protein. Of these pre-packed foods, moist, meaty preparations are the ones most suitable for cats. Dried foods in the form of small biscuits can be dangerous (especially for cats that do not drink a great deal) and may cause bladder problems. They are the feline equivalent of junk food – made tasty with additives, but they are so far from a cat's natural, wild food that, if used as a major part of the diet, they can cause serious damage. Many cat experts insist that, in addition to packaged food, some fresh meat should be given from time to time. And all cats must have access to fresh (untreated) grasses for an occasional vitamin chew (see separate entry for Grass).

There has recently been a well-meaning but misguided attempt to introduce vegetarian diets for cats. Cats are carnivores and cannot survive on a vegetarian or vegan diet. Given a meatless diet they will rapidly become ill and will then die a painful death. Anyone who cannot bear to

contemplate giving pet cats a carnivorous diet should keep rabbits or canaries. Those who ignore the cat's nutritional requirements and insist on using a vegetarian cat food may one day find themselves prosecuted for cruelty to animals.

There are three key facts to consider. First, cats need an amino-acid called taurine to prevent them from going blind. Without it the retinas of their eyes would rapidly deteriorate. Some animals can manufacture taurine from other sources, but the cat cannot do so. It can only obtain it by eating animal proteins. So without a meat diet, a cat would lose its sight.

Second, cats must have animal fats in their diets because they are incapable of manufacturing essential fatty acids without them. Some other animals can manage to convert vegetable oils into these fatty acids, but cats lack this ability. Without animal fats to eat, cats would, among other serious problems, find it difficult to achieve reproduction, blood-clotting and new cell production.

Third, unlike many other animals, cats are unable to obtain Vitamin A from plant sources (such as carrots) and must rely instead for this crucial substance on animal food such as liver, kidney or fish oils.

These facts alone underline the folly of recent attempts to convert cat owners to vegetarian regimes for their pets.

Dilute

Coat Pattern. The term 'dilute' is used in the names of certain pedigree colour patterns, when they appear in a paler version.

Many of the subtle, modern coat colours created by breeders are the result of a dilution gene working on a darker colour. If the mutant gene *'d'* is present, it reduces the strength of a particular colour. In this way black become blue, red becomes cream and chocolate becomes lilac. Such animals are referred to simply as red, cream, or lilac, but if the colours being diluted exist as a pattern, such as tortoiseshell, rather than as a single colour, then the cat is named as a 'dilute tortoiseshell'.

Examples of the use of this term include the following: (1) Dilute Cameo; (2) Dilute Cameo Smoke; (3) Dilute Cameo Tabby; (4) Dilute Tortoiseshell; (5) Dilute Shaded Tortoiseshell; (6) Dilute Chinchilla Shaded Tortoiseshell; (7) Dilute Tricolour (blue + cream + white); (8) Van Dilute Calico (white with blue and cream extremities).

Dinah

Lewis Carroll's Alice playing with her black kitten, called Kitty. Her pet cat, Dinah, had two kittens, this one and a white one named Snowdrop.

Fictional Cat. A mother cat with two kittens who appears as Alice's pet cat in both *Alice's Adventures in Wonderland* (1865) and *Through the Looking-Glass* (1872) by Lewis Carroll. As she is falling down the rabbit-hole at the start of her adventures in Wonderland, Alice worries aloud about Dinah, the family cat she has left behind and debates with herself the question 'Do cats eat bats?' At both the start and the end of the looking-glass adventure, Dinah's two kittens, a black one called Kitty and a white one called Snowdrop, play an important role in the story, and are featured in the Tenniel illustrations.

Doe-cat

Feline Term. An early name for a female cat. It was replaced by 'she-cat', although this is rarely employed today. The only female feline term commonly used in English at present is 'queen', for a pedigree breeding female.

Domestication

Feline History. We know for certain that 3,500 years ago the cat was already fully domesticated. We have records from ancient Egypt to prove this. But we do not know when the process began. The remains of cats have been found at a Neolithic site at Jericho dating from 9,000 years ago, but there is no proof that those felines were domesticated ones. The difficulty arises from the fact that the cat's skeleton changed very little during its shift from wild

to tame. In countries where wild cats were common, we can only be sure that the transformation from wild cat to domestic animal had taken place when we have specific records and detailed pictures – as we do from ancient Egypt. Ancient bones alone can be misleading and may reflect no more than wild-cat eating rather than tame-cat keeping.

Luckily, however, we do have one intriguing feline record from a country where there were no wild cats – the island of Cyprus. In 1983, excavations at the ancient site of Khirokitia on the south coast of Cyprus unearthed a feline jawbone. The only possible explanation for its presence there, in that early human settlement, is that it belonged to a tame cat taken over to the island from the nearby mainland. It is unthinkable that settlers would have taken a savage wild cat with them. A spitting, scratching, panic-stricken wild feline would have been the last kind of boat companion they would have wanted. Only tame, domesticated animals could possibly have been part of the goods and chattels of that early band of pioneers.

This slender piece of evidence from Cyprus dates from 6,000 BC, which means that we can hazard a guess that the cat had been domesticated at the very least by 8,000 years ago. How much earlier we cannot say, until future excavations bring more evidence to light.

One thing is clear: there would have been no taming of the cat before the Agricultural Revolution (in the Neolithic period, or New Stone Age). In this respect the cat differed from the dog. Dogs had a significant role to play even before the advent of farming. Back in the Palaeolithic period (or Old Stone Age) prehistoric human hunters were able to make good use of a four-legged hunting companion with superior scenting abilities and hearing. But cats were of little value to early man until he had progressed to the agricultural phase and was starting to store large quantities of food. The grain stores, in particular, must have attracted a teeming population of rats and mice almost from the moment that the human hunter settled down to become a farmer. In the early cities, where stores were great, it would have become an impossible task for human guards to ambush the mice and kill them in sufficient numbers to stamp them out or even to prevent them from multiplying. A massive infestation of rodents must have been one of the earliest plagues known to urban man. Any carnivore that preyed on these rats and mice would have been a godsend to the harassed food-storers.

AN EARLY ILLUSTRATION of a domestic cat, from Thomas Bewick's *A General History of Quadrupeds,* first published in 1790.

It is easy to visualize how one day somebody made the casual observation that a few wild cats were approaching the grain stores and picking off the mice. For these cats, the scene must have been hard to believe. There, all around them, was a scurrying feast on a scale they had never encountered before. Gone were the interminable waits in the undergrowth. All that was needed now was a leisurely stroll in the vicinity of the vast grain stores and a gourmet supermarket of plump, grain-fed rodents awaited them. From this stage to the keeping and breeding of cats for increased vermin destruction must have been a simple step, since it benefited both sides.

With modern methods of pest control available to us, it is difficult for us to imagine the significance of the cat to those early civilizations. In ancient Egypt it rapidly rose to become, not merely a highly valued pet, but a feline deity, a sacred animal to be adored and worshipped. From there, it spread out across the Middle East, the Mediterranean and eventually, thanks to the Romans, to the whole of Europe. Everywhere it was highly esteemed for its role as a pest controller. As the centuries passed, it spread further and further, wherever mankind voyaged, working as a ship's cat to control the rodents that infested the early sailing vessels. Jumping ship in faraway places it soon established itself worldwide.

It has retained its role as an important pest-killer right down to the present day, most farmers, worldwide, still giving homes to working cats around their barns and stores. The domestication of the cat has been one of the great animal success stories. Their numbers now outstrip those of all the wild cats put together and, in their new, additional role of house-pets, their popularity is soaring to even greater heights.

How has this long domestication process changed the cat? The simple answer is: very little. Unlike the domestic dog, the modern cat has remained close to its ancestral form. Both in anatomy and behaviour it is still remarkably like its ancestor – the African Wild Cat.

Most of the changes have been superficial. Coat colour and hair length have been altered, but beneath the surface even the most pampered of pedigree cats is still the same predatory pest-killer that protected the food stores in ancient Egypt.

One of the few significant alterations has been a stepping up of the breeding cycles of the domesticated breeds. Modern pet cats can easily go through three reproductive cycles in a year, whereas the wild type will only breed once, in the spring. This tripling of the breeding rate accounts to a large extent for the dramatic way in which cat populations can explode in modern urban areas.

A second change is towards a slightly smaller body size than is found among the wild specimens. Whether this was a deliberate step taken by early cat-keepers in ancient times to make their new-found animal partners easier to handle, or whether it was the result of a great deal of inbreeding, is hard to say, but it is nevertheless a significant feature of feline domestication.

Third, modern domestic cats are slightly more 'juvenile' than their wild ancestors. This is the result, almost certainly, of unplanned selection by centuries of cat-owners. Animals that remain playful even as adults suit us better, so we favour them. They are the ones that we are the most likely to breed. They have the advantage that they look upon their human owners as pseudo-parents. This means that they will also look upon the human home as their 'nest' long after they have ceased to be kittens. And this means that they will be more likely to return home repeatedly for parental reassurance after each of their territorial forays. Less juvenile cats would be more inclined to wander off, abandon the parental site, and seek an entirely new territory to call their own. This is what wild kittens do when they become mature. But the domestic kitten must stay put and live out its life as a split personality, part-breeder and mouse-killer, and part pseudo-kitten towards its human family. This process has gone further and further in recent years as cats have become more important as house pets than as pest destroyers. The new, man-handled cat must be prepared for a great deal of interference. Human hands will repeatedly reach out to stroke and cuddle it. Only the kitten inside the adult cat will tolerate this. It is therefore perhaps true to say that the most important change in the 8,000 years of feline domestication is the creation of this infantile–adult feline.

The cat remains, nevertheless, highly adaptable and can switch to being a full-blooded wild cat with great speed. If kittens are born to a domestic cat that has turned her back on human protection, they will grow up as untame as any truly wild ones. A farm kitten that has never seen a human being during its formative weeks will become a ball of spitting fury if cornered when it is half-grown. Great patience is needed then to convert it into a friendly adult. So the cat has it both ways: it has the capacity to be a domestic kitten-cat and has retained the option of becoming a wild killer-cat if its circumstances change. No wonder it has been so successful during the past few thousand years.

Domestic Shorthair Cat

Domestic Breed. An obsolete American term, this was an early name for what is now referred to as the 'American Shorthair'.

At the first major cat shows, on both sides of the Atlantic, home-grown cats with short coats were known simply as 'Shorthairs'. During the final decades of the 19th century they had pride of place, but by the start of the 20th century they had lost ground to the exotic foreign breeds. The Shorthairs were soon in a small minority, but managed to survive as pedigree show cats, thanks to the efforts of a few passionate enthusiasts. The 'Short-haired Cat Society' was formed in England in 1901 to promote and protect them.

At about the same time, in America, the Shorthairs appearing at cat shows there were given a more specific name, being officially classified as 'Domestic Shorthairs'. This did not, however, help their cause because the word 'domestic' made them sound more like household 'moggies' than pedigree cats. Consequently, in the 1960s, it was decided to change their title to the more chauvinistic 'American Shorthairs'.

Today a clear distinction is made between these American Shorthairs, the British Shorthairs and the (Continental) European Shorthairs. Inevitably, slight differences have developed between the three lines, but the same basic body form and personality have been retained.

DRAIN CAT

DOMESTIC BREED. This was a name given to the small breed of cat found in the streets of Singapore before it acquired its official pedigree title of 'Singapura'. It is said that the human occupants of Singapore were not unduly fond of cats and frequently persecuted them, with the result that many of them retreated to the city sewers for safety. When foreign visitors became interested in the breed and began exporting examples to the United States, it was felt necessary to invent a more exotic title for them and the name of 'Drain Cat' was discreetly dropped.

DRINKING

FELINE BEHAVIOUR. Cats drink by converting their long tongues into spoons. They squat low over the water and then start lapping up the liquid at a steady rate. The tip of the tongue is curled backwards to create a hollow shape that acts like the bowl of a spoon, and the animal then dips this into the water and flips it back and up, towards the open mouth. This flicks small quantities of liquid towards the rear of the mouth. The cat does not swallow with each lap, but only after about every fourth or fifth, when it feels that enough liquid has accumulated at the back of its mouth.

WATER: If domestic cats are eating a natural diet of small rodents they drink very little. Their kidneys are far more efficient than ours at ridding the body of waste products. (To be precise, they are two and a half times better.) This reflects their ancestral origins. The North African Wild cat *(Felis sylvestris lybica),* from which they are descended, inhabits a particularly arid region and during the course of evolution would have been forced to develop unusually efficient kidneys if it were to survive.

The situation changes if cats are fed on commercially prepared foods. Cats kept on the semi-moist, canned food do need a fresh water bowl alongside the food bowl. Cats fed on modern dried food, which may be tasty but which is far from ideal for them, must have fresh water always available to them and must drink large quantities of it if they are to survive. Individual cats that, for some idiosyncratic reason, prefer to drink very little will soon suffer kidney damage if they are kept on dried foods.

PUDDLES: A number of owners have noticed, to their dismay, that their feline pets seem to have a passion for drinking from puddles in the garden. The animals do this despite the fact that on the kitchen floor there is an immaculately clean dish of pure tap water awaiting them. For some reason they ignore this carefully provided hygienic supply and go padding off to a stagnant pool to lap up the filthy water there. At first sight, this behaviour seems inexplicable, but there is a simple, chemical reason for it.

When fresh water is supplied in a bowl, the chances are that the water has come from a tap and that the bowl has been washed in some kind of modern detergent. Today, fresh tap water is heavily treated with chemicals and often chlorinated strongly enough actually to have a chemical smell. The cat's sensitive nose cannot stand this. To make matters worse, the dish probably has some traces of detergent still clinging to it when it is filled with this water. With food dishes, the odour of the food is strong enough to mask this, but with water dishes it is not. Unless this is the cat's only source of water, it will be inclined to reject this sanitized offering. The stale water in the puddles and pools outside is much more attractive. It may be full of microbes and rotting vegetation, but these are natural and organic and only give it an attractive flavour.

Sadly, modern puddles are not always as organic as they used to be. Environmental pollution – and garden pesticides and weedkillers – can cause problems. It is therefore safer to try to make the water bowl more appealing, by rinsing off the detergent traces more efficiently and by letting the tap water stand for some time before offering it to the cat, to allow the chemicals

to dissipate. Cats are many times more sensitive to chemical contamination than humans are, and this fact has often been overlooked in the past.

Milk: Despite popular belief to the contrary, milk is not a suitable source of water for adult cats. If they drink it, it is because they are attempting to increase their fat intake, not to quench their thirst. If milk is offered, a bowl of water should be given alongside it. Then the cat can balance its fat and water needs, rather than be forced to use the milk as a source of liquid.

Many adult cats actively dislike milk and for some, especially Siamese Cats, it can cause gastric upsets. If milk is given without alternative water, such cats are liable to suffer from diarrhoea. The problem is caused largely by the milk sugar lactose which some cats can accept, but others cannot tolerate.

Alcohol: Some owners are amused by the fact that their pet cats may enjoy a shot of alcohol in their milk. Unfortunately some cats, like some people, can quickly become addicted to booze and, as there is no Cats Anonymous organization available to help them, they soon die of liver disease. Most cats do not get that far. If their milk is laced with alcohol they may, after even only a moderate dose, start to vomit, collapse or go into a coma. This is because the feline digestive system is inferior to the human one when it comes to detoxifying the dangerous substances contained in alcoholic beverages. There is no escaping from the fact that sobriety suits the domestic cat.

Anti-freeze: If a pet cat has access to a garage where someone has been filling the car's radiator system with anti-freeze at the onset of winter, the animal may see a small puddle on the floor where some has spilled. This is extremely dangerous because, unfortunately, it tastes sweet and cats like the flavour of it. If the animal laps up a little, the ethylene glycol may cause irreversible kidney damage. The cat may even fall into a deep coma. Sadly, the pool of liquid usually forms underneath the car, where it is difficult to mop up, but where it is easy for a cat to crawl. All too frequently, when a much loved pet cat falls ill, we think first of diseases and infections, when in reality the cause is simple chemical poisoning against which the cat has no natural defence.

Duchess

Cartoon Cat. In Walt Disney's 1970 cartoon feature *The Aristocats*, Duchess is the elegant, sophisticated Parisian cat who is abducted and taken to the French countryside.

Dune Cat

Wild Feline. An alternative name for the Sand Cat *(Felis margarita)* of North Africa, which is also sometimes called the Sand-dune Cat. (For details see Sand Cat.)

Dusty

Pet Cat. Reputed to be the most prolific female cat in the world, by 1952 Dusty of Bonham in Texas had produced a total of 420 kittens.

Dutch Rex Cat

Domestic Breed. One of the later breeds of Rex Cat.

Appearance: Said to have a coarser wavy coat, with a more bristly texture, than the better-known Rex Cats.

History: First reported from Holland in 1985.

Ears

Feline Anatomy. The cat's ears are much more sensitive that those of its owners, which is why cats hate noisy homes. Loud music and shouting are torture to its delicate hearing apparatus.

It is the specialized hunting behaviour of cats that has resulted in their improved hearing. Although dogs have a much greater acoustic range than humans, cats exceed even dogs in their ability to hear high-pitched sounds. This is because humans and dogs rely most on chasing and trapping their prey, whereas cats prefer to lurk in ambush and listen very carefully for the tiniest sound. If they are to succeed as stealthy hunters, they must be able to detect the most minute rustlings and squeaks and must be able to distinguish precise direction and distance to pinpoint their intended victims. This requires much more sensitivity than we possess, and laboratory tests have confirmed that domestic cats do, indeed, possess a very fine tuning ability.

At the lower level of sounds, there is little difference between humans, dogs and cats – this is not where it counts if you are a hunter of small rodents and birds. At the higher levels, humans in the prime of life can hear noises up to about 20,000 cycles per second. This sinks to around 12,000 cycles per second in humans of retirement age. Dogs can manage up to 35,000 or 40,000 cycles per second, so that they are able to detect sounds that we cannot. Cats, on the other hand, can hears sounds up to an astonishing 100,000 cycles per second. This corresponds well to the high pitch of mouse sounds, which can be emitted up to this same level. So no mouse is safe from the alert ears of the predatory cat.

This acoustic ability of pet cats explains why they sometimes appear to have supernatural powers. They hear and understand the ultrasonic sounds that precede a noisy activity and respond appropriately before we have even realized that something unusual is going to happen. Even while taking a nap, the cat's ears are in operation. If something exciting is detected, the cat is awake and responding in a split second. Perhaps this is why it sleeps twice as long as we do – making up in length of slumber for what it lacks in depth.

Deafness in cats is not uncommon, especially among very old animals. This makes them prey to fast cars, which are upon them before their ears have warned them of the danger. Also, kittens are deaf for the first few weeks of life, because their ear canals do not open immediately after birth. In addition, there is a genetic deafness in most blue-eyed white cats. This is caused by a malformation of the inner ear. This condition is irreversible, but many blue-eyed white cats manage to survive well enough by becoming extra alert in other ways. Cats in which only one eye is blue are only deaf in one ear. (For details see Deafness.)

Ear Signals

Feline Behaviour. The external ears of cats can be rotated to improve hearing and they can also be used as signals to indicate the emotional condition of the animal. There are five basic ear signals:

Relaxed: The apertures of the ears point forwards and slightly outwards, as the animal quietly listens for interesting sounds over a wide range.

Alert: When a cat focuses on some exciting detail in its surroundings, the ear position changes into the 'alert mode'. As it stares at the point of interest, its ears become fully erect and rotate so that the apertures point directly forward. The ears are kept pricked in this way as long as the cat remains gazing straight ahead. The only variation occurs if there is a sudden noise away to the side of the animal, in which case an ear may be permitted a brief rotation in that direction without a shift in gaze.

Agitated: An agitated cat, suffering from a state of conflict, frustration or apprehension, often displays a nervous twitching of the ears. In some species of wild cat this response has been made highly conspicuous by the evolution of long ear-tufts, but the domestic cat lacks this refinement and the ear-twitching itself is less common. Slight tufting does occur in some breeds, especially the Abyssinian where there is a small dark hairy point to the ear, but compared with the huge ear-tufts of a species such as the Caracal Lynx, this is a very modest development.

Defensive: A defensive cat displays fully flattened ears. They are pressed tightly against the head as a way of protecting them during fights. The torn and tattered ears of battling tom-cats are a vivid testimony to the need to hide this delicate part of the anatomy as much as possible when the claws are out. The effect of flattening the ears to the sides of the head is to make them almost invisible when the animal is viewed from the front and to give its head a more rounded outline. The Scottish Fold Cat, a breed which has permanently flattened ears, has a continually defensive look, regardless of its true mood. What effect this has on the cat's social life is hard to imagine.

Aggressive: An aggressive cat which is hostile without being particularly frightened has its own special ear posture. Here, the ears are rotated but not fully flattened. The *backs* of the ears become visible from the front, and this is the most dangerous ear signal any cat can transmit. In origin, this posture is halfway between alert and defensive – in other words, halfway between pricked forward and flattened backward. In effect, it is a 'ready for trouble' position. The animal is saying, 'I am ready to attack, but you don't frighten me enough to flatten my ears protectively.' The reason why this involves the showing off of the backs of the ears is because they must be rotated backwards before they can be fully flattened. So the rotated ears are in a 'ready-to-be-flattened' posture, should the aggressive cat's opponent dare to retaliate.

This aggressive ear posture has led to some attractive ear-markings in a number of wild cat species, especially the Tiger, which has a huge white spot ringed with black on the back of each ear. When a Tiger is angry, there is no doubt at all about its mood, as the pair of vivid white spots rotates into view. Again, domestic cats lack these special markings.

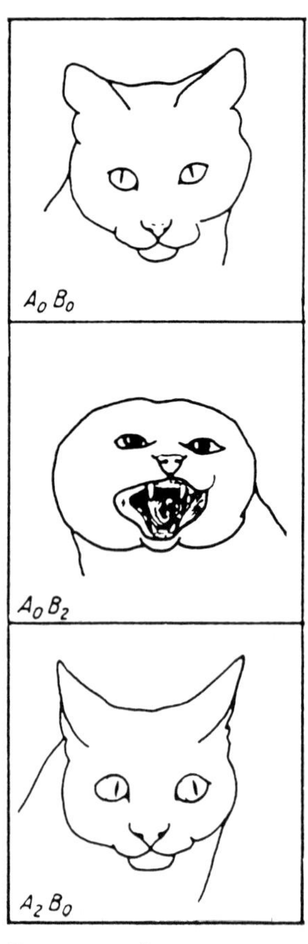

The position of a cat's ears clearly expresses its changing emotions. These three examples, taken from Paul Leyhausen's classic study of feline behaviour, show *(top, Ao Bo)* 'relaxed', *(middle, Ao B2)* 'defensive', and *(bottom, A2 Bo)* 'aggressive'.

Earthquakes

Feline Behaviour. It has been established beyond doubt that cats are capable of predicting earthquakes, but it is still not certain how they manage to do this. They may be sensitive to vibrations of the earth so minute that our instruments fail to detect them. It is known that there

is a gradual build-up to earthquakes, rather than one sudden, massive tremor. It may be that cats have an advance warning system.

A second possibility is that they are responsive to the dramatic increase in static electricity that apparently precedes earthquakes. In humans there is also a response to these changes, but it is rather vague and unspecific. We speak of tenseness or throbbing in the head on such occasions, but we cannot distinguish these feelings from times when we have had a stressful day at work or perhaps when we are coming down with a cold. So we cannot read the signs accurately. In all probability cats can.

A third explanation sees cats as incredibly responsive to sudden shifts in the earth's magnetic field. Shifts of this type accompany earthquakes. Perhaps all three reactions occur at once – detection of minute tremors, electrostatic activity and magnetic upheavals. One thing is certain, cats have repeatedly become intensely agitated just before major earthquakes have struck. Cat-owners recognizing their pets' fears may well owe them their lives. In many cases cats have been observed suddenly rushing about inside the house, desperate to escape. Once the doors are opened for them they flee in panic from the buildings. Some females even rush back and forth carrying their kittens to safety. Then, a few hours later, the quake strikes and levels the buildings. This has been reported time and again from the most vulnerable earthquake areas and now serious research is under way to analyse precisely which signals the cats receive.

Similar responses have been recorded when cats have predicted volcanic eruptions or severe electrical storms. Because of their exceptional sensitivity they have often been foolishly credited with supernatural powers. In medieval times this was frequently their undoing, and many cats met a horrible death by burning at the hands of superstitious Christians because they appeared to be possessed of 'unnatural knowledge'. The fact that we now know this knowledge to be wholly natural makes it no less marvellous.

Eastern Cats

Domestic Cats. An early name for Long-haired Cats, in use in Victorian times. Writing in 1976, Gordon Stables comments: 'There are, first, the European or Western cat, a short-haired animal; and secondly, the Asiatic or Eastern cat – called also Persian or Angora.' Again, in 1895, Rush Huidekoper says, 'The Long-haired Cats, otherwise known as the Astiatic or Eastern Cats vary only slightly in conformation.'

Ebony

Coat Colour. An alternative name for black, used in America for certain types of 'modified black' in the Oriental Shorthair category. The following variants have been recorded: (1) Ebony Silver (undercoat white with a mantle of black tipping); (2) Ebony Silver Tabby (ground colour pale clear silver; markings dense black); (3) Ebony Smoke (white undercoat, deeply tipped with black); (4) Ebony Tabby (ground colour coppery brown; markings dense black); (5) Ebony Tortoiseshell (black mottled or patched with red and/or cream).

Egyptian Cats

Legendary Cats. Few people are unaware that the cat was important to the ancient Egyptians, but there is often confusion about its precise role. This is because it did, in fact, have several quite distinct roles. Writing in 1990, Jason Morris separated out five major categories, based on depictions in the art of ancient Egypt, as follows:

The Cat as Household Companion: In about a dozen cases, the cat is depicted as a small, domesticated animal positioned beneath the chair of its owners. Amazingly, although these pictures are very similar to one another in design, they span nearly 800 years and nine dynasties (roughly from 2000 to 1200 BC). In each case, the cat is shown in close proximity to its female owner, usually under her own chair. This means either that cats were the pets of Egyptian women, rather than men, or that the close juxtaposition of the two in pictures had some special, perhaps sexual significance.

In several cases, these household cats are shown performing a naturalistic activity. One of them strains at its leash as it tries to get at a bowl of food; another devours a fish on the floor; a third sits apprehensively still on its owner's barge as it glides along; another strikes out at a bird with its paw; another has its mouth open and its tongue hanging out, as if it is over-heating at a banquet; another is holding a duck while a pet monkey leaps over its head; another gnaws at a bone held in its paw; another shows a cat striking out at a threatening goose.

These natural actions contrast with the highly traditional positioning of the cat beneath the chair in each case. They clearly show that these were lively, real cats, taking part in the everyday life of the household. Several of them are wearing some kind of decorative collars, suggesting that they were special pet cats rather than mere working mousers.

The cat in its role as a hunting companion in the marshlands of the Nile. This drawing of an exceptionally efficient bird-catching cat shows a detail from an Ancient Egyptian wall painting in the British Museum.

The Cat as Hunting Companion: Only the Egyptians, who were amazingly adept at domesticating a whole range of animal species, attempted to use the cat as a hunting companion. Everywhere else in the world, this role was reserved for the dog, but Egyptian art shows with great clarity and detail the way in which owners took their cats with them on hunting trips in the marshlands of the Nile, when in pursuit of fish or birds.

There are several such scenes dating from 1880 to 1450 BC. One shows a cat hunting birds while its master spears fish from his barge; another shows a cat on a barge pawing impatiently at its master's clothes, as the man hurls a throwing-stick at a cluster of birds on the shore; another shows a cat flushing out game for its master; another shows a cat in the midst of a cluster of startled birds, snatching and grabbing at them as best it can, while its master, on a barge, is in the act of hurling a throwing-stick.

The Cat as Humorous Figure: Roughly between 1300 and 1000 BC, there are a number of humorous cats, depicted almost in the style of modern cartoon cats. They show the cat in various satirical roles, probably illustrating well-known legends and stories of the day. Among these, there is one in which mice are shown besieging a fortress defended unsuccessfully by cats; in another, there is a duel between a cat and a mouse, presided over by an eagle; in another, cats are shown dancing attendance on an enthroned mouse and bringing her gifts; in another, cats assist at the toilet of a Queen Mouse; in yet another, mice bring food and drink to a cat to bargain for peace; and others show cats driving flocks of geese.

The Cat as Serpent-slayer: In the New Kingdom period (roughly 1500–1000 BC) the great Sun-God Re is often depicted as a cat attacking the evil serpent of darkness, Apopis, and slicing off its head. This symbolizes the battle between darkness and light. If the cat does not succeed, the sun will not rise again and darkness will cover the land for ever. There are at least four well-known depictions of this struggle, each showing the cat wielding a pointed knife and with the serpent heaving its coils into the air. The knife is in the act of severing the snake's head. (See separate entry for Re.)

The Cat as a Goddess: From roughly 1500 BC to 30 BC, the cat in Egypt became sacred. As the goddess Bastet, she was worshipped in great temples, mummified by the million and endlessly modelled in bronze. The cult of Bastet grew from a local cult to a nationwide obsession and huge crowds gathered to celebrate the deity, with much feasting and drinking (and, for good measure, orgiastic, ritual frenzies). The main centre of this cult was at a town called Bast, later given the Greek name of Bubastis, which lies north-east of Cairo. Today the great temple there is a ruin – a mere heap of rubble – at a place now called Tell Basta.

In its role as Bastet, goddess of fertility, the ancient Egyptian cat is nearly always depicted in a squatting position, with back legs bent and front legs straight.

Bastet was a goddess of fertility, pleasure, music and dance, and it was doubtless this central role in licentious celebration that led to so much misery for cats in later centuries at the hands of pious, tight-lipped Christians. The idea that sacred ceremonies could be fun was soon to be crushed by a miserable new puritanism, and suppressed for ever. (See separate entries for Bastet and Mummified Cats.)

Bibliography:

1940. Langton, N. & Langton, B. *The Cat in Ancient Egypt.* Cambridge University Press.

1990. Morris, J. *The Cat in Ancient Egypt.* Unpublished thesis, Ashmolean Museum.

1993. Malek, J. *The Cat in Ancient Egypt.* British Museum, London.

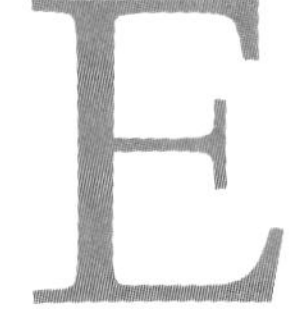

The Egyptian Mau, a spotted breed which has been selected to look like the domesticated feline of the Ancient Pharaohs. The word 'Mau' is Egyptian for 'Cat'.

Egyptian Mau

Domestic Breed. A cat with spots or very short stripes that looks like the domesticated felines depicted in the art of ancient Egypt. There are two forms, one artificially created and the other a natural breed taken from the streets of modern Egypt.

Appearance: The artificial form of this breed has the build and personality of a Siamese, but with a tabby coat. The natural form of this breed has a rounder head and a less exaggerated, more muscular body.

History: The Egyptian Mau has two distinct origins that must be considered separately:

1 In the 1960s a British breeder, Angela Sayer, decided to initiate a programme that would re-create the cat of the ancient Pharaohs. The appearance of the domesticated Egyptian cat was well known from wall paintings dating from the second millennium BC (see Egyptian Cats, above). It was shown as a long-legged, slender-bodied, big-eared animal with a coat covered in markings that were intermediate between stripes and spots. Each mark was a dash, or very short stripe, and these were sometimes shown, not only on the body but also on the legs, the tail and even the ears. In some cases, these short stripes were reduced to spots and in other cases they were elongated to create full striping, but these two extremes were the exceptions. The common form was always the 'dash' or abbreviated stripe.

To sum up, this ancient Egyptian cat looks to us today rather like a mackerel-tabby Siamese, and it was this type that Angela Sayer was seeking to reconstitute. The idea arose when, during a programme designed to produce a Tabby-pointed Siamese, certain individuals appeared with all-over short stripes. They were rejected from the programme, but Mrs Sayer decided to take one of them, a female called Panchusan Zerina, and use her as the foundation queen for her new project. Using back-crosses with Siamese and Havanas, she aimed to complete her Egyptian programme by the early 1970s.

At an earlier date (see page 170), a second, quite separate attempt had been made to re-create the Egyptian cat, and this was eventually to overshadow the Sayer project. The name

'Egyptian Mau' was kept for the cat developed from this other line, and Sayer's cat became known by the less romantic title of 'Oriental Spotted Tabby'. (In some countries it is called the 'Oriental Shorthair Tabby' or the 'Spotted Oriental'.)

2 In 1953, a Russian expatriate, Princess Natalie Troubetskoy, who was living in Rome, became fascinated by a pair of spotted cats belonging to the Egyptian Ambassador to Italy. These cats, a silver female and a smoke male, were being kept not for breeding, but as mascots. The female was, in fact, spayed, so breeding was out of the question. With the help of the Ambassador, she did, however, manage to acquire a similar one from Cairo, a silver female kitten called Baba. When Baba was successfully mated with the Ambassador's male cat, Geppo, two bronze-coloured male kittens were obtained, called Jude and Joseph. Jude died, but Joseph, nicknamed Jo-Jo, was mated back to its mother to produce a female kitten called Lisa. Baba, Jo-Jo and Lisa were the first ever Egyptian Maus to be exhibited. This happened in Rome at the International Cat Show in 1955. Late in December 1956 the Princess left Italy to live in the United States and took her three cats with her. These were to form the basis of the breed in America. In 1957, Lisa was the first Mau to be shown there (at the Empire Cat Show) and quickly attracted the attention of other breeders. By 1968 the breed had gained Championship status with the CFF. Other cat organizations were soon to follow. By 1978, this line of Egyptian Maus finally arrived in Britain.

In the United States a special organization has been formed to promote this breed, called the Egyptian Mau Breeders and Fanciers Association.

Regarding the name of the cat, it should be mentioned that Princess Troubetskoy stated that she preferred the title 'Egyptian Cat' for this breed because the word Mau simply means 'cat' in Egyptian and should be translated as such. She was ignored, probably because the name had already become so widely accepted, but it is worth pointing out that to call this breed by the full name of the Egyptian Mau Cat is an error, because this is, in effect, to call it the Egyptian Cat Cat.

Comparing the cats from these two lines – the British and the Italian – it is clear that there are slight differences. The British line is effectively a Siamese with fine spotted-tabby markings, whereas the Italian line is closer to a spotted Abyssinian. Strangely, it is the artificial British breed that looks more like the ancient Egyptian cat as depicted in some of the early wall paintings. The Italian breed, which is descended from Cairo alley cats, which were presumably themselves directly descended from the cats of the Pharaohs, is ironically slightly less convincing, being almost too elegant and too perfectly spotted. (See Spotted Cats (1) for further details.)

Several authors make reference to a possible additional source for Egyptian Maus. They report that the first ones to reach America were a pair called Gepa and Ludol, and that they arrived there in 1953. If correct, this would put them three years ahead of the arrival of the Troubetskoy cats, but it seems more likely to be an error, with 'Gepa' being a garbled version of the original male 'Geppo'. Writing in 1995, American breeder Len Davidson mentions that further examples of Maus were later imported into the United States and were used to enlarge the gene pool of the breed. He comments: 'Traditionally, obtaining more Maus from Egypt has been nearly impossible. It was not until the early 1980s, when Cathie Rowan exported 13 beautiful cats, that additional Egyptian Maus were brought to the United States . . . Because no other allowable out-crosses exist, these efforts helped save the breed. In 1991 I brought four more Maus into the United States.'

Personality: Terms used to describe this breed include: good-tempered, calm, hardy, shy, agile, healthy, robust, reserved, quiet, good-tempered, loyal, affectionate, active, intelligent and with good memories. It is claimed that they can be walked on a collar and lead. Originally they were said to be unpredictable, aloof, excitable, fiery and wild, but after generations of selective breeding their temperament has clearly improved.

Colour Forms:

GCCF: (Accepts the British version under the title Oriental Spotted Tabby. See under that name for colour details.)

CFA: Silver (with charcoal markings); Bronze (with dark brown markings); Smoke (with jet black markings).

Breed Club:

National Egyptian Mau Club. Address: 52 Gregory Road, Framingham, MA 01701, USA.

Elsa

Pet Lion. The most famous lion in history, Elsa was a cub whose mother was shot by Kenyan Game Warden George Adamson in 1956. His wife, Joy, hand-reared the newborn cub. When it was 27 months old, the tame lion was set free in a game reserve. The Adamsons spent a year training Elsa to hunt and kill. She eventually mated with a wild lion and in December 1959 gave birth to three cubs of her own. When they were six weeks old she started bringing them to the Adamsons' camp, retaining her links with her human foster-parents even though she was now living the life of a wild lioness. She died young, of a parasitic infection, in 1961 and the Adamsons then captured her cubs and moved them for safety to the Serengeti reserve.

Elsa was made famous by a series of books, films and television programmes, beginning with the worldwide best-seller *Born Free* in 1960. In 1965, Columbia made a feature film version of *Born Free,* starring Virginia McKenna and Bill Travers. In 1972 they made a sequel based on *Living Free,* starring Susan Hampshire and Nigel Davenport.

Joy Adamson's writings made a major impact on the public attitude towards lions. In a survey carried out just before her work was published, the lion appeared in the lists of both the top ten animal loves and the top ten animal hates. It was loved for its dignity and beauty, but hated for its savagery. After *Born Free* had appeared, the survey was repeated. There was only one significant difference from the earlier figures: although the lion appeared again in the top ten animal loves, it had disappeared from the top ten animal hates.

There was an irony in the way the Adamsons died. Despite living most of their lives in close bodily contact with adult African lions, it was African humans who proved to be more dangerous. In 1980 Joy Adamson was murdered by a Turkana servant she had sacked. In 1989 George Adamson was murdered by Somali bandits.

Actors Bill Travers and Geoffrey Keen in Africa in 1965, filming *Born Free,* Joy Adamson's famous story about her pet lioness, Elsa.

The complete bibliography of the Adamson saga is as follows. It includes books on how, in addition to Elsa, they reared a cheetah and a leopard. There are also several autobiographical and biographical volumes.

Bibliography:

1960. Adamson, J. *Born Free*. Collins Harvill, London.
1961. Adamson, J. *Living Free*. Collins Harvill, London.
1961. Adamson, J. *Elsa; the Story of a Lioness*. Collins Harvill, London
1962. Adamson, J. *Forever Free*. Collins Harvill, London.
1965. Adamson, J. *Elsa and her Cubs*. Collins Harvill, London.
1966. Jay, J.M. *Any Old Lion*. Leslie Frewin, London.
1966. McKenna, V. & Travers, B. *On Playing with Lions*. Collins, London.
1968. Adamson, G. *Bwana Game*. Collins Harvill, London.
1969. Adamson, J. *The Spotted Sphinx*. Collins Harvill, London.
1970. Adamson, J. *Pippa the Cheetah and her Cubs*. Collins Harvill, London.
1971. Bourke, A. & Rendall, J. *A Lion Called Christian*. Collins, London.
1972. Adamson, J. *Pippa's Challenge*. Collins Harvill, London.
1972. Couffer, J. *The Lions of Living Free*. Collins Harvill, London.
1978. Adamson, J. *The Searching Spirit*. Collins Harvill, London.
1980. Adamson, J. *Queen of Shaba*. Collins Harvill, London.
1981. Adamson, J. *Friends from the Forest*. Collins Harvill, London.
1986. Adamson, G. *My Pride and Joy*. Collins Harvill, London.
1991. Patterson, G. *Lion's Legacy*. Robson Books, London.
1992. Cass, C. *Joy Adamson*. Weidenfeld & Nicolson, London.
1993. House, A. *The Great Safari*. Harvill/Harper Collins, London.
1995. Patterson, G. *With My Soul Amongst Lions*. Hodder & Stoughton, London.

Eponine

Pet Cat. A green-eyed, black cat belonging to French poet and novelist Théophile Gautier. Her habits are recorded in his work *La Ménagerie Intime*. A 'sensitive, nervous and electric animal', she was so intelligent and sociable that she had a place set for her at the author's table. If we are to believe Gautier, Eponine's behaviour during meals was exemplary. She was always promptly in her seat (no doubt with a little help from his servants) at the moment when he entered his dining-room. She sat there, he reported, with 'her paws folded on the tablecloth, her smooth forehead held up to be kissed, and like a well-bred little girl who is politely affectionate to relatives and older people'. The author and his cat then proceeded to dine together, the animal first lapping up soup (with some reluctance, he admits) and then feasting on fish. 'She went right through the dinner, dish by dish, from soup to dessert, waiting for her

Eponine, the adored black cat belonging to the French poet Théophile Gautier and featured in his 1871 work *La Ménagerie Intime*. The illustration is by Mrs William Chance, taken from her 1899 English translation of his book.

turn to be helped, and behaving with such propriety and nice manners as one would like to see in many children.'

Bibliography:

1899. Gautier, T. *A Domestic Menagerie.* Eliot Stock, London. (An English translation by Mrs William Chance of *La Ménagerie Intime.*)

Esmeralda

Cartoon Cat. A black-striped, strip-cartoon cat who first appeared on 3rd December 1933, in a Sunday comic strip by Al Smith called *Cicero's Cat.* A clever, cunning cat, Esmeralda appeared regularly for 30 years, outwitting a variety of other animals in her slapstick adventures.

ESP

Feline Behaviour. Many people believe that cats are capable of some kind of extra-sensory perception, but they are not. It has become popular to explain anything puzzling as being due to some sort of supernatural power, but this can easily become a short-cut to complacency. The scientific truth is often much more fascinating, but serious investigation is easily stifled if every unusual occurrence is relegated to the dustbin of 'mystic forces'.

ESP is a contradiction in terms. Anything that is perceived is, by definition, something which operates through one of the sense organs. So, if something is extra-sensory, it cannot be perceived. Therefore there cannot be any such thing as ESP.

If a cat performs some very strange action – finds its way home over a long distance, predicts an earthquake, or senses the return of its owners – then it becomes a challenge to find out which sensory pathway was involved. To put the feat down to ESP simply stops any further enquiry. It says the cat has magical powers, and that is an end to it. Much more stimulating is the idea that everything cats do is capable of logical explanation, if only it were possible to find out how the behaviour mechanism operates.

If it is discovered that magnets attached to cats will upset their ability to find their way home, then this may be a start to understanding the amazing homing abilities the animals have evolved over a long period of time. If it is found that cats are sensitive to very small vibrations or changes in static electricity, then this might assist in analysing how they can predict earthquakes. And if it is possible to learn more about their sensitivity to ultrasonic sounds, it may help to clarify how they can 'know' that someone is approaching from a great distance.

This does not mean that it will be possible to explain everything a cat does. We may have to wait for much more advanced technology before it is possible to do that. But ultimately it should be possible, and the 'mysterious cat' will be mysterious no more. And if and when this happens, the cat will, because of our detailed knowledge of its abilities, be more fascinating than ever before. To explain something is not to explain it away, and to understand something is not to underestimate its value.

If, despite – or perhaps because of – these comments, there is a desire to investigate further the 'mysteries' of the cat, the following references may be of interest:

Bibliography:

1940. Mellen, I.M. *The Science and Mystery of the Cat.* Scribner's, New York.
1973. Epton, N. *Cat Manners and Mysteries.* Michael Joseph, London.
1974. Necker, C. (Editor) *Supernatural Cats.* Warner Books, New York.
1989. Gettings, F. *The Secret Lore of the Cat.* Grafton, London.
1989. Shuker, K.P.N. *Mystery Cats of the World.* Robert Hale, London.

Eurasian Lynx

Wild Feline. An alternative name for the Northern Lynx *(Lynx lynx).* This title accurately describes the range of the species, but Northern Lynx is usually preferred today because it draws attention to the fact that there is a separate, southern species (the Spanish Lynx, *Lynx pardinus*). (For details see Northern Lynx.)

European Burmese Cat

Domestic Breed. In the United States the colour forms of the Burmese are more restricted than in Europe. The CFA recognizes only four colour forms: the original sable brown and its dilutions, known as champagne, blue and platinum. Because some American breeders have imported pedigree Burmese with other colours from Europe, a separate class has been established by the CFA for 'European Burmese', in the following colour forms: brown, blue, chocolate, lilac, red, cream, seal tortie, blue tortie, chocolate tortie and lilac tortie.

European Cat

Domestic Breed. A name sometimes given to the non-pedigree forms of the European Shorthair Cat. In 1957, Dechambre defined the term as follows: 'This is the name given to a number of varieties of domestic cat with short hair and varied colourings, which live in close proximity to man not only in Europe, but also in almost all other parts of the world. It is the commonest breed in town or country. Breeding is only too often left to chance mating. From time to time fine specimens do occur, but it is not easy to establish them on a heredity basis.'

European Lynx

Wild Feline. *(Lynx lynx)* The European Lynx was once considered a distinct species, but it is now known to range from Europe right across northern Asia. Today it is instead referred to either as the Eurasian Lynx, or more commonly, as the Northern Lynx. (See Northern Lynx.)

European Shorthair Cat

Domestic Breed. The modern pedigree European Shorthair has been developed from the ordinary working cats and pet cats of Continental Europe, with careful, selective breeding replacing the casual breeding that had been going on for centuries.

Appearance: A stocky cat with a round, longish head, rather thick, strong legs and a medium-length tail. In fact, this is generally a rather 'medium' breed in most respects, which is not so surprising, bearing in mind its incredibly mixed ancestry.

The European Shorthair Cat. Until 1982 this pedigree cat was not separated from the very similar British Shorthair, but in that year a distinction was made for show purposes.

History: Until 1982 no distinction was made between the British Shorthair and the European Shorthair, but then they were formally separated for show purposes. Since then they have been diverging slightly, although it is still easy to confuse them. The European breed has a less stocky body, longer legs, a slightly longer head and larger ears.

The most confusing aspect of this breed is that it is possible to find three separate definitions of it, according to the kind of author writing about it. It has been defined as:

1 Any domestic short-haired cat living as a household pet in Europe (by authors writing about the history of cats in general).
2 Any British Shorthair Cat living on the mainland of Continental Europe (by British authors writing about British pedigree breeds).
3 A distinct breed of pedigree cat not to be confused with the British Shorthair Cat (by authors writing about international breed classifications).

Personality: Terms used to describe this breed include: hardy, rugged, quiet, untemperamental, adaptable, moderate, sensible, active, intelligent, shrewd, inquisitive, brave and lively.
Colour Forms: Essentially the same as the British Shorthair. A huge variety of colour forms is available. (For details see British Shorthair.)

European Wild Cat

Wild Feline. *(Felis sylvestris sylvestris)* Commonly known simply as the Wild Cat, this animal requires the more detailed name of European Wild Cat to distinguish it from its African and Asiatic cousins, which were once each thought of as separate species but are now considered to be no more than sub-species. All three today are classified as a single species *(Felis sylvestris).* (For details see Wild Cat.)

The European Wild Cat looks very similar to the typical domestic cat, but is slightly larger, heavier, stockier and more thickly furred. Also, the ringed tail has a blunt, rounded end. Its personality differs markedly from the domestic pet cat. Attempts to tame it have nearly always failed. It has a secretive, shy and – if pushed into a corner – intensely aggressive character. Its African relative is much more amenable to human proximity, and it is that sub-species from which it is believed the domestic cat originated in ancient Egypt. However, the European Wild Cat will readily cross-breed with domestic cats after these have reverted to a feral condition. It is believed that, centuries ago, such crosses between the originally imported, tame 'Egyptian Cats' and the indigenous European Wild Cats would have given rise to the founding stock of what we now call the European Shorthair Cats. Such animals would have enjoyed the double benefit of inheriting the friendly personality of the African animals and the heavier, cold-climate bodies of the European cats.

In terms of hunting, social, sexual and parental behaviour, there appears to be little difference between the European Wild Cat and the domestic cat except that the latter breeds more frequently.

Over the years there have been so many crossings between European Wild Cats and feral domestic cats, that it is hard to say how many 100 per cent pure Wild Cats remain and how many of those have been properly studied.
Size: Length of Head + Body: 47–75 cm (18½–29½ in). Tail: 21–35 cm (8–14 in). Weight: 4–8 kg (9–17½ lb).
Distribution: The regions of Europe that are most removed from human influence, in northern Scotland, Spain, Portugal, France, Italy, Germany, Switzerland, Austria, Czech Rep., Slovakia, Poland, Hungary, Croatia, Serbia, Bosnia-Herzegovina, Romania, Bulgaria and Greece.
Bibliography:
1896. Hamilton, E. *The Wild Cat of Europe.* Porter, London.
1974. Dudley, E. *Scrap, the Gentle Wildcat.* London
1975. Dudley, E. *The Wild Cat.* Frederick Muller, London.
1977. Tomkies, M. *My Wilderness Wildcats.* MacDonald & Jane's, London.

The European Wild Cat *(Felis sylvestris sylvestris).* It is thought that this race may have interbred with the less stocky, tame African Wild Cats that were brought to Europe from ancient Egypt, creating a heavier breed of northern domestic cat.

1987. Tomkies, M. *Wildcat Haven.* Jonathan Cape, London.
1993. Stahl, P. et al. *Seminar on the Biology and Conservation of the Wildcat.* Council of Europe Press, Strasbourg.

Evolution

Feline Biology. The earliest cat-like carnivores, which were to evolve into the family *Felidae,* appeared between 30 and 40 million years ago, in the Late Eocene and Early Oligocene. Two main branches developed: the Sabre-tooths and the True Cats.

The first of these had evolved gigantic, curved canine teeth, used for killing their prey. They include the animal often referred to in popular writing as the Sabre-toothed Tiger. Some species were larger than modern Lions. They were immensely powerful, but slow-moving. They could only prey on large, cumbersome animals, and when their prey vanished, they too became extinct. The last of the Sabre-tooths is thought to have died out 12,000–15,000 years ago.

The True Cats had started to evolve during the long reign of the Sabre-tooths, but did not become what we would call a typical cat until about 20 million years ago. They became specialized as medium-sized ambush-killers of smaller prey. Their populations spread out across the Bering land-bridge to North and then South America, with the small cats of the New World and Old World evolving in a parallel way over a period of some millions of years.

The surviving, modern members of the cat family have been divided into three sub-families:

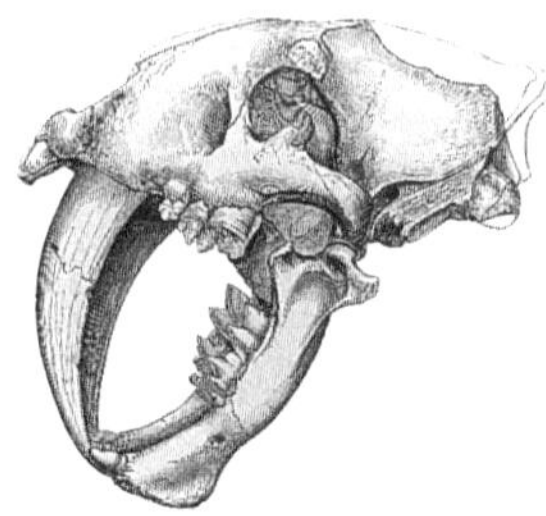

The skull of the so-called Sabre-toothed Tiger. Its huge upper canines were three times the length of those of the modern Lion, but it became extinct more than 12,000 years ago.

1 The Small Cats (Sub-family *Felinae;* 30 species)
2 The Big Cats (Sub-family *Pantherinae;* 5 species)
3 The Cheetah (Sub-family *Acinonychinae;* 1 species)

These 36 species of modern cats are found over a vast range from Asia, through Europe and Africa to the Americas. However, they are under pressure from human intervention almost

everywhere and it is highly likely that a number of them will have become extinct before the end of the twenty-first century. (For details see general entry for Wild Species and separate entries for each of the 36 wild felines.)

Exotic Shorthair Cat

Domestic Breed. The short-haired version of the Persian Cat, first developed in the 1950s. The name 'Exotic' was introduced by American breeders in 1966.

Many people wished to own a cat with the docile, serene personality of the Persian, but without having to suffer the endless grooming problems created by their exceptionally long fur. The solution was to shorten the hair genetically, but without altering the character of the cat. Once this had been done, the new breed quickly became immensely popular. It has sometimes been referred to as the 'Easy-care Persian'.

Appearance: A 'chunky' cat, it retains the heavy head, the flat face, the stocky body and the short legs and tail of the Persian, but it has a thick, soft, plush, luxuriant, short coat, giving it an appealing 'teddy bear' look.

History: The breed originally arose because of attempts to strengthen the quality of the American Shorthair Cat. This was done by introducing Persians into Shorthair breeding programmes in the United States. This soon gave rise to a new, 'improved' American Shorthair which was so different from the traditional Shorthair that it was decided to give them two separate breed names. In 1966, Jane Martinke suggested the title 'Exotic Shorthair' for the newer type. The first 'Exotic' was shown under that name in 1967. Two years later, two Americans, Bob and Nancy Lane, started the first Exotic Breed Club, and began more carefully orchestrated breeding programmes.

Other short-haired breeds were occasionally involved in the crosses in the early days, including Abyssinians, Burmese and Russian Blues, but once the Exotic breed had been firmly established, only out-crosses using American Shorthairs and Persians were permitted.

The Exotic Shorthair Cat is essentially a short-haired version of the Persian Cat. For those who want a docile cat that does not require endless grooming, this is the ideal breed.

The appealing pug-face of the Exotic Shorthair Cat, a breed first developed in the United States in the 1950s and which has been steadily growing in popularity ever since. By the 1990s it had become the eighth-most popular pedigree cat in America.

Similar crosses were made in Britain, using British Shorthairs, where the results were sometimes referred to as 'British Exotics' to distinguish them from their American counterparts. Two clubs were formed: the 'Exotic Cat Club' in 1983 and then the 'Exotic Shorthair Breeders Society' in 1984.

The arrival of this breed has caused some controversy, since some cat organizations classify them as short-haired cats (because of their fur) and others as long-haired (because they are Persian in every other respect). This difference of opinion serves to underline the unfortunate state in which pedigree cat classifications find themselves today.

Personality: Terms used to describe this breed include: quiet, placid, tranquil, home-loving, hardy, intelligent, alert, bright, inquisitive and playful.

Colour Forms: Almost all colours are known in this breed. In fact, no fewer than 96 different colour forms are listed by the Exotic Shorthair Breeders Association.

Bibliography:

1993. Green, J. 'What is an Exotic?' In: *Cat World Annual 1993*. p.62-63.

Breed Clubs:

Exotic Cat Club. Address: 6 Oakwell Crescent, Ilkeston, Derbyshire, DE7 5GX, England.

Exotic Shorthair Breeders Society. Founded in 1984. Issues a half-yearly *Journal*. Address: The Cottage Cattery, Mill Road, West Walton, Nr. Wisbech, Cambs., PE14 7EU, England.

Note: There is an additional breed publication, *Exotic Thoughts*. Address: P.O. Box 52, Verona, PA 15147, USA.

Eyes

Feline Anatomy. The cat has magnificent eyes which are very large in relation to its skull. They provide the animal with a wider visual field than ours (295 degrees instead of only 210). They also give it a slightly wider binocular field (130 degrees instead of 120). This frontal, three-dimensional vision is especially important for a hunter, which must be able to judge distances with great accuracy.

The cat's greatest visual asset, however, is its ability to see well in very dim light. This ability is made possible by an image-intensifying device at the rear of the eyes. It is a complex, light-reflecting layer called the *tapidum lucidum* (meaning literally 'bright carpet'), which acts rather like a mirror behind the retina, reflecting light back to the retinal cells. It is this that makes the cat's eyes 'glow' in the dark and gives them what, to some, is a sinister nocturnal appearance.

With this special layer, the cat can utilize every scrap of light that enters its eyes. With our eyes we absorb far less of the light that enters them. Because of this difference cats can make out movements and objects in the semi-darkness which would be quite invisible to us.

Despite this efficient nocturnal ability, it is not true that cats can see in complete darkness, as some people seem to believe. On a pitch black night they must navigate by sound, smell and the sensitivity of their amazing whiskers.

Another major difference between human and feline eyes is the way in which cats reduce their pupils to vertical slits. This gives them a more refined control over how much light enters the eyes. For an animal with eyes sensitive enough to see in very dim light, it is important not to be dazzled by bright sunlight, and the narrowing of the pupils to tight slits gives a greater control over light input. The reason cats have vertical slits rather than horizontal ones is that they can use the closing of the lids to reduce the light input even further. With these two slits – the vertical one of the pupil and the horizontal one of the eyelids – working at right angles to one another, the feline eye has the possibility of making the most delicate adjustment of any animal, when faced with what would otherwise be a blinding light.

Confirmation of the fact that the nocturnal sensitivity of the cat's eyes is linked with the contraction of the pupils to slits, is found in the observation that lions, which are daytime killers, have eyes that contract, like ours, to circular pinpricks.

One way in which cats' eyes are inferior to ours is in their ability to see colours. In the first half of the 20th century scientists were convinced that cats were totally colour-blind and one authority reworked a popular saying with the words: 'Day and night, all cats see grey.' That was the prevailing attitude as late as the 1940s, but since then more careful research has been carried out and it is now known that cats can distinguish between certain colours, but not, apparently, with much finesse.

The reason earlier experiments failed to reveal the existence of feline colour vision was that in discrimination tests cats quickly latched on to subtle differences in the degree of greyness of colours; they then refused to abandon these clues when presented with two colours of exactly the same degree of greyness, so the tests gave negative results. Using more sophisticated methods, recent studies have been able to prove that cats can distinguish between red and green, red and blue, red and grey, green and blue, green and grey, blue and grey, yellow and blue, and yellow and grey. Whether they can distinguish between other pairs of colours is still in dispute. For example, one authority believes that they can also tell the difference between red and yellow, but another does not.

Whatever the final results of these investigations, one thing is certain: colour is not as important in the lives of cats as it is in our own lives. Their eyes are much more attuned to seeing in dim light, where they need only one-sixth of the light that we do to make out the same details of movement and shape.

Eye Signals

Feline Behaviour. Certain changes in the cat's eyes can act as signals of its shifting emotional moods. The animal's pupils become greatly enlarged when it sees something extremely appealing or something intensely threatening. In other words, a state of strong emotional arousal, whether pleasant or unpleasant, causes an exaggerated pupil expansion. Tests have shown that when this happens the area of the pupils may increase to between four and five times their previous size in less than one second.

This dramatic change is part of the cat's mood-signalling system, but it is only one of the ways in which the eyes alter their expression. In addition to pupil changes there is also the

possibility of signalling mood by the degree of opening or closing the eyelids. An alert cat has fully opened eyes and this is the condition that is always maintained in the presence of strangers, who are not entirely trusted by the cat. If the animal switches to half-closed eyes, this is an expression of total relaxation signalling complete trust in the friendship of its owners.

Full closure of the eyes only occurs in two contexts: sleep and appeasement. When two cats are fighting and one is forced into submission, it often performs what is called 'cut-off', where it turns away from its tormentor and shuts its eyes, trying to blot out the frightening image of its dominant rival. This is basically a protective action, an attempt to save the eyes from possible danger, but it has also become a way of reducing the unbearable tension of the moment. In addition, the victor sees it as a sign of capitulation by his opponent.

The obvious opposite of this behaviour is the prolonged, direct stare. This is a hostile signal in the world of feline body language, a fact that is worth remembering when encountering a sensitive cat for the first time.

The Eyra *(Felis yaguarondi)*, better known today as the Jaguarundi. The least typical member of the cat family, it is a small, plain-coloured, long-faced feline from South America.

Eyra

Wild Feline. An early, alternative name for the small, South American cat now known as the Jaguarundi *(Felis yaguarondi)*. The coat colour of this species is highly variable, and some authors used to make a special distinction between the different colour forms. The grey, black and brown ones were called Jaguarundis, while the fox-red ones were referred to as Eyras. They were originally considered to be separate species, but later it was discovered that the different types could appear in the same litter, and the distinction had to be dropped. When this happened, most authorities called all colour forms Jaguarundis, and this remains the generally accepted title today, but a few preferred to persist with the name Eyra for them all. (For further details see Jaguarundi.)

Fables

Folk-tales. Over the centuries many fables have been told that involve cats in one way or another. The earliest are those attributed to the Greek author Aesop, who is supposed to have lived in the sixth century BC. It is not certain whether he actually existed, because it was several hundred years before 'Aesop's Fables' were collected together in written form. They appear to be an amalgam of ancient tales gathered from many sources. In the late 17th century, the French poet Jean de La Fontaine (1621–1695) adapted and amplified Aesop's Fables and published twelve books containing a total of 230 animal tales. From these sources, examples of stories with a feline theme include the following:

Belling the Cat: A colony of mice decide that the only way to protect themselves from a predatory cat is to hang a bell around its neck, so that they can hear when the cat is coming. Unfortunately no mouse can be found that is willing to carry out the task of putting the bell in place.

The Cat and the Cock: The cat pounces on the cock and holds him tight, ready to kill and eat him. But first he feels he needs some excuse to do so. He decides that the terrible noise the cock makes every morning, disturbing the peace and quiet, is sufficient reason. But the cock argues that he is the world's alarm clock and that without him men will be late for their work. The cat listens to this reasonable defence but then ignores it and eats the cock anyway.

The Cat and the Fox: The fox is boasting to the cat about the hundred different ways it can escape attacks from dogs. The cat says it has only one trick. Just then a pack of dogs arrive and the cat employs its one trick by running up a tree. The fox considers all its various options but this takes so long that the dogs catch it and kill it.

The Cat and the Hen: When the hen is ill the cat pays her a visit to ask if there is anything it can do to help. The hen replies that there is indeed something it can do, namely to go away and leave her in peace.

The fable of the cat and the fox.

The Cat and the Mice: One old cat decides to use a trick to attract mice, so that it will not have to chase after them. It hangs itself upside-down from the wall, looking as though it is dead, and the mice start to come near. But a wise old mouse warns the younger ones to keep away, because a cat is not to be trusted, even if it is stuffed with straw.
The Cat, the Weasel and the Rabbit: The rabbit and the weasel go to the elderly cat Raminagrobis to ask him to settle a dispute. They start to make their respective cases to him, but he complains of being deaf and asks them to come close enough for him to be able to hear what they are saying. When they do this, he lashes out at them, kills them, and settles their disagreement by eating them both.
The Eagle and the Cat: An eagle, a cat and a sow live together in a tree. The eagle has a nest for its young at the top of the tree. The sow and her piglets live at the foot of the tree. And the cat and her kittens live in a hollow halfway up the trunk of the tree. One day the cat tells the eagle that the sow is undermining the tree and it will collapse, and tells the sow that the eagle is about to attack her piglets and carry them off for food. Both the eagle and the sow are so terrified that they refuse to leave their young, even to look for food, and eventually all starve to death. The cat then feasts on their bodies.
Venus and the Cat: A female cat falls in love with a young man. Venus, the goddess of love, agrees to turn the cat into a beautiful girl. The young man marries the girl, but Venus wants to know whether her character has changed as well as her body and so she introduces a live mouse into the couple's bedroom. The girl, forgetting herself, instantly pounces on the mouse, much to her husband's dismay. Seeing this, Venus decides that she will have to turn the girl back into a cat again.

(See also the following entries: Belling the Cat; Cat's Only Trick; Raminagrobis; Rodilard; and The White Cat.)

Faeces

Feline Behaviour. One of the most characteristic actions of a domestic cat is its habit of using a paw to cover over its dung, scraping the surrounding earth over the freshly deposited faeces until they are invisible. In an indoor litter tray, the same action is observed. (And sometimes, as a critical comment concerning its tinned cat food, the animal will attempt to do the same thing with the contents of its food-bowl.)

This action of dung-covering is always referred to as an indication of the fastidious tidiness of the cat. Owners of messy dogs are often regaled with this fact by cat-owners insisting on the superiority of felines over canines. This favoured interpretation of faeces-burying as a sign of cat hygiene does not, however, stand up to close investigation.

The truth is that cats bury their faeces as a way of damping down their odour display. Faeces-burying is the act of a subordinate cat, fearful of its social standing. Proof of this was found when the social lives of feral cats were examined closely. It was discovered that dominant tom-cats, far from burying their faeces, actually placed them on little 'advertising' hillocks, or any other raised points in the environment where their odour could be wafted abroad to the maximum effect. It was only the weaker, more subdued cats that hid their faeces.

The fact that our pet cats always seem to carry out such a careful burying routine is a measure of the extent to which they see themselves dominated by us (and also perhaps by other cats in the neighbourhood). This is not really so surprising. We are physically stronger than they are and we completely dominate that all-important element in feline life – the food supply. Our dominance is in existence from the time of kittenhood onwards, and never in serious doubt. Even big cats, such as lions, can be kept in this subordinate role for a lifetime, by their friendly owners, so it is hardly surprising that the small domestic cat is permanently in awe of us and therefore always makes sure to bury its faeces.

Burying the faeces does not, of course, completely switch off the odour signal, but it does reduce it drastically. In this way the cat can continue to announce its presence through its scents, but not to the extent that it transmits a serious threat.

FANCHETTE

FICTIONAL CAT. Appears in Colette's *Claudine à l'école* (1900) and *Claudine à Paris* (1901), where she is described as 'the most intelligent cat in the world'. She had a powerful sexual urge and was eventually provided with a mate because 'the poor darling wanted it so cruel'.

FAWN

COAT COLOUR. A light, pinkish-cream coat. This is a dilution of cinnamon and has been described by one authority as a pale, warm colour, a 'light lavender with pale cocoa overtones'.

It has been recorded in the following variant forms: (1) Fawn Shaded; (2) Fawn Smoke; (3) Fawn Silver; (4) Fawn Silver Tabby; (5) Fawn Tabby; (6) Fawn-Cream; (7) Fawn-Cream Shaded; (8) Fawn-Cream smoke; (9) Fawn-Cream Calico; (10) Fawn-Cream Van Calico.

FEATHERS

PET CAT. When Karl van Vechten began writing his feline classic *The Tiger in the House* (1920), he acquired a new Persian kitten called Feathers. She was described by him as: 'a tortoise-shell and white smoke tabby queen, with seven toes on each front paw'. By the time he had completed the manuscript, 14 months later, Feathers was fully grown and was already pregnant. He writes: 'When I began this book she was a kitten, a chrysanthemum-like ball of tawny, orange, white and black fuzzy fur, and now she is about to become a mother.' She was, in effect, the 'Tiger' in the title of his famous work, and the dedication at the front of the book reads: 'For Edna Kenton . . . and Feathers'.

AUTHOR KARL VAN VECHTEN and his pet cat, Feathers, to whom he dedicated his classic work *The Tiger in the House* (1920). He described Feathers as 'A Tortoiseshell and White Smoke Tabby Queen'.

FECUNDITY

FELINE REPRODUCTION. The breeding rate of domestic cats is so high that they can rapidly become overpopulated. This is partly because domestication has increased their breeding rate. Wild cats only breed once a year, but domestic cats can easily go through three reproductive cycles annually. Also, domestic females come into heat sooner that wild females (six to eight months instead of ten months).

Litter size varies considerably. Four to five is the average domestic litter size (compared with two to four for wild cats), but some exceptional litters have been huge. The record is held by a four-year-old Burmese named Tarawood Antigone who, after mating with a half-Siamese, produced a litter of 19 kittens, 15 of which survived. Another impressive litter was born to a Persian female called Bluebell, who gave birth to 14 kittens, all of which survived.

The most prolific domestic queen was a tabby called Dusty, who produced a total of 420 kittens during her lifetime. The oldest feline mother, Kitty, was 30 years old when she produced her last litter, bringing her lifetime total to 218. Clearly the potential for population growth among domestic cats is enormous.

How quickly can a feline population grow? A simple calculation, starting with a single breeding pair of domestic cats, and allowing for a total of 14 kittens in each three-litter year, reveals that in five years' time there will be a total of 65,536 cats. This assumes that they will all survive, that males and females are born in equal numbers and that they all start breeding when they are a year old. In reality, the females might start a little younger, so the figure could be higher. But against this is the obvious fact that many of the animals would perish from disease or accident.

This paints a grim picture for the aspiring house mouse, a nightmare world of wall-to-wall cats. But it never materializes because there are enough responsible human owners to ensure that breeding restraints *are* applied to their cats, to keep the numbers under control. Neutering of both males and females is now commonplace and it is estimated that more than 90 per cent of all toms have suffered that operation. Females that are allowed to breed may have their litter size reduced to one or two, the unfortunate kittens being painlessly killed by the local vet.

In some areas there are fairly ruthless extermination programmes for feral and stray cats, and in certain countries there have even been oral contraceptive projects, with the stray cat

population given food laced with 'the pill'. Israel, for example, claims to prevent about 20,000 kittens a year by using this technique.

Despite these attempts, however, there are still well over a million feral and stray cats in Great Britain at the present time. It has been estimated that there are as many as half a million in London alone. In addition there are more than seven million pet cats, making a massive feline population of roughly one cat per ten humans.

Fédération Internationale Féline

Feline History. FIFe was founded in France in 1949 by Mrs M. Ravel, but today has Switzerland as its home base. Its aim is to be considered as the United Nations of the pedigree cat world and, to that end, it has established a federation of 31 nations, with a member association in each. Notable exceptions are the United States, Canada, Australia, New Zealand and Japan.

The members of the Federation agree to follow common rules concerning breeds, showing and judging. The general assembly works on a democratic, 'one nation, one vote' principle. FIFe acknowledges three official languages: English, French and German. The current President is Alva Uddin.

The 31 member countries are: Argentina, Austria, Belorus, Brazil, Croatia, Czech Republic, Denmark, Estonia, Finland, France, Germany, Great Britain, Hungary, Iceland, Italy, Latvia, Liechtenstein, Lithuania, Luxemburg, Malaysia, Mexico, The Netherlands, Norway, Poland, Portugal, Russia, Slovakia, Slovenia, Spain, Sweden, Switzerland. Provisional members: Belgium, Ukraine, Uruguay. (For further details see Cat Societies.)

Feline Advisory Bureau

Cat Welfare. The FAB is a British charity dedicated to the health and welfare of cats. It was formed in 1958 by a group of breeders and veterinarians who wished to improve the specialized knowledge of feline medicine. The Bureau brings together information on the treatment, care, welfare, and management of cats and makes it available to veterinary surgeons and nurses, breeders, cattery proprietors and cat owners. It has also established the first lectureship of Feline Medicine in the world, at Bristol University in England. It issues a list of FAB-approved catteries, holds an annual conference, and publishes a quarterly colour magazine. Address: FAB Office, 235 Upper Richmond Road, Putney, London, SW15 6SN, England. Tel: 0181-789 9553.

Feline Anatomy

Feline Anatomy. The external anatomy of the cat is discussed under a number of separate headings. For further details, see the following entries: Cat Colours and Markings; Claws; Ears; Eyes; Haws; Nose; Nose Leather; Paws; Points of the Cat; Tail; Teeth; Tongue; Whiskers.

The first major publication in English on the subject of the cat's anatomy was by St. George Mivart in 1881. Books on the subject include those listed in the following bibliography.

Bibliography:

1845. Strauss-Durckheim, H. *Anatomie descriptive et comparative du Chat.* Paris. (2 vols)

1881. Mivart, St. George. *The Cat.* John Murray, London.

1882. Wilder, B.G. and Gage, S.H. *Anatomical Technology as Applied to the Domestic Cat.* Barnes, New York. (Enlarged edition in 1886)

1895. Gorham, F.P. and Tower, R.W. *A Laboratory Guide for the Dissection of the Cat.* Scribners, New York.

1901. Reighard, J. and Jennings, H.S. *Anatomy of the Cat.* Holt, New York. (Enlarged edition in 1935)

1903. Davidson, A. *Mammalian Anatomy with Special Reference to the Cat.* Rebman, London.

1914. Winkler, C. and Potter, A. *An Anatomical Guide to Experimental Researches on the Cat's Brain.* Versluys, Amsterdam.

1932. Reighard, J. and Jennings, H.S. *Dissection of the Cat.* Holt, New York.

1940. Stuart, R.R. *The Anatomy of the Cat.* Denoyer-Geppert, Chicago.

1946. Leach, W.J. *Functional Anatomy of the Mammal (Dissection of the Cat).* McGraw-Hill, New York.
1948. Horsburgh and Heath. *Atlas of Cat Anatomy.* Stanford University Press.
1950. Field, H.E. *An Atlas of Cat Anatomy.* University Press, Chicago. (Enlarged and revised edition in 1969)
1968. Gilbert, G.S. *Pictorial Anatomy of the Cat.* University of Washington, Seattle.
1969. Crouch, J.E. *Text-Atlas of Cat Anatomy.* Lea & Febiger, Philadelphia.
1976. Booth, E.S. *Laboratory Anatomy of the Cat.* (5th edition)
1993. Hudson and Hamilton. *Atlas of Feline Anatomy for Veterinarians.* Saunders.

Feline Genetics

Feline Biology. Genetically, cats are far less variable than dogs. There are no feline equivalents of Great Danes or Chihuahuas, Mastiffs or Whippets. There is a historical reason for this. Dogs have been required to carry out a whole variety of tasks in their long partnership with mankind. Among their many roles they have been hunting partners, dogs of war, fighting dogs, guard dogs, herders, retrievers, setters, pointers, terriers, sight-hounds, scent-hounds, racers and lap dogs. By contrast, the cat has had only one official role, namely that of pest-controller.

To be a good rodent-destroyer required little or no modification of the wild cat's anatomy. A supreme carnivore, it has evolved as a highly efficient, specialized hunter. That was all that was being asked of it, so there was no pressure to change its shape. All that was needed for the domestication process to be successful was to reduce its natural shyness. Wild cats are notoriously retiring and secretive and, when cornered, become highly aggressive. In ancient Egypt, these qualities had to be removed for the cat to become a bold and friendly participant in human affairs. This must have been achieved by repeatedly hand-rearing wild kittens and by genetically selecting for those individuals that were more juvenile in their behaviour, even when they became adult. This would have created a cat that was a perpetual kitten towards its new, human companions, while at the same time remaining a savage predator towards rodents.

This modified kitten-cat must soon have become an animal very similar to the one with which millions share their homes today. But the changes involved were only behavioural. The visual images we have of domestic felines from the arts of ancient Egypt show us a cat that is physically almost indistinguishable from the North African Wild Cat. It would probably have stayed that way, but humans have always liked to vary the colours and markings of their domestic livestock – for individual identification and to distinguish them from their wild relatives. So, over the centuries, colour variations were favoured and retained for breeding. Gradually the domestic cat became a cat of many coats and colours. As it spread into colder regions, longer fur and stockier bodies must have developed as a natural response to the freezing winters.

In the 19th century, when high-status cat-keeping became a popular new pursuit, and cat shows began, there were already several types of pet cat available for competitive exhibition. There were tough, heavily built European short-haired cats, exotic long-haired cats from further East, and delicate, slender, hot-country cats from the Orient. And they came in a variety of attractive colours and coat patterns. There were no extremes of shape or size, but there was enough variation already present to create a number of separate pedigree types and classes. And so began a century of competitive genetic manipulation which saw the few early types blossom into nearly a hundred breeds, and the thousands of colour combinations that exist today.

Even so, despite strong pressure to find exciting new breeds, the cat has nearly always resisted any dramatic genetic alterations. Furthermore, on the rare occasions when these have occurred, they have encountered widespread hostility. The words 'deformity', 'atrocity' and 'abomination' are bandied about. Recently, when a short-legged cat was introduced, it caused an outrage of a kind that no Dachshund, Corgi or Basset Hound has ever had to face. Part of the reason for this is that the basic design of the cat is so graceful and so beautifully balanced that it seems almost sacrilegious to interfere with it. The body-design of the primitive dog is, by comparison, much more 'general purpose', and specialized breeding often seems to improve

on the original shape in a way that is difficult to achieve in the world of felines. As a result, the efforts of breeders have been largely confined to creating more exquisite colour-tones or coat patterns, with dramatic alterations in body-shape very much in the minority.

The details of feline genetics are too technical for a general encyclopedia of this kind, but here is a brief summary of the main genetic features and mutations:

Body Genes:

Manx (M): Dominant. Shortens the tail and spine to varying degrees.
Polydactyl (Pd): Dominant. Increases the number of toes, especially on front feet.
Japanese Bobtail (jb): Recessive. Shortens the tail without affecting the rest of the spine.
Scottish Fold (Fd): Dominant. Folds the ears forward.

(Other body genes include: the leg-shortening of the Munchkin; the ear-curling of the American Curl; the tail-shortening of the American Bobtail and the American Lynx.)

Hair Genes:

Long-haired (l): Recessive. Increases hair-length in the Persian, Angora, Maine Coon and others.
Rex (Cornish) (r): Recessive. Creates a short, curly coat with no guard hairs. (The same gene is found in the German Rex.)
Rex (Devon) (re): Recessive. Short, curly coat, with all hairs reduced.
Rex (Oregon) (ro): Recessive. Creates a short, curly coat with no guard hairs.
Wirehair (Wh): Dominant. Creates a stiff, wiry coat, as seen in the American Wirehair breed.
Sphynx (hr): Recessive. Creates a hairless cat.

(Other hair genes, yet to be fully investigated, include the other various Rex breeds, which may or may not be genetically distinct from the above three, and the new 'La Perm' mutation which creates tight ringlets of hair.)

Colour Genes:

Black (B): Dominant. A very, very dark brown hair colour which appears black to human eyes. It combines with the agouti gene (see below) to create tabby.
Dark Brown (b): Recessive to black. It dilutes black to dark brown. Cat breeders usually refer to this colour as either chestnut or chocolate.
Light Brown (bl): Recessive to both black and dark brown, it dilutes the coat to pale brown. Cat breeders often refer to this colour as cinnamon.
Orange (O): Dominant. Converts black and brown to orange and favours the agouti gene so that all orange cats are automatically tabbies. This is a sex-linked gene, almost all orange cats being males. The extremely rare females are usually sterile. Although, in genetics, orange is the official name for this colour, it has also in the past been called yellow, ginger, marmalade and red. All these names refer to the same gene, but the 'red' examples are sometimes improvements on the original form. The intensifying of the red colour is achieved by the addition of rufous polygenes, the minimizing of the tabby contrast-markings and the spreading-out of the blotches of the classic tabby pattern. Among pedigree cats these changes can greatly enhance the richness of the reddish coloration.
Dilution (d): Recessive. Reduces the density of the colour in each hair, creating a paler coat. The result may be grey, tan, beige or cream. The colours are often given special names by cat breeders: grey = blue; tan = lavender or lilac; beige = fawn. Together with black, dark brown, light brown and orange, this gives the pedigree cat eight basic colours.
Burmese (cb): Recessive. Creates a slight albinism that reduces black to sable.
Siamese (cs): Recessive. Creates an intermediate albinism giving the cat a pale body with dark extremities. The albinism of this gene can only operate on the warmer parts of the body. The cooler extremities (or 'points') are not influenced by it and retain their dark colour.

Blue-eyed Albino (ca): Recessive. Creates an almost total albinism. The cat has a pure white coat but does not have the typical pink eyes of the full albino.
Albino (c): Recessive to full-colour and also to all the partially albino colours. Creates a white coat with pink eyes. In cats this is a rare condition.
Agouti (A): Dominant. Creates a coat of banded or ticked hairs.
Solid (a): Recessive. The non-agouti gene which, in the absence of the orange gene, results in a self-coloured cat.
Tabby (Mackerel) (T): Dominant. Creates a coat pattern of thin, dark lines on an agouti background. This is the original wild cat camouflage pattern. The Spotted Tabby is a Mackerel Tabby with its lines broken up into spots by the action of polygene interference.
Tabby (Classic) (tb): Recessive. Creates large dark blotches and swirls on an agouti background.
Tipping (I): Dominant. Tipped hairs are produced by the action of a colour-inhibitor gene that leaves only the ends of the hairs darkened. The inhibition expresses itself in varying degrees. Slight inhibition, with the darker area of each hair extending quite a way down the hair is called 'Smoke'; moderate inhibition is called Shaded; and stronger colour-inhibition, with only the very ends of the hair darkened, is called 'Shell' or 'Chinchilla'.
White-spotting (S): Dominant. Creates variable areas of white that mask other colours. Most likely to affect the lower regions of the cat.
White (W): Dominant. Suppresses all colours to produce an all-white coat. Cats with the dominant white gene and blue eyes frequently suffer from hearing difficulties. In a recent study, 54 per cent of such animals were discovered to be deaf.
Van (Wv). Is a variant of the previous one, suppressing colour everywhere except on the tail and parts of the head, as seen in the Turkish Van Cat.

These are some of the main characteristics that are of particular interest in the genetics of domestic cats. New information is being gathered all the time, just as new mutations are being discovered by observant cat specialists. (For further details see separate entries on Hair, Coat Colours and Markings, and the various individual colours.)

Bibliography:

More detailed information can be obtained from two standard works on feline genetics:
1955. Jude, A.C. *Cat Genetics*. All-Pets Books, Fond du Lac, Wisconsin.
1971. Robinson, R. *Genetics for Cat Breeders*. Pergamon Press, Oxford. (Second, enlarged edition in 1977)

Note: There is also an excellent, illustrated section on this subject in *The Book of the Cat* (1980. Edited by Michael Wright and Sally Walters. Pan Books, London, pages 19–49).

Felis

Feline Term. *Felis* is the scientific name for the genus that contains all the species of small cats. It is Latin in origin and has two possible derivations. The first is from *fe*, meaning to bear young, and referring to the cat's reputation for fecundity. (The words *fecund* and *foetus* come from the same root.) The second is from *fell*, referring to the cat's role in 'felling' mice. We will probably never know for sure whether *Felis* was meant to be 'the bearer of young' or 'the feller of mice', but this is perhaps less interesting than the fact that the word has given us the valuable and widely used term *feline*.

Felix, the famous cartoon cat. He appeared in the first ever 'talkie' film cartoon and dominated the 1920s. He was clearly the inspiration for the figure of Mickey Mouse, who did not appear until 1928.

Felix

Cartoon Cat. Felix the Cat was the first of the three famous animated cartoon cats. He appeared as early as 1919 in *Feline Follies* for Paramount. He went unchallenged for many years until MGM introduced Tom and Jerry in 1939 and Warner Brothers launched their rival, Sylvester, in 1945. Created by Pat Sullivan and animated by Otto Messmer, Felix dominated the film cartoons of the 1920s. His character was that of a resilient survivor in a hostile world. His

name was derived from 'felicity' and he was deliberately designed to be a black cat who was also a hero, in order to counteract the hostile superstitions that still linked such cats to witchcraft and evil. Marcel Brion wrote of him: 'He is honest, generous, fearless, and optimistic. He is ingenious and fertile in resourcefulness . . . [He has] two mental attitudes: astonishment and curiosity. The virtues of poets and scholars.'

Felix appeared in several hundred animated films and had the distinction of starring in the first ever 'talkie' cartoon, even before the birth of Mickey Mouse, who was clearly a derivative figure. He also became the first moving image to be seen on television, having been used in an experimental test by NBC in 1928. In addition, he was immensely popular in strip-cartoon form in newspapers and comic books, a separate career that he began in 1923. In the 1960s he made a comeback on television, in a modernized form, with a further 260 episodes of *Felix the Cat.*

Bibliography:

1991. Canemaker. J. Felix. *The Twisted Tale of the World's Most Famous Cat.* New York.

Feral Cat

Domestic Cat. Ever since the African Wild Cat was domesticated by the ancient Egyptians, individual animals have reverted to the semi-wild state. Some have wandered off, others have been abandoned. With their natural hunting instincts undiluted by the domestication process, these feral cats have been able to survive and establish territories and social groupings.

In many urban centres there are whole communities of such cats, feeding on city rodents and anything they can find in human garbage. Such animals are frequently in poor condition, but many of them survive well enough to breed and to continue the process of increasing independence from human aid. In rural areas similar trends have occurred, with feral cats frequently interbreeding with the local wild cats.

It is estimated that worldwide there are literally millions of feral cats eking out an existence at the present time. Because domestication has involved a dramatic increase of the feline breeding rate, these cats quickly become overpopulated. True wild cats, with their much slower breeding rates, do not suffer from this problem.

Many animal welfare organizations do what they can to help this situation. Some organize the routine feeding of feral cat communities, although this approach is more often taken by helpful private individuals, who become attached to particular local groups of 'alley cats'. Others regularly trap feral cats, house them, give them veterinary care, neuter them and then find homes for them.

One scheme has employed the strategy of releasing such neutered cats back into their original city haunts. The logic behind this plan is that the neutered cats will occupy territories without breeding. Without their presence, other cats would quickly fill the vacuum left when they were trapped and removed. The neutered cats will continue to defend their territories for years, without the overall feline population growing. In that way they will be able to survive well enough and the spectre of teeming masses of half-starved cats will be avoided. Another technique has been to organize regular feeding of feral cats with food laced with contraceptives.

In some areas feline benefactors have offered sanctuary to large numbers of feral cats and cared for them as best they can. Mutsugoro's 'Cats Kingdom' in Japan is an example of this approach. However, when the fate of feral cats is viewed as a worldwide problem, such attempts, brave as they may be, do not begin to solve the situation as a whole. That remains a task for the future, and the struggling feral population exists today as a permanent reminder of the way in which we have broken our contract with the cat – an animal we originally enlisted as a highly valued pest-controller and then gradually devalued until we were prepared to abandon it in huge numbers, leaving it to fend for itself as a wild animal, after we had made it tame.

Bibliography:

1946. Wilding, J.F. *Domestic Wild.* Animal Pictorial Books. (a photographic record of domestic cats living in the wild)

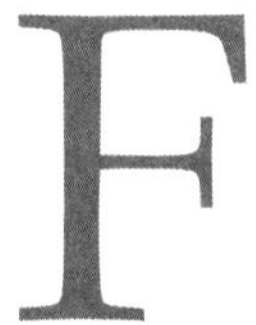

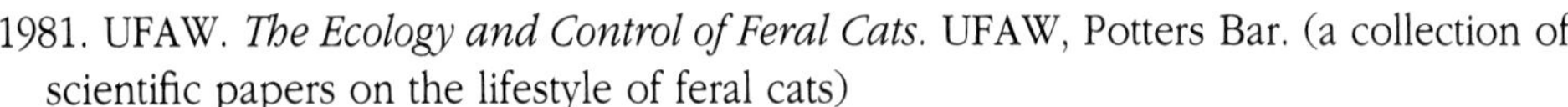

1981. UFAW. *The Ecology and Control of Feral Cats.* UFAW, Potters Bar. (a collection of scientific papers on the lifestyle of feral cats)
1982. Allaby, M. & Crawford, P. *The Curious Cat.* Michael Joseph, London. (a report on feral cats living in a farming community in Devon)
1982. Berkeley, E.P. *Maverick Cats. Encounters with Feral Cats.* New England Press, Vermont. (observations of feral cats in rural Vermont)
1983. Tabor, R. *The Wild Life of the Domestic Cat.* Arrow Books, London. (a study of feral cats in urban environments in Britain)
1985. Angel, J. *Cats' Kingdom.* Souvenir Press, London. (a history of life in a large sanctuary for feral cats in Japan)
1989. UFAW. *Feral Cats: Suggestions for Control.* UFAW, Potters Bar.

Fettered Cat

Wild Feline. An early, alternative name for the Egyptian race of the Wild Cat *(Felis sylvestris),* now obsolete. The Fettered Cat was originally thought to be a separate species and was given the scientific title of *Felis maniculata.* The more usual name for the Egyptian Wild Cat was the Caffer Cat. It was also sometimes referred to as the Egyptian Cat, the Gloved Cat, or Rüppell's Cat, but in the 19th century, when these names were in common use, there was considerable confusion about how many species of wild cat existed. These names are now obsolete and all the forms of wild cat to which they referred are considered local subspecies of a single species.

The Fettered Cat *(Felis maniculata),* as illustrated in Edward Hamilton's 1896 book *The Wild Cat of Europe.* The name is now obsolete and the Fettered Cat is today thought of as merely a local Egyptian variant of the Wild Cat *(Felis sylvestris).*

Figaro

Cartoon Cat. Figaro appears as a lively kitten belonging to the wood-carver Gepetto, in Walt Disney's 1940 feature-length cartoon film *Pinocchio.*

Fighting

Feline Behaviour. Under wild conditions cat-fights are a rarity because there is plenty of space, but in the more crowded urban and suburban areas feline territories become squashed together and frequently overlap. This means that a great deal of squabbling and serious physical duelling occur, especially between rival tom-cats. Occasionally there are even killings or deaths resulting from battle injuries.

The primary objective of an attacking cat is to deliver a fatal neck-bite to its rival, employing much the same technique as when killing a prey. Because its opponent is of roughly the same size and strength, this lethal bite is hardly ever delivered. Indeed, the most craven and cowardly of rivals will defend itself to some extent, and a primary neck-bite is almost impossible to achieve.

Even the most savage and dominant individual, as he goes in to the attack, is fearful of the consequences of a 'last-ditch-stand' by his terrorized underling. Driven into a corner, the weakling will try anything, lashing out with sharp claws and possibly injuring the dominant cat in a way that may pose a serious threat to his future hunting success and therefore his very survival. So even an out-and-out attacker shows fear mixed with his aggression, when the final crunch of physical contact arrives.

A typical sequence goes as follows: the dominant animal spots a rival and approaches it, adopting a highly characteristic threat posture, walking tall on fully stretched legs so that it suddenly appears bigger than usual. This effect is increased by the erecting of the hairs along its back. Because the crest is greater towards the rear end of the animal, the line of its back slopes up towards the tail. This gives the attacking cat a silhouette which is the exact opposite of the crouching shape of the weaker rival, whose rear end is held low on the ground.

With the backs of his ears showing and a great deal of howling, growling and gurgling, the attacker advances in slow motion, watching for any sudden reaction from his cringing enemy. The noises made are startlingly hostile and it is hard to understand how anything so totally aggressive can ever have been misnamed as the tom-cat's 'love-song'.

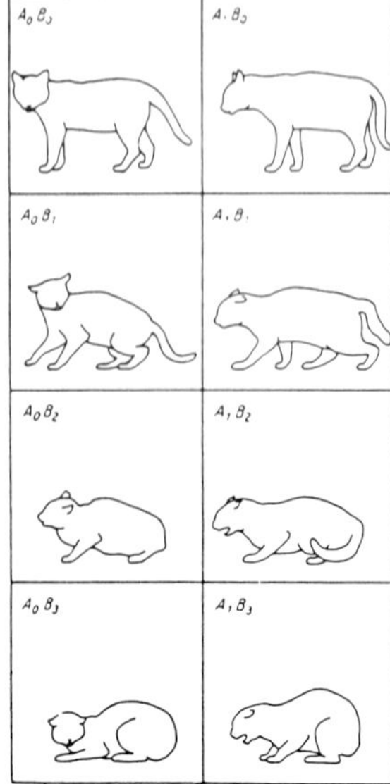

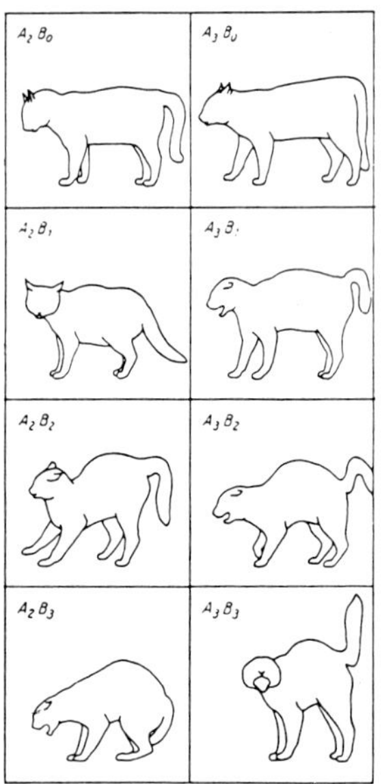

The varying aggressive postures of the cat, from Paul Leyhausen's classic study *Cat Behavior* (1979). Symbols: A = offensive mood; B = defensive mood; 1–4 = weak to strong motivation.

As the attacking cat comes very near to its rival, it performs a strange but highly characteristic head-twisting action. At a distance of about a metre (three feet) it raises its head up slightly and then tilts it over to one side, all the time fixating the enemy with its eyes. Then the attacker takes a slow step forward and tilts its head the other way. This may be repeated several times and appears to be a threat of a neck-bite to come, the head twisting into the biting position as much as to say 'this is what you will get'. In other words, the attacker acts out the 'intention movement' of the assault typical of the species.

If two cats of equal status meet and threaten one another, a long period of deadlock may follow, with each animal performing exactly the same slow, hostile approach, as if displaying in front of a mirror. The nearer they get, the slower and shorter are their movements, until they become frozen in a prolonged stalemate which may last for many minutes. Throughout this they will continue to give vent to their caterwauling howls and moans, but neither side will be prepared to capitulate. Eventually they may separate from one another in incredibly slow motion. To increase their speed would be tantamount to admitting weakness and would lead to an immediate attack from the rival, so they must both withdraw with almost imperceptible movements to retain their status.

Should these threats and counter-threats collapse into a serious fight, the action begins with one of the adversaries making a lunging attempt at a neck-bite. When this happens the opponent instantly twists round and defends itself with its own jaws, while at the same time striking out with its front feet, clinging on with its forepaws and then kicking wildly with its powerful back feet. This is the point at which the 'fur flies' quite literally, and the growling gives way suddenly to yowls and screams as the two animals roll and writhe around, biting, clawing and kicking.

This phase does not last for long. It is too intense. The rivals quickly pull apart and resume the threat displays, staring at one another and growling throatily once again. The assault is then repeated, perhaps several times, until one of them finally gives up and remains lying on the ground with its ears fully flattened. At this point the victor performs another highly characteristic display. It turns at right angles to the loser and, with great concentration, starts to sniff the ground, as though at that very moment there is an irresistibly delicious odour deposited there. The animal concentrates so hard on this sniffing that, were it not a regular feature of all fights, it would have the appearance of a genuine odour-check. But it is now only a ritual act, a victory display which signals to the cowering rival that its submission and capitulation have been accepted and that the battle is over. After the ceremonial sniffing the victor saunters slowly off and then, after a short while, the vanquished animal slinks away to safety.

Not all fights are conducted at such high intensity. Milder disputes are settled by 'paw-scrapping' in which the rivals swipe out at one another with extended claws. Slashing at their rival's head in this way, they may be able to settle their disagreement without the full ritual battle and all-in wrestling described above.

Films

Feline History. A number of feature films have employed cats in their titles, or used them as their central theme. In most cases – indicated by an asterisk (*) – there is a genuine feline element in the films, but in some the use of the word 'cat' in the title is merely symbolic or metaphorical. It is a sad commentary on surviving feline mythology that so many cat films involve elements of mystery, killing and horror, as though the earlier witchcraft associations of cats have yet to be completely obliterated. The films include the following:

1927 The Cat and the Canary (USA, B/W, silent): The original 'house of horror' comedy thriller, that spawned an entire genre.

1930 The Cat Creeps (USA, B/W, Universal): The first of three remakes of the silent classic 'The Cat and the Canary'.

1933 The Cat and the Fiddle (USA, B/W, MGM): A light musical comedy starring Jeanette Macdonald.

1934 *The Black Cat (USA, B/W, Universal): Horror film loosely based on the story by Edgar Allen Poe, starring Boris Karloff and Bela Lugosi.

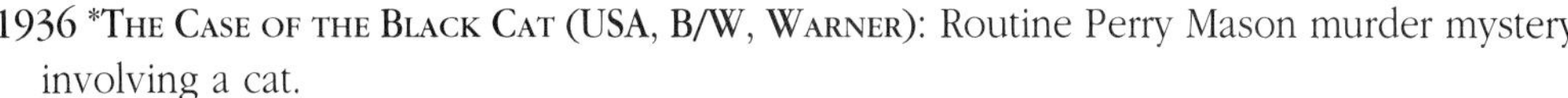

1936 *The Case of the Black Cat (USA, B/W, Warner): Routine Perry Mason murder mystery involving a cat.

1936 The Cat's Paw (USA, B/W): Harold Lloyd comedy about a Chinese gang war.

1939 The Cat and the Canary (USA, B/W, Paramount): A remake of the silent classic, starring Bob Hope and Paulette Goddard.

1941 *The Black Cat (USA, B/W, Universal): Murder mystery about a cat-loving recluse, starring Basil Rathbone and Gladys Cooper.

1942 *Cat People (USA, B/W, RKO): Horror classic about a beautiful girl being transformed into a lethal panther. The first monster film not to show its monster, relying entirely on suggestion. Starring Simone Simon.

1942 The Panther's Claw (USA, B/W, PRC): A routine blackmail and murder mystery.

1944 *The Curse of the Cat People (USA, B/W, RKO): A sequel to the 1942 classic, with the central figure a child who is haunted by the Cat People. Starring Simone Simon.

1946 The Cat Creeps (USA, B/W, Universal): A routine murder mystery, involving Egyptian curses and reincarnation. Unrelated to its earlier (1930) namesake.

1946 Catman of Paris (USA, B/W, Republic): Horror film about a mad killer who prowls the streets of Paris by night.

1948 *The Cat that Hated People (USA, MGM): A cartoon film about a Manhattan cat taking a trip to the moon.

1949 *The Big Cat (USA): Film drama set in the great outdoors, about families combining to defeat a maurading Mountain Lion, starring Preston Foster and Forrest Tucker.

1951 *Rhubarb (USA, Paramount): A comedy about a millionaire who leaves his entire fortune, including his baseball team, to a ginger cat called Rhubarb. Starring Ray Milland.

1952 *Androcles and the Lion (USA, B/W, RKO): In ancient Rome, a slave helps a lion by removing a thorn from its paw. Later, in the arena, the now captive lion refuses to devour the slave. Based on the play by Shaw and starring Victor Mature and Jean Simmons.

At the cinema, cats have all too often featured as savage killers, frequently with supernatural powers. To the hero of *The Incredible Shrinking Man* (1956), a sudden encounter with an ordinary tabby house-cat is a terrifying experience.

AUDREY HEPBURN, with her ginger tom co-star in *Breakfast at Tiffany's* (1961). In the film the animal was simply called Cat, but in real life he was a temperamental professional feline named Orangey.

1953 CAT WOMEN OF THE MOON (USA, B/W, 3-D PICTURES): Renowned as one of the worst films ever made, this is the story of astronauts finding the moon inhabited solely by savage cat women.

1954 TRACK OF THE CAT (USA, WARNER): A remake of The Big Cat, about a farming family menaced by a marauding Mountain Lion, symbolizing evil. Starring Robert Mitchum.

1958 *BELL, BOOK AND CANDLE. (COLUMBIA, USA): A romantic comedy about a modern-day witch and her familiar, a Siamese Cat called Pyewacket. Starring James Stewart and Kim Novak.

1958 CAT AND MOUSE (GB, B/W, ANVIL): Thriller directed by Paul Rotha.

1958 CAT GIRL (GB): An attractive girl develops predatory feline qualities.

1958 CAT ON A HOT TIN ROOF (USA, MGM): Tennessee Williams melodrama, starring Paul Newman and Elizabeth Taylor. (The victory of a cat on a hot tin roof is, in the author's words, 'just staying on it'.)

1961 *BREAKFAST AT TIFFANY'S (PARAMOUNT, USA): New York romantic comedy starring Audrey Hepburn as Holly Golightly and her cat called simply 'Cat'. The feline role was played by a ginger tom named 'Orangey'.

1961 *PUSS IN BOOTS (MEXICO): A Mexican interpretation of the well-known fairy-tale.

1961 *SHADOW OF THE CAT (GB, B/W, U-I): Another 'old dark house' horror story in which the murderers of the cat's mistress are brought to justice by the animal itself.

1963 *THE INCREDIBLE JOURNEY (USA, DISNEY): Three family pets, a Siamese Cat and two dogs, are stranded and must make their way home over 400 km (250 miles), experiencing many adventures on the way.

1963 *One Day, A Cat. (Czechoslovakia): A fantasy about a cat that wears spectacles, and the effect he has on the village where he lives when he removes them.

1963 *The Three Lives of Thomasina (USA, Disney): A children's film about a cat belonging to the daughter of a vet. Starring Susan Hampshire and Patrick McGoohan.

1963 *A Tiger Walks (USA, Disney): A children's film about a tiger that escapes from a circus. Starring Sabu.

1963 *Under the Yum Yum Tree (USA, Columbia): A lecherous landlord is followed around by a cat as he tries to seduce a college student, in a comedy starring Jack Lemmon and Carol Lynley.

1965 *Born Free (GB, Columbia): Based on the true-life story of Joy Adamson and her tame lioness, Elsa, in Africa, starring Virginia McKenna and Bill Travers.

1965 Cat Ballou (USA, Columbia): The use of the word 'cat' in the title is misleading, as it refers to an abbreviation of Catherine, the heroine of the film, played by Jane Fonda.

1965 * Clarence the Cross-eyed Lion (USA, MGM): An adventure comedy set in Africa and starring an amazingly well-trained, gentle, cross-eyed lion called Clarence, who went on to star in the television series Daktari.

1965 *That Darn Cat! (USA, Disney): A small town comedy with a Siamese Cat playing the central role, helping to trap bank robbers. Starring Hayley Mills.

1965 What's New Pussycat? (USA/France, UA/Famous Artists): Woody Allen comedy in which the 'pussycats' are the girls pursued by Peter O'Toole. Also starring Peter Sellers and Ursula Andress.

1966 *Cat! (USA): Children's film about a friendship between a boy and a wildcat. The boy's kindness to the cat is later rewarded when the animal saves him from danger.

1968 The Pink Panther (USA, UA): Inspector Clouseau comedy about a famous jewel thief, starring Peter Sellers and David Niven.

1969 *Eye of the Cat (USA, Universal): A cat-hating nephew attempts to murder his wealthy cat-loving aunt, but she is saved by her colony of loyal felines. Starring Eleanor Parker, Michael Sarrazin and Gayle Hunnicutt.

1969 *Robinson Crusoe and the Tiger (Mexico, Avco Embassy): Based on the novel by Defoe, but with the the addition of a pet tiger for the shipwrecked hero.

1970 *The Aristocats (USA, Disney):
Cartoon feature-length film about an attempt to rob two cats of their rightful inheritance.

1971 *Fritz the Cat (USA, Fritz Productions): Adult, feature-length cartoon film notorious for its obscenity and violence, concerning the adventures of a New York alley cat called Fritz.

1972 *Living Free (GB, Columbia): Sequel to 'Born Free', continuing the dramatized biography of Joy Adamson and her tame lions in Africa, starring Susan Hampshire and Nigel Davenport.

1972 *The Night of the Thousand Cats (Mexico): A horror film about a mad aristocrat living in a castle containing a colony of man-eating cats whose favourite diet appears to be beautiful young women.

1972 *Shamus (Columbia, USA): A routine murder mystery starring Burt Reynolds, Dyan Cannon and the famous TV cat 'Morris'.

1973 The Cat (France, Danon): Drama concerning a trapeze artist and his wife, starring Jean Gabin and Simone Signoret.

1974 *Harry and Tonto (USA, TCF): An elderly widower makes an epic trip across America with his pet cat Tonto, following his eviction from his New York apartment. Starring Art Carney in an Oscar-winning performance.

1974 The Return of the Pink Panther (GB, UA): A sequel to the hugely successful 'Pink Panther' of 1968, starring Peter Sellers and Herbert Lom.

1975 *I Am A Cat (Japan): A cat's-eye-view of a human family in turn-of-the-century Japan.

1976 The Pink Panther Strikes Again (GB, UA): A second sequel in the 'Pink Panther' series, again starring Peter Sellers and Herbert Lom.

Donald Pleasance as the arch-villain Blofeld, with his pampered Chinchilla in the James Bond thriller *You Only Live Twice* (1967). The cat's name was Solomon.

1977 *The Uncanny (Canada/GB, Rank/Cinevideo/Tor): A collection of three horror stories about 'evil' cats, starring Peter Cushing and Ray Milland.

1978 *The Cat from Outer Space (USA, Disney): A live-action Disney feature film concerning a super-intelligent extra-terrestrial cat that finds itself stranded on Earth. Starring Roddy McDowall and and Sandy Duncan.

1979 The Cat and the Canary (GB, Gala): A second remake of the silent classic, starring Honor Blackman and Edward Fox.

1980 *Our Johnny (Austria): The disruptive impact of a cat on an ordinary, peaceful family.

1981 *Roar (USA, Noel Marshall): Animal adventure story involving a large number of tame lions. Starring Tippi Hedren.

1982 *Cat People (USA, Universal): A remake of the earlier classic horror film. Whenever she makes love, a beautiful girl changes into a lethal feline and must kill in order to return to human form. Starring Nastasia Kinski and Malcolm McDowell.

1982 Trail of the Pink Panther (GB, MGM): The third sequel to the 'Pink Panther', starring Peter Sellers and Herbert Lom.

1983 The Curse of the Pink Panther (GB, MGM-UA): The final film in the 'Pink Panther' series, starring Herbert Lom and David Niven.

1985 *The Black Cat (Italy): A paranormal mystery about a cat in an English village that may be causing the deaths of villagers.

1985 *Cat's Eye (USA, Famous Films): A collection of three horror stories involving cats, starring James Woods and Drew Barrymore.

1992 *Dangerous Desire (Canada, Tomcat Productions): A male dancer with a genetic disease is treated by being injected with DNA from a domestic cat. As a result, he becomes increasingly acrobatic, sexually voracious and predatory.

1992 *Sleepwalkers (USA, Columbia): A Stephen King horror story. A sleepwalker is defined as 'a nomadic shape-shifting creature of human and feline origin'. To survive, the creature must suck the life out of virgins and to accomplish this they must first change into the shape of a big cat. A tabby cat called Clovis comes to the virgin's rescue with the help of other local cats.

1993 *The Black Cat An adaptation of Edgar Allen Poe's horror story about a man's hatred for his wife's cat.

1994 *The Lion King (USA, Disney): A feature-length cartoon film in the Walt Disney tradition, telling the story of the trials of a young lion cub called Simba, following the death of his father.

Fire Cat

Wild Feline. An early, alternative name for the Flat-headed Cat *(Felis planiceps)*, of tropical, southern Asia.

Fishing Cat

Wild Feline. *(Felis viverrina)* In earlier days it was referred to as the Large Tiger Cat but this was abandoned because of possible confusion with the South American species now widely called the Tiger Cat *(Felis tigrina)*.

A nocturnal hunter that prefers dense cover, the Fishing Cat is rarely observed in the wild. It lives mostly among the reed beds and long grasses of riverbanks, marshes and swamps. It is not, apparently, a good climber.

It is a rather nondescript, spotted cat, with average, if somewhat clumsy proportions including rather short legs and heavy head. The backs of the ears carry 'eye-spots', with a white patch inside a black ring. The claws are only semi-retractile.

It is a powerful, assertive, medium-sized cat which, despite its name, takes a wide variety of terrestrial as well as aquatic prey. On land, it has a macabre reputation for carrying off unattended human infants, while their mothers are working nearby.

The Fishing Cat *(Felis viverrina)* at the water's edge. This short-legged species has partially webbed feet and is an excellent swimmer, capable of catching quite large fish.

It appears to attack anything it can overpower, including sheep, calves and feral dogs. On one occasion, when a Fishing Cat was being pursued by a trio of hunting dogs, their intended victim eventually turned on them with spectacular results. One dog was thrown to the ground, another was struck so hard with a forepaw that its jaw was broken, and the third was carried off and eaten. In the water, the Fishing Cat can swim strongly, not only on the surface, but also submerged, with its eyes open. It uses this last ability to enable it to approach waterfowl, especially ducks, and grab them from below. It also lives up to its name by occasionally catching fish. In addition, it is believed to eat snakes, frogs and crustaceans.

Size: Length of Head and Body: 75–86 cm (29½–34 in). Tail: 25–33 cm (10–13 in). Weight: 8–14 kg (17½–31 lb).

Distribution: The Fishing Cat has a wide range in southern Asia, from India through Nepal, Burma, Thailand, Malaysia, Indonesia and southern China to Taiwan.

Although this species has attracted the fur-trade, it is impossible to say how rare it is today because it is so little known in the wild. It certainly appears to be rare, but this may simply reflect its ability to remain invisible to the human eye.

Flame Point

Coat Colour. Flame point is an alternative name for red point. The term 'flame' is only used instead of red when it occurs in a colourpoint pattern. One variant has been recorded: in America, a cat with extremities showing red and orange tabby markings is sometimes called a Flame Lynx Point.

Flat-Headed Cat

Wild Feline. *(Felis planiceps)* In the 19th century it was sometimes called the Fire Cat. It is known locally as the Kucing Hutan. A rare, elusive and little known fishing cat about the size of a domestic cat, it has a heavy coat of long, soft hairs. The colour of its ticked coat is described as 'dark brown with a silvery tinge'. The lower parts of the body are whitish in colour, with

THE FLAT-HEADED CAT *(Felis planiceps)* of South-east Asia, is an unusual, little-known cat, with small rounded ears and huge dark eyes. It favours the river-banks of thickly forested regions, where it hunts for fish and frogs.

some spotting. It has a characteristic, flattened and pointed skull, small ears set low on the sides of the head, short legs and a very short, heavily furred tail. Its claws are only semi-retractile.

It lives in low country, favouring riverbanks in forests. A nocturnal hunter, this feline is said to prey mainly on fish, frogs and crustaceans. Captive specimens have been seen to 'wash' food like raccoons. They were so aquatic that they would take a piece of fish with their heads submerged well below the surface. They ignored live sparrows even though these were easy to catch.

Size: Length of Head + Body: 40–60 cm (15½–6½ in). Tail: 15–20 cm (6–8 in). Weight: 5–8 kg (11–17½ lb).

Distribution: Confined to southern Thailand, the Malay Peninsula, Sumatra and Borneo.

FLEHMEN

FELINE BEHAVIOUR. Every so often a cat can be seen to pause and then adopt a curious sneering expression, as if disgusted by something. When first observed, this reaction was in fact called an 'expression of disgust' and described as the cat 'turning up its nose' at an unpleasant smell, such as urine deposited by a rival cat.

This interpretation is now known to be an error. The truth is almost the complete opposite. When the cat makes this strange grimace, known as the *flehmen* response, it is in reality appreciating to the full a delicious fragrance. We know this because tests have proved that urine from female cats in strong sexual condition produces powerful grimacing in male cats, while urine from females not in sexual condition produces a much weaker reaction.

The response involves the following elements: the cat stops in its tracks, raises its head slightly, draws back its upper lip and opens its mouth a little. Inside the half-opened mouth it is sometimes possible to see the tongue flickering or licking the roof of the mouth. The cat sniffs and gives the impression of an almost trancelike concentration for a few moments. During this time it slows its breathing rate and may even hold its breath for several seconds, after sucking in air. All the time it stares in front of it as if in a kind of reverie.

If this behaviour were to be likened to a hungry man inhaling the enticing smells emanating from a busy kitchen, it would not be too far from the truth, but there is an important difference: the cat is employing a sense organ that human beings lack. The cat's sixth sense is to be found in a small structure situated in the roof of the mouth. It is a little tube opening into the mouth just behind the upper front teeth. Known as the vomero-nasal, or Jacobsen's organ, it is about 1.2 cm (½ inch) long and is highly sensitive to airborne chemicals. Best described as a taste–smell organ, it is extremely important to cats when they are reading the odour-news deposited around their territories. During human evolution, when we became increasingly dominated by visual input to the brain, we lost the use of our Jacobsen's organs, of which only a tiny trace now remains, but for cats it is of great significance and explains the strange, snooty, gaping expression they adopt occasionally as they go about the social round.

Flyball

Fictional Cat. The hero of Ruthven Todd's *Space Cat* (1952), Flyball was an intelligent, resourceful cat who saved his human companion's life during their first trip to the moon. He learned to communicate telepathically with his Captain and even managed to mate with the last of the Martian cats, a horizontally striped female by the name of Moofa, producing an interplanetary litter of kittens.

Fontanier's Cat

Wild Feline. An earlier name for Temminck's Cat *(Felis temminckii)*. Originally it was recorded as a separate species *(Felis tristis)*, but it now thought to be no more than a local race.

Food Preparation

Feline Behaviour. Packaged cat food may be carefully balanced nutritionally, but it lacks the complexity of the 'kill' and makes it impossible for the cat to exhibit its specialized food-preparation activities, behaviour that has evolved over millions of years as part of the feline predatory pattern. To observe this, it is necessary to take a close look at exactly what happens after the prey has been dispatched.

Immediately after the kill, a cat goes through a strange routine of 'taking a walk'. Unless it is starving, it paces up and down for a while, as if feeling the need to release the tension of the hunt-and-kill sequence. Only then does it settle down to eating the prey. This pause may be important for the cat's digestion, giving its system a chance to calm down after the adrenalin-excitement of the moments that have just passed. During this pause a prey that has been feigning death may try to escape and, on very rare occasions, succeeds in doing so before the cat can return to the hunting mood.

When the cat finally approaches its prey to eat it, there is the problem of how to convert it for easy swallowing. Small rodents cause no difficulties. They are simply eaten head first and the skins, if swallowed, are regurgitated later. Some cats separate out the gall-bladder and intestines and avoid eating them, but others are too hungry to care and gobble down the entire animal without any fuss.

Birds are another matter because of their feathers, but even here the smaller species are eaten in their entirety, with the exception of tail and wing feathers. Birds the size of blackbirds and thrushes are plucked a little before eating, but then the cat impatiently starts its meal. After a while it breaks off to remove a few more feathers, before eating further. It repeats this a number of times as the feeding proceeds. Bigger birds, however, demand more systematic plucking, and

if a cat is successful at killing a pigeon or something larger, it must strip away the feathers before it begins to eat.

To pluck a pigeon, a cat must first hold down the body of the bird with its front feet, seize a clump of feathers between its teeth, pull its jaw-clamped head upwards with some force, and then finally open its mouth and shake its head vigorously from side to side to remove any clinging plumage. As it shakes its head, it spits hard and makes special licking-out movements with its tongue, trying to clear its mouth of stubbornly attached feathers. It may pause from time to time to lick its flank fur. This last action puts grooming into reverse. Normally the tongue cleans the fur, but here the fur cleans the tongue. Any last remnants are removed and then the next plucking action can take place.

The urge to pluck feathers from a large bird appears to be inborn. This was revealed by tests with wild cats living in zoo cages where they had always been given chunks of meat as their regular diet. When offered dead pigeons for the first time in their lives they set about plucking them without any hesitation. One cat became so excited at seeing a fully feathered bird that its ecstatic plucking session went on and on until the bird was completely naked. Instead of settling down to eat it, the cat then turned its attention to the grass on which it was sitting and began plucking that, too. Time and again, it tugged out tufts of grass from the turf and shook them away with the characteristic feline bird-plucking movements until eventually, having exhausted its long-frustrated urge to prepare its food, the cat finally bit into the flesh of the pigeon and began its meal. Clearly, plucking has its own motivation and can be frustrated by captivity, just like other, more obvious drives.

The strangest feature of feather-plucking is that small cats from the Old World perform it differently from those from the New World. In his classic study of feline predation, the German zoologist Paul Leyhausen discovered that all the Old World species he tested perform a zigzag tugging movement leading to the full shake of the head, while those from the Americas tug the feathers out in a long vertical movement, straight up, and only then perform the sideways shake. It appears that, despite superficial similarities between the small cats from the two sides of the Atlantic, they do in reality have some significant differences, suggesting that they belong to two distinct groups.

Food Rejection

Feline Behaviour. Pet cats sometimes approach a dish of food, sniff it, and wander off. This rejection of an apparently attractive meal has puzzled many cat-owners. Assuming the cat is healthy and the food is fresh and nutritious, there are five possible reasons for the 'finicky' response of the domestic cat.

The first has to do with the natural size of cat meals. Cats prefer to eat small meals on frequent occasions. Considering the size of their natural prey – mice and voles – this is not so surprising. Unfortunately for domestic cats, their human owners rarely have the time to offer them mouse-sized meals, preferring to spoon out big dishfuls of cat food at mealtimes. If the amount of meat on a mouse is compared with that placed on a cat's food dish, it is clear that the average pet cat meal is the equivalent of about five mice. Although this is convenient for busy human owners, it is too much for the cat to eat at once. Usually, the cat eats a mouse-worth of food and then strolls off to digest it, returning later for another rodent-sized portion, and so on, until all the food is gone. If a cat refuses to touch a new dish of food, it may simply be that the animal is not, at that moment, ready for its next 'kill'.

A second reason has to do with the cat's mood. When sex rears its head, a domestic cat will temporarily go off its food. If the weather becomes hotter or more humid the same loss of appetite occurs.

Third, many cats 'adopt' subsidiary owners. Neighbours are often solicited by wandering cats for tasty titbits and if these become plentiful, the cat's appetite at its original home may suffer. Cats that do the rounds of friendly humans often show fluctuations in their hunger levels that are inexplicable to their true owners.

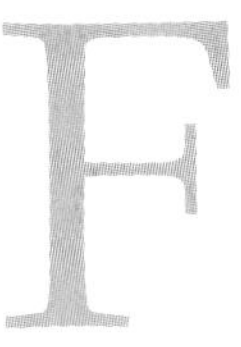

Fourth, a cat may be receiving its food in a place where it is uneasy about eating. Cats do not like to feed in a spot that is too brightly lit, too noisy or too busy. In such cases, moving the food dish to a quieter position may make all the difference.

Finally, there may be a 'food variety mechanism' at work. Cats, like many animals (including humans), like to switch from one type of food to another from time to time. In the wild this prevents them from becoming totally dependent on one particular source of food and also gives them a slightly more varied and therefore nutritionally safer diet. This may explain why, on certain days, they reject the 'same old food' and why pet food manufacturers have been so attentive in recent years to the business of creating a wide variety of packaged dishes.

FOREIGN

DOMESTIC CATS. In the world of pedigree cats, the term 'Foreign' has a specific meaning. It is one of the seven main categories of pedigree cat at British cat shows (along with Longhair, Semi-Longhair, British Shorthair, Burmese, Oriental and Siamese). It describes a type of cat that has a long slim body, long slender legs, a long pointed tail and a wedge-shaped head with large ears.

The category 'Foreign Cats' forms a group of the following breeds: Abyssinian; Somali; Russian Blue; Korat; Cornish Rex; Devon Rex; Asian; Tonkinese.

The GCCF defines cats of the Foreign Group as follows: 'They have a lithe elegance, intermediate in type between the chunky solidity of the Persians and British Shorthairs and the elongation of the Siamese and Orientals.'

FOREIGN SHORTHAIR

DOMESTIC BREED. This was the original name given to Siamese Cats that lack the typical points markings (of pale coat with darker extremities). They were first given this name by British breeders in the 1920s, at a time when self-coloured Siamese were in need of a new title to

A FOREIGN SHORTHAIR, the Foreign White Cat is a self-coloured Siamese Cat lacking the usual coloured points. This cat illustrates the confusion that exists over the names of some breeds. In America it is known simply as the white colour form of the Oriental Shorthair.

distinguish them from the traditional Siamese. They gained full recognition in Britain in the 1960s. Recognition in the United States was soon to follow, although there they were given a new name – Oriental Shorthairs. In Britain, the GCCF followed suit and adopted this name-change in the early 1990s. They switched the names of specific colour forms from Foreign Shorthair to Oriental Shorthair in all breeds except the Foreign White (see entry).

It is said that these cats have an unusual personality, in that they are prepared to walk on a collar and leash with their owners and find physical restraint less disturbing than other cat breeds. This makes them especially suited to travelling and showing. (For further details see Oriental Shorthair.)

Foreign White Cat

Domestic Breed. Essentially, this is a pure white Siamese. A dramatically elegant breed, it was created by crossing Siamese with white short-haired cats.

In the United States the Foreign White is classified as just another colour form of the Oriental Shorthair, but in Britain the GCCF still treats it as a separate breed. There is a reason for this. When, in the early 1990s, the GCCF decided, for reasons of clarity, to abandon the use of the word 'Foreign' for certain Oriental breeds, the breeders of the Foreign White objected, insisting that they wanted to keep their time-honoured name. This request was granted and so the Foreign White became the only one of the many Oriental Shorthair colours to retain its old name.

Although it is a white cat with blue eyes, a combination that is usually associated with deafness, the Foreign White does not suffer from this disability. (For further details see entry for Oriental Shorthair.)

Breed Club:

Foreign White Cat Society. Address: 17 George Street, Bletchley, Bucks., MK2 2NR, England.

Foss

Pet Cat. The much-loved companion of Victorian artist and humorist Edward Lear, Foss was a less than beautiful feline with a startled expression, a bloated body and a greatly abbreviated tail. He became famous through the delightful cartoons of him drawn by Lear, who even went to the lengths of showing him a range of heraldic postures, such as couchant, passant, rampant, and regardant. Lear published that series of drawings under the title *The Heraldic Blazon of Foss the Cat*.

A striped tom-cat, Foss arrived in the Lear household as a kitten in 1873. His tail was cut off by a servant called Giorgio because he believed that if a cat left its tail in a house, it would never stray from there.

Lear was so concerned over his cat's comfort that when, late in life, he was moving to a new house in San Remo, he instructed his architects to design his new abode as an exact replica of his old one. This, he felt, would assist the cat to make the transition to the new house with the minimum of disturbance to its feline routine.

Edward Lear's striped tom-cat, Foss, immortalized by his owner's delightful sketches. The end of the cat's tail had been cut off by a superstitious servant, who believed that this would stop the animal from straying.

When Foss died in 1887, he was honoured with a full burial in a grave in Lear's Italian garden, topped by a large tombstone informing the world (incorrectly) that he had lived to the ripe old age of 31. Why Lear chose to exaggerate his cat's lifespan in this way is not at all clear. He even confirmed the error in a letter in which he said: 'whoever has known me for 30 years has known that for all that time my cat Foss has been part of my solitary life.' In reality, the cat was only 14 when he died. Perhaps Lear, who himself died two months later at the age of 76, was becoming confused in his final days.

Frank, Anne

Cat Owner. Three cats – Tommy, Boche and Mouschi – became the wartime companions of Anne Frank, the German Jewish girl who, with the posthumous publication of her *Diary of a Young Girl* in 1947, became a symbol of Jewish suffering during World War II. Having fled with her family to Amsterdam to escape Nazi persecution, the 13-year-old girl was forced to go into

hiding in a warehouse attic in 1942. She and her family shared their secret hiding place with the cats for three years before being betrayed by informers.

When she first arrived at her hiding place she found two of the cats already there. One was an aggressive warehouse cat which was always the first to attack, so she called it Boche. The other, an attic cat, was repeatedly forced to retaliate, but always won in the end, so she called it Tommy. The third was Mouschi, the pet of the 15-year-old son of some family friends, who eventually joined the Franks in hiding in the attic.

French Cats

Domestic Breeds. In the middle of the 19th century, Long-haired Cats, as a group, were sometimes referred to as 'French Cats' because so many were being imported to England from France, where they had become popular as high-status pets. Later, when the English breeders had developed them further, the term was dropped and never used again.

Freya's Cats

Legendary Cats. The great chariot of the blue-eyed, blonde goddess Freya was drawn through the heavens by a pair of magnificent cats. These legendary felines symbolized the twin qualities of their Scandinavian mistress, namely fecundity and ferocity. Like real cats they were normally affectionate and loving, but were fierce if roused.

Freya, the Viking goddess of sex and fecundity, riding one of her magnificent cats through the skies. From a wall-painting in the Schleswig Cathedral.

Freya (or Freyja) was originally the Viking goddess of sex, love and fertility. She wept golden tears and roamed the night skies in the form of a she-goat. She wore a special necklace, a symbol of her sexuality, which she obtained by sleeping with each of the four dwarfs who fashioned it. She was the patroness of a witchcraft cult that involved trances, foretelling the future, and the performance of orgiastic rites.

In 15th-century Germany the cult of Freya enjoyed a revival that was ultimately to cause thousands of innocent cats untold pain and misery. Because of the ancient association between Freya and her felines, the German followers of her cult used to round up as many cats as possible and forcibly introduce them into the ceremonies at their wild nocturnal orgies. Not surprisingly, this led to a powerful connection, in the popular mind, between cats and witchcraft. Then, when Pope Innocent VIII formally condemned the followers of Freya, the unfortunate cats were caught in the same net. In his edict of 1484 he declared that all women who worshipped Freya should be burned at the stake, and their cats burned with them.

According to one source, the holocaust that followed led to the deaths by fire of ten per cent of the entire female population of Germany. Inevitably, it also led to the torture and killing of a vast number of cats. This nightmare phase of feline history persisted through the 16th, 17th and 18th centuries, the onslaught spreading out from Germany across the whole of Europe and even to the New World. It did not die out until the 19th century, when, at last, Victorian England began to take a more enlightened attitude towards animal life. (For further details see Norwegian Forest Cat and Witchcraft.)

Fritz

Cartoon Cat. Fritz first appeared in 1965 in strip cartoon form in underground comic books. He was created by the artist Robert Crumb, who based Fritz on his family cat Fred. Originally, as a teenager, he had made drawings of Fritz for private amusement, but later, in the liberated atmosphere of the 1960s, they began to appear publicly. They were sexually outrageous and caused considerable controversy. Fritz was as different from a Disney cat as it is possible to be. He mouthed endless four-letter words and added to his obscenities by undertaking blatant sexual adventures. An expert on Comic Book history described the cat as 'a con-man, a sex maniac, and totally incorrigible'.

Fritz developed a huge cult following, especially in the hippie sub-culture of the 1960s. Despite the anger he caused, Crumb was solemnly described as 'a kind of American Hogarth . . . who gave back to cartooning the scatological exuberance it had during the Regency.'

Fritz the Cat, the outrageously obscene cartoon character who developed a cult following in the 1960s. Fritz starred in the first-ever X-rated cartoon film.

In 1971 a young film animator called Ralph Bakshi turned Fritz into an adult film star. His cinema feature called *Fritz the Cat* was the first ever X-rated cartoon film, full of sexually explicit material. One critic described it as 'a fast-moving orgy of outrage'. Another described it as 'a bitter and snarling satire that refuses to curl up in anyone's lap'. When Crumb saw what Bakshi had done, he was so furious that he tried to have the film banned. When this failed he took revenge (and neatly prevented any sequel) by drawing a cartoon strip in 1972 called *Fritz the Cat 'Superstar'* in which Fritz is murdered by a deranged ostrich who drives an icepick through the lecherous cat's skull.

Frost

Coat Colour. Frost Point is an American name for Lilac Point.

Garfield

Cartoon Cat. Garfield is a strip cartoon cat whose great appeal depends entirely on the fact that he is a complete slob. Created by Jim Davis in 1977, he is a fat, greedy, lazy, selfish and sometimes aggressive animal, but he is quite unrepentant. 'Grovelling,' he says, 'is not one of my strong suits.' He gets his own way, bites the postman, attacks dogs, hates jogging, refuses to diet, hangs from the ceiling, sleeps too much, watches too much television, hates cat food, loves lasagne, knocks things over and never apologizes. With charm like that it was inevitable that he would soon become a best-seller (*Garfield at Large*, 1980) and would be syndicated in 700 newspapers.

Gautier, Théophile

Cat Owner. The French Romantic author Théophile Gautier (1811–1872) was a fanatical cat lover who shared his life with a succession of unusual cats. He describes some of them in his book *La Ménagerie Intime: Childebrand* was a splendid gutter-cat, striped black and tan . . . with a distant tigerish look. *Madame Théophile* was a red and white cat who stole food from the author when morsels were 'on their way from my plate to my mouth'. (See separate entry.) *Don Pierrot de Navarre* was an immaculate white cat that watched the author's pen closely as he wrote, and 'would snatch the pen out of my hand' as if to take over the writing himself. *Séraphita* was another pure white cat, who was dreamy, reserved, luxuriating and addicted to perfume. Don Pierrot and Séraphita produced three jet black kittens called *Enjoras, Gavroche* and *Eponine,* named after characters in Victor Hugo's *Les Miserables*. Eponine (see separate entry) regularly dined at table with her master. *Zizi* was a magnificent Angora who enjoyed making music by walking up and down the keyboard of Gautier's piano. *Cléopatre* was Eponine's daughter, a tawny-black cat that liked to stand on three legs, 'her fourth lifted up like a classical lion that has lost its marble ball'.

An illustration by Mrs William Chance to her (1899) English translation of Théophile Gautier's *La Ménagerie Intime*.

Gautier is said to have loved cats so passionately that, at times, 'he cared for nothing else', and his writings about them clearly reveal the extent of his obsession.

Geoffroy's Cat

Wild Feline. *(Felis geoffroyi)* Also known in the past as the Spotted Tiger-cat. Referred to locally as the Gato Montés. It was named after the French naturalist Geoffroy St. Hilaire.

A small, spotted South American cat, it is about the same size as a large domestic cat, but with a slightly shorter tail and a slightly longer head. The dark spots are small and lack pale interiors. On the back of each ear there is an 'eye-spot' with a black ring around a white centre.

A small, nocturnal hunter of small mammals and birds, this is the 'cooler' of the South American cats, preferring the less tropical, more temperate regions of the continent, where it inhabits broken woodland rather than dense forest. It is said to be a good swimmer and climber and it is believed to sleep in trees. It has been observed to act 'like a miniature jaguar', lying in ambush in the branches of a tree and then leaping down on to its prey. The home range of a female that was tracked in the wild, using a radio-collar, proved to be 2.8 sq km (1.1 sq miles).

Geoffroy's Cat *(Felis geoffroyi)*, a small South American feline that has suffered greatly at the hands of fur-trappers. Literally hundreds of thousands of pelts of this attractive little spotted cat have been exported for the fur trade, year after year.

Geoffroy's Cat has suffered more than most at the hands of the fur-trappers. To give one example, it is recorded that in the three years between 1976 and 1979, Argentina alone exported no fewer than 340,000 pelts of this species. In one year, Paraguay exported 78,000 skins. Initially it was the Ocelot and the Margay that the trappers favoured, but as these became over-hunted, they then turned their lethal attention more and more to Geoffroy's Cat.

Size: Length of Head + Body: 42–66 cm (16½–26in). Tail: 24–36 cm (9½–14 in). Weight: 2–4 kg (4½–9 lb).

Distribution: Geoffroy's Cat is restricted to South America where it is found from Bolivia and southern Brazil down to Paraguay, Uruguay, Chile and Argentina, right to the southern-most part of the continent.

Geography of Domestic Breeds

Domestic Breeds. The 80 breeds of pedigree domestic cats originated in the following countries:

Australia: (1) Australian; (2) Spotted Mist.

Britain: (1) British Shorthair; (2) Colourpoint Shorthair; (3) Oriental Shorthair; (4) Cornish Rex; (5) Havana Brown; (6) British Angora; (7) Javanese (also in USA); (8) Devon Rex; (9) Scottish Fold; (10) Colourpoint British Shorthair; (11) Coupari; (12) Tiffanie; (13) Burmilla; (14) Seychellois; (15) Rexed Maine Coon; (16) Suqutranese.

Burma: (1) Birman.

Canada: (1) Cymric; (2) Sphynx.

Egypt: (1) Egyptian Mau.

Ethiopia: (1) Abyssinian.

France: (1) Chartreux.

Germany: (1) Prussian Rex; (2) German Rex.

Holland: (1) Dutch Rex.

Iran: (1) Persian.

Isle of Man: (1) Manx.

Italy: (1) Italian Rex; (2) Colourpoint European Shorthair; (3) European Shorthair.

Japan: (1) Japanese Bobtail; (2) Japanese Bobtail Longhair.

Kenya: (1) Sokoke Forest.

Norway: (1) Norwegian Forest.

Russia: (1) Siberian Forest; (2) Russian Blue; (3) Urals Rex.

Singapore: (1) Singapura; (2) Wild Abyssinian.

Thailand: (1) Burmese; (2) Korat; (3) Siamese.

Turkey: (1) Angora; (2) Turkish Van.

USA: (1) Maine Coon; (2) Mexican Hairless; (3) Himalayan; (4) Karakul; (5) Peke-faced Persian; (6) Balinese; (7) Ohio Rex; (8) Kashmir; (9) Tonkinese; (10) Bombay; (11) California Rex (Marcel); (12) Oregon Rex; (13) American Bobtail; (14) Javanese (also in Britain); (15) Ragdoll; (16) Snowshoe; (17) Bengal; (18) Ocicat; (19) American Shorthair; (20) American Wirehair; (21) Exotic Shorthair; (22) Somali; (23) Tiffany; (24) California Spangled; (25) American Lynx; (26) Malayan; (27) American Curl; (28) York Chocolate; (29) Ojos Azules; (30) La Perm; (31) Si-rex; (32) Selkirk Rex; (33) Nebelung; (34) Munchkin; (35) Ragamuffin.

Geography of Wild Species

Feline Biology. The 36 living wild species of cats are distributed in the major geographical zones as follows:

Europe: (1) Wild Cat (also in Africa and Asia); (2) Spanish Lynx; (3) Northern Lynx (also in Asia).

Africa: (1) Wild Cat (also in Europe and Asia); (2) Jungle Cat (also in Asia); (3) Sand Cat (also in Asia); (4) Black-footed Cat; (5) Serval; (6) African Golden Cat; (7) Caracal (also in Asia); (8) Leopard (also in Asia); (9) Lion (also in Asia); (10) Cheetah.

Asia: (1) Wild Cat (also in Europe and Africa); (2) Sand Cat (also in Africa); (3) Chinese Desert Cat; (4) Jungle Cat (also in Africa); (5) Pallas's Cat; (6) Leopard Cat; (7) Flat-headed Cat; (8) Rusty-spotted Cat; (9) Fishing Cat; (10) Marbled Cat; (11) Bay Cat; (12) Temminck's Cat; (13) Caracal (also in Africa); (14) Northern Lynx (also in Europe); (15) Clouded Leopard; (16) Snow Leopard; (17) Leopard (also in Africa); (18) Tiger; (19) Lion (also in Africa).

North America: (1) Canadian Lynx; (2) Bobcat; (3) Puma (also in South America).

South and Central America: (1) Tiger Cat; (2) Margay Cat; (3) Ocelot; (4) Pampas Cat; (5) Geoffroy's Cat; (6) Kodkod; (7) Mountain Cat; (8) Jaguarundi; (9) Puma (also in North America); (10) Jaguar.

Note: For details of these species, see separate entries.

The German Rex Cat, first discovered wandering in the ruins of East Berlin in the 1940s. Genetically it appears to be very similar to the Cornish Rex, although it has a slightly different body form.

German Rex Cat

Domestic Breed: Discovered in 1946 (some authors say 1947 or 1948, but the early date seems most likely) in East Germany. Taken up by serious breeders in 1951, following the discovery of the Cornish Rex Cat in England in 1950.

Appearance: Its coat is very similar to that of the Cornish Rex: it has no guard hairs and the awn hairs and undercoat are both unusually short. However, it differs from the Cornish Rex coat in having awn hairs that are a little thicker than those of the undercoat, and this gives it a fuller, woollier look.

History: The first German Rex was a black female feral cat seen wandering in the gardens of the Hufeland Hospital in the ruins of East Berlin, shortly after the end of World War II. She was rescued by a Dr R. Scheuer-Karpin, who named her 'Lammchen'(= Lambkin). She was found to be carrying the same wavy-hair gene as the Cornish Rex Cats. This was designated GEN 1. Rex. No. 33, as distinct from the wavy-hair gene of the Devon Rex Cat, which was designated GEN 2. Rex. No. 33a.

Lammchen had many litters and, when she was ten years old, in 1957, she was mated with one of her sons. This mating produced a litter of Rex kittens. During the next few years more German Rex litters were born and eventually, in 1960, two female German Rex Cats, called Marigold and Jet, were taken to the United States for breeding purposes. In 1961 a black male called 'Christopher Columbus' followed them and these three cats, in conjunction with the already imported Cornish Rex Cats, formed the basis of the Rex breed in America.

For many years (until 1979), the American CFA only recognized one form of Rex Cat – the one forged from crosses between the German and the Cornish – and ignored the other main breed, the Devon Rex.

Since, genetically, the German and Cornish breeds share the same Rex gene and are therefore, in one sense, virtually the same animal, it was only a matter of time before one eclipsed the other. The German breed was still being shown in Germany in the 1980s, and in 1982 some European breeders came to regard it as a separate breed, not because of its Rex gene, but because it had a body form that differed from that of the Cornish Rex and was closer to the European Shorthair. Despite this, however, fewer and fewer of them appeared in shows and eventually the line seems to have almost disappeared, while the Cornish has gone from strength to strength.

There is a report of an even earlier example of a German Rex Cat being found, back in the 1930s in East Prussia, but details are scanty. (See Prussian Rex Cat.)

Gestation

Feline Reproduction. The pregnancy of the domestic cat averages just over nine weeks – about 65 days. The variation around this figure is considerable, however, normal pregnancies occurring anywhere between 58 and 72 days. If the pregnant female who is about to produce a litter is severely stressed (as when environmental conditions are unsuitable for her kittens) she can delay giving birth for several days.

The average periods of time between mating and giving birth in other members of the cat family are as follows:

Feline Gestation Times

Cat	Time (days)	Cat	Time (days)
African Wildcat	58	Caracal	71
Canadian Lynx	61	Serval	73
Sand Cat	61	Tiger Cat	75
Indian Desert Cat	62	Geoffroy's Cat	75
Bobcat	63	Ocelot	75
Fishing Cat	63	Clouded Leopard	88
[Domestic Cat]	[65]	Cheetah	92
Jungle Cat	66	Puma	93
Leopard Cat	66	Leopard	96
Black-footed Cat	67	Snow Leopard	99
Jaguarundi	67	Jaguar	101
European Wild Cat	68 (63–68)	Tiger	103
Northern Lynx	69	Lion	110

Gib

Feline Term. A male cat. According to Charles Ross (1868) the name 'Gib Cat' or 'Gibbe Cat' preceded 'Tom-cat', especially in northern England. (It was pronounced with a hard 'g'.) It fell into disuse when Tom-cat became popular, but was still employed in north-east England as late as the 1860s. The word was a contraction of the name Gilbert that was used for a male cat in earlier times.

The phrase 'Gibbe our Cat' is used by Chaucer in *Romance of the Rose*. Gibbe is also found in Shakespeare, where it refers to an 'old, worn-out animal.'

Gilbert

Feline Term. A male cat. An early name used to describe a tom-cat. The Old French equivalent for Gilbert was *Tibert, Thibert,* or *Tybert*. Apart from 'Gib Cat' (see Gib), abbreviations sometimes employed for Gilbert and Tibert were 'Gil Cat' and 'Tib Cat'.

Ginger (1)

Coat Colour. Ginger is the popular term for the coat colour that geneticists used to call 'yellow', but now call 'orange'. To confuse matters further, pedigree cat breeders call it 'red', and storytellers call it 'marmalade'. The ginger gene has the effect of eliminating all black and brown pigment from the hairs of the cat.

When present, the ginger colour is always attached to a tabby pattern, so that the full name for a ginger cat should be 'a ginger tabby'.

Ginger is a sex-linked character and nearly all ginger cats are male. When females do occasionally occur, they are usually sterile.

Ginger (2)

Fictional Cat. A yellow tom-cat created by Beatrix Potter for her story *Ginger and Pickles* (1909). Pickles is a terrier with whom Ginger runs a small village shop for the other animals. The problem is how to avoid alarming the customers. The problem is solved by the terrier always serving the mice and the cat always attending to the rabbits.

The two owners were extremely generous, but gave so much credit that they soon went out of business.

Gloved Cat

Wild Feline. According to Dechambre, writing in 1957, this was a name given to the race of the African Wild Cat *(Felis sylvestris libyca)*, which is generally thought to be the ancestor of the European domestic cat.

Golden

Coat Colour. A golden sheen can be created in one of two ways. In one form there are brown-tipped white hairs. In the other there are black-tipped golden hairs.

There are three variants: the Chinchilla Golden, the slightly darker Shaded Golden and the Golden Tabby.

Golden Persians used to be known as 'Brownies', when they first appeared in litters of silver kittens, in the 1920s. At first they were rejected, but later were prized and developed. The first recorded Golden was a kitten called 'Bracken', who was registered as a Sable Chinchilla in 1925.

Golden Cat

Wild Feline. *(Felis temminckii)* An alternative name for Temminck's Cat. It is also known as the Asian or Asiatic Golden Cat. It is superficially similar to the African Golden Cat, from which it can better be distinguished by using the now preferred name of Temminck's Cat. It is a medium-sized species from tropical Asia, with a rich golden coat and attractive facial markings in white, grey and brown. (For details see Temminck's Cat.)

Golden Flower

Legendary Cat. In Japan it was red cats, rather than black ones, that used to be feared for their magical powers. Known as 'Golden Flowers' *(kinkwa-neko)*, they were thought to be able to transform themselves into beautiful women. Although this might appear to be an improvement on 'ugly old witches', the alluring form that these supernatural cats took made them even more dangerous. In a famous legend, one of these glamorous cat-women causes the downfall of a powerful feudal lord.

Golden Siamese

Domestic Breed. The original name given to the cross between Siamese and Burmese that was later named the Tonkinese. It was first developed through five generations in the 1950s by American breeder Milan Greer, but was then taken over by other breeders and renamed. (For details see Tonkinese.)

Governing Council of the Cat Fancy

Feline History. The Council was formed in May 1910 when a need arose to settle disputes between rival factions in the quickly developing world of pedigree cats and cat shows. The functions of the Council were to exercise disciplinary powers, to license cat shows and appoint judges, to introduce rules for the cat shows, to provide registration facilities and issue certified pedigrees, to draw up standards of points for judging, to classify cat breeds and to protect the welfare of cats and the interests of cat owners. The council has been doing this ever since and remains, even today when there are so many new societies and clubs, the most prestigious of all feline organizations.

In 1953 the GCCF held its first cat show – previously these had been run by affiliated clubs – and another in 1960. Then, in 1976 it was decided to institute an annual 'Crufts for the Cat Fancy', and the GCCF's Supreme Show was born. This has grown in size and popularity each year until today there are around 1,400 entries.

In 1983 the GCCF opened a headquarters at Bridgwater in Somerset and began to transfer its records onto a computer system. Before World War II there had only been about 1,000 registrations each year, and written records were kept with comparative ease. In 1940, with the advent of war, the figure dropped to only 400. Then, after hostilities were over, the numbers grew higher and higher until, by 1990, there were as many as 36,000. There are now 119 affiliated clubs – either breed clubs or local clubs. Three times a year these send delegates to GCCF meetings at which issues central to the organization of cat shows and pedigree cats can be discussed.

Grass-eating

Feline Behaviour. Domestic cats occasionally eat grass, if given the chance. Indoor cats with no access to grass have been known to chew houseplants as a substitute. Clearly the grass has some value as a subsidiary element in the feline diet, but precisely what this might be has been much debated in the past. The following suggestions have been put forward at various times:

1 Cats use grass as a laxative to help them pass troublesome hairballs lodged in their intestines.
2 Cats eat grass to make them vomit up their hairballs.
3 Cats eat grass because they are feeling sick and the grass makes them vomit, ridding themselves of any poisons they may have swallowed.
4 Cats eat grass to relieve throat inflammation.
5 Cats eat grass to relieve stomach irritation.
6 Cats eat grass as a way of adding roughage to their diets.

None of these explanations fits the facts. If one observes the way in which a cat eats grass it is clear that it is not swallowing any appreciable quantity of vegetable matter. What it is doing is biting, chewing and taking in a little juice from long, fresh grass stems. Clearly it is the juice that is important, not the grass itself.

We now know that the juice of grasses contains *folic acid*, a vitamin that is vital to cats because it plays a role in the production of haemoglobin. This essential chemical substance is missing from a modern, purely meat diet and the cats are driven to search for it to complete their diet. In the wild they would obtain it in the stomach contents of the small rodents they devour whole, but when it is missing, they add it by going straight to the fresh grass stems.

If a cat is deficient in folic acid its growth will suffer and it may become anaemic. This is a major problem for indoor cats with no access to a garden. Owners of such cats can avoid damaging the health of their pets by planting a small tray of grasses and keeping it in their apartments for their cats to chew on when the mood takes them.

Note: If garden grasses have been treated with weedkiller or other horticultural chemicals, these may be poisonous to cats.

Green Cat

Feline Mutation? In November 1995 it was reported that a green-coloured domestic cat had been discovered in North-west Denmark. Mrs Pia Bischoff discovered the green animal – a tiny kitten – in a hayloft and was astonished at its unique colouring. Adopting it as a pet, she tried

to wash out the green colour, but failed. From its photograph, the kitten appears to be a grey cat with a distinct greenish tinge. A veterinary examination proved that the kitten was perfectly healthy but that it had 'a copper patina, apparently present since birth, from the tip of its fur to the hair follicles'. Investigations are now being carried out to discover whether the colouring is genetically controlled or the result of some kind of exposure to copper. If the cat retains its green colouring into adulthood and then passes it on to its offspring, a startling new breed of cat will have to be added to the world of pedigree cats. It seems much more likely, however, that copper pollution will turn out to be involved and the unique colouring will disappear in one generation.

Greeting

Feline Behaviour. When a pet cat greets its owners after a period of separation, it usually does one of three things: it may rub up against their legs, hop up on its hind legs, or roll over on to its back. Each of these actions has a particular significance in the body language of cats.

Rubbing against human legs takes a characteristic form. It starts with the animal pressing with the top of its head or the side of its face. Then it leans over slightly and rubs with the side of its body, all along one of its flanks. Finally it may try to twine its tail around the vertical leg. After this, it looks up and then repeats the process, sometimes several times. If a hand reaches down to stroke the animal, it increases its rubbing, often pushing the side of its mouth against the hand, or nudging upwards with the top of its head. Then eventually it wanders off, its greeting ritual complete, after which it sits down and washes its fur.

All these elements have special meanings. Essentially what the cat is doing is implementing a scent-exchange between its owners and itself. There are specialized scent glands on the temples and at the gape of the mouth. (Close examination of the temple region reveals a slightly 'bald' patch there on either side of the forehead, which is the site of these temple glands.) Another scent-gland is situated at the root of the tail. Without its owners realizing it, their pet has marked them with its scent from these glands.

The feline fragrances are too delicate for human noses, but it is important that friendly members of the cat's adopted family should be scent-sharing in this way. This makes the cat feel more at home with its human companions. And it is important, too, for the cat to read the human scent signals. This is achieved by the flank-rubbing element of the greeting, followed by the cat sitting down and 'tasting' its owners with its tongue – through the simple process of licking the fur it has just rubbed so carefully against the human legs.

Some cats elaborate their greeting ritual by hopping up on their hind legs. This is a brave attempt to compensate for the difference in size between the pet cats and their human companions. If human bodies were cat-sized, the animals would rub faces with them in a typically feline greeting, but humans are so tall that all the cats can do is to struggle to increase their own body height, by rearing up on their hind legs. The greeting hop is therefore a token survival of a head-to-head contact.

The typical greeting ritual of the domestic cat, rubbing against its owner's leg. In making this contact, the cat is effecting a scent-exchange, depositing its own scent and at same time acquiring some of the fragrance of its human companion.

A clue to this interpretation comes from the way in which small kittens sometimes greet their mother when she returns to the nest. If they have developed to the point where their legs are strong enough for the 'hop', the kittens will perform a modest version of the same movement, as they push their heads up towards that of the mother cat. In their case there is not far to go, and she helps by lowering her own head towards theirs, but the incipient hop is clear enough.

Some cats use their initiative to recreate a better head contact when greeting their human friends. Instead of the rather sad little symbolic hop, they leap up on to a piece of furniture to the human and employ this elevated position to get themselves closer for a more effective face-to-face rub.

Other cats adopt a different tactic. Instead of rushing towards a returning human companion, they stay where they are and roll over on to their back. This is the cat's ways of offering a passively friendly reaction and it is something which is done only to close family intimates. Few cats would risk such a greeting if the person entering the room were a stranger, because the belly-up posture makes the animal highly vulnerable. Indeed, this is the essence of friendliness. The cat is saying, in effect, 'I roll over to show you my belly to demonstrate that I trust you enough to adopt this highly vulnerable posture in your presence.' A more active cat would use the rubbing display, but a cat in a lazy or sleepy mood prefers the belly-roll display.

It is not always safe to assume that a cat making this belly display is prepared to allow its soft underside to be stroked. It may appear to be offering this option, but frequently an attempt to respond with a friendly hand is met with a swipe from an irritated paw. The belly region is so well protected by the cat that it finds contact there unpleasant, except in relationships where the cat and the human owner have developed an exceptionally high degree of intimacy. Such a cat may trust its human family to do almost anything to it. But the more typical, wary cat draws the line when a human hand approaches its softer parts.

Gregory the Great

Cat Owner? St. Gregory the Great (540–604) – Pope Gregory I – was a man whose mildness, tolerance and joy in pastoral simplicity were completely out of character with the epoch in which he lived. Originally a Roman civil servant, he so hated the chaos of his world that he retired into a monastery where he spent what he described as the happiest days of his life. When he emerged three years later he was eventually to rise to the highest office in the church, but in the peace of the monastery he lived a quiet, serene existence with a feline companion. His biographer, Jacobus Diaconus, records that 'he possessed nothing in the world except a cat, which he carried in his bosom, frequently caressing it, as his sole companion'.

That is the official story, but it seems that, over the centuries, it has suffered considerably in the retelling. In an alternative version, which may be closer to the truth, it is recorded that a hermit, whose only possession was a cat, was told in a dream that he would 'be in the same place as Pope Gregory'. The hermit was unhappy about this because he did not want to be associated with such a wealthy man as the Pope. But then he had another dream in which the Lord ticked him off for being so proud of his poverty: 'Since a man is not rich by reason of what he owns, but of what he loves, how dare you compare your poverty with Gregory's wealth, when you can be convicted of showing more affection for that cat of yours, fondling it every day and sharing it with no one, than he does for all his riches, which he does not love, but lavishes on all?'

If the story of the hermit is true, then it would seem that Pope Gregory was a cat-lover and cat-owner, not in person, but only by association with an ailurophilic hermit who spiritually identified himself with the great man.

Grey

Coat Colour. In domestic cats, the grey colour is a dilution of black. Although grey is a common enough colour among pedigree cats, the word is almost taboo. By a harmless conspiracy of mutual deception, all cat breeders refer to their conspicuously pure grey cats as 'blue'. Thus we have the Russian Blue and the British Blue, and the many blue variants of other breeds.

This convention is rarely broken, although there was once a coat pattern referred to as the 'Grey-spotted Tabby'. Even this usage now seems to have vanished and a quick check through the index of a recent volume describing the various cat breeds reveals the following number of times that the words blue and grey are mentioned: Blue: 86 times; Grey: 0.

Grimalkin

Feline Term. A 17th-century word meaning 'a cat', especially an old female cat. It also came to stand for 'a jealous or imperious old woman'. Its oldest known usage is in the opening scene from Shakespeare's *Macbeth* (1605), where one of the three witches cries out, 'I come, Graymalkin,' implying that the cat was one of her familiars. This led to a definition of Grimalkin as 'a fiend supposed to resemble a grey cat'.

An early 18th-century definition describes the term as follows: 'Grimalkin to domestic vermin sworn an everlasting foe.'

The derivation of the word has been explained as follows: Grimalkin = Grey + Malkin. Malkin = Maud + kin. Maud = abbreviation of Matilda. Maltilda = slang term for a slut. This makes the word Grimalkin = grey-slut-kin. Or, a grey being related to a slut. This may all be connected to the association of cats with witches, but there are few hard facts to go on.

Writing in 1969, Brian Vesey-Fitzgerald, who took special pleasure in debunking accepted wisdom, had no doubts on this matter, stating boldly, 'The true cat of witchcraft, the true familiar of the witch, was the grey cat, Grimalkin.' He rejects the widely held idea that, in the era of witch-burning, black cats were considered especially 'evil'. He says, 'It is often stated that this was so and that many innocent old women were burnt or hanged at the height of the persecution because their cats were black. There is not a shred of evidence to support that allegation. It is true that many innocent old women were burnt or hanged, but this was not because their cats were black: it was simply because they had cats.'

While it is true that all kinds of cats were persecuted during the witch-hunting years, the early illustrations of witches with their familiars nearly always do show a jet black cat, so it is hard to accept this view. However, it may well have been that grey-coloured cats, in addition to black cats, had a special role in the medieval annals of feline 'wickedness'. (See also Black Cat.)

Keeping the fur well-groomed is vitally important for a cat. Grooming removes dirt and dead hair, improves the coat's insulating properties, increases vitamin intake, reinforces the cat's personal odour and improves the waterproofing of the fur.

Grooming

Feline Behaviour. Grooming the fur is of great importance to cats. It takes two forms: autogrooming and allogrooming. Autogrooming is when a cat grooms itself; allogrooming is when one cat grooms another. (For details see Allogrooming and Autogrooming.)

Guiña

Wild Feline. An alternative name for the Kodkod *(Felis guigna)*, the smallest of the South American wild cat species. (See Kodkod for details.)

Gus

Fictional Cat. Gus was an elderly theatre cat, well into his anecdotage, who loved to reminisce nostalgically about the good old days 'When I made history as . . . the Fiend of the Fell.' He appears in T.S. Eliot's *Old Possum's Book of Practical Cats.* His full name was Asparagus.

Hair

Feline Anatomy. A wild cat has four kinds of hairs: down hairs, awn hairs, guard hairs and vibrissae. There may be as many as 200 hairs per millimetre, giving the cat an excellent fur coat that can protect it from even the most severe night air.

The *down hairs* are the ones closest to the skin and it is their primary task to keep the animal warm and to conserve its precious body heat. These are the shortest, thinnest and softest of the hairs. They have roughly the same diameter down their whole length, but instead of being straight they have many short undulations, making them appear crimped or crinkled when viewed under a magnifying lens. It is the soft and curly quality of this undercoat, or underfur, that gives it its excellent heat-retaining property.

The *awn hairs* form the middle-coat. They are intermediate between the soft underfur and the guard hairs of the topcoat. Their task is partly insulatory and partly protective. They are bristly with a slight swelling towards the tip, before the final tapering-off. Some authorities subdivide them into three types – the down-awn hairs, the awn hairs and the guard-awn hairs – but these subtle distinctions are of little value.

The *guard hairs* form the protective topcoat. They are the longest and thickest of the ordinary body hairs and serve to protect the underfur from the outside elements, keeping it dry and snug. These hairs are straight and evenly tapered along their length.

The *vibrissae* are the greatly enlarged and toughened hairs employed as sensitive organs of touch. These specialized tactile hairs form the whiskers of the upper lips, and are also found on the cheeks and the chin, over the eyes and on the wrists of the forelegs. Compared with the other types of hair there are very few of them, but they play a vital role when the cat is exploring in poor light, or is hunting.

Of the three types of general body fur on the wild cat, the down hairs are the most numerous. For every 1,000 down hairs there will only be about 300 awn hairs and 20 guard hairs. But these ratios vary enormously with the different breeds of pedigree cats. This is because these felines have been carefully selected for their special kinds of coats. Some are fine and thin, others short and coarse, or long and fluffy. The differences are due to exaggerations and reductions of the different types of hair.

Pedigree long-haired cats, for example, have excessively lengthy guard hairs, measuring up to 13 cm (5 inches), and greatly elongated down hairs, but no awn hairs. Some short-haired breeds have guard hairs that are less than 5 cm (2 inches) in length, sparse awn hairs and no down hairs. Wirehair cats have all three types of body hair, but they are all short and curly. The strange Cornish Rex Cat has no guard hairs and only very short, curly awn and down hairs. The Devon Rex has all three types of body hair, but they are all reduced to the quality of down hairs. The amazing naked cat – the Canadian Sphynx – lacks both guard hairs and awn hairs and has only a soft fuzz of down hairs on its extremities.

So selective breeding has played havoc with the natural coat of the cat, producing types of animals that would not all thrive in the wild today. Some would suffer from the cold, others from the heat, and still others would become badly matted and tangled without their daily grooming. Fortunately for these pedigree breeds there are usually plenty of human helpers to tend to their needs and, should the worst happen, and the animals be forced to fend for themselves as strays, changes would soon take place. They themselves might suffer from the climate, but if they managed to survive and interbreed, the chances are that in a few generations their offspring would have reverted to wild-type coats once again, as a result of the inevitable mixing that would occur among the stray cat colonies.

Hairless Cat

Feline Mutation. From time to time a natural mutation has occurred giving rise to a naked cat, lacking all or most of its hair. One of the earliest reports of hairless cats, dating from 1830, is found in *A Natural History of the Mammals of Paraguay* by the German naturalist Rudolph Rengger. Later, in 1902, an American couple living in New Mexico acquired a pair (see entry for Mexican Hairless Cat), but never bred from them.

Other examples were reported from a wide range of geographical locations including France, Czechoslovakia, Austria, Morocco and Australia. None of these became established as breeding lines, vanishing almost as soon as they had become known. Then, in 1966, a hairless cat was born in a litter of otherwise normal kittens in Canada. This time, a concerted effort was made to keep the line alive. This has succeeded, although the cat remains rare. Under the name of the Canadian Sphynx Cat, it has aroused a great deal of interest, and some controversy, in both North America and Europe. In the 1990s one cat society (TICA) accepted it and gave it championship class status (see Sphynx Cat). This is the first time that a breed of hairless cats has been officially recognized.

It is claimed that felines looking very much like the modern Sphynx Cat can be found among the stone engravings on the walls of ancient pre-Columbian buildings in Central and South America, but little is actually known about the significance of these particular animals in those early cultures.

Hamilcar

Fictional Cat. Hamilcar was the acutely observed Angora Cat belonging to Bonnard in Anatole France's novel *Le Crime de Sylvestre Bonnard* (1881).

Hamlet

The signature of Hamlet, the Algonquin Cat.

Working Cat. Hamlet is the subject of a book called *Algonquin Cat* by Val Schaffner (1980). A cat of mixed parentage, white with grey blotches and a tabby tail, he was for many years cat-in-residence, mascot and pest-controller of the famous Algonquin Hotel at 59 West 44th Street in Manhattan. Hamlet was the replacement for Rusty, the tortoiseshell tom who presided at the hotel during its famous literary 'Round Table' in the 1920s and '30s, days when it was the

HAMLET was for many years the mascot of the famous Algonquin Hotel in Manhattan. The cream of the New York wits gathered here to gossip. One of them, Dorothy Parker, when asked how to kill a cat, replied, 'Try curiosity.'

meeting place of the great wits of New York, including Dorothy Parker, Alexander Woollcott, James Thurber and Robert Benchley. Each Algonquin cat becomes a special character in its own right and uses Rusty's original cat-door. The latest recruit, in the 1990s, is an adopted stray called Matilda who, during one of her nocturnal Manhattan prowls, was mugged and had her collar stolen, an event perhaps symptomatic of her decade.

HARDY, THOMAS

CAT OWNER. The great English novelist Thomas Hardy (1840–1928) was so passionate about his pet cat that, when it died, he buried it under a small mound beneath its favourite tree and composed a long obituary poem to it, declaring: 'Never another pet for me! Let your place all vacant be.' He was good to his word, refusing to have another for many years until, as an old man, he was given a grey Persian Cat with deep orange eyes called 'Cobby' that he could not resist. He adored Cobby and the cat stayed loyally by his side until Hardy died, when it vanished without trace.

An intriguing explanation of Cobby's strange disappearance has recently been provided by author Frank Smyth. If true, it must surely rank as one of the oddest tales of a pet cat's relationship with its owner. It seems that, when Hardy died, a conflict arose concerning where his body should rest. For the nation, it had to lie in Poet's Corner at Westminster Abbey, but since, during his life, he had given his heart (metaphorically) to the village of Stinsford, near Dorchester, it was decided that, in death, his heart would (literally) be given to that village. Two small bronze urns were prepared, one to contain his ashes for the Abbey and the other to hold his heart, to be buried in a grave at St. Michael's Church in the village. A doctor was called in and quickly removed the heart, and it was indeed buried, with appropriate formalities, in the village graveyard. The tombstone can be seen there to this day, proclaiming 'Here Lies the Heart of Thomas Hardy'. But matters were not quite as simple as they seemed.

What actually occurred, according to Frank Smyth, is that the heart was removed from Hardy's body while his corpse was still lying in his house. It was carefully wrapped in a tea

towel and the towel was then placed in a biscuit tin. The tin was left beside the body. Cobby the cat had loved to stay close to the old man during his final days, and probably expected to be fed there. So he can hardly be blamed if, sniffing what appeared to be a tin full of meat, he did his best to open it. He must have been puzzled by the old man's refusal to help him, but he struggled on and eventually managed to remove the lid. Inside the tin was a new kind of cat food, but he ate it up greedily, having no doubt been somewhat neglected in all the drama surrounding the great author's demise. All Cobby left uneaten were a few valves and gristly bits.

The next day, the undertaker arrived to collect the heart for burial. All he found were an open biscuit tin, a few scraps of heart and a plump, contented cat. It was his solemn duty to bury Hardy's heart in the village graveyard and so it was clear to him what he must do. Without a moment's hesitation, he quickly strangled the cat, put it inside the biscuit tin and then proceeded as planned, as though nothing unusual had happened. The only strange feature of the subsequent church ceremony was that, standing before the alter in the church, in place of the small bronze urn that had been promised, there was a 'polished wooden box, about the size and shape of a biscuit tin'.

No explanation was given for this last-minute change, the service took place normally and the box was duly laid to rest, containing Hardy's heart as formally required. However, the congregation was spared the news that the revered organ was nestling, not in a neatly wrapped funeral cloth, but instead inside the stomach of his much loved pet cat, old Cobby, an animal of whom it truly could be said, he stole the old man's heart in more ways than one.

When archaeologists come to explore Hardy's tomb a thousand years from now, they will doubtless reach the conclusion that the skeleton of a cat found there proves conclusively that the famous novelist (who was in reality a down-to-earth atheist) was involved in some form of sinister Bubastic cat worship.

Harimau Jalor

Mystery Cat. In the Malaysian state of Trengganu, the local people speak of a giant tiger with horizontal stripes instead of the usual vertical ones. They call it the Harimau Jalor and repeatedly tell of its existence, but since there is no living or dead specimen to support their stories, their reports have been ignored and the animal is still considered to be an imaginative fiction rather than a scientific fact.

Harlequin

Coat Pattern. A term that is occasionally used to describe the coat of a bi-colour cat which has more white than non-white fur. Technically, to be a Harlequin coat the pattern must be 50–75 per cent White and 50–25 per cent Coloured.

Havana (Brown) Cat

Domestic Breed. Sometimes referred to simply as the Havana. Despite its title, this breed did not originate in Cuba. It is in reality an all-brown cat created in England in 1952. There are two theories as to how it acquired its name. One suggests that it was inspired by the colour of Havana Cigars, and the other that it was borrowed from the Rabbit Fancy, where there is a Havana breed with the same coat colour. However, even if the second theory is correct, it does not invalidate the first, because the Havana Rabbit itself was named after the 'Havana Brown' colour of Cuban cigars.

After a few years (in the late 1950s) it was decided to rename the breed. This was done, against the breeders' wishes, because it was feared that the name 'Havana' might give the false impression that this home-grown British breed had originated in the West Indies. Its new name was to be more mundane: the Chestnut Brown. It was exhibited in England under the full title of Chestnut Brown Foreign Shorthair until about 1970, but then, owing to popular demand, the original name resurfaced and has been used ever since.

The elegant Havana Brown Cat *(opposite)*. Because it was developed in England rather than Cuba, a committee decided to alter its name to Chestnut Brown Foreign Shorthair, a title that only a committee could love. By popular demand this was later abandoned and Havana reinstated.

There were a number of precursors for the breed which failed to survive: the Swiss Mountain Cat (an all-brown Siamese first shown in 1894 but soon forgotten) and the Brown Cat (shown in 1930).

Two discarded names for the breed were the Berkshire Brown and the Reading Brown. They were suggested because of the geographical location of the 1952 foundation stock, but were soon rejected in favour of Havana. Another rejected name used in the early days of the breed was Oriental Chocolate Cat.

Appearance: In Britain, because of repeated back-crossings to Siamese, this cat is now essentially an all-brown Siamese. In the United States, Canada and Japan, however, crossings with Siamese were outlawed and there, as a result, the breed has a slightly different, less Oriental build, closer to its original 1950s shape, with a rounder face and a shorter nose.

History: The Havana was the unexpected result of a mating between a Seal Point Siamese male called Tombee and a black short-haired female (which was half Seal Point Siamese and half Black Persian) called Susannah. One of the kittens resulting from this cross was a Self-Brown male which was named 'Elmtower Bronze Idol'. This was the first Havana Cat, born on 24th October 1952. He was soon joined by a female, 'Elmtower Brown Study', resulting from a further mating between the Siamese stud and the black cat.

This foundation stock was created by Mrs Munro-Smith of Reading in Berkshire, although she had, in fact, been trying to obtain something quite different – namely, a Colourpoint Persian. The Havana Brown was merely a lucky accident, but she was quick to realize its value.

The Havana was first exhibited in Britain in 1953 and was given championship status in 1958.

In 1956 a pair of kittens, a male called Laurentide Brown Pilgrim and a female called Roofspringer Mahogany, were exported to a Californian breeder in the United States and became the foundation stock for the breed in North America. The Havana was given official recognition there as early as 1959.

Personality: Terms used to describe this breed include: intelligent, active, affectionate, lively, considerate, playful, mischievous, lordly, home-loving and outgoing. Because of the stronger Siamese element in the British Havana, it is more vocal than its American counterpart.

Colour Form: A rich, warm, chestnut brown. No variant colours are allowed.

Breed Clubs:

Havana and Oriental Lilac Cat Club. Address: Talisker Cottage, Tadwick, Near Bath, BA1 8AH, England.

Havana Brown Fanciers. Address: 2250 24th Street, Apt. 129, San Francisco, CA 94107, USA.

Havana (Brown) Preservation Society. Address: 40 Clinton Street, Brooklyn Heights, NY 11201, USA.

Havana, Foreign and Oriental Cat Association. Address: 26 Lethe Grove, Colchester, Essex, CO2 8RG, England.

International Havana Brown Society. Publishes a magazine, *Havana Happenings.* Address: 185 Bridgeside Circle, Danville, CA 94506-4452, USA.

Haws

Feline Anatomy. The haw is the cat's third eyelid. It is situated at the inner corner of the eye and comes into action to protect the delicate organ from damage or to lubricate the corneal surface by spreading the cat's tears evenly across it. When the haws are activated, they move sideways across the eye and then return to their resting position. In this respect the cat has an advantage over the human species, for we are unable to move our third eyelids, which exist only as small pink lumps at the inner point of each eye.

The cat's haw – or nictitating membrane, to give it its technical name – is not normally conspicuous, but if the cat is in ill health, undernourished, or about to succumb to a major disease, it may become permanently visible, giving the cat's eye a 'half-shuttered' look. When this happens, it is an important clue that the animal is in need of veterinary assistance. The appearance of the haws in these circumstances is caused by the fact that there are shock

absorber pads of fat behind the eyeballs which start to shrink if the animal's health is below par. This shrinkage means that the eyes sink into the head slightly, and this in turn causes the haws to move forward and half cover the corneal surfaces. When the cat returns to full health, the fat pads are replenished and the eyes pushed forward again, hiding the haws once more.

Heathcliff

Cartoon Cat. Heathcliff is a strip-cartoon cat, created in 1973 by artist George Gately, who commented: 'Before him, cats were depicted as either stupid or sinister, but cats are smart. Heathcliff represents the anti-hero, like Humphrey Bogart. He's a tough little mug.' Named after the character in Emile Brontë's *Wuthering Heights,* Heathcliff steadily grew in popularity until, by 1981, he was syndicated in more than 700 newspapers. He also appeared in Saturday morning animated cartoons on ABC TV and was the subject of two books: *Heathcliff Banquet* (1980) and *Heathcliff Feast* (1981).

Hemingway, Ernest

Cat Owner. The tough, outdoor, huntsman, man-of-action image created by American author Ernest Hemingway (1898–1961) is strangely at odds with his private love of cats. At home, one would expect to see him accompanied by faithful, subservient gundogs and hounds, but instead he is found surrounded by a whole colony of pampered felines. He wrote *For Whom the Bell Tolls* at a desk covered in cats.

The Hemingway house, on a hilltop in Havana, was overrun with no fewer than 30 pet cats and such was the chaos that his wife, Mary, insisted on building them a separate 'White Tower', complete with special feeding, sleeping and maternity facilities. Even after it was completed, several of the cats, including Crazy Christian, Friendless Brother and Ecstasy were soon back in the main house with their besotted master. It is reported that, when he was working on *A Farewell to Arms,* the cat-count had risen to 34. At one stage he began crossing local Cuban cats with Angoras in an attempt to create a new Hemingway breed.

The author had such trust in his cats that, in earlier days when living in Paris, he and his wife allowed their yellow-eyed cat called 'F. Puss' to baby-sit for them. Friends were horrified because they were convinced that the cat would lie on the baby and suffocate it. Needless to say, F. Puss proved them wrong. When he slept in the cradle he always distanced himself from the face of the sleeping baby.

Hemingway also had a home full of cats in Florida. When he shot himself in 1961 he left behind a whole colony of these cats. Fortunately for them this house (address: 907, Whitehead Street, Key West, FL 33040) was turned into a Hemingway Museum and the offspring of his original cats are now sold off as 'celebrity kittens'. Some of his cats had strange feet and today the price tag of the 'celebrity kittens' depends on how many toes they have – the seven-toed ones being the most expensive.

Heraldic Cats

Feline History. Domestic cats are uncommon in heraldry, where the only felines to hold a prominent position are lions and leopards. The reason is not hard to find. Throughout the Middle Ages the cat was so detested by the Christian Church that it was difficult for it to be displayed as a noble image. Even at other times it was not particularly favoured in this role. There were exceptions, however, including the following:

1 In the Temple of Liberty which Rome owed to Tiberius Gracchus, the goddess was shown with a cat at her feet representing liberty.
2 The Vandals and the Suevi carried a cat sable upon their armorial bearings
3 St. Clotilda (470–545), daughter of Chilperic, King of Burgundy, and wife of Clovis, King of the Franks, had a cat sable upon her armorial bearings, in the act of springing at a rat.
4 A Catanach book plate shows a cat beneath the words 'Touch not the Cat Gloveless'.

Heraldic Cats

5 The Katzen family shield shows, on azure, a cat sable holding a mouse sable in its mouth.
6 In Scotland, the Clan Chattan, whose chief was known as Mohr au Chat (great wild cat) used a cat as its emblem, with the words 'Touch not the cat but [without] the glove'.
7 In the 16th century, Melchior Sessa, the Venetian printer, adopted the device of a cat holding a rat in its jaws.
8 The Chetaldie family, in the Limoges country, bore, on azure, two cats argent.
9 The Neapolitan noble house of Della Gatta bore, on azure, a cat argent with a lapel gules in chief.
10 The Chaffardon family bore, on azure, three cats, or two full-face.
11 St. Ives, the patron of lawyers, is shown accompanied by a cat, which is therefore seen as the symbol of the officials of justice.
12 The armorial bearings of Scotsman Peter Duguid-M'Combie of Aberdeen show a cat rearing up in the sejant erect position.
13 The armorial bearings of Alfred Scott Scott-Gatty, with the motto 'Cate at Caute', show two cats in the rampant guardant position.
14 The armorial bearings of 'Cluny' Macpherson show a cat in the sejant proper position, beneath the words 'Touch not the Cat Bot [without] a Glove'.
15 The armorial bearings of Joseph Andrew Keates show three cats in the passant guardant position, beneath a tiger in the same posture.
16 The coat-of-arms of Madame Myrtle Farquharson of Invercauld, Chief of the Clan in 1936, shows two Scottish wild cats embracing a central lozenge.
17 The Arms of the Royal Burgh of Dornoch, granted in 1929, carry the motto 'Without Feare' above a striped wild cat showing aggressively lowered ears.

The shield of the Katzen family, showing, on azure, a cat sable holding a mouse sable in its mouth.

A Merchant's Mark, from a print at the British Museum.

Hiddigeigei

Fictional Cat. The sable-coated tom-cat featured in Joseph Viktor von Scheffel's famous poem *Der Trompeter von Säckingen* (1854), which ran to over 250 editions. Hiddigeigei takes a superior view of the human race – 'contemptuous mortals' – and considers the struggle and strife of their lives quite absurd. He himself prefers the contemplative life, sitting serenely on a roof, watching the world go by. Perhaps echoing this philosophy, a restaurant in Capri was named after him.

Highland Fold Cat

Domestic Breed. The name given to the long-haired version of the Scottish Fold Cat by the American Cat Fanciers' Association in 1991, when according this breed championship status. The idea behind the choice of this name is presumably that the Scottish Fold Cats with the thicker coats would be more suited to the colder Highlands of Scotland, than they would to the milder Lowlands. However, since the breed did in reality originate at the village of Coupar Angus in the Lowlands, British breeders have preferred to use the name Coupari for this attractive cat.

The Cat Fanciers Federation, which also gave the long-haired breed championship status in the United States in 1991, employed the more descriptive name of 'Longhair Fold'.

Breed Club:

The Longhair Clan - Longhair Scottish Fold Breed Club. Address: 49 Hancock Street, Salem, MA 01920, USA.

Himalayan Cat

Domestic Breed. This is the American name for a Persian Cat with Siamese colourpoint markings. Its popular nickname is the 'Himmy' or 'Himmie'. It is sometimes referred to as a 'Colourpoint Persian'. In Britain it is officially called a 'Colourpoint Longhair'.

In the 1920s references occur to a breed called the 'Malayan Persian'. This appears to have been an early, alternative name for the Himalayan which was soon abandoned. In 1947, the

name 'Masked Silver' was given to certain Persians which carried Siamese markings – presumably yet another (now obsolete) name for the Himalayan.

Appearance: Almost exactly as for the Persian Cat, with snub nose, flat face, broad head, short body and thick, heavy, very long-haired coat. The only difference is that this breed shows the colourpoint coat pattern of the Siamese.

History: In the 1920s and 1930s, breeders in several countries were striving to produce a cat with a typical Persian body, but with Siamese markings. The idea was to borrow only the coat pattern from the Siamese and nothing else. In 1924, Dr T. Tjebbes was making Persian/Siamese crosses in Sweden. In 1930, Dr Clyde Keeler and Virginia Cobb started a serious breeding programme in the United States with the same aim. After six years, the first true Himalayan kitten was born. It was appropriately named 'Debutante'. In September 1936 Miss Cobb was able to write an article for *The Journal of Heredity* describing the successful progress of their programme.

After World War II, the development of the Himalayan was taken up in earnest by Marguerita Goforth of San Diego. As the years passed, great improvements were achieved and the breed was finally given official recognition in the United States in 1957.

In Britain, similar breeding experiments were being carried out by Brian Stirling-Webb at Richmond in Surrey. Although his cats were condemned to the unimaginative title of 'Colourpoint Longhairs', their quality was so impressive that they gained official recognition as early as 1955 – two years before the American Himalayans.

Even today, some cat organizations still do not like to give this breed its own separate name. The fact that they carry a genetic contribution – admittedly a relatively small one – from Siamese Cats seems to be sufficient to justify the separate title, but in the end it is simply a matter of taste.

Personality: Terms used to describe this breed include: docile, gentle, intelligent, outgoing, devoted, affectionate and demanding. The voice is slightly louder than that of the full Persian, but much quieter than the Siamese. Because of their mixed ancestry it is inevitable that they will show some characters derived from both their Persian and their Siamese backgrounds. Not

The Himalayan Cat, a breed that displays the attractive combination of a Persian Cat body with Siamese Cat markings. In Britain it is known officially by the more cumbersome name of Colourpoint Longhair.

surprisingly, they are closer to the Persian than the Siamese. One author commented that Himalayans 'are a rest cure to an owner who has endured the domineering ways and boisterous and violent affections of the Siamese'. On the other hand, Himalayans are said to be more enterprising than full Persians, perhaps borrowing a small slice of the Siamese vigour.

Colour Forms:

GCCF: For colour forms, see under their British name of Colourpoint Longhair.

CFA: Himalayan (point) Pattern: Chocolate Point, Seal Point; Lilac Point; Blue Point; Flame (Red) Point; Cream Point; Tortie Point; Blue-Cream Point; Chocolate Tortie Point; Lilac-Cream Point.

Himalayan Lynx (point) Pattern: Seal Lynx Point; Blue Lynx Point; Flame (Red) Lynx Point; Cream Lynx Point; Tortie Lynx Point; Blue-Cream Lynx Point; Chocolate Lynx Point; Lilac Lynx Point; Chocolate Tortie Lynx Point; Lilac-Cream Lynx Point.

Bibliography:

1976. Brearley, J.M. *All About Himalayan Cats.* TFH, New Jersey.

1979. Manton, S.M. *Colourpoint Longhair and Himalayan Cats.* Ferendune and Springwood.

Breed Club:

The Colourpoint Cat Club publishes a twice-yearly magazine. Address: 11 Chestnut Avenue, Ravenshead, Notts., England. Tel: 01623 793980.

Note: There are also two breed publications: *Cat Tracks.* Address: 167 West Genesee Street, Chittenango, NY 13037, USA; and *The Western Edition.* Address: 1575 Hurlburt lane, Sebastopol, CA 95472, USA.

Himbur Cat

Domestic Breed. A new experimental breed based on a cross between Himalayan and Burmese Cats. This is a long-haired cat with Tonkinese markings (the Tonkinese itself being a cross between Burmese and Siamese, displaying a dark brown body with even darker extremities).

Himmy

Pet Cat. Himmy holds the world record for the heaviest domestic cat. He was a neutered tabby cat belonging to Thomas Vyse of Redlynch, Cairns, Queensland, Australia. According to *The Guinness Book of Records* he weighed in at 21.3 kg (46 lb, 15.25 oz). Himmy died of respiratory failure, aged ten, in 1986.

In 1991 an American magazine held a contest to see if there was an American cat who could outweigh Himmy, but they failed to find one. The mightiest feline they could locate was a tabby in Iowa called Spike, and he only managed a modest 16.8 kg (37 lb). They repeated the contest in 1992, but could only come up with a Kansas tom-cat called Morris, who, at 15.9 kg (35 lb), could not even match Spike. For the time being, Himmy's dubious record appears to be safe.

Hinse

Pet Cat. Hinse was a tyrannical tom-cat belonging to Scottish novelist Sir Walter Scott. He constantly terrorized the author's huge dogs and at dinnertime clouted any hound that got in his way. Eventually, in 1826, he met his match. Tormenting a bloodhound called Nimrod once too often, he roused the animal into a violent retaliation and was killed in the ensuing fight. Scott wrote: 'cats are a mysterious kind of folk. There is more passing in their minds than we are aware of.'

Hissing

Feline Behaviour. It seems likely that the similarity between the hiss of a cat and that of a snake is not accidental. It has been claimed that the feline hiss is a case of protective mimicry. In other words, the cat imitates the snake to give the enemy the impression that it too is venomous and dangerous.

The quality of the hissing is certainly very similar. A threatened cat, faced with a dog or some other predator, produces a sound that is almost identical to that of an angry snake in a similar situation. Predators have great respect for venomous snakes, with good reason, and often pause long enough for the snake to escape. This hesitation is usually the result of an inborn reaction. The attacker does not have to learn to avoid snakes. Learning would not be much use in such a context, as the first lesson would also be the last. If a cornered cat is capable of causing alarm in an attacker by triggering off this instinctive fear of snakes, then it obviously has a great advantage, and this is probably the true explanation of the way the feline hiss has evolved.

Supporting this idea is the fact that cats often add spitting to hissing. Spitting is another way in which threatened snakes react. Also, the cornered cat may twitch or thrash its tail in a special way, reminiscent of the movements of a snake that is working itself up to strike or to flee.

Further, it has been pointed out that when a tabby cat (with markings similar to the wild type, or ancestral cat) lies sleeping, curled up tightly on a tree-stump or rock, its coloration and its rounded shape make it look uncannily like a coiled snake. As long ago as the 19th century it was suggested that the markings on a tabby cat are not direct, simple camouflage, but rather are imitations of the camouflage markings of a snake. A predator, seeing a sleeping cat might, as a result of this resemblance, think twice before attacking.

Hodge

Pet Cat. Hodge was a much loved and pampered cat owned by the great 18th-century lexicographer Dr Samuel Johnson. Dr Johnson's biographer, James Boswell, a confirmed cat-hater, was clearly surprised at the trouble Dr Johnson took over his cat, and he records that the great man himself would go out on errands to buy oysters for Hodge, rather than send his staff, 'lest the servants having that trouble should take a dislike to the poor creature'. It seems likely that Johnson was sensitive not only to his staff having to run such errands, but also to the thought that, by doing so, they might start making unfortunate comparisons between their diet and the cat's.

Like many cat-owners, Dr Johnson imagined that his pet understood his thoughts. On one occasion, he was remarking that he had had better cats than Hodge, but then, sensing Hodge's disapproval, quickly added 'but he is a very fine cat, a very fine cat indeed'.

Homing

Feline Behaviour. Over short distances each cat has an excellent visual memory, aided when close to home by familiar scents. Over longer distances cats are also capable of finding their way home, even over distances of several miles, and there has been much debate as to how they achieve this.

Some years ago, a German zoologist borrowed a number of cats from their owners, who lived in the city of Kiel. He placed them in covered boxes and drove them round and round the city, taking a complex, winding route to confuse them as much as possible. Then he drove several miles outside the town to a field in which he had installed a large maze. The maze had a covered central area with 24 passages leading from it. Looked at from above, the passages fanned out like compass points, at intervals of 15 degrees. The whole maze was enclosed, so that no sunlight or starlight could penetrate to give navigation clues to the cats. Then each cat in turn was placed in the maze and allowed to roam around until it chose an exit passage. In a significant number of cases, the cats selected the passage which was pointing directly towards their home.

This result was so puzzling that some critics felt that the cats had somehow managed to retain a memory map of their whereabouts, calculating every twist and turn they had taken. This doubt was removed by some other tests with cats done in the United States. There, the cats were given doped food before the trip, so that they fell into a deep, drugged sleep throughout the journey. When they arrived they were allowed to wake up fully and were then tested. Astonishingly, they still knew the way home.

Since then, many other navigation tests have been carried out with a variety of animals and it is now beyond doubt that many species, including human beings, possess an extraordinary

sensitivity to the earth's magnetic field which enables them (and us) to find the way home without visual clues. The experimental technique which clinched this was the one in which powerful magnets were attached to the navigators. The magnets disrupted the animals' homing ability.

It is still not clear how this homing mechanism works. It seems likely that iron particles occurring naturally in animal tissues are the vital clue, giving the homing individuals a built-in biological compass. But there is obviously a great deal more to discover.

At least it is now possible to accept some of the incredible homing stories that have been told in the past. Previously they were considered to be wildly exaggerated anecdotes, or cases of mistaken identity, but now it seems they must be treated seriously. Cases of cats travelling several hundred miles to return from a new home to an old one, taking several weeks to make the journey, are no longer to be scoffed at.

The latest tale of a remarkable feline homing feat comes from Russia, where a female cat called Murka was sent away to live with the owner's mother. After two days she set off for her original home, arriving there one year later 'dirty, hungry, pregnant and minus the tip of her tail'. The distance travelled was 640 km (400 miles).

Honeybear Cat

Domestic Breed. This is an experimental breed developed as a variant of the Ragdoll Cat. It is not, as yet, accepted by any official cat organization.

Hong Kong Cat

Mystery Cat. In 1976 more than 20 dogs were slaughtered by an unknown feline in the New Territories of Hong Kong. According to local villagers it was 120 cm (4 feet) long and had blackish-grey fur and a long tail. Its identity was never established.

Howel the Good

Feline History. In the year 936, the then Prince of Wales, Hywel Dda, now generally known as Howel the Good, made himself famous in feline history by introducing special laws to protect domestic cats. This is a rare enough event at any time in human history, but in tenth century Europe it was truly remarkable. Howel clearly felt, with good reason, that an animal of such value to agriculture, in its role as a pest-controller, should be more highly respected. He therefore introduced a scale of prices for kittens and cats and fixed penalties for stealing or killing a cat. The prices varied according to the animal's age and killing skills: '1. The worth of a kitten from the night it is kittened until it has opened its eyes is a legal penny. 2. And from that time, until it shall kill mice, two legal pence. 3. And after it shall kill mice, four legal pence.'

The rules laid down by Howel the Good were so precise that, if a cat failed to kill mice, or if it was a female that failed to rear its kittens, the buyer could claim back one-third of the price paid for it. And the penalties for killing or stealing a cat were, to say the least, imaginative: 'The worth of a cat that is killed or stolen; its head to be put downwards upon a clean even floor, with its tail lifted upwards, and thus suspended, whilst wheat is poured about it, until the tip of its tail be covered; and that is to be its worth; if the corn cannot be had, a milch sheep with her lamb and her wool, is its value; if it be a cat which guards the king's barn.'

The cat's value was also equated with that of other livestock: 'There are three animals whose . . . lives are of the same worth: a calf; a filly . . . ; and a cat . . . ' Sadly, this sensible respect for an important working animal was soon to be eclipsed by the savage superstitious persecutions of the medieval Christian Church.

Hugo, Victor

Cat Owner. The favourite cat of the great French novelist and dramatist, Victor Hugo (1802–1885), was a 'magnificent Angora' called Gavroche. The cat was his companion when he was living on the island of Guernsey with his wife and his mistress, while waiting for the fall of

Napoleon III, so that he could safely return to France. This cat was later renamed Chanoine – the canon – because it was so indolent (there being a French expression 'to lead an easy life, like a canon').

Victor Hugo marvelled at the companionship of a cat, commenting: 'God has made the cat to give man the pleasure of caressing the tiger.'

HUMPHREY

WORKING CAT. A long-haired black and white cat called Humphrey, an adopted stray, arrived at No. 10 Downing Street in 1989 as the Prime Minister's official mouser during the premiership of Margaret Thatcher. He outlasted Mrs Thatcher and remained at his post during John Major's occupancy. When he was accused of killing and eating four baby robins in the garden of No. 10, he was defended by his new owner, who announced on television that 'it is quite certain that Humphrey is not a serial killer'. Then in 1995 he disappeared. In September it was assumed

HUMPHREY, the Downing Street Cat, whose fame grew when his death was incorrectly announced in *The Times,* was an adopted stray who had become the Prime Minister's official mouser.

that he had gone away to die in a quiet corner, probably from kidney failure due to his habit of consuming large quantities of civil service biscuits. When his probable death was published in *The Times* the staff of the Royal Army Medical College, situated just over 1.5km (one mile) from No. 10, realized that the cat they had adopted and christened PC, and had fed for some months, was no ordinary stray. He was quickly returned and welcomed back (with international television coverage) to his official role as the First Mouser of the British Isles. Like his namesake (Sir Humphrey in the BBC TV series *Yes, Minister*), he is clearly a survivor.

Bibliography:

1995. Brawn, D. *A Day in the Life of Humphrey the Downing Street Cat.* HarperCollins, London.

HUNTING

FELINE BEHAVIOUR. Of all the carnivores, the cat has become the most snake-like in its hunting techniques. Instead of rushing this way and that, snorting and snuffling and prodding and probing, it is silent, stealthy and still. Above all, it is patient. Using its highly sensitive organs of

All members of the cat family are superb hunters with highly refined skills, whether they are pursuing birds *(right),* rodents *(below),* or fish *(opposite).* In each of these three cases there is a specially adapted 'final strike-action'.

smell, sight and hearing, it selects the best spot and there it waits, making careful use of any cover available.

Even the slightest rustle or tiniest movement is detected. The hunting cat may respond to it by freezing or by stalking. If the signs are that the prey will, unwittingly, come very close, it makes no move; but if this appears unlikely, it will move forward, barely making a sound, often in short, quick advances, interspersed with frozen pauses.

Crouched low, it tenses itself and then, at the very last moment, it attacks. The attack itself varies according to the circumstances. If the prey is nearby, the cat simply pounces on it, grabs it with its razor-sharp front claws, holds it down and delivers a killing bite to the back of its neck. If the prey is a short distance away, the cat breaks cover and makes a high-speed dash before the final pounce. If the prey is a long distance away, the hunter will probably ignore it for, unlike dogs, cats are not marathon runners who gradually wear down their desperately fleeing prey.

When a hunting cat is about to make its final pounce, it sometimes sways its head rhythmically from side to side. This is a device employed by many predators blessed with binocular vision (and is most clearly seen in owls). The head-sway is a way of checking the precise distance at which the prey is located. The cat does this to refine its judgement, because when the rapid pounce forward is made it must be absolutely accurate or it will fail.

It may also reveal its intentions by a slight twitching of its tail. This is a sign of incipient movement, rather like a bull pawing the ground before charging. The tail is primarily a balancing organ, and its wagging movements in the seconds before the attacking leap or sprint are simply signs that the cat's body is getting ready for the power-move. Normally, this tail-swishing is invisible to the prey, because in nature the cat makes maximum use of cover. But the situation changes when a domestic cat is seen stalking a bird on the immaculate lawn of a suburban garden. There the wagging of the tail looks ridiculously conspicuous, and may even alert the bird to the hunter's approach. This has often puzzled human observers, because it appears to be a weakness in the feline stalking technique. But of course there are no neatly

trimmed lawns in nature and during the evolution of the cat there has been no 'lawn-factor' to eliminate this reaction. So the tail action remains, exposed now for all to see, including the prey. For this reason the lawn-hunting cat is rarely successful.

If it does manage to catch a bird, however, another aspect of its hunting technique is revealed. It has three different kinds of 'final strike', depending on the type of prey it is attacking. With mice, the pounce is a simple, downwards action. With birds it is more complicated. Here, the cat anticipates that the prey will fly upwards to escape. As it closes in, it is ready for this and performs an upwards air-leap, swiping at the rising bird with both front feet at once. If it is quick enough to trap the bird's body in this pincer movement of its front legs, it pulls it down to the ground to deliver the killing-bite. With fish, the cat lies in wait by the water's edge. Then, when an unwary fish swims near, it dips a paw swiftly into the water and slides it rapidly under the fish's body, flipping it up out of the water. The direction of the flip is back and over the shoulders of the cat. This flings the prey clear of the water. As the startled fish lands on the grass behind the cat, the hunter swings round and pounces. If the fish is too large to be flipped with the claws of just one front foot, then the cat may risk plunging both front feet into the water at once, grabbing the fish from underneath with its extended talons and then flinging the prey bodily backwards over its head. (In a Dutch study, it was found that if kittens were allowed to hunt fish regularly from their fifth week of life, even in the absence of their mother, they became successful anglers by the age of seven weeks. Pet goldfish beware.)

These three different actions can often be seen in the play of kittens, when they may pounce on a ball (= a mouse), fling it up into the air and leap after it (= a bird), or flip it over the shoulder and spin round to trap it (= a fish). All these special killing actions are programmed into the brain of the kitten, awaiting further development as it matures, and in the meantime revealing themselves as exciting, and highly predictable play-patterns.

This play behaviour of kittens is very different from the apparently playful actions of an adult cat when it has caught and half-killed a prey animal. To human eyes the cat appears to be torturing the prey, but this is not the case. The reason adult cats sometimes 'play' with their prey before devouring them, engaging in hit-and-chase or trap-and-release, is that, if they are well-fed pet cats, they are not hungry enough to start eating immediately, but do have a powerful (and often frustrated) hunting urge that drives them on, again and again, to pounce and pause, pounce and pause.

With wild cats, this type of action is far less common, but even there it can occasionally be seen and then requires a different explanation, since wild or feral cats are usually all too hungry. In their case, the delay in killing may simply be due to fear. If their prey happens to be a rat rather than a mouse, they may be apprehensive about the savage bite a cornered rat can deliver. They will therefore swipe at the rat, trying to stun it, then swipe again and again, until they are sure that the victim is safe to grab and bite. Alternatively, if the cat in question happens to be a female with kittens, she may simply be inhibiting her killing bite and 'half-killing' the rodent, in preparation for carrying it to her offspring, as part of their feline education in the act of killing.

Hunting Leopard

Wild Feline. This was the name generally used for the Cheetah *(Acinonyx jubatus)* until recent times. It was abandoned simply to avoid confusion with the true Leopard *(Panthera pardus)*. The reason for its early popularity was that in the 19th century the Cheetah was widely employed in Asia for hunting game. Local rulers kept large numbers of tame Cheetahs for use on hunting expeditions, training them like coursing greyhounds, walking them on a collar and leash like pet dogs, and hooding them like birds of prey.

According to Richard Lydekker, writing in 1896, these Hunting Leopards were greatly valued and were carefully transported to the hunting field: 'carried either on an Elephant or on horseback on a pad behind the rider, but more generally on a cart made for the purpose, drawn by oxen . . . On approaching the game, the animal is unhooded and slipped . . . ' This practice

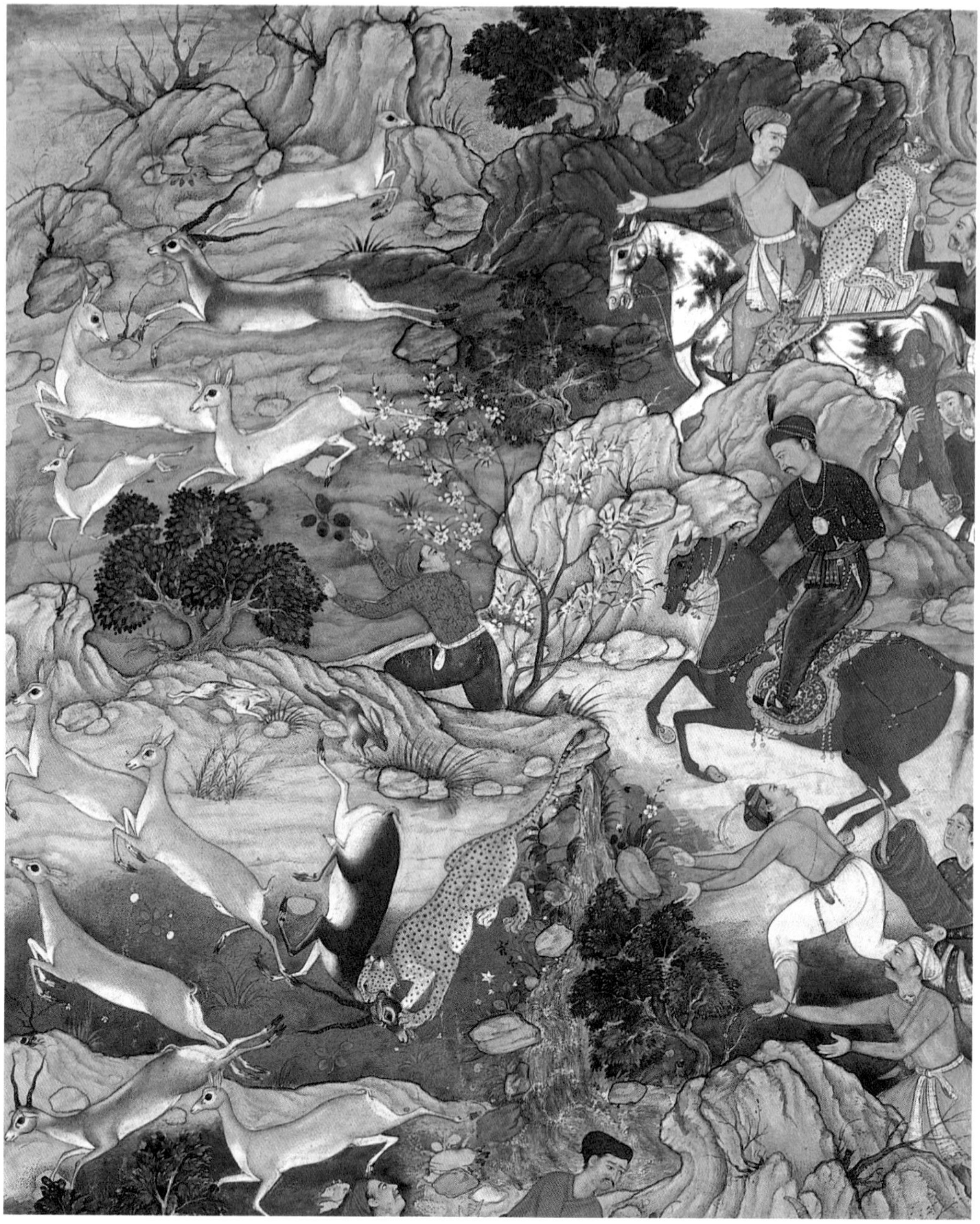

THE HUNTING LEOPARD was the early name given to the animal we know today as the Cheetah. It was hooded and used in the hunting field much as birds of prey are employed today.

dates back at least to the Mogul Empire when 'it is said that some of the emperors, in their great hunting expeditions, were accompanied to the field by a thousand Hunting Leopards'.

The Indian and Persian fashion for hunting with Cheetahs spread to Europe via Armenia and Turkey and became a popular form of exotic pastime at the royal courts. It is recorded that, when it was raining too hard to hunt out of doors, Louis XI of France would let loose his favourite pet Cheetah in the royal apartments, so that it would chase down the huge rats that were infesting them.

Ikimizi

Mystery Cat. In Rwanda the local people speak of a mystery cat they call the Ikimizi, which looks like a cross between a leopard and a lion. It is said to have a spotted grey coat and a beard under the chin.

Although hybrids have been created between leopards and lions (and called Leopons) in the artificial confines of zoos, there is no authenticated record of such a hybrid occurring naturally where the two species co-exist in the wild. It is therefore highly unlikely that the Ikimizi really exists.

However, it must be admitted that the belief in the existence of such an animal is firmly held in a number of quite separate cultures in tropical Africa. In the Cameroons, it is known as the Bung Bung; in Ethiopia it is called the Abasambo; in the Central African Republic it goes by the name of Bakanga; and in Uganda it is the Ntarargo.

Taken together, these local names suggest that there is perhaps, after all, something to be explained. The answer may lie in the direction of the Spotted Lion (see separate entry). This is known to exist, if only from a few skins, and only as a freak mutant. Local people, seeing a Spotted Lion, might naturally assume that it was a cross between a leopard and a lion, rather than an adult lion that had failed to lose its juvenile spotting (although this latter explanation makes much more sense scientifically).

The Indian Cat that appears in the 1903 book *Rabbits, Cats and Cavies*, by Charles Lane, looks remarkably like an early Abyssinian. As a breed, the Indian Cat has long since vanished.

Indian Cat

Domestic Breed. An early type of Long-haired Cat referred to by several Victorian authors, but which soon disappeared from pedigree cat records. Writing in 1893, cat show judge John Jennings comments: 'Indians partake a great deal of the Persian, except that in India we have what is well known there as a "Tiger cat" (not the wild Tiger cat . . .), with striped markings of red and black; it has long hair, but coarser in texture than either of the other long-haired

varieties, and its ears are larger and less furred internally than the Persian, whose tail, however it closely resembles.'

Little more appears to be known about the Indian Long-haired Cat. Either it vanished without trace, contributing nothing to the gene pool of pedigree cats, or it was used in the rather random crossings that took place in the 19th century between the various forms of long-haired cat then in vogue. If it was involved in these matings, and became part of the genetic mixing that was eventually to see the Persian type gain the upper hand, it may have made a minor genetic contribution before sliding into obscurity.

Some confusion is created by the existence of an animal also called an 'Indian Cat' that is illustrated in the 1903 book *Rabbits, Cats and Cavies* by Charles Lane. This is clearly a different type of cat, being short-haired and having the typical colouring and markings of an Abyssinian Cat. It was a pale chestnut red, paler on the underside, with a ticked coat and with light striping on the legs and tail. Like other domestic Indian Cats, it was said to have been an animal 'derived from crosses with some of the smaller wild breeds found in that country'. It was called 'Indischer Fürst' and was owned by a Mrs H.C. Brooke. It is difficult to understand how an animal that looks so much like an Abyssinian Cat could have arrived in England from India at that date, unless, of course, it was taken on board a ship at an appropriate point on a returning voyage. Reading its personal history perhaps gives a clue. Writing in 1903, the cat's owner gives the following astonishing account of its voyage to England:

'This cat . . . was stolen from a hotel in Bombay by an English sailor. He [the cat] twice fell overboard . . . He also suffered shipwreck . . . On arriving nearer home he disappeared and was only after several days' absence discovered in the bowels of the ship, as black as the coal amongst which he had been sojourning . . . His last exploit was to fall in the docks, after which the sailor handed him over to a shoemaker in Leytonstone, where he was discovered by his present owner.' It is obvious from this account that the cat that left Bombay may not have been the same one that arrived in London, so the precise origin of this intriguing animal must remain an open question.

Indoor Cats

Domestic Cats. Many pet cats now spend their entire lives inside their owners' houses. In the last 20 years 'indoor cats' have become increasingly common, especially in the United States, so much so that in 1981 an American author published an entire book (*Indoor Cat* by Curtis) on the subject. The book's message was that 'a cat CAN live happily forever indoors if the owner recognizes and provides for its unique needs'.

Clearly, for anyone living in a New York skyscraper, or any other form of high-rise housing, there is no choice. If they wish to own a cat, the cat must suffer the loss of the great outdoors. This means that they will never know the sensation of stretching out on a sunny lawn or the excitement of creeping stealthily through a shrubbery, sniffing the landscape of changing fragrances, patrolling their territorial boundaries, or occasionally hunting down a small rodent. There is however, one major compensation. According to a recent report, half of all cats are killed in road accidents, and records show that, on average, indoor cats live twice as long as outdoor cats.

The problem for the indoor cat's owners is to make sure that their pet is not 'environmentally deprived' – in other words, that it is not bored stiff and unable to fulfil its feline urges. Ideally, an indoor cat should not be a solitary one. Either it should have a feline companion, with which it can interact, or its owners should spend more time with it than usual. It must also have its own special sleeping place, with a snug bed, a climbing device, a claw-stropping surface and a litter-tray that is positioned well away from its usual feeding and sleeping areas. Suitable toys and hiding places are also a great advantage to the incarcerated cat.

Without a garden, the indoor cat will need a bowl planted with fresh, growing grasses for it to chew on occasionally, to obtain its folic acid supplement (See Grass-eating). And without exposure to sunlight it will require regular vitamin supplements, especially vitamin D, if its coat is to remain healthy. A wire screen over an open window, or a wired-in balcony will allow direct sunlight onto the cat's coat and will also, incidentally, allow wafting fragrances to pass over the cat's sensitive nose, without there being any risk of the animal falling to its death, or escaping onto a busy road.

The indoor life is not ideal for an animal like the inquisitive, territorial feline, but compared with the modern urban alternatives, it is perhaps not so bad.

Ingonyama

Wild Feline. This is the Zulu name for the Lion *(Panthera leo),* its other important African tribal title being the Swahili name of Simba. (For details see Lion.)

Inn Signs

Feline History. In the British Isles, inns, taverns and pubs have for centuries displayed their presence by pictorial sign-boards. Cats rarely featured on the earlier examples of these, probably because the buildings date from the period when felines were being widely persecuted. A number did exist, however, and some of those early ones can still be seen today. The dates given below indicate known references to particular inns:

Cat: A London tavern in Long Lane (1636)

Cat: A London tavern in Rose Street. (1730s–1744)

Cat and Bagpipes: A London tavern on the corner of Downing Street,Westminster, where the clerks of the Foreign Office used to drink. (1810–26) Its name comes from the nursery rhyme: 'A cat came fiddling out of a barn, with a pair of bagpipes under her arm.'

Cat and Bagpipes: A pub near Moate, Kings Co., Ireland. (1866)

Cat and Fiddle: A London tavern in Shire Lane near Temple Bar. (1702–14) The name is thought to be a corruption of a 13th-century French phrase: *Caton Le Fidèle,* meaning 'The Faithful Knight'. The name 'Caton' was given by the French to a knight who successfully defended the town of Calais for Edward I. An alternative explanation is that *Cat and Fiddle* is derived from *La Chatte Fidèle,* meaning *The Faithful Cat,* which was the name given by a Frenchman to his hotel, in honour of his cat Mignonette. A third explanation is that the old game of 'Tipcat', played with a stick and a bat, was accompanied by music played on fiddles. This may later have given rise to the 'Hey Diddle Diddle, the Cat and the Fiddle' rhyme in the 16th century.

Le Catt Cum le Fiddle: A London tavern in Bucklersbury. (1501); renamed *The Catte and the Fiddle* (1536–1660)

Catt and Fiddle: A London tavern in St. Lucknors Lane. (1663)

Catt and Fiddle: A London tavern in Fleet Street. (1568–1660s)

Cat and Kittens: A London tavern near Eastcheap. (1823)

Cat and Lion: An inn at Stockport. (before 1866) The name is explained by the following lines: 'The lion is strong, the cat is vicious, My ale is strong, and so is my liquors.'

Cat and Wheel: A pub at Castle Green, Bristol. (1866)

Cat Head: A village inn at Chiselborough, Somerset. (today)

Cats Head: A London tavern in Orchard Street, Stable Yard, Westminster. (before 1761)

Catt: A London tavern in Old Fish Street. (1633–34)

Catt: A London tavern in Salisbury Court. (1648–60s)

Salutation and Cat: A London tavern in Newgate Street. (1744–71; 1794) This name sometimes appears elsewhere as the *Cat and Salutation*. It originates from the idea that a cat was present at the moment when the angel Gabriel greeted Mary with the news that she was to bear Christ. This greeting was known as the 'Angelic Salutation'.

Whitingtons Cat: A London tavern in Long Lane, West Smithfield. (1657)

Whittingtons Cat: A London tavern in Church Row, Bethnal Green. (1826–27)

Whittington & Cat: A London tavern at 35 High Street, Whitechapel. (1809–27)

Whittingtons & Cat: A London tavern in Golden Lane, Clerkenwell. (1668)

With modern British pubs, cats are more popular. According to Janice Anderson, recent examples with feline names include the following: *Black Cat; Cat and Cracker; Cat and Custard Pot; Cat and Mustard Pot; Cat and Lion; Cat and Mutton; Cat and Tiger; Cat's Whiskers; Cat in the Basket; Cat in the Cage; Cat in the Wall; Cat in the Well; Cat in the Window; Civet Cat; Ginger Tom; Laughing Cat; Mad Cat; Old Cat; Poplar Kitten; Puss in Boots; Rampant Cat; Red Cat; Romping Cat; Salutation and Cat; Squinting Cat; Tabby Cat.*

According to Geraldine Mellor, there is also a pub called the *Burmese Cat* at Melton Mowbray in Leicestershire, and one called the *Cheshire Cat* at Ellesmere Port in Cheshire. In France there is a *Hunchback Cat* at Lille and a *White Cat (Chatte Blanche)* at Lyons.

Bibliography:

1987. Anderson, J. *Cat-a-logue.* Guinness Books, Enfield, Middlesex.

1866. Larwood, J. & Hotten, J.C. *The History of Signboards.* Hotten, London.

1972. Lillywhite, B. *London Signs.* Allen & Unwin, London.

1988. Mellor, G. 'At the Sign of the Cat'. In: *Cat World Annual 1988.*

Iriomote Cat

Wild Feline. *(Felis bengalensis iriomotensis)* Also known to the local people as the Pingimaya.

When first discovered, this small, spotted cat was thought to represent an entirely new species, but is now generally considered to be merely a local race of the Leopard Cat.

When it was first encountered, as recently as 1967, by the Japanese zoologist Yoshinori Imaizumi, it caused great excitement. The idea that a new species of feline could be discovered in the second half of the 20th century seemed amazing. It was located on the small island of Iriomote near Taiwan. Although, with its spotted coat, long trunk and round ears with 'eye-spots' on their backs, it looked remarkably like a Leopard Cat, Imaizumi found that it had only 28 teeth instead of the usual 30. In place of three pre-molars on each side of the upper jaw, it had only two.

Writing in 1968, he commented: 'Although they are quite different when they are adult, the newly born leopard cat and feral cat have skulls which are very similar to those of the Iriomote

The painfully rare Iriomote Cat *(Felis bengalensis iriomotensis)*, of which there are fewer than 80 still surviving. It is confined to a small island near Taiwan and may well become extinct within a few decades.

cat . . . The likeness disappears as they develop and lose their juvenile characteristics.' The Iriomote cat 'on the other hand, retains its juvenile skull characters into adulthood.' In other words, the Iriomote cat is a neotenous variant.

On the strength of this, it was not only given its own species, but even its own genus *(Mayailurus)*. This over-enthusiastic reaction to its discovery has not been sustained, but it is certainly a most interesting sub-species of Leopard Cat and one that deserves protection for further study. Unfortunately, it is a popular food item among the local people, and agricultural development is also robbing it of its sub-tropical rain-forest strongholds. It is now estimated that there are only between 40 and 80 individuals left. These dramatically low numbers must make it one of the rarest forms of wild feline in existence.

Intriguingly, the Iriomote islanders also speak of another, larger cat that they insist lurks deep in their rain forests. This one is called the Yamamaya to distinguish it from the little Pingimaya, and is said to be 'the size of a sheepdog and looks like a tiger'. It remains to be seen whether Science and the Yamamaya ever come face to face.

Size: Length of Head + Body: 50 cm (20 in). Tail: 23 cm (9 in). Weight: 5.5 kg (12 lb).

Distribution: Found only on the tiny, 292 sq km (113 sq mile), Japanese-owned island of Iriomote, 100 km (62 miles) east of Taiwan.

Italian Rex Cat

Domestic Breed. First discovered in Italy in 1950, this wavy-haired cat was clearly carrying the Rex gene, but was not used for a serious breeding programme and seems to have vanished in one generation.

Jaguar

Wild Feline. *(Panthera onca)* Also known locally as El Tigre, or simply Tigre. Less commonly used local names include: Onça, Onça Pintada, Otorongo, Penitigri and Zacbolay. The word 'Jaguar' itself comes either from the Guiana Indian word 'Yaouar', or 'Jaguara'. (For explanation of the meaning of the name *onca,* see entry for Snow Leopard.)

The biggest of the New World cats, the Jaguar is the third-largest of all cats, exceeded in size only by the Tiger and the Lion. It is the least well known of the Big Cats. Wildlife cameramen have exposed in detail the social lives of the Old World species – the Tiger, the Lion, the Leopard and the Cheetah – but the Jaguar has remained elusive in its Amazonian forest strongholds.

To many people the Jaguar and the Leopard look remarkably alike, with their heavily spotted, orange coats, but there are several key differences. The most obvious diagnostic difference lies inside the spots. In both animals there is a pale interior to many of the large spots, but in the Jaguar some of these spots always have small black dots *inside* the pale interior. Also, the Jaguar is generally heavier and stockier than the Leopard. It has shorter, thicker legs, bigger paws, a shorter back, a larger head and more powerful teeth and jaws.

As one author put it, the Jaguar is powerful rather than graceful, strong rather than speedy. Its impressive physical power is well illustrated by an incident in which a Jaguar was observed to have dragged a freshly killed, fully grown horse a distance of over 1.5 km (about a mile). Even more impressive is the fact that, during this long journey, it had at one point to pull its heavy prey across a river. It is interesting to contemplate how many men would have been needed to carry out such a task, even using ropes.

So strong is this Big Cat that it seems to use a slightly different killing technique when dealing with big prey. The other large felines usually knock their prey down and then apply a throat bite, clamping their jaws onto the victim's neck until it suffocates. But the Jaguar uses a more direct approach – it simply bites straight through the skull, driving its huge fangs right into the victim's brain.

Although the Jaguar climbs well, most of its hunting is done at ground level at night, using both stalk-and-rush and ambush techniques. Its prey varies considerably, from tapirs, peccaries

JAGUAR

THE JAGUAR *(Panthera onca)*, the largest cat of the Americas, is very similar to the Leopard that is found in Africa and Asia. It can be told apart by the presence of small black dots inside some of its large ring-spots. These never occur in the Leopard.

and capybaras to crocodilians, turtles, large birds and even fish. The Jaguar is fond of water and spends a great deal of time in and around rivers and streams.

This species is solitary and territorial. The territories of the males are twice as large as those of the females and each male has a range which overlaps with those of several females. When the female comes into heat, she wanders far and wide, mating with the territorial males she encounters. The breeding season differs from region to region, starting, for example, in March in Argentina and in December in Brazil. The litter of one to four cubs is weaned at between five and six months of age and the young animals become mature when they are three years old.

One special feature that Jaguars have in common with Leopards is the high frequency of black individuals that appear in the wild population. In certain areas they are even said to be more common than the spotted form.

Size: Length of Head + Body: 110–185 cm (43½–73in). Tail: 45–75 cm (18–29½ in). Weight: up to 138 kg (304 lb).

Distribution: The Jaguar is found today from Mexico south to Argentina. Its last stronghold is Amazonia and it is rare everywhere else. It used to be found in the southernmost parts of North America, but is now extinct there. And it is believed that there are only a few hundred left in the whole of Central America. Because of its forest habitat it is difficult to estimate its total numbers with any accuracy, but it is safe to say that it is an endangered species because of deforestation, persecution as a result of its attacks on domestic animals and, above all, fur-trapping. The fur trade records show that, as recently as the 1960s, there was an annual slaughter of no fewer than 15,000 Jaguars in Amazonian Brazil alone. Today, 15,000 is probably not too far from the figure for the total world population.

Bibliography:

1970. Perry, R. *The World of the Jaguar*. David & Charles, Newton Abbot.
1987. Rabinowitz, A. *Jaguar*. Collins, London.

THE JAGUAR has a heavier head, more powerful jaws, shorter legs and bigger paws than its close relative, the Leopard. Today it is extremely rare outside its last stronghold, the Amazonian rain-forest.

JAGUARETE

THE JAGUARETE is a mysterious cat about which little is known. It is not even certain that it actually exists, although it has been illustrated in early Natural Histories. This picture comes from Thomas Bewick's *General History of Quadrupeds* (1790).

JAGUARETE

MYSTERY CAT. The early naturalists Buffon and Bewick both refer to this mysterious animal, which they also called the 'Couguar noir' or 'Black Tiger'. They describe it as having a dusky coat, sometimes with black spots, but usually plain. The undersides of the animal are pale and the upper lip and paws are white. It has sharply pointed ears. A large, powerful cat, it is 'cruel and fierce' and much feared by the local people. Frequenting the seashore, it feeds on turtles' eggs. It also takes large reptiles and fish. Its hunting methods are remarkable: 'In order to catch the alligator, they lie down on their belly at the edge of the river, strike the water to make a noise, and as soon as the alligator raises its head above the water, dart their claws into its eyes and drag it on shore.'

It would seem from this description that the animal in question is no more than a melanistic Jaguar or Puma – possibly both, confused and amalgamated in local stories. But its pale underparts and white paws do not fit with this explanation, as melanistic cats tend to be black all over.

The plot thickens with the comment by another early naturalist, Thomas Pennant, that two Jaguaretes were actually exhibited in London in the 18th century. Precisely what they were remains a mystery at present, but the most likely explanation is that they were some kind of mutant Jaguar.

JAGUARUNDI

WILD FELINE. *(Felis yaguarondi)* There are three alternative spellings of its common name: Jaguarundi/Jaguarondi/Yaguarundi. Among local people it is known as the Gato Moro, Gato Pardo, Gato Eyra, Gato Cerban, Gato Mourisco, Tigrillo Negro or Tigrillo Congo. The name Jaguarundi is a local (Tupi) word meaning 'Little Jaguar', but in reality this small cat looks nothing like its massive, spotted cousin.

One of the most unusual of the small cats, the Jaguarundi is sometimes called the 'Weasel Cat' because of its long neck, pointed head, small, rounded ears, slender body and short legs. Its elongated shape gives it the look of an animal that is halfway between a cat and a mustelid.

THE AMERICAN JAGUARONDI *(Felis yaguarondi)* is one of the most unusual of all wild felines, looking rather like a cross between a cat and a mongoose, with its long, pointed head, short legs and dark, self-coloured coat.

This, its round pupils, and its plain, unspotted coat, give it the appearance of a primitive proto-cat and visually set it apart from all other living cat species.

Its colour forms show wide variation. It may be black, brown, grey, red or tawny yellow. It used to be thought that the red form was a separate species which was then called the Eyra. It is now known that the red and grey forms can occur in the same litter.

A ground-dwelling species, it is less nocturnal than other small cats and feeds on small mammals, birds and reptiles and hunts over a huge home range. Despite its short legs it is a fast runner and can make rapid darts towards its intended prey. It has also been said to eat various fruits, such as green figs, although captive specimens seem to show little interest in such foods. A strong swimmer, in some regions such as Mexico the Jaguarundi has sometimes been referred to as an Otter Cat.

It is said to become reasonably tame when kept in captivity, at least until it catches sight of a plump bird, when it becomes transformed into an uncontrollably enthusiastic hunter. Its voice is a bird-like chirrup and it purrs like a domestic cat when friendly. In pre-Columbian times, it is thought to have been partially domesticated as a rat-catcher.

Size: Length of Head + Body: 55–77 cm (21½–30½ in). Tail: 33–60 cm (13–23½ in). Weight: 5 – 9 kg (11–20 lb).

Distribution: The Jaguarundi is found over a wide range in South and Central America, but is uncommon everywhere. In the north it just reaches into the most southernmost parts of North America (in southern Arizona and Texas), but is extremely rare there. In the south it reaches northern Argentina.

The habitat of this essentially lowland cat varies from rain forest to secondary forest and scrubland.

Jake

Film Cat. An extraterrestrial cat of superior intelligence, equipped with a magic collar, who is forced to land his spacecraft on the planet Earth for urgent repairs. Jake stars in a 1978 Walt Disney film comedy featuring Roddy McDowall and Sandy Duncan. A professional feline called Rumple plays the role of the alien cat.

Japanese Bobtail Cat

Domestic Breed. A stump-tailed Eastern cat, sometimes referred to as the *Mi-Ke* Cat (pronounced mee-kay). Among their owners, these cats are affectionately known as 'Bobs' or JBTs. In Holland the breed is known as the *Japanse Stompstaartkat.*

Appearance: A short-haired cat with a lean, muscular body and slender legs. The hind legs are a little longer than the front legs, giving an upward tilt to the rump region. The unique tail is a stump 5–10 cm (2–4 inches) long, tightly curved on itself and with restricted movement. The hair covering of the tail is thick and fluffy, giving it a pompom-like quality. The delicate head is slightly pointed, with slanted eyes.

Despite its superficial resemblance to the Manx Cat, the two breeds are genetically quite distinct.

History: This is an ancient breed which, although now thought of as exclusively Japanese, originally appears to have been observed in many regions of the Far East, including Malaysia, Burma and Thailand. There are 19th-century references to a breed called the Malay Cat, which from its description sounds identical. (See Malay Cat.)

There is some disagreement as to the precise date at which the Bobtail arrived in Japan. Some authorities claim that it was introduced from China about a thousand years ago, probably at the instigation of the cat-loving Japanese Emperor Ichijo. Others put the date even earlier, in the ninth, eighth, seventh or even sixth century, because of the existence of very early woodcuts and paintings of cats, especially those from the Gotokuji and Niko Temples.

For centuries the Bobtails were the exclusive pets of the nobility, who used to walk them on a collar and lead, and it was not until the beginning of the 17th century that they were allowed

Japanese Bobtail Cat

The Japanese Bobtail Cat, with its characteristic pom-pom tail, is an ancient Oriental breed. Although today it is strongly associated with Japan, it seems to have had a much wider range in the past, from Burma and Thailand, through Malaysia.

to spread to the general population. The reason for this change of heart was that it was officially decreed that all the noble cats had to be set free to act as badly needed pest-controllers. From this point onwards it became known as the *Kazoku Neko,* the Family Cat of Japan.

The Bobtail has been pictured in Japanese works of art from many epochs. The most famous representation is in the woodcut 'Cat in Window' by the 19th-century artist Ando Hiroshige.

The favoured type is the *Mi-Ke* (meaning three-coloured, or, literally, 'three fur') which is white with bold patches of black and red. It was believed that to own such a cat would bring good luck, and it has become identified with the legendary 'Beckoning Cat' (see entry).

An additional factor that may help to account for the popularity of this short-tailed cat is the existence of a folk-myth in Japan which warns that long-tailed cats can change into human form and bewitch their owners.

The breed attracted the attention of the West when the American soldiers of the occupying army encountered it at the end of World War II. In 1968, an American called Judy Crawford, who had been living in Japan for 15 years and who had been breeding these cats during most of that time, sent a pair to the United States. The pair consisted of a tortoiseshell and white female called Madame Butterfly and a red and white male called Richard. They were sent to the well-known breeder Elizabeth Freret, who had already discovered the breed and become intrigued by it. (She also received a third one, a cinnamon tabby female, which she did not keep.) The pair soon produced kittens, which Mrs Freret took to an American cat show in 1969, where they aroused great interest. Judy Crawford herself was soon to return to America, accompanied by 38 of her Japanese Bobtails. There she continued to breed her cats and to create a circle of enthusiasts. In 1970 the International Japanese Bobtail Fanciers Association was formed and the breed was well on the way to acceptance as an exciting addition to the world of pedigree cat showing. In 1978 the CFA granted it full recognition.

Despite its growing popularity in America, the Japanese Bobtail did not arrive in Great Britain until the 1970s, when a single female Bobtail was brought to England from Japan by its owner.

A long-haired version also now exists (see separate entry).

Personality: Terms used to describe this breed include: friendly, loyal, intelligent, affectionate, playful, outgoing, lively and inquisitive.

Vocally, they are said to have a 'melodious chant' unique to their breed, which they use when they are pleased.

Colour Forms: The following are the favoured ones, although many other combinations are accepted: Black, red and white (Mi-Ke); Black, red and cream (tortoiseshell); Black and white; Red and white; Tortoiseshell and white; White; Black; Red.

Bibliography:

1995. Edwards, A. 'The Japanese Bobtail'. In: *All About Cats,* July 1995. p.13-21.

Breed Club:

Japanese Bobtail Breeders Society. Address: 1272 Hillwood Lane, Vineland, NJ 08360, USA.

Note: There are also two breed publications: *Bobs.* Address: 1069 Gridley Street, Bay Shore, NY 11706, USA; and *Pom!* Address: P.O. Box 338, Napanee, IN 46550-0338, USA.

The Japanese Bobtail Longhair Cat is a recent offshoot of the ancient breed. Originally ignored in favour of the traditional short-haired examples, the Longhair has only been taken seriously in the second half of the 20th century.

Japanese Bobtail Longhair Cat

Domestic Breed. In 1954 the Japanese began to develop a long-haired version of the Bobtail as a distinct breed. Previously, long-haired specimens had been frequently seen as street cats in the northern provinces, but had been ignored as undesirable oddities by the pedigree cat world. Then it was decided to isolate and pure-breed them and they soon gained a considerable following.

In America, they were accepted as a separate breed by TICA in 1991 and at the same time the standards for the ordinary, short-haired Bobtail were slightly revised.

Javanese Cat

Domestic Breed. A long-haired version of the Siamese Cat, closely related to the Balinese Cat. The definition of the Javanese is confusing, to say the least. The name has different meanings in different regions:

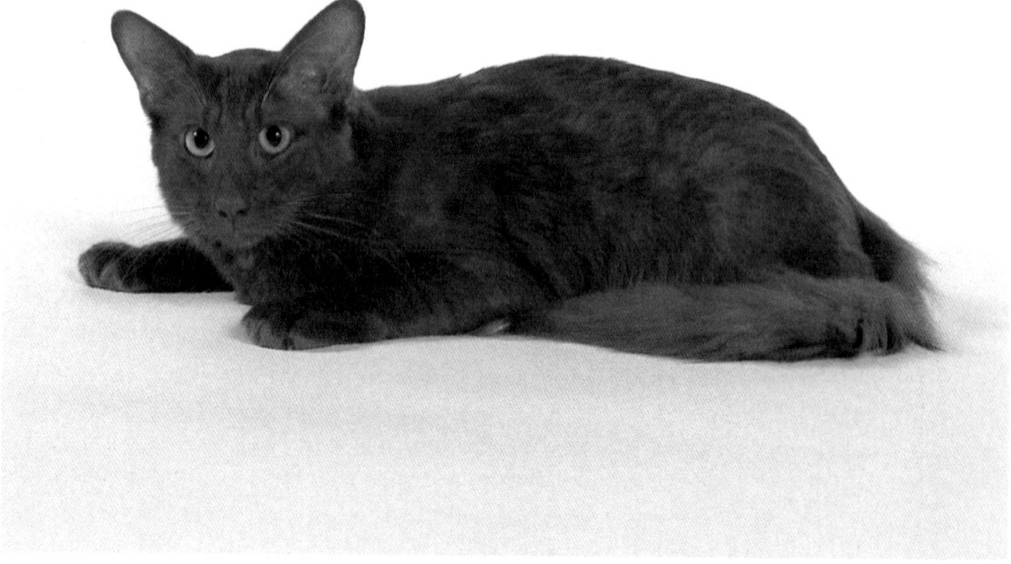

The elegant, elongated, Javanese Cat. There has been considerable confusion about precisely what constitutes a Javanese, and the breed is treated differently in different countries. In essence, it is a long-haired Siamese without colourpoints.

1 In the United States, long-haired Siamese Cats are called Balinese if they show one of the four basic Siamese colourpoint patterns (Seal, Chocolate, Blue, or Lilac) and Javanese if they show any other colour pattern. (Some American cat societies do not make this distinction, however, calling them all Balinese.)
2 In New Zealand, long-haired Siamese Cats are called Balinese if they show any colourpoint pattern, and Javanese if they have spotted or self-coloured coats.
3 In Britain, long-haired Oriental cats, originally bred to recreate the Angora, are now known as Javanese.

Appearance: The elegant, angular, elongated body, the wedge-shaped head, the large ears and the blue eyes are all typically Siamese. The Javanese only differs from the Siamese in the possession of a long, silky coat. And it only differs from the Balinese in the colours of that coat.
History: In America those breeders who were concentrating on developing the Balinese breed in the 1960s found that, from time to time, kittens were born with unusual colour patterns. If these colours did not conform to the basic Siamese colours, they were not accepted as true Balinese. Instead of discarding them, they were placed into a new category, that of the Javanese.

In Britain in the 1960s and 1970s attempts were being made to re-create the Angora Cat, using long-haired variants of Oriental Shorthairs. In 1989 these artificially reconstituted Angoras were given a new name to avoid confusion with the true Turkish Angoras; the name chosen was Javanese, despite the fact that the American Javanese was already well known. Adding more confusion, some breeders referred to this British form of Javanese as the Cuckoo Cat and formed a breed club called 'The Cuckoo Cat Club'. Making matters even more complicated, certain breeders in Holland renamed the British form of the Javanese Cat, calling it the Mandarin Cat. This name has also been taken up in Germany.

Just as the Balinese Cat had never existed in Bali, so the Javanese Cat had never seen Java – the name was merely an exotic-sounding Oriental location.
Personality: As for Siamese.

Colour Forms: Generally speaking, the American Javanese can appear in any colour seen in the Colourpoint Shorthair. Colours listed by the Cat Fanciers' Association are as follows:
CFA: Red Point; Cream Point; Seal Lynx Point; Chocolate Lynx Point; Blue Lynx Point; Lilac Lynx Point; Red Lynx Point; Chocolate-Tortie Lynx Point; Blue-Cream Lynx Point; Lilac-Cream Lynx Point; Cream Lynx Point; Seal-Tortie Lynx Point; Seal-Tortie Point; Chocolate-Tortie Point; Blue-Cream Point; Lilac-Cream Point.

Outside America, Javanese colours are related instead to those of the Oriental Shorthair.

Jennie

Fictional Cat. A scrawny, stray tabby featured in the work of author Paul Gallico, first appearing in his story about a boy who had been turned into a cat, *The Abandoned* (1950). Jennie (full name Jennie Baldrin) teaches the boy how to behave like a cat – how to fall on his feet, catch a mouse, kill a rat and defend himself.

Jeoffry

Pet Cat. Jeoffry belonged to the tragic 18th-century poet Christopher Smart. A distinguished Cambridge scholar and fellow of Pembroke College, he ran into debt, sank into poverty and then became seriously ill. This affected his mind and he ended up in the living hell of solitary confinement in Bedlam. He languished in his dark, rat-infested cell in the London madhouse for several years and during this time the cat Jeoffry was his only companion.

Smart wrote a long, meandering poem which included some haunting lines about his pet: 'For I will consider my cat Jeoffry . . . For he is of the tribe of tiger . . . For he will not do destruction, if he is well-fed, neither will he spit without provocation . . . For he is an instrument for the children to learn benevolence upon . . . For every house is incompleat without him . . . For he is the cleanest in the use of his fore-paws of any quadrupede . . . For he is the quickest to the mark of any creature. For he is tenacious of his point. For he is a mixture of gravery and waggery . . . For there is nothing sweeter than his peace when at rest. For there is nothing brisker than his life when in motion . . . For he is hated by the hypocrite and miser . . . For he is good to think on, if a man would express himself neatly . . . ' Smart eventually died in a debtors' prison in 1771.

Jeoffry washing himself. Jeoffry was the sole companion of the tragic poet Christopher Smart when he was confined to a dank cell in Bedlam.

Jones

Film Cat. The orange tabby 'ship's cat' who lives on board the space-ship 'Nostromo' in the science fiction classic *Alien* (Twentieth Century Fox, 1979), featuring Sigourney Weaver and John Hurt.

Jungle Cat

Wild Feline. *(Felis chaus)* Also known as the Chaus; the Swamp Cat or Swamp Lynx; the Reed Cat or Reit-Kat; and the Jangli-billi (in India). German: *Rohrkatze;* French: *Chat de Marais*.

This highly successful, adaptable feline is a cat for all seasons and almost all habitats. The only environments it shuns are the two extremes of dense rain forest and arid desert. It is a cat of moderation in all things, not only environment, but also colour, size, shape and diet. A flexible, all-purpose cat, it has thrived through its determined lack of specialization.

Its short, pale brown coat varies from sandy-grey to rich tawny-red. From a distance there appear to be no markings on it at all, but closer inspection reveals a few faint bands on the legs and tail. The ears are sharply pointed, with long black hairs at their tips creating small ear-tufts. The tail is rather short for a cat.

A long-legged animal, the Jungle Cat is a fast-moving species that has been timed at 23 km (14 miles) per hour. Although it can climb well, it prefers to remain at ground-level whenever possible. Its habitats include reed beds, grasslands, thickets, broken woodland and even some forests. It is less shy of approaching human habitation than many other wild cat species. As a precaution, it often has more than one den available to it at any one time, giving itself flexibility

The Jungle Cat *(Felis chaus)* has a wide range, spanning no fewer than 25 countries, from Egypt to China. It usually has a very plain brown coat, but in some regions, as with this specimen from Israel, dark markings are more conspicuous.

even in retreat. As a hunter, it is more diurnal than most other small cats. The preferred diet consists of rats, mice, lizards and frogs.

The breeding season varies in different parts of its wide range and in captivity it will breed at any time of the year. Courtship and mating activities are very similar to those of the domestic cat. Like some other wild felines, the Jungle Cat female provides a snug, fur-lined nest for its litter, which usually consists of three or four kittens.

Surprisingly, considering the size difference, fertile female hybrids have successfully been produced between captive Jungle Cats and domestic cats. In this connection, it is interesting to recall that the ancient Egyptians mummified this species as well as the ordinary African Wild Cat. Of 190 skulls of mummified cats examined by the Natural History Museum in London, 187 turned out to be ordinary Wild Cats and three proved to be Jungle Cats. This may be a very small proportion of Jungle Cats, but it nevertheless suggests that the early Egyptians had tried their hand at domesticating this larger species as well as the smaller one. The tawny-coloured, ticked coat of the Jungle Cat is so reminiscent of the coat of the domesticated Abyssinian Cat that it is tempting to see a connection here and to suggest that, perhaps, the Jungle Cat did play a minor role in the development of our modern domestic cats. At present, however, this is pure speculation and it would require a sustained interbreeding programme to test the point further.

Size: Length of Head + Body: 50–75 cm (19½–29½ in). Tail: 22–29 cm (8½–11½ in). Weight: 7–16 kg (15½–35 lb).

Distribution: This species has a remarkably wide range, from N.E. Africa right through to the Orient. Between these two extremes it is found in the following countries: Egypt, Israel, Syria, Iraq, Iran, Afghanistan, S. Russia, Nepal, India, Sri Lanka, Pakistan, Burma, Thailand, Vietnam and W. China. It is not restricted to any particular elevation, being found both at sea level and up in the highlands.

Kallibunker

Pet Cat. Kallibunker was the founding father of the Cornish Rex breed. A red tabby with an unusual curly coat, the only one in his litter of five to have such a coat, he was born on 21st July 1950 in an old farmhouse on Bodmin Moor in Cornwall. His owner, Mrs Nina Ennismore, mated Kallibunker back to his mother, a tortoiseshell farm cat called Serena, and in this way began the in-breeding programme that was to secure the Cornish Rex Cat for the future. Sadly, in 1956, when her collection of Rex Cats had risen to about 40, she had to reduce the numbers for economic reasons. Kallibunker, although still young, was among those she had put to sleep, but enough of his offspring survived to continue his line.

Kangaroo Cat

Feline Mutation. On two separate occasions, at different localities, a bizarre mutation has appeared among domestic cats, giving them dramatically shortened front legs. This condition is known to be inherited, because it has been seen in at least four litters. The animals in question exhibit a hunched-up gait and, when sitting up, adopt a posture that makes them look like miniature kangaroos.

This mutation appears to be related to the one seen in the Munchkin Cat, where all four legs are shortened.

Karakul Cat

Domestic Cat. It is reported that in the 1930s curly-coated mutations occasionally occurred among short-haired cats in the United States. These individuals were referred to as Karakul Cats, but no attempt appears to have been made to study them or to use them to establish a new breed. They were obviously isolated precursors of the Rex breeds that were developed after World War II.

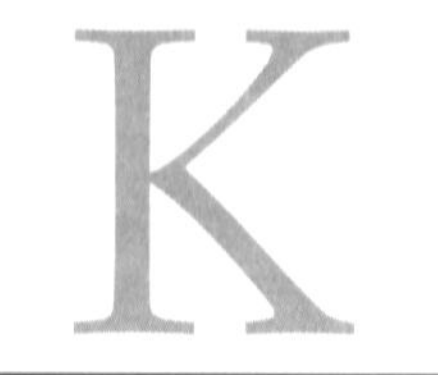

Karelian Bobtail Cat

Domestic Breed. Similar to the Japanese Bobtail Cat, but with a longer coat. Little is known about this breed. In 1995 international judge Alan Edwards commented: 'In Germany last year, I encountered a new variety called the Karelian Bobtail, a semi-longhaired cat from Russia. Its Standard of Points includes: "as many bents in the tail as possible".'

Karoun

Pet Cat. The 'King of Cats' ('deaf to orders, to appeals, to reproaches') to whom his owner, French author Jean Cocteau (1889–1963) dedicated his work *Drôle de Ménage*.

He also used a long-haired grey cat of his acquaintance as the model for the feline costume worn by The Beast in his classic film *Beauty and the Beast*.

Kashmir Cat

Domestic Breed. A solid-coloured version of the Himalayan Cat developed in North America. It has no connection with Kashmir. The name is based on the fact that this breed is close to the Himalayan breed and that Kashmir is close to the Himalayas.

Appearance: A Persian Cat with solid chocolate or lilac fur.

History: In the 1930s, breeding programmes were started to obtain a Persian cat with Siamese markings. This colourpointed Persian, called the Himalayan, was given championship status in the 1950s (1955 in Britain and 1957 in the United States). During the course of creating the Chocolate Point and Lilac Point versions of this breed, occasional specimens appeared with solid colours. Some breeders decided that these all-over Chocolate and all-over Lilac individuals should be given separate breed status under the name Kashmir. There was considerable opposition to this on the grounds that this was just another minor colour variation and did not justify a separate title. One author described the Kashmir as 'a taxonomist's daydream and a superfluous breed division'. Another says it is 'unnecessary splitting . . . simply in order to create another breed'. As a result, it remains controversial, welcomed by some but ignored by many. The Canadian Cat Association is one of the few major organizations to accept it as a separate category. For most others, the cats are merely Chocolate Persians or Lilac Persians.

Technically, the justification for calling these cats by a separate name is this: when the Himalayan Cats were being developed from traditional Persians, they acquired their Siamese colourpoints from an introduction of Siamese genes into the breeding programme. When a few self-coloured individuals arose by accident in this programme, they may have lacked the colourpoints, but still carried a Siamese genetic element in their make-up. They are therefore not pure Persians, even though they may look like them. In other words, this is a cat that is given a separate breed name, not for what you see when you look at it, but for what is hidden in its genetic make-up. For some authorities this is simply not enough.

Personality: Terms used to describe this breed include: gentle, intelligent, outgoing, calm, self-confident, devoted, demanding and affectionate.

Kaspar

Talismanic Cat. A black cat carved in wood, Kaspar is the famous 'lucky cat' employed by the Savoy Hotel in London to occupy the 14th seat at dinner parties when the guests unexpectedly form a group of 'unlucky 13'. For some people, the superstition about not sitting down to dinner as a member of a party of 13 is held so strongly that it can create something of a crisis for a top restaurant. The Savoy suavely solves the problem by ceremoniously placing the figure of Kaspar in an extra chair. The wooden cat, carved by Basil Ionides in 1926, has been used by many famous guests including, on several occasions, that great cat-lover Sir Winston Churchill.

In origin, the fear of the number 13 dates back to Norse mythology when 12 gods were joined at a feast by an evil spirit, who proceeded to cause havoc. Later, the idea of 'unlucky 13' was taken up by Christian mythology and given a new boost by the number of guests present at 'The Last Supper'.

In the case of the Savoy Hotel, this superstition had acquired extra significance when one of its guests, who had been forced to sit down as host of a party of 13 because one of his guests cancelled at the last moment, was later shot dead in his office. After that, the hotel always provided a member of their staff, if an extra place at the table was needed to avoid a group of 13. However, some dinner parties involved confidential conversations, and so Kaspar was born as a 'silent 14th'. When he was placed at the table, a napkin was tied around his neck and waiters were always careful to change his place-settings for each course of the meal. Even today this tradition persists.

Kattestoet

Feline History. In the Belgian city of Ypres there is a curious Cat Festival on the second Sunday in May, called the *Kattestoet*. It is curious because it originated in a epoch when cats were suffering severe persecution and involved extreme cruelty to them, whereas today this same ceremony, with minor but significant modifications, is seen as a festival to celebrate the cat and is attended by thousands of cat-lovers.

In its earliest form it consisted of a feast, the culmination of which was the throwing of live cats from the top of the tall tower in the city centre. The crowd cheered as the cats fell to their deaths because the unfortunate animals were seen as devilish creatures and the pious Christians who took part in these events felt that, by destroying the cats, they were defeating the Devil. Astonishingly, some of the cats survived their great fall and managed to crawl away after they landed. This started a new superstition. If a cat survived, it must have been an innocent one and its charmed life meant that there would be a good harvest that year.

Amazingly, these cruelties persisted until the 19th century and were not stopped until the year 1817. In the 1930s, the good citizens of Ypres were missing their annual festival and it was decided to start it up again, but this time using only dummy cats. Abandoned during World War II, the Festival of Cats was not begun again until the 1950s and since then has grown and grown both in scale and popularity until today it is a major spectacle – a feline Mardi Gras. In fact, it has grown so big that it can no longer be held annually, but only at intervals of three years.

A strange feline scene in a side street of the Belgian city of Ypres, as the inhabitants prepare for the famous Cat Festival, or Kattestoet. When they march in procession through the city centre, it takes three hours for the parade to pass.

One of the most recent festivals – the 37th in the modern phase – was held on Sunday, 7th May 1994. The official festival programme for that day gives a flavour of the events:

11.00 am: Aperitif Concert

14.00 pm: Introduction to the Parade

15.00 pm: 37th Cats' Parade begins

18.00 pm: Cat Throwing (Belfort Tower)

20.30 pm: Evening spectacular: 'Witches' Brew', including Witch Burning in the Great Market

22.30 pm: Grand Musical firework display

The parade is now so vast that it takes three hours to pass. It consists of enormous feline floats and cat effigies representing every phase of the cat's long history, starting with Cat Worship in Ancient Egypt and ending with a lively display by modern 'Cheercats' (young females with feline make-up, complete with cheerleaders' costumes and pompoms). The giant floats are accompanied by thousands of adults and children, dressed as cats of one type or another, with marching bands and orchestras to serenade them.

Although many of the towering cat figures are antique and impressively atmospheric, the combination of ancient cat persecution and modern cat celebration has about it a peculiar contradiction, as though Walt Disney had been asked to mount his version of the Spanish Inquisition.

The many floats include the following set-pieces: (1) The Cat in Egypt; (2) The Cat in Celtic Times; (3) The Cat in Germanic Times; (4) Cat Proverbs; (5) Tybaert the Tom-cat; (6) Puss-in-Boots; (7) Because of the Grease; (8) A Bird for the Cat; (9) They are Burying a Big Cat; (10) Catty Kwabette and the Emperor Karel; (11) The Siege of The Cat's Stronghold; (12) The Condemnation of the Cat and the Witch.

The final burning of the witches may today be purely theatrical, but it is a sobering thought that it is re-enacted on the very spot in the city centre where, between 1561 and 1595, 300 witches were, in reality, brought to face the Inquisition and a hideous death in the flames.

Kellas Cat

Hybrid Cat. The Kellas Cat is a melanistic hybrid between feral black domestic cats and Scottish Wild Cats. In the 1980s there were a number of reports of a wild-living, long-legged, black cat in Scotland, in the region east of Inverness. In the mid-1980s, specimens were obtained from near the hamlet of Kellas and some of these were examined at the Natural History Museum in London. The animal is slightly larger than a domestic cat and less stocky than a Scottish Wild Cat. Its presence gave rise to the romantic suggestion that there was an unknown, wild member of the cat family roaming the more remote parts of Scotland. Four rival theories were put forward, suggesting that this cat was:

(1) a new species of wild cat; (2) a feral domestic black cat; (3) a melanistic Scottish Wild Cat *(Felis sylvestris);* (4) a hybrid between a feral domestic black cat and a Scottish Wild Cat.

Anatomical measurements of the few Kellas Cat specimens known support the fourth suggestion. In all but one case, they show certain features of domestic cats and others of wild cats. Their impressive size is doubtless due to hybrid vigour. In a single, exceptional case, the measurements match those of the wild cat, suggesting that, in addition to the hybrids, there exists the occasional melanistic Scottish Wild Cat.

The presence of these Kellas Cats may explain the tales of a fairy cat called the *'cait sith'* in Scottish Highland folklore.

Bibliography:

1989. Shuker, K. *Mystery Cats of the World.* Robert Hale, London.
1993. Francis, D. *My Highland Kellas Cats.* Jonathan Cape, London.

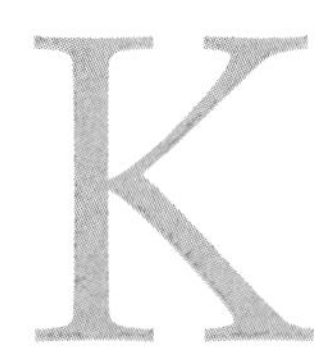

Khmer Cat

Domestic Breed. A rare, long-haired breed with Siamese colouring. It is similar to the Birman, except that it lacks the Birman's white feet.

Kiki-la-Doucette

Pet Cat. One of the many cats belonging to the French author Colette. Her passion for cats created a feline cult among the French intelligentsia at the turn of the century. Kiki was a grey male Angora who also appeared as a fictional, talking cat in *Sept Dialogues de Bêtes* (1903) (translated as *Barks and Purrs* in 1913). In the book Kiki debates life with a French bulldog called Toby-Chien: 'The cat is a guest and not a plaything . . . Try to imitate my serenity.' (See also entry for Colette.)

The French novelist Colette with her beloved cat, Kiki-la-Doucette. Her devotion to cats was so strong that she influenced French society and created a whole new 'Cult of the Cat'.

Kilkenny Cats

Legendary Cats. The expression 'to fight like Kilkenny Cats' means to fight to the bitter end. It stems from a legend about two cats tortured by soldiers in 18th-century Ireland. The soldiers were supposed to have tied two cats together by their tails and hung them over a line to watch them fight to the death. However, one soldier decided to release them. He could only do this by cutting off their tails, whereupon the tailless cats immediately fled. The soldier was still holding their severed tails when an officer arrived and asked what had happened. The soldier invented the story that two cats had been fighting savagely and had devoured each other except for their tails.

Kimono Cat

Folklore. According to Japanese folklore, a cat which is born with a special kind of black mark on its back is a spirit-bearing cat. If the shape of this black mark resembles a woman wearing a kimono, then the animal is believed to contain the spirit of one of the owner's ancestors. Should such a cat be born, it has to be carefully protected. It was common practice to send it to a temple for safe-keeping, but occasionally one was stolen and removed from its native homeland.

It is known that such a theft took place at the beginning of the 20th century, when a Chinese servant stole a Kimono Cat from a temple and smuggled her on to a ship bound for England. Her loss created a public scandal, but she reached London safely and went to live with a family in Putney. Called Kimona, she was well looked after and lived a suitably protected life until her death in 1911. A photograph of her reveals that she was a black and white cat with a black saddle marking on her back that could, with a little imagination, be interpreted as a fat lady wearing a kimono.

Kindle

Feline Term. Kindle is a special term for a litter of kittens. Originally, the word was used as a verb to denote a small animal giving birth, but it then came to refer to the result of the 'kindling' – the offspring themselves. In the famous *Book of St. Albans*, an early treatise on hunting published in 1486, there is the phrase 'a kyndyll of yonge cattes'.

King Cheetah

Wild Feline. An incipient forest race of the Cheetah *(Acinonyx jubatus)*, with large black blobs on its coat in place of the usual small spots. Along the back, these blobs fuse to create several thick, dark stripes, giving the animal a very different appearance from the typical Cheetah.

When the King Cheetah was first discovered, in the 1920s, it created great excitement and was recorded as a dramatic new species. It was given the scientific name of *Acinonyx rex*, but within ten years had been relegated to nothing more than a local mutation of only superficial interest.

However, in the years that followed, more and more examples of King Cheetahs were found. By 1987 no fewer than 38 specimens had been authenticated, all from the same area of Africa,

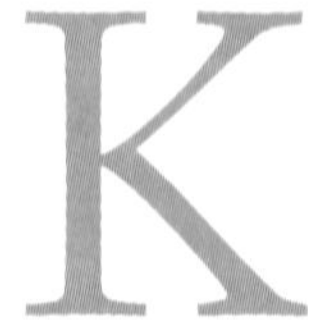

The King Cheetah *(Acinonyx jubatus)*, with its heavily blotched coat, appears to be an emerging race of the Cheetah, developing in one small region of Africa where it is found in a forest habitat, in contrast to the usual open plains.

in the region where Zimbabwe, South Africa and Botswana meet. Intriguingly, the recessive gene that created the blotched-and-striped coat markings also seemed to affect the texture of the fur, which differed from that of the common Cheetah. In addition, the King Cheetahs had a more distinct mane. Furthermore, these animals preferred the forests to the open plains and were more nocturnal in their habits.

It would appear, after all, that the King Cheetah is more than an isolated freak. Instead, it looks as though it is a new race of forest-dwelling Cheetahs in the making, with its darker markings revealing that it is adapting to a different form of camouflage more suited to its forest habitat.

Bibliography:

1987. Bottriell, L.G. *King Cheetah: The Story of a Quest.* Brill, Leiden.

1989. Shuker, K.P.N. *Mystery Cats of the World.* Robert Hale, London.

King of the Cats

Legendary Cat. In an old Irish legend there is a huge cat who ruled over all the other cats. His name was Irusan and he lived in a cave at Knowth. His end came when, learning that a poet had made satirical remarks about cats, he carried the poet off and, as he did so, was killed by a saint who drove a red-hot bar through his body.

There is an old Irish folk-tale that makes reference to the importance of the King of Cats to other felines: A man was killing a cat but before it died it told him to go home and say he had just killed the King of Cats . . . This he did, but when his own pet cat heard the news, it leapt up from its resting place by the side of the fire and tore him to pieces.

Kirlee

Pet Cat. The founding father of the Devon Rex breed. The curly-coated Kirlee was born in 1960 in a field near a disused tin mine in Devon and was rescued by Miss Beryl Cox. He was used in breeding experiments with Cornish Rex cats, but the matings failed to produce curly-coated offspring. It was then realized that Kirlee possessed a new Rex gene and an in-breeding programme was started that led to the establishment of the Devon Rex as a distinct breed. Kirlee sired many litters before he was eventually killed in a road accident in 1970.

KITTEN

FELINE TERM. A young cat. The technical definition varies from country to country. In Britain a domestic kitten is defined as a young cat up to the age of nine months.

In origin, it is thought that the term 'kitten' derives from the general word for cat in the Turkish language, which is *keti* or *kedi*. Its earliest recorded use in the English language dates from 1377.

The average number of kittens in a domestic litter is four. The record for the largest litter was 19, of which only 15 survived (see entry for Tarawood Antigone).

At birth, kittens measure about 13 cm (5 inches) in length. They weigh about 115 grams (4 oz). This will double in the first week. By the age of seven weeks they will weigh roughly 800 grams (28 oz).

When they are born, the kittens are blind and deaf, but have a strong sense of smell. They are also sensitive to touch and soon start rooting for the mother's nipples. By day four, they have already started the paw-treading action which helps to stimulate the mother's milk-flow. Their eyes do not begin to open until they are roughly a week old, and it will be another two weeks after that before they are fully open. By this stage they have started to crawl about and will soon be able to stand shakily on their small legs.

As they approach the end of their first month of life, they show the first signs of playing with one another. Whatever colour their eyes will be later in life, at this age all kittens are blue-eyed and remain so until they are about three months old. Their teeth are beginning to break through at the age of one month.

At roughly 32 days, they eat their first solid food, but they will not be weaned until they are two months old. (Wild cats take longer to wean their kittens – about four months.) During their second month of life they become very lively and intensely playful with one another. Inside the

FOUR YOUNG Lilac British Shorthairs demonstrating the irresistible appeal of the kitten.

house, pet kittens will use their mother's litter-tray by the time they are 1½ months old. Play-fighting and play-hunting become dominant features at the end of the second month.

In their third month of life the kittens are in for a shock. The mother refuses to allow them access to her nipples. They must make do entirely with solids and with liquids lapped from a dish. Before long their mother will be coming into oestrus and concentrating on tom-cats again.

In their fifth month the young cats begin to scent-mark their home-range. They are shedding their milk teeth and exploring their exciting new world in a less playful manner. The chances are that their mother is already pregnant again by now, unless her human owners have kept her indoors against her will.

At six months, the young cats are fully independent, capable of hunting prey and fending for themselves.

Swiss artist Paul Klee was fascinated by cats and they frequently appeared in his paintings and drawings, including this painting, *Idol for House Cats* (1924). Such was his interest that a whole book was written about his felines, both real and imaginary.

Klee, Paul

Cat Owner. Swiss artist, Paul Klee (1879–1940) was so fond of cats that Marina Alberghini was able to write a whole book – *The Cosmic Cats of Paul Klee* – devoted to the subject. In it we meet a number of Klee's own pet cats, some of them photographed by himself: Mys, in 1902, a dark, long-haired cat; Nuggi, in 1905, a long-haired kitten; Fritzi, in 1921, a mackerel tabby; and Bimbo, in 1931, a white, long-haired cat. And we see the way he celebrated them in line and in paint. There are cats hunting by moonlight, cats dreaming of birds and, looming over the tiny humans below, a giant cat presiding over its sacred mountain. It is clear that Klee, the subtle, sensitive artist, was also sensitive to the subtleties and nuances of feline existence.

Bibliography:

1993. Alberghini, M. *Il Gatto Cosmico di Paul Klee.* Felinamente, Milan.

Kodkod

Wild Feline. *(Felis guigna)* Also known by the local name of Guiña or Gato Guigna. (Some authorities refer to it as the Kokod, but this appears to be an error.)

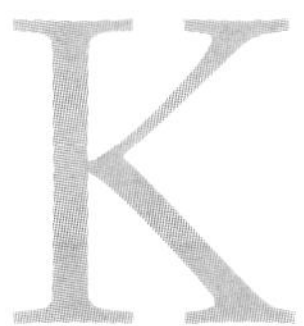

The Kodkod *(Felis guigna) (left)*, is one of the least known of the small cats of South America. It is confined to a small region of Chile and Argentina, where habitat destruction means that it is now a threatened species.

This little-known cat is one of the smallest felines in the New World. It has a spotted coat with dark markings on a grey-brown background. The tail has black rings, and there are also black bands on the chest region. As with several other species of small cats, there are 'eye-spots' on the backs of the ears. Black individuals have been recorded on a number of occasions.

The most unusual feature of the Kodkod, apart from its very small body size, is to be found in its feet. It has disproportionately large claws. This suggests either that it has specialized in catching a particular type of prey that requires improved grasping during the kill, or that the cat is, for some reason, an improved climber of difficult trees. At present, we have no direct observations of this species in the wild to help us answer this question.

In some areas, it favours scrubland – semi-open country where there are occasional bushes and trees for cover. In others, it is found in moist, coniferous forests. It hunts small mammals and birds. There is an early report by a German naturalist that 'parties of Kodkods raided chicken houses at Valdivia'. Based on this isolated case, some authors have rashly proposed that this is a 'pack-hunting' species. This idea is so out of keeping with the behaviour of small cats all over the world, that it requires further verification.

Size: Length of Head + Body: 39–49 cm (15–19 in). Tail: 19–23 cm (7½–9 in). Weight: 2–3 kg (4½–6½ lb).

Distribution: A South American cat with a limited distribution, it is found only in central and southern Chile and in the Andean lakes district of Argentina.

A rare photograph of a Kodkod in the wild *(above)*, clearly showing that, although it has a small body, it possesses huge feet. Understanding the function of this unusual feature must await more detailed observations in the wild.

Korat Cat

Domestic Breed. An ancient domestic breed from Thailand. Known there as the Si-Sawat, its existence is recorded in *The Cat Book Poems* written in the Ayudhya Period, some time between 1350 and 1767, and now lodged in the Bangkok National Library. In the 1970s, a Thai cat expert, Pichai-Ramadi Vasnasong, described this cat as one of the eight types of 'Siamese Cats' (using the term in an unusually broad sense) known to exist in Thailand: '1. The Koraj. This is better known as the Si Sawat (purple grey, the colour of the Sawat nut).' This Thai spelling, Koraj, has been changed to Korat by European breeders because the Thai pronunciation of 'j' is equivalent to our soft 't'.

Appearance: A trim, medium-sized, muscular, short-haired cat with tall ears and a heart-shaped head. The luminous green eyes are unusually large and prominent. The silver-blue coat is glossy and fine, lying close to the body – essentially a hot-country coat. The hairs have a delicate, silver tipping, eloquently known in the East as 'sea-foam'.

History: In its native Thailand, where to own one is thought to bring good fortune, the Korat has been a highly prized cat for centuries. The symbolism of their colours has led to their being used in rain-making ceremonies. At the end of the dry season they are taken in procession and water is poured over them to bring the rains. They have sometimes been called the 'Cloud-coloured Cat' and, because their eyes are the colour of young rice, they have been thought to help in producing a good crop. Traditionally, a pair of Korats was given to a bride on her wedding day to bring her prosperity in the years ahead. Because of the sheen on their coats, they were said to symbolize a gift of silver.

It is said to have acquired its present name from King Chulalongkorn at the turn of the century, when he asked where such beautiful cats came from. He was told that they were found in Korat *(Cao Nguyen Khorat),* one of the eastern provinces of the country. It was this same king, also known as Rama V, who commissioned a monk (with the catchy name of Somdej Phra Buddhacharn Buddhasarmahathera) to paint a copy of the ancient *Cat Book Poems,* with its revealing illustrations of the different types of local cats. This *Smud Khoi* (papyrus book) is on view in the Minor Arts Room at the National Museum in Bangkok and carries a lyrical description of the Korat breed: 'The hairs are smooth, with roots like clouds and tips like silver./ The eyes shine like dewdrops on a lotus leaf.'

This book also says of the Korat: 'The cat "Ma-led" has a body colour like "Doklao".' The word 'Ma-led' is used to describe the silvery-grey seed of a wild Thai fruit called the 'Look Sawat'. 'Doklao' refers to the silvery-tipped flower of a local herb. The name 'Si-Sawat' means 'Colour of the Sawat Seed'. This insistence of the specific hue of the Korat makes it clear that, for this particular breed, any individual animal deviating from the traditional coat colour would cease to be a true Korat.

Because this breed was valued so highly, it was never sold. As a result, exported examples were extremely rare. Only occasionally was one presented as a special gift to honour some dignitary or aristocrat.

The first record of a Korat Cat being seen in the West dates from 1896, when one was exhibited in London at the Holland House Show. According to the well-known cat judge, C.A. House, writing some years later, it was entered by a Mr Spearman, a young Englishman just back from Siam. It is not clear how he obtained it, although it is clear that he had brought it personally from its country of origin. Sadly, despite his protestations that it was a distinct and separate breed, the judge of the day, the famous cat artist Louis Wain, disqualified it because, in his ignorance, he foolishly considered it to be a poor specimen of a blue Siamese.

After this, the breed then disappeared without trace for many years. It was not heard of again until 1959, when a pair, called Nara and Darra, was presented to the American Ambassador to Thailand. They were sent to Mrs Jean Johnson in the United States, who had become fascinated by the breed when she had visited what was then Siam in 1947. She had been searching for a typical Siamese Cat, but was shown the Korats and told that these, and not the local colourpointed varieties, were the most important local felines. Twelve years later she now had a pair of these 'special cats' and was able to use them to start a breeding programme. In the early 1960s more Korats were obtained and brought safely back to the United States. In 1965 a Korat Cat Fanciers' Association was formed in America and published a quarterly newsletter called *Mai Pen Rai.* It insisted that, to be accepted as a true Korat, a cat must have a pedigree stretching back to an origin in Thailand. Others clubs were also formed, including the Si-Sawat Society, the *Sa-Waat-Dee* and the Korat Fanciers of the East. The Korat was eventually recognized as a pedigree breed there in 1966.

The Korat Cat, an ancient Thai breed known locally as the Si-Sawat because it has the unusual, purple-grey colour of the Sawat nut. In modern times it was developed in the West in the 1960s by the American breeder Jean Johnson.

Korat breeding stock did not reach Britain until the 1970s – to be precise, at 10.30 am on the morning of 11th March 1972: a five-weeks pregnant female called Saeng Duan and an unrelated male kitten called Sam. The female gave birth to six kittens in quarantine on Easter Sunday – the first Korats ever born in Britain. Twelve years later the breed was given full recognition and granted championship status.

Personality: Terms used to describe this breed include: intelligent, inquisitive, gentle, active, soft-voiced, cautious, shy, powerful, faithful, shy, reserved, calm, friendly, intuitive, swift, agile and playful.

Korat Cat males are said to make good fathers if left with their kittens. They are unusually territorial and will hiss and growl at unknown intruders. According to legend, the males were sometimes taken into battle on the shoulders of the warriors and would launch themselves ferociously at the enemy.

Colour Forms: All Korats are a slate blue/grey colour.

Breed Clubs:

The Korat Cat Association. Publishes a regular newsletter. Address: 25 Stapleford Road, Whissendine, Oakham, Leics., LE15 7EY, England.

Korat Cat Fanciers' Association. Formed in 1965. Address: 1601 North Federal Highway, Lake Worth, FL 33460-6695, USA. The KCFA publishes a quarterly newsletter, *Mai Pen Rai.* Address: 2790 Newberry Avenue, Green Bay, WI 54302, USA.

Si-Sawat Circle. Address: 23 Kingsway Avenue, West Point, Manchester, M19 2DH, England.

Si-Sawat (Korat) Society. Publishes a *Newsletter.* Address: 251 Connell Ct., Reynoldsburg, OH 43068, USA.

Krazy Kat

Cartoon Cat. Krazy Cat was a slightly surrealist strip cartoon feline invented by George Herriman in 1910. The strip broke many conventions and was never a major commercial success for the artist, but did gain him critical acclaim and considerable respect from literary quarters.

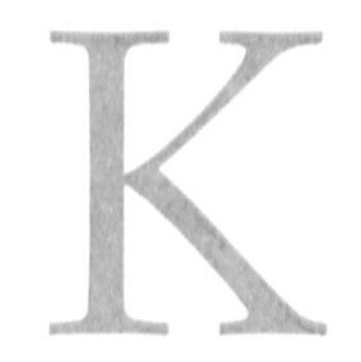

President Woodrow Wilson was a devoted follower and in 1922 John Carpenter made the cat the subject of a full-length ballet. The poet e.e. cummings wrote: 'Krazy Kat is a living ideal. She is a spiritual force, inhabiting a merely real world, and the realer a merely real world happens to be, the more this living ideal becomes herself.' The strip continued for over 30 years, until Herriman's death in 1944.

Bibliography:

1986. McDonnell, P. *Krazy Kat. The Comic Art of George Herriman*. New York.
1990. Herriman, G. *The Komplete Kolor Krazy Kat*. Vol.1. 1935–1936.
1991. Herriman, G. *The Komplete Kolor Krazy Kat*. Vol. 2. 1936–1937.

Lady Jane

Fictional Cat. A rather sinister, large grey cat that appears in the 1853 novel *Bleak House,* by Charles Dickens.

Langbourne

Pet Cat. Jeremy Bentham (1748–1832), the English philosopher who preached that human actions should be aimed at 'producing the greatest happiness for the greatest number' – a concept that has since become the norm for democratic societies – had a much-loved cat named Langbourne. Despite his public concern for 'the greatest number' of people, in private life he seemed not to care for the company of even a small number of them. He was described as 'suffering few persons to visit him, rarely dining out'. Instead he preferred the company of his adored cat and honoured the animal in a curious way by bestowing titles on him. From simple Langbourne, he became Sir John Langbourne, and was finally awarded a doctorate in divinity by his besotted owner, being given the title of The Reverend Sir John Langbourne, D.D.

Langton, Blanche

Cat Art. In the years between the two World Wars, Gloucester-born Blanche Langton began to assemble an outstanding collection of carved and modelled cats, from sources in both Europe and the Orient. With her husband, Neville Langton, she also made special collecting trips to Egypt, to seek out some more ancient examples. She called these older feline figures her 'B.C. Cats', and her later ones her 'A.D. Cats'.

She continued to add to her collection, known affectionately as 'Mrs Langton's Cats', for over half a century, endlessly searching antique markets, galleries and salerooms for exciting new specimens. She found Meissen, Staffordshire, Worcester, Rockingham and Lowestoft ceramic cats, Chinese Jade and Japanese Netsuke, selecting each piece with an expert eye.

Just before her death in 1974, she donated her A.D. cats (94 of them) to the Castle Museum in Norwich, where the whole collection is on public display.

The B.C. Cats – an incomparable collection of 336 ancient Egyptian cats – went to London University's Petrie Museum in Gower Street. Illustrated catalogues of both collections have been published (see below).

Bibliography:

1940. Langton, N. & B. *The Cat in Ancient Egypt. Illustrated from the collection of Cat and other Egyptian figures formed by N. and B. Langton*. Cambridge University Museum, Cambridge.

1982. Cheetham, F. *Mrs Langton's Cats*. Castle Museum Catalogue. Norfolk Museums Service. p.1-6.

La Perm Cat

Domestic Breed. A new, curly-coated breed from the United States. Its full title is 'The Dalles La Perm', after the place in Oregon where it was discovered as an isolated mutation.

Appearance: A cat with a tightly curled coat. In short-haired examples it has an 'Afro' look, but in longer-haired versions the coat forms into very tight ringlets. Referred to as 'The Cat with the Permanent Curl', it has also been called the Alpaca Cat (see entry).

History: Described by its discoverer as 'The Cat for the '90s', the first example of this exciting new breed was found among ordinary, short-haired American barn-cats by Linda Koehl of The Dalles, Oregon, in 1986. She noticed that one of the kittens had been born bald and she thought it would die. But it survived and two months later began to grow a unique, curly coat. This animal – a brown tabby female, predictably named 'Curly' – became the foundation cat of a breeding programme to foster the unusual hair mutation. The La Perm has already gone though seven generations and in September 1995 was accepted as a New Breed by TICA. All colours are allowed. Bald kittens still appear occasionally but are no longer common. It is estimated that by early 1996 there were about 60 cats of this breed in existence. In personality it is described as extremely affectionate and easy-going.

The Dalles La Perm from the United States is a new breed of curly-coated cat that is destined for a great future because of its exceptionally attractive, shaggy appearance. It was discovered among Oregon barn-cats in 1986.

Breed Club:
There is as yet no breed club, but until one is formed, enquiries are directed to 2945 Dry Hollow Road, The Dalles, OR 97058-9551, USA.

Lavender

Coat Colour. This pinkish-grey colour is a diluted form of chocolate. In America, the name lavender is preferred for some breeds, while lilac is used for others, but the two colours are essentially the same. In Britain, lavender is not employed in pedigree descriptions.

Variants of the colour include the following: (1) Lavender Cream; (2) Lavender Cream Calico; (3) Lavender Cream Van Calico; (4) Lavender Cream Shaded; (5) Lavender Cream Smoke; (6) Lavender Shaded; (7) Lavender Silver; (8) Lavender Silver Tabby; (9) Lavender Smoke; (10) Lavender Tabby.

Leo

Film Cat. The trademark lion of MGM productions, who roars an introduction at the start of each film. The first time Leo appeared was in 1928, with MGM's first sound movie, called *White Shadows in the South Seas.* The idea of using a feline emblem in this way came from a young advertising executive called Howard Dietz.

Several male lions have been used in this role in the history of the company, starting with one called Slats, then Jackie and finally, in colour, one named Tanner. Jackie, who was born in the Los Angeles Zoo, was perhaps the most famous of these, having had a long performing career, appearing in more than 250 films. He acted as Leo the Lion for MGM for nearly 18 years.

Leopard

Wild Feline. *(Panthera pardus)* Also known in earlier days as the Panther or the Pard. In India it has been called the *Tendwa, Adnára, Karda, Honiga* or *Búrkál;* in Malaya, the *Harimau Bintang;* in Tibet, the *Sik;* in Africa, the *Luiperd;* German: *Leopard;* French: *La Panthère d'Afrique*; Swahili: *Chui;* Afrikaans: *Luiperd.*

The heavily built Leopard is the largest spotted cat in the Old World, matched in size only by the New World Jaguar. Its coat is covered in black spots which become bigger in the trunk region. There, each spot becomes a dark rosette with a pale interior. These rosettes differ slightly from those of the Jaguar. In the case of the Leopard there are never any dark marks within a rosette, whereas in the Jaguar it is always the case that some of the rosettes have small black dots *inside* their pale interior.

As with the Jaguar, the Leopard's typically dark-spotted, orange coat is sometimes obliterated by a melanistic condition in which the whole pelt becomes black. These 'Black Panthers' as they are usually called, occur only in the hottest, most humid parts of its range.

Leopards prefer hilly, wooded country, where there are rocky retreats, but they will accept almost any kind of habitat if necessary, from thick forest to semi-desert. Both males and females establish territories and will defend them against other individuals of the same sex as themselves. As a result, the population density averages about one animal to 30 sq km (11 sq miles). However, if the food supply is particularly rich, this spacing out can be greatly reduced, with the population density rising to as much as one individual per square kilometre (247acres).

They are solitary, nocturnal hunters and only come together when breeding. During the day they can often be seen lying asleep in a tree. If there are rock cavities or caves available to them, they will retreat there from the heat of the day. The 'roar' of the Leopard is highly characteristic and has been aptly described as being like the sound of a man rhythmically sawing wood.

Unlike the Cheetah, the Leopard is essentially a stalking, pouncing killer. Its body is built for strength rather than fast sprinting. Whereas the Cheetah will set off on a run of over 200 metres (220 yards), the Leopard rarely exceeds 30 metres (33 yards) when attempting a kill. It nearly always dispatches its prey with a throttling neck-grasp, unless the victim is too small for this, in which case it will apply a lethal bite to the back of the head.

Its main prey are various kinds of medium to small antelope. Compared with the Lion, the average size of its prey is not so impressive – rarely more than 70 kg (154 lb) in weight – and it frequently pursues large rodents and small monkeys. The carcass is often carried up into a tree, away from the other earth-bound predators and scavengers, and stored there. Sometimes, if an unusually large prey has been killed, this storing activity requires amazing strength. One Leopard, for example, was seen to carry a young giraffe weighing 100 kg (220 lb) (which was more than its own body weight) high up into a tree before eating it. If no suitable trees are available, a Leopard will store its food in cavities at ground level.

Female Leopards produce a litter of two or three cubs about every year and a half. There is no particular breeding season. When a female comes on heat, she consorts with a nearby male and they mate every 15 minutes throughout one night. The cubs are born about 100 days later. Usually there are two or three cubs in a litter, the female having located a suitably secure cavity for her den or lair. Always alert to the safety of her cubs, the mother will move them to a new site every few days until they become active. Altogether, she will probably suckle them for 100 days.

When they are able to follow her, she walks in front of them with her tail curved upward, displaying its white underside as a flag. As they grow older they are allowed to accompany her on the hunt, but she has a special call that instructs them to stay back when she undertakes the final pounce-and-kill. Young Leopards start to kill prey themselves when they are about one year old, and they become sexually mature at about 2½ years, or a little more. Long after they have become completely independent, they will occasionally take part in a friendly reunion with their mother.

They can expect a lifespan of between 20 and 30 years if they are lucky enough to be left alone by their only major enemy – the human being.

Size: Length of Head + Body: 90–190 cm (35½–75 in). Tail: 58–110 cm (23–43½ in). Weight: 30–90 kg (66–198 lb).

Distribution: The Leopard has the widest distribution of any of the Big Cats. It is found throughout most of Africa; in parts of the Middle East; and in Asia, from Siberia in the north to

THE LEOPARD *(Panthera pardus)* is one of the five living 'Big Cats' (along with the Lion, Tiger, Jaguar and Snow Leopard). It can be distinguished from the Jaguar by the absence of any small black dots inside its ring-spots.

Sri Lanka and Malaysia in the south, and on into the Far East. Despite this huge geographical range, the species has become increasingly rare everywhere. Not so long ago there were hundreds of thousands of them, but today the fur-trade (taking as many as 60,000 skins a year in the 1960s) and widespread poisoning by local farmers, has reduced their numbers drastically. In the 1970s alone, their populations sank by as much as 90 per cent in many regions. In some areas, such as Sri Lanka, where there are now only a few hundred left, they are rapidly heading for extinction. Tourists on safari in 'Leopard Country' in Africa count themselves lucky if they have seen a single specimen by the end of their visit.

Bibliography:

1955. Denis, M. *Leopard in my Lap.* W.H. Allen, London.
1965. Burke, N. *Eleven Leopards.* Jarrolds, London.
1967. Kemp-Turnbull, P. *The Leopard.* Cape Town.
1980. Adamson, J. *Queen of Shaba: the Story of an African Leopard.* Collins Harvill, London.
1982. Singh, A. *Prince of Cats.* Jonathan Cape, London
1991. Hes, L. *The Leopards of Londolozi.* New Holland, London.
1992. Hinde, G. *Leopard.* HarperCollins, London.
1993. Bailey, T.N. *African Leopard. Ecology and Behaviour of a Solitary Felid.* Columbia University Press.

Leopard Cat

Wild Feline. *(Felis bengalensis)* Also known as the Bengal Cat. In Malaya it is the Kuching Batu. In China it is called the 'Money Cat', because its spots are thought to resemble Chinese coins.

A small, tawny cat with a black-spotted coat, about the same size as a domestic cat, this species has a wide distribution right across southern Asia. Its ears are long and rounded, and there is a vivid 'eye-spot' on the back of each ear. Its tail is heavily spotted, with a black tip. The coat is short and thin.

Its success seems to be due to its flexibility. It is at home as much on the ground as it is in the trees, as much in the highlands as in the lowlands, as much in the day as at night, as much near to human habitation as far from it. It swims well, climbs well and runs fast. It breeds all the year round. Its adaptability is a sharp contrast to several of its close relatives that have much more specific demands, and therefore much more limited geographical ranges. Because of its wide range of habitats it is not surprising to find that it varies in both size and coat colour, being larger and paler in the northern, cooler regions (almost silver-grey in certain areas) and darker and smaller in the hot, humid, more southern regions (with a brownish ground colour in some areas).

Its prey consists largely of birds and rodents, such as mice, rats and squirrels. It may also take lizards, frogs and even bats (which they catch when they fall onto the floors of caves). Its boldness around human settlements means that it often attacks small domestic stock such as poultry. Unlike some of its extremely shy relatives, it will even enter villages at night to carry out these raids.

It has been reported that, unusually for wild cats, the Leopard Cat may form breeding pairs, with the male sharing the parental duties. This may be another reason for its success, compared with other species of wild cat, since the extra parental care must give the kittens a better chance of survival.

Its excellent swimming abilities mean that it has managed to populate a number of small, off-shore islands, which other wild cat species have failed to colonize. In fact, the very first Leopard Cat ever caught was found swimming in the Bay of Bengal – which explains why the Leopard Cat's specific name is *bengalensis*.

This species has been crossed with domestic cats deliberately on a number of occasions, to create a spotted domestic cat. In recent years breeders have been successful in developing these crosses into an exciting new breed they have called the Bengal Cat. It is surprising that such a cross should produce fertile offspring and this throws into doubt the validity of a recent

The Leopard Cat *(Felis bengalensis)* of Asia, a wide-spread cat whose success has depended on its flexibility. It is at home in almost any habitat and eats almost any kind of small animal.

re-classification of small cats, in which this species was taken out of the genus *Felis* (the genus to which the domestic cat belongs). For obvious reasons, this re-classification has not been followed here.

Size: Length of Head + Body: 44–60 cm (17–23½ in). Tail: 30–40 cm (12–16 in). Weight: 3–4 kg (6½–9 lb).

Distribution: A huge range, from Siberia, Tibet and India, through Burma, Thailand, to China and south to Sumatra, Java, Borneo and the Philippines.

Leopon

Feline Hybrid. A Leopon is a cross between a male Leopard and a Lioness. These hybrids have been bred on a number of occasions in zoos. They have been recorded at zoos in both Italy and Japan. In Japan they have been exhibited at the Koshien Zoo and the Hanshin Park Zoo.

Let the Cat out of the Bag

Feline Saying. The origin of this phrase, meaning 'he gave away a secret', dates back to the 18th century when it referred to a market-day trick. Piglets were often taken to market in a small sack, or bag, to be sold. The trickster would put a cat in a bag and pretend that it was a pig. If the buyer insisted on seeing it, he would be told that it was too lively to risk opening up the bag, as the animal might escape. If the cat struggled so much that the trickster let the cat out of the bag, his secret was exposed. A popular name for the bag itself was a 'poke', hence that other expression 'never buy a pig in a poke'.

Leyhausen, Paul

Cat Authority. One of the world's leading experts on the behaviour of small cat species, German ethologist Dr Paul Leyhausen's classic work, *Verhaltensstudien an Katzen,* was first published in 1956. The most detailed study ever made of feline behaviour, it surprisingly remained untranslated for almost a quarter of a century. Eventually it did appear in English in a greatly enlarged form in 1979, as *Cat Behavior*. Leyhausen's lengthy and meticulous observations provided many new insights into feline activities and established him as the foremost student of cat behaviour in the world. He was known in Germany as the 'Katzen-professor', and his research was carried out at a custom-built institute at Wuppertal where he was able to study domestic cats and a wide range of small wild cat species in specially designed glass-fronted enclosures.

Bibliography:

1956. Leyhausen, P. *Verhaltensstudien an Katzen*. Paul Parey, Berlin.

1979. Leyhausen, P. *Cat Behavior. The Predatory and Social Behavior of Domestic and Wild Cats*. Garland Press, New York.

Library Cats

Feline History. Attacks by mice on valuable books have often proved a hazard for libraries. In the vast library of one of the palaces of St. Petersburg the problem was so great that no fewer than 300 Russian cats were employed to control the rodent population. In more recent times, so many public libraries in the United States have kept a resident cat, that in 1987 a group of librarians formed 'The Library Cat Society' (LCS) and issued a quarterly newsletter called *The Library Cat*. The society's creed was simple: 'We advocate the establishment of cats in libraries and recognize the need to respect and to care for library cats.'

This demand for respect for library cats might seem a trifle unnecessary, but the peaceful silence of the public library is sometimes disturbed by the arrival of a virulent ailurophobe. One such cat-hater created a scandal when she demanded a tax rebate because she was unable to enter her public library in Woodford, Connecticut, since she was allergic to the library cat, a black and white female called Fred. The library staff resisted the demand that 'Fred must go!' and the matter went as high as the state Governor. Then a local schoolgirl started a 'Save Fred'

The Leopard Cat *(opposite)* is unusually bold. Most of the smaller wild cats are shy and secretive, but the little Leopard Cat is prepared to enter villages at night in search of prey and is not scared off by the presence of humans.

competition which quickly involved everyone in the town, then in the state and finally internationally, with signatures coming from as far away as Switzerland and the Philippines. Fred stayed, and became a star, appearing on American television, and being written about in *People* magazine and *The New York Times*. She became a major tourist attraction until her death in 1986 at the age of 14. The following year a tree was planted outside the library in Fred's memory. Appropriately, it was a Pussy Willow.

Bibliography:

1992. Lahti, P. (Editor) *Cats, Librarians and Libraries*. Haworth Press, New York.

Specialist Club:

Library Cat Society. Address: P.O. Box 274, Moorhead, MN 56560, USA.

Lifespan

Feline Biology. The expected lifespan for the domestic cat is between nine and 15 years. With improved feeding regimes today, 16 years is not unusual. The longest lifespan ever claimed for a domestic cat is 36 years. This exceptional record is held by a tabby cat called 'Puss', which lived from 1903 to 1939, and seven years longer than the record for any kind of domestic dog.

A better documented case is that of a female tabby called 'Ma' who is known to have lived for 34 years, from 1923 to 1957.

It is claimed that pedigree cats do not live as long as non-pedigree ones, but there has been at least one that lived beyond 30 years: a Seal Point Siamese called Sukoo, living in southern England, reached the age of 31 in 1989.

Neutered tom-cats, on average, live three years longer than entire ones. This is thought to be because they are less likely to become embroiled in damaging fights and because they are, for some reason, more resistant to infection.

As regards breeding, tom-cats have been known to produce offspring at the advanced feline age of 16 years. This is equivalent to a human male becoming a father in his late 70s.

Female cats have been know to give birth when 12 years old. For a human female this would be like having a baby in her mid-60s. This means that cats remain fertile longer than humans do, in relative terms.

Not to exaggerate the cat's breeding abilities, it must be recorded that from the age of eight until 12 years there is a gradual decline in the number of kittens produced in each litter, so the reproductive apparatus is beginning to show signs of slowing down at this stage, and only the strongest and healthiest of moggies can stay the full course. Pedigree cats, because they so often lack 'hybrid vigour', are not so long-lasting.

The following table gives a rough comparison between human ageing and feline ageing:

Comparison of Cat and Human Ages

CAT AGE	HUMAN AGE	CAT AGE	HUMAN AGE
1	15	10	60
2	25	15	75
4	40	20	105
7	50	30	120

Many owners fail to notice that their cats have reached 'old age', as senility has little effect on the feline appetite. Because they continue to eat greedily, and with their usual vigour, it is thought that they are still 'young cats'. But there are certain tell-tale signs of ageing. Leaping and grooming are the first actions to suffer, and for the same reason. Old age makes the cat's joints stiffer and this leads to slower movements. Leaping up on to a chair or a table, or outside up on to a wall, becomes increasingly difficult. Very old cats actually need to be lifted up on to a favourite chair. As the supple quality of the young cat's flexible body is lost, it also becomes increasingly awkward for the animal to twist its neck round to groom the more inaccessible parts of its coat. These areas of fur start to look dishevelled and at this stage a little gentle grooming by the animal's owner is a great help, even if the cat in question is not one that has generally been fussed over with brush and comb in its younger days.

As the elderly cat's body becomes more rigid, so do its habits. Its daily routine becomes increasingly fixed and novelties cause distress now, where once they may have aroused acute interest. The idea of buying a young kitten as a companion to cheer up an old cat simply does not work. It upsets the elderly animal's daily rhythm. Moving house is even more traumatic. The kindest way to treat an elderly cat is therefore to keep as much as possible to the well-established pattern of the day, but with a little physical help where required.

Luckily these changes do not occur until late in the lives of most cats. Their declining years are mercifully brief. For the average cat, the period of senile decline should be no longer than the final year of its lifespan.

Liger

Hybrid Cat. A Liger is a cross between a male Lion and a female Tiger. According to Richard Lydekker, writing in 1896, the first recorded Ligers were a litter of two males and a female born to a captive tigress at Windsor on 24th October 1824. They were shown to King George IV, who christened them Lion–Tigers, a name that was later shortened to Ligers.

Since then a number of zoos have, from time to time, produced a Liger (or a Tigon – a cross between a male Tiger and a female Lion) and it has always been assumed that these hybrid animals would be infertile. However, according to Armand Denis, writing in 1964: 'about twenty years ago a fifteen-year-old female Liger in the Munich Zoo produced a female cub after being mated with a Lion.' If this is true, it goes to show how closely related the Lion is to the Tiger.

Lilac

Coat Colour. Lilac is the name given to the dilute version of brown or chocolate. It bears the same relationship to brown that blue does to black.

Lilac has been described variously as pinkish dove-grey, as warm lavender with a pinkish tone, or (rather differently) as frost grey. Its appeal lies in the fact that it is a warmer, softer shade of blue.

In the United States, with some breeds, the name lavender is used in place of lilac, but this is not done in Britain.

Lilac-cream

Coat Pattern. The lilac-cream combination is a diluted form of tortoiseshell. A 'Lilac-cream Point Cat' is a colourpoint cat with a white body and lilac points with patches of cream.

Lion

Wild Feline. *(Panthera leo)* German: *Löwe;* French: *Le Lion;* Swahili: *Simba;* Afrikaans: *Leeu.*

The lion is at once the most famous and the least typical member of the cat family. Other cats are solitary hunters; the lion is a co-operative group hunter. Other cats live alone, the lion lives in prides. In its level of sociability it comes closer to the wolves and wild dogs than to the other cat species. In addition, with other cats the male and female do not look conspicuously different; with lions, the huge, dark mane of the male sets him clearly apart from the maneless female. Another small difference: the lion is the only cat species to have a knob-like tuft of dark hair at the tip of its tail.

There is a second paradox. In surveys of animal popularity, the lion is the only animal in the world that appears among both the top ten loves and the top ten hates. It is loved because it is perceived as proud, dignified, handsome and powerful – the 'lord of the jungle' – and it is hated because it is a killer of appealing animals such as antelope and zebra.

In a typical pride of lions there are between five and ten adult females with their cubs, and several adult males. The females do most of the hunting, while the males do most of the fighting. The cubs pass most of their waking hours playing. When the food supply is plentiful the whole pride spends a great deal of time resting and sleeping. On average a lion sleeps for 16 hours out of every 24. The pride usually has special resting places – in the shade of a large tree, or on a rocky outcrop. Sometimes, they climb onto the large branches of a tree and sprawl out there, gaining the advantage of any slight breeze that might be blowing and which will cool them in the heat of the day.

When the lionesses set off on a hunt at dusk, they approach their prey, such as a herd of zebra or antelope, with great caution, fanning out sideways and gradually encircling them. When they eventually break cover and make the final, high-speed charge, they may briefly travel as fast as 64 km (40 miles) an hour. Any lioness that manages to catch up with a fleeing animal, strikes it down with a blow from a front leg and then falls upon it, grabs it by the throat with its jaws and, holding firm, quickly suffocates it.

During this final stage of the hunt, the individual lionesses work on their own. They launch the final attack on the prey without reference to the actions of their companions. Indirectly, however, they do help one another because of the confusion they create. With attacks coming from all directions at once, the prey does not know which way to flee and with no clear flight path, in the hesitation of the moment, they are struck down. This hunting strategy works well but, even so, lions are normally only successful in making a kill in one out of four hunts.

Because lions tend to attack large prey animals, the kill usually produces a sudden surplus of food, and all members of the pride can share in the feast, even those that have not been involved in the hunt itself. There may be a few status squabbles during the course of this sharing process, but in the end the entire group will probably be bloated with food and, after a visit to a water-hole, will rest once again.

The males defend their pride against rivals until they are too old or sick to do so. New males will then take over the breeding group and, in the process, will kill any existing cubs. When this happens, the females will soon come into heat again and will then produce cubs that are fathered by the new males. Elderly male lions that have been deposed in this way must live out their final years as solitary individuals hunting for smaller game.

Lions advertise their presence in their defended territories by leaving scent signals – either by depositing their droppings, or by spraying urine onto landmarks – and also by loud roaring sessions, especially at dusk.

In 1975 it was estimated that there were still about 200,000 wild lions left in the world, making it easily the most successful of all the big cats. However, by 1984 a more careful analysis gave a much lower figure – only 50,000. Nearly all of these were in tropical Africa. It has been calculated that this number will continue to shrink at a steady rate and it is reassuring to know that, in addition to wild lions, there is also a sizeable captive population, this species being the easiest of all feline species to breed in zoos and wildlife parks.

Size: Length of Head + Body: 140–250 cm (55–98½ in). Tail: 70–105 cm (27½–41½ in). Weight: males –150–225 kg; (330–500 lb); females 110–150 kg (243–330 lb).

Distribution: In comparatively recent times, the lion had a much wider distribution than it does today. Lions once roamed most of Europe. The last ones in Britain were killed off by Stone Age man about 50,000 years ago, and those living on Continental Europe followed them into extinction soon afterwards. Only in Greece did they manage to survive the slaughter and were still living wild there until about 2,000 years ago. The North African or Barbary Lion was reduced to small numbers by the ancient Romans, seeking livestock for the displays in the Colosseum and other such arenas. The remaining leonine survivors in that part of the world were finally exterminated within the last century. In the Middle East, the last lion to be seen was recorded in 1941. Since that time there has been no authenticated sighting in that region.

Further east, the once common Asiatic Lion is still surviving, but only in one small game reserve. Throughout the 19th century, sportsmen, hunters and local farmers decimated the eastern lions, rapidly reducing their huge numbers to a mere handful. So efficient was this purge that, by the year 1900, there were only 100 lions left in the whole of Asia. By 1913 that figure

The lion *(Panthera leo) (opposite),* the most sociable member of the entire cat family. Most cat species, both big and small, are solitary in their habits and the lion's tendency to live in prides is unique among felines.

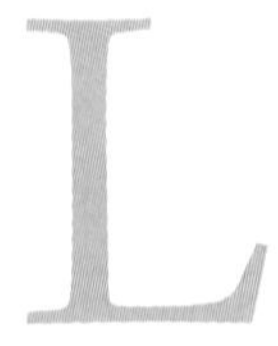

LION

CONTRARY TO POPULAR OPINION, the lion hardly exists now as a truly wild animal. Although there are reckoned to be about 50,000 left 'in the wild', the truth is that they are nearly all in carefully protected game parks in Africa.

had dropped to a mere 20 animals and extinction beckoned. These survivors were all concentrated in one small reserve in the Gir Forest in western India. There, they at last found some protection and their numbers gradually started to rise again. At the last count there were about 300 of them, and breeding programmes are being designed to re-introduce them to other areas. (See separate entry for Asiatic Lion.)

The one remaining stronghold for the lion today is tropical Africa, below the Sahara. Even there, where thousands of lions still roam freely, their days may be numbered because the human population of Africa is doubling every two decades. Even today most of the lions appear to be confined to National Parks and Game Reserves. In the whole of South Africa, for example, not a single truly wild lion now exists. Nearly all the South African lions are now guests of just one reserve – the huge Kruger National Park.

Game reserves where African Lions can be seen today include the following: (1) Amboseli (2) Arusha (3) Chobe (4) Etosha (5) Garamba (6) Gemsbok (7) Hluhluwe/Umfolozi (8) Hwange (9) Kafue (10) Kalahari (11) Kidepo (12) Kruger (13) Lake Manyara (14) Mana Pools (15) Marsabit (16) Masai Mara (17) Meru (18) Moremi (19) Murchison Falls (20) Nairobi (21) Ngorongoro (22) Queen Elizabeth (23) Ruaha (24) Samburu (25) Serengeti (26) South Luangwa (27) Upemba (28) Virunga.

Bibliography:

1933. Wells, E.F.V. *Lions Wild and Friendly.* Cassell, London.
1961. Guggisberg, C.A.W. *Simba: The Life of the Lion.* Bailey Bros & Swinfen, London.
1962. Carr, N. *Return to the Wild. A Story of Two Lions.* Collins, London.
1964. Kay, J. *Wild Eden.* Hutchinson, London.
1972. Schaller, G. *The Serengeti Lion.* University of Chicago Press, Illinois.
1972. Schaller, G. *Serengeti, Kingdom of Predators.* Knopf, New York.
1973. Rudnai, J.A. *The Social Life of the Lion.* Medical and Technical Press.
1973. Schaller, G. *Golden Shadows, Flying Hooves.* Knopf, New York.
1977. McBride, C. *The White Lions of Timbavati.* Paddington Press, London.

1978. Bertram, B. *Pride of Lions.* Dent, London.
1981. McBride, C. *Operation White Lion.* Collins Harvill, London.
1982. Jackman, B. & Scott, J. *The Marsh Lions.* Elm Tree Books, London.
1992. Scott, J. *Kingdom of Lions.* Kyle Cathie, London.
Note: See also extensive bibliography for Elsa.

Lion Cat

Domestic Breed. Known from ancient Chinese paintings, this was an early long-haired breed similar to the Persian. These cats were thought to bring good luck to their owners and were pampered favourites of the Chinese courts, especially during the Ming dynasty (1368–1644 AD). They were fed from exquisite bowls, given honours and titles, decorated with necklaces and even given funeral rites. One Emperor loved his favourite cat so much that, when it died, he had it buried in a specially made gold coffin.

The most precious form of the Lion Cat was the Star-seal variety, which had predominantly white fur. Its important markings were a black patch on its forehead and a black tail.

Little Spotted Cat

Wild Feline. An alternative name for the Tiger Cat *(Felis tigrina)* from South America. It is preferred to the more traditional name by some authors because it is more accurately descriptive of this species. *Felis tigrina* is spotted and not striped like a tiger, and it is the smallest of the New World species. However, the name can cause confusion because the Black-footed Cat of Africa *(Felis nigripes)* is sometimes called the Small Spotted Cat. So, for the sake of clarity, the old name of Tiger Cat is preferable. (For details of this species, see Tiger Cat.)

Long-haired Cats

Domestic Breeds. Long-haired breeds of domestic cat have been known for centuries, but their popularity did not reach a peak until the Victorian era when Queen Victoria herself owned two, and they became the star attractions at the earliest cat shows.

Writing on the subject of Long-haired Cats in 1889, Harrison Weir, the organizer of the very first cat show in 1871, comments: 'There are several varieties – the Russian, the Angora, the Persian, and Indian. Forty or fifty years ago they used all to be called French cats, as they were mostly imported from Paris.'

A few years later, in 1893, John Jennings slightly increased this list of long-haired varieties: 'The several varieties which range under *Long-hair* embrace Persian, Angora, Chinese, Indian, French, and Russian.'

Of these six early forms of Long-haired Cats, little is known about the Chinese, Indian or Russian. The Chinese was said to be similar to the better-known Persian, except that it had pendulous ears (which seems highly unlikely). The Indian was also said to be close to the Persian, but with striped markings of red and black. In India it was said to be called the domestic 'Tiger cat', not to be confused with the wild Tiger Cat. The Russian was described as 'by far the most woolly of cats' with a comparatively coarse and very thick coat. As designated breeds, these three types soon vanished, although much later it was thought that perhaps the early Russian type was the ancestor of all the others, its long fur having developed as an adaptation to the intense cold of the Russian winter. This would certainly make more sense than suggesting that our modern long-haired breeds have originated from hot countries such as Turkey and Iran.

Of the other three forms, the Angora, with its lithe, long-bodied look and its plumed tail and exaggerated ruff, was the earliest of the long-haired breeds to be seen in Western Europe, where it first appeared in the 16th century. Later, in the 17th century and especially at the end of the 18th century, it was joined by the much more rounded and fluffy-coated Persian, which quickly became the top favourite. The type referred to as the 'French cat' was not a true breed, but was simply a name given to all long-haired cats in the middle of the 19th century because so many of them at that time were being imported into England from France, where they had gained

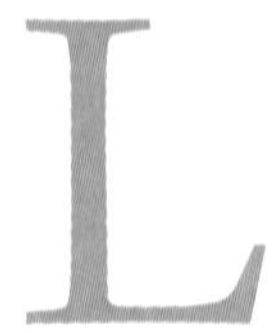

Long-haired Cats

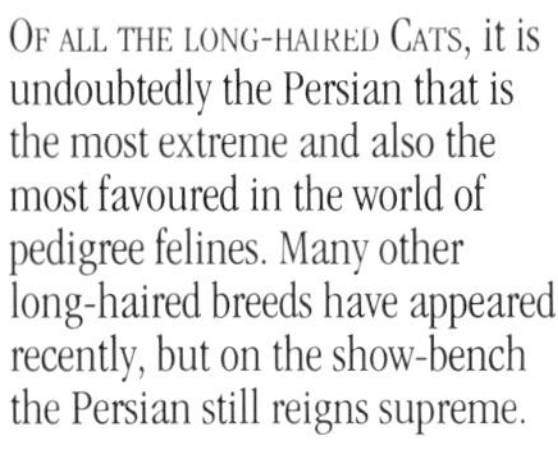

Of all the long-haired Cats, it is undoubtedly the Persian that is the most extreme and also the most favoured in the world of pedigree felines. Many other long-haired breeds have appeared recently, but on the show-bench the Persian still reigns supreme.

considerable popularity. By the end of the 19th century, English and American breeders had become so serious in their interest in these breeds that they were no longer thought of as 'French Cats', and the name was dropped.

At the turn of the century, when cat shows were gaining in strength, there was great competition to produce the most exaggerated of long-haired specimens. Little attempt was made to keep the different long-haired breeds apart as pure lines. They were mixed together to create the softest, heaviest coats obtainable. Inevitably, this meant that the Persian breed became the most dominant element in the mixing, because its fur was thicker than that of the Angora and softer than that of the Russian.

By the early part of the 20th century, the Angora and Russian had been swamped out and the preferred long-haired type was predominantly Persian. For most people, this was a good-enough reason to refer to all long-haired cats simply as 'Persians'. The pedigree-cat authorities in England, however, took a different view. Because these cats were the result of a mixture of early types, they took the purist view that long-haired cats should be called simply that, and the name 'Persian' was eliminated from official documents. The rest of the cat world ignored this somewhat academic decision and has persisted in using the term 'Persian'. Even in England, ordinary cat-owners still use the term Persian Cat rather than Long-haired Cat, when talking about these animals.

In recent decades, new breeds of cat with long hair have been discovered or developed and today the official use of the name 'Long-haired Cat' to refer to a Persian Cat is not merely confusing, it is now also misleading, especially as both the Angora and the Russian have been 'rediscovered' and re-introduced (as the Turkish Angora and Siberian Forest Cat respectively).

At the present time, there are the following distinct long-haired breeds:

1 Persian ('Longhair' in GB)
2 Himalayan ('Colourpoint Longhair' in GB)
3 Peke-Faced (Flat-faced Persian developed in America in the 1930s)

4 **Balinese** (Long-haired Siamese, developed in the 1940s)
5 **Japanese Bobtail Longhair** (Long-haired version, developed in the 1950s)
6 **Kashmir** (Persian variant developed in America in the 1950s)
7 **Maine Coon** (Long-haired American breed, popularized in the 1950s)
8 **Turkish Van** (Related to the Angora and developed in the 1950s)
9 **American Bobtail** (New American breed discovered in the 1960s)
10 **Birman** (Long-haired Burma breed, popularized in the 1960s)
11 **British Angora** (Reconstituted Angora created in GB in the 1960s)
12 **Cymric** (Long-haired Manx Cat, developed in the 1960s)
13 **Ragdoll** (New American breed developed in the 1960s)
14 **Somali** (Long-haired Abyssinian, developed in the 1960s)
15 **Tiffany** (Long-haired American breed, discovered in the 1960s)
16 **Turkish Angora** (Rediscovered in Turkey in the 1960s)
17 **Javanese** (Long-haired breed developed in the 1970s)
18 **Norwegian Forest** (Long-haired Scandinavian breed, popularized in 1970s)
19 **American Curl** (New American breed discovered in the 1980s)
20 **Coupari** (Long-haired Scottish Fold, developed in the 1980s)
21 **La Perm Longhair** (New American breed discovered in the 1980s)
22 **Siberian Forest** (Russian Long-haired Cat, rediscovered in the 1980s)
23 **Tiffanie** (Long-haired Burmese, developed in the 1980s)
24 **Longhair Rex** (New Eastern European breed, reported in the 1990s)
25 **Nebelung** (Long-haired Russian Blue, developed in the 1990s)
26 **Ragamuffin** (New American breed developed in the 1990s)
27 **Suqutranese** (White long-haired Abyssinian, developed in the 1990s)

Clearly, the term 'Long-haired Cat' is now only appropriate in its broad, descriptive sense, as a term to embrace all these breeds. Its continued use in the narrow sense, in Britain, is increasingly difficult to justify.

Bibliography:
1933. Buckworth-Herne-Soame, E. *Cats: Long-Haired and Short.* Methuen, London.
1968. Pond, G. *The Long-haired Cats.* Arco, London.
1974. Pond, G. and Calder, M. *The Longhaired Cat.* Batsford, London.
1983. Pond, G. *The Long-haired Cats.* Batsford, London.

Longhair Fold Cat

Domestic Breed. The name given to the long-haired version of the Scottish Fold Cat by the Cat Fanciers Federation (CFF) in the United States, when they accorded it championship status in 1991. Confusingly, this breed has four different names with four different cat societies. Eventually one of these titles will probably become entrenched and will then eclipse the other three, but at present – the breed being so new – they are still competing with one another.

The other three names are: The Highland Fold – with the American Cat Fanciers Association (ACFA): The Scottish Fold Longhair – with the Cat Fanciers' Association of America (CFA); and The Coupari – with British breeders.

Longhair Rex Cat

Domestic Breed. According to a 1994 German report, a long-haired version of the Rex Cat has recently been created by Eastern European breeders by crossing Rex Cats with Persians.

Longhair Siamese Cat

Domestic Breed. The original name given to the breed now known as the Balinese Cat. When long-haired Siamese individuals first appeared in litters they were looked upon as oddities and discarded from breeding programmes. Then, in the 1940s and '50s, a few American breeders

decided to develop them as a distinct breed and gave them the obvious name of Longhaired Siamese. This annoyed other Siamese breeders and so in the 1960s the name was dropped in favour of Balinese. In Australia, however, they have the alternative name of Oriental Longhairs.

Lop-eared Cat

Domestic Breed. The original name given to the Scottish Fold Cat in the 1960s by the breed's discoverer, the Scottish shepherd William Ross. He was later persuaded to change the name because the folding down of the ear is quite different from that of the Lop-eared Rabbit.

The mysterious 'Chinese Cat' mentioned in the 18th and 19th centuries was reputed to have long, pendulous ears, but this was never confirmed, and is highly unlikely. It may, however, have had folded ears similar to those of the Scottish Fold Cat.

Lucifer

Cartoon Cat. Walt Kimball, one of Walt Disney's animators, owned a large Calico Cat, and this cat was used as the model for Lucifer, the house cat, in Disney's feature-length cartoon, *Cinderella* (1950).

Lynx (1)

Coat Pattern. In the world of pedigree cats the term 'lynx' is applied specifically to the points of the colourpoint coat pattern. In the original version of the colourpoint coat, first seen in the earliest Siamese Cats, the points were always 'seal' coloured – very dark brown. As the years passed and new variants were produced, a number of different types of dark point appeared. Among these was a tabby-patterned point. In Britain this was given the obvious name of Tabby Pointed coat, but in the United States the more glamorous name of Lynx Point was preferred.

Colour variants of Lynx Points listed by American breeders include the following: (1) Blue-Cream Lynx Point; (2) Blue Lynx Point; (3) Chocolate Lynx Point; (4) Chocolate-Tortie Lynx Point; (5) Cream Lynx Point; (6) Lilac-Cream Lynx Point; (7) Lilac Lynx Point; (8) Red Lynx Point; (9) Seal Lynx Point; (10) Seal-Tortie Lynx Point; (11) Tortie Lynx Point.

Lynx (2)

The short-tailed, tufted-eared, medium-sized Lynx, depicted here in an early drawing from Thomas Bewick's *General History of Quadrupeds* of 1790.

Wild Feline. This is the name given to medium-sized wild cats with stocky bodies, tufted ears and very short tails. In origin the word *Lynx* comes from the Greek *leukos,* meaning white or bright, referring to the light colouring of the coat and the bright eyes.

Four species are recognized today: (1) *Lynx canadensis* (the Canadian Lynx from North America; (2) *Lynx lynx* (the Northern Lynx from N. Europe and N. Asia; (3) *Lynx pardinus* (the Spanish Lynx from the Iberian peninsula; (4) *Lynx rufus* (the Bobcat from North America).

In addition there is: (5) *Caracal caracal* (the Caracal – often called the Caracal Lynx – from Africa and southern Asia). This species has frequently been linked with the other, true lynxes. It has the external features of a lynx, but there is still debate as to how genuinely close it is to the other species.

Ma

Pet Cat. A female tabby cat who holds the official record for the oldest known domestic cat. According to *The Guinness Book of Records,* she was 34 years old when she had to be put to sleep in 1957. She was owned by Alice Moore of Drewsteignton, Devon. (A tabby cat called 'Puss', said to have lived for 36 years, has also laid claim to the world record lifespan, but its case is less well documented.)

Maau

Feline Term. In ancient Egypt the cat was known as Maau, Mau-Maï, Maon, or Mau.

Macavity

Fictional Cat. Macavity was the mystery cat in T.S. Eliot's *Old Possum's Book of Practical Cats.* More a cat burglar than a cat, he was a tall, thin, ginger cat who always managed to disappear at the crucial moment: 'For he's a fiend in human shape, a monster of depravity./ You may meet him in a by-street, you may see him in the square – / But when a crime's discovered, then *Macavity's not there!*'

Mackenzie, Compton

Cat Owner. The best-selling British author Sir Compton Mackenzie (1883–1972) was devoted to cats throughout his long life and wrote several books on the subject. His fascination with Siamese Cats led to his becoming the President of the Siamese Cat Club, a post which he held for nearly half a century – from 1928 until his death. At one time he owned no fewer than 11 Siamese. Of the intimacy between this breed and its human owners, he wrote in 1934: 'Nobody who has once been admitted into this intimacy can ever love any other animal so dearly.' He went on to say that he admired Siamese Cats for 'their sense of humour, their fidelity, their

dauntless courage (except of the unknown), their playfulness, their conversational powers, their awareness of themselves, their honesty (by which I mean they will take a lobster off a table in front of you), their continuous passionate interest in all that is going on around them, and their depth of affection .'

Bibliography:
1960. *Cat's Company.* Elek Books, London.
1961. *Catmint.* Barriet Rockliff, London.
1963. *Look at Cats.* Hamilton, London.
1965. *Little Cat Lost.* Macmillan, New York. (Juvenile)

Mackerel Tabby

Coat Pattern. The Mackerel Tabby pattern is the one closest to the markings seen on the ancestral Wild Cat. It consists of dark streaks on a paler background. These streaks are long, thin, curving and largely vertical. They tend to break up into short bars and spots. It is these breaks that are thought to have been exploited and exaggerated by breeders to create the domestic spotted breeds. By contrast, those wishing to exhibit a champion Mackerel Tabby worked in the opposite direction, trying to make the streaks as long, fine and unbroken as possible. (See also the entry for Striped.)

Maculate

Coat Pattern. An alternative name for a spotted coat. The term comes from the Latin *macula,* meaning a spot.

Madagascar Cat

Mystery Cat. In 1939 there was a French report of a giant, cave-dwelling cat rather like a lion, that inhabited remote, unexplored areas of the island of Madagascar. It was romantically suggested that this represented a remnant population of sabre-toothed felines. The report was published by Paul Cazard in *Le Chasseur Français.* He suggested the mounting of an expedition to search for this unknown cat, but no action was ever taken and the Madagascar Sabre-tooth must remain in the mystic realms of the 'Mystery Cat'.

Madame Théophile

Pet Cat. One of the many cats belonging to the French author Théophile Gautier (1811–1872). A 'red cat, with white breast, pink nose, and blue eyes', she was given her unusual name because she always shared the author's bed. She had a strange reaction to human music (see entry for Music), strongly disliking the high A note. Once, on encountering a pet parrot, she began to stalk it and was just moving in for the kill when the parrot spoke to her in a clear human voice, asking her if she had had her breakfast. This so unnerved the cat that she sneaked under the bed and refused to come out again that day.

Madame Vanity

Pet Cat. She belonged to the brilliant French essayist Michel de Montaigne (1533–1592), who wrote the following words about her in 1580: 'When I am playing with my Cat, who knows whether she has more sport dallying with me than I have gaming with her. We entertain one another with mutual apish tricks. If I have my hour to begin or to refuse, so has she hers.' He was making a plea, far ahead of its time, for a less arrogant attitude when comparing ourselves with other animals.

He writes with great modesty: 'Shall we say we have seen the use of a reasonable soul in no other creature but in man?' . . . and he complains of man 'that he ascribes divine conditions to himself, that he selects and separates himself from out the rank of other creatures . . . How does he know, by virtue of his understanding, the inward and secret emotions of beasts? By what comparison from them to us does he conclude the brutishness he ascribes to them? . . . The

defect which hinders the communication between them and us, why may it not as well be in us, as in them? . . . may they as well esteem us beasts, as we them?'

It is tempting to think that it was his relationship with his cat that inspired Michel de Montaigne to such humility.

Magpie Cat

Domestic Breed. At early pedigree shows, cats with bold black and white markings were often referred to as 'Magpie Cats'. Today this term has disappeared and such animals would be looked upon as no more than Black and White Bi-colour forms of one breed or another. Originally, they were seen as a distinct, separate breed in their own right. Back in 1951, the international cat judge Kit Wilson remarked: 'Then, too, there has been that fascinating breed, the Magpie Cat, a black and white cat marked like a Dutch Rabbit.' A little later, in 1955, Rose Tenent used the term as an alternative name for the Black and White Persian Cat: 'Often known as the Magpie Cat, the Black-and-White Persian can be very pretty when the markings are symmetrical.'

Moving with the times, one breeder who specializes in this type of cat today refers to them (informally), not as Magpie Cats, but as 'Panda Cats'.

Maine Cat

Domestic Breed. An early name for the Maine Coon Cat, used by Frances Simpson in 1903.

Maine Coon Cat

Domestic Breed. One of the first truly American breeds, the Maine Coon Cat is a big, tough, outdoor, cold-country cat, similar to the Norwegian Forest Cat and the Siberian Forest Cat from the Old World. It has also been called the Maine Cat, the Maine Trick Cat, the American Longhair, the American Forest Cat, the American Shag and the American Snughead. It has been described as a 'gentle giant with the face of a lynx'. This is a powerful working cat with physical beauty as a bonus.

A Brown Mackerel Tabby and White example of the impressively built Maine Coon Cat from North America. A splendidly tough, sturdy, long-haired, cold-country cat that is rapidly gaining in popularity.

Appearance: One of the largest of all domestic breeds. Long-bodied but with a relatively small head. Well-muscled and strong-boned. The protective coat is long, heavy and silky, with a large ruff and bib and, above all, a magnificently luxuriant tail.

History: As with all early breeds, there are a number of alternative explanations concerning the origin of the Maine Coon Cat:

1 It is a cross between a house-cat (or a wild cat) and a raccoon. Although this is zoologically impossible, the legend could at least have given the breed its distinctive name. The idea first arose because the original Maine Coons were tabbies with ringed tails and were fond of climbing trees. This made them look raccoon-like and sparked imaginative speculations concerning their unlikely parentage.

2 It is a cross between a house-cat and an American Bobcat or Canadian Lynx. This is another preposterous theory which was seriously considered by some authors. Although it is true that a variety of feline hybrids have occurred in the past, there is nothing about the anatomy or behaviour of the Maine Coon that suggests any non-domestic genetic elements.

3 It is descended from six Angora cats that belonged to the Queen of France, Marie Antoinette. A Captain Samuel Clough of Wiscasset, Maine, is said to have brought the cats to Maine on board his ship, *The Sally*, along with other precious belongings of the beleaguered Queen. It is claimed that she was planning an escape from the dangers of the French Revolution and had sent all her most treasured possessions on ahead of her, including furniture, cloth, wallpaper, china, silver, ornaments and her six beloved long-haired cats. She herself never followed because she was beheaded before she could leave. Her cats broke free, or were turned loose in Maine, and began to fend for themselves in the New England countryside. Her other belongings were disposed of, and it is claimed that some of the furniture is still to be seen in Wiscasset. Without more detailed, documented evidence, all one can say in favour of this story is that a cross between Angoras and local tabby cats would probably result in something approaching a Maine Coon in appearance.

4 It is descended from Norwegian Forest Cats, or Skogkatts, that were sent to America by Marie Antoinette during the French Revolution, when she hoped to escape to the New World. The reason the French Queen might have owned Norwegian Skogkatts is that one of her most devoted admirers at the French court was the Swedish diplomat Count Axel von Fersten, who would have had access to Scandinavian felines and might have offered her some as an exotic gift. Sadly, there is no hard evidence to support this.

5 It is descended from Angora Cats sent to America by Marie Antoinette during the American War of Independence. She is said to have made a gift of some to the Marquis de Lafayette on one of his voyages.

6 It is descended from Persians and Angoras brought to New England by an English sea captain by the name of Coon. In his trading vessel, he is reputed to have been a regular visitor to the ports up and down the coast and was always accompanied by his feline 'army'. Whenever he went ashore, some of his cats managed to follow suit and fraternize with the local cats. In this way, they founded the long-haired cat population of North America – a population that was named after him. (In some versions of this story, Captain Coon is identified as Chinese.)

7 It is descended from Norwegian Skogkatts brought to North America as ships' cats at a very early date by the Vikings. To believe this, you have to accept the controversial view that Vikings were regularly visiting North America in the 500 years before Columbus 'discovered' the New World. (It is claimed that Columbus was only able to make his voyage successfully because he had set eyes on some of the early Viking maps of North America.) In support of this theory it has been pointed out that the Norwegian Forest Cat and the Maine Coon Cat are remarkably similar in appearance. One expert cat judge, seeing both breeds together at a show in Berlin, remarked that in her opinion they belonged to the same breed. (It could, however, be argued that it is only similar climatic conditions which have made them look the same – both breeds being well protected from the cold.)

THE OFFICIAL EMBLEM of the Maine Coon Cat Club.

A SILVER TORTIE SMOKE AND WHITE MAINE COON CAT. This breed has the unique distinction of being the only one to boast its own glossy colour magazine: *Maine Coon International*.

8 It is a descendant of Russian Steppe Cats (Russian Long-haired Cats) that were brought to Maine by sailors on trading ships.
9 It is a descendant of a French breed from the mountains of the Pyrenees known as the 'French Domestic', which looks very similar to the Maine Coon. It is thought that early French explorers first brought these long-haired cats to the New World to trade with the local Indian tribes as valuable rodent-destroyers. (The North American Indian tribes had no domestic cats available to them before the arrival of Europeans.)
10 It is a cross between local house cats that were running wild in the New England forests and Angora Cats that had been imported as exotic novelties by New England sailors and had escaped. The custom in the early days of sea travel was for sailors to bring back unusual 'curios' from faraway places for sale in their home ports. Angora Cats could have been acquired on voyages to Turkey any time from the 17th century onwards.
11 It is a result of British sailors bringing Angoras over as ships' cats in the 1850s. When these cats escaped and mated with the local cats, the outcome was the Maine Coon. The weakness of this idea is that ships' cats would almost certainly have been the tough, local British shorthairs, rather than the then highly valued long-haired imports from Turkey.
12 It is the descendant of local house-cats that became semi-wild and, as a result of living in the cold forests, gradually developed a heavier body and a thicker coat as a natural protection against the cold.

Of all these various explanations the last one is the simplest, but there may well have been occasional injections of long-haired cats from abroad, by one or other of the routes mentioned.

Whichever origin is the true one, we do know that Maine Coons have the remarkable distinction of being the very first cats ever to be exhibited in competitive cat shows. The first official cat show in the world is usually dated at 1871, in London. The first in North America is usually given as 1895, in New York. But Maine Coon shows had been taking place regularly before either of these. From the early 1860s, New England farmers had been holding an annual cat show at the Skowhegan Fair. Maine Coons were brought there from all over the region to compete for the title of 'Maine State Champion Coon Cat'.

When the bigger shows began at the end of the century, the Maine Coons had a considerable advantage, having already been exposed to over 30 years of competitive showing. As a result they were extremely popular and highly successful in those first days of major, national pedigree competition. But it was not to last. As cat shows became more and more popular, the exotic Persians and Siamese began to appear and gradually took over the show scene, as they had done in Europe. The Maine Coons were eclipsed and gradually vanished.

The problem was familiarity. As one Maine Coon enthusiast put it, early in the 20th century: 'The Maine people having had them so long, it is difficult to arouse any great enthusiasm about them.' The farmers may have taken pride in them, but these new cat exhibitions were city affairs. The recently arrived breeds from overseas were rare novelties and therefore much more appealing to the sophisticated urbanites who were flocking to the big shows.

Interest in the New England breed did, however, return in the 1950s and a Maine Coon Cat Club was formed in 1953. In 1968 the Maine Coon Breeders and Fanciers Association was established and in 1976 this was joined by the International Society for the Preservation of the Maine Coon. From this point onwards, the breed began a full revival and in the 1980s its fame started to spread abroad. It arrived in Britain in 1983/84 (although the first Maine Coon in Europe was a pregnant female sent to Austria in 1953/54). (See also Rexed Maine Coon.)

Personality: Terms used to describe the breed include: hardy, rugged, dignified, reserved, amiable, gentle, elegant, loving, faithful, self-confident, responsive, durable, affectionate, playful, intelligent, resourceful, shy, good-tempered, soft-voiced, active and healthy.

Colour Forms: Traditionally, this is a tabby cat, but today almost any colour is allowed, including all solids, tabbies, shadeds and smokes, Bi-colours and Parti-colours. The British Maine Coon Cat Club lists no fewer than 64 colour forms. Specifically excluded are: Chocolate, Lilac and Siamese Points; blue or odd eyes in cats of a colour other than white; and Bi-colour or Parti-colour cats with more than one-third of the fur white.

Bibliography:

1981. Hornridge, M. *That Yankee Cat: The Maine Coon.* Harpswell Press, Gardinar, Maine.

1983. Bass, S.P. *This is the Maine Coon Cat.* TFH, New Jersey.

Breed Clubs:

British Maine Coon Cat Club was founded in 1985. In 1995 it published a guide to the breed: *Introducing the Maine Coon.* Address: 12 St Joseph's Road, Handsworth, Sheffield, South Yorkshire, S13 8AU, England.

Internationaler Maine Coon Cat Club (IMCCC). Address: Ziegelleiweg 18, 51149 Köln, Germany.

Maine Coon Fanciers of Great Britain. Address: Woodsview Cottage, Fowley Lane, High Hurstwood, East Sussex, TN22 4BG, England

Maine Coon Breeders and Fanciers Association. Address: 4405 Karrol S.W., Alburquerque, NM 87121, USA; or 2669 Skeel Street, Brighton, CO 80601, USA.

Maine Coon Club. 59 Ninth Street, Wyoming, PA 18644, USA.

United Maine Coon Cat Association. 7 Mason Drive, Milford, MA 01757, USA.

Note: In 1994, the Maine Coon had the unique distinction of being the only breed to have its own glossy colour magazine: *Maine Coon International* has been published quarterly since then by MCI Group, P.O. Box 59, Uckfield, East Sussex, TN22 4ZY, England.

Maine Wave

Domestic Breed. A new name suggested for the wavy-coated Maine Coon Cats that carry a Rex gene. Writing in 1995, British breeder David Brinicombe made the following comment about his Rexed Maine Coons:

'I exhibited my three recently (billed as 'Maine Waves' or just 'Waves') and received an overwhelmingly positive reaction to them, with very few adverse comments.' (For details see Rexed Maine Coons.)

Malayan Cat

Domestic Breed. An alternative name for certain types of Burmese Cats. Some cat organizations have accepted the whole range of Burmese colour forms as 'Burmese'. Others have refused to include the more recent colour forms, such as blue, champagne and platinum, under the title of Burmese. Purist breeders felt that a Burmese Cat is, by definition, a brown cat, and that any other colour must therefore be classified separately. To satisfy them, the name 'Malayan Cat' was introduced in 1980 to cover all non-traditional Burmese colour variants.

Malayan Persian

Domestic Breed. In 1924, in America, attempts to produce a Colourpoint Persian cat by crossing Siamese with White Persians resulted in animals that were christened 'Malayan Persians'. For some reason this line disappeared and it was not until after World War II that Colourpoint Persians were successfully established. In America these cats became known as Himalayans. (For further details see Himalayan.)

Malay Cat

Domestic Breed. Victorian zoologist St. George Mivart, discussing the various breeds of domestic cats known to him in 1881, comments: 'In Pegu [part of Lower Burma], Siam and Burmah, there is a race of cats – the Malay Cat – with tails only of half the ordinary length, and often contorted in a sort of knot, so that it cannot be straightened . . . Its contortion is due to deformity of the bones of the tail.' This information is repeated by Lydekker in 1896.

Judging by the description of the tail, it seems likely that the Malay Cat was related to, or identical with, the Japanese Bobtail Cat. It is thought that the Bobtail originally arrived in Japan from China about a thousand years ago. Burma borders Western China and it seems likely that this stump-tailed breed was originally found right across that region. (For further details see Japanese Bobtail.)

Maltese Cat

Domestic Breed. A short-haired, blue-grey cat is said to have existed on the Mediterranean island of Malta in earlier centuries. It is first mentioned by François Moncrif in 1727, in his book *Les Chats*. He says that a traveller from the East discovered that 'Like those in the Orient, there are beautiful slate-grey cats on the island of Malta.' It has recently been suggested by French author Jean Simonnet, an expert on the history of blue cats, that it was these Maltese Cats that were brought to Europe centuries ago where, in France, they became the ancestors of the Chartreux.

Other authors have taken a different view. They believe that all the various breeds of blue-grey cat are in reality one and the same, with only trivial, minor differences in body build. In 1895, Rush Huidekoper, for example, lumps them all together with the following words: 'The Blue Cat is called the "Maltese" in America. It was first shown as the "Archangel Cat", then called the "Russian Cat", also the "Spanish Blue", and "Chartreuse Blue", and recently has been called the "American Blue". This latter name is probably due to the fact that the Maltese for some years has been a very favourite cat in America.'

The American connection for the Maltese is confirmed by Frances Simpson who, writing in 1903, says, 'A great deal of interest has been taken in England in the subject of blue cats in

America, which are often called Maltese, and really among the rank and file of the public this is the name they go by.' The Chartreux Cat itself did not arrive in the United States as a pedigree cat until the 1970s, but it looks as though the Maltese was the first blue-grey cat to become popular there, nearly a century earlier.

In some circles in America the name 'Maltese' became so entrenched that it eventually became synonymous with 'blue'. In this way, even a long-haired cat that had blue-grey fur was referred to as having 'Maltese colour'. In Robert James's 1898 book on the Angora Cat, he shows an illustration of a long-haired cat with a plumed tail, labelled as 'Maltese Male Cat'.

Confirmation of the popularity of the name 'Maltese Cat' at the turn of the century comes from a surprising source – an 1898 story about a polo pony by Rudyard Kipling. The heroic pony at the centre of the tale is called 'The Maltese Cat' because it is feline in its movements and grey in colour. (For further details see Russian Blue Cat.)

Mandarin Cat

Domestic Breed. When Dutch breeders Ed and Helen van Kessel acquired a blue Angora (= Javanese) from the English breeder Janet Pitman, they gave it a new breed name: Mandarin. This name has since become popular in Germany where, judging by recent publications, it is now preferred to Javanese.

Maneki Neko

Legendary Cat. The Japanese name for the famous 'Beckoning Cat'. In the form of a painted pottery figure, showing a white cat with its right paw raised in the air, the Maneki Neko has become a popular good luck charm in modern Japan. It is displayed in many shop windows to invite customers to enter and it is felt that its presence will bring prosperity. For full details of the legend, see Beckoning Cat.

The Manul Cat, now generally know as Pallas's Cat. This early illustration fails to do justice to this remarkably beautiful species. For confirmation of this, see the photograph of Pallas's Cat on page 324.

Manul Cat

Wild Feline. An alternative name for Pallas's Cat *(Felis manul)*. Like the other early name for this species – the Steppe Cat – this is rarely used today. (For details see Pallas's Cat.)

Manx Cat

Domestic Breed. An old breed, famous for being tailless, originally found on the Isle of Man in the Irish Sea, between Northern England and Northern Ireland. Now kept as a pedigree cat all over the world. Outside the Isle of Man, it appears to be more popular in the United States than in Europe.

Appearance: A sturdy, rounded, thick-coated short-haired cat with short front legs and long back legs. The tailless rump is higher than the shoulders. The head is large and broad. There are four recognized categories of Manx Cat:

1 'The Rumpy', completely tailless. This is the true Manx Cat, with a small hollow where its tail should be.
2 'The Rumpy Riser', with one, two or three vertebrae fused to the end of the spine, giving the animal a tiny knob where the tail should be.
3 'The Stumpy', with one, two or three normal tail vertebrae, giving the animal a short but movable tail-stump.
4 The Longy', with an almost full-length tail.

In addition, there is a fifth type – the fake Manx Cat – created by ruthless dealers who have been known to amputate the tails of ordinary kittens to produce tailless adults that can be passed off as expensive pedigree Manx Cats. This is not a recent practice. It was recorded as long ago as 1903, when visitors to the island were offered tailless cats on the landing pier at Douglas, the capital of the Isle of Man. A commentator at the time remarks wryly that 'many

The controversial Manx Cat, much loved and hallowed by its long history, but now under fire as a 'genetic abnormality'. Its tailless condition can indeed cause medical problems but it is claimed that these can be avoided with proper breeding controls.

more tailless cats and kittens than ever were born have been sold to tourists eager to carry home some souvenir of the island'.

The typical, traditional Manx Cat has a short, thick coat, but there is also a longhaired version, called the Cymric, which first appeared in Canada in the 1960s.

History: The Manx Cat from the Isle of Man is one of the oldest breeds of domestic cat. During its long history a rich assortment of fanciful legends has grown up around it, including the following:

1 The Manx Cat is the result of mating between domestic cats and rabbits. According to this myth, this cross accounts, not only for the reduced tail, but also for the fact that the Manx Cat has a strange gait, caused by its unusually long back legs. (In some individuals the gait is so strange that they are called 'hoppers', but this 'Manx Hop' may actually be an indication of spinal deformity.)

2 The Manx Cat was the last animal to enter Noah's Ark. A pair of them insisted on one last mousing trip as the flood waters were rising and they kept putting off the moment when they would have to go aboard the Ark. Finally, when heavy rain began to fall, they rushed on board, just as Noah was closing the door. As they squeezed through, the heavy door slammed shut on their beautiful bushy tails and severed them, so that although the cats themselves were saved from the flood, their tails were lost for ever.

3 The Manx Cat was a survivor from the Spanish Armada. According to this legend, several tailless cats managed to avoid drowning when a galleon from the defeated Armada was shipwrecked in 1588 on rocks off the coast of the Isle of Man, in the extreme south-west of the island. There they managed to find shelter until low tide when they were able to clamber ashore at a location now known as 'Spanish Head'. Finding themselves isolated from other cats on this small island, they began to reproduce and established themselves as a distinctive, tailless cat. (Unfortunately for this and the next story, there is no record of a ship from the Spanish Armada ever coming near the Isle of Man.)

4 According to yet another legend, the ancestor of the Manx Cat was originally a (fully tailed) temple guardian in Tibet. He travelled from there to Spain, where he went aboard a Spanish galleon. This galleon was part of the Armada and was sunk near the Isle of Man. The cat swam ashore and settled on the island, where it produced a large number of kittens. Like the founding father of their breed, they all had long bushy tails. Because of these beautiful appendages, the kittens were repeatedly stolen and killed by Irish soldiers, who needed cats' tails as lucky mascots. (In a variant of this legend, the tails were taken by Viking invaders to adorn their helmets.) As a way of stopping this, the mother cats hit on the idea of biting off the tails of their kittens when they were born. The soldiers then lost interest, and the tailless Manx Cat breed came into existence.
5 In a variant of this last legend, the tails of the native cats of the Isle of Man were sliced off by Viking invaders, who wanted them as decorations for their helmets.
6 A mythological tale describes how Samson was taking a little light exercise by swimming the length of the Irish Sea. As he swam close to the Isle of Man, he was caught by a cat which nearly drowned him with its long tail. To defend himself, he severed the tail and from that day onwards, the cats of the Isle of Man had no tails.
7 A traditional Manx poem describes how Noah's dog bit off the tail of a cat as the Ark rested on Mt. Ararat, after the flood. The mutilated cat leaped through a window and started swimming. It went on swimming until eventually it arrived at the Isle of Man, where it came on to land and made its home.
8 The Manx Cat arrived at the Isle of Man on board trading ships coming from the Orient. (It has even been suggested that it was the Phoenicians who brought back tailless cats from Japan, over two thousand years ago.) This story is probably inspired by the fact that there has been a short-tailed domestic cat in Japan – the Japanese Bobtail Cat – since early times. Genetically, however, the two breeds are quite unrelated.
9 A variant of this last explanation has the breed arriving as a 'couple of kittens' brought home to the Isle of Man from the East Indies by a returning sailor.
10 A feudal lord increased his revenues by placing a tax on cats' tails. The population of the Isle of Man rebelled against this by cutting off the tails of all their cats. From then on, the cats remained tailless and no tax was paid.

Few breeds of domestic cat can have acquired such an amazing variety of speculative or nonsensical tales concerning their origins. The plain and far less colourful truth, however, is that the Manx gene almost certainly cropped up as a local, random mutation on the Isle of Man, centuries ago, and then became established there through prolonged in-breeding on the restricted island habitat.

Today Manx Cats have become so strongly associated with the Isle of Man that they have become a popular emblem there, appearing on local postage stamps and coins. At one point, the Tynwold (the Manx Parliament) became concerned that, although the Manx Cat was being bred all over the world, there was a risk that it might die out in its homeland. It was therefore decided to establish a government cattery to preserve a nucleus of breeding stock for all time. This was first done at Knockaloe Farm, where a group of 20 females and three males were installed. Then, in order to make the cats more available as a tourist attraction, a new cattery was built at Noble's Park in the capital, Douglas. With approximately 30 cats and kittens on display, this was opened to the public in July 1964.

In its home territory, the Isle of Man, the Manx Cat has become an important emblem, appearing on coins, stamps and all kinds of advertising and tourist documents.

Personality: Terms used to describe this breed include: active, hardy, lively, mischievous, playful, faithful, affectionate, speedy, patient, shy, docile, calm, quiet, doleful, undemanding and intelligent. It is said to be dog-like in some respects, will play a fetching game and will even accept the imposition of being taken for a walk on a leash. It is amenable to training and is good with children and other animals. One author describes it as a study in contradictions: 'quiet but active, shy but friendly, witty but reserved, clever but trusting'. Another called it a 'feline clinging vine' that will never leave you alone.

Critics of the breed see the loss of a tail as a deformity which robs the animals of one of their principal means of expression. Aldous Huxley commented: 'The Manx Cat is the equivalent of a dumb man.'

Breeding: The Manx Cat has never been particularly common, partly because the litters are rather small. There are usually only two to four kittens. An analysis of 237 litters gave an average figure of 3.4 kittens.

There is also the problem that the Manx gene is semi-lethal. If a Rumpy Manx Cat is mated with another Rumpy, the kittens die at an early stage of development. So there can never be a true-breeding Manx Cat. To create a completely tailless show cat, breeders usually mate a Rumpy with a partially tailed or fully tailed Manx.

The problem for Manx Cats is that the effect of the 'tailless gene' does not stop at the base of the tail. It modifies the whole of the spinal column, with the modification increasing from front to rear. The front parts show little more than a slight decrease in the length of the individual vertebrae, but towards the rear there is not only decrease in size, but also in number, and an increase in fusion. In the most extreme cases there is a condition similar to spina bifida, and interference with defecation because of a narrowing of the anal opening. Because of this the Manx Cat requires more careful and expert treatment on the part of breeders, than any other kind of domestic cat.

It has been said that, if the Manx Cat was a new breed, it would not be given pedigree status, and that it survives as a show cat only because of its long-established history. (A specialist breeders' club for Manx Cats was established as long ago as 1901.) This is unfair to modern breeders who have worked for years to improve the Manx Cat and to reduce the deformities without losing the essential, tailless condition. Some authors suggest that deformities are common but this is no longer the case. In two recent studies of spina bifida in Manx Cats, this condition was found in only 15 out of 806 and 2 out of 417 kittens. Other deformities, such as anal restrictions, deformed legs and a hopping gait, were also rare. It is claimed that, bred with care, the vast majority of Manx kittens are perfectly healthy today, thanks to intelligent selective breeding programmes, and that the breed is now safe for the future.

A pure white form of the Manx Cat. Serious breeders claim that the deformities once associated with the Manx have now been reduced to the level of extreme rarities as a result of careful, selective breeding programmes.

Colour Forms:

GCCF: All patterns and colours are accepted, except for Siamese markings. Those specifically listed are: White; Black; Chocolate; Lilac; Red Self; Blue; Cream; Silver Tabby (ten variants) (Classic and Mackerel); Red Tabby (Classic and Mackerel); Brown Tabby (nine variants) (Classic and Mackerel); Tortie; Chocolate Tortie; Lilac Tortie; Tortie and White; Blue Tortie and White; Chocolate Tortie and White; Lilac Tortie and White; Blue-Cream; Brown Spotted (ten variants); Silver Spotted (ten variants); Black and White Bi-colour (six variants); Black Smoke and White (ten variants); Brown Tabby and White (ten variants); Silver Tabby and White (ten variants); Black Smoke (ten variants); Black Tipped (ten variants).

CFA: All colours are permitted (except those involving chocolate, lavender or the Himalayan pattern). Specifically listed as accepted colours are: White, Black, Blue, Red, Cream, Chinchilla Silver; Shaded Silver; Black Smoke; Blue Smoke; Classic Tabby Pattern; Mackerel Tabby Pattern; Patched Tabby Pattern; Brown Patched Tabby; Blue Patched Tabby; Silver Patched Tabby; Silver Tabby; Red Tabby; Brown Tabby; Blue Tabby; Cream Tabby; Tortie; Calico; Dilute Calico; Blue-Cream; Bi-color.

Bibliography:

1961. Todd, N.B. 'The Inheritance of Taillessness in Manx Cats'. In: *Journal of Heredity,* 52, p.228-232.

1964. Kerruish, D.W. *The Manx Cat.* Kerruish, Douglas, Isle of Man.

1964. Todd, N.B. 'The Manx Factor in Domestic Cats'. in: *Journal of Heredity,* 55, p.225-230.

1979. Hellman, J. 'The Manx Cat'. In: *The Manx Cat,* 6, No. 11, p.15-19.

1987. Swantek, M. *The Manx Cat.* TFH, New Jersey.

1991. Hartman, J. *Memories of Manx Cats.* Hart-Manx Cattery.

Breed Clubs:

American Manx Club. Address: P.O. Box 15053, Colorado Springs, CO 80935-5053, USA.

International Manx and Cymric Society. 254 S. Douglas, Bradley, IL 60915, USA.

NOTE: There is also a breed publication: *Manx Lines.* Address: 19324 2nd Avenue, N.W. Seattle, WA 98177, USA.

THE MARBLED CAT *(Felis marmorata)* from Asia looks like a smaller version of the Clouded Leopard because it shares the same kind of large-blotched markings. Whether they are closely related or merely superficially similar remains to be seen.

M

Marbled Cat

Wild Feline. *(Felis marmorata)* Known in Malaya as the Kuching Dahan. In earlier times it was called the Marbled Tiger Cat, but that name has become obsolete.

Little larger than a domestic cat, it has a thick, soft coat with blotched markings on the trunk, spotted markings on its long legs and streaks and spots on its very long, black-tipped, bushy tail. The ears are small and rounded. It has been described superficially as a 'smaller edition of the Clouded Leopard'.

A little known, arboreal forest-dweller from Asia, the Marbled Cat has rarely been observed in the wild. Its diet consists of squirrels, small primates, rats, lizards, frogs and, above all, birds. It has on one occasion been seen hunting by creeping along a branch.

The few captive specimens that have been taken are reported to have been 'the fiercest of all cats'. They are reported to adopt an arched back posture much more frequently than other species.

Size: Length of Head + Body: 45–60 cm (18–23½ in). Tail: 40–55 cm (16–21½ in). Weight: 5 kg (11 lb).

Distribution: It has a wide range, from Nepal in the north to Borneo and Sumatra in the south. Through this range, it has been recorded in Sikkim, Assam, Burma, Malaysia and Thailand.

The Marbled Cat as it appears in George Mivart's classic study, *The Cat,* in 1881.

Marbled Tabby

Coat Pattern. This is a rarely used, alternative name for the Blotched or Classic Tabby.

Marcel Cat

Domestic Breed. A long-haired Rex Cat discovered in California in 1959. Also known as the 'California Rex Cat'.

Appearance: This cat has the wavy-haired coat of the typical Rex Cat, but with longer fur, giving it the look of 'marcel-waving', hence its name.

History: This breed originated from two cats found in an animal shelter in San Bernadino, California – an odd-eyed tortoiseshell female called 'Mystery Lady' and her son, a red tabby. They were rescued by a Mrs Blancheri and acquired by cat breeders Bob and Dell Smith, who mated the female with her son to produced a wavy-coated offspring – a red tabby – with even longer, silkier hair. The Marcel Cat, as the Smiths christened it, was later used in crossing experiments with shorthaired Rex Cats, but there seems to have been a general lack of interest in the breed in its own right.

Margate

Pet Cat. Margate was a stray black kitten who appeared on the doorstep of No. 10 Downing Street on 10th October 1953 and was immediately adopted by Prime Minister Winston Churchill, who saw it as a sign of good luck. He had just successfully delivered an important speech at Margate and named the kitten after the town. Ten days later, Margate had managed to progress to a place of honour on his new master's bed.

Margay Cat

Wild Feline. *(Felis weidii)* It has also been called the Marguey, the Long-tailed Spotted Cat, and the Little Ocelot. This last name describes it well and it is highly likely that this tree-living species has evolved as a miniature form of the heavier, more ground-dwelling Ocelot. Locally it is known as the Gato Pintado or the Gato Brasileiro.

The Margay is a small, spotted, New World cat now considered rare throughout its range. The attractive markings on its tawny coat consist of large spots with paler interiors and black edges. On the back of each ear there is a large white spot ringed with black. Seen from behind, these two marks create the impression of a pair of vivid 'eye-spots'. The cat's own eyes are impressively large and dark. Its tail is exceptionally long and acts as a crucial balancing aid when the animal is moving fast through the branches.

THE MARGAY CAT *(Felis weidii)* from Central and South America is like a miniature Ocelot. Despite its wide range, it has become increasingly rare because its beautifully marked coat is so favoured by the fur-trade.

Living in dense forests, it is the most arboreal of all cats, with several unique features. It can leap through the trees almost as acrobatically as a monkey. It can run down a tree-trunk head-first, aided by the fact that it, alone among cats, can rotate its hind feet through 180 degrees. It can even run along the underside of branches and can hang from branches by its hind feet like a squirrel. It is so adapted to an arboreal existence that it hunts, nests and mates above ground. Its prey are arboreal small mammals, birds, lizards and tree-frogs. The female gives birth to a single, large kitten (rarely two).This is the smallest litter size in the entire cat family and is, once again, consistent with an arboreal life, where a mother would find it almost impossible to control, protect and care for a nest full of a whole group of squirming kittens. Significantly, unlike other female cats, she only has one pair of nipples.

The rarity of this species has been increased by widespread illegal hunting for its beautiful pelt, and by massive deforestation that reduces its favoured habitat.

Size: Length of Head + Body: 50–70 cm (20–27½ in). Tail: 33–51 cm (13–20 in). Weight: 3–5 kg (6½–11 lb).

Distribution: The Margay Cat is usually said to have a wide range extending from southern Texas to northern Argentina, but this is misleading. The North American presence amounts to nothing more than a single specimen recorded many years ago, and in the Mexican region there are very few genuine sightings. The true distribution of this rare, forest-dwelling cat is more accurately described as stretching from tropical Central America to the south of Brazil.

MARRIAGE

FELINE HISTORY. It may be hard to believe, but there have been occasions when a formal marriage ceremony has been conducted for pairs of cats. In his *First Pet History of the World,* David Comfort reports that 'Dawn Rogers, a California Pet Pastor, ordained in the Universal Life Church, performed seventeen marriage ceremonies for dogs, cats, horses, goldfish and frogs in 1986'. One small advantage of being a cat-owner, rather than a dog-owner, was that the cost of a feline wedding was only $300, compared with $500 for canine nuptials.

THE MARGAY CAT *(opposite)* is the most arboreal of all feline species and it is capable of climbing actions to which no other cat can aspire. Uniquely it can rotate its hind feet through 180 degrees.

Masked Silver

Coat Colour. Writing about colour forms of Persian Cats in 1947, Milo Denlinger says: 'Masked silvers are a "new" variety, and at present very few are bred . . . The ideal masked silver is a very beautiful animal; in colouring or, I should say, marking, they should resemble the Siamese Cat; that is to say, they should have a black mask or face, black feet and legs. The body should be as pale a silver as possible . . . the eyes deep golden or copper.' Apart from the eye colour, it would appear from this description that the 'Masked Silver' was very similar to what is now known as the Himalayan Cat, or Colourpoint Persian.

In 1964 Jeanne Ramsdale adds this comment: 'About 1900 there was a colour of Persian called Masked Silver which is not seen any more. From their pictures, these cats seemed to resemble Silvers having black faces and legs, similar to the "points" of a Siamese.'

Mason, James

Cat Owner. James Mason had the distinction of being the only major film star to write a book about his pet cats and to illustrate it with his own drawings. He and his wife, Pamela, took a whole colony of cats (mostly Siamese) with them when they moved from England to Hollywood via New York in the 1940s. There were many disasters along the way, but they persevered, even when it meant spending long hours searching the streets for lost cats.

An elegant drawing by film actor James Mason of one of his much-loved Siamese Cats, a female called Sadie or Flower-face. When he left England for Hollywood, his colony of cats went with him.

In Los Angeles it emerged that many of their famous neighbours were also addicted to felines. Hollywood cat-owners they encountered included Fred Astaire, Lucille Ball, Charles Chaplin, Van Heflin, Katharine Hepburn, Charles Laughton, Ida Lupino and Elizabeth Taylor. The film director Max Ophuls owned a magnificent white Persian. Tallulah Bankhead, characteristically, had to outdo the others: her pet cat was a lion cub.

James Mason is quoted as saying: 'The happiest houses are those in which kitten-bearing is held over as a permanent attraction.'

Bibliography:

1949. Mason, P. and Mason, J. *The Cats in Our Lives.* Michael Joseph, London.

Master's Cat

Pet Cat. When Charles Dickens's cat, Williamina, produced a litter and insisted on moving it into his study, the great man decided not to keep the kittens, but relented over one little female who was allowed to stay on and became known as the Master's Cat. She is said to have tried to gain his attention by snuffing out his reading candle with a deft paw.

Matagot

Legendary Cat. The Matagot is a good luck cat. Any family sheltering, feeding and caring for such an animal will attract immense wealth to their house. The Matagot is always a black cat and it has strange, magical powers.

The name is used in the South of France, where there is a special formula for becoming rich with the aid of this 'magician-cat': because the Matagot is greedy, you must lure him with a plump chicken. Once you have hold of his tail you must put him into a sack and, without once looking back over your shoulder, you must secretly take him to your home. When you arrive there, you must place him in a large chest and offer him the first mouthful of every meal you have. If you do all this, you will find a gold coin deposited next to the chest each morning.

This belief was especially strong near Marseilles, where a nickname for the Matagot was 'Coste'. To this day, according to Fernand Mery, there are still people living in Provence with the surname of 'Coste-Matagot'.

In Brittany the Matagot is known as the 'Chat d'argent', a black cat that can serve nine masters at once (presumably with its nine lives) and make them all rich.

This legend of a cat that can bring riches to its owner is found in the folklore of many countries, including Denmark, Italy and Iran. In England it was the basis of the legend of Dick Whittington and his Cat (see separate entry).

Maternal Care

Feline Behaviour. After she has given birth and settled down with her new litter of kittens, the mother cat faces two months of intensive maternal duties. For the first few days she hardly leaves the nest at all. If she does, she does not go far and returns quickly. A pet cat prefers to be fed close to her nest at this time, and keeps a close eye on it even while eating. As the days pass, the time she will spend away from her kittens increases slightly. A feral cat, at this stage, will have to start hunting again.

Every time she returns to the nest the mother examines each kitten in turn, licks and cleans it, and when they have all been formally greeted in this way, settles down once more to feed them. Any kitten that is bold enough to stray from the centre of the nest is gently but firmly retrieved in her jaws. If the nest is approached by anyone or anything that she feels is a threat to her kittens, the mother will defend them bravely and ferociously.

So, during these first weeks, the mother provides three essentials: milk, warmth and security. She also has an additional task, namely stimulating urination and defecation, neither of which the very young kittens can manage on their own. Without her help in this matter they would die. She comes to their rescue by licking each kitten's genital region at regular intervals. This stimulates them to evacuate and she consumes what they produce, in this way keeping the nest dry and clean. This form of maternal care continues until the young animals have started to eat solid foods.

As they move into their second month of life, the kittens become much more mobile and start to take an interest in the mother's food dish when she is eating. They begin to taste the solid foods and gradually the weaning process gets under way. If they are pet cats, they will simply imitate her feeding behaviour. In the wild, they will have to wait for her to bring back freshly caught prey. For the wild or feral mother, this means catching and killing an animal and then suppressing her natural urge to devour it all on the spot. Instead she must carry it, still warm, back to her kittens, place it before them and, uttering a special feeding cry, invite them to join her in the feast. She will make sure that the prey is still warm, because cold food can cause problems for the kittens' sensitive digestive systems. (Because of this, pet cats always need their food warmed at this phase of motherhood.)

As the kittens grow older, the mother will bring them live prey, and this is the first phase of their education as hunters. If a female cat has no kittens of her own, she may, from time to time, bring live prey back for her human companions, treating them momentarily as substitute kittens. Having never seen her humans catch and kill a mouse, she assumes that they might benefit from her help, and is often deeply puzzled when this educational programme she has instigated results in human panic or even hostility.

The first live prey she brings back for her kittens she will play with in front of them, enabling them to see how she deals with it. She will then kill it herself and let them share her meal. After further weeks have passed, a wild-living mother cat will set off on the hunt with her kittens following behind and learning as they go, until they themselves have become efficient hunters.

When her litter enters its third month of life, the mother finally refuses to provide any more milk, thus forcing the kittens to fend for themselves. She may still keep an eye on them, but her maternal duties are now coming to an end, and she will soon, if given the chance, start to seek out tom-cats for another mating session.

Simply by watching the above series of events, as a mother cat rears her kittens, it is impossible to tell just how much actual maternal 'teaching' is taking place. It certainly appears to be happening, but this may be deceptive. How well would the kittens have managed if their mother had not 'trained' them in killing and hunting? Only specific tests can give the answer.

Experiments have proved that, although kittens do not need to learn how to perform the killing actions, it does indeed help them if they get some instruction from their mother. Kittens reared by scientists, in isolation from the mother cat, were able to kill prey when given live rodents for the first time, but not all the kittens succeeded. Out of the 20 tested, only nine killed and only three of those actually ate their kills. Kittens reared in a rodent-killing environment,

Constant vigilance is required of the mother cat in the first couple of months of the kittens' lives.

where they could witness kills but never saw the prey being eaten, were much more successful. Eighteen out of 21 such kittens tested were killers and nine of these actually ate their kills.

Interestingly, of 18 kittens reared in the company of rodents, only three became rodent-killers later on. The other 15 could not be trained to kill later by seeing other cats killing. For them, the rodents had become 'family' and were no longer 'prey'. Even the three killers would not attack rodents of the same species as the one with which they were reared. Although it is clear that there is an inborn killing pattern with kittens, this pattern can easily be damaged by unnatural rearing conditions.

Conversely, really efficient killers have to experience a kittenhood which exposes them to as much hunting and killing as possible. In experiments, the very best hunters are those which, as youngsters, were able to accompany their mother on the prowl and watch her dealing with prey. Also, at a more tender age, they benefited from her bringing prey to the nest to show them. If the mother does not bring prey to the kittens between the sixth and the 20th week of their lives, they will be far less efficient as hunters in later life. So, to sum up, although kittens have an inborn killing urge, their mother's example can have great value for them and is an important part of feline maternal care. (For further details see Birth, Suckling and Milk.)

Mating

Feline Behaviour. Cats spend a great deal of time building up to the mating act, and their prolonged 'orgies' and promiscuity have, over the centuries, given them a reputation for lasciviousness and lust. This is not because the mating act itself is lengthy or particularly erotic in form. In fact, the whole process of copulation rarely exceeds ten seconds and is often briefer than that. What gives the felines their reputation for lechery is the superficial resemblance between their sexual gathering and a gang-rape. There is a female, spitting and cursing and swiping out at the males one moment and writhing around on the ground the next. And there is a whole circle of males, all growling and howling and snarling at one another as they take it in turns (apparently) to rape the female.

The truth is slightly different. Admittedly the process may involve hours, even days, of almost non-stop sexual activity, but it is the female who is very much in charge of what is happening. It is she who calls the tune, not the males.

It begins when the female comes on heat and starts calling to the males. They also respond to her special sexual odours and are attracted from all around. The male on whose territory she has chosen to make her displays is initially strongly favoured, because other males from neighbouring territories will be frightened to invade his ground. But a female on heat is more than they can resist, so they take the risk. This leads to a great deal of male-to-male squabbling (and accounts for most of the noise – which is why the caterwauling and howling is thought of, mistakenly, as sexual, when in reality it is purely aggressive). But the focus of interest is the female and this helps to damp down the male-to-male fighting and permits the gathering of a whole circle of males around her.

She displays to them with purring and crooning and rolling on the ground, rubbing herself and writhing in a manner that fascinates the male eyes fixating upon her. Eventually, one of the males, probably the territory owner himself, will approach her and sit close to her. For his pains, he is attacked with blows from her sharp-clawed forepaws. She spits and growls at him and he retreats. Any male approaching her too soon is seen off in this way. She is the mistress of the situation and it is she who will eventually choose which male may approach her more intimately. The male who succeeds in this may or may not be the dominant tom present. That is up to her. But certain male strategies do help the toms to succeed. The most important one is to advance towards her only when she is looking the other way. As soon as she turns in his direction, the male freezes – like a child playing the party game called 'statues'. She only attacks when she sees the actual advance itself, not the immobile body that has somehow, by magic, come a little nearer. In this way a tom with finesse can get quite close. He offers her a strange little chirping noise and, if she gives up spitting and hissing at him, he will eventually risk a contact approach.

He starts by grabbing the scruff of her neck in his jaws. This bite on the back of her neck may look savage, like a cartoon caveman grabbing his mate, but this is not the case. It is, in reality, a desperate ploy on the part of the male to protect himself from further assault. But it is not a matter of forcibly holding down the female so that she cannot twist around and attack him. She is too strong for that. Instead it is a 'behaviour trick' played by the male. All cats, whether male or female, retain a peculiar response to being grabbed firmly by the scruff of the neck, dating back to their kitten days. Kittens have an automatic response to being held in this way by their mother. She uses it when it is necessary to transport the kittens from an unsafe to a safe place. It is crucially important that the kittens do not struggle on such occasions, when their very lives may be at stake. So felines have evolved a 'freeze' reaction to being taken by the scruff of the neck – a response which demands that they stay quite still and do not struggle. This helps the mother in her difficult task of moving the litter to safety. When cats grow up they never quite lose this 'immobilization response' and it is the trick that the courting toms apply to their potentially savage females. As long as they hang on with their teeth, they have a good chance that the female will be helplessly transformed into a 'kitten lying still in its mother's jaws'. Without such a behaviour trick the tom would return home with even more scars than usual.

Still firmly gripping the female's neck, the male then mounts her. If she is ready to copulate she flattens the front of her body and raises her rump up into the air, twisting her tail to one side. This is the 'lordosis' posture and is the final invitation signal to the male, permitting him to copulate.

As the male finishes the brief act of copulation, the female twists round and attacks him, swiping out savagely with her claws and screaming abuse at him. When he withdraws his penis and dismounts he has to move swiftly, or she is liable to injure him. The reason for her savage reaction to him at this point is easily understood by examining photographs of his penis taken under the microscope. Unlike the smooth penis of so many other mammals, the cat's organ is covered in sharp, backward-pointing spines. This means that the penis can be inserted easily

THE LIVELY COURTSHIP and mating activities of cats have inspired several artists including, here in *The Cats' Rendez-vous,* the French painter Édouard Manet.

enough, but when it is withdrawn it brutally rakes the walls of the female's vagina. This causes her a spasm of intense pain and it is this to which she reacts with such screaming anger. The attacked male, of course, has no choice in the matter. He cannot adjust the spines even if he wanted to do so. They are fixed and, what is more, the more sexually virile the male, the bigger the spines. So the sexiest male causes the female most pain.

There is a special reason for this. The female cat can *only* ovulate after she has been mated by a male. Under natural conditions, no virgin cat ever ovulates. And it is the intense pain she experiences at the climax of the mating act that triggers off her ovulation process. (Technically, this is referred to as 'induced ovulation'.) That violent moment acts like the firing of a starting pistol which sets her reproductive hormonal system in operation. Within 25–30 hours of the first mating act she is shedding her eggs, ready to be fertilized.

It is not exaggerating to describe the female cat's sexual behaviour as 'masochistic' because, within about 30 minutes of having been hurt by the first male penis, she is actively interested in sex again and ready to be mated once more, with a repeat performance of the scream-and-swipe reaction. Indeed, she becomes even more interested than before, and will accept one male after another.

As time goes on, the 'orgy' changes its style. The males becomes satiated and are less and less excited by the female. She, on the other hand, seems to become more and more lustful. One might imagine that, having worked her way through male after male at comparatively short intervals for perhaps several days, she too would be satiated, but this is not so. As long as her peak period of heat persists she will want to be mated, and the toms now have to be encouraged. Instead of playing hard to get, she now has to work on the males to arouse their interest. She does this with a great deal of crooning, rubbing and especially writhing on the ground. The males still sit around watching her, and from time to time manage to muster enough enthusiasm to mount her once more. Eventually it is all over, and the chances of a female cat returning home unfertilized after such an event are utterly remote.

Matisse, Henri

Cat Owner. The French artist Henri Matisse (1869–1954) loved the company of felines and, confined to bed for long periods with poor health towards the end of his life, was often comforted by the presence of his favourite black cat.

Matou

Feline Term. The French name for a tom-cat.

May Kittens

Folklore. There is a curious early European tradition that kittens born in the month of May should be destroyed, because if they are allowed to grow they will become 'dirty cats'. This bizarre idea is summed up in an old English proverb which baldly states: 'May chets bad luck begets, and sure to make dirty cats.' The explanation reaches back into antiquity when, apparently, it was considered incorrect to indulge in sexual intercourse, or to marry, in this particular month. This was because people were supposed to be purifying themselves in readiness for the great midsummer celebrations in June.

Mehitabel

Fictional Cat. New York columnist Don Marquis (1878–1937) invented a literate cockroach called 'archy' who wrote, with great difficulty on Marquis's typewriter, a series of poems and stories about a female alley cat called 'mehitabel'. The cockroach was not heavy enough to be able to create capital letters or punctuation, which gave the writings a highly characteristic style. For example, the song of mehitabel is introduced by archie with these words:

this is the song of mehitabel/of mehitabel the alley cat/as I wrote you before boss/metihabel is a believer /in the pythagorean/theory of the transmigration/of the souls and she claims/that formerly her spirit/was incarnated in the body/of cleopatra/that was a long time ago/and one must not be/surprised if mehitabel/has forgotten some of her/more regal manners'

The adventures of 'archy and mehitabel' appeared in countless newspaper columns over many years and were published in book form in three volumes that appeared in many editions from the late 1920s onwards.

Bibliography:

1927. Marquis, D. *archy and mehitabel.* Doubleday Page, New York.
1933. Marquis, D. *archy's life of mehitabel.* Doubleday Doran, New York.
1935. Marquis, D. *archy does his part.* Doubleday Doran, New York.

Mexican Hairless Cat

Domestic Breed. An apparently extinct breed known from the turn of the century.

Appearance: Similar to the modern Sphynx Cat, with a long body and tail, a wedge-shaped head and large ears. They did, however, differ from the Sphynx Cat in two ways: in the winter they managed to grow a little hair on their backs and tails, though this was shed in the summer; also, they had long whiskers.

History: In 1902 an American couple, Mr and Mrs F.J. Shinick, living in Albuquerque, New Mexico, were presented with a pair of hairless cats by local Pueblo Indians. They were told by Jesuit priests that these cats were the last survivors of an ancient Aztec breed of cat.

The male was called Dick and the female Nellie. Mrs Shinick reported that 'Nellie has a very small head, large amber eyes, and long whiskers and eyebrows . . . Dick was a very powerful cat and could whip any dog alone. His courage, no doubt, was the cause of his death . . . one night he got out and several dogs killed him.' This happened before the male had become sexually mature, so that the pair were never able to breed. Mrs Shinick searched all over New Mexico for a hairless mate for Nellie, but without success. Sadly, she was forced to conclude, 'I fear the breed is extinct.'

The extraordinary Mexican Hairless Cats, photographed at the turn of the century. Known as Dick and Nellie, they failed to launch a naked feline dynasty because brave Dick was killed by a pack of dogs.

For some reason, it did not occur to her to mate Nellie with a normally haired male and then back-cross to her in an attempt to continue the line. Nor is it clear what she did with Nellie, although a report in the following year, 1903, suggests that she may have sold the female to an English cat-lover. In that year Charles Lane, in his book *Rabbits Cats and Cavies,* shows an illustration of a Mexican Hairless Cat called Jesuit, with the caption: 'Believed to be the only specimen ever exhibited in England. Owner, Hon. Mrs McLaren Morrison.' He says he hopes this 'may prove they are not quite extinct'. It seems likely that 'Jesuit' was in reality a renamed Nellie, brought to England at great expense to cause a sensation at major cat shows. This view is strengthened by the comments in a letter, dated 1902, sent by the Shinicks to an English cat exhibitor: 'I have priced Nellie at $300. She is too valuable a pet for me to keep in a small town. Many wealthy ladies would value her at her weight in gold if they knew what a very rare pet she is. I think in your position she would be a very good investment to exhibit at cat shows and other select events, as she doubtless is the only hairless cat now known.'

If Nellie did cross the Atlantic and become Jesuit, she may well have introduced a wider public to the Mexican Hairless breed, but there are no records that she was ever used for breeding, and it would appear that, after her day, the Mexican Hairless Cat finally vanished without trace.

Some authors referred to this breed as the 'New Mexican Hairless' because earlier hairless examples of domestic cats from Latin America had been described by naturalists as far back as 1830. As in several other instances, in different parts of the world (including France, Czechoslovakia, Austria, Morocco and Australia), these naked mutant cats appeared and then soon vanished. Only the modern Sphynx Cat (see separate entry) has been treated seriously as a potential pedigree breed.

Micetto

Pet Cat. Micetto had the rare distinction of being raised by a Pope. A big, black-striped, greyish-red cat, he was born in the Vatican, became the adored pet of Pope Leo XII (1760–1829) and was frequently seen nestling in the folds of the Pope's white robes. Also known as 'The Pope's Cat', he was the Pontiff's most intimate companion in the final years of his life. Micetto outlived his master and was adopted by Chateaubriand, the French ambassador to the Vatican, who took him back to France where he lived to a serene old age, 'bearing his weight of honours with graceful propriety, and hardening into arrogance only when forced to repel the undue familiarity of visitors'.

Mickey

Working Cat. Mickey was a tabby cat belonging to Shepherd and Sons of Burscough, Lancashire, England. A champion mouser, he died in 1967 aged 23, after killing an estimated 22,000 mice. His record was finally broken by a tortoiseshell cat called Towser, who dispatched over 28,000 at a Tayside Distillery before he died in 1987.

Mike

Working Cat. Mike the Museum Cat (1908–1929) assisted in keeping the main gate of the British Museum in London for 20 years, from February 1909 to January 1929. His arrival at the Museum was unusual. An old Museum cat by the name of Black Jack, notorious for sharpening his claws on valuable book bindings, one day deposited at the feet of the Keeper of Egyptian cat mummies, a small object that he had been carrying in his jaws. It turned out to be a tiny kitten, which was taken in and cared for by the Museum staff.

Christened Mike, he flourished and grew and eventually made friends with the gatekeeper, who allowed him to make a second home in his lodge. Mike became an adept pigeon-stalker and frequently took a flapping bird to present to his human companions. They always rescued the bird, rewarded Mike with a slice of meat, fed and watered the pigeon and then let it go. Mike continued to live this life of a working cat for year after year, and no one liked to disillusion him. Even during the austere years of World War I, the Keeper of Mummified Cats (perhaps because of some unspoken superstition) made sure that he was properly fed. Wallis Budge, the famous archaeologist observed that 'he preferred sole to whiting, and whiting to haddock, and sardines to herring; for cod he had no use whatever.'

A long obituary poem written by one of the British Museum officials ended with the words: 'Old Mike! Farewell! We all regret you / Although you would not let us pet you, of cats, the wisest, oldest, best cat / This is your motto – Requiescat.'

Mi-ke

Domestic Breed. Japanese name for Japanese Bobtail Cat. It is pronounced ME-KA and means 'three colours'.

Milk

Feline Reproduction. Most female cats are such good mothers that hand-rearing kittens is rarely necessary. However, in the rare event that an abandoned kitten has to be fed artificially, it is important to know that cat's milk is very different from human or cow's milk. It is much richer, having more protein and more fat, but less sugar. In an emergency, to imitate this, the nearest easy source is unsweetened condensed milk. It is preferable, however, to obtain veterinary advice concerning a more precise formula.

Figures given for the contents of cat's milk are as follows: protein 6–9 per cent; fat 3–4 per cent; lactose 4 per cent.

Because her milk is so rich and her growing litter so demanding, a mother cat needs extra food, both in quantity and quality, when she is nursing. However, since domestic cats can never consume huge meals at one sitting this means increasing the number of meals a day, rather than increasing their size. Four meals, ideally supplied warm rather than cold, will give her the best support during her maternal phase.

Milk-treading

Feline Behaviour. When kittens are feeding at the nipple, they can be observed to make characteristic kneading movements with their front paws. First one paw presses down on the mother's body, then the other. They alternate in this way very slowly, at a rate of approximately one stroke every two seconds. The actions are accompanied by loud purring. These milk-treading, trampling, or kneading movements help to stimulate the mother cat's milk-flow and are an important aid to successful suckling.

These actions are also observed occasionally in adult cats when they are sitting on their owners' laps. In this context they reflect the infantile side of the pet cat, when it is treating its owner as its foster-mother. It would seem that, when the owner sits down in a relaxed manner, signals are given off saying to the cat, 'I am your mother lying down ready to feed you at the breast.' The adult cat then proceeds to revert to kittenhood and squats there, purring contentedly and going through the motions of stimulating a milk supply. It emphasizes its mood by drooling and dribbling as it does so.

From the cat's point of view this is a warm, loving moment, but when the human lap on which it is pressing becomes pricked with sharp claws and dampened with cat-dribble, the contented animal sometimes finds itself unceremoniously placed on the floor. This bodily removal by a claw-pricked owner must be quite inexplicable to it. No good cat mother would behave in such a negative way. To the cat, people are clearly maternal figures, because they do supply milk (in a saucer) and other nourishment, and they do sit down showing their undersides in an inviting manner, but once the juvenile reaction of milk-treading is given, they suddenly and mystifyingly become upset and thrust the pseudo-infant from them.

This is a classic example of the way in which interactions between humans and cats can lead to misunderstandings. Many can be avoided by recognizing the fact that an adult domestic cat always remains a kitten in its behaviour towards its pseudo-parental owner.

Minerva

Television Cat. Fictional character featured in the television programme *Our Miss Brooks*.

Mink

Coat Colour. American breeders specializing in the Tonkinese breed have introduced the name 'mink' into their coat colours. There are the following variants of mink: (1) Blue Mink (soft, blue-grey with darker slate-blue points); (2) Champagne Mink (beige or buff-cream with medium brown points); (3) Honey Mink (ruddy brown with darker brown points); (4) Natural Mink (warm brown with darker brown points); (5) Platinum Mink (pale silvery-grey with darker grey points).

Minnaloushe

Fictional Cat. 'Minnaloushe creeps through the grass/ Alone, important and wise/ And lifts to the changing moon/ His changing eyes.' wrote the Irish poet W.B. Yeats in his 1919 poem *The Cat and the Moon*.

The reverence in which Yeats held cats is clear from the story told of him that, on one occasion, finding a cat asleep on his fur coat when he went to collect it at the Abbey Theatre in Dublin, he emulated the prophet Mohammed and cut off a piece of the coat rather than disturb the animal's slumbers.

Minna Minna Mowbray

Pet Cat. British publisher Michael Joseph was passionate about cats and wrote many books about them. According to him, Minna was a small, graceful, exquisitely proportioned, short-haired tortoiseshell tabby, with tiny white paws to match her piquant white face. In his book *Cat's Company*, he devotes a whole chapter to her, beginning with the words: 'Among all my cats, past and present, Minna Minna Mowbray was an outstanding personality.' Michael Joseph's cat books include those listed in the following bibliography.

Bibliography:

1930. *A Book of Cats*. Covici-Friede, New York.
1938. *Kittens and Cats*. Whitman, Wisconsin.
1943. *Charles: The Story of a Friendship*. Michael Joseph, London.
1946. *Cat's Company*. Michael Joseph, London.
1952. *Best Cat Stories*. Faber & Faber, London.

Minon

Fictional Cat. Minon is the enchanted cat in Charles Lamb's poem *Prince Dorus* (1811).

Mistigris

Fictional Cat. The cat who appears in Balzac's story *Le Père Goriot* (1835).

Misty Malarky Ying Yang

Pet Cat. Male Siamese cat belonging to American President Jimmy Carter's daughter Amy. Lived as 'First Cat' in the White House for four years (1976–1980).

Mitla

Mystery Cat. The explorer Colonel Percy Fawcett wrote of his observations in the Bolivian forests: 'In the forests were various beasts still unfamiliar to zoologists, such as the Mitla, which I have seen twice, a black dog-like cat about the size of a foxhound.' There is no such cat known to science and it was later suggested that what Fawcett has seen was in fact the rather strange-looking South American Bush Dog *(Speothos)*. Karl Shuker, in his scholarly study of Mystery Cats of the World, has offered an alternative candidate, namely the little-known Small-eared Dog *(Atelocynus)*, which he points out moves in a rather feline way, with graceful actions that are not typically dog-like. Ultimately, as he says, the 'dog-like cat' may prove to be no more than an already identified 'cat-like dog'.

Mivart, St. George

Cat Authority. Zoology lecturer Dr St. George Mivart (1827–1900) published the first major study of the anatomy and biology of the cat in 1881. Running to 557 pages, it was a milestone in the history of feline knowledge. Commenting on it in 1903, Frances Simpson wrote: 'The great scholar and eminent writer, St. George Mivart, has given the world a wonderfully comprehensive work on the cat, and has used the maligned feline as his type for an introduction to the study of back-boned animals.'

Bibliography:

1881. Mivart, St. George. *The Cat. An introduction to the study of backboned animals especially mammals.* John Murray, London.

Mngwa

Mystery Cat. In the coastal forests of Tanzania, a huge, grey-striped cat known locally as the Mngwa or Nunda, which has apparently been featured in African native songs for over 800 years, is still believed by some to be surviving in remote corners. Because of its night-time attacks on humans it is widely feared.

Various identities have been suggested, including a giant version of the African Golden Cat *(Felis aurata),* but there is no scientific evidence to support this or any other zoological explanation. This may, in fact, be just another savage legendary cat invented to explain the violent nocturnal deaths of human rivals.

Moggie

Feline Term. A non-pedigree dog is always referred to as a mongrel and, strictly speaking, this is the correct term for a non-pedigree cat, but few people use it in this way. They are much more likely to call their pet feline a 'moggie' (sometimes spelt 'moggy').

In origin, the term 'moggie' began life as a local dialect variant of the name 'Maggie' meaning a dishevelled old women. In some regions it was also the name given to a scarecrow and the essence of its meaning was that something was scruffy and untidy. By the start of the present century its use had spread to include cats. This seems to have begun in London where there were countless scruffy alley-cats whose poor condition doubtless led to the comparison with 'dishevelled old women'.

By the inter-war period the word moggie had been abbreviated to 'mog' and in the 1920s and 1930s schoolboy slang referred to dogs and cats and 'tikes and mogs'. For some reason, this shortened form fell into disuse after World War II and the more affectionate 'moggie' returned as the popular term for the ordinary, common-or-garden cat.

Mombasa Cat

'Domestic Breed'. In 1890, Charles Darwin reported that a certain Captain Owen, R.N., in his *Narrative of Voyages,* described how he had visited the port of Mombasa on the east coast of Africa, where he observed that 'all the cats are covered with short stiff hair instead of fur'. In 1896, Richard Lydekker developed this theme, speaking of an unusual breed of domestic cat seen in Africa: 'The Mombasa Cat, from the Eastern coast of Africa, near Zanzibar, is reported to have the fur short and stiff, instead of the ordinary structure.' Frances Simpson, writing seven years later, goes a step further: 'A cat called the Mombassa Cat, from the East of Africa, is said to have a short coat of a wiry texture.'

What began as a local population of hot-country cats with adaptively short coats, had grown, by exaggerated repetition, into a special breed of cats with wiry fur. This is the way in which many early feline stories developed, with small embellishments being added as each author copied an earlier statement.

Had they read the full Darwin text they might have had second thoughts because he goes on to quote the redoubtable Captain Owen as saying that a cat 'which had been kept on board for some time . . . was left for only eight weeks in Mombasa, but during that short period it underwent a complete metamorphosis, having parted with its sandy-coloured fur.' The fact that this ship's cat took a mere two months to join the local 'breed' of Mombasa Cats puts the whole matter into perspective.

Moncrif, François-Augustin Paradis de

Cat Authority. The French author, poet, musician, dramatist and actor Francois-Augustin Paradis de Moncrif (1687–1770), has been justly described as 'the first genuine chronicler of cats'. His now famous book *Les Chats,* published in 1727, is the first complete volume seriously devoted to the subject. It consists of 11 letters to a Madame la M. de B** and ten poems.

The book was written to please his noble patrons. In it, he vigorously defends the cat against its many critics and persecutors: 'One has heard since the cradle that Cats are treacherous by nature, that they suffocate infants; that perhaps they are sorcerers. Succeeding reason may cry out in vain against these calumnies . . . You know, Madame, . . . there is none among the animals who can bear more brilliant titles than those of the Cat species.'

He ends the letters on an optimistic note: 'one day we shall see the merit of Cats generally recognized. It is impossible that in a nation as enlightened as our own the prejudice in this regard should prevail much longer over so reasonable a statement.'

Moncrif was described as witty, handsome, seductive and fastidious. The son of a Scottish mother and French father, he was a debonair figure at the court of Louis XV. However, when his cat book was published, Moncrif was lampooned and his ideas were met with ridicule. Savage skits and biting satires appeared. Two years later, when he was being admitted to the

An engraving from Moncrif's classic work, *Les Chats* (1727), the first important cat book ever published. He was savagely ridiculed for devoting a whole volume to this subject and eventually withdrew it from circulation.

French Academy, a fellow Academician let a live cat loose at the ceremony. During Moncrif's maiden speech, the terrified cat miaowed pitifully and the audience of pompous Academicians mimicked its cries. Influenced by the ridicule he had to bear, Moncrif eventually withdrew *Les Chats* from circulation and from his collected works. The irony is that today all his other works – not to mention those of his fellow Academicians – are forgotten, while his little book in praise of cats is prized as the forerunner of modern feline literature.

Bibliography:

1727. Moncrif, F-A. P. de. *Les Chats*. Gabriel-Francois Quilleau, Paris.
1961. *Moncrif's Cats*. Translated by Reginald Bretnor. Golden Cockerel Press, London. (Limited to 400 copies.)
1969. *Moncrif's Cats*. Translated by Reginald Bretnor. Barnes, New York. (A re-issue of the 1961 edition.)

Monsieur Tibault

Fictional Cat. In Stephen Vincent Benét's story *The King of Cats* (1929), Monsieur Tibault is the amazing feline who, when conducting an orchestra, faces the audience and uses his tail as a baton.

Moon Cat

Domestic Breed. An alternative name for the naked Sphynx Cat that was discovered in Canada in 1966. It was also known originally as the Canadian Hairless Cat, but it is the name 'Sphynx' that has survived and become generally accepted.

Moppet

Fictional Cat. Moppet was the title cat in Beatrix Potter's 1906 children's story *The Story of Miss Moppet*. She also appears in the 1907 story *The Tale of Tom Kitten*.

Morris

Television Cat. Morris was a large, stray ginger tom discovered in an animal shelter in a Chicago suburb in 1968. Professional animal trainer Bob Martwick paid five dollars for him, which rescued him from 'death row'. Twenty minutes later and it would have been too late.

The 'big orange tiger' was estimated to be about seven years old and was chosen for his haughty, unflappable personality. He appeared arrogantly calm, as though he owned the place, and was not alarmed even when Martwick deliberately dropped a metal dish nearby.

At first he was appropriately named 'Lucky' but when he was chosen to promote a brand of cat food on television in 1969 he was renamed Morris. He appeared in 40 commercials during the next ten years, before his death in 1978, and became nationally famous throughout the United States. His gimmick was that he was exceptionally finicky over his food, and would eat only the very best.

His rags to riches life story appealed to the American public and Morris was treated like the great star he had become. He travelled by limousine, guested on TV talk shows, attracted a huge fan mail, ate out at exclusive restaurants in the company of attractive young (feline) queens, visited the White House, met the Hollywood elite, and even had an outrageously expensive Louis Vuitton litter-tray. In 1972 he starred in a Hollywood movie called *Shamus* with Burt Reynolds and Dyan Cannon. In 1973 he was awarded a 'Patsy', the animal equivalent of an Oscar and in 1974 was the subject of a biography by Mary Daniels. He died in 1978 and was replaced by Morris II after a nationwide search that took two and a half years.

Morris II, who was also discovered at an animal rescue shelter, looked exactly like the original Morris, and shared his stoical, patiently aloof personality. He was so similar that it was hard to tell them apart on the screen, and the commercials could continue once more. Morris II also had his biography written, this time by Barbara Burn, who was astonished at the long lines of people queuing in the rain to see the cat star at book signings during the launch of her book.

In 1988 Morris II became a candidate for the Presidency of the United States, on the grounds that he was better known than almost any of the other candidates. On August 18th, he held a press conference in Washington to announce his candidacy and outline his political platform, which had a great deal to say on the subject of feline rights. Despite a spirited 'Morris for President' campaign, he was beaten by a whisker. Although high hopes that he might at last bring a more civilized, elegant air to the Oval Office were dashed, all was not lost, because his brief entry into politics indirectly gave a great boost to his reputation in the field of cat-food advertising. And with $1.4 billion spent on cat food annually in the USA, such a career is not to be sneered at.

Bibliography:
1974. Daniels, M. *Morris. An Intimate Biography.* William Morrow, New York.
1980. Burn, B. *The Morris Approach.* New York.

Moumoutte Blanche

Pet Cat. Moumoutte Blanche and her companion, Moumoutte Chinoise, were the subject of a book called *Lives of Two Cats* by the French novelist Pierre Loti (1850–1923). The book, which first appeared in English in 1900 and ran into many later editions, told the story of the author's lives with his two cats. Blanche, a black and white Angora, had been with him for some years when he returned home from China with a stowaway kitten he called Chinoise. When the two cats were introduced, they attacked one another so savagely that Loti had to pour a jug of water over them to separate them, after which they never fought again.

Mountain Cat

Wild Feline. *(Felis jacobita)* Also known as the Andean Cat, the Andean Mountain Cat, or the Andean Highland Cat. Locally referred to as the Gato Andino.

One of the least known and least understood of all the cats, the Mountain Cat lives on the treeless, arid, rocky slopes of the Andes, where it hunts large rodents such as Chinchillas and Vizcachas. Records suggest that it does not occur below 3,000 metres (10,000 feet) and that it

The strange little Andean Mountain Cat *(Felis jacobita)*, photographed here at the southern end of its range, in Northern Chile, on one of the high, rocky slopes where it makes its home.

can reach an elevation of as much as 5,000 metres (16,000 feet), or even higher. It has been seen occasionally right up in the snow region.

It has sometimes been placed alone in a separate genus of the cat family because of its unique skull anatomy. Superficially, it resembles a smaller version of the Snow Leopard.

Living in the colder regions of South America, it is not surprising to find that this cat has longer, softer, finer fur than the other South American species. The coat is essentially silvery-grey in colour, but is adorned with short stripes, blotches and spots of brown and orange. The backs of the ears are dark grey and the bushy tail is ringed with black.

Size: Length of Head + Body: 60–90 cm (23½–35½ in). Tail: 35–40 cm (14–16 in). Weight: 3–7 kg (6½–15½ lb).

Distribution: Exclusively South American, it is confined to the mountainous regions of S. Peru, S. Bolivia, N.W. Argentina and N.E. Chile. It is considered to be a rare species, but even this is not known for certain because of the nature of its terrain.

Mountain Lion

Wild Feline. An alternative name for the Puma *(Felis concolor)*. Because it was a large cat with a plain, uniform coat colour, the first Westerners to meet this species referred to it as an American Lion. And because it was most often encountered in the Rocky Mountains, it was called the Mountain Lion. It is still known by that name to the local people who live in the Rockies. It is also known as the Cougar and many other local names, but its generally accepted title nowadays is that of Puma. (For details see Puma.)

Mountain Tiger

Mystery Cat. In northern Chad, the local people speak of a 'Tigre de Montaigne' which is described as being larger than a Lion, having a terrifying roar, being cave-dwelling, having red fur banded with white stripes, no tail, large hairy feet and teeth that protrude from its mouth. It is said to hunt large antelope.

In the south-west of Chad a similar beast is known as the Hadjel. In the Central African Republic it is called the Coq-ninji, the Gassingram or the Vassoko. The romantic view is that these creatures could perhaps represent a surviving remnant population of the Sabre-toothed Tiger. Although this is so unlikely as to be hardly worth considering, it is nevertheless difficult to guess what could have inspired such a widespread legend. For the moment, the Mountain Tiger of Africa must remain on the list of unproven 'mystery cats'.

MTM Kitten

Television Cat. The kitten appears in the logo of the Mary Tyler Moore television production company, as a parody of the famous MGM roaring lion, Leo.

Muezza

Pet Cat. Muezza was the favourite cat of the prophet Mohammed. He is said to have loved his cat so much that he sacrificed his robe to the animal. Meuzza was asleep on the sleeve of this robe one day when Mohammed was called to prayer and, rather than disturb the cat's serene slumber, he cut off the sleeve and left the animal snoozing peacefully. After he returned, the cat awoke and bowed in thanks. Mohammed stroked the animal three times and Muezza was thus given a permanent place in the Islamic Paradise. Ever since, cats have been left unmolested, and are even permitted inside mosques. (In Mohammedan countries a Muezzin is the public crier who proclaims the regular hours of prayer from the minaret.)

According to a popular legend, the reason Mohammed loved cats so much was that one had once saved his life. A snake had crawled in the sleeve of his garment and refused to leave. The cat was consulted and asked the snake to show its head, so that the matter of its departure could be discussed. When the snake did this, the cat pounced on it and carried it off. After this it was officially decreed that no cat should ever be hit with anything except a ball of cotton.

M

It has been claimed that Mohammed preached with a cat in his arms, that he purified himself with water from which a cat had been drinking, and that his wife ate from a dish that had previously been used by a cat.

Mummified Cats

Feline History. Millions of domestic cats were mummified and buried in ancient Egypt. In the earliest times, this process was uncommon and special. In later periods it became routine and the cat mummies were 'mass-produced'.

The oldest known example of cat burials dates from the 12th Dynasty (1991–1778 BC). In a tomb at Abydos there were 17 cat skeletons thoughtfully supplied with a row of milk dishes. Later, in the 18th Dynasty (1567–1320 BC) Prince Tuthmosis provided his beloved pet cat, Tamyt, with a magnificent limestone sarcophagus. The inscriptions refer to her as Osiris, the Lady Cat, indicating how highly she was valued by her owner. The writing on the lid informs us that she wishes to become an 'imperishable star' – in other words, that she hopes to ascend into the heavens. To help her along on her great journey, she is supplied with a roast duck on a table in front of her. Clearly this was a special cat of a special man and her treatment was exceptional. But it does show that, even at this very early date, pet cats were revered, if not actually deified.

An impressive example of a mummified cat from Ancient Egypt. Most examples are undecorated, but this one, dating from the Late Period (664–332 BC), which is now in the Louvre in Paris, is carefully stuccoed and painted.

About a thousand years later, the situation had changed radically. At this stage there were mass burials and literally millions of mummified cats were laid to rest, carefully wrapped in linen bindings and often wearing specially made feline masks. These have been found at many sites throughout Egypt and reflect a widespread practice of making votive offerings to the cat goddess, Bastet (see separate entry). Once such a cat was buried, it became an intermediary between its owner and the gods, operating a ghost-cat information service to let the gods know about the prayers and needs of the earthbound citizens.

Because these mummified cats were so helpful in solving personal problems by persuading the gods to listen to the needy, it followed that a much loved family pet cat did not always die at the best moment. This little problem was neatly solved by the priesthood at the holy temples who, in effect, became feline factory farmers. They established 'dead cat supermarkets' near to the great shrines, where they kept vast numbers of sacred felines. These they bred, housed, fed, reared to near-adulthood and then systematically killed, embalmed, and encased in suitable wrappings for the pious pilgrims to purchase on their visits to the cult centres.

The scale of this operation must have been enormous, its organization and execution elaborate. At times, the demands of the believers were so great that, even with their careful planning, the priests could not keep up with the demand. Pondering this problem, it occurred to them that, since the faithful always bought carefully wrapped mummies of cats, they would never know precisely what was inside the wrappings. So they started to cut corners. X-ray examination of surviving cat mummies reveals that some of them were made up of cats' skulls with human bones, or cats' bones mixed up with those of jackals, birds or even reptiles. One 'cat' mummy was made entirely from frog bones.

Clearly, there was a commercialism bordering on the cynical in this priestly industry. What was worse, none of these cats had been allowed to enjoy a long life. Examination of their teeth reveals that most of them were either between two and four months old or between nine and 12 months old. Only four per cent of them were over two years old when they 'passed away'. The way they passed was also rather suspicious. Many had had their necks broken; some had been strangled; and still others had been drowned.

Hundreds of thousands of cats died and were mummified in this way in a country where, paradoxically, the cat was sacred, revered and worshipped. We read of whole families going into deep mourning when the family cat died, of the imposition of the death penalty for 'murdering' a cat, and of a Roman solider being stoned to death because he killed a cat. This may well reflect the attitude of the ordinary populace, but it certainly did not reflect the conduct of the crafty priesthood. Either the ordinary believers were ignorant of the priestly cat industry, or they knew about it but somehow managed to develop a mental double-standard, seeing the killing of temple cats as 'sacrifices' rather than murders.

Whatever the truth of these matters, one thing is certain – all along the Nile from Thebes to Bubastis, cat burials took place on a staggering scale. One cat cemetery alone was almost a kilometre (half a mile) long. In 1888, an Egyptian farmer, digging up a piece of land that had not been cultivated before, discovered 300,000 cat mummies. These were sold as fertilizer to British buyers. One consignment of 19 tons, made up of the mummified bodies of about 80,000 cats, was shipped to Liverpool in England, where it was auctioned off at £4 a ton, to be spread on local fields, to encourage the crops to grow. It is said that, during the sale, the auctioneer used the body of one of the embalmed cats as his gavel.

This bizarre and undignified end to the story of the Sacred Cat of Ancient Egypt has a final, intriguing twist. On the farming land all around Liverpool, from time to time, Egyptian jewellery is brought to the surface by the ploughs of bewildered farm-hands. Beads, scarabs and other small decorative artefacts that once adorned the mummified cats lie scattered there, awaiting the watchful eye, though few of the finders have the faintest idea how they came to rest on the cold alien soil of northern England.

Munchkin Cat

Domestic Breed. Short-legged American cat discovered in the 1990s. Viewed as a freak by most cat societies. Also referred to as the American Munchkin, the Munchkin Mutant, the Wiener Cat, the Dachshund Cat, the Minikat, or the 'Ferret of the Feline World'. It was named after the 'little people' who appear in *The Wizard of Oz*.

Appearance: This is a short-haired cat with a dominant gene for reduced leg-length, the front legs being even shorter than the back legs. The length of the front legs is no more than 7.5 cm (3 inches).

History: This unusual mutant feline is the first short-legged cat to be taken seriously as a breed. It parallels the Dachshund and the short-legged terrier breeds of dog, but there is a fundamental difference between them. The Dachshund and the short-legged terriers were bred for a specific

The startling new, short-legged breed called the Munchkin Cat has caused an uproar in the cat world. Many see it as a degradation of feline grace, while others argue that it is no more unusual that a Dachshund or any other short-legged breed of dog.

purpose – to go to earth. Their short legs were an advantage to them in entering burrows. But the Munchkin Cat has been developed purely as an oddity, whose modified legs offer the animal no serious, practical advantage.

It emerged as a chance mutation in the United States in 1983, when a short-legged stray cat was discovered and became the foundation stock for the breed. Despite its clumsy appearance, it appears to have found favour among those who prefer to own an undemanding indoor cat. It first came to the notice of American cat breeders at a TICA show in Madison Square Garden in 1991. The original Munchkin was a black female called 'Blackberry' and the early examples came from Lousiana.

The breed has been developed in Virginia Beach, Virginia, by the American breeder Penny Squires, who insists that they are not deformed. She points out that, for their owners, they offer the advantage that 'they can't jump on to kitchen counters'. The only benefit she can envisage for the cats themselves is that 'they can chase things under the bed'.

According to one report, the Munchkin is capable of turning faster than longer-legged breeds and is able to run backwards.

Critics of this breed, and there are many, point out that, apart from its lack of lithe feline grace, the Munchkin has great difficulty in grooming itself and also runs the risk of suffering from premature ageing of its unnaturally long spine. Despite the claims made for it by Penny Squires, these critics feel it is unlikely that this new breed will ever obtain wide popularity as a pedigree show cat.

Short-legged cats have appeared before, the first in England in the 1930s. They lasted for several generations but apparently died out during the chaos of World War II. After the war, one was reported in Russia in Stalingrad (now St. Petersberg) in 1953, but, like the English ones, this line did not survive.

Breed Club:

The International Munchkin Society. Tel (USA): 413-736 6381.

Music

Feline Behaviour. The feline response to musical sounds appears to be idiosyncratic. Some cats show no interest, while others seem to detest it and still others adore it. At first glance, it is hard to make any sense out of the reports that are to be found in the cat literature.

The French writer Théophile Gautier, for example, observed that his female cat Madame Théophile would always listen attentively to the singer that he accompanied on the piano. The cat was not happy, however, when high notes were struck. They probably reminded her too closely of sounds of feline distress and she did her best to silence them. Whenever a female singer reached a high A, the cat would reach out and close the songstress's mouth with her paw. There must have been something especially feline about that particular note, because Gautier carried out experiments to see if he could fool the cat, but she always responded with her critical paw precisely when the note reached high A.

A more severe music critic was one of the cats owned by Frenchman C.C. Pierquin de Gembloux. This animal's reaction to certain sequences of notes was to throw itself into uncontrollable convulsions. A second cat, present at the same time, responded in a totally different way. Instead of having a fit, it jumped up and sat on the piano, listening to the same music with great interest.

The composer Henri Sauguet was astonished to discover that his cat, Cody, became ecstatic when it heard Debussy being played on the piano. It would roll around on the carpet, then leap on to the piano and then on to the pianist's lap, where it would start licking the hands that played the magic notes. When these same hands gave up playing under the onslaught of feline affection, the cat would wander off, but if they then began to play again, the cat immediately dashed back and resumed its licking.

In the 1930s two doctors by the names of Morin and Bachrach discovered to their surprise that the note E of the fourth octave had the effect of making young cats defecate and adult ones

become sexually excited. It was also noted that extremely high notes could cause agitation in many cats.

It is likely that these seemingly varied reactions to human music all have some underlying connection with the special sound signals that are given in feline 'language'. The mewing of a distressed kitten, for example, is at a particular pitch, and if a musical note hits that pitch then it will disturb an adult cat, especially a female one. This may explain why Gautier's cat touched the mouths of the singers with her paw when they hit the particular note. She must have thought, at that moment, that each singer was a 'kitten' in distress, and she was no doubt trying to help in her own way.

Similarly, Sauguet's cat probably thought that his owner needed help, and rushed over to lick the hands from which the sounds appeared to be coming, as a way of comforting him – just as a mother cat would rush across to lick the fur of one of its kittens if the young animal appeared to be in distress.

The convulsions and sexual excitement of other cats are probably no more than erotic responses to sounds that remind felines of the courtship tones of their species. And fear induced by very high-pitched musical notes could simply be the natural panic reaction to what the cat hears as squeals of pain.

In other words, the musical sense of cats is a feline myth. All they are doing – and with some remarkable individual variation – is responding to selected notes from the great array that music offers them, according to their own instinctive system of sound signals. Some musical notes trigger off parental feelings, others sexual ones and still others self-protection. The cats are mistaking our messages and we, in the past, have reciprocated by misunderstanding theirs.

Myobu No Omoto

Pet Cat. The Emperor Ichijo (986–1011), an early Japanese ruler, was so enamoured of his cat that when Myobu No Omoto (which means Omoto, lady-in-waiting) was chased by a dog, he had the unfortunate canine exiled and its human companion imprisoned.

The Emperor had begun his love affair with cats at an early age. When he was only 13, he had taken possession of a litter of kittens and had become so attached to them that he insisted on his 'Left and Right Minister' rearing them and tending for them in specially prepared boxes, at the Imperial Palace in Kyoto. They were given clothes and fed delicacies and rice. A court lady, known as Uma No Myobu, was appointed as their wet-nurse.

Mysouff I

Pet Cat. Mysouff belonged to French novelist Alexandre Dumas (1802–1870). In his *Histoire de mes Bêtes* (1867) he describes how the cat greeted his return each evening as if it were a dog: 'The moment I set foot in the Rue de l'Ouest, he used to dance about my legs just like a dog; then careering along in front, and turning back to rejoin me, he would start back for the house.'

Dumas declared himself the 'defence lawyer' for all the homeless cats that he befriended. He founded a group called the 'Feline Defence League', along with Baudelaire, Maupassant and Anatole France.

Mysouff II

Pet Cat. When Alexandre Dumas's cat, Mysouff II, the black and white successor to Mysouff I, was discovered in the cellar by his cook, it became an immediate favourite. But then, one day, it unfortunately ate Dumas's entire collection of exotic birds. Instead of banishing the hungry feline, he gave it a fair trial before his guests the following Sunday. One guest pleaded the animal's defence on the grounds that the aviary door had been opened by Dumas's pet monkeys, and this was considered to be 'extenuating circumstances'. The sentence agreed upon was that the unfortunate cat should serve five years' imprisonment with the monkeys in their cage. Luckily for Mysouff II, however, Dumas was shortly to find himself financially embarrassed. As a result, he had to sell the monkeys, and the cat regained its freedom.

Mystery Cats

Feline History. In addition to all the scientifically accepted cat species, there have for many years been reports of 'mystery cats' from various parts of the world. Some of these shadowy felines are pure fancy; others are merely odd variants of otherwise well-known species; still others are genuine mysteries – perhaps even new species awaiting full scientific discovery. Zoologist Karl Shuker has assiduously tracked down all of these 'sightings' and assembled the evidence in a book.

Among the most interesting examples of the mystery animals he has discussed are the following: British Big Cat; Kellas Cat; Red Tiger; Blue Tiger; Black Tiger; Harimau Jalor; Hong Kong Cat; Spotted Lion; Ikimizi; Mngwa; Wobo; Mountain Tiger; Madagascar Cat; Santer; Blue Lynx; Onza; Ruffed Cat; Paraguyan Ghost Jaguar; Jaguarete; Waracabra Tiger; Mitla; Siemel's Cat; Water Tiger. (For further details see separate entries.)

Bibliography:

1989. Shuker, K.P.N. *Mystery Cats of the World*. Robert Hale, London.

Nebelung Cat

Domestic Breed. A new American breed, the recently developed long-haired version of the Russian Blue.

Appearance: Similar in all respects to the Russian Blue, except for the coat length which is long and soft to the touch. The blue-grey double coat has guard hairs that are silver-tipped, giving the cat a lustrous look.

History: This new long-haired cat was developed in the 1980s by American breeder Cora Cobb from a foundation pair called Siegfried and Brunhilde. Their ancestry can be traced back to a black female called Terri who produced a litter that appeared to be carrying Angora genes. One of her daughters, named Elsa, was mated to a Russian Blue male. They produced two litters including the male Siegfried in the first litter and the female Brunhilde in the second. These were then acquired by Cora Cobb and used for further careful breeding to stabilize the new 'Long-haired Blue'. In 1987 it was finally given official recognition by TICA and looks set for a successful future.

Personality: Terms used to describe this breed include: calm, reserved, gentle, quiet, timid, affectionate, loving, adaptable and intelligent.

Colour Forms: Only two are recognized so far: Blue (light blue-grey, with a slight silvery sheen); White (pure, glossy white).

Necker, Claire

Cat Authority. Chicago zoologist Claire Necker is the leading bibliographer on domestic cats. Her painstaking 1972 volume *Four Centuries of Cat Books* has become the classic reference work for the subject. It lists 2,293 titles and provides invaluable information for anyone researching a feline theme or assembling a feline library. Her 1973 sequel *The Cat's Got Our Tongue* is a fascinating, scholarly study of every word, phrase and proverb associated with cats.

Bibliography:
1969. Necker, C. (Editor) *Cats and Dogs.* Barnes, New Jersey.
1970. Necker, C. *The Natural History of Cats.* Barnes, New Jersey.
1972. Necker, C. *Four Centuries of Cat Books. A Bibliography,* 1570–1970. Scarecrow Press, New Jersey.
1973. Necker, C. *The Cat's Got Our Tongue.* Scarecrow Press, New Jersey.
1974. Necker, C. (Editor) *Supernatural Cats.* Warner Books, New York.

Nemo

Pet Cat. A Seal Point Siamese Cat belonging to former British Prime Minister Harold Wilson and his wife, Mary, living with the Wilson family at 10 Downing Street. Nemo always accompanied them on their annual holiday to the Scilly Isles – which was as far 'abroad' as they could go without running into quarantine problems. The name was taken from a boat in the Scilly Isles.

Nepaul Cat

Wild Feline. Writing in 1834, William Jardine listed this cat as a distinct species *(Felis nepalensis),* but it was later discovered to be no more than a variant form of the Asiatic Leopard Cat *(Felis bengalensis).*

Lydekker, in 1896, believed that the Nepaul Cat (or, as he spelled it, the Nipal Cat) might have been a cross between the wild Leopard Cat and a domestic cat. He commented: 'The so-called Nipal Cat *(Felis nipalensis)* was founded on a grey phase, which there is some reason to believe may have been a hybrid.' Bearing in mind that such hybrids are not only possible, but are now thought to have been quite common, this is a reasonable explanation. (See Leopard Cat and Bengal Cat.)

Nest-moving

Feline Behaviour. With domestic cats, when the kittens are between 20 and 30 days old, their mother usually moves them to a new nest site. Each kitten is picked up firmly by the scruff of the neck and, with the mother's head held as high as possible, is carried off to the fresh location. If it has to be transported over a long distance, the mother may grow tired of the weight and let her head sag, switching from carrying to dragging. The kitten never objects, lying limp and still in its mother's jaws, with its tail curled up between its bent hind legs. This posture makes the kitten's body as short as possible and reduces the danger of bumps as it is unceremoniously shunted from old nest to new one.

In this famous photograph, a mother cat stops the busy traffic of downtown Manhattan as she laboriously transfers her kittens to a new nest.

As soon as the mother arrives at the new site she has chosen, she opens her jaws and the kitten drops to the ground. She then returns for the next kitten and the next, until the whole litter has been transported. After the last one has been moved she makes a final trip to inspect the old nest, making doubly sure that nobody has been left behind. This suggests that counting kittens is not one of the cat's strong points.

It is usually stated that this removal operation is caused by the old nest becoming fouled or because the kittens have outgrown it. These explanations seem logical enough, but they are not the true reason. A cat with a large, clean nest is just as likely to set about moving its litter. The real answer lies with the wild ancestors of the domestic cat. In the natural environment, away from canned cat food and dishes of milk, the mother cat must start bringing prey back to the nest, to arouse the carnivorous responses of her offspring. When the kittens are between 30 and 40 days old they will have to begin eating solids, and it is this change in their behaviour that is behind the removal operation. The first, old nest had to be chosen for maximum snugness and security, as the kittens were helpless then and needed protection above all else. But during the second month of their lives, after their teeth have broken through, they need to learn how to bite and chew the prey animals brought by the mother. So a second nest is needed to facilitate this. The primary consideration now is proximity to the best food supply, reducing the mother's task of repeatedly bringing food to her young.

This removal operation still occurs in domestic cats – if they are given half the chance – despite the fact that the feeding problem has been eliminated by the regular refilling of food dishes by their human owners. It is an ancient pattern of maternal feline behaviour which, like hunting itself, refuses to die away simply because of the soft lifestyle of domestication.

In addition to this 'food-source removal pattern', there are, of course, many examples of a cat quickly transporting her litter away from what she considers to be a dangerous nest-site. If human curiosity becomes too strong and prying eyes and groping hands cannot keep away from the 'secret' nest, strange human smells may make it an unattractive abode. The mother cat may then search for a new home, simply to get more privacy. Moves of this kind can take place at any stage of the maternal cycle. In wild species of cat, interference with the young at the nest may result in a more drastic measure, the mother refusing to recognize them as offspring anymore, and abandoning them or even eating them. What happens, in effect, is that the alien smells on the kitten's body make it into an alien 'species' – in other words, into a prey species – and the obvious response to such an object is to eat it. Domestic cats rarely respond in this way, because they have become so used to the scents and odours of their human owners that they do not class them as alien. Kittens handled by humans therefore usually remain 'in the family', even if they have acquired new scents.

Neutering

Feline Reproduction. Neutering of domestic cats is now commonplace and it has been estimated that 90 per cent of all toms alive today have suffered the operation. The castrating of males and the spaying of females have become almost automatic where pet cats are concerned.

This is a practice that can be traced back to the end of the 19th century, when pedigree cat showing was in its infancy. Writing in 1903, Frances Simpson encourages her readers to have their pets neutered, commenting: 'For a home pet there is, of course, nothing to come up to a fine neuter cat who will not roam, who does not attract amorous females, and who is content to lie for hours stretched out on the drawing-room rug or the kitchen hearth, the admired of all admirers.'

Neuters became so popular that they were included in the early cat shows where they were at first judged by their weight. Simpson recalls: 'I remember some specimens exhibited at the Palace that really looked like pigs fatted for market.' This was changed in 1886, to Miss Simpson's relief: 'Though neuters should be big, massive cats, yet they should not, and need not, be lumps of inert fat and fur.'

In addition to making domestic cats bigger and lazier, neutering also had several other effects. It made them more affectionate and more playful. Altogether they were less demanding and more convenient to keep as household pets. As an added bonus, their lifespan was two to three years longer than that of 'entire' cats.

The main attraction, however, was the reduction in breeding activities. There were no more smelly, spraying, yowling, ear-torn toms and no more kitten-factory females. Neutering converted the full-bloodied feline into a furry, living toy. It is not exaggerating to say that the rise of the cat as a pet, rather than as a pest-controller, was largely due to the increasing popularity of the neutering operation.

Some owners, who feel uneasy about robbing their cats of their reproductive rituals, but who at the same time are rightly concerned about the feline population explosion, have sought to render them infertile without the severe mutilation of full castration or spaying. For the female cat this means cutting her fallopian tubes. For the male it means a vasectomy – the cutting of his sperm ducts. These operations are far less severe and leave the cats with the ability to engage in the excitements of feline sexual behaviour, but without creating any unwanted kittens. Unfortunately, veterinary surgeons are routinely trained in full neutering, but not in these more delicate operations and it usually proves difficult to find one who will carry out these procedures. As long as owners prefer to settle for the docility of the neutered cat, it is doubtful whether this situation will change.

Nichols, Beverley

Cat Owner. The English author, composer and playwright, Beverley Nichols (1898–1983), who wrote over 50 books on a wide variety of topics, was passionate about cats and wrote several volumes specifically about them. Although he admitted to being a 'cat-lover' he disliked the title because it implied he did not like other animals. Throughout his cat books he therefore used the expressions 'F' and 'Non-F' 'indicating a person who is basically feline or non-feline by nature.

His own pet cats were, rather oddly, given numbers instead of names. In this he was influenced by the success of the perfume Chanel No. 5, as a result of which, he felt, 'numbers have acquired a subtle elegance of their own'. He called his first Siamese kitten 'Number One', and went on from there until he came to Six. There he had a problem because, when calling out 'Six', it sounded like 'Sicks', so he skipped that number and went straight to Seven. He also had trouble with 'Eight' because it had already been named Oscar before it arrived at his home. But at the time of writing about his cats, he was still doggedly (if that is an appropriate word) looking forward to the arrival of 'Nine, Ten, Eleven and Twelve, who are sleeping somewhere in the womb of Time'.

Beverley Nichols is quoted as saying: 'I have a catholic taste in cats, in the sense that almost anything feline on four legs goes straight to my heart.'

Bibliography:

(No date). Nichols, B. *Beverley Nichols's Cat Book.* Nelson, London.

1960. Nichols, B. *Beverley Nichols's Cats' A.B.C.* Jonathan Cape, London.

1961. Nichols, B. *Beverley Nichols's Cats' X.Y.Z.* Jonathan Cape, London.

1962. Nichols, B. *Cats in Camera.* Andre Deutsch, London.

1974. Nichols, B. *All about Cats.* Orbis, London.

Nightingale, Florence

Cat Owner. The 'Lady of the Lamp', the founder of modern nursing, Florence Nightingale (1820–1910), owned 60 cats during her lifetime. They were all large Persians and she refused to travel anywhere without her current favourites. She named them after the famous men of her day, such as Disraeli, Gladstone and Bismarck.

She is quoted as saying, 'I learned the lesson of life from a little kitten of mine.' She goes on to describe how one of her little kittens stays put when approached aggressively by her biggest cat: 'the little one stands her ground; and when the old enemy comes near enough kisses his nose and makes the peace. That is the lesson of life; to kiss one's enemy's nose always standing one's ground.'

Nine Lives

Feline Saying. The phrase 'a cat has nine lives' is well known but few people understand its origin. It is obviously based on the fact that the cat is unusually resilient, but that does not explain the *nine* lives. The answer is to be found in early religious beliefs, where a 'trinity of trinities' was thought to be especially lucky, and therefore ideally suited for the 'lucky' cat.

Nitchevo

Fictional Cat. Appears in Tennessee Williams's 1948 story 'The Malediction'.

Non-pedigree Cat

Domestic Cat. This is the official name given to all cross-bred, moggie, or mongrel cats. To encourage non-specialists to participate in major cat shows, it is the custom to include special classes for Non-pedigree Longhair and Non-pedigree Shorthair Cats. To quote a recent show catalogue: 'The essential qualities of these non-pedigree pets are that they are happy, much loved examples of the non-pedigree cat being shown in sparkling, tip-top condition . . . they are all beautiful in the eyes of their owners.'

Norsk Skaukatt (or Skogkatt)

Domestic Breed. Norwegian name for the Norwegian Forest Cat. (See separate entry.)

Northern Lynx

Wild Feline. *(Lynx lynx)* Also known as the Eurasian Lynx. It was originally called the European Lynx, but since the species is also found right across northern Asia, this was obviously inappropriate and was eventually dropped in favour of a more general name.

This is the medium-sized cat of the northern forests. It has a stocky body with big, broad paws, long, powerful legs, a very short, black-tipped tail and tufted ears. There is faint spotting all over the body, and black and white facial lines.

The tail has probably been shortened as a protection against the extreme cold that this lynx must often face during the long northern winters, but what the animal loses in conspicuous tail-signals, it makes up for with movements of its tufted ears and its remarkable neck-ruff. This ruff, with black and white markings, which looks like a pair of throat tassels, is fanned opened when the animal hisses and clearly acts as an aggressive visual signal.

The Northern Lynx is driven by its harsh environment to eat anything it can catch, but it specializes in rabbits and hares, which make up most of its diet, along with occasional small deer, chipmunks, rats, mice and lemmings. Because of the scarcity of food, each individual covers a large territory, sometimes as vast as 300 sq km (over 100 sq miles).

The New World counterpart of the Northern Lynx, the Canadian Lynx *(Lynx canadensis),* is thought by some authorities to belong to the same species. Others, however, have pointed out that the Canadian Lynx is only about half the size of the Eurasian form, lacks the spotting on the body, and has an even shorter tail. As a result, the two lynxes are now generally considered to be two separate species.

The Northern Lynx *(Lynx lynx),* has an enormous range, right across Eurasia, from Norway to Mongolia. It is the largest of the four species of Lynx and today survives in only the harshest of environments.

Size: Length of Head + Body: 80–130 cm (31½–51 in). Tail: 11–24 cm (4½–9½ in). Weight: 20–38 kg (44–84 lb).
Distribution: Western Europe, Scandinavia, Asia Minor and northern Asia, including the following countries: Norway, Sweden, Finland, Greece, Turkey, Iran, Iraq, Russia, Mongolia, Manchuria and northern China. It has recently been re-introduced into Germany, the former Yugoslavia, Switzerland, Italy and Austria.

Norwegian Forest Cat

Domestic Breed. The Viking cat. A large, long-haired Norwegian breed. In its homeland it has been known as the Skaukatt or Skogkatt, or more formally as the Norsk Skaukatt or Norsk Skogkatt. Its Norwegian nickname is the 'Wegi' or 'Wegie'. They are also often referred to as 'Skogs' or 'Norgies'. In 19th-century Norwegian folk-tales it is an enchanted cat and is referred to as the 'Fairy Cat'. In France it is called the *Chat de Bois Norvégian,* the *Chat des Forêts Norvégiennes,* or simply the *Norvégien;* in Germany it is the *Norwegische Waldkatze.*
Appearance: A large, powerfully built cat with long hair, a full ruff, tufted ears and a bushy tail. The front legs are slightly shorter than the hind legs. It is a giant among cats, similar in size to the American Maine Coon. The long outer coat is glossy and water-resistant, while the thick undercoat adds protection against the cold. The winter coat is even thicker than the summer one. Inevitably, this means a heavy moult once a year.
Legendary History: Norse folk-tales often speak of huge cats, perhaps inspired by the genuinely impressive bulk of the real-life Norwegian Forest Cat. One legendary cat was so heavy that even the god Thor could not lift it off the ground. The wagon of Freya, the blue-eyed, blonde-haired goddess of love and beauty, was drawn by two powerful cats. Any mortals who placed pans of milk in their cornfields for her cats to drink would have their crops protected by her. It was Freya who gave us Friday ('Freya's day') and this became a popular day for marrying. If the sun shone on her wedding day it was said of the bride 'she has fed the cat well', meaning that she had not offended the feline favourite of the goddess, who, in return, had bestowed upon the bride the good weather.

The impressive Norwegian Forest Cat, with its magnificent, heavy coat, is one of the largest of all domestic breeds. An ancient breed, it has recently grown in popularity all over the world.

Cats were chosen to serve the goddess Freya because their fecundity reflected hers. The early Christians declared her a witch and banished her to the mountains. From their association with her, her cats were also seen as evil forces and were thereafter condemned to torture and death at the hands of the pious.

Factual History: The true story of how the Forest Cat came to be in the Norwegian countryside may never be known. There are six current theories:

1 Long ago, Viking ships brought Scottish Wild Cats to Norway, where they gradually changed into the Forest Cats we see today. (There are no indigenous wild cats in Scandinavia.)
2 Domestic cats from Europe reached Scandinavia on board trading ships. Once there, they escaped and hybridized with the imported Scottish Wild Cats, in the process gaining a thicker coat and larger bone structure.
3 Angora Cats were carried by boat from the Middle East to the ports of the Mediterranean and from there to Scandinavia in the 16th century, where they crossed with the descendants of the imported wild cats, creating a bigger-boned, heavier-coated Angora.
4 Angora Cats, arriving by ship and escaping into the freezing Norwegian countryside, simply became bigger and bigger, with a thicker and thicker coat, as an adaptation to the climate, without the intervention of any imported wild cat stock.
5 Long-haired Russian Cats (modern Siberian Forest Cats) found their way to Norway on board ships plying the Baltic and North Sea routes.
6 Ordinary local domestic cats that became feral and lived rough slowly became bigger and more heavily furred.

Of these various theories, those involving Scottish Wild Cats seem to be the least likely. Any breed of domestic cat exposed to sub-arctic conditions will soon become larger and thicker-coated if it is to survive. A more elaborate explanation of the origin of this breed is hardly necessary.

We are certain of one thing, however, namely that, whichever way it may have arrived, the Norwegian Forest Cat lived in Norway for centuries as a farmyard cat, without any particular attention being paid to it. Then, in 1912, the first named Norwegian Forest Cat, a male called Gabriel Scott Solvfaks, was recorded by the Norwegian Cat Society. Nothing much more was heard about the breed for a while until, in the 1930s, cat enthusiasts began to take a greater interest. Planned breeding programmes followed, and the first Norwegian Forest Cat Club was formed in 1938, but further progress was interrupted by World War II.

Thanks to the tireless efforts of the Norwegian enthusiast Carl-Fredrik Nordane, the Forest Cat found favour again in the 1970s and before long was being seen at cat shows in many different countries, where its impressive size, elegant shape and magnificent coat made a great impact. It was given the international name of Norwegian Forest Cat in 1972, and it gained international championship status in 1977. In a few years it had been exported as a pedigree cat to the United States and most European countries, although it was late arriving in England, a breed club there not being formed until 1987. In 1995 it was estimated that there were approximately 1,000 of these cats in the British Isles.

Personality: Terms used to describe this breed include: rugged, sturdy, intelligent, agile, confident, calm, quiet, athletic, strong, quick, bold, mischievous, outgoing, affectionate, good-natured, playful, alert, responsive, inventive, independent, adventurous, adaptable, brave and loving. A skilful tree-climber, this is definitely not an indoor cat.

Colour Forms: In Norway, the most popular colour form is the Black and White. Outside Norway, the tabby is generally favoured. According to one source, all colours except chocolate, lilac and Siamese pointing are acceptable; according to another source, all colours except chinchilla and Siamese pointing are acceptable. Colour combinations that have been bred so far include: Black Smoke and White, Blue Tabby and White, Blue Tortie Smoke and White, Brown Tabby and White.

The official club emblem of the Norwegian Forest Cat in Denmark.

Breed Clubs:

Norwegian Forest Cat Club. Address: 9 Sundridge Road, Woking, Surrey, GU22 9AU, England.

National Norwegian Forest Cat Club. Address: 17 Ashwood Road, Trenton, NJ 08610-1328, USA.

Norsk Skogkattering, Danmark. Formed in 1975. A Danish breed club with 400 members worldwide. It issues a quarterly magazine in Danish – *Huldrekatten* – and an English newsletter. Address: Hermelinvaenget 8, DK-2880 Bagsvaerd, Denmark.

Norwegian Forest Cat Breeders Consortium. Address: 1859 Vintage Court, Corinth, TX 76205, USA.

Norwegian Forest Cat Fanciers' Association. Address: 2094 Sandpiper Court, Ponte Vedra Beach, FL 32082, USA, or 2507 Ocean Drive S., Jacksonville Beach, FL 32250, USA.

Nose

Feline Anatomy. Like most mammals, the cat has a good nose, well equipped to detect minute changes in fragrance. Internally, it is a maze of complex nasal cavities. One section of these cavities is covered with a nasal lining called the olfactory mucosa, which contains 200 million special olfactory cells. This mucosa is twice as large as the one inside the human nose and this reflects the huge importance of fragrance-detection in the feline world.

It has been estimated that the cat's sense of smell is roughly 30 times better than that of a human being, and a great deal of feline communication is carried out through the medium of scent-marks. Cats leave their scent signals in their environment by means of spraying urine, depositing faeces, rubbing against objects with their scent glands and scratching at surfaces with their feet in such a way as to deposit scent from their paw-pads. They renew these scents at regular intervals, keeping them fresh and 'announcing' any changes that may have occurred in their condition since the last time.

This explains why house-cats are always asking to go out, and then soon asking to come back in again. Each visit is a 'scent-check' to see who and what has been entering their territory. They feel a strong urge to keep up to date with this information, an urge that demands a constant opening and closing of doors for them, if no cat-flaps are available.

Nose Leather

Feline Anatomy. The visible patch of naked skin around the nostrils of the cat is known as the 'nose leather'. In the world of pedigree cats, the precise colour of this patch of skin is considered to be aesthetically significant, and many subtle distinctions are made between one shade and another. Nose leather colours given in modern breed standards include the following: black, seal, brown, chestnut, chocolate, brick red, tile red, cinnamon pink, deep rose, old rose, rose, rosy pink, salmon, flesh, pink, coral pink, lavender pink, lavender, pale fawn, blue, slate blue.

Nubian Cat

Wild Feline. The African Wild Cat *(Felis sylvestris lybica)* was sometimes referred to as the Nubian Cat, especially when discussing its domestication by the Egyptians. For example, Rose Tenent, writing in 1955, comments: 'there is every reason to believe that the original Abyssinian Cat was one and the same as the Nubian Cat, which was domesticated by the Ancient Egyptians. This cat, a small tawny-coloured creature with lighter flanks and white stomach, came from North Africa . . . Paintings and murals which have been preserved show a definite similarity between the skulls of the Nubian Cat and the Sacred Cat of Ancient Egypt.'

Ocelot

Wild Feline. *(Felis pardalis)* It is also known locally as the Tigrillo, Mano Gordo, Gato Onza, Chibi-Guazu, or Ocelote. Its scientific name, *pardalis,* means, literally, 'related to the leopard' – presumably because the Ocelot looks like a smaller version of that species. The name Ocelot itself was originally given to the animal by the French, who took it from a local (Nahuatl) name for the Jaguar: *ocelotl.*

A medium-sized, spotted cat from the American tropics, the Ocelot has one of the most beautiful coats in the entire cat family, a fact that has led to its mass slaughter for the fur trade. It is now classified as an endangered species.

A nocturnal, ground-dwelling cat, it will occasionally take to the trees, but prefers to move about on the forest floor. It is reported to be a strong swimmer.

The Ocelot is much larger than its arboreal relative, the Margay Cat, and has a shorter tail. The spotting of the coat is extremely variable. Each spot has a pale interior ringed with dark edges, but these spots are frequently joined together to make long, horizontal chains that almost become stripes. On the back of each ear there is a vivid white patch surrounded by a black ring, creating the impression of an eye-spot.

The prey consists largely of medium-sized rodents, hares and small deer. Smaller rodents, birds and reptiles, including iguanas, are also taken. Ocelots are usually solitary hunters, employing great stealth.

According to some authorities, the male Ocelots live in pairs with the females and assist in feeding the young, bringing food to the den where the mother is caring for her litter. Others have failed to observe this and doubt whether it occurs, suggesting instead a social system of overlapping male and female territories, with the females solely responsible for parental care. There does not appear to be a breeding season, or, if one does exist locally, it varies considerably from region to region.

The Ocelot *(Felis pardalis)*, is perhaps the most beautiful of all the spotted wild cats. This has been its undoing because, as a result, it has become a prime target for ruthless fur-trapping and extensive hunting.

The importation of Ocelot skins into the United States was banned in 1972, which may have helped to slow down its decline in the wild. It is recorded that, in 1969 alone, the United States imported 133,069 pelts. With that figure representing only part of the annual slaughter for the fur trade, it is surprising that the species has not already become extinct.

In some parts of the world, as late as the 1980s, Ocelot fur coats were selling for up to $40,000 each. However, the outcry against the killing of wild felines has since reached such proportions that fur coats are no longer as popular as they once were, and the wild populations of the Ocelot may yet thrive again – assuming that there are any untouched forests left for them in the American tropics.

Size: Length of Head + Body: 70–90 cm (27½–35½ in). Tail: 30–45 cm (12–18 in). Weight: 11–16 kg (24–35 lb).

Distribution: The Ocelot has been reported from the southernmost parts of the United States, in southern Texas, along the border with Mexico, but is extremely rare there. A 1986 survey reported that only 120 wild Ocelots still existed in the United States at that time. It is also extremely rare in Mexico, where it is thought that fewer than 1,000 now survive.

Its range spreads right through the tropics of Central and South America, as far south as northern Argentina, but it is common nowhere today.

Ironically, the recent craze for keeping pet Ocelots in the United States, which has depleted the wild population even more, has had one unexpected side-benefit: pet escapes (or releases) in Florida have led to a small, wild-living population, which is apparently growing in size, becoming established there.

Bibliography:

1975. Travers, J. *Starting from Scratch: Our Island for Ocelots.* Taplinger, New York.

Ocicat

Domestic Breed. A recent American breed of spotted cat. It was originally a mixture of three-quarters Siamese and one-quarter Abyssinian, with later additions of American Shorthairs. The

name is a combination of 'Ocelot' and 'cat'. Two other names were used in the early days of the breed: 'Ocelette' because it looked like a small Ocelot and 'Accicat' because the first one appeared as a lucky accident in another breeding programme. The breed has been described as 'a purr wrapped in polkadots'.

Appearance: A large, muscular, spotted, short-haired cat with an 'average' body shape, showing no extremes of either stockiness or angularity. In other words, a domestic cat with a 'wild-type' appearance. Despite the strong Siamese element in its original make-up, later breeding programmes, taking it away from the Siamese type of body, have meant that it has not inherited the lean, elongated Oriental look.

History: The first Ocicat appeared in 1964, bred by Virginia Daly of Michigan. It was an accidental by-product of a breeding programme that was attempting to create an Abyssinian-pointed Siamese. It resulted from a mating between a champion Chocolate Point Siamese male and a hybrid female. This female was a cross between a Seal Point Siamese male and an Abyssinian female.

Among the offspring, unexpectedly, was a golden-spotted male kitten. He was named Tonga, and was the first ever Ocicat. However, because he was not part of the official breeding programme, he was sold as a pet and was neutered. Virginia Daly's interest in the idea of developing a spotted cat grew, however, and when she repeated the mating and obtained further spotted kittens, she kept these and used them to create the foundation stock for what was to become an exciting new breed.

Another American breeder, Tom Brown, then took up the Ocicat and initiated a long-term programme. By 1970 he had seen it through five generations. Other breeders improved the type by introducing crosses with American Shorthair Cats. This increased the body size of the Ocicat and made it into the impressive animal we see today. It achieved championship status in the United States in 1987, and in the late 1980s the first ones were introduced into the British Isles, where their numbers have been growing ever since.

In the 1980s a separate line of Ocicats was developed in Germany by Karen Dupuis. The foundation animal for the European Ocicat, born in 1984, was named Nadir.

The Ocicat is one of the new domestic breeds of spotted cat that attempt to recapture the 'wild look' while retaining the friendly domestic temperament. It was first developed in the United States in the 1960s.

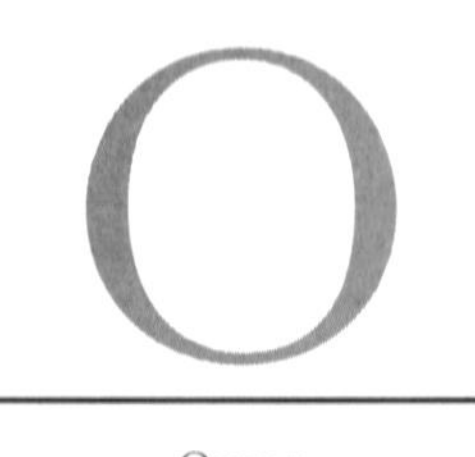

Personality: Terms used to describe this breed include: affectionate, friendly, companionable, athletic, active, acrobatic, attentive, intelligent, loyal, even-tempered and sweet-natured. It is said to be unusually easy to train.

Colour Forms: The typical colouring is light brown or tawny, imitating the coat of a wild cat species. Variant colours include:

CFA: Tawny (Brown Spotted Tabby); Chocolate; Cinnamon; Blue; Lavender; Fawn; Silver; Chocolate Silver; Cinnamon Silver; Blue Silver; Lavender Silver; Fawn Silver.

Breed Clubs:

Ocicat & Bengal Cat Club. Address: Moonfleet, Bakers Lane, Shutlanger, Towcester, Northants., England.

Ocicat Club. Publishes a twice-yearly newsletter, *The Ocicat Muse*. Address: Woodlands, Mounters Lane, Chawton, Alton, Hampshire, England.

Ocicat International. Formed in 1984. Address: P.O. Box 606, Great River, NY 11739, USA, or 865 Sycamore, Boulder, CO 80303, USA.

Ocicats of North America. Address: Route 1, Box 190, Harrison, AR 72601, USA, or 1320 Hilltop Road, Susana Knolls, CA 93063, USA.

Ohio Rex Cat

Domestic Breed. One of the American Rex Cats (the others being the Oregon Rex, the California Rex, the Selkirk Rex and the Missouri Rex), it first appeared in Ohio in 1953.

History: The first Ohio Rex Cat, a male kitten named 'Toni', was an unexpected mutation in an otherwise normal litter born to normal-coated domestic cats owned by Miss Mary Hedderman of Plainsville, Ohio. Toni died young, but was followed by three more Rex kittens from the same parents. No long-term breeding programme was pursued with these, however, and the Ohio Rex strain died out.

According to one authority, this breed was first discovered in 1944, but was ignored owing to wartime preoccupations.

Ojos Azules

Domestic Breed. A recent American discovery from New Mexico. The Spanish name means, literally, 'Blue Eyes'.

Appearance: A tortoiseshell cat with intensely blue eyes. The colouring of the eyes is even more intense than that found in Siamese. There is no deafness or squint associated with this particular blue-eyed gene.

History: The first example of this new breed was found in New Mexico in 1984. She was a tortoiseshell female called 'Cornflower'. Her vivid blue eyes were a spontaneous mutation and subsequent breeding from her has proved that the blue-eyed gene is dominant. All her kittens displayed the same dramatic eye colour.

The Ojos Azules remains a rare breed. As recently as 1992 only ten had been registered.

Ollie

Cartoon Cat. An orange cat with large feet, created by Harry Hargreaves in 1951 for his strip-cartoon *Ollie the Alley Cat*.

O'Malley

Cartoon Cat. O'Malley is the wily alley cat who falls in love with the beautiful 'Duchess' in Walt Disney's 1970 feature-length cartoon film *The Aristocats*.

A new breed of cat *(opposite)*, the Ojos Azules, meaning 'Blue Eyes'. The extraordinary, intense blue eyes have no squint and are not linked to any problems with deafness, as has happened in other cases in the past.

Oncilla

Wild Feline. An alternative name for the Tiger Cat *(Felis tigrina)* from South America. It is also known as the Little Spotted Cat because it is the smallest of the New World felines. (For details see Tiger Cat.)

Onza

Mystery Cat. It has long been claimed that a large cat exists in Mexico which is neither a Puma nor a Jaguar. Locals have named this animal the Onza and describe it as a 'Cheetah-like Puma'. It is said to be similar to a Puma except for the following: (1) There are horizontal stripes on the insides of the front legs. (2) The body is much more slender. (3) The legs are longer and stronger. (4) The claws are non-retractile. (5) The paws are narrower and more elongated.

The animal is said to be confined to the Sierra Madre Occidentale mountains in Mexico, only rarely descending to the lowlands. It lives in regions that are impassable to vehicles and difficult even for horses. This is said to explain the fact that it has gone largely undetected, even in modern times. It is reputed to hunt deer as its main form of prey.

A female Onza was shot by a deer-hunter in 1986 and a detailed examination of its body revealed an animal that was 186 cm (73 inches) long, of which 73 cm (29 inches) was tail. Its weight was 27 kg (59½ lb). A colour photograph of the carcass shows a skinny animal that looks like an emaciated, sub-adult Puma in very poor condition. The leg-stripes are not at all clear and the claws on the front feet appear to be sheathed. The protruding claws on the hind paws appear to have been added to the photograph in ink. However, it does have rather long, pointed ears for a typical Puma and its dissection did prove that, although it was extremely slender, it was not starving or abnormally emaciated, despite appearances.

On the strength of this evidence, it seems likely that the Onza is, at best, an unusual, slender-bodied race of the ordinary Puma, but not a separate species. The biggest drawback to its credibility is that all its specializations point towards a Cheetah-like way of life – hunting on open plains, where the lanky, long-limbed body would be at such an advantage in high-speed pursuits of fleet-footed prey. Yet, the Onza lives in difficult mountain terrain – precisely the wrong type of habitat for an animal with that kind of build. For the moment, therefore, despite the existence of a carcass, the Onza must remain firmly on the list of 'Mystery Cats'.

Bibliography:

1961. Marshall, R. *The Onza.* Exposition Press, New York.

Opal Cat

Domestic Breed. The new name for the Apple-head Siamese. Some American breeders recently set out to re-create the original, less angular, less elongated form of the Siamese Cat. This type was generally referred to as the Apple-head Siamese, but a group that was formed to promote the 'new' breed decided to also give it a special title of its own – the Opal Cat. They formed a club called FOCUS – Fanciers of the Opal Cat of the United States – with the motto 'One man's apple is another man's Opal'. (For further details see Apple-head Siamese.)

Orange

Coat Colour. 'Orange' is the geneticist's name for the coat colour that is called 'red' by cat breeders, 'ginger' by the general public, and 'marmalade' by story-tellers. To confuse matters further, in the early days it was also called 'yellow'. Geneticist Roy Robinson describes the orange gene in the following way: 'The recognized symbol for the gene is "O". The action of the "O" gene is to eliminate all melanic pigment (black and brown) from the hair fibres.'

In earlier days, the term 'orange' was also applied to various pedigree cats by breeders, before they switched to the official term 'red'. Some examples of early 'orange' cats were: Orange Tabby Short-hair (1887); Orange Persian (1903); Orange and White Persian (1903); Orange and Cream Persian (1907). (For further details see Ginger and Red.)

Orangey

Film Cat. A professional cat who performed in a number of feature films, including the title role in *Rhubarb* (1951), a Ray Milland comedy about a cat that inherits a fortune. He also appeared in *Breakfast at Tiffany's* (1961) with Audrey Hepburn, where he was known simply as 'Cat'. Orangey was a long-haired ginger cat with a fiery temperament, who often required many 'doubles' for difficult scenes. He won a Patsy, the animal equivalent of an Oscar, in 1952 and again in 1962. He died in 1963.

Ordos Cat

Wild Feline. A long-haired race of the Wild Cat *(Felis sylvestris)*. This little known cat comes from the cold, easternmost part of the Wild Cat's geographical range, in the Ordos region of N.W. China, where it borders on Mongolia. Guggisberg, writing in 1975, comments that 'the Ordos Cat (subspecies *vellerosa*) . . . is quite unmarked and almost as long-haired as an Angora Cat'. (See also Asiatic Steppe Cat and Wild Cat.)

Oregon Rex Cat

Domestic Breed. First appeared in 1959 in the USA. It is one of four recorded American Rex Cat strains, the others being the Ohio Rex, the California Rex and the Selkirk Rex.

History: In 1959 Mrs M. Stringham of Warrenton, Oregon, a well known cat-breeder, found a wavy-haired black-and-white female kitten among an otherwise normal-haired litter, from a normal-haired tortoiseshell queen. This solitary Rex kitten was named 'Kinky Marcella' and became the founding female of a new strain of Rex Cats.

Crosses between this breed and the better known Cornish Rex and Devon Rex have produced only straight-haired kittens, revealing that the Oregon Rex gene is distinct from both. It has therefore been assigned a separate gene symbol: 'ro'.

According to one authority, this breed was first discovered in 1944, but died out because of wartime preoccupations.

Oriental Chocolate Cat

Domestic Breed. An alternative name for the Havana, abandoned at an early date.

Oriental Longhair Cat

Domestic Breed. This is a recently developed, long-haired version of the Oriental Shorthair. It is sometimes called the Mandarin Cat. It is a long-haired cat of Siamese body-type, but without the typical Siamese point-markings. The true source of the long-haired gene is not clear. By the early 1990s the new breed had been officially recognized by TICA in America, with other societies showing increasing interest. The colour forms are the same as for the Oriental Shorthair (see entry).

Note: Rather confusingly, in Australia 'Oriental Longhair' is an alternative name for the Balinese Cat (see entry).

Oriental Shorthair Cat

Domestic Breed. This is, quite simply, a Siamese Cat without the typical Siamese coat markings. It has been called the 'greyhound of cats'.

Appearance: As for Siamese, but with non-pointed coat colours.

History: When Siamese Cats were first introduced to the West they had a variety of colour patterns. Very early on (in the 1920s), it was decided to concentrate on one particular kind of colouring. The official, pedigree Siamese Cat was to display a Seal Point coat – that is, a pale coat with dark brown extremities – and intense blue eyes. Other forms were rejected and soon vanished. Over the years, the colour of the Siamese points was varied, but the basic pattern – of pale ground colour with darker extremities – was always retained. As time passed, this pattern became synonymous with the breed, and any cat without points could no longer even be called a Siamese.

When, in the 1950s, certain breeders decided to resurrect the original non-pointed type of colouring in their Siamese, they had to find a new name for their cats. The first type they sought was the all-brown cat which was eventually given its own name – the Havana. Other solid (or 'self') colours that were developed were referred to as 'Foreigns'. The more complicated

colours, involving patterns such as tabby, spotted or tortoiseshell, were the ones called 'Oriental Shorthairs'.

In America, this distinction between Foreigns and Oriental Shorthairs was not made; there, they were all called Oriental Shorthairs.

The method used to create these cats has been to introduce various other short-haired breeds into Siamese stock. This had to be done in such a way that only the colouring of these other breeds was added, and the Siamese type, with its slender, elongated build, was retained.

Personality: As for Siamese.

Colour Forms: All colours are acceptable except the typical Siamese-pointed coat pattern. The list of colours already developed has grown and grown. To simplify it, the colours are grouped into convenient categories.

GCCF: Oriental Self: Havana (= Brown); Lilac; Foreign White (the only colour form still using its older title of 'Foreign'); Black; Blue; Red; Cream; Cinnamon; Caramel; Fawn.

Oriental Tortie: Black; Blue; Chocolate; Lilac; Cinnamon; Caramel; Fawn.

Oriental Smoke: Black; Blue; Chocolate; Lilac; Red; Tortie; Cream; Blue Tortie; Chocolate Tortie; Lilac Tortie; Cinnamon; Cinnamon Tortie; Caramel; Caramel Tortie; Fawn; Fawn Tortie.

Oriental Shaded: Black; Blue; Chocolate; Lilac; Red; Tortie; Cream; Blue Tortie; Chocolate Tortie; Lilac Tortie; Cinnamon; Cinnamon Tortie; Caramel; Caramel Tortie; Fawn; Fawn Tortie; Black Silver; Blue Silver; Chocolate Silver; Lilac Silver; Red Silver; Tortie Silver; Cream Silver; Blue Tortie Silver; Chocolate Tortie Silver; Lilac Tortie Silver; Cinnamon Silver; Cinnamon Tortie Silver; Caramel Silver; Caramel Tortie Silver; Fawn Silver; Fawn Tortie Silver.

Spotted Tabby: Brown; Blue, Chocolate; Lilac; Red; Tortie; Cream; Blue Tortie; Chocolate Tortie; Lilac Tortie; Cinnamon; Cinnamon Tortie; Caramel; Caramel Tortie; Fawn; Fawn Tortie; Black Silver; Blue Silver; Chocolate Silver; Lilac Silver; Red Silver; Tortie Silver; Cream Silver; Blue Tortie Silver; Chocolate Tortie Silver; Lilac Tortie Silver; Cinnamon Silver; Cinnamon Tortie Silver; Caramel Silver; Caramel Tortie Silver; Fawn Silver; Fawn Tortie Silver.

Classic Tabby: (as for Spotted Tabby)

Mackerel Tabby: (as for Spotted Tabby)

Ticked Tabby: (as for Spotted Tabby)

CFA: Solid: Blue; Chestnut; Cinnamon; Cream; Ebony; Fawn; Lavender; Red; White.

Shaded: Blue Silver; Chestnut Silver; Cinnamon Silver; Cream Silver; Ebony Silver; Fawn Silver; Lavender Silver; Parti-color Silver; Red Silver.

Smoke: Blue Smoke; Cameo Smoke; Chestnut Smoke; Cinnamon Smoke; Dilute Cameo Smoke; Ebony Smoke; Fawn Smoke; Lavender Smoke; Parti-color Smoke.

Tabby: Classic Tabby Pattern; Mackerel Tabby Pattern; Spotted Tabby Pattern; Ticked Tabby Pattern; Patched Tabby Pattern; Blue Silver Tabby; Blue Tabby; Cameo Tabby; Dilute Cameo Tabby; Cinnamon Silver Tabby; Cinnamon Tabby; Chestnut Silver Tabby; Chestnut Tabby; Cream Tabby; Ebony Tabby; Fawn Tabby; Fawn Silver Tabby; Lavender Silver Tabby; Lavender Tabby; Red Tabby; Ebony Silver; Tabby.

Parti-color: Blue-Cream; Cinnamon Tortie; Chestnut Tortie; Fawn-Cream; Lavender-Cream; Ebony Tortie.

Breed Clubs:

Oriental Cat Association. Publishes a *Yearbook* and a series of pamphlets on various colour forms. Address: 3 Ownstead Gardens, Sanderstead, South Croydon, Surrey, CR2 OHH, England.

Oriental Shorthair Breed Council. Publishes a *Newsletter.* Address: P.O. Box 250066, West Bloomfield, MI 48325-0066, USA.

Note: There is also a breed publication, *Tailes of the Orient.* Address: 7828 Citadel Drive, Severn, MD 21144, USA.

The Oriental Shorthair Cat *(opposite)* – a Siamese Cat without the typical Siamese markings. This breed is now available in a bewilderingly large range of colour forms.

Yet another colour form of the Oriental Shorthair Cat, the Oriental Spotted Tabby. This one is given separate consideration here because the original intention was to develop it into a completely new breed. This plan was later abandoned.

Oriental Spotted Tabby Cat

Domestic Breed. A Siamese Cat with spotted tabby markings. This was an attempt by British breeders to re-create the ancient-Egyptian ancestor of the domestic cat. Although this is just one of the many colour variants of the Oriental Shorthair Cat, it requires separate consideration because it was originally intended to become a distinct breed and was called the 'Egyptian Mau'. This title was later dropped in order to avoid confusion with the new American breed of the same name. (For colour forms, see Oriental Shorthair Cat. See Spotted Cats (1) for further details about spotted domestic breeds.)

Ounce

Wild Feline. An early, alternative name for the Snow Leopard *(Panthera uncia)*. It has become obsolete because it was used in different ways in different countries and therefore caused confusion. (For example, in France, 'Once' means Snow Leopard, but in Spain 'Onza' means Jaguar.) The name 'Ounce' itself is derived from the ancient noun that also gave us the word 'Lynx'. For further details see Snow Leopard.

Painter

Wild Feline. A local, American name for the Puma *(Felis concolor)*. Many of the early white settlers in North America referred to the Puma as the 'American Panther' and in some regions the word 'panther' was corrupted into 'painter'. This became the popular pronunciation in many rural districts of the mid-western and eastern United States. In 1913, James Whitcomb Riley made the name famous when he wrote: 'Yes – and painters, prowlin' 'bout,/ Allus darkest nights. Lay out/ Clost yer cattle. – Great, big red/ Eyes a blazin' in their head . . . '

Pale Cat

Wild Feline. An early, alternative name for the rare Chinese Desert Cat *(Felis bieti)*, from the border country between Tibet and China. When it was given the name of Pale Cat, or Pale Desert Cat, back in the 19th century, it was then known by the scientific name of *Felis pallida*. (For details see Chinese Desert Cat.)

Pallas's Cat

Wild Feline. *(Felis manul)* Named after the German zoologist and explorer, Professor Peter Pallas (1741–1811), this species of cat is also sometimes known as the Manul. In earlier days it was sometimes called the Steppe Cat or the Black-chested Wild Cat. The word *manul* is Mongolian for a small wild cat.

In appearance this cat looks rather like a wary, crouching Persian cat with an Abyssinian coat. Its legs are short, its typical posture is always rather flattened, and its fur is very thick – the thickest in the entire cat family. Together, these features give its body a massively wide shape. The stocky effect is increased by its low, broad head with small, blunt ears set down and to the sides. Its huge eyes give it an owl-like expression. It is clear from its shape and the thickness of its fur that this is a species that must endure intense cold at some time in its natural habitat.

The amazing Pallas's Cat *(Felis manul)*. In appearance this is one of the most dramatic of all small wild felines, with its low-slung ears, its white beard and its strangely human eyes.

The Pallas's Cat prefers open terrain and has been observed living at elevations of up to 4,000 metres (13,000 feet). It is equally at home in deserts, steppe country, or on the rocky slopes of mountains. It stays close to the ground, but is a deft climber on steep rocky surfaces. It usually makes its den in rock cavities and often 'borrows' the homes of other species, such as marmots. Because of the generally open country in which it lives, it is essentially an ambush hunter, lying in wait, ready to pounce on small mammals or birds. Its flattened shape may help it to remain concealed while watching for prey.

Little is known about its sexual behaviour except that it has a strange call that sounds not unlike the barking of a small dog. It is thought to produce large litters, usually of about five or six kittens.

According to Pallas, the original discoverer of the species, they like to mate with domestic cats, and he suggested that such crossings could explain the arrival of the thick-coated Persian Cats. Recent, more sophisticated studies have refuted this suggestion, but it is not clear on what grounds. They may well be right to reject Pallas's idea, but it would certainly be of great interest to put them to the test and try to create some new hybrids that could be examined more closely.

Size: Length of Head + Body: 50–65 cm (20–25½ in). Tail: 21–31 cm (8½–12 in). Weight: 3–5 kg (6½–11 lb).

Distribution: This is a southern Russian cat which extends its range down into Afghanistan and Iran, and across to Tibet, Mongolia and W. China. Despite its wide geographical distribution it is nowhere common and is generally considered to be yet another rare species of wild cat. It was reported that in the 1980s 2,000 skins of this cat were sold to the fur trade each year and that this annual slaughter is creating a gradual decline in numbers.

Palomino Cat

Domestic Breed. A new, experimental breed from North America.

Pampas Cat

Wild Feline. *(Felis colocolo)* Known locally as the Colocolo, Gato Pajero, Gato de Pajonal, the Paja-cat, or the Grass Cat.

A mainly terrestrial cat, it is typically found in the long grasses of the Pampas, where it can hide and hunt. It does, however, have a wider range of habitats than most South American felines and in some regions becomes much more arboreal. In certain areas, for example, it inhabits humid forests and in others it may be found in quite mountainous regions, although not as high up as its close relative, the South American Mountain Cat. It is a nocturnal hunter, seeking out small mammals, especially guinea-pigs, and ground-living birds. There are small litters of only one to three kittens. Little else is known about its life in the wild, and it is notoriously difficult to keep in captivity.

The Pampas Cat is a robust animal, with a broad face and pointed ears. Its body is little bigger than that of an ordinary domestic cat. Its spotted coat is soft and long, and some of its spotted markings run into one another, creating dark diagonal lines. There are strong bands of dark fur around its legs and tail.

As with so many feline species, the Pampas Cat has suffered heavily at the hands of fur-trappers. One record, for example, shows that in the three years between 1976 and 1979, Argentina alone exported no fewer than 78,000 skins of this species.

Size: Length of Head + Body: 60–70 cm (23½–27½ in). Tail: 29–32 cm (11½–12½ in). Weight: 4–7 kg (9–15½ lb).

Distribution: Restricted to South America, the Pampas Cat is found in Ecuador, Peru, Brazil, Bolivia, Chile, Paraguay, Uruguay, and Argentina.

The Pampas Cat *(Felis colocolo)*, from the grasslands of South America, from an old print. Because of its long, thick coat, it has been heavily hunted.

One advantage of the lengthy coat of this species, the South American Pampas Cat, is that, when alarmed, the cat can erect the fur on its back, as it is doing here, and make itself appear suddenly much larger and more threatening.

Pangur Bán

Pet Cat. When an anonymous eighth-century Irish scholar wrote a poem about his pet cat, Pangur Bán, with whom he shared his study, he was unaware that it was the first ever mention of a pet cat in European literature. His first verse reads: 'I and Pangur Bán my cat / 'Tis a like task we are at / Hunting mice is his delight / Hunting words I sit all night.'

Panther

Wild Feline. Most commonly used as an alternative name for the Leopard *(Panthera pardus)*. It is no longer popular because it led to confusion, since several other species of large cats have, at certain times in the past, been called 'Panthers', including the Puma, the Jaguar and even the Clouded Leopard. Today, it is still occasionally employed when referring to a melanistic specimen of a large cat as a 'Black Panther', although in such cases the precise species involved is never clear.

Paraguayan Ghost Jaguar

Mystery Cat. There have been many reports by local people of a very pale Jaguar sometimes glimpsed in the dense forests of Paraguay. The animal, which is regarded with fear, is said to be like a Jaguar, but without any visible markings and with a greyish-white coat. It has been dismissed in the past as local superstition rather than scientific fact, but it should be remembered that Black Jaguars, like Black Leopards, are not uncommon, and if it is easy for a melanistic form to appear, there is no good reason why an albino or semi-albino one should not crop up. Even if it appeared only rarely, that would be enough to create a local legend of a Ghost Cat. However, until a pelt or a live specimen has been exposed to scientific examination, the Paraguayan Ghost Jaguar must remain on the list of 'Mystery Cats'.

Paraguay Cat

Domestic Breed. A 'dwarf' domestic cat from Paraguay. In his *Handbook of the Carnivora*, published in 1896, Richard Lydekker includes a section on domestic cats and lists the various breeds known to him. In addition to well-known and authentic examples such as the Persian, Siamese and Manx, he mentions several mysterious breeds that have never been seen since, such as the Chinese Cat with pendulous ears. He ends his varied list with the following comment:

'Finally, we have the Paraguay Cat of South America, which is but one-fourth the size of the ordinary domestic breed, and is further characterized by its elongated body, and its covering of short, shiny, and close-lying hair, more especially on the tail.'

Sadly, there is no hard evidence to confirm the existence of this remarkable, miniature feline, which is not surprising because it appears to be no more than a figment of Lydekker's clumsy copying from Charles Darwin. Six years earlier, in 1890, Darwin had written about a Paraguay Cat observed by the German explorer Rengger in 1830. These are Darwin's precise words: ' . . . the domestic cat, which has been bred for 300 years in Paraguay, presents a striking difference from the European cat; it is smaller by a fourth . . . '

Needless to say, 'smaller by a fourth' is not the same as 'one-fourth the size'. With inaccuracies like this, legends are born. Which is sad, because a genuine, dwarf cat would be a delightful companion for the cramped lifestyle of the modern urbanite. (See also South American Dwarf Cat.)

Pard

Wild Feline. An obsolete, alternative name for the Leopard *(Panthera pardus)*. It was in common use in earlier epochs, but by the beginning of the 19th century it had been overtaken by the words 'panther' and 'leopard', and was already employed only as a poetic term. In 1821, for example, Shelley talks of 'A pard-like Spirit beautiful and swift', but William Jardine, in his popular scientific volume on the cat family in 1834, speaks only of the Panther or the Leopard.

Parti-colour

Coat Pattern. A term sometimes applied to those cats which have more than one colour. Some American authorities group bi-colours, tortoiseshells and calicos together under this general heading. It is a rarely used term today, but the following variants can be found among the lists of pedigree colour forms: (1) Parti-colour Blue-Cream; (2) Parti-colour Silver; (3) Parti-colour Smoke; (4) Van Parti-colour Tabby and White.

Patched Tabby (= Torbie)

Coat Pattern. This is the two-tone version of the tabby pattern. The standard colouring is Brown Tabby/Red Tabby. The dilute version is Blue Tabby/Cream Tabby.

Colour variants include the following: (1) Blue Patched Tabby; (2) Blue Patched Tabby and White; (3) Blue Silver Patched Tabby; (4) Brown Patched Tabby; (5) Brown Patched Tabby and White; (6) Patched Tabby and White; (7) Dilute Patched Tabby and White; (8) Silver Patched Tabby; (9) Silver Patched Tabby and White.

Paternal Care

Feline Behaviour. As a father, the tom-cat has a bad reputation. For centuries he has been looked upon as a sex maniac whose only interest in kittens is to kill them if he gets half a chance. This image of the male owes its origin to the writings of the great historian Herodotus, following his visit to ancient Egypt 2,500 years ago. Amazed by the Egyptians' extreme devotion to their cat population, Herodotus felt inspired to comment on certain aspects of the behaviour of the felines.

Among his observations is the following assessment of the sexual cunning of the tom-cat: 'As the females when they have kittened no longer seek the company of the males, these last, to obtain once more their companionship, practise a curious artifice. They seize the kittens, carry them off, and kill them; but do not eat them afterwards. Upon this the females, being deprived of their young and longing to supply their place, seek the males once more, since they are particularly fond of their offspring.'

In other words, the sex-mad tom-cats destroy the litters of kittens in order to get the female back on heat again more quickly. This story has lasted well during the past two millennia, and many people still believe it, so that tom-cats are nearly always kept carefully away from nursing mother cats and their young kittens, in case the urge to commit lust-inspired infanticide overcomes them. Nobody has commented on any possible biological advantage of such a reaction on the part of tom-cats, or why males should want to eliminate their own genetic progeny. So what is the truth?

Observations of European Wild Cats, which belong to the same species as the domestic cat, reveal that, far from being kitten-killers, the males sometimes actively participate in rearing the young. One tom was seen to carry his own food to the entrance of the den in which his female had given birth and place it there for her. Another tom did the same thing, supplying his female with food while she was unable to leave the nest during the first days after producing her litter. He also became very defensive and threatened human visitors in a way that he had not done before the young were born. Both these cat families were in zoos, where the proximity of the male was forced upon the female and where, if anywhere, one might have expected to see tom-cat aggression towards the young.

In the wild, where cats have huge territories, the chances of a tom-cat coming across a female in her den with her kittens is remote, so there is little opportunity for either paternal care or paternal infanticide. In the crowded conditions of the zoo or the human city, greater proximity increases the likelihood of tom-cat/kitten encounters and when these happen one of four reactions occurs: (1) The male simply ignores the kittens. (2) The male behaves paternally towards them, as in the case of the zoo cats. (3) The female attacks the male as soon as he approaches her nest and drives him away before he can reveal how he would have responded to the kittens. (4) The male kills the kittens.

Although this fourth reaction is the traditionally accepted one, it is in reality extremely rare. Nearly all the encounters end in one of the other three ways. But clearly the old tale from Herodotus would not have survived 2,500 years without any supporting evidence whatsoever, so the rare cases that have helped to keep the story alive do require some explanation.

The answer seems to be that a female cat sometimes experiences a 'false heat' a few weeks after she has given birth. If a tom-cat is nearby, this excites him tremendously, but the female usually fights with him and drives him off. Now in a great state of sexual arousal, the frustrated tom is desperate. If he meets a small kitten at this stage he may try to mount it and mate with it. The low, crouched posture of the kitten is similar to that of the sexually responsive adult female cat. This, and the kitten's inability to move away quickly when the male mounts it, act as sexual signals to the over-excited tom-cat and seal the fate of the unfortunate kitten. The male does not attack it, but, when mounting the tiny animal, simply performs the perfectly normal neck-bite that he employs when copulating with a female. To the kitten this feels just like its mother's maternal grabbing, so it does not struggle. Indeed, it responds by remaining very still. This is the specific sexual signal from the adult female and tells the male that she is ready to mate. The misunderstanding causes disaster when the male discovers that the kitten is too small for mating. He cannot manoeuvre himself into the correct position. His response to this problem is to grip the kitten's neck tighter and tighter, as if he is dealing with an awkward adult mate. In the process he may accidentally crunch the kitten's tiny, delicate head and kill it.

If this happens, the kitten's body may now trigger off a new reaction. Dead kittens are often devoured by their parents, seemingly as a way of keeping the nest clean. So the victim of the tom-cat's sexual frustration may now be eaten, as the final act of the gruesome misfiring of the feline reproductive sequence. It is these rare cases that have led to stories of tom-cat cannibalism – and to stories that paint the male feline as a savage monster bent on slaughtering and consuming his own children.

As with so many animal fallacies, it is the rare event that becomes established as the 'norm' in popular folklore. And usually, as in this case, the animal motives involved are luridly exaggerated or distorted.

It should be mentioned that in one species of wild feline – the lion – infanticide is far less rare. But there is a special reason for this. When an elderly or injured male lion is no longer capable of protecting his pride against the interest of a younger male, he may be attacked by his rival and driven away. The young male will then take over the pride and acquire the females. He will also inevitably acquire the cubs that had been sired by the older male. In this situation he may react by killing the cubs, rather than waste his time rearing the offspring of his departed rival. When he does this, the females will, indeed, come into heat again more quickly, and can then be made pregnant, so that they now carry the offspring of the new male.

Careful studies in Africa have revealed that, following a male take-over of a pride, the females will, on average, come on heat again after 244 days. Without a male take-over, the full rearing process would have taken 560 days. So infanticide by the new male lion can speed up his reproductive activities by nearly a year. Bearing in mind that the average duration of 'owning a pride' is only about two years, this is clearly an important consideration if a male lion is to perpetuate his genes.

This ruthless strategy works well enough for lions, where there is clear ownership of females and cubs by particular, ruling males. But with small cats the situation is very different. With overlapping territories and female promiscuity, any kittens a male may meet are likely to be his already. Certainly, he will not know whether they are his or belong to some other, nearby, rival male. So there is no genetic advantage for him in killing the kittens. It has even been suggested that one of the main reasons why female domestic cats will mate with all the tom-cats that surround her during a typical feline 'orgy' is precisely because this causes 'paternal uncertainty'. If any of these males do happen to encounter her later on, with her litter of kittens, they cannot be certain that they are not the father. As a result, they are less likely to cause the mother cat any problems.

P

Patripatan

Legendary Cat. A white cat was dispatched by his princely master to pluck a flower from a tree in heaven. The cat found heaven so enchanting that the days and weeks flew by. After 300 years had passed, Patripatan remembered his task and knew he must return. He had been such pleasant company that the gods gave him, not just a single flower, but a whole flowering branch of the wonderful tree, to take back with him to Salangham, his home in India. While he had been away his prince and the people of Salangham had not aged at all and, on his return, their country became a land of serenity and beauty.

Paws

Feline Anatomy. When Oscar Wilde spoke of the 'Velvet Paw' he was conjuring up an image of the surprisingly gentle softness of a cat's foot when its claws are sheathed. The feline paw, sharp and savage when tensed for action, smooth and rounded when relaxed, lives a double life. Claws out, it is a lethal hunting weapon, an acrobatic climbing device and a fighting tool; claws in, it is a padded, silent shock-absorber.

Beneath each front paw there lie seven small pads, separated by tufts of fur. There are five *digital pads,* one per claw. The first of these is the pad for the rudimentary thumb, which carries a dew claw. The others lie beneath the four, sharp retractile claws. In the centre of the underside of the foot is the largest of the seven pads, called the *plantar pad.* This has three lobes and is the main support-point for the animal's leg, protecting the weight-bearing leg-bones. Finally there is a small wrist-pad called the *pisiform pad* ('pisiform' means 'pea-shaped', and refers to the shape of the wrist-bone beneath the pad).

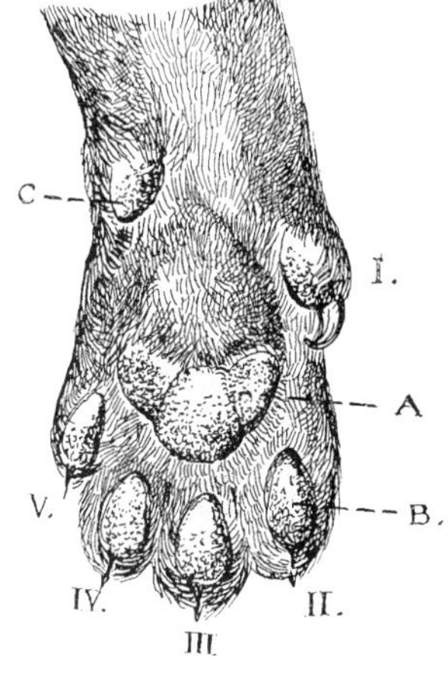

The underside of a cat's paw, showing the arrangement of the seven pads. A: the large central, plantar pad. B: one of the five digital pads. C: the small wrist-pad, the pisiform pad. I–V are the five claw-bearing digital pads.

On each hind foot there are only five pads – the four main digital pads and the one large, central plantar pad. The hind foot is much stronger and stiffer than the front foot and must bear the greater burden during locomotion, especially when the cat is jumping.

All these pads are soft, smooth and spongy in indoor cats. By contrast, in outdoor, roaming cats, they are tough and leathery, echoing the difference between the hands of office-workers and farmers.

Cats' paws exhibit one rather common form of genetic abnormality, a condition known as *polydactylism,* in which extra toes are present. Slippers, the famous White House cat belonging to President Teddy Roosevelt, was a cat of this kind, having six toes on each foot. Some of Ernest Hemingway's cats had as many as seven toes.

Biologists in Boston, Massachusetts, have discovered that their city has been the centre for the spread of many-toed domestic cats in North America. In Boston, of 311 cats examined, 39 had extra toes. This is a higher percentage than anywhere else in America. When cats in other cities were studied, it emerged that those locations which had received most (human) ex-Bostonians into their population during their past history also had the biggest percentage of many-toed cats. By their distribution, these cats were, in effect, acting as a measure of human cultural movements. Cities where there has been very little influx of Bostonians had only very small percentages. For example: Boston: 12 per cent; New York: 0.5 per cent; Chicago: 0.4 per cent; Columbus, Ohio: 0.4 per cent; Philadelphia: 0.2 per cent.

A final point of interest about cats' paws: although we are all aware that human beings are either left-handed or right-handed, it is not generally known that many cats are also either left-pawed or right-pawed. Careful tests have revealed that, of every hundred cats, approximately 40 are left-pawed, 20 are right-pawed and 40 are ambidextrous. These findings contrast strikingly with the human situation, where only 10 individuals are left-handed for every 90 who are right-handed.

Peke-faced Cat

Domestic Breed. A flat-faced breed developed in America, with head proportions similar to those of the Pekinese Dog. The depressed nose gives the breed an appealing facial configuration, but critics believe this is achieved at the expense of causing breathing difficulties.

THE CONTROVERSIAL Peke-faced Cat. The face of the Persian cat has grown flatter and flatter over the years, and the Peke-face is the ultimate expression of this trend. Although appealing, it can easily suffer from breathing problems.

Appearance: The Peke-faced Cat is essentially a Persian Cat with a face that is even flatter than usual. According to the standard for the breed, the nose should be 'short, depressed and indented between the eyes'. Unlike the Persian, which appears in many colour forms, the Peke-faced cat is only known in red and red tabby colours.

History: This variant of the ordinary Persian appeared spontaneously in litters of ordinary Reds. The earliest records of Peke-faced individuals date from the 1930s. They became highly valued by American and Canadian breeders and often won prizes at cat shows, being seen, in effect, as 'Super-Persians'. In Europe they have remained unpopular because of the physical abnormalities that are associated with them.

Abnormalities: Because of its excessively flattened face, this breed is likely to suffer from blocked tear-ducts which cause runny eyes, a poor bite when its mouth is closed, and respiratory difficulties due to the reduced size of its nasal cavities. The respiratory problems increase with age. Breeders are attempting to reduce these faults, but may not be able to do so without abandoning the extreme flattening of the face – the very feature which makes these cats so anthropomorphically appealing.

Personality: Terms used to describe this breed include: calm, affectionate, polite, friendly and sociable. Claimed to be 'the ideal indoor cat'.

PENNY

PET LEOPARD. Penny was a female African Leopard cub reared by Joy Adamson and then returned to the wild in the Shaba Reserve in Kenya. Adamson had already reared and returned a Lion (Elsa) and a Cheetah (Pippa), and Penny completed her trio of Africa's great cats. Penny was the most difficult of the three. Although she took Adamson to see her cubs after she had mated with a wild Leopard she was unpredictable and several times bit or clawed her foster-mother.

Bibliography:

1980. Adamson, J. *Queen of Shaba.* Collins Harvill, London.

(For a full Adamson bibliography, see the entry for Elsa.)

Pepper

Film Cat. The very first film star cat, Pepper was a grey alley cat who appeared in early Mack Sennett comedies with Charlie Chaplin, Fatty Arbuckle and the Keystone Cops. She appeared one day on the set of a film and was promptly written into the story. After many starring roles, she went into decline following the death of her favourite co-star, a Great Dane called Teddy. She refused all replacements for Teddy and soon vanished as mysteriously as she had arrived.

Persian Cat

Domestic Breed. One of the oldest breeds of domestic cat, the exceptionally long-haired Persian became popular as soon as competitive cat showing began, at the end of the 19th century. Although its origins are obscure, the breed quickly became clearly defined and standardized.

As the glamorous 'luxury' breed of pedigree cat, it is still known throughout the world today by the name 'Persian', with one inexplicable exception. Among the officials of the British cat fancy, it is confusingly referred to simply as the 'Longhair'. This is done despite the fact that (1) outside feline officialdom, the entire British public (like the rest of the world) calls it the Persian, and (2) it creates considerable confusion with domestic cat classification systems, because of all the other, quite different, long-haired breeds that now exist.

In France it is known as the *Persan;* in Germany as the *Perser, Perserkatzen* or *Persisch Langhaar;* and in Holland as the *Perzisch*.

Appearance: The Persian has a uniquely rounded shape, with a thick woolly coat, short neck and body, stocky legs, thick bones, bushy tail and massive, broad head with small, tufted ears set low on the head. The face has become much flatter in modern specimens, when compared with the profile seen a century ago. The thick fur has a dense, woolly undercoat.

History: As with most early breeds, there is considerable argument concerning the origin of the Persian. The truth is that detailed information is lacking, so that authors can speculate freely. No less than nine different views (some nonsensical, some plausible) have been expressed in the past; they are as follows:

A Blue and White Bi-colour Persian. One of the oldest of domestic breeds, the Persian Cat is by far the most spectacular and has retained its dominant position at cat shows throughout the 20th century.

1 It is descended from the long-coated wild cat called Pallas's Cat *(Felis manul)*.
2 It is descended from the long-coated wild cat called the Sand Cat *(Felis margarita)*.
3 It is descended from a cross between Pallas's Cat (or the Sand Cat) and local domestic cats in the Middle East.
4 It is descended from the European Wild Cat *(Felis sylvestris)*.
5 It is descended from a cross between Pallas's Cat and the European Wild Cat.
6 It is descended from the Russian Longhair Cat. It has been suggested that the 'Persian' is not really Persian at all, but that it is simply the thick-coated, cold-country cat from the north of Russia that was somehow accidentally associated with Persia. This could have happened if these cats were first seen in the West when they arrived on board ships from the Middle East.
7 It is descended from a cross between the Russian Longhair and local domestic cats in the Middle East.
8 It is descended from a cross between the Russian Longhair and the Turkish Angora. The appeal of this theory is that it explains the nature of the Persian coat, the thickness coming from the Russian cat and the long flowing silkiness from the Angora.
9 It is a long-haired mutant that appeared spontaneously in the Iranian region of the Middle East. This is the simplest theory, but it fails to explain why a long-haired mutant should have been successful in the intense heat of the Iranian region. The only suggestion offered so far to overcome this objection is that the mutation occurred in the most mountainous regions of Iran where lower temperatures do occur.

Of these nine suggestions, the first five, involving wild species, can almost certainly be discounted. The sixth overlooks specific reports of cats being brought to Europe from Persia. Of the other three, each is plausible enough. The most likely idea would seem to be that, one way or another, thick-coated cats from the frozen north were brought south where they managed to survive the amazing temperature contrasts of what is now Iranian territory.

The idea of an indigenous, long-haired breed arising inside Persia cannot, however, be discounted. The German author Hermann Dembreck has assembled a fairly detailed historical account of such an origin, but it is not entirely clear how much is based on precise records, and how much on his imagination. In summary, he claims the following:

When King Cambyses of Persia conquered Egypt in 525 BC, the invaders took large numbers of the sacred Egyptian cats home with them. There, the winters were much more harsh and, as the generations passed, these cats began to develop longer and longer coats. In 331 BC, Alexander the Great invaded Persia, and King Darius and his court fled to the mountains, taking with them their valuable cats. About 2,000 metres (7,000 feet) up, they built their strongholds and there, in the even colder air, generations of cats gradually grew even longer fur. Their main centre was north-west of the present-day city of Meshed, in the Chorassan district of Eastern Persia. These mountainous regions were heavily forested and in the forests roamed local wild cats, which mated with the domesticated castle cats and created a stockier, sturdier build. By AD 247, these Parthian lords had established a culture of their own and began to export some of their precious cats. By the eighth century, Islam was expanding and invaded Persian territory. They took some of the cats they found there and passed them on to other Islamic regions. By the 15th century they had reached Anatolia and were to be found in Angora, where they changed their shapes again, becoming slightly sleeker. Some of these Angoras Cats were then exported west to Europe, where they created a sensation, being the first long-haired cats ever seen there. A little later, the even fluffier cats from Persia itself were taken to the West.

Whichever theory one cares to follow, it is clear that, by the 17th century, a remarkable breed of thick-coated cat had somehow developed in what was then Persia. It was at that time that the Italian traveller, Pietro della Valle, first encountered it and was so impressed by its beauty that he brought breeding stock back to Europe with him. He set sail from Venice in 1614, travelling to Persia via Egypt, the Holy Land and Arabia. He spent five years in Persia before returning to Italy in 1626, via India, Mesopotamia and the Levant. (Some authors have reported that he brought Angora Cats back from Turkey, but he does not appear to have visited that country, so this is probably an error.) Of the cat he met in Persia, he recorded the following description: 'There is in Persia a cat of the figure and form of our ordinary ones, but infinitely more beautiful in the lustre and colour of its coat. It is of a blue-grey, and soft and shining as silk. The tail is of great length and covered with hair six inches long.'

It is not clear how well his breeding plans fared, but we do know that, by the 19th century the Persian had become a highly desirable breed, especially in France. Its only serious long-haired rival at that time was the Angora from Turkey.

The Persian's impact on the first cat shows in Britain was such that it quickly came to dominate the scene. Its long-haired Turkish rival was soon eclipsed. Already, by 1903, Frances Simpson was able to say: 'In classing all long-haired cats as Persian I may be wrong, but the distinctions . . . between Angoras and Persians are of so fine a nature that I must be pardoned if I ignore the class of cat commonly called Angora, which seems gradually to have disappeared from our midst.' She then goes on to devote no fewer than 127 pages to the various colour forms of Persians. Clearly, by the turn of the century, the Persian had won the day. It was soon being referred to as 'the aristocrat of the cat family'.

As the years passed, more and more colours and patterns were added to the Persian repertoire, until there were more than 60 different coat variants on show. At the same time, the Persian body-type was made more and more extreme, with even longer coats and flatter, broader faces. The degree to which these changes have been taken has varied from country to country, with the result that international judging of pedigree Persians at cat shows sometimes leads to strong disagreements and much heated debate.

Personality: Terms used to describe this breed include: docile, quiet, intelligent, aloof, gentle, easygoing, good-tempered, sweet-natured, affectionate and friendly. In this respect, it would seem that selective breeding during the last hundred years has greatly modified the breed. Writing in 1889, Harrison Weir paints a very different picture of the character of the Persians he encountered at the early cat shows: 'My attendant has been frequently wounded in our

The dramatic appearance of the Persian Cat has created many thousands of slaves to its undeniable beauty, owners who must daily devote themselves to hours of laborious grooming.

P

Persian Cat

In the early days of cat-showing, the few known colour forms of the Persians were each classed as a separate breed. Now that there is a huge number of colours available, that antique arrangement requires revision.

endeavour to examine the fur, dentition, etc., of . . . the Persian.' He goes on to say that 'I find this variety less reliable as regards temper than the short-haired cats . . . In some few instances I have found them to be of almost a savage disposition, biting and snapping more like a dog than a cat.' This forms a striking contrast with the temperament of the modern Persian, which is now generally thought of as the most placid of breeds.

Colour Forms: Uniquely and strangely, in Britain, the different colour forms of the Persian have been classed as different breeds since the early days of cat-showing. Separate breed colour clubs were established and the cats were treated as though there was much more than a mere colour-gene difference between them. Back in the days when there were only a few colour forms available, this did not matter, but today, when almost every colour and coat pattern imaginable has been created for the Persian, the idea of judging some of these variants as distinct breeds requires re-examination.

GCCF: Self: Black; White; Blue; Red Self; Cream; Chocolate; Lilac.

Smoke: Black Smoke; Blue Smoke; Chocolate Smoke; Lilac Smoke; Red Smoke; Tortie Smoke; Cream Smoke; Blue-Cream Smoke; Chocolate Tortie Smoke; Lilac Tortie Smoke.

Chinchilla: Chinchilla; Golden Persian; Shaded Silver.

Cameo: Red Shell Cameo; Red Shaded Cameo; Tortie Cameo; Cream Shell Cameo; Cream Shaded Cameo; Blue-Cream Cameo.

Pewter: Pewter.

Tabby (classic pattern only): Silver Tabby; Brown Tabby; Blue Tabby; Chocolate Tabby; Lilac Tabby; Red Tabby.

Tortie Tabby: Tortie Tabby; Blue Tortie Tabby; Chocolate Tortie Tabby; Lilac Tortie Tabby.

Tortie: Tortie; Blue-Cream; Chocolate Tortie; Lilac-Cream.

Tortie and White: Tortie and White; Blue Tortie and White; Chocolate Tortie and White; Lilac Tortie and White.

Tortie Tabby and White: Tortie Tabby and White; Blue Tortie Tabby and White; Chocolate Tortie Tabby and White; Lilac Tortie Tabby and White.

Bi-colour Solid: Black and White Bi-colour; Blue and White Bi-colour; Chocolate and White Bi-colour; Lilac and White Bi-colour; Red and White Bi-colour; Cream and White Bi-colour.

Bi-colour Tabby: Brown Tabby and White; Blue Tabby and White; Chocolate Tabby and White; Lilac Tabby and White; Red Tabby and White; Cream Tabby and White.

Van Bi-colour: Black and White Van; Blue and White Van; Chocolate and White Van; Lilac and White Van; Red and White Van; Cream and White Van.

Van Tricolour: Tortie and White Van; Blue Tortie and White Van; Chocolate Tortie and White Van; Lilac Tortie and White Van.

Note: For GCCF Colourpoint versions see Colourpoint Longhair.

CFA: Solid: White; Blue; Black; Red; Peke-face Red; Cream; Chocolate; Lilac.

Silver and Golden: Chinchilla Silver; Shaded Silver; Chinchilla Golden; Shaded Golden.

Shaded and Smoke: Shell Cameo; Shaded Cameo (Red Chinchilla); (Red Shaded); Cream Shell Cameo (Cream Chinchilla); Cream Shaded Cameo (Cream Shaded); Shell Tortie; Shaded Tortie; Shell Blue-Cream (Blue-Cream Chinchilla); Shaded Blue-Cream; Black Smoke; Blue Smoke; Cream Smoke; Cameo Smoke (Red Smoke); Tortie Smoke; Blue-Cream Smoke.

Tabby: Classic Tabby Pattern; Mackerel Tabby Pattern; Silver Tabby; Silver Patched Tabby; Blue Silver Tabby; Blue Silver Patched Tabby; Red Tabby; Peke-face Red Tabby; Brown Tabby; Brown Patched Tabby; Blue Tabby; Blue Patched Tabby; Cream Tabby; Cameo Tabby; Cream Cameo Tabby.

Parti-color: Tortie; Blue-Cream; Chocolate Tortie; Lilac-Cream.

Bi-color: Calico; Van Calico; Dilute Calico; Van Dilute Calico; Chocolate Calico; Chocolate Van Calico; Lilac Calico; Lilac Van Calico; Bi-color; Van Bi-color; Smoke and White; Van Smoke and White; Tabby and White; Van Tabby and White.

Note: For CFA Colourpoint versions, see Himalayan.

Bibliography:

1936. Linden, M. *Pasha the Persian.* Kendall, New York.

1956. Anon. *Persian Cats as Pets.* TFH, New Jersey.

1956. De Churchill. *On All Fours.* New York. (Anecdotal)

1960. Ramsdale, J.A. *Persian Cats.* TFH, New Jersey.

1964. Ramsdale, J.A. *Persian Cats and Other Longhairs.* TFH, New Jersey.

1965. Tenent, R. *Persian Cats and other Longhairs.* W. H. Allen, London.

1968. Pond, G. *The Long-haired Cats.* Arco, London.

1974. Pond, G. and Calder, M. *The Longhaired Cat.* Batsford, London.

1976. Ramsdale, J.A. *Persian Cats and Other Longhairs.* (2nd, enlarged edition) TFH, New Jersey.

1980. Pond, G. *Persian Cats.* Foyles, London.

1982. Esarde, E.E. *Persian Cats.* TFH, New Jersey.

1983. Pond, G. *Longhaired Cats.* Batsford, London.

1989. Schneider, E. *A Step-by-Step Book About Persian Cats.* TFH, New Jersey.

1990. Müller, U. *Persian Cats.* Barron's Educational Series, Hauppauge, New York.

1993. Single, D.J. *Silver and Golden Persians.* TFH, New Jersey.

1993. Thompson, W. and Wickham-Ruffle, E. *The Complete Persian Cat.* Howell, New York.

Breed Clubs:

Persian Bi-color and Calico Society. Address: 187 N. Madison Drive, S. Plainfield, NJ 07080, USA.

United Silver (Persian) Fanciers. Address: 663 N. Dayton Lakeview Road, New Carlisle, OH 45344, USA.

Note: In the United States there is a quarterly magazine which is devoted exclusively to the Persian Cat: *Persian Quarterly.* Address: 4401 Zephyr Street, Wheat Ridge, CO, USA. There is also a publication called *Persian News.* Address: 746 North Crescent Drive, Hollywood, Florida 33021, USA. And specifically for Silver Persians there is *Silver Lining.* Address: 491 Valencia Lane, Vacaville, CA 95688, USA.

Persian Longhair Cat

Persian Longhair Cat

Domestic Breed. This is an alternative name for the Persian Cat. Use of the title 'Persian Longhair' to describe this particular breed is a diplomatic solution to a difficult problem. Since the British feline authorities stubbornly insist on calling the Persian Cat the 'Longhair', while everyone else in the world calls it the Persian, some authors opt for a compromise. By calling it the 'Persian Longhair' they hope to keep British officialdom happy without mystifying the general reading public.

Persian Variants

Domestic Breeds. The Persian has been used as the ancestral cat for several recent breeds, each modifying the original form in some way. These modern descendants of the traditional Persian include the following (see separate entries for further details):

1 Himalayan (Longhair Persian with Colourpoint coat pattern)
2 Peke-faced (Longhair Persian with flattened face)
3 Exotic (Shorthair Persian)

Since its earliest days in ancient Egypt, the main function of the domestic cat has been to control the vermin that have perennially infested the settlements of mankind.

Pest Control

Feline History. Before the cat became elevated to the level of a companion and pet for friendly humans, the contract between man and cat was based on the animal's ability to destroy pests. From the time mankind first started to keep grain in storage, the cat had a role to play and carried out its side of the bargain with great success.

Not so long ago it was thought that the best way to get farm cats to kill rats and other rodent pests was to keep the feline hunters as hungry as possible. This seemed obvious enough, but it was wrong. Hungry farm cats spread out over a huge hunting territory in search of food and killed fewer of the pests inside the farm. Cats that were fed by the farmer stayed nearer home and their tally of farm pests was much higher. The fact that they had been fed already and were not particularly hungry made no difference to the number of prey they killed each day, because the urge to hunt is independent of the urge to eat. Cats hunt for the sake of hunting. Once farmers realized this they were able to keep their cats close by the farm and reduce the damage done to their stores by rodent pests. A small group of farm cats, well looked after, could prevent any increase in the rodent population, providing a major infestation had not been allowed to develop before their arrival.

Two champion mousers were Mickey and Towser (see separate entries). Mickey was a male tabby who killed an estimated 22,000 mice at the factory where he was employed. Towser was a female tortoiseshell whose tally was even greater – over 28,000 mice at the distillery where she made her home.

The world's champion ratter was a female tabby who used to earn her keep at the White City Stadium in London. Over a period of only six years she caught no fewer than 12,480 rats, which works out at a daily average of five to six. This is a formidable achievement and it is easy to see why the ancient Egyptians went to the trouble of domesticating cats and why, in ancient Egypt, the act of killing one was punishable by death.

Petrarch

Cat Owner. The pet cat much loved by Petrarch (1304–1374), the Italian poet who is recognized as the leading scholar of his age, was described as 'her master's joy in the sunshine, his solace in the shade'. According to Agnes Repplier, writing in 1901: 'When she died, her little body was carefully embalmed; and travellers who visited Arquà, the poet's home, hidden among the Euganean Hills, have stared and mocked and wondered at this poor semblance of cathood, this furless withered mummy, which, more than five hundred years ago, frolicked softly in the joyousness of youth. Upon the marble slab on which she lay were cut two epigrams . . . one of which gracefully commemorated the rival passions that shared Petrarch's heart.

(Translated from the Latin, it read: "I was the greatest passion, second only to Laura.") Doubtless of these conflicting emotions, the more simple and sincere was the poet's affection for his cat.'

There are two other, alternative versions of this story. According to Timothy Bay, after Laura had died from the plague, one year after the poet had met her, 'Petrarch took the dead cat of his beloved Laura, embalmed it in the Egyptian manner, and placed it over his doorway, where it was to remain in protective vigil until his death'.

Louise Caldi, an art historian writing in 1976, paints a different picture: 'Petrarch's chief companion was his cat. When the poet died, the cat was put to death and embalmed. Today, the mummified body of the cat lies in a niche decorated with a marble cat and bearing a Latin inscription, said to have been written by the poet himself.'

Of the three versions, the first is the most convincing.

Pewter

Coat Colour. Pewter is the name sometimes used to describe a Blue-Silver Tabby coat. It lacks the rich warmth of the Blue Tabby.

Picasso, Pablo

Cat Art. In the early part of his career, according to the diaries of his mistress, Fernande Olivier, Pablo Picasso (1881–1973), the Spanish artist, owned two cats, a dog and a monkey. A photograph shows that at least one of these cats was a Siamese.

He observed many cats during his long life and on a number of occasions incorporated them into his paintings. They were usually portrayed in a predatory role and it was clearly the cat as an independent, stalking hunter, rather than as a soft, purring lap-cat, that fascinated Picasso.

He is quoted as saying: 'I want to make a cat like those true cats that I see crossing the road. They don't have anything in common with house pets; they have bristling fur and run like demons. If they look at you, you would say that they want to jump on your face and

Cat Chasing Bird by Pablo Picasso. To Pablo Picasso the realm of the cat was a world full of violence, as this 1939 painting by him reveals. As a Spaniard reared on the savagery of the bullfight, he ignored the soft gentleness of his feline subjects and made them instead harsh and predatory beings.

scratch your eyes out. The street cat is a real wild animal. And have you ever noticed that female cats – free cats – are always pregnant. Obviously they don't think of anything but making love.'

Bibliography:

1995. Cox, N. and Povey, D. *A Picasso Bestiary*. Academy Editions, London.

Piebald

Coat Pattern. The term Piebald or Pied is not commonly used today for cats, but was mentioned by Dechambre in 1957, as follows: 'By a pied cat is meant any cat with large patches of colour on a white background . . . Although extremely interesting, this variety has not so far been precisely selected and it is not admitted as a special breed at exhibitions.'

Later, in 1970, Claire Necker uses the term Piebald in the following way: *'White Spotting (Piebald)* The degree of white spotting ranges from a few white hairs on the throat to a completely white cat.' She goes on to explain how the white areas tend to favour the frontal parts of the cat's body and its undersides.

In the past, piebald cats have sometimes been referred to as 'Magpie Cats', but today they are more often called Bi-colours. (For further details see Bi-colour.)

Pious Cat

Folk-tale. In 14th-century Persia, the poet Obaid-e Zakani wrote a children's story called *Mush u Gurba* (Cat and Mouse) that was to last for 600 years. It is still read by Iranian children today, but was little-known in the West until Basil Bunting's delightful translation of it was published in 1986, under the title of *The Pious Cat*. Beneath the superficial simplicity of the children's fable lies a serious warning about the duplicity and tenacity of tyrants.

The devious cat Tibbald attacking the mice in the 14th century Persian tale *Mush u Gurba* (Cat and Mouse), recently translated by Basil Bunting and published under the title of *The Pious Cat*.

Briefly, the story tells how the devious cat Tibbald went to pray forgiveness for having killed and eaten a mouse. He offers a gift of compensation to every surviving relative of the mouse he has just eaten. The mice are delighted and they all flock to see him, bringing him gifts. For their pains, he kills and eats all but two of them, who manage to escape. They run to the Mouse King, crying: 'Once on a time that ravenous ratter ate/ his daily mouse at a steady flat rate,/ but since he took to prayers and pieties,/ he bolts us down in whole societies.'

The Mouse King musters a huge army and war breaks out between the mice and the cats. Tibbald is caught and condemned to die on the gallows, but he manages to escape and swallows the Lord Chief Justice.

That is where the story ends, a salutary tale of the triumph of despots, and it is easy to see why it has retained its popularity, century after century, in a Middle East as infested by tyranny today as it was in Obaid-e Zakani's 14th century.

Pippa

Pet Cheetah. In Joy Adamson's book *The Spotted Sphinx,* Adamson describes the way in which she reared a pet Cheetah called Pippa and then returned her to the wild. Released in the Meru National Park in Kenya, Pippa mated successfully and produced four sets of cubs before she died as a result of a fight. Most of her cubs also survived and produced their own offspring.

Bibliography:

1969. Adamson, J. *The Spotted Sphinx*. Collins Harvill, London.

1970. Adamson, J. *Pippa the Cheetah and her Cubs*. Collins Harvill, London.

Note: For a full Adamson bibliography, see entry for 'Elsa'.

Platinum

Coat Colour. An American name for the pale grey/fawn of one of the dilute colours of the Burmese Cat. The full description of the coat is as follows: 'a pale silvery gray with pale fawn undertones, shading almost imperceptibly to a slightly lighter hue on the underparts.' It is similar to the colour called lilac in Britain.

Play

Feline Behaviour. Kittens exhibit four basic play patterns:

Play-fighting: This is the earliest form of play to develop. At about three weeks the kittens start to engage in rough-and-tumble actions with their litter-mates. They jump on one another, roll over on their backs and grapple. No one gets hurt. This is because at first they lack the strength to hurt, and when they do acquire it they quickly learn that a too powerful play-attack ends the enjoyable encounter. So they perfect the art of inhibited assault. By the age of four weeks the play-fighting becomes more elaborate, with chasing, pouncing, clasping with the front legs and vigorous kicking with the hind legs. And now the other main play-themes are added, each connected with a different kind of prey-hunting:

The Mouse-pounce: This involves hiding, crouching, creeping forward, and then rushing and pouncing on an imaginary rodent, usually its mother's twitching tail or a small object lying on the ground.

The Bird-swat: This includes the same approach, but then ends with an upward leap and a sharp blow with the front feet. The stimuli that trigger this action are usually moving objects that hang down from above, or toys that are thrown to the kittens by their owners.

The Fish-scoop: This occurs when the object lying on the ground is very static. The kitten suddenly flings out a paw and scoops the object up into the air and backwards over its shoulder. It then turns and pounces on it triumphantly, as if a fish scooped up from a river or stream has been landed on the bank and must be secured before it wriggles its way back to the safety of the water.

During these play bouts the kitten's imagination is put to full use. Anything small that moves easily may be accepted as a victim. The ideal toy is very light, so that only a little effort moves it a long way, and very soft, so that sharp feline claws and teeth can sink into it in a satisfying way. This means that the most exciting objects for play are also the simplest and cheapest. A piece of silver wrapping-paper rolled up into a tight ball, or the traditional ball of wool, provides the greatest reward.

All cats show the four basic patterns mentioned here, but in addition each pet feline may develop its own special games, which persist even after the animal has become adult. These games become almost like rituals as the cat grows older – little routines that reward it because they involve it in a social interaction with its owners or their guests.

For example, one young tom-cat developed the habit of jumping on the shoulders of dinner-guests and refusing to get down until it was given a morsel of food. The animal was not hungry – its reward was the shock impact of its actions. Another cat developed the game of running at newspapers its owner had placed on the tiled floor to keep the surface clean on wet days. Once on the papers, the cat braked and went into a long skid. It then returned and waited, time and again, for a chance to repeat the experience. Another cat learned to knock coins off a sideboard one at a time. Eventually its owner was able to train it to knock off a coin every time he clicked his fingers.

The more one talks to individual cat-owners, the greater the variety of cat personalities one finds. It is true that all cats share many features of their behaviour, down to the tiniest detail. But when it comes to playtime, each cat seems to have its own personal, idiosyncratic way of embellishing its playful interactions with its owners. If it is lucky, it will have owners who are of an equally playful frame of mind.

Such owners have existed for many centuries. Edward Topsel, writing in the 17th century, waxed lyrical about feline play: 'Therefore how she beggeth, playeth, leapeth, looketh, catcheth, tosseth with her foot, riseth up to strings held over her head, sometimes creeping, sometimes lying on her back, playing with one foot, sometimes on the belly, snatching now with the mouth, and anon with the foot . . . '

Michel de Montaigne, the great French essayist of the 16th century, commented: 'When I play with my cat who knows whether she diverts herself with me, or I with her. We entertain one another with mutual follies . . . and if I have my time to begin to refuse, she also has hers.' These

remarks reveal the irresistible appeal of the playful cat even in an epoch when felines were generally considered to be evil and dangerous, and were being widely persecuted.

Pluto

Fictional Cat. A tormented pet that features in the macabre tale *The Black Cat* (1843) by American author Edgar Allen Poe. At first loved and protected, the cat is later treated more and more cruelly, as its owner sinks into drunkenness and madness. When, being harshly grabbed, it responds by biting its owner's hand, he reacts by cutting out one of its eyes. Eventually he kills the unfortunate animal and is afterwards haunted by an avenging, demonic black cat who brings him to justice for the murder of his wife.

The title was used for a famous 1934 horror movie, starring Boris Karloff and Bela Lugosi, but little of Poe's original tale survived the Hollywood treatment.

Poetry

Cat Literature. There is a voluminous body of feline poetry, some incisive and illuminating and some quirky and amusing. Most, however, is unashamedly sentimental. Individual poems are to be found in the many anthologies of cat writings, but there are also a number of books devoted exclusively to feline poetry. They include the following:

1891. Brown, H. *Catoninetails. A Domestic Epic.* Lawrence and Bullen, London.
1892. Tomson, G. *Concerning Cats.* London.
1931. marquis, d. *archy and mehitabel.* Faber & Faber, London.
1939. Eliot, T.S. *Old Possum's Book of Practical Cats.* Faber & Faber, London.
1946. Gooden, M. (Editor) *The Poet's Cat.* Harrap, London.
1947. Pitter, R. *On Cats.* Cresset Press, London.
1949. Fyfe, H. *Poems in Praise of Cats.* Bannisdale, London.
1974. Carr, S. (Editor) *The Poetry of Cats.* Batsford, London. (Enlarged edition in 1980)
1984. Elson, D. *Cats! Cats!* Windmill Press, Kingswood, Surrey.
1986. Zakani, O. (Translated by Basil Bunting) *The Pious Cat.* Bertram Rota, London.
1987. Joseph, M. *A Book of Cats.* Ashford Press, Southampton.
1991. Anon. *101 Favourite Cat Poems.* Contemporary Books, USA.
1992. Aldiss, B. *Home Life with Cats.* Grafton, London.
1993. Dean, J. *Tabby Tales.* Kipper Press, Lancing, West Sussex.

The Poet's Cat, an engraving by Stephen Gooden from Mona Gooden's 1946 anthology of the same name.

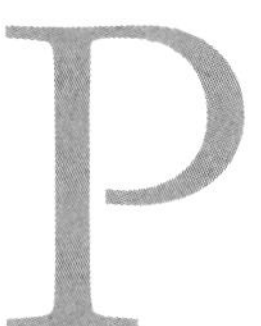

Poezenboot

Cat Sanctuary. De Poezenboot is the Dutch name for the famous 'Pussycat-boat' that is permanently moored alongside one of the canals in the centre of Amsterdam. It houses stray and unwanted cats which are then found new homes. It is open to the public from 1 pm to 3 pm every day. (Address: Singel T/O Nr 40, NL-1012 VL Amsterdam, Holland.) (See also Amsterdam Cats.)

The official emblem of the famous Dutch cat sanctuary, the 'Pussycat-boat', in the centre of Amsterdam.

Pointed Cats

Domestic Breeds. In the world of pedigree cats, the word 'points' carries two completely different meanings. 'Points' refer to the marks given for each part of a cat's anatomy (see Points of the Cat) and 'Points' also refer to the darkened extremities of certain coat patterns. When used in this second sense, the cats are usually referred to as the 'Colourpoint Breeds', but this is sometimes abbreviated to 'Pointed Breeds'. (For details see Colourpoint.)

Points of the Cat

Feline Anatomy. At cat shows each cat is assessed by its anatomical features. Points are awarded for each feature, according to a set scale. This scale varies from breed to breed.

There are some General Points which are the same in all cases. These include: body and tail = 10 points; head and neck = 10; ears = 10; legs and paws = 5; quality of coat = 10; condition = 5.

In addition, there are Special Points for colouring. Cats that are black, white or blue: coat = 25; eyes = 25. Cats that are cream: coat = 35; eyes = 15. Cats that are tortoiseshell, tortoiseshell and white, or tabby: coat = 50.

Pond, Grace

Cat Authority. Grace Pond (1910–) is the most prolific of all cat authors, with more than 20 cat books to her credit. She was the Organizer of the UK National Cat Club Show, the largest cat show in the world, for 40 years, from 1953 to 1993, and was responsible for introducing special classes for non-pedigree pet cats – a brave innovation for which she was strongly criticized. She has since been the President of many cat clubs, including the Governing Council of the Cat Fancy (GCCF). She was also famous as a breeder and as an International Show Judge. She gave up breeding in 1979, but continued to add to her long list of books about cats.

She was given her first cat – a Black Persian – when she was four years old and this began a lifelong involvement with long-haired cats, on which she became a world expert.

Bibliography:

1959. *The Observer's Book of Cats.* Warne, London.
1962. *Cats.* Arco, New York.
1964. *Persian Cats.* Foyles, London.
1966. *Cat Lovers' Diary.* Museum Press, London.
1966. *The Perfect Cat Owner.* Museum Press, London.
1968. *The Long-haired Cats.* Arco, London.
1969. *Complete Cat Guide.* Pet Library, London.
1969. *The Batsford Book of Cats.* Batsford, London.
1970. (with Elizabeth Towe) *Cats.* Cassell, London.
1972. (with Catherine Ing) *Champion Cats of the World.* Harrap, London.
1972. (with Alison Ashford) *Rex, Abyssinian and Turkish Cats.* Gifford, London.
1972. (Editor) *The Complete Cat Encyclopedia.* Heinemann, London.
1974. (Editor) *The Cat Lover's Bedside Book.* Batsford, London.
1974. (with Muriel Calder) *The Longhaired Cat.* Batsford, London.
1976. (with Angela Sayer) *Cats.* Bartholomew, Edinburgh.
1977. (with Angela Sayer) *The Intelligent Cat.* Davis-Poynter, London.
1979. (with Ivor Raleigh) *A Standard Guide to Cat Breeds.* Macmillan, London.

1980. *Pictorial Encyclopedia of Cats.* Rand McNally, New York.
1982. *The Cat. The Breeds, the Care and the Training.* Exeter Books, New York.
1983. *Longhaired Cats.* Batsford, London.
1985. (with Mary Dunnill) *Cat Shows and Successful Showing.* Blandford Press, Poole, Dorset.

Poodle Cat (1)

Domestic Breed. In the British popular press, the Cornish Rex Cat has sometimes been referred to as 'The Poodle Cat'.

Poodle Cat (2)

Domestic Breed. According to a 1994 report from Germany, a new type of Rex Cat has recently been developed by breeder Dr Rosemarie Wolf. Called the *Pudelkatzen,* or Poodle Cat, it was created by crossing Devon Rex with Scottish Fold to produce a breed with a lambswool coat and folded ears.

The new Poodle Cat, created by crossing a Devon Rex with a Scottish Fold to produce a wavy-coated feline with folded ears.

Popes

Feline History. The Vatican's attitude towards cats has varied from savage cat-hating to gentle cat-loving. Sadly, the overall balance has been against cats. Several Popes have issued instructions that led to the torture and slaughter of millions of innocent felines, whereas the few cat-loving Popes have only shown affection towards their own personal pets. Six Popes appear in the feline literature. They are:

Pope Gregory I (540–604): Reputed to be a cat-lover, but the true ailurophile may have been a hermit who identified himself with the Pope.

Pope Gregory IV (1147–1241): Issued a Papal Bull in 1233 declaring black cats diabolical, initiating centuries of cat hatred.

Pope Innocent VII (1336–1415): Demanded an increase in the persecution of cats, leading to millions of feline deaths.

Pope Innocent VIII (1432–1492): Issued a Papal Bull in 1484 insisting that witches and their cats should both be burned to death, causing widespread suffering.

Pope Leo XII (1760–1829): His beloved cat Micetto was born in the Vatican. He was raised by the Pope and was often seen nestling in his robes.

Pope Pious IX (1792–1878): His pet cat waited patiently while his master dined, after which the Pope himself would serve a special meal to the animal, at the Papal table. Despite this, he refused permission for the opening of an animal protection office in Rome on the grounds that 'man owed duties to his fellow men, but none to the lower animals'. His legacy, regarding animals, is summed up by the following passage from the *Catholic Dictionary* of 1897: 'They [animals] have no rights. The brutes are made for man, who has the same right over them which he has over plants and stones . . . it must also be lawful to put them to death, or to inflict pain upon them, for any good or reasonable end . . . or even for the purpose of recreation.'

Poppa

Pet Cat. According to *The Guinness Book of Records*, Poppa was the second-heaviest cat ever. An 11-year-old male tabby from Newport in Wales, belonging to a Gladys Cooper, he tipped the scales at 20.19 kg (44½ lb). The only cat to outweigh him was an Australian tabby called Himmy, who reached nearly 21.3 kg (47 lb).

Population

Feline Biology. It is impossible to give a precise figure for the total number of cats alive in the world today, but it is clear that domestic cats outnumber, many times over, the entire wild cat population. In 1995, cat authority Dr Peter Neville gave a rough figure of 400 million domestic cats, of which he estimated that 100 million are pet cats and 300 million are strays and feral animals. Attempts have been made to provide slightly more precise estimates for certain countries. Although it is difficult to verify their accuracy, the following figures have been published in recent years:

In 1987 the number of domestic cats in the U.S. was given as 56.2 million. It was said that, for the first time, they outnumbered domestic dogs (of which there were then only 51 million).

In 1995 the cat figure had risen to 62.4 million. It was reported that 25 per cent of American adults owned one or more cats. Of these, 78 per cent owned one cat, 17 per cent owned two cats, and 5 per cent owned more than two.

According to another recent report there are 7.5 million cats in Great Britain (1995). This is the highest figure ever recorded, there having been a steady increase, year by year:

British Cat Population

YEAR	NUMBER OF CATS	YEAR	NUMBER OF CATS	YEAR	NUMBER OF CATS
1885	350,000	1986	6.2 million	1991	6.9 million
1982	5.3 million	1987	6.5 million	1992	7.0 million
1983	5.4 million	1988	6.7 million	1993	7.1 million
1984	5.9 million	1989	6.9 million	1994	7.2 million
1985	6.1 million	1990	6.8 million	1995	7.5 million

In 1993, the cat population of Britain exceeded the dog population for the first time (dogs having dropped from a peak of 7.4 million in 1990 to 6.9 by 1993). The reason given for this change is that cats suit the new lifestyle of British families more than dogs. With so many couples both going out to work, an animal that is content to be left behind in the house is more suitable as a pet.

The 7.2 million cats of the 1994 survey are estimated to live in 4.6 million homes, showing that although cats may have to spend part of the day without the presence of their human owners, they do in many cases have another feline as a companion.

Additional facts concerning the feline population, gathered from various studies in North America, are as follows:

41% of the cat population is owned; 59% of the cat population is stray or feral.

Sex ratio of owned cats is 50/50 male/female; sex ratio of unowned cats is 65/35 male/female.

Average lifespan of owned cats is 7 years; average lifespan of unowned cats is 2-3 years.

42% of feral kittens die by the age of two months; 67% of feral kittens die by the age of one year.

1-3% of owned cats become strays each year.

97% of owned cats are non-pedigree animals; 3% of owned cats are pure-bred pedigree animals.

86-87% of owned adult cats have been neutered.

Postage Stamps

A recent postage stamp from Cuba depicting, appropriately, a Havana Brown.

Cat Art. Designs for postage stamps have frequently included cats of one kind or another and these have become the subject of thematic collections for many philatelists.

The first cat seen on a stamp was issued back in 1887 by the German State of Bergedorf. It depicts a cat with a fish in its mouth. The first modern cat stamp dates from 1930. Issued in Spain to commemorate Lindbergh's famous transatlantic flight, it shows Charles Lindbergh's black cat called Patsy. She accompanied him during the first leg of his epic journey, from San Diego to New York. Since then, 115 different countries have issued stamps showing domestic cats of one kind or another.

The first set of stamps devoted exclusively to cats was offered by Poland in 1964. Since then, special sets of feline stamps showing various breeds of cat have been issued by many other countries including the following: Albania, Bulgaria, Cuba, Equatorial Guinea, Fujeira (Trucial States), Great Britain, Guinea-Bissau, Guyana, Jersey, Kampuchea, Korea, Manama, Marshall Islands, Moçambique, Mongolia, Nicaragua, Oman, Romania, St. Vincent, Sharjah, Tanzania, the United States and Vietnam.

There is now a specialist organization devoted to this subject, the 'Cats on Stamps Study Unit' (Address: 1300 Crescent Drive, Elizabeth City, NC 27909, USA), which issues a publication called *Cat Mews*.

Bibliography:

1951. Way and Standen. *Zoology in Postage Stamps.*

1977. James, A. (Editor) *The Stanyon Book of Cats.* Random House, New York. (illustrated with cat stamps)

1980. Ladd, F & Ladd, N. *Illustrated Cat Stamp* Checklist.

1994. Schuessler, R. 'Cats on Stamps'. In: *Cat World Magazine,* February 1994. p.28-29.

Post Office Cats

Feline History. It is not generally known that there are official Post Office Cats, employed to protect letters and sacks of mail from the attacks of rats and mice. These government employees have existed in Britain for over 120 years and there has been a long, official correspondence concerning them, which has been delightfully gathered together by the author Russell Ash.

Because, in earlier days, it was a common practice to send food parcels through the mail, rodents quickly became a major hazard. It was dangerous to scatter rat poison around the letters and parcels that were going to end up in people's homes – often on their kitchen tables. Traps were also a risk, especially in confined areas where so much sorting and handling of material was going on. Cats were the only solution.

In the summer of 1868, a large number of money orders were eaten by mice and the Controller of the Money Order Office promptly put in a formal request for three cats to be officially appointed to prevent this from happening again. He asked for two shillings a week to cover this, but was beaten down to one shilling by the Secretary of the Post Office, who pointed out that the animals should not be overfed, or they would not catch their quota of mice. He added that if they failed in their duties, their allowance would be further reduced. This type of correspondence – nearly always quibbling over the feline rates of pay – continued for year after year, with the full weight of bureaucratic precision behind it. A century later, the weekly cost of a cat had risen to ten shillings. By the mid-1980s the figure had risen to £2 a week.

Generally, the feline task force appears to have proved a success and it is recorded that, at one time, a total of no fewer than 25,000 cats were employed in the Post Office Service throughout the country. Their minimum wage was always a problem, however, and the staff concerned frequently had to make their voices heard. One official complained that the collecting of the cats' food was a heavy burden to bear and that 'wear and tear of shoe leather in going to and fro will cost at least one-fourth of the proposed allowance' and that whatever may be left over will not 'compensate him for the loss of dignity in carrying the cats' food through the streets in Her Majesty's uniform'. Such are the hazards of working with government-appointed felines.

Bibliography:

1986. Ash, R. *Dear Cats. The Post Office Letters.* Pavilion Books, London.

Practical Cats

Fictional Cats. These are the cats invented by the poet T.S. Eliot in 1939 in his famous publication *Old Possum's Book of Practical Cats.* They include such well-known feline personalities as Macavity, Mungojerrie and Rumpelteazer, and the Rum Tum Tugger.

Presidential Cats

Pet Cats. A number of felines have graced the White House in Washington, as pets of various American Presidents or their families, including the following:

16th President, Abraham Lincoln (1809-1865): Tabby
19th President, Rutherford Hayes (1822-1893): Siam
26th President, Theodore Roosevelt (1858-1919): Slippers / Tom Quartz
29th President, Calvin Coolidge (1872-1933): Smokey / Tiger
35th President, John Kennedy (1917-1963): Tom Kitten
38th President, Gerald Ford (1913-): Shan
39th President, Jimmy Carter (1924-): Misty Malarky Ying Yang
40th President, Ronald Reagan (1911-): Several unnamed cats
42nd President, Bill Clinton (1946-): Socks

American Presidents, like most men who enjoy power, have, on balance, preferred dogs as pets, but there have been a few exceptions, as Ronald and Nancy Reagan demonstrate here.

Proverbs

Feline Sayings. There are many proverbs referring to cats. The following are the best-known ones. They are arranged in the order in which they were first recorded:

One day as a tiger is worth a thousand years as a sheep. (Ancient)
The cat knows whose lips she licks. (1023)
The cat would eat fish but would not wet her feet. (1225)
As the cat plays with a mouse. (1340)
He is like a cat; fling him which way you will, he'll light on his legs. (1398)
When the cat's away the mice will play. (1470)
Beware of cats that lick from the front and claw from behind. (15th century)
A cat has nine lives. (1546)
A cat may look at a king. (1546)
All cats are grey in the dark. (1546)
A cat in gloves catches no mice. (1573)

PROVERBS

Good liquor will make a cat speak. (1585)
Never was a cat drowned that could see the shore. (1594)
An old cat laps as much milk as a young. (1605)
A muzzled cat was never good mouser. (1605)
The scalded cat fears cold water. (1611)
The cat has kittened in your mouth. (1618)
A baited cat may grow as fierce as a lion. (1620)
As nimble as a blind cat in a barn. (1639)
An old cat sports not with her prey. (1640)
Like a cat on hot bricks. (1678)
The more you rub a cat on the rump, the higher she sets up her tail. (1678)
Cats eat what hussies spare. (1683)
To put the cat among the pigeons. (1706)
He that plays with cats, must expect to be scratched. (1710)
He who hunts with cats will only catch rats. (1712)
None but cats are allowed to quarrel in my house. (1732)
Cats hide their claws. (1732)
The cat invites the mouse to a feast. (1732)
To let the cat out of the bag. (1760)
Watch which way the cat jumps. (1825)
Enough to make a cat laugh. (1851)
The cat shuts its eyes while it steals cream. (1853)
There are more ways of killing a cat than choking her with cream. (1855)
The cat and dog may kiss, yet are none the better friends. (1855)
A cat's walk: a little way and back. (1869)
When the cat of the house is black, the lasses of lovers will have no lack. (1878)
As busy as a cat in a tripe shop. (1890)
Like a cat in a bonfire, don't know which way to turn. (1895)
The trouble with a kitten is that eventually it becomes a cat. (1940)

A 15TH CENTURY GERMAN WOODCUT illustrating the proverb, 'Beware of cats that lick from the front and claw from behind.'

PRUSSIAN REX CAT

DOMESTIC BREED. Discovered in East Prussia in the early 1930s but not developed. Little is known about the Prussian Rex except that, like other Rex Cats, it carried the wavy-hair gene. According to one report, it was the offspring of a Russian Blue/Angora cross, was owned by a Frau Schneider and was called Munk. It is the earliest recorded example of a Rex Cat, but does not appear to have been used in a systematic breeding programme, and soon vanished. (See also German Rex Cat.)

PUDLENKA

PET CAT. Karel Capek (1890–1938), the Czech playwright, felt himself to be magically infested with cats. On the very day his Angora tom-cat died of poison, an avenging female cat appeared on his doorstep. Its mission, he mused, was to 'revenge and replace a hundredfold the life of that tomcat'. Christened Pudlenka, she set about this task with a reproductive verve that staggered him, producing in a very short space of time no fewer than 26 kittens. One of her daughters, called Pudlenka II, continued with the 'plot', presenting Capek with 21 more kittens before she was killed by a dog. And then one of *her* daughters, named Pudlenka III, in turn continued what he called 'The Great Task' of creating a host of cats to seize power 'to rule over the universe'.

Bibliography:

1940. Capek, K. *I had a Cat and a Dog*. Allen & Unwin, London.

PULCINELLA

PET CAT. Pulcinella was the name of the cat belonging to the Italian composer Domenico Scarlatti (1685–1757). Pulcinella's special claim to fame rests with his habit of leaping up on to the keyboard of the composer's harpsichord and walking up and down on the keys. On one occasion this inspired Scarlatti to compose a fugue (Fugue in G Minor: L499) which became generally known as 'The Cat's Fugue'. Scarlatti recorded his comments on this co-operative effort, as follows:

'My cat . . . would walk on the keys, going up and down from one end to the other. Sometimes he would pause longer on one note listening closely until the vibration ceased. One evening, while dozing in my armchair, I was roused by the sound of the harpsichord. My cat had started his musical stroll, and he really was picking out a melodic phrase. I had a sheet of paper to hand, and transcribed his composition.'

PUMA

WILD FELINE. *(Felis concolor)* The Puma has attracted many different names, more possibly than any other cat in the world. Apart from the now generally accepted standard name of Puma, it has also been known as: (2) Cougar; (3) Panther; (4) Painter; (5) Mountain Lion; (6) American Lion; (7) Mexican Lion; (8) Catamount; (9) Deer Tiger; (10) Red Tiger, (11) Leon; (12) Leopardo; and by various Indian tribes as (13) Chim Blea; (14) Yutin; (15) Mitzli; (16) Pagi; (17) Mischipichin; (18) Ingronga; (19) Ingonga-Sinda; (20) Schunta-Haschla; and (21) Ig-mu-tank-a. The scientific name *concolor* refers to the fact that the animal's coat is all of one colour.

The Puma is the second largest of the New World cat species, exceeded only by the Jaguar. Unlike the Jaguar, however, it is not confined to tropical South and Central America, but occurs throughout the Americas, from Argentina to Canada. In North America, therefore, it is the biggest of all wild cats and has naturally attracted a great deal of attention, originally from hunters and more recently from conservationists.

Apart from the Lion, the Puma is the only large unspotted cat, and it is easy to see how it acquired the name of 'Mountain Lion'. Although its cubs are fully spotted, in the adult there is a highly characteristic coat of uniform, greyish fur. The long, lithe body has powerful legs, a small head with rounded ears, and a very long balancing tail. It is a powerful, muscular, athletic cat, built to cope with a variety of habitats.

Over its huge range it varies enormously in size. Up in the far north, the Canadian Pumas are massively built against the rigours of the cold climate and some are as big as Leopards. Down in the tropical regions of South America, it is a much smaller animal – less than half the weight of the Canadian specimens. If only these two extremes survived today, with all the intermediate forms having been exterminated (as they nearly have been) by man, we might reasonably look at these two and decide that they must belong to two different species, the Great Puma and the Lesser Puma. But we know, from those that have survived in the intermediate regions, that there is, in reality, a very gradual change from the big northern to the modest southern form. We can be certain, therefore, that this is a single, variable species.

A solitary, mostly nocturnal hunter, with a large territory, the Puma takes a wide variety of prey. The home range of each individual is so extensive, that after the animal has made a kill and moved on, it is unlikely to return to the same spot for some time, leaving it undisturbed until the next lethal visit. On average, the Puma makes about one large kill per week. It prefers to hunt small deer, but is also willing to attack peccary, beaver, opossum, raccoon, hare and even porcupine.

If a kill is too large to consume at one sitting, the Puma will drag it into cover and then conceal it by dragging sticks and leaves across it, using a front paw to scoop the surrounding litter over the carcass. During the course of evolution, the Puma appears to have borrowed this behaviour pattern from the action of faeces-burying, which is common in so many cat species.

Size: Length of Head + Body: 95–196 cm (37½–77 in). Tail: 53–78 cm (21–31 in). Weight: 36–103 kg (79½–227 lb).

Distribution: North, Central and South America.

Bibliography:

1946. Young, S.P. *The Puma: Mysterious American Cat.* Constable, London. (reissued in 1964 by Dover Books, New York.)

1967. Brock, S.E. Leemo: *A True Story of a Man's Friendship with a Mountain Lion.* Taplinger, New York.

1968. Brock, S.E. *More About Leemo. The Adventures of a Puma.* Taplinger, New York.

THE PUMA *(Felis concolor),* is the largest cat to be found in North America. The huge range of this highly successful species also extends down into Central and South America, where its size is exceeded only by the Jaguar.

P

The size of the Puma varies considerably. The South American examples are much smaller than those from the United States and this one, from the far north in Canada, is one of the biggest types found.

1976. Sitton, L. et al. *California Mountain Lion Study*. California Department of Fish and Game, Sacramento.
1978. Hancock, L. *Love Affair with a Cougar*. Doubeday, Toronto.
1983. Shaw, H. *Mountain Lion Field Guide*. DFG, Phoenix.
1989. Shaw, H. *Soul among Lions: the Cougar as Peaceful Adversary*. Johnson, Boulder.
1992. Hansen, K. *Cougar: The American Lion*. Northland, Flagstaff.

Purring

Feline Behaviour. There are two theories as to how a cat purrs:

The False Vocal Cord Theory: This sees purring originating in the cat's voice-box, or larynx. In addition to the ordinary vocal cords, the cat possesses a second pair of structures called vestibular folds, or false vocal cords. The presence of the second pair of cords is thought to be the secret behind the extraordinary purring mechanism that permits the animal to produce the soft, rumbling sound for minutes and even hours on end, without any effort and without opening its mouth. This theory regards purring as little more than noisy breathing of the type humans sometimes indulge in when they are asleep – in other words, snoring. With every inhalation and exhalation, air passes over the false vocal cords and makes the *rrrrrr* noise of the purr. To produce this characteristic sound, air has to be interrupted by the contraction of the laryngeal muscles about 30 times a second.

The Turbulent Blood Theory: This says that the cat's voice box has nothing whatever to do with purring. Instead, it is argued that when the cat's blood-flow through its main veins into the heart is increased, turbulence is created. This is greatest at the point where the main vein, carrying blood from the animal's body back into the heart, is constricted as it passes through the animal's chest. The swirling blood is thought to make the purring noise, the diaphragm acting as an amplifier of the vibrations. The noise thus created is thought to be passed up the animal's windpipe and into the sinus cavities of the skull, where it resonates to produce the purring sound. Some authorities believe that it is the arching of the back of the purring cat that

increases this blood turbulence to create the purring sound, while others see the increase as being more to do with emotional changes affecting the animal's blood flow.

Of the two, the false vocal cord theory seems to have more to commend it, but we still cannot be certain which is the true explanation.

There is also some confusion as to *why* a cat purrs. To most people, it simply means that a cat is contented, but there is more to it than that. Repeated observation has revealed that cats in great pain, injured, in labour and even dying often purr loud and long. These can hardly be called contented cats. A slightly different definition is needed.

Essentially a cat purrs as a sign of friendship – either when it is contented with a friend, or when it is in need of friendship – as with a cat in trouble. Purring first occurs when kittens are only a week old and its primary use is when they are being suckled by their mother. It acts then as a signal to her that all is well and that the milk supply is successfully reaching its destination. She can lie there, listening to the grateful purrs, and know without looking up that nothing has gone amiss. She in turn purrs to her kittens as they feed, telling them that she, too, is in a relaxed, co-operative mood. The use of purring among adult cats (and between adult cats and humans) is almost certainly secondary and is derived from this primal parent–offspring context. For further details, see the entry for Voice.

Looking at the wild species, there is a clear distinction between small cats and large ones. All small cats can purr, but the big cats, like the lion and the leopard, cannot. The tiger will greet you with a friendly 'one-way-purr' – a sort of juddering splutter done while exhaling – but it cannot produce the two-way purr of the domestic cat. In this respect, the small cats are one up on their giant relatives, but big cats can roar, which is something small cats can never do.

Puss (1)

Feline term. Colloquial name for a cat. Thought to be derived from the Egyptian word 'Pasht', but possibly taken from the Latin for a little boy *(Pusus)* or a little girl *(Pusa)*. The Rumanian name for the cat *(pisica)* may have a similar origin.

The French equivalent of Puss/Pussy is *minet/minette*.

Puss (2)

Pet Cat. According to *The Guinness Book of Records,* the claim for the longest-lived of all domestic cats was on behalf of a tabby cat called 'Puss' who died in 1939 at the amazing age of 36 years and a day. The case was not fully documented, however, and the official record has now been transferred to a female tabby called 'Ma', who is known to have survived for a fully authenticated 34 years.

Puss in Boots

Folk-tale. The story of *The Master Cat, or Puss In Boots,* in its present form, dates from the end of the 17th century. The French lawyer and author Charles Perrault (1628–1703), who was a leading member of the Académie Française, wrote a number of tales to amuse his children, including Little Red Riding Hood, Cinderella, Sleeping Beauty and Puss in Boots. These were half-forgotten, traditional folk-tales of uncertain origin that he retold in a simple and attractive form and published as *Histoires ou Contes du Temps Passé or Contes de ma mère l'Oie* in 1697. They first appeared in English in 1729.

Gustave Doré's version of *Puss in Boots,* with the ingenious feline striking an elegant pose in this French engraving of 1899.

There is a bronze statue of Perrault with Puss in Boots in the Tuileries gardens in Paris. The publication of the story, which depicts the cat, not as an evil creature, but as a clever animal, proved to be a major influence in changing and improving the cat's image in a Europe still bent on persecuting it as a witch's familiar and an embodiment of the devil.

The simple story tells of a young man who is so poor that his cat is his only possession. He decides he has no choice but to eat the cat and wear its skin. The cat, however, persuades the young man that all will be well if only he will have a pair of boots made for him and give him a small pouch to carry. This is done and the cat takes to the woods, where he snares a young

The 17th century folk-tale becomes a Victorian theatrical entertainment. *Puss in Boots* as an English pantomime in 1874.

rabbit. This he presents to the king from the 'Marquis of Carabus', a name he has invented for his master. After he has pleased the king by taking him a number of gifts, he arranges a meeting between his master and the king's beautiful daughter. They fall in love and the king is delighted to give the couple his blessing because he believes the young man to be such a generous nobleman. The pair live happily ever after and Puss in Boots retires from his task of mouse-catching and becomes a figure of great fame and importance.

This concept of a cat bringing his master good fortune undoubtedly influenced the development of the fanciful tale of Dick Whittington's Cat (see separate entry). Although Whittington was a real person, the story of his cat was a later fiction invented long after his death. Similar, early folk-tales of 'lucky cats' have been traced all over Europe, Africa, India, Indonesia and the West Indies.

A psychological analysis of the tale sees the cat as a symbol of man's native cunning – an intuitive cleverness that is used to gain success in life.

Pussy-cat

Fictional Cat. Edward Lear's nonsense cat in 'The Owl and the Pussy-cat', who 'danced to the light of the moon', inspired by the author's own much loved cat, 'Foss'.

Pussycat Princess

Cartoon Cat. In a comic strip created by Grace Drayton in 1935, Pussycat Princess was a kitten that ruled a domain called Tabbyland. The strip was soon taken over by Ruth Carroll, who continued with it until it finally ceased in 1947.

Pussy Willow

Folk-tale. There is an early Polish legend about the Pussy Willow that is found along riverbanks. It concerns a grey mother cat whose kittens were thrown into the river by a farmer who felt he already had enough cats to worry about. Their mother wept so loudly that the willows agreed to stretch themselves down into the water to rescue the drowning kittens. The kittens grabbed hold and were saved from a watery death. Ever since then, each spring, in memory of that event, the Pussy Willows grow soft grey furry buds which, to the touch, feel just like the fur of newborn kittens.

Pyewacket

Film Cat. In the 1959 film *Bell, Book and Candle* (originally a 1950 Broadway play by John van Druton), Pyewacket is the Siamese Cat familiar of a modern witch. The witch sets about seducing her neighbour by supernatural means. She does this by stroking Pyewacket while uttering magic spells. The cat playing the role won a Patsy Award, the animal equivalent of an Oscar, for his performance. His supporting cast included James Stewart, Kim Novak and Jack Lemmon.

Queen

Feline Term. A female cat. The term is used especially in the context of breeding. Breeders refer to their females as Queens and their males as Studs. In origin the word is said to be a debased form of the Saxon word 'Wheen', meaning the female sex. One of its earliest uses is in John Ray's writings in 1691, where the term Wheen-Cat is equated with Queen Cat.

The term has probably remained popular because it seems an appropriate title for a female who, when she is on heat, 'lords it over her males'. They must gather round her like a circle of courtiers, must approach her with great deference and are often punished by her in an autocratic manner.

Ra

Legendary Cat. In ancient Egypt the great Sun-God Ra took the form of a cat in his nightly battle with the monstrous serpent Apopis. Every night he won this battle and the sun rose again in the morning. Among Egyptologists, the preferred spelling is usually Re (see entry).

Rabbit Cat

Domestic Breed. A popular name given to the American domestic Bobtail Cat. Writing in 1940, zoologist Ida Mellen comments that the 'Bobtail Cat of the New England and Middle Atlantic States (called also the Rabbit Cat) traces its ancestry to the Manx Cat'. (For further details see American Bobtail Cat.)

At the turn of the century, the name of Rabbit Cat was sometimes given to what we now call the Abyssinian Cat. This was because the Abyssinian's ticked, pale brown fur is reminiscent of the coat of a wild rabbit. The existence of two completely different kinds of 'Rabbit Cat' can lead to confusion when reading some of the earlier cat books.

Racekatte

Domestic Breed. A long-haired Danish breed, almost identical with the Siberian Forest Cat. Its Swedish equivalent is the *Rugkatt*.

Ragamuffin Cat

Domestic Breed. A recent American breed, similar to the Ragdoll (see separate entry), but in a new range of colours.

Appearance: A luxuriant, long-haired breed, it is described as 'the new rag-type cat with the coat of many colours . . . [a] large cat with silky, plush non-matting fur and large, expressive oval eyes'.

The Ragamuffin Cat, an American breed developed in the 1990s, is in essence a Ragdoll Cat in unusual colours. It appears to signal a split between two groups of breeders, with one camp supporting Ragdolls and the other favouring Ragamuffins.

History: One of the newest of all breeds, the Ragamuffin was created in 1994. Pat Steckman describes how this came about: 'Ann Baker founded an organization, the International Ragdoll Cat Association, whose cats are not shown. In early 1994 a group of breeders from IRCA formed a new group and breed called the Ragamuffin, which has been accepted as an experimental breed by ACFA.' According to another source, the Ragamuffin is already recognized for competition by the United Feline Organization in America and can be registered with the American Cat Fanciers' Association, although not, as yet, shown with them.
Personality: Terms used to describe this breed include: docile, quiet, affectionate, intelligent, playful, placid and loving.
Colour Forms: On the subject of Ragamuffin colour, Judy Thomas, writing in 1996, comments: 'The conformation and pattern standards for the Ragamuffin are virtually identical to that of the Ragdoll, but Ragamuffins include many more colors. All varieties of pointed color, including Lynx Point, Tortie Point and Red Point, all the Mink and Sepia colors produced by the introduction of the Burmese gene and all the colors of the Persian Cats are accepted in Solid, Mitted and Parti-color varieties . . . Seal, Blue, Chocolate and Lilac Pointed, Mitted and Parti-color Ragamuffins are virtually indistinguishable from Ragdolls; the other colors resemble Ragdolls in conformation but differ in color.'
Breed Clubs:
Ragmuffin Associated Group. Describes itself as 'the parent club of the Ragamuffin'. Address: 5759 Cypress Cir., Tallahassee, FL 32303, USA.
Ragamuffin Fanciers Association. Address: RR 1, Box 185, LeRoy, IL 61752, USA.

Ragdoll Cat

Domestic Breed. A controversial new American breed that acquired its name because, when held, it goes limp and becomes completely relaxed and floppy, like a feline ragdoll.
Appearance: A large, long-haired cat similar to a Birman except for certain details of its colouring and its heavier body.

Legendary History: This cat is unique in that it is a recent breed with a legendary history. All other breeds that can boast a legendary beginning are ones which have an ancient origin 'lost in the mists of time', to quote a well-worn phrase. The Ragdoll myth can only be traced back to the early 1960s, when a pregnant white Persian-style cat called Josephine, belonging to Californian Ann Baker, was involved in a road accident. She broke her pelvis when struck by a car, and it was claimed that this injury resulted in her subsequent offspring being abnormally limp and having no reaction to physical pain. Genetically this was nonsensical, but the story was retold endlessly and was believed by the gullible. Ann Baker reinforced the myth when she tossed one of her Ragdolls across the room for television cameras. As a result, the breed became notorious overnight, and many cat organizations rejected it on the grounds that it was vulnerable to abuse. If the kittens showed no response to being hurt, they were clearly at risk. The legend – which appealed to the romantic and created a wide interest in the breed – also worked against it in the world of serious pedigree breeding.

Factual History: As far as can be ascertained, this breed resulted from a 1960s mating between the white 'Persian' female Josephine and a male Birman. There is a certain vagueness about this, however. Some authorities think that the female may have been more of an Angora than a Persian, and that a sable Burmese was also involved somewhere in the early stages of the making of the Ragdoll.

According to Ann Baker, two of Josephine's sons, called Blackie and Daddy Warbucks, which were sired by different males, are to be considered as the 'founding fathers' of the Ragdoll breed. The mitted Daddy Warbucks (the epitome of the Ragdoll breed) was mated with one of Blackie's daughters to produce the kittens that were to become the first 'official' Ragdolls, called Tiki and Kyoto.

The female Josephine may well have been involved in a road accident, but that event would have had no effect whatever on the genetic constitution of her offspring. The fact that they and subsequent generations were all remarkably relaxed when being handled can only be due to what might be called an intensifying of the 'docility factor' already present in the foundation stock. Both Persian and Birman breeds are well known for their gentleness and, by bringing

The Ragdoll Cat, a controversial American breed developed in the 1960s. Essentially a mixture of Birman and Persian, it is famous for its extreme docility, which some critics fear may lead to its being treated as a 'living toy'.

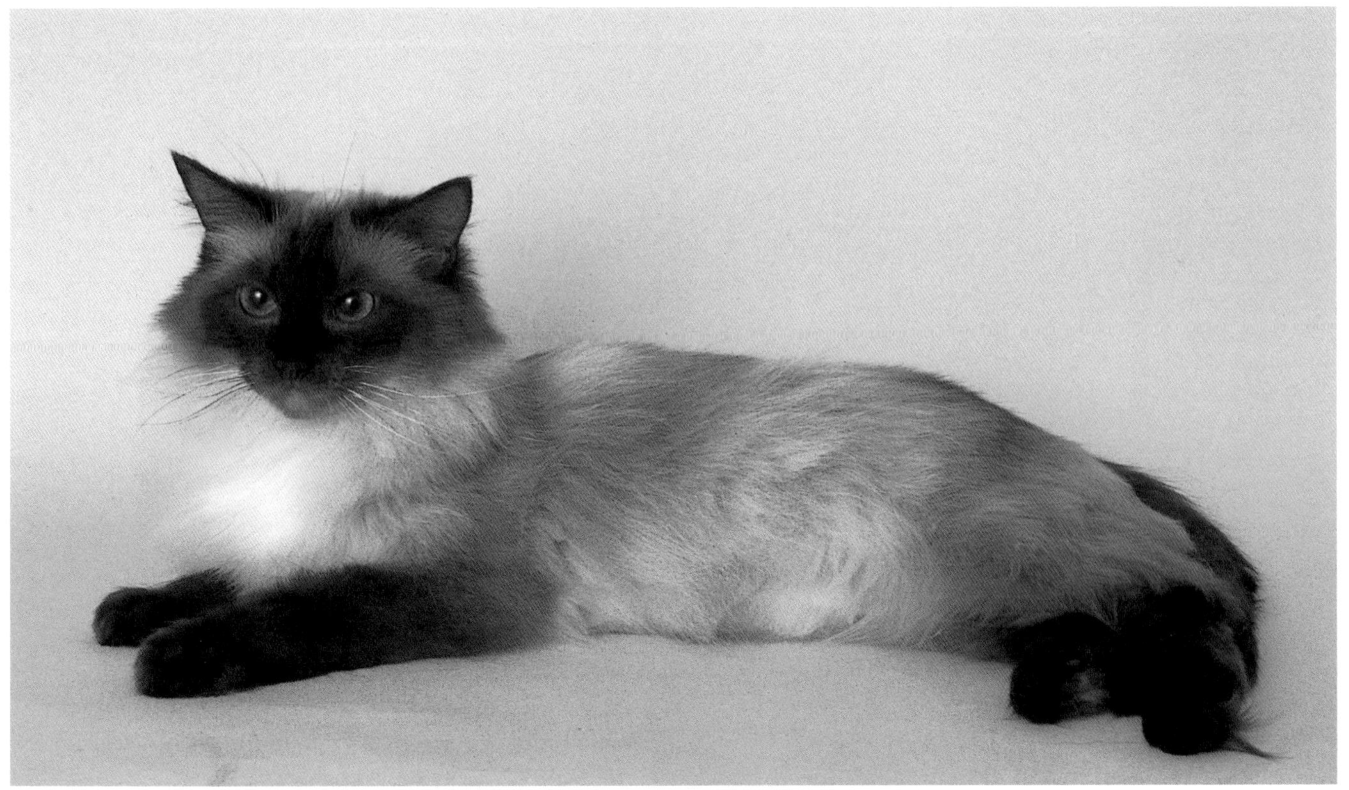

these two breeds together, Ann Baker, the originator of the Ragdoll, accidentally created an abnormally mild-mannered cat.

There is, however, a great difference between a cat that is tolerant of manhandling and one that is unable to experience pain. In reality the Ragdoll is an attractive breed that is genetically sound and ideal for urban, indoor living. It is excessively good-natured and makes an ideal and undemanding companion. As soon as this was realized, its popularity soared and it was gradually accepted by more and more cat societies.

Californian cat breeders Denny Dayton and his wife were responsible for developing the breed and worked hard to acquire championship status for it, which they eventually succeeded in doing. In 1981, the Norwich cat breeder Lulu Rowley purchased four Ragdolls (called Prim, Proper, Lad and Lass) from the Dayton cattery and introduced the new breed to Britain, where its numbers have since increased rapidly. By the winter of 1995 there were an estimated 3,000 Ragdolls in the country.

In the 1990s, three variant breeds have been developed from the Ragdoll Cat: the Cherubim, the Honeybear and the Ragamuffin. The Ragamuffin is already making headway (see entry), but it remains to be seen whether the other two will eventually also gain official recognition.

Personality: This is the most docile of all cat breeds. Whatever its true genetic history may prove to be, it cannot be denied that the Ragdoll is the most relaxed, mild-mannered cat in the world. To its supporters this is extolled as a virtue of the breed, but to critics it is seen as the creation of a 'living soft toy', a 'cushion cat', the 'denigration of the spirit of the cat'.

It has been reported that Ann Baker does not consider the British Ragdolls to be true Ragdolls, because they are not sufficiently 'floppy'. According to her, the 'flop-factor', which was strong in her original stock, has been diluted in the British-bred animals. (Some authorities have voiced their opinion that this is an advantage rather than a shortcoming.)

Colour Forms:

GCCF: There are three basic pattern-types: Colourpoint, Mitted and Bi-colour, and four colours: Seal; Blue; Chocolate; Lilac. The three pattern types have been defined as follows: (1) Colourpoint: dark points on mask, ears, tail, legs, feet; (2) Mitted: dark points on mask, ears, tail, legs; feet are white; (3) Bi-colour: dark points on mask, ears, tail; legs and feet are white.

Bibliography:

1995. Wallace, L. et al. *The Definitive Guide to Ragdolls.* Available from: Ragdoll World UK, 60 Knottingley Road, Pontefract, West Yorkshire, WF8 2LD, England.

Breed Clubs:

British Ragdoll Cat Club. Address: 1 Glyn Way, Threemilestone, Truro, Cornwall, TR3 6DT, England.

International Ragdoll Cat Association (IRCA). Established by Ann Baker, with strict rules about the future breeding of the Ragdoll Cat.

National Ragdoll Cat Association. Address: 9 Tadmarton, Downhead Park, Milton Keynes, Bucks, MK15 9BE, England.

Progressive Ragdoll Breed Cat Club. Formed in 1993. Address: 85a Burrows Road, Kensal Green, London, NW10 5SJ, England.

Ragdoll Club. Formed in 1992; publishes a quarterly magazine, *The Ragbag.* Address: 38 Faraday Road, Beechdale Estate, Walsall, West Midlands, WS2 7ER, England.

Ragdoll Fanciers Club. Address: 7320 Normandy Drive N.E., Cedar Rapids, IA 52402, USA, or 15700 Riley Street, Holland, MI 49424, USA.

Note: There is also a breed publication called *Rag Sheet.* Address: 18977 48th Avenue, North Loxahatchee, FL 33470, USA.

Raining Cats and Dogs

Feline Saying. This phrase became popular several centuries ago at a time when the streets of towns and cities were narrow and filthy and had poor drainage. Unusually heavy storms produced torrential flooding which drowned large numbers of the half-starved cats and dogs

The Ragdoll Cat *(opposite).* The example on the previous page was a Colourpoint Ragdoll, while this one is a Bi-colour. Intermediate between these two types is the Mitted.

that foraged there. After a downpour was over, people would emerge from their houses to find the corpses of these unfortunate animals, and the more gullible among them believed that the bodies must have fallen from the sky – and that it had literally been raining cats and dogs.

A description of the impact of a severe city storm, written by Jonathan Swift in 1710, supports this view: 'Now from all parts the swelling kennels flow, and bear their trophies with them as they go . . . drowned puppies, stinking sprats, all drenched in mud, dead cats, and turnip tops, come tumbling down the flood.'

Some classicists prefer an ancient explanation, suggesting that the phrase is derived from the Greek word for a waterfall: *catadupa*. If rain fell in torrents – like a waterfall – then the saying 'raining catadupa' could gradually have become converted into 'raining cats and dogs'.

Ram-cat

Feline Term. An early name for a male cat. An alternative name was 'boar-cat', but both were replaced by 'tom-cat' in the 18th century.

Raminagrobis

Fictional Cat. In La Fontaine's 17th-century fables, this fat, reclusive cat appears in several tales, always allowing simple, predatory greed to overcome the finer points of philosophy. When two animals ask him to settle a dispute for them, he solves their problem by eating them both. When asked by a young mouse to wait until it is a bigger and therefore better meal, he declines the offer. When a mouse asks some rats to save him, Raminagrobis already has the small rodent halfway down his throat by the time the rats' protest group has arrived. La Fontaine (1621–1695) borrowed the name of his cat from the earlier works of Francis Rabelais, where Raminagrobis was 'a Man that is both Old and a Poet', who is approached for a wise judgement.

Raton

Fictional Cat. Another of La Fontaine's cats, this one appears in the famous cautionary tale of the monkey and the cat. The monkey flatters the cat into pulling hot chestnuts out of the fire with its paw. As it is doing so, the monkey quickly eats them. The animals are then disturbed and have to flee, leaving the cat pondering the value of flattery.

Re

Legendary Cat. In ancient Egypt, during the New Kingdom (1567–1085 BC), the great Sun-God Re took the form of a cat every night to do battle with the powers of darkness in the shape of a gigantic serpent, called Apopis. Every night Apopis would lie in wait for Re, hoping to attack and kill him and thus prevent the sun from rising. And every night, the great cat Re had to defeat the snake. He managed this every time, and the sun rose again, but on very rare occasions he suffered a serious temporary defeat, causing an eclipse.

The battle between the cat and the snake is depicted a number of times in the art of ancient Egypt, and for 500 years follows essentially the same pattern. The cat Re is shown squatting on his haunches, holding a sharp, pointed knife with a curiously tapered blade in one of its front paws. With this weapon he is seen in the act of decapitating the fiendish serpent of darkness. The body of the serpent is always shown thrown up into vertical coils, as if writhing from the savage attack. Despite these nightly decapitations, Apopis somehow manages to keep his head for the next assault, and the confrontation goes on, night after night, for eternity.

The cat itself is shown either as a mackerel-striped tabby, or as a spotted cat, or as a dark, plain cat with a white ruff, face and paws. This last variant suggests that the model in that instance was a Jungle Cat *(Felis chaus),* rather than the usual domestic cat. (See also Ra.)

Reading Brown Cat

Domestic Breed. An alternative title for the Havana, derived from the fact that the breed was first developed in England at Reading in Berkshire. The name was abandoned at an early stage.

RED

COAT COLOUR. Red is the cat breeder's name for the colour that geneticists call orange. All the various 'red-tone' colours, such as yellow, marmalade, orange and red, are controlled by a single sex-linked gene, designated 'O' (for orange). The effect of this gene is to convert all black pigment to orange. This means that it converts an ordinary tabby pattern into orange tabby. In earlier days this always gave rise to the familiar 'ginger cat', but years of pedigree selective breeding have improved on the colour quality of that animal, creating a deeper, more luxurious red. This is done in several ways. First, there are 'rufous polygenes' that can be added genetically to strengthen the coat's redness. Second, the tabby contrast-markings can be minimized by careful breeding programmes. Third, the blotched (or classic) tabby patches can be selectively bred in such a way that they spread and congeal into extensive red zones. The combined effect of these changes is to produce an evenly spread, 'de-tabbied', intensified red that now graces some of the most appealing of all modern pedigree cats.

The following variant forms of red have been listed by pedigree breeders: (1) Red Chinchilla (= Shell Cameo); (2) Red Shaded (= Shaded Cameo); (3) Red Silver; (4) Red Smoke Cameo (= Cameo); (5) Red Tabby; (6) Red Tabby and White; (7) Red (Flame) Lynx Point; (8) Van Red and White; (9) Black, Red and Blue (= Tricolour).

RED LYNX

WILD FELINE. An early name, now obsolete, that was confusingly used for both the American Bobcat *(Lynx rufa)* and the African Caracal *(Felis caracal)*. Each acquired the title because of the reddish tinge of its coat.

RED TIGER

MYSTERY CAT. White Tigers are no longer a mystery. These pallid mutants exist and have been exhibited and bred in a number of zoos. But there was also a report in 1936 of a plain Red Tiger – one with the usual background colour but no stripes. This uniformly reddish-brown animal was said to inhabit a region of open sandy tracts, where it was thought that its plain colour would act as better camouflage. Its existence, however, has never been scientifically verified.

REED CAT

WILD FELINE. An alternative name for the Jungle Cat *(Felis chaus)*. It has been called the Reed Cat, or Reit-Kat, in certain regions because one of its favourite habitats is the reed bed zone near river systems. (For details see Jungle Cat.)

REFRIGERATOR CATS

WORKING CATS. Refrigerator Cat is the name that was given to a special breed of felines developed in Pittsburgh in the late 19th century to control the rodent pests in large commercial refrigeration plants. Arguing that some species of wild cats, such as the Canadian Lynx, live in the frozen north, it was felt that a breed of domestic cat could be developed that would be able to survive at very low temperatures. This was deemed necessary because a race of rats had managed to do just this and were causing havoc with the stored food. The experiment was successful, American authorities reporting: 'This hardy race of Eskimo cats cannot stand the daylight nor normal temperature, but due to the cold have acquired heavily furred coats, thick tails like Persians, and tufted ears, with altogether a northern and lynxlike appearance.' They even managed to breed in the icy conditions and the offspring were then supplied to other cold-storage warehouses.

REPELLENTS

FELINE BEHAVIOUR. There are times when both cat-lovers and cat-haters alike would prefer to keep the animals away from certain objects or areas. Cats damage soft furnishings and can sometimes be a nuisance in gardens. House-proud owners and meticulous gardeners often wish

to find some kind of repellent that will drive cats away. This is not a new problem. Searching back through the long history of feline deterrents, there appear to have been only three smelly substances that achieved a measure of success.

The first of these is the oil of the crushed leaves of a small aromatic plant called 'rue'. As long ago as the first century AD, the Roman author Pliny, in his monumental Natural History, suggested that placing branches of this shrub around an object would keep the cats away from it. This advice was still being offered 1,200 years later, in the Middle Ages, when an expert on herb gardens wrote, 'Behind the turf plot let there be a great diversity of medicinal and aromatic herbs, among which Rue should be mingled in many places for its beauty and its greenness, and its bitterness will drive poisonous animals away from the garden.' Some modern gardeners report that handling the leaves of this plant can cause a blistering rash on sensitive skin, so it must obviously be treated with respect, but there is a good chance that oil of rue would prove to be a successful repellent for most misbehaving cats. For some reason this ancient piece of folk-wisdom seems to have been largely forgotten, but it is worth reviving in cases where ordinary measures have failed. Modern tests have shown that the broken leaves of this plant, offered to a curious cat, will cause it to jump backwards and then attempt to vomit.

A second and perhaps easier suggestion is the use of onions. By rubbing a raw onion over the area to be protected, a cat can usually be deterred, and the smell, although unpleasant for humans at first, soon goes unnoticed. Most cats, however, continue to find it distasteful long after the human occupants of the rooms have forgotten about it.

The most effective deterrent, however, is that simple household substance, vinegar. Cats loathe it. The acid fragrance upsets their delicate nasal passages and they avoid anything smeared with it for long periods of time. Short of buying special, commercially prepared cat-repellent sprays from a local pet shop, it is the best weapon available.

It must be added, though, that cats are stubborn animals and often consider such chemical warfare as a kind of challenge. Their first reaction will be to shift the location of their activities. If this fails, after a while they may manage to overcome their distaste for a particular substance and then it is necessary to change one's tactics. Ultimately, the best solution is to try to defeat the cat's damaging ways by using understanding and intelligence rather than foul-smelling chemicals. If the behaviour behind the unwanted feline activity can be analysed, it may be possible to find a psychological solution which, in the long run, will always be more successful.

Repplier, Agnes

Cat Owner. The American essayist Agnes Repplier (1855–1945), author of a total of 26 books on a wide variety of subjects, was one of the first writers to publish a serious historical study of the domestic cat – *The Fireside Sphinx* (1901). It was her ninth book, and the one she enjoyed the most: 'I adore it – quite impersonally – and don't dare pick it up, lest I waste my time rereading it. That comes of doing – once in a lifetime – something one wants to do.' The book is dedicated to her cat Agrippina who, after presenting her with many offspring, eventually died in kitten-birth. Miss Repplier, a lifelong spinster, commented: 'I preached virginity to Agrippina until I was blue in the face. But she'd howl, so I'd kiss her and put her out in the alley!' There, she was able to meet her lover, an old black tom-cat of uncertain ownership.

Agnes Repplier had a strong dislike of neutered toms and recalled the days when, as a convent school girl, she had misheard 'altered cats' as 'altar cats' and assumed they must have some mysterious, sacred role. In amused tones she openly envied Agrippina's beauty and sex appeal, observing that she herself was unlucky in love because she had 'nothing but brains'. She also owned cats by the names of Banquo, Banshee, Nero and Carl, but it was Agrippina who was special to her and whose friendly ghost continued to sit on her desk as she wrote.

Bibliography:

1901. Repplier, A. *The Fireside Sphinx*. Gay & Bird, London.

1949. Stokes, G.S. *Agnes Repplier. Lady of Letters*. University of Pennsylvania Press, Philadelphia. (Reprinted by Greenwood Press, Westport, Connecticut in 1970)

The Missouri Rex, the latest in a long line of curly-coated mutants. There are now records of at least 17 different Rex Cat lines. Some have been taken seriously and developed as new breeds. Others have vanished in a single generation.

Rex Cats

Domestic Breeds. Rex cats have been reported from many places at different times, but in most cases the individual animals with the sparse, wavy 'Rex coat' have not been used for breeding and their genetic properties have died with them. In several cases, however, they have been developed systematically to start new 'pure-breeds'. The following are cases that have been specifically recorded. (See also separate entries.)

1930/1931. Prussian Rex Cat: Discovered in East Prussia, but not developed.
1930s. Karakul Cat: Recorded in America, but not developed.
1946. German Rex Cat: Discovered in the ruins of East Berlin after World War II. Used in successful crosses with the Cornish Rex, but apparently no longer preserved as a distinct breed.
1950. Italian Rex Cat: Not developed as a breed. Vanished in one generation.
1950. Cornish Rex Cat: Discovered in a litter of farm cats in Cornwall and carefully in-bred to develop the breed. Remains a popular Rex breed today.
1953. Ohio Rex Cat: Born in an otherwise normal litter, but not developed as a breed.
1959. Oregon Rex Cat: An American strain which seems to have been overshadowed by the popular Cornish Rex.
1959. California Rex Cat. Found in an animal shelter. Because of its longer, wavy coat it was called a 'Marcel Cat'.

1960. Devon Rex Cat: Discovered in Devon and developed into a popular breed. Although geographically close to the Cornish Rex, the Devon Rex depends on a different gene for its curly coat.

1972. Victoria Rex Cat: Cat carrying curly-coated Rex gene found in Victoria, London, the offspring of feral cats in that district.

1985. Dutch Rex Cat: A recent addition to the Rex breeds, the Dutch version has a coarser wavy coat, with a more bristly texture.

1987. Selkirk Rex Cat: Another American Rex strain, this one was discovered in Wyoming. Its curly coat is thicker than typical rex breeds.

1988. Rexed Maine Coon Cat: Rare cases of Maine Coon Cats with wavy, Rex hair have recently been reported by British breeders.

1991. Urals Rex Cat: Discovered in Russia.

1990s. Longhair Rex: Eastern European breeders are reported to have crossed Rex Cats with Persians to create a long-haired Rex.

1990s. Poodle Cat: A new breed of Rex Cat with folded ears, created by crossing Devon Rex with Scottish Fold.

1990s. Missouri Rex: The latest Rex discovery from the United States..

History: The genes for the sparse, short, curly hair of all the Rex breeds are recessives that seem to crop up as random mutations in different parts of the world. If left alone, they soon vanish, but if carefully inbred to intensify them, can be used to start a new form of pedigree cat. Most of the 'founding felines' of the various Rex breeds have been local strays or farm cats, spotted by enthusiasts, rescued and employed as foundation breeding stock. At least two genes appear to be involved: Gene 1. Rex. No. 33 (the Cornish and German); Gene 2. Rex. No. 33A (the Devon only).

The new Selkirk Rex appears to be a third, and the Rex gene observed in Maine Coons may also be a different one.

Unusual Features: The wavy fur of these cats, lacking the usual guard hairs (which make up the topcoat) of other breeds, gives them a strange, unsleek appearance which is exaggerated by their slender, leggy bodies. The tight curling of their coats has given them the popular name of 'Poodle Cats'. In the world of show cats, the Rex breeds have caused heated arguments and divided experts into two rival groups. The pro-Rex faction sing the praises of Rex Cats because of their delightful personalities. They remain more affectionate, playful and inquisitive than other cats, the adults behaving more like kittens. The anti-Rex faction claim that the wavy coats are 'imperfect' and that they give the animals a diseased look even when they are healthy. They also feel that the thinness of the coats of most Rex breeds makes the cats look unduly angular, awkward and lacking in typical feline grace. Despite these criticisms, some of the Rex breeds, at least, appear to have a strong enough following to ensure their future in the realm of pedigree cats and cat shows.

Breed Clubs:

Rex Society International. Formed in 1962 to promote the breeds.

Rex Breeders United. Formed in 1969 and affiliated to the American CFA, it publishes a quarterly magazine, *The Forum*. Address: 446 Itasca Court N.W., Rochester, MN 55901, USA.

Rex Cat Association. Formed in 1989. Address: 37 Leycroft Gardens, Slade Green, Kent, DA8 2PA, England.

Rex Cat Club. Formed in 1964. Address: Darby House, Sunbury-on-Thames, Middlesex, TW16 5PJ, England.

Rexed Maine Coon Cat

Domestic Breed. A wavy-haired mutation of the long-haired Maine Coon Cat. Also known as the Maine Wave.

THE REXED MAINE COON CAT, or 'Maine Wave'. It is reported that the Rex gene occurs in about one in every 200 Maine Coon births. Some breeders reject Rexed kittens, but others are encouraging them.

The Rex gene was first reported in the Maine Coon by British breeder Di Everett. In 1994 she commented: 'The first Rexed Maine Coon in Britain was born, as far as we know, in our household in 1988 . . . We have produced a total of four rexed kittens, from three different mothers, all mated to the same male.' Tests proved that the mutation concerned was neither the Devon Rex gene nor the American Wirehair gene, and there were some indications that the Cornish Rex gene was probably not involved either.

She investigated the occurrence of the Maine Coon Rex gene and found that 'out of some 4,000 registrations in Britain, we only have approximately 20 rexed kittens.' Because some of the rexed animals died young she feared that it might be a semi-lethal gene in this breed, but other Maine Coon breeders disagreed, pointing out that their own rexed animals were 'bounding with health', and suggesting that the early deaths were probably not related to the special hair condition.

Some Maine Coon breeders see the Rex gene as a problem to be eliminated, while others consider it to be an intriguing new variant. Breeder David Brinicombe reported positive reactions: 'I exhibited my three recently (billed as 'Maine Waves' or just 'Waves') and received an overwhelmingly positive reaction to them with very few adverse comments. I have just heard there is interest being shown in them from Italy, so this may not be the end of the story.'

RHUBARB

FICTIONAL CAT. In the 1946 satire *Rhubarb,* by American author H. Allen Smith, a cat of this name inherited a fortune including a New York baseball team. In 1951 Paramount turned the novel into a feature film, with a professional acting cat called Orangey playing the title role. Orangey made a good Rhubarb, but was a difficult and temperamental star. His co-star was the seasoned actor Ray Milland, to whom the animal took an instant dislike. Milland had to suffer the indignity of being smeared with meat paste and catnip to keep the cantankerous feline close enough to complete the filming. Orangey won a Patsy (the animal equivalent of an Oscar) for his part in the film. Despite his gallant efforts and extreme tolerance, Mr Milland won nothing.

Richelieu, Cardinal

Cat Owner. Known as 'the King of the King', because of his powerful influence over his monarch Louis XIII, the French statesman Cardinal Richelieu (1585–1642) was devoted to his many pet cats. They lived in a special room of their own next to his bedroom and were often allowed to sleep on his bed. He was, however, guilty of a strange double standard. Despite his passionate love for his own cats, he was an enthusiastic persecutor of witches and their feline familiars.

When he was dying he still owned 14 cats and made generous provision for them in his will, arranging pensions both for them and for their two attendants. We not only know the names of these cats, but also something about them as individuals.

There was *Mounard le Fougueux,* quarrelsome, capricious and worldly; *Soumise,* his favourite, a soft, gentle cat that often slept on his lap; *Gazette,* an indiscreet little cat; *Ludovic le Cruel,* a savage rat-killer; *Mimi-Paillon,* an Angora; *Felimare,* who was striped like a tiger; *Lucifer,* black as jet; *Ludoviska,* a Polish cat; *Rubis sur l'Ongle,* who drank her milk to the last drop; *Serpolet,* who loved to sun himself in the window; *Pyrame* and *Thisbe,* so-named because they slept entwined in one another's paws; and finally *Racan* and *Perruque,* who were named after a bizarre incident at court. (This incident involved an absent-minded academic called Racan. His own cat had given birth in his discarded wig, which made an excellent nest for her newborn kittens. Racan put the wig on without noticing them and set off to see Richelieu. After talking for a while, he complained about palpitations in his head, scratched his wig and the kittens fell out at Richelieu's feet. The great statesman was so amused that he insisted on keeping them and christened them Racan and Perruque, which is French for wig.)

When the Cardinal died, his wishes concerning the future of these much loved cats were brutally ignored. As soon as he was in his grave, the soldiers of his Swiss Guard slaughtered the animals, burning them to death just as he had caused so many witches' cats to be put to the torch during his lifetime.

Rimau-dahan

Wild Feline. The Malay name for the Clouded Leopard *(Neofelis nebulosa),* meaning literally 'Tiger of Tree-fork', or 'Tree-Tiger'. In the earliest works to mention this wild species, it was usually referred to by its Malay name but by the end of the 19th century this had been superseded by its English title. (For details see Clouded Leopard.)

Rodent-scarers

Feline History. In Europe as late as the 18th century, cats were regularly being placed inside the walls of new houses as a way of supposedly protecting the buildings against invasions by rats and mice. It is unlikely that these unfortunate cats were deliberately walled up alive in hollow cavities, to achieve this form of symbolic pest-control. Recent studies suggest that this was not the case, and that they were dead before being immured in this way.

Several examples of these early rodent-scarers, or 'vermin-scares', have come to light where it is clear that a cat was 'prepared' before being sealed up. The cats in question were carefully posed, often with a rat or a mouse placed in the mouth. Sometimes a bird was used in the role of prey. These manufactured cat-catching-rodent tableaux were probably sold to new house-owners as magic cures for rodent infestation, and carefully placed in a wall cavity before the house was occupied. In some cases they were placed under floorboards or doorsteps.

Examples of these rodent-scarers have been found in the London areas of both Bloomsbury and Southwark, and also in the Tower of London during renovations there in 1950 in an area untouched for 200 years. They have also been unearthed at a cottage in Essex, where a cat and her kittens were found plastered into a wall; in a medieval building at King's Lynn in Norfolk; in Cambridge, during building work on an old wall in 1811; in Dublin, where one was found hidden behind the organ in Christchurch Cathedral; in France, at an old charnel house in Rouen; and in Switzerland in the walls of a house at Rans, in the canton of Saint-Gall. In addition there

is an example from Gibraltar, put in place by Spanish masons. And in Sweden one was found under an entrance door in a house constructed as recently as 1920.

The strangest case concerns a 300-year-old mummified cat found hidden in an old house in Sudbury in Suffolk. When this building was being converted into a hotel in the early 1980s, the cat was removed, but there then followed a series of disasters including two fires and a structural collapse at the very spot where the cat had been walled up. In the face of this ill-fortune, ancient superstition once again reared its head and the owners had a special, glass-topped casket made for the cat, which they reburied near its original resting place. In its casket sunk into the floor of the hotel lounge, and visible to any visitor who wishes to inspect it, the cat once again protects its ancient site. At the reopening of the establishment, now called the Mill Hotel, a priest was called in to perform a special blessing ceremony, and since then there has been no further mishap.

Rodilard

Fictional Cat. In two of La Fontaine's 17th-century fables, the cunning, predatory cat Rodilard is doing battle with a colony of mice. In one tale, they take council and decide that the only solution is to put a bell around his neck, so that they can hear when he is approaching. The only problem is, which one of them is going to 'bell the cat'? In the other tale, Rodilard plays dead to catch the mice and then camouflages himself with flour. Both his stratagems are successful. The name of La Fontaine's cat was borrowed from the even earlier writings of Rabelais (see entry for Rodilardus).

One of the cunning stratagems of the wily predatory cat, Rodilard *(above)*, as he does battle with an infestation of mice.

Rodilardus

Fictional Cat. In the remarkable writings of Mr Francis Rabelais (1494–1553), there appears a large, furry cat called Rodilardus (the name being a Latin rendering of 'I gnaw bacon'). In the chapter entitled 'How Panurge beray'd himself for Fear, and of the huge Cat Rodilardus, which he took for a puny devil' Rabelais describes how, when the guns of the vessel in which Panurge is sailing are fired in salute, he is below decks. Both he and the cat appear to have reacted badly to the sudden noise, because: 'Panurge like a wild addle-pated giddy Goat, sallies out of the Bread-room in his Shirt, with nothing else about him but one of his Stockings, half on half off, about his Heel, like a rough-footed Pigeon, his Hair and Beard all bepowdered with Crums of Bread, in which he had been over Head and Ears, and a huge and mighty Puss partly wrapt up in his other stocking.' As he stands there 'scar'd, appall'd, shivering, raving, staring, beray'd, and torn with the Claws of the famous Cat Rodilardus,' he is asked about the cat. He replies: 'With this cat . . . the Devil scratch me, if I did not think it had been a young Soft-chin'd Devil which, with this same stocking instead of Mitten, I had snatched up in the great Hutch of Hell . . . ' With this 'he threw the Boar-Cat down', blaming Rodilardus for his dishevelled state, rather than his own panic.

Royal Cat (of Siam)

Domestic breed. An early name for the Siamese Cat, used by many of those who were involved in exhibiting the breed when it first arrived in England, in the late Victorian period. It was then generally believed that the Siamese Cat was an exclusively regal breed, although later information has cast serious doubt on this. Despite this knowledge, May Eustace – as late as 1968 – felt inclined to revert to the older name for her book on the Siamese Cat. (*The Royal Cat of Siam*. Pelham Books, London.)

An early Siamese Cat pictured in 1889 when the breed was usually referred to as 'The Royal Cat of Siam'.

Ruddy

Coat Colour. This was the name given to the coat colour of the original form of the Abyssinian Cat. It is a reddish-brown, burnt sienna, ticked coat reminiscent of the coats of several species of wild cat. The ticking is in bands of darker brown or black. During the early breeding history of the Abyssinian Cat, this was the only colour form known and it was some years before it was joined by a red variant and then, much later, by other variant forms. But for most people, it is the original, ruddy coat that is synonymous with this particular breed, a fact which explains why, in Europe, the coat name 'usual' is employed instead of 'ruddy'.

RUFFED CAT

MYSTERY CAT. In 1940 the zoologist Ivan Sanderson was travelling in the mountains of N.W. Mexico when he came across the skin of a very strange cat, which was being offered for sale by local trappers. The head and body measured 180 cm (71 inches) and the comparatively short tail another 45 cm (18 inches). It was clear from the pelt that the animal had a short face, long legs and big paws. The brown fur had wavy stripes on the flanks and upper legs. The tail and lower legs were a darker brown that the rest. Amazingly, this cat also had a large ruff of fur around its neck. In great excitement, Sanderson bought the pelt of what appeared to him to be a new species of large feline, but before he could return home it was lost in a hurricane and flood. He did see another similar skin for sale later, in a market at Colima, but could not, by then, afford the very high price being asked for it.

If his description is accurate, it is clear that this skin did not belong to any previously recognized cat. Although Sanderson was known to his friends as having a rather active imagination, he was too good a zoologist to have imagined all these unusual details. Sadly, Sanderson is now dead and the mystery of his Ruffed Cat remains to be resolved.

RUGKATT

DOMESTIC BREED. A long-haired Swedish breed, almost identical to the Siberian Forest Cat. Its Danish equivalent is the *Racekatte*.

RUMPEL

PET CAT. Robert Southey (1774–1843) the English author and poet who was an early figure in the romantic movement, had such regard for his cat that he insisted on giving it a formal name that makes even the most elaborate pedigreed name seem economical. The cat's full title was: The Most Noble the Archduke Rumpelstizchen, marquis Macbum, Earle Tomemange, Baron Raticide, Waowler, and Skaratchi. Known as Rumpel to his friends, his death caused the whole household, servants included, to mourn his passing, Southey remarking that the sense of bereavement was greater than any of them liked to admit.

A DRAWING of a Russian Longhair Cat made by Harrison Weir in 1889. It has also been referred to as the Russian Angora.

RUSSIAN ANGORA CAT

DOMESTIC BREED. Alternative name for Russian Longhair Cat.

RUSSIAN BLUE CAT

DOMESTIC BREED. An early breed of short-haired cat that has enjoyed many names: Blue, Russian, Maltese, Maltese Blue, Archangel Blue, Chartreuse Blue, Foreign Blue, American Blue, Russo-American Blue, Spanish Blue, Blue Russian and Russian Shorthair. The official title of Russian Blue was finally agreed in the 1940s. It has sometimes been referred to as 'The Connoisseur's Cat'. In France it is the *Bleu Russe;* in Holland the *Russisch Blauw;* in Germany the *Russisch Blau*.

Appearance: Originally a robust cat with a strong build and rather average proportions, but more recently modified by the introduction of Siamese genes, making it more elongated and angular. Its diagnostic feature is its lustrous, plush, dense, but short coat of grey fur. It has a characteristic wedge-shaped head.

History: Like other domestic cats with a long history, there are a variety of theories about the supposed origins of this breed:

1 The oldest tradition, and the one which gave the cat its geographical name, states that the breed originated in the cold northern regions of Russia. It adapted to this harsh climate by

developing, not a long furry coat, but a short, thick, seal-like one. It is, in fact, a double coat, there being an outer coat of remarkably strong guard hairs and an inner coat of unusually water-resistant down hairs. The breed was hunted for its pelt in early times and may even have been kept, not so much as a pet or vermin-destroyer, but as a valuable source of clothing in the cold north. In this role, it is thought to have spread west through Scandinavia and became a favourite of the Vikings, eventually travelling with them to Britain and many other locations.

2 An alternative version sees these animals being taken as ships' cats from the port of Archangel (now known as Archangel'sk), on the White Sea, to Sweden and from there to Britain.

3 Another variation on this theme suggests instead that they came to Britain from Northern Norway. The earliest blue cats to reach England were certainly from that region, but they may not have been true Russian Blues. They were described at the time as 'Shorthaired Blue Tabbies' and were also known as 'Canon Girdlestone's breed'.

4 Another story envisages them being collected from Archangel by visiting British sailors who acquired them for sale in their home country. One version of this story depicts them being brought back at a very early date – during the reign of Elizabeth I, in the 16th century. Another version suggests the much later date of 1860.

Whichever origin is the true one, we do know that by the end of the 19th century, the Russian Blue had become a popular short-haired breed at the early cat shows. Writing in 1889, Harrison Weir commented that he thought it might be just another form of Blue British Shorthair, but he had 'to admit that those that came from Archangel were of a deeper, purer tint than the English cross-breeds . . . they had larger ears and eyes, and were larger and longer in the head and legs, also the coat of fur was excessively short, rather inclined to woolliness, but bright and glossy.'

Frances Simpson, writing in 1903, reported on the continuing clash between the British Blues and the Russian Blues. One owner complained that there should be separate classes: 'it is disappointing for a Russian owner, who seeing "Russian Blue" only given in the schedule, enters his cat accordingly and gets beaten by a short-haired blue failing in just the points that the Russian is correct in.' Simpson provided a detailed description of the two breeds and the

The Russian Blue, one of the earlier breeds of show cat, which has been exhibited for well over a century. It is famous for its plush, dense coat of bluish-grey fur.

Russian Blue was eventually given a separate class in 1912. Arguments about its origins, however, had it reduced to the official title of 'Foreign Blue'. Russian Blue breeders were not happy about this, but it was not until 1939 that the name Russian Blue was officially reinstated.

During World War II, the Russian Blue nearly disappeared in Europe. In Britain, only one breeder, Marie Rochford, managed to keep a pure line going, and it was from her stock that the post-war redevelopment of the breed began. Unfortunately, because of the small numbers of pure Russian Blues available, it was decided to introduce other lines, supposedly to improve the breed. Blue Point Siamese were favoured and the result was that the Russian Blue became increasingly lanky and angular and less and less like the heavy, tough cat it had been in its early days. By 1950 the official description of the breed had to be rewritten, making the cat little more than an all-blue Siamese.

In 1965/1966 British breeders decided to reverse this trend and to work back towards the original type of the Russian Blue. The extent to which this reversal has succeeded has varied in different parts of the world, creating some minor inconsistencies in the breed, worldwide, at the present time. (For example, the British version is today slightly heavier and has a rounder head than the American.) In Britain, a Russian Blue Association was founded in 1867.

The Russian Blue arrived early in the United States and Canada, appearing there around the turn of the century. Some give the date as between 1888 and 1890, but others place it a little later. The first one for which there is a specific record is a male called 'Blue Royal', which was imported by Clinton Locke of Chicago in 1907. As in Britain, there was at first some confusion between the Russian Blue and the local blue shorthair.

For some reason, after being shown at early cat shows in the United States, the breed disappeared from the American scene. When the 'orientalized' Russian Blues started to cross the Atlantic in the late 1940s, there was a new surge of interest in the breed and in 1950 a Russian Blue Club was formed by a group of American enthusiasts led by C.A. Comaire of Buda in Texas, who had imported post-war stock from both Britain and Denmark.

According to one author, this breed was 'a cherished pet both at the courts of the Russian Tsar and of Queen Victoria of England'.

Personality: Terms used to describe this breed include: affectionate, shy, pensive, intelligent, tranquil, timid, reserved, serene, placid, hardy, obliging, independent, unintrusive, quick-witted, acrobatic, elegant, resourceful, sensitive, temperamental, quiet, sensitive and loyal.

Colour Forms: The so-called blue colour is in reality a silvery-grey. In some countries there are three other, minor colour forms – White, Black and Red – but the creation of these variants seems rather perverse in a breed that is specifically named for its colour.

Bibliography:

1983. Urcia, I. *This is the Russian Blue*. TFH, New Jersey, USA.

Breed Clubs:

Russian Blue Breeders Association. Address: 53 Percy Road, Shirley, Southampton, Hants, SO1 4LP, England.

Russian Blue Society. Address: 1602, Southbrook Drive, Wadena, MN 56482, USA.

Russian Cat

Domestic Breed. An early name for the Russian Blue Cat, used by Huidekoper in 1895. Confusingly, it was also an early name for the Russian Longhair Cat, used by Harrison Weir in 1889. Although some authors still like to refer to the Russian Blue simply as the Russian Cat, this is best avoided because of its ambiguous, double usage in earlier days.

Russian Longhair Cat

Domestic Breed. One of the original longhair breeds introduced into the pedigree cat world at the end of the 19th century.

Appearance: The Russian breed differed from the Turkish (Angora) and the Persian in several respects. It had a larger body with shorter legs. Its heavy coat was described as being 'of a

woolly texture, with coarse hairs among it'. It had a large mane and a short, thickly furred tail.
History: In the Victorian era, when it first appeared in the West, the Russian Longhair Cat was crossed with the other long-haired breeds popular at the time, such as the Angora and the Persian, and its separate identity was soon lost. By the early part of the 20th century it had been eclipsed by the softer-coated Persian and before long had vanished from the pedigree cat scene.

It was not heard of again till 1987, when a pair of long-haired cats were found in St. Petersburg and taken to Berlin. They bred there and by 1990 a number of them had been registered in Germany and elsewhere in Europe, using the name of Siberian Cat, or Siberian Forest Cat.

It has recently been reported that, although they have long since vanished from the cat shows in the West, these Longhair Cats have been well known in Russia for many years. They have apparently been overlooked outside Russia because their presence has been undocumented.

As Russia was probably the original source of all domestic long-haired cats, before they were taken to Turkey and Persia and thence to the rest of the world, the re-appearance of these northern cats is to be welcomed. A close study of their genetics may help to unravel some of the uncertainties concerning the origins of the other pedigree long-haired breeds.

According to the Fauna Cat Lovers Association in Moscow, the only conspicuous difference between Turkish Angoras and Russian Longhair Cats is that the latter are more likely to have green eyes. For this reason, one recent author has referred to them simply as 'Russian Angoras'.
Personality: The original Russian cats were said to be hardy, preferring to be outdoors even in the coldest weather, less agile, and less affectionate towards their human companions, than other breeds. The latest (Siberian) ones are reported to be charming, quiet, gentle and slightly shy.

Russian Shorthair Cat

Domestic Breed. An alternative name for the Russian Blue Cat.

Rusty-spotted Cat

Wild Feline. *(Felis rubiginosa)* Looking like a smaller edition of the Leopard Cat, this tiny species, with its rusty-coloured spots, is found in forest and scrubland, hunting for small birds

The Rusty-spotted Cat *(Felis rubiginosa)* of southern India is a smaller version of the Leopard Cat. It used to be considered as no more than a local race of its larger relative but is now thought to be a distinct species in its own right.

and mammals at night and retreating during the day into dens in hollow logs or bushy thickets. It is not quite as big as a domestic cat, but is more agile when climbing.

Its resemblance to the Leopard Cat is more than superficial and these two cats are clearly very closely related. The bigger Leopard Cat, which has a wide range throughout southern Asia, is replaced by the Rusty-spotted Cat as one travels south through India. Until recently it was probably no more than a local race, but it now appears to have evolved into a separate, distinct species. It seems to have adapted to more arid conditions, in dry grasslands and open dry forests. Strangely, however, in Sri Lanka, where the Leopard Cat is absent, the Rusty-spotted species prefers the more humid regions of the south and ignores the drier north. This contradiction is hard to explain.

It is said that this species will hybridize with local domestic cats.

Size: Length of Head + Body: 35–48 cm (14–19 in). Tail: 15–25 cm (6–10 in). Weight: 1–2 kg (2–4½ lb).

Distribution: Southern India and southern Sri Lanka.

Rutterkin

Talismanic Cat. By definition a talisman is a charm that brings good luck, but it can also be used by its owner specifically to bring bad luck to others. This was allegedly the case with Rutterkin, the reputedly evil black cat (with eyes like burning coal) that was the familiar of the 17th-century English serving-woman Joan Flower, who was condemned for practising witchcraft. Joan and her two daughters worked for the Earl of Rutland at Belvoir Castle and stood accused of bewitching his family. Both his sons had died and his wife had become barren, probably from quite independent causes, but a scapegoat had to be found and the three 'Belvoir Witches' were accused of causing these calamities with the help of their pet cat, Rutterkin.

Rutterkin (seen here on the ground to the right of this 17th century woodcut) was described as an evil cat, a familiar of the witch Joan Flower, pictured here with her two daughters, Margaret and Phillipa.

The accusation was that the daughters had stolen intimate objects from the Rutlands and given them to their mother, who rubbed them ceremonially over Rutterkin's magical fur, uttering curses. This was supposedly done with the glove of the eldest son, who promptly died; next with the glove of the younger son, who also died; then with feathers from the bed of the Earl's wife, who subsequently became barren.

Joan Flower's two daughters were hanged for these crimes in 1617 and Joan herself, still protesting her innocence, mysteriously choked on some food and died in prison before she could be executed. Nothing is recorded concerning the fate of Rutterkin himself, although it seems unlikely that he survived the Earl's vengeful persecution of the Flower household.

Sable

Coat Colour. Frances Simpson introduced the term 'sable' into cat colours in 1903: 'With the "sable" cat, be it understood, I have no fault to find; I can forgive him even his white chin, because he is such a magnificent animal; but he is not a tabby, and should not be shown as such.'

A different description appears in 1957, when Dechambre defines it as 'a variety which has been created in America, where it is known as the Burmese. It is better to call them Zibelines or Sables, because of their coat, and to distinguish them from the true Burmese. These cats without doubt derive from the crossing of a Siamese with one or two more breeds . . . It is a short-haired cat of self colour, chocolate brown, with green eyes and a long tail.'

Today, the term Sable Cat is not used as a breed name; the Burmese is still called the Burmese. The original colour form of this breed – the dark brown – is, however, called a 'Sable Burmese' in the United States (in contrast to Europe, where it is known simply as a 'Brown Burmese').

Sacred Cat of Burma

Domestic Breed. Another name for the Birman Cat. According to several reports, this breed was kept as a holy animal by temple priests in Burma who believed that, in order to gain entrance to paradise, they would first have to be reincarnated in the body of one of the temple cats. (For details see Birman Cat.)

Safari Cat

Domestic breed. A new experimental breed.

Saha

Fictional Cat. Saha was 'The Cat' in the title of Colette's novel *La Chatte* (1933). The story is based on the concept of 'love me, love my cat'. Saha, a magnificent pedigree Russian Blue Cat, is so disliked by her owner's new wife that disaster is guaranteed. The wife tries to kill the cat by pushing her off a ninth-floor balcony, but the falling animal is saved by an awning. The husband discovers what has happened and promptly goes home to mother, taking his beloved cat with him.

SALT DESERT CAT

WILD FELINE. A small, spotted cat that inhabits the arid wastelands of western Argentina, near the foothills of the Andes. It was once considered to be a distinct, separate species, but since the 1950s it has been looked upon as no more than a local race of Geoffroy's Cat *(Felis geoffroyi)*. (For details see Geoffroy's Cat.)

SAM

FICTIONAL CAT. Yet another horror story about cats, Walter de la Mare's *Broomsticks* tells how a black cat called Sam, belonging to a Miss Chauncey, starts to act strangely whenever there is a crescent moon, insisting on going outside. Miss Chauncey hears cackling and other strange noises. In the morning there is the impression of a broomstick on the ground.

SAND CAT

WILD FELINE. *(Felis margarita)* Also known as the Sand-dune Cat or Dune Cat. German: *Sandkatze,* or *Saharakatze;* French: *Le Chat des Sables*. The scientific title of *margarita* was taken from the name of a French officer, Général Margueritte, who was serving in Algeria in the 1850s.

This small, pale, sandy-coloured cat is easily recognized by its amazingly broad head and huge, wide-set ears. Its short legs and compact body give it the appearance of being permanently crouched. The longish tail has a black tip and a few black rings near the tip. The fur is long, soft and dense.

It has hairy feet, with long tufts growing between the pads. Although it is nocturnal, hunting in the cool of the desert night, this hairy padding on its feet means that, should it be driven out

THE SAND CAT *(Felis margarita)*, a small, sandy-coloured wild cat from the Sahara and the deserts of the Middle East. A stealthy hunter, it emerges from its burrows in the cool of the night to prey on desert rodents.

onto the painfully hot sand during the day, its sensitive paw-pads would be protected. These tufts of hair also, incidentally, give it a unique set of feline tracks, its footprints completely lacking any of the usual sole-pad markings.

As a protection against exposure, the Sand Cat is an efficient burrower and can dig out its own den in the sand. One such den, that was carefully excavated, proved to be 4.5 metres (15 feet) long and about 14 cm (5½ inches) wide at the entrance – a considerable burrowing achievement for a small cat.

A strictly nocturnal, ground-living hunter, the Sand Cat preys on any small desert rodents, reptiles, or large insects that it can find in its hostile environment, relying to a great extent on its incredibly sensitive hearing. It has been known to feast on locusts, but its staple diet consists largely of jerboas, gerbils and other desert rodents. Unlike many cat species, the Sand Cat is able, if necessary, to survive without drinking, obtaining all the liquid it needs from its prey.

Its main enemies are venomous snakes and desert birds of prey.

Size: Length of Head + Body: 45–58 cm (18–23 in). Tail: 28–35 cm (11–14 in). Weight: 2–4 kg (4½–9 lb).

Distribution: Found in the rocky, sand-dune regions of the deserts of northern Africa and western Asia. It has been recorded from many parts of the Sahara. Specific countries where its presence has been confirmed include (roughly from west to east): Morocco, Algeria, Niger, Tunisia, Libya, Egypt, Sudan, Israel, Saudi Arabia, Yemen, Qatar, Oman, Iran, Southern Russia (Turkmenistan and Uzbekistan) and Pakistan.

SANTER

MYSTERY CAT. At the end of the 19th century a mystery cat called the Santer terrorized the farming communities of North Carolina, killing livestock and causing a flurry of newspaper articles and public statements. It was described as being the size of a large dog, grey in colour, and 'striped from the end of its nose to the end of its tail'. Its true identity was never established and by the end of the century it had vanished, never to reappear.

SAYER, ANGELA

CAT AUTHORITY. Angela Sayer is the President of the Cat Association of Great Britain, Vice-President of the Cat Survival Trust, an international show judge, a major figure in cat breeding, and a breed innovator, having introduced several new breeds to Britain. She has also organized the annual Kensington Cat Show, been editor of *Cat World* magazine, run a feline quarantine station and organized wildlife safaris to Africa. In addition, she is professional animal photographer (under the name Solitaire) and has run her own company: Animal Graphics Ltd., She has written many books on feline subjects (some as Angela Sayer, others as Angela Rixon) including those listed in the following bibliography.

Bibliography:

1976. Pond, G. & Sayer, A. *Cats.* John Bartholomew, Edinburgh.
1977. Pond, G. & Sayer, A. *The Intelligent Cat.* Davis-Poynter, London.
1979. Sayer, A. *The Encyclopedia of the Cat.* Octopus Books, London.
1982. Sayer, A. *The World of Cats.* Optimum Books, London.
1983. Sayer, A. *Cats: A Guide to Breeding and Showing.* Batsford, London.
1984. Sayer, A. *The Complete Book of the Cat.* Octopus Books, London.
1990. Sayer, A. (co-author) *The Noble Cat.* Merehurst, London.
1995. Rixon, A. *The Illustrated Encyclopedia of Cat Breeds.* Blandford, London.

SCHALLER, GEORGE

CAT AUTHORITY. George Schaller was the first modern zoologist to make prolonged, analytical observations of big cats in the wild. His pioneering studies of Tigers in India, Lions in Africa and Snow Leopards in the Himalayas became models for the many field investigations that were to follow. Before he began his work in the 1950s, observations of big game animals were largely anecdotal or personal. Most of them relied on the experiences of scouts, trackers and hunters, or of those who had enjoyed the company of a tame or captive animal. They had learned a great deal, but it was not organized, systematically collected information. Schaller brought a new, objective approach to the subject and his reports gave us the first detailed information about the life history and behaviour of the greatest members of the cat family. It was his goal to reveal the animals as they really were, rather than as human fears, emotions and sentimentality had painted them in the past. As he put it, 'when humans observe an animal they mainly see the fiction they have invented for it'. Schaller's aim was to replace that fiction with fact.

Bibliography:

1967. Schaller, G. *The Deer and the Tiger.* University of Chicago Press, Illinois.
1971. Schaller, G. & Selsam, M.E. *The Tiger. Its Life in the Wild.* World's Work, London.
1972. Schaller, G. *The Serengeti Lion.* University of Chicago Press, Illinois.
1972. Schaller, G. *Serengeti, Kingdom of Predators.* Knopf, New York.
1973. Schaller, G. *Golden Shadows, Flying Hooves.* Knopf, New York.
1977. Schaller, G. *Mountain Monarchs.* University of Chicago Press, Illinois.

Scottish Fold Cat

Domestic Breed. A recently discovered mutation with a unique ear shape.

Appearance: The small ears are folded downwards and forwards, giving the animal's head a smoothly rounded silhouette. The appeal of this shape is clearly that it gives the breed a more humanoid look. A stocky cat with a wide face and large round eyes, the Scottish Fold can exist in any colour and with either a short or a long coat.

The ear-shape starts to develop at about 25 days. This is the point at which the cartilage in a normal kitten's ears starts to harden and the ears stand upright. With the Scottish Fold, this change does not occur. Today there are variations in the degree of this folding, some individuals having a single fold, while others have a double fold. With the double fold, the ear tips almost touch the fur of the head.

There is also a long-haired version of this breed (see Longhair Fold Cat, Highland Fold Cat, or Coupari.)

History: The first Scottish Fold appeared on a farm in Perthshire, Scotland, near the village of Coupar Angus 21 km (13 miles) north-east of Perth, in 1961. A local shepherd noticed that a short-haired white female cat, playing in a nearby farmyard, had strangely folded ears. He pointed this out to the cat's owners, Mr and Mrs McRae. They knew very little about the animal's ancestry, but it seemed fairly certain that the other kittens in her litter had been perfectly normal. The conclusion was that the strange one must be an isolated, spontaneous mutation. The McRaes promised the shepherd a kitten from any litter she might produce in the future.

Two years later, this cat, now called Susie, herself gave birth and produced two more folded-eared kittens. One, a male, was given to a neighbour who had it neutered and kept it as a pet. The other was a white female, looking exactly like its mother, and this one was given to the shepherd and his wife – William and Mary Ross.

Within three months, Susie herself was dead, killed by a car on the road near her home, and the survival of the breed now rested entirely with the Rosses. Fortunately, they had a special interest in pedigree cats and already owned a fine Siamese. They were fascinated by the potential of their new kitten. They named her Snooks, bred from her and began to think seriously about developing their 'new breed', which at this stage they were referring to as 'Lop-eared Cats'. A cat show judge suggested that they should contact a London breeder by the name of Pat Turner, who was interested in feline genetics. This they did in 1967 and Turner visited them at their Scottish home. She borrowed a male called Snowdrift, took him back to London, and began a serious experimental breeding programme. It was she who persuaded the Rosses to change the name of the breed from Lop-eared to Fold, pointing out that the pendulous ears of the Lop-eared Rabbit were anatomically very different from the folded-over ears of the cat, and that the name was therefore misleading.

The Scottish Fold Cat. An attractive but controversial breed discovered by a Scottish shepherd in the 1960s. Its forward-folded ears give its head a more rounded and therefore more human outline, adding to its appeal.

Snowdrift was destined to become the founding father of the breed, with 76 descendants in three years, 42 of which had the typical folded ears. He soon became famous, appearing on television and creating something of a controversy. Many experts condemned the new breed as a deformity and before long the feline authorities formally decreed that 'no applications for registration or show entries may be accepted for the Lop-eared (Fold-eared) cats'.

With opposition continuing in England, three of Snowdrift's descendants crossed the Atlantic and, in 1970, became the focus of a special study by geneticist Neil Todd in Newtontown, Massachusetts. When he eventually lost interest, a Pennsylvania breeder called Sally Wolfe Peters took on the task of developing the breed. As a result of her programme, the first Scottish Fold Cat was registered in the United States in 1973. In 1974 she formed 'The International Scottish Fold Association' and by 1978 the breed had gained championship status at American cat shows. By the 1990s, despite the disapproval it still attracts elsewhere, it ranked among the top ten most popular pedigree breeds in America.

It has been claimed that cats with folded ears have also been observed in both Germany and Belgium, but it seems that in neither country has this mutant form been developed.

Abnormalities: Sadly, the gene that causes the folded ears of this attractive breed appears to be linked to certain physical abnormalities. It is a single dominant gene that causes problems when it is present in double strength (that is, in the homozygous condition). If one Scottish Fold is mated to another Scottish Fold, the kittens all have folded ears, but they are also liable to suffer from two serious defects: (1) a thickened tail caused by the fusing of the tail vertebrae, and (2) thickened legs, with cartilage growing around the paws, making walking difficult.

As a result of this unfortunate genetic link, Scottish Fold breeders only ever put their animals with non-folded mates. The kittens resulting from such a cross have the ear-folding gene only in single strength (the heterozygous condition), and they are then free from these defects. So Scottish Fold breeders must always out-breed if they are to succeed with this unusual form of cat. Some have bred with short-haired mates and some have preferred long-haired ones, giving rise to two basic types of Scottish Fold Cat.

Because of the ever-present threat of physical abnormalities should two folded cats get together and mate, there has been strong resistance to this breed on the part of certain feline authorities and it is banned altogether, by law, in Germany.

In England the main authority, the GCCF, has refused to accept the breed for competition. The GCCF's formal objection was worded as follows: '[The ear configuration] will almost certainly lead to an increased incidence of ear disease on account of the poor natural ventilation of the ear canal and difficulty in cleaning and applying any medication'. Supporters of the breed felt that this sounded like a lame excuse for opposing the new breed. They insisted that the Scottish Fold is no more prone to ear disease than any other breed and that its ears are just as easy to keep clean. One British organization eventually agreed with them, and in 1983 the GCCF's rival, the Cat Association, eventually recognized the breed, and the Scottish Fold Cat is now seen regularly at their cat shows.

As with Manx Cats and other controversial breeds, careful attention to the problems of genetically linked abnormalities by responsible breeders can avoid most of the difficulties. Outright banning of these unusual and intriguing breeds seems a rather heavy-handed response, although it is easy to understand the caution of the authorities concerned. (See entry for Abnormal Breeds.)

An additional defect from which this breed has been said to suffer is deafness. This problem does not, however, have any connection with the folded ear gene. The deafness is genetically linked, not to the ear shape but to the pure white coats of some of the Scottish Fold individuals.

Personality: Terms used in connection with this breed include: affectionate, alert, intelligent, optimistic, sensible, perceptive, good-tempered, undemanding, placid, courteous, reserved, sweet, gentle, peaceable, well-balanced, soft-voiced, slow-moving, persistent, resilient, nosy and rugged.

Colour Forms:

CFA: White; Black; Blue; Red; Cream; Chinchilla Silver; Shaded Silver; Shell Cameo (Red Chinchilla); Shaded Cameo (Red Shaded); Black Smoke; Blue Smoke; Cameo Smoke (Red Smoke); Classic Tabby Pattern; Mackerel Tabby Pattern; Patched Tabby (= Torbie) Pattern; Spotted Tabby Pattern; Silver Tabby; Blue Silver Tabby (Pewter Tabby); Blue Silver (Pewter); Red Tabby; Brown Tabby; Blue Tabby; Cream Tabby; Cameo Tabby; Tortoiseshell; Calico; Dilute Calico; Blue-Cream; Bi-color (= Black and White; Blue and White; Red and White; or Cream and White).

Other colours recorded include: Black Smoke and White; Blue-Cream and White; and Tortie and White.

Bibliography:

1993. Maggitti, P. *Scottish Fold Cats.* Barron's, Hauppauge, N.Y.

Breed Club:

Scottish Fold Association. Publishes a magazine: *International Scottish Fold.* Address: 12500, Skyline Drive, Burnsville, MN 55337-2920, USA.

Seal Point

Coat Pattern. This is the original Siamese Cat colouring, with a fawn to cream body and the dark extremities a deep seal brown. It was first recognized in 1871 and remained the only Siamese colour form until the 1930s, when other extremity-colours were introduced.

Seal variants (recognized in 1966) include: (1) Seal Lynx Point (the seal brown on the extremities shows a tabby pattern); (2) Seal Tortie Point (the seal brown on the extremities shows a tortoiseshell pattern); (3) Seal Tortie Tabby Point (a combination of the previous two patterns).

Searle, Ronald

Cat Art. The British artist, Ronald Searle (1920–), created a collection of delightfully rotund, hairy cats in a long series of humorous cartoons which were eventually collected together in book form.

Bibliography:

1969. Searle, R. *Searle's Cats.* Dobson Books, London.

Sebala Cat

Wild Feline. An earlier name for the small, spotted Black-footed Cat *(Felis nigripes)* of Africa. It was a local tribal name for this species that became widely used in the fur trade, where there are frequent references to 'Sebala Skins'.

Self-coloured

Coat Pattern. This type of coat was accurately defined as long ago as 1895, by Rush Huidekoper: 'The Self-coloured cats are those which are entirely of one solid colour, which may vary its hue or tint, but must not have any intermixture of white or of any other colour. The Self-coloured Cats are the Black, the Blue, the Red and the Yellow.'

Since then, various other self-colours have been added to that early list, but the definition remains unaltered. (An alternative name for 'selfs' is 'solids'.)

Selima

Pet Cat. Selima was a tortoiseshell tabby cat owned by the English man of letters Horace Walpole (1717–1797). With his friend, the poet Thomas Gray, he made the Grand Tour of Europe and when his beloved cat was drowned in a goldfish bowl, Gray wrote a poem to commemorate the event, called *Ode on the Death of a Favourite Cat Drowned in a Tub of Gold Fishes* (1748).

Selkirk Rex Cat

Domestic Breed. Appeared in Wyoming in 1987 and quickly developed as a new Rex breed. Aptly described as 'The Cat in Sheep's Clothing', or a 'Sheepcat'.

Appearance: It has the characteristic curly coat and curled whiskers of a Rex Cat, but unlike the other Rex breeds, the Selkirk has a bulky appearance with a rectangular, muscular body. The head is wide and rounded with a short muzzle. The ears, which have ear-tufts, are smaller than those of a typical Rex Cat. Coarse guard hairs are present and these, as well as the awn and down hairs, are curled. Selkirk kittens are born with curly coats, but these disappear at about six months, to be replaced by a temporary covering of sparse, wiry hair. Then, at about ten months, the plush, thick, curly adult coat appears.

History: The first Selkirk Rex was spotted in 1987 as a curly-coated, dilute calico female kitten in an otherwise normal, straight-haired litter of non-pedigree cats. This litter, along with their straight-haired mother, had been deposited in an animal shelter as unwanted pets.

The curly kitten was noticed as something out of the ordinary by Peggy Voorhees of the Bozeman Humane Society in Wyoming. Because the animal's coat was so unusual, she was adopted by Jeri Newman, a Montana breeder of pedigree Persian Cats. When 14 months old, this young female, now known as Miss De Presto, was mated with Newman's champion Black Persian called Photo Finish, and on 4th July 1988 produced a litter of six kittens. Half of these displayed their mother's curly coat. One was a black and white male, another was a black female and a third was a tortie female.

The Selkirk Rex, a shaggy-coated cat discovered in 1987. It has a heavier build than the more familiar, long-established Rex Cat breeds. It acquired its name because it first appeared near the Selkirk Mountains in Wyoming.

It was soon clear to those involved that they were witnessing the birth of an exciting new breed and it was decided to give it the name of Selkirk, after the Selkirk Mountains in Wyoming, which were near to the spot where the foundation cat, Miss De Presto, had been discovered.

Further matings, including back-crosses to Miss De Presto, were organized. There were also out-crosses to various short-haired breeds as well as long-hairs. Other Rex breeds are not, however, to be introduced into the Selkirk development programme, because it is clear that the Selkirk is the only type of Rex that is genetically dominant. This means that the Selkirk Rex cannot be related to any of the other Rex genes, and there is therefore no point in mixing them.

Encouraged by the success of the Selkirk programme, the breeders involved formed a Selkirk Rex Society and in August 1990 two American cat associations agreed to give official recognition to this new breed. There is now also a Selkirk Rex Breed Association in Canada.

Personality: Terms used to describe this breed include: patient, tolerant, laid-back, cuddly, playful.

Colour Forms: Those recorded so far include: Black Tortie Smoke; Blue-Green; Tortie. Pointed coats are known, inherited from the foundation cat, and Burmese and 'mink' colours have also been recorded.

Breed Clubs:

Selkirk Rex Breed Club. Publishes a quarterly newsletter, *Woolgathering*. Address: 3555 South Pacific Highway No. 3, Medford, OR 97501, USA.

Selkirk Rex Breeders. Address: P.O. Box 21282, Concord, CA 94521-0208, USA.

Selkirk Rex Society. Address: 231 South D Street, Livingston, MT 59047, USA.

Semi-Longhair Cats

Domestic Cats. This name is sometimes used as a group title for all the long-haired cats *other than the Persian.* It is a clumsy and unnecessary term that has come into existence for historical reasons.

To understand why it was invented, it is necessary to go back to the time when long-haired cats were first imported into the West. The first to arrive was the Angora, followed by the Persian. These two were more or less indiscriminately interbred, but eventually the Persian type swamped out the Angora. By the start of the 20th century the Angora had virtually ceased to exist as a pure breed. Because of the mixing that had occurred, the British pedigree cat authorities decided to introduce the name 'Longhair' for the predominantly Persian animal. Officially the name Persian was dropped, but in the popular mind it refused to die. At first, this did not create much of a problem because it was the only type of long-haired cat available. British officials used the name Longhair and everyone else called it the Persian. But then additional long-haired breeds became popular and the original Angora was rediscovered. For most people, it was obvious these should all be called longhairs, like the Persian, but for the pedigree authorities this was impossible, as they were now reserving the name 'longhair' exclusively for the Persian. To solve their problem they introduced the term 'semi-longhair' for all the non-Persian longhairs, arguing that the Persian had longer hair than anything else.

For most people, these historical arguments are meaningless and they simply divide all cats neatly into either longhairs or shorthairs.

Breed Club:

Semi-Longhair Cat Association. Address: 99 Porchester Drive, Eastfield Chase, Cramlington, Northumberland, NE23 9QQ, England.

Sepia

Coat Colour. A colour name that is rarely used for cats. It is mostly applied to the Singapura Cat, whose coat is described as follows: 'Sepia Agouti only . . . dark brown ticking on a warm old ivory ground colour.'

Serval

Wild Feline. *(Felis serval)* German: *Servalkatze;* French: *Le Serval,* or *Chat-tigre;* Swahili: *Mondo, Kisongo, Marara,* or *Tschui Mbara;* Afrikaans: *Tierboskat.* The origin of the name serval is strange. It comes from a Portuguese word meaning 'deer-wolf'.

Long, lean and lanky, the Serval has a remarkably dainty, elongated body and legs. Its small head is perched on a slender neck and surmounted by huge bat-like ears. The tawny coat is covered in small black spots, and the short tail is marked with dark rings and has a black tip.

The medium-sized Serval is an African predator that prefers to live among the long grasses and scrubland near riverbanks. It favours open country to dense forest, but only where there is plenty of cover.

Although it will take a wide variety of prey animals including birds, fish, frogs, lizards and large insects, this species is, above all, a specialized rodent-hunter. It uses its enormous ears to detect the sounds of rodents above or below ground. If they are above ground, it pounces on them with a curious vertical leap, rising high in the air and then landing on top of them, a technique that seems to bewilder the prey, making it difficult for them to know which way to flee. If the prey are below ground, the Serval makes use of its long front feet to probe into recesses, grab the victims with its claws, and hook them out into the open. Sometimes it uses yet another technique, waiting and watching for a rodent to break cover. If it detects one moving about just below ground, it will stand very still over the entrance to the burrow, with one paw raised up ready to strike. Like a statue it will hold this position until the rodent believes that the coast is clear. Then, as soon as it emerges, it is scooped high up into the air with a single deft movement of the Serval's long front leg. As the rodent falls to the ground it is snatched and killed.

The Serval *(Felis serval)* is a medium-sized African grassland species with enormous ears. With these it is able to detect the presence of rodents even when they are in their underground burrows.

Size: Length of Head + Body: 70–100 cm (27½–39½ in). Tail: 36–45 cm (14–17½ in). Weight: 14–18 kg (31–40 lb).
Distribution: The Serval is confined to Africa, but occurs over most of the continent, avoiding only the extremes of wet – in the western rain forests – and the extremes of dry – in the Sahara. It never strays far from water.

Servaline Cat

Wild Feline. This used to be considered a distinct species *(Felis servalina),* but is now thought to be no more than a race of the Serval (see separate entry). It differs from the typical Serval in being slightly smaller and having a coat with a paler ground colour and much smaller spots. However, when intermediate forms were found it was realized that the Servaline Cat is only a local variation of the Serval and of little importance.

Sexual Maturity

Feline Biology. Domestic cats become sexually mature when they are nearly one year old. There are slight variations, however. For toms, the youngest recorded age for sexual maturity is six months, but this is abnormal. Eight months is also rather precocious, and the typical male does not become sexually active until he is between 11 and 12 months of age. For toms living rough, it may be considerably longer – more like 15 to 18 months, probably because they are given less chance in the competition with older males.

For females, the period can be relatively short, six to eight months being usual, but very young females only three to five months old have been known to come into sexual condition. This early start seems to be caused by the unnatural circumstances of domestication. For a wild cat, ten months is more usual.

The European Wild Cat, for instance, starts its breeding season in March. There is a gestation period of 63–68 days and then the kittens appear in May. By late autumn they strike off on their own and, if they survive the winter, they themselves will start to breed the following March when they are about ten months old, producing their own litters when they are a year old. For these wild cats there is only one season a year, so young toms may have to be patient and wait for the following season before they go into action.

This wild cycle is obviously geared to the changing seasons and the varying food supply, but for the protected pet there are no such problems. With its hunting ears finely tuned to the metallic sound of a can-opener and with central heating humming gently in the background, the luxuriating house cat has little to fear from the annual cycle of nature. As a result, its breeding sequences are less rigid than those of its wild counterpart. It may breed as early as the second half of January, producing a litter by the beginning of April. Two months later, with its kittens weaned and despatched to new homes, it may well start off again with another breeding sequence, producing a second litter in the late summer. With this loss of a simple annual rhythm, there is a wide scatter of ages among young domestic cats, leading to the variations in the stages at which they become sexually active.

Cases have been recorded of wild cats producing a second litter in August, but it is suspected that this only occurs where there has been interbreeding between the wild animals and feral domestic cats. (Such crossing is thought to be more and more common and zoologists who are studying the European Wild Cat are becoming concerned that pure-bred ones are becoming increasingly rare.)

SEYCHELLOIS CAT

DOMESTIC BREED. A new experimental breed created in England in the 1980s.

Appearance: Oriental build, with slim, elegant body, long neck and legs, and wedge-shaped head with large ears. The coat is white with splashes of colour. There are both short-haired and long-haired versions. The eyes are blue. The markings are divided into three types:

SEYCHELLOIS SEPTIÈME: White, with a coloured tail, and large patches of colour on the head, body and legs.

SEYCHELLOIS HUITIÈME: White, with a coloured tail, and small patches of colour on the head and legs.

SEYCHELLOIS NEUVIÈME: Almost entirely white, with a coloured tail and only small patches of colour on the head.

History: A report on the cats of the Seychelles was the inspiration for this breed. British breeder Pat Turner of Milton Keynes, Buckinghamshire, set about re-creating the Seychelles coat pattern which consisted of a white ground colour with small splashes of colour and a fully coloured tail. Her breeding programme began in 1984, in co-operation with another British breeder, Julie Smith. As foundation stock, they used two female tortie and white Persians and two male Siamese. By back-crossing the offspring of these matings to Siamese and Oriental cats, the Seychelles pattern was improved, and has been further strengthened with each subsequent generation. The first fully developed Seychellois Cats in the programme were named Félicité, Victoria, Amirante and Thérèse and the first two of these were used to introduce the breed at a cat show in 1988 – the first to be exhibited under the new name. In 1989 a Seychellois Cat Society was formed and the future of the breed was assured.

Personality: Terms used to describe this breed include: athletic, scatter-brained, demanding and demonstrative.

THE SEYCHELLOIS is a comparatively new breed, displaying a white coat splashed with colour. It was developed in England in the 1980s.

SHADED

COAT PATTERN. A shaded coat is one that is made up of pale hairs each of which has a dark tip. The darkened portion of the tip reaches a *moderate* distance down the length of the hair. In the Shell Pattern, the darkened portion is very restricted. In the Smoke Pattern, the darkened portion reaches much further down the length of each hair. In other words, the Shaded Pattern is intermediate, between the Shell and the Smoke Patterns, in its visual effect.

There are the following colour variants of this pattern: (1) Shaded Blue; (2) Shaded Blue-Cream; (3) Shaded Blue Silver; (4) Shaded Cameo; (5) Shaded Cream Cameo; (6) Shaded

Chinchilla Tortoiseshell (= Shell Tortoiseshell); (7) Dilute Shaded Chinchilla Tortoiseshell (= Dilute Shell Tortoiseshell); (8) Shaded Chocolate; (9) Shaded Chocolate Tortoiseshell; (10) Shaded Cinnamon; (11) Shaded Cinnamon Tortoiseshell; (12) Shaded Fawn; (13) Shaded Fawn-Cream; (14) Shaded Golden (see separate entry for details); (15) Shaded Lavender; (16) Shaded Red (= Shaded Cameo); (17) Shaded Silver (see entry below for details); (17) Shaded Tortoiseshell; (18) Dilute Shaded Tortoiseshell.

Shaded Golden

Coat Colour. On a cat with a Shaded Golden coat, each hair is apricot or pale brown with a dark brown tip. This is the darker version of the Chinchilla Golden, just as the Shaded Silver (see entry) is the darker version of the typical Chinchilla.

Shaded Golden cats exist in both long and short-haired versions, as Shaded Golden Persians and Shaded Golden Exotics. They are also seen in two other breeds: The American Curl and the Norwegian Forest Cat.

Shaded Silver

Coat Colour. On a cat with a Shaded Silver coat, each individual hair is silvery-grey with a black tip. The overall effect is of a light grey cat with a shimmering silvery texture.

Originally there was much confusion between Shaded Silver and Chinchilla. In the 19th century Chinchillas were slightly darker than they are today and it was almost impossible to distinguish between the two forms. They were sometimes lumped together as 'silvers'. But then, as the years passed, the Chinchilla cats became paler and paler, each hair becoming pure white with a dark tip. So today it is easy to tell Shaded Silver cats from Chinchillas.

Shaded Silver cats exist in both long and short-haired versions, as Shaded Silver Persians and Shaded Silver Exotics. They are now also seen in the following breeds: American Curl, American Shorthair, American Wirehair, Maine Coon, Manx, Norwegian Forest, Cornish Rex, Devon Rex and Scottish Fold.

Shan

Pet Cat. Shan was one of those rare felines to inhabit the White House as American 'First Cat'. Most Presidents, being men who enjoy power, prefer the more slavish devotion of a dog. Cats usually enter the White House as pets of the President's children and Shan was no exception, being the Siamese cat pet of President Gerald Ford's daughter Susan.

Shasta

Talismanic Cat. Shasta, a Cougar or Puma, imported from Mexico, was the living mascot of the University of Houston's football team, who were known as the Cougars. Shasta was retired in 1963, to be replaced by a younger animal.

Shaw's Cat

Wild Feline. An obsolete species, originally called *Felis shawiana*. It was known only from a few skins and a skeleton, collected in Eastern Turkestan. It is now considered to be no more than a local variant of the Wild Cat *(Felis sylvestris)*.

Sheik Mohammed Al-fassi

Cat Owner. A nobleman from Saudi Arabia, the Sheik kept over a hundred stray cats in his multi-million-dollar Florida mansion. He employed a staff of nine, including a private vet, to look after them in a suite of seven large rooms of their own. He had been horrified to discover that cats were frequently put to sleep when they were unwanted and vowed to stop this to the best of his ability, even to the extent of having doomed cats flown to his mansion from faraway American cities. Had he known the true extent of the problem he might have given up before he began, but happily for a hundred cats he did not.

SHELL

COAT PATTERN. When a coat is made up of pale hairs with dark tips it is called either a Shell, Shaded or Smoke Pattern. The shell version has a very restricted darkening of the tip – less than the other two. Today a shell pattern is very similar to a 'shaded chinchilla'.

The following pedigree colour variants of this pattern have been recorded: (1) Shell Cameo (= Red Chinchilla); (2) Cream Shell Cameo; (3) Shell Tortoiseshell (= Shaded Chinchilla Tortoiseshell); (4) Dilute Shell Tortoiseshell (= Dilute Shaded Chinchilla Tortoiseshell).

SHERE KHAN

FICTIONAL CAT. In Rudyard Kilping's classic story *The Jungle Book* (1894), Shere Khan is the lame tiger who repeatedly attempts to carry off and devour the man-cub Mowgli, but without success. In the end he is killed by Mowgli, who corners him in a ravine where he is trampled to death by cattle.

BECAUSE MOST non-pedigree house-pets have short hair, a special name was required to distinguish their carefully bred, pedigree show-cat relatives. The solution was to give the latter the name British Shorthair, European Shorthair or American Shorthair. The example shown here is a European Shorthair.

SHORTHAIR CAT

DOMESTIC BREED. At the earliest cat shows, in the final decades of the 19th century, all cats with short coats were lumped together as 'Short-haired Cats'. Some were named simply by their fur colour, while others were distinctive breeds, such as the Siamese or Manx. As time passed, the distinctive breeds were more strongly recognized as such and this left a mixed bag of short-haired cats, separated from one another purely by their coat colour. These cats then needed a more precise name to establish them as a particular breed. In Britain they acquired the title of the British Shorthair. On the Continent, they became the European Shorthair and in the United States, the American Shorthair. (See separate entries.)

Bibliography:

1963. Wolfgang, H. *Shorthaired Cats.* TFH, New Jersey.

1981. Lauder, P. *The British, European and American Shorthair Cat.* Batsford, London.

1992. Urcia, I. *American Shorthair Cat.*

S

Siam

Pet Cat. Siam, a gift from the American Consul in Bangkok to the wife of the American President, Rutherford B. Hayes, in 1878, was the first Siamese Cat ever to reach the United States. (For details see Siamese Cat.)

Siamese Cat

Domestic Breed. The best known of the ancient cats of Siam (now Thailand), it appears in *The Cat Book Poems* written some time between 1350 and 1767 (most probably in the 1500s) in the old Siamese capital of Ayudhya. It is depicted as a pale-coloured cat with black tail, ears, feet and lower face. Known as the *Vichien Mat,* it was only one of 17 varieties that appeared in the poems. It later acquired the name 'Siamese' (rather than a more specific title) because it was the first, and most strikingly unusual one to be seen in the West. Because of its traditional association with Siamese royalty, it has sometimes also been called 'The Palace Cat', 'The Royal Siamese', or 'The Royal Cat of Siam'. In France is it known as the *Siamois;* in Germany as the *Siamkatzen;* and in Holland as the *Siamees.*

An early sketch of a Siamese Cat, from 1903, when the breed was little known in the West and was referred to as having a colour 'in accord with the ideas of a pug-dog' and 'with a short twisted tail, something like a badly carried pug's tail'. It has changed dramatically since those days.

Appearance: The blue-eyed Siamese has a highly characteristic shape, being slim, elongated and angular. The earliest examples of this breed to reach the West had two additional, unusual features: a crooked, kinked tail and inward-squinting eyes. Both these features were soon removed by selective breeding. The angularity of the breed, on the other hand, has been retained and greatly exaggerated during recent times, creating an extreme type of Siamese which some feel has moved too far from its original form.

The diagnostic feature of the Siamese Cat has always been its unique coat pattern. The body of the animal is light in colour, but its extremities are dark. This configuration, which is referred to as a 'colourpoint' pattern, or 'points' pattern, develops in an unusual way. To understand this, it is best to think of this cat as a dark-coated animal carrying a gene which inhibits the pigmentation of its fur if its body temperature rises above a certain level. So, where the cat's surface is coolest – on its extremities – the pigment is able to develop normally. But where its surface is hottest – around the main trunk of its body – the pigment is unable to develop and the coat remains pale.

Needless to say, when Siamese kittens are born, emerging from the heat of the womb they are hot all over and therefore pale all over. But then, as they grow older, their extremities gradually become cooler and darken. In elderly Siamese, the whole body becomes slightly cooler and all the fur then darkens a little.

It is easy enough to confirm that the fur of the Siamese is temperature-dependent. Any Siamese that has, say, a foot injury which needs bandaging for a long period of time will eventually show a pale foot where the bandages increased the heat of that extremity. Any Siamese that suffers a high-temperature fever will also eventually develop paler fur.

Legends: There are several popular fables connected with the special features of the Siamese:

1 The kinked tail and the squinting eyes of this breed, which so intrigued those who first encountered the early specimens, are said to be the result of escapades of an intoxicated monk. This particular monk, who served in a temple that housed a golden goblet once used by the Great Buddha, was in the habit of disappearing for days on end, leaving his pair of Siamese Cats to guard the sacred goblet. Eventually the male Siamese decided to seek a replacement for the monk and set out in search of another holy man. The female Siamese Cat stayed behind to guard the precious goblet on her own and she stared at it so hard and so long that she developed a permanent squint. As the days passed she became so exhausted that she wrapped her tail around the goblet and sank into a deep sleep. When the male cat finally returned with a new monk, they found the female, still protecting the goblet, but now surrounded by a litter of five kittens, all with crossed eyes and kinked tails.

2 The kinked tail was the result of a Buddhist monk tying a knot in his cat's tail to prevent him from forgetting something important.

A modern Grand Champion Seal Point Siamese (*opposite*), in all its graceful, elongated splendour. Throughout the 20th century the breed has become increasingly angular and slender.

3 The kinked tail was the result of a Royal Princess, preparing to bathe in a stream, threading her rings on her cat's tail and then tying a knot in its tip to stop them sliding off.
4 A variant of this last story omits the tying of the knot. In this version it is the cat itself that deliberately kinks its own tail to prevent the loss of its mistress's rings.
5 The blue eyes of the breed were gained as a result of the devoted courage of these cats when defending a sacred altar. When raiders had driven the priests from their temple, the intruders were confronted by menacing cats, sitting on the altar steps. Frightened of the teeth and claws of the loyal felines, they left the altar untouched. When the priests were able to return to the temple, they marvelled at the cats' loyalty and from that day forward, the fiery red of the animals' eyes was turned into a heavenly blue, reflecting the way in which they has served heaven in their stand against the barbarians.

History: There are five theories concerning the possible origin of this ancient breed:

1 The Siamese is descended from an Oriental wild cat species, thus giving it a different zoological origin from all other domestic cats and thereby explaining its striking differences in voice and personality. Although this has been put forward as a serious suggestion as recently as 1992, there is no scientific evidence to support it.
2 Egyptian traders took their domestic cats with them to the Far East, where they developed directly into the Siamese breed, without any European influence on the way. This direct route might be sufficient to explain the special features of the breed.
3 An extremely rare and greatly prized, pure white cat was given to the King of Siam as a special gift and from this animal the Siamese breed was developed by crossings with the dark-furred temple cats.
4 During the victory of the Siamese and Annamese people over the Cambodian Empire of the Khmers about 300 years ago, Annamese Cats were imported into Siam, where they crossed with specimens of the Sacred Cat of Burma to produce what we now call the Siamese Cat.
5 Centuries ago, a natural mutation occurred in the local cats of Siam in which an all-over dark brown coat became temperature-dependent in such a way that it resulted in a dark-pointed coat pattern.

In the absence of any hard evidence, it is impossible to decide between these five alternative theories, and it is unlikely that we will ever know, with complete certainty, the true origin of this breed of cat.

It is often stated that the Siamese Cat was of such elevated status that it was confined solely to the Royal Palace of the King of Siam and that the theft of one was punishable by death. Such a strict degree of confinement is certainly an exaggeration. A modified view suggests that this type of cat was also present in many princely homes, in the mansions of the Siamese aristocracy, and in the precincts of the sacred temples. This view insists that, although it may not have been an exclusively royal cat, it was nevertheless a cat of high social standing.

According to one frequently repeated tale, the role of this breed was not merely to rid the palaces and mansions of rodents, but to provide a repository for the souls of the human occupants when their earthly lives ended. When a member of the royal family died, one of their favourite cats would be entombed with them. This was not as cruel as it may sound because there were a number of holes in the roof of each tomb, through which an athletic feline could make its escape. When it did so, it was considered that the dead person's soul was now successfully reincarnated in the cat.

In this sacred role the animal was said to have played a vital part in the religious lives of the people and, for this reason, it was supposed to be highly unusual for a foreign visitor to be allowed to take away any Siamese Cat. Only if it was felt necessary to pay some great tribute to honour a foreigner, would one of these cats be offered as a special gift. It follows that, if this was true, the number of these cats leaving the country was extremely small.

There are early records of occasional ones being exhibited as curiosities at European zoos. And we know that a few must somehow have been obtained as pets because of their presence at the very first of the British cat shows, held in 1871. Unfortunately there are no detailed records of these cats. How they came to be there remains a mystery.

Part of the problem with these very first references to Siamese Cats is that, at that time, individual animals were often named by their country of origin. In other words, a 'Siamese Cat' would simply mean one that came from Siam, without saying anything about its appearance. The earliest confirmation we have of the exhibition at a cat show of a true Siamese, with typical coat pattern, dates from 1879, when an article in the London *Daily Telegraph* refers to a 'couple of juveniles of Siamese extraction, with black muzzles, ears, feet and tail setting off a close yellowish drab coat . . . the exhibitor of these curiosities being a Mrs Cunliffe-Lee'.

The next specific reference to the breed appears in St. George Mivart's classic work on feline anatomy, *The Cat*, published in 1881. There he mentions that: 'The Royal Siamese Cat is of one uniform fawn colour, which may be of a very dark tinge. There is a tendency of a darker colour about the muzzle . . . It also had remarkable blue eyes [and] a small head.'

A little later we have the following comment from Harrison Weir in 1889: 'it will be seen how very difficult it is to obtain the pure breed, even in Siam, and on reference to the Crystal Palace catalogues from the year 1871 to 1887, I find that there were *fifteen* females and only *four* males, and some of these were not entire; and I have always understood that the latter were not allowed to be exported, and were only got by those so fortunate as a most extraordinary favour, as the King of Siam is most jealous of keeping the breed entirely in Siam as royal cats.'

The first fully documented export of a Royal Siamese bears out Weir's words, for it was a special gift to the White House in Washington: a present for Lucy Webb Hayes, the wife of the American President, from David Stickles, the American Consul in Bangkok. A female called Siam, she started her long sea journey in 1878 by being sent from Bangkok to Hong Kong. From there she was shipped to San Francisco after which she had to travel by land across America. Arriving at the White House early in 1879, she did not survive long. She fell ill in September of the same year and died in October, despite being offered the finest cuisine the White House kitchens could provide. In her short spell at the presidential home she did, however, become immensely popular and created great interest in this exotic new breed.

The earliest properly documented case of Siamese Cats being exported to Britain dates from the year 1884, when Mr Edward Blencowe Gould, an Acting Vice-Consul (not the Consul General as usually stated) at Bangkok, acquired a pair. It is claimed that he obtained them directly from King Chulalongkorn (who ruled from 1868 to 1910 and who was the son of the King of Siam so well known in the West as the central figure in the musical *The King and I*). Apparently, when the Vice-Consul paid his farewell call on the King, he was offered any gift he liked from the Royal Palace, to take away with him. He chose a pair of the magnificent royal cats. The king was dismayed, but reluctantly honoured his obligation.

Some authors take a sceptical view of this incident, viewing it as pure invention designed to add glamour to the new breed. Brian Vesey-Fitzgerald flatly rejects it with the words: 'We can dismiss the "direct gift from the King" story straightaway.' Milo Denlinger is particularly scathing: 'There is no record that Mr Gould, himself, claimed that these two cats were a present, reluctantly made to him, by the King of Siam, but much romantic drivel has been printed about his difficulty in obtaining them. It seems more likely that they were merely purchased at some bazaar in Bangkok, like any other commodity.'

The official emblem of the Siamese Cat Club, one of the earliest of all breed clubs, founded in January 1901.

A partial confirmation of this unromantic view is to be found in a letter written by Gould's sister, Mrs Lilian Velvey, for whom the cats were a gift. Many years later, in 1930, she wrote: 'It is curious to note now that my original queen, Mia, a very beautiful cat, only cost my brother three ticals or about 7/6d.' However, although this seems to destroy at least half the legend, it should be remembered that no mention is made in this letter concerning the male cat, who was called Pho. So it is still possible, though unlikely, that Gould did acquire the male from the King and then purchased the female from a less noble source to make up a breeding pair.

However he obtained them, we do know that the Vice-Consul gave these two cats to his brother, Owen Gould, who brought them to England as a gift for their sister. These are the oldest 'official' Siamese and are recorded as 1a and 2a in the Siamese Cat Register. They produced a litter, and the kittens, who were given the exotic names of Duen Ngai, Kalahom and Karomata, were exhibited by Mrs Velvey at the 1885 Cat Show at Crystal Palace. They enjoyed great success there, winning both the 'best shorthaired cat' prize and the 'best cat in show', out of 480 entries. This created a huge demand for Siamese Cats and, in the final decade of the 19th century, the royal embargo (if it ever existed) was weakened and many more were imported and shown. Mrs Velvey herself was involved in the importation of many of these Siamese between 1885 and 1890, a fact that is perhaps not entirely unrelated to the report that her brother, the Consul, had by then built his own cattery in Bangkok.

Despite Mrs Velvey's triumph in 1885 (or perhaps because of it), when more Siamese Cats began to appear at cat shows in Britain, they met with a mixed reception. One critic, who had seen the breed at one of the first exhibitions, had called it 'an unnatural nightmare kind of cat'. Another, writing in a magazine in 1889 commented that 'all our informants agree in confessing that almost any other cat is pleasanter and safer to live with'. However, Harrison Weir, who organized the early shows, declared (also in 1889) that: 'Among the beautiful varieties of the domestic cat brought into notice by the cat shows, none deserve more attention than "The Royal Cat of Siam".'

In January 1901, the Siamese Cat Club was formed to promote and protect the breed. Without delay, its members contacted the Siamese Legation in London to find out a little more about their favourite feline. The Legation's reply, dated 17th September 1901, held a few surprises for them: 'the fawn-coloured animal with the dark points and blue eyes is rare in all parts of the country. In Bangkok because there are more leisured people who can devote time to hobbies of the sort, these cats are bred a good deal . . . The King of Siam does not keep any special breed, nor are there any specially preserved in his palace . . . There is no Royal Cat of Siam . . . Nor does any religious sanctity attach to any cat of Siam . . . These ideas have probably arisen from the fact that the Siamese generally are fond of animals, cats included.'

If these statements are true, and not merely the unverified comments of a snobbishly dismissive Legation bureaucrat, then they contradict all the earlier stories concerning the exotic background of this breed. A similar and equally unromantic view was offered 30 years later by a Dr Hugh Smith: 'I was well acquainted with cats in Siam . . . There are no "palace" cats . . . There are no "royal" cats . . . Any person can have a Siamese Cat, and as a matter of fact there are many people outside the palaces and many foreigners who keep such cats as household pets . . . There are no "temple" cats . . . '

However, whether true or not, these negative comments had little impact on the cat world and were soon forgotten. The romantic legends of the Siamese Cat, both regal and sacred, stubbornly survived and are still being told retold to this day.

For those who find the unromantic dismissals depressing, there is a glimmer of hope in remarks made by a Mr A.N.M. Garry who, in 1930, visited Siam and remarked that: 'Having been a contemporary of the then King [of Siam] at Eton, I got a special permit to see the Bangkok Palace . . . and I saw one or two of these "Royal" cats . . . ' So perhaps there was something feline in the Royal Palace, after all. And a Major Walton of the Rice Purchasing Commission, who became a personal friend of the Prince Regent of Siam in the 1940s, tends to confirm this because, before leaving Siam, he was presented with a pair of Siamese as a special gift from the Prince Regent. This again suggests that the breed had some sort of royal connections. But more solid, historical evidence is needed before we can be sure of this.

Returning to the earlier days of the cat fancy, at the very end of the 19th century a few of the famous European Siamese Cats found their way across the Atlantic. Under the aegis of Mrs Clinton Locke of Chicago, the 'Mother of the American Cat Fancy', they were soon appearing in cat shows there, also with great success. In 1899 she founded the Beresford Cat Club, and in the club's first stud book published in 1900, the first two American Siamese Cats recorded were a champion male called Siam and a female called Sally. Their full names were Lockhaven Siam and Lockhaven Sally Ward, which indicates that they were owned by Mrs Locke herself.

Among these early Siamese there was a high mortality. Despite this, rich Americans were paying as much as $1,000 at the turn of the century to import a British-bred Siamese Cat. Translated into today's monetary value, this would make an early Siamese one of the most expensive felines of all time. Presumably this also gave them a certain glamour and they soon became favourites in American high society. By 1909 the Siamese Cat Society of America had been formed and the breed was firmly established as an important new type of show cat.

From that point onwards, on both sides of the Atlantic, the Siamese went from strength to strength. Throughout the 20th century its popularity has continued to spread worldwide as it has progressed to becoming one of the most celebrated of all pedigree breeds.

Personality: Terms used to describe this breed include: unpredictable, demanding, noisy, thieving, mischievous, determined, lively, active, agile, demonstrative, domineering, graceful, loyal, affectionate, devoted, intelligent and resourceful.

Perhaps the most unusual feature of the Siamese, that sets it apart from other breeds, is its voice. No other cat is quite so noisy. As one owner commented plaintively: 'He is so vocal with his incessant yowling and mewing that he drives a person forced to listen to him almost to distraction. He talks all the time he is awake . . . with his raucous and always persistent voice. There are frequent alterations in the tone, pitch, timbre and volume of that voice.' For some this may be an irritant, but for many Siamese owners it is one of the qualities that helps to give this unusual breed its unique charm.

Several authors have referred to the Siamese as 'more like a dog than like a cat'. Although this is an exaggeration, it is fair to say that, of all the various cat breeds, the Siamese is the one nearest to the dog in personality.

Colour Forms: When it first arrived in the West, the Siamese Cat displayed only one colour pattern: *Seal Point*. This was to be the only colour form recognized for half a century – from 1871 until the 1930s. Even today, when there are many different variants, it has remained in the public mind as 'the' Siamese colour.

To the general public there is only one Siamese colour pattern – the Seal Point, shown here. To modern Siamese specialists, however, this is just one of many variants.

The history of the development of the other Siamese colours is complex. In the early days, when a variant occurred, it was usually written off as 'poor seal'. From time to time, however, a particular breeder would become attached to one of these alternative colour forms and start a serious breeding programme. Then, after a while, the variant would be given official recognition and become registered as a distinct breed. For example, the *Blue Point*, first noticed as early as 1894, was not recognized as a breed by the GCCF until 1936. (In America it was recognized a little earlier, in 1932.) Another early variant, the *Chocolate Point* was not given the official blessing until 1950. The *Lilac Point* had to wait until 1960. (To avoid confusion, it should be mentioned that the Lilac Point had already been accepted in America in 1954 under the title of Frost Point.)

The *Tabby Point*, mentioned as early as 1902, was finally recognized in 1966, along with the *Cream Point*, *Red Point* and *Tortie Point*. However, these four breeds (and other, later ones) are not considered true Siamese in the United States. There, they are called Colourpoint Shorthair Cats. (For details see separate entry.)

In recent years many other colour combinations have been added until, today, there is a huge variety from which to choose, including the following:

GCCF: Seal Point; Chocolate Point; Blue Point; Lilac Point; Cinnamon Point; Caramel Point; Fawn Point; Seal Tabby Point; Blue Tabby Point; Chocolate Tabby Point; Lilac Tabby Point; Red Tabby Point; Cream Tabby Point; Cinnamon Tabby Point; Caramel Tabby Point; Fawn Tabby Point; Seal Tortie Tabby Point; Blue Tortie Tabby Point; Chocolate Tortie Tabby Point; Lilac Tortie Tabby Point; Cinnamon Tortie Tabby Point; Caramel Tortie Tabby Point; Fawn Tortie Tabby Point; Red Point; Seal Tortie Point; Blue Tortie Point; Chocolate Tortie Point; Lilac Tortie Point; Cinnamon Tortie Point; Caramel Tortie Point; Fawn Tortie Point; Cream Point.

CFA: Seal Point; Chocolate Point; Blue Point; Lilac Point.

Bibliography:

This is undoubtedly the most extensively documented of all breeds.

1907. Rideout, H.M. *The Siamese Cat*. McClure, Phillips, New York. (Fiction)
1928. Underwood, L. *The Siamese Cat*. Brentano, New York. (Fiction)
1929. Morse, E. *The Siamese Cat*. Dutton, New York. (Juvenile)
1934. Wade, P. *The Siamese Cat*. Methuen, London.
1935. Becker, M.L. *Five Cats from Siam*. McBride, New York. (Juvenile)
1947. Sim, K. *These I Have Loved*. London. (Anecdotal)
1949. Joseph, M. *Charles. The Story of a Friendship*. London (Anecdotal)
1950. France, S. W. *Siamese Cats*. Cats and Kittens Publications, Derby.
1950. Hart, E. A. *Practical Handbook of the Siamese Cat*. Privately printed, London.
1950. Holdworth, I. *Little Masks*. London. (Anecdotal)
1950. Lauder, P. *Siamese Cats*. Williams & Norgate, London.
1950. Tenent, R. *The Book of the Siamese Cat*. Rockliff, London.
1950. Tute, W. *Chico*. London. (Anecdotal)
1950. Williams, K.R. *The Breeding and Management of the Siamese Cat*. Williams, London.
1952. Baker, H.G. *Your Siamese Cat*. Verschoyle, London.
1952. Denlinger, M.G. *The Complete Siamese Cat*. Denlinger's, Richmond, Virginia.
1953. Lauder, P. *New Siamese Cats*. Williams & Norgate, London.
1956. Anon. *Siamese Cats as Pets*. TFH, New Jersey.
1956. Nelson, V.M. *Siamese Cat Book*. All-Pet Books, Wisconsin.
1958. Chetham-Strode, W. *Three Men and a Girl*. London (Anecdotal)
1960. Colfer, E. *Cucumber*. USA. (Anecdotal)
1960. Van der Meid, L.B. *Siamese Cats*. Sterling, New York.
1960 Williams, K.R. *Siamese Cats*. Foyle, London.
1962. Eustace, M. *Cats in Clover*. Michael Joseph, London. (Anecdotal)
1963. Lauder, P. *Siamese Cats*. Ernest Benn, London.
1963. Roth, B. Beulah. *The Cosmopolitan Cat*. New York. (Anecdotal)

WITH ITS LIVELY, demanding personality, the Siamese Cat has become the subject of many books and has, without question, acquired the longest breed bibliography of all.

1963. Smyth, J. *Beloved Cats.* London. (Anecdotal)
1964. Naples, M. *This is the Siamese Cat.* TFH, New Jersey.
1964. Warner, E.R. *Siamese Summer.* Viking, New York. (Juvenile)
1967. Hindley, G. *Siamese Cats Past and Present.* The Wharf, Goldalming, Surrey.
1968. Denham, S. and Denham, H. *The Siamese Cat.* Arco, London.
1968. Eustace, M. *The Royal Cat of Siam.* Pelham Books, London.
1971. King, F.D. *Siamese Pussies.* Stockwell, Ilfracombe, Devon. (Juvenile)
1971. Lauder, P. *The Siamese Cat.* Batsford, London.
1974. Lauder, P. *The Batsford Book of the Siamese Cat.* Batsford, London.
1974. Dunhill, M. *The Siamese Cat Owner's Encyclopedia.* Pelham Books, London.
1975. Eustace, M. *A Hundred Years of Siamese Cats.* Research Publishing, London.
1976. Stranger, J. Kim. *The True Story of a Siamese Cat.* London.
1981. Reagan, R. *Siamese Cats.* TFH, New Jersey.
1983. Dunhill, M. *Siamese Cats.* Batsford, London
1989. Naples, M. *A Step-by-Step Book about the Siamese.* TFH, New Jersey.
1992. Collier, M.M. *The Siamese Cat; A Complete Cat Owner's Guide.* Barron's, Hauppauge, New York.
1993. Burns, B.S. *All About Siamese Cats.* TFH, New Jersey.
1995. Franklin, S. *The Complete Siamese.* Ringpress Books, Gloucester.

Breed Clubs:

National Siamese Cat Club. Address: 5865 Hillandale Drive, Nashport, OH 43830, USA.

Siamese Cat Association,. Publishes a *Journal.* Address: Wrenshall Farmhouse, Walsham Le Willows, Bury St Edmunds, Suffolk, IP31 3AS, England.

Siamese Cat Club. One of the oldest of all breed clubs, founded in 1901. It issues a twice-yearly *Newsletter.* Address: Fistral, 10 Noak Hill Close, Billericay, Essex, CM12 9UZ, England.

Siamese Cat Society of America. Publishes a *Siamese News Quarterly.* Address: 304 S.W. 13th Street, Fort Lauderdale, FL 33315, USA.

Siamese Cat Society of the British Empire. Woodlands Farm, Bridford, Exeter, Devon, EX6 7EW, England.

SIAMESE VARIANTS

DOMESTIC BREEDS. The Siamese has been used as the ancestral cat for a number of recent breeds, each modifying the original form in one way or another. These modern descendants of the Siamese include the following:

1 BALINESE (Longhair Siamese with points)
2 JAVANESE (Longhair Siamese with new-colour points)
3 ORIENTAL LONGHAIR (Longhair Siamese without points)
4 ORIENTAL SHORTHAIR (Shorthair Siamese without points)
5 COLOURPOINT SHORTHAIR (Shorthair Siamese with new-colour points)
6 HAVANA (Shorthair Siamese with solid brown coat)
7 FOREIGN WHITE (Shorthair Siamese with all-white coat)
8 SEYCHELLOIS (Shorthair Siamese with splashed white coat)

In addition there are three breeds that have an important Siamese element in their make-up, but which also have a strong 'rival' element present:

9 OCICAT (Shorthair Siamese/Abyssinian)
10 SNOWSHOE (Shorthair Siamese/American Shorthair Bi-colour)
11 TONKINESE (Shorthair Siamese/Burmese)

(See separate entries for further details. Some of these names, especially the Javanese, are used slightly differently in different countries.)

NOTE: Because modern show Siamese have developed such an extreme body-type, there has recently been a movement to return to the old-style Siamese with a less angular body and more rounded head. These types of Siamese have been given a number of different names, including the following: Applecat; Apple-head Siamese; Classic Siamese; Old-fashioned Siamese; Opal Cat; Thai Cat; Traditional Siamese. (For further details see Apple-head Siamese, Thai Cat and Traditional Siamese.)

SIBERIAN FOREST CAT

DOMESTIC BREED. An ancient long-haired breed now believed to have been ancestral to all modern long-haired cats including both the Angora and the Persian. Sometimes referred to simply as the 'Siberian Cat' or the 'Siberia'. Most commonly found in Northern Russia, especially around St. Petersburg where its thick fur protects it from the harsh winters. In Germany it is known as the *Sibirische Katze*.

Appearance: A strongly built, long-bodied cat with a broad, round head and powerful legs. The long fur has a dense, heavy under-coat. There is a thick ruff and a bushy tail. In many respects it is similar to the Norwegian Forest Cat, to which it is no doubt closely related.

History: It would seem that this breed has been present in Russia for centuries. At the end of the 19th century a few were imported into Britain and appeared at the first cat shows, but by the beginning of the 20th century they had vanished, overtaken by the more popular Persian. Those early examples were known as Russian Long-haired Cats.

The breed presumably continued to thrive in its homeland but was taken for granted to such an extent by the local people that nobody bothered to develop it as a pedigree cat. (A recent survey revealed that 64 per cent of the cats in St. Petersburg carried the long-haired gene.) The result was that, in the world of cat shows, it became a forgotten breed. Even today it remains rare outside its homeland. However, this seems set to change. In 1987 a young male and female were collected from the region of St. Petersburg and taken to Germany by enthusiasts who invented the new name 'Siberian' and started a serious breeding programme. The male was called Tima and the female Mussa. The female was discovered in a city market. Within a few months they had produced their first litter.

THE SIBERIAN FOREST CAT is similar in appearance to the better-known Norwegian Forest Cat. Coming from cold northern regions, both are large cats with heavy coats. The Siberian Forest Cat is thought by some to be the original ancestor of all our long-haired breeds.

Since then there has also been increased interest in Russia itself, as pedigree cat breeding has at last started to flourish there. There is now a birth registry for Siberian Forest Cats at the Kotofej Cat Club in St. Petersburg.

The breed was first imported into America in 1990 and the first litter was born there in October of that year. It was exhibited at the International Cat Show in New York in 1991.

Personality: Terms used to describe this breed are slightly contradictory. They include: shrewd, docile, lively, shy, rugged, affectionate, devoted, gentle, relaxed and active. It is vocally quiet, like the Persians.

Colour Forms: The typical colouring is tabby, usually with a white ruff and white paws, but now that Russian breeders are taking an interest in it, many new colours are being developed.

Breed Club:

Comrade Cat Club (Siberian Cat). Address: RR 1, Box 2460, Bowdoinham, ME 04008, USA.

Siemel's Cat

Mystery Cat. There is a record from the early part of the 20th century that the big-game hunter Sacha Siemel, while on an expedition to the Mata Grosso, shot a large cat that he claimed was a cross between a Jaguar and a Puma. It had the ground colour of a Puma but the spots of a Jaguar and was very heavily built. For such a hybrid to occur in the wild is so unlikely as to be hardly worth serious consideration, but the identity of the animal remains a mystery.

Silkworm Cat

Talismanic Cat. Images of cats were placed on the walls of the houses of Chinese silkworm breeders to protect their silkworms from harm during the breeding season. It was believed that these pictures would have the power to frighten off the rats that often plagued the farmers. Some, more practical farmers also collected together as many live cats as they could to carry out the task, at the most sensitive time of the year.

Silver

Coat Colour. The silver effect is created by a coat of hairs each of which is pale at the base and dark at the tip. (See also Chinchilla.)

Modern variants of this colour include: (1) Blue Silver; (2) Blue Silver Tabby; (3) Blue Silver Tabby and White; (4) Blue Silver Patched Tabby; (5) Blue Chinchilla Silver; (6) Blue Shaded Silver; (7) Chestnut Silver; (8) Chestnut Silver Tabby; (9) Chinchilla Silver; (10) Chocolate Silver; (11) Chocolate Silver Tabby; (12) Cinnamon Silver; (13) Cinnamon Silver Tabby; (14) Cream Silver (= Dilute Cameo); (15) Cream Silver Tabby; (16) Ebony Silver; (17) Ebony Silver Tabby; (18) Fawn Silver; (19) Fawn Silver Tabby; (20) Lavender Silver; (21) Lavender Silver Tabby; (22) Parti-colour Silver; (23) Red Silver (= Cameo); (24) Shaded Silver; (25) Silver Tabby; (26) Silver Patched Tabby; (27) Silver Tabby and White.

Silver Lace Cat

Domestic Breed. An alternative name for the cat now generally known as the Snowshoe Cat. (See separate entry.)

Simba

Wild Feline. The Swahili name for the Lion *(Panthera leo)*. It was used by Guggisberg as the title for his book on this species.

Bibliography:

1961. Guggisberg, C.A.W. *Simba*. Bailey Bros. & Swinfen, London.

Simpkin

Fictional Cat. One of Beatrix Potter's feline characters, Simpkin appeared in *The Tailor of Gloucester* in 1903.

Simple J. Malarkey

Cartoon Cat. An unpleasant feline who arrived at the infamous Okefenokee Swamp in 1953, in Walt Kelly's comic strip *Pogo*. He was a bobcat with a nasty smile and was based on the right-wing, witch-hunting Senator McCarthy, as part of Kelly's savage political satire.

Simpson, Frances

Cat Authority. By the end of the 19th century, competitive cat shows had become established and great interest had arisen in the subject of pure lines of pedigree cats. In 1903, Frances Simpson, a prominent cat breeder, show manager and judge, produced a major reference work on the subject that was to have lasting value. As recently as 1972, Claire Necker had special praise for Simpson's *The Book of the Cat:* 'Although dated, this book is still considered the most comprehensive on cat breeds, at least from the historic angle. A classic in its field.' In 1985, Grace Pond commented: '*The Book of the Cat* by Frances Simpson . . . is one of the most comprehensive books on the early days of the Cat Fancy that has ever been written. It has been published worldwide and is a never-ending source of interest.'

Bibliography:

1902. Simpson, F. *Cats and all about them.* Isbister, London.
1903. Simpson, F. *The Book of the Cat.* Cassell, London.
1905. Simpson, F. *Cats for Pleasure and Profit.* Pitman, London.

Singapura Cat

Domestic Breed. A recently acknowledged cat from Singapore. A small, short-haired breed that was known locally as the 'Drain Cat of Singapore' (because it is reputed to take shelter in the city drains, during the dry season, when suffering from human persecution), or the 'Singapore River Cat' (because it is supposed to have originated on the banks of the river system there).

There is no mystery over its internationally recognized name, Singapura: it is simply the Malay term for Singapore. This was the title originally given to the city in 1299, by a visiting Sumatran Prince.

Today this cat is known by yet another name in Singapore. It is called 'Kucinta, the Love Cat of Singapore'. This is not, however, an old traditional name, but a recently promoted one. It was introduced in 1991 by the Singapore Tourist Board as part of a worldwide promotional campaign for the city.

In 1993 the Singapura Cat became the official symbol of Singapore and two pedigree specimens were returned there to act as models for statues of 'Kucinta' that will be positioned on the Singapore River, where the breed supposedly began its existence.

Appearance: This is one of the smallest of all the pedigree breeds. It is a muscular cat with a very short, fine, satiny coat that lies close to the body. The ground colour of the breed is ivory, each hair being ticked with two or more bands of dark brown. (The only other pedigree cats with ticked, or agouti hair are the Abyssinian, the Somali, the Wild Abyssinian and the Ceylon.) The tail tip is black. The eyes and ears are large. The legs are strong, but the feet are small.

History: There has been considerable controversy about the origins of this attractive breed. The usual story, as reported in most cat publications (but now known to be incorrect in several respects), goes as follows:

The founders of the breed, an American couple called Hal and Tommy Meadow, discovered it in Singapore in 1974. There they heard about an unusually small breed of cat that lived in the streets and sewers of the city. They acquired a kitten which they called 'Pusse' and later an adult pair called 'Tickle' and 'Tessa'. They started breeding from these cats while still in Singapore and then, in 1975, took five of them, including the original three, back to the United States. There they set about establishing the Singapura as a new addition to the list of pedigree cat breeds.

In a 1988 interview, Mrs Tommy Meadow added the following details to this version of the Singapura's origin: 'In April [1975] Saigon fell and in July I was moving back to the United States,

The exquisitely delicate Singapura is one of the smallest of all breeds of domestic cat. Incorrectly described as 'Singapore drain cats', they were in reality ships' cats discovered in the harbour of Loyang in the north-east of Singapore.

with my husband Hal following a few days later. With me I brought my orchids, ten hooded rats . . . and six cats. Of the six cats, five were cats that acquired the breed name of Singapura while in Singapore and had been registered with the Singapore Feline Society . . . the oldest one was Pusse who had been found near the Goldhill Building in the centre of the 225 square mile island. The next in age were a male, Tickle, and his little sister Tessa found near the waterfront. George and Gladys, named after members of the Singapore Feline Society, were 4 month old kittens travelling with mum Pusse and had been sired by Tickle. These 1975 immigrants into the United States were joined in 1980 by a cat named Chiko who had been located at the SPCA by another American cat breeder vacationing in Singapore. Subsequently Chiko was shipped to a Singapura breeder [Barbara Gilbertson] in the State of Washington.'

That was the official story of the origin of the new breed and was accepted by everyone until, a few years later, another American breeder, Jerry Mayes, visited Singapore in search of new blood, only to make a surprising discovery. To his astonishment he found that there was documentary evidence to prove that Mr and Mrs Meadow had *imported* Pusse, Tickle and Tessa into Singapore from the United States.

The story of them being found 'near the Goldhill Building' and 'on the waterfront' was an elaborate deception. But why?

One theory was that Mrs Tommy Meadow had deliberately concealed the true origin of the Singapuras in order to give them a more romantic heritage. It was pointed out that she had previously owned both Burmese and Abyssinians, and that a cross between those two breeds can look remarkably like a Singapura. If she had created such a cross in America, taken the progeny to Singapore, 'discovered' them in the streets of the city, and then brought them back to the United States as an exotic new breed from the Orient, she would have pulled off a remarkable subterfuge to become the founder of a delightful 'Eastern' breed that was rapidly gaining popularity on the show benches. Critics of the original version of the Singapura 'history' felt that this was the true story of what had happened, and their scepticism forced Tommy Meadow to make a new statement, correcting her earlier comments.

In a 1994 interview, she admitted that there were inaccuracies in the way she had told the original version of the story. Her new account ran as follows:

During a previous marriage, she had been a successful exhibitor of Siamese, Burmese and Abyssinian Cats. In 1970 she had met Hal Meadow, a geophysicist whose work for an oil company took him repeatedly to the Far East, including Singapore. Hal had always been fascinated by cats, and through Tommy he developed an interest in the cat fancy and pedigree breeds. When he was on one of his trips to Singapore, in 1971, he spotted some local cats that he realized at a glance were unusual. He was particularly struck by the fact that they had a ticked coat like an Abyssinian's, but with a more silvery colour. Never having seen such a colouring before, he arranged to have four of these 'strange coloured Abys' shipped back to his wife in the United States. The group consisted of a male and three females, and in Tommy's care they soon began breeding.

Mrs Tommy Meadow, the moving force behind the establishment of the Singapura breed, with two of her cats.

Then in 1974, after Hal and Tommy had married, they travelled to Singapore together, accompanied by a group of her cats, including three grandchildren of the original quartet. These three were called Pusse, Tess and Ticle. (Slightly different spellings are given in this version of the story.) The Meadows continued breeding from these cats while still in Singapore. They had intended to stay there for ten years but, following the fall of Saigon in July 1975, and the collapse of the American involvement in Vietnam, they returned earlier than expected to the United States. They took five Singapuras with them, including the original three, plus Gladys and George, who had been born there in the meantime. Once back home, they set about firmly establishing the new breed and gaining official recognition for it.

From this point onwards there is no controversy about what happened. In late 1975, Tommy Meadow started exhibiting her Singapuras at American cat shows. In the years that followed, the Singapura was formally recognized by more and more cat societies in America and in 1980 a United Singapura Society was formed to support the breed. By 1988 it was estimated that there were over 500 of these cats in North America and by the mid-1990s this had risen to about 2,000.

The first Singapura in Britain was a pregnant female called Faye Raye, who arrived on 25th July 1988 and gave birth a few weeks later, while still in quarantine. British interest in the Singapura developed in the 1990s and a Singapura Cat Club was formed to promote the breed. By 1995 there were an estimated 30 cats of this breed in the British Isles.

The question remains as to what drove Tommy Meadow to 'simplify' the history of the breed by pretending that she and her husband had picked up Pusse, Tessa and Tickle in the streets of Singapore. Were these three cats, as some critics were now suggesting, American-born hybrids between Abyssinians and Burmese, or were they truly the grandchildren of those original Singapore cats discovered by Hal Meadow in 1971? When this question was put to Tommy Meadow, she defended her 'revised' version of events in the following way:

It had been necessary to conceal the information about the original quartet of cats sent to her from Singapore by Hal Meadow in 1971, because at the time (to quote her) 'he was involved in "sensitive" work and his presence in Singapore could not be revealed'. The cats were perfectly genuine and had originated in Singapore, but for reasons quite unconnected with the animals themselves, it had been advisable to omit the earliest phase of their discovery.

Additional information obtained directly from Hal Meadow himself in 1996 confirms this. He was in Singapore to carry out confidential marine surveys for an oil company and was operating out of a port called Loyang in the north-east of the island. One day he noticed three ships' cats on one of the marine survey vessels and was surprised by their unusual appearance. They looked to him like odd-coloured Abyssinians and, as he had never seen anything like them before, he arranged for them to be shipped back to Houston on one of the work boats. About six months later, he saw a fourth cat of this type, also in the harbour at Loyang, which he managed to obtain from a local sailor. This, too, he had shipped back to the United States. Tommy took in all four cats and began to breed from them. When the Singapore cats arrived, her other cats were all neuters and she was not at that stage engaged in breeding programmes with anything else. She kept the Singapore cats pure and took them through two generations before she set off for Singapore with Hal in 1974, taking with her the soon-to-be-famous trio of Pusse, Tessa and Tickle.

The fact that, in July 1975, when Saigon fell, the Meadows returned unexpectedly to the United States was due to the rapid change in the economics of oil company activities in the Orient, caused by the sudden ending of the war in Vietnam.

Based on this more detailed explanation, it is safe to assume that the Singapura is, after all, a true-blue Eastern cat that developed naturally over a long period in the streets of Singapore. Certainly, it is the general view among most Singapura breeders that a cat of this type has been present in Singapore for at least 300 years, and that it is a well-established, ancient breed.

Furthermore, supporters of this 'ancient Singapura' view believe that there is a perfectly good explanation as to why some critics have favoured the rival idea that the breed is a more recent hybrid between Abyssinian and Burmese Cats. They point out that attempts by unscrupulous dealers to mass-produce inexpensive 'fake Singapuras' using crossings of this type, could easily have led to the incorrect belief that all Singapuras were created like this. It is pointed out that Mrs Meadow has been quite open about the fact that she did introduce other breeds in the early days of her Singapura breeding programme, but that these crossings were merely 'test-matings to eliminate known recessive genes from Singapura breeding stock'.

The best way to settle the matter of the breed's origin is for a detailed check to be made of the feral cat population of Singapore today, to see if pockets of typical Singapuras are still present there. A recent attempt to do this by Sarah Hartwell, during a brief stay in the city, proved inconclusive. She scoured the streets for pure specimens, but reports that 'although I saw numerous nervous cats of Oriental or Bobtail type, I found no Singapuras . . . During my stay I saw tabbies, bi-colours and self-colours, but not a single cat with "ticked fur the colour of old ivory", though this might simply mean that Kucinta is a shy and elusive creature. Having scoured the river area and not managed even a glimpse of Kucinta, I eventually began to wonder "are there any Singapuras in Singapore?".'

It seems likely that she was looking in the wrong districts. Perhaps if she had searched in the harbour region in the north-east of the island, where Hal Meadow discovered the original foundation stock for the breed in 1971, she might have been more successful. Obviously, a more careful search is indicated, although it must be borne in mind that, according to a new report, the Singapore authorities have recently introduced a policy of 'clearing the streets of stray cats', so it may already be too late.

Personality: Words used to describe this breed are slightly contradictory and include: playful, sociable, lively, responsive, undemanding, calm, even-tempered, quiet, gentle, alert, good-natured, placid, inquisitive, mischievous, active, intelligent, friendly and fearless. Some describe them as outgoing, but this is denied by others who say they are shy, demure and reserved. They have also been called 'aggressively affectionate'.

THE OFFICIAL EMBLEM of the Singapura Cat Club.

Colour Form: Only one colour is accepted: Sepia Agouti (sometimes called Brown Ticked).

Bibliography:

1988. Meadow, T. B. 'The Singapura Cat in the United States'. In: *Cat World*, September 1988, p.8-9 and October 1988, p. 34-35.

1994. Flavia, C. 'Tommy Meadow: "Discoverer" of the Singapura'. In: *Cat World*, June 1994, p. 12-13.

1995. Edwards, A. 'The Singapura; The Cat with a Coat of Antique Ivory'. In: *All about Cats*, March 1995. p.13-21.

1995. Van Den Berg, D. 'Spotlight on a New Breed: The Singapura'. In: *The Journal of the Chinchilla, Silver Tabby and Smoke Cat Society*, Autumn 1995. p.13-15.

1996. Hartwell, S. 'Kucinta – The Love Cat of Singapore and the Bobtails of Malaysia'. In: *Cat World Annual*, 1966. p.44-45.

Breed Clubs:

International Singapura Alliance. Address: P.O. Box 32218, Oakland, CA 94604, USA.

Original Singapura Breeder's Network. Address: P.O. Box 1457, Solvang, CA 93464, USA.

Singapura Cat Club. Issues a quarterly *Mewsletter*. Address: 437 Whippendell Road, Watford, Herts., WD1 7PS, England.

Singapura Fanciers' Society. Address: 82 W. Catalina Drive, Oakview, CA 93022, USA.

United Singapura Society. Address: 2135, Edison, Santa Ynez, CA 93460, USA, or 5520 Dublin Avenue, North Little Rock, AR 72118, USA.

Singhasep

Domestic Breed. In the ancient Thai Book of Poems (from the Ayudhya Period, 1350–1767), where 17 early Eastern breeds are described and illustrated, there is a black cat with a white collar called Singhasep.

Sinh

Legendary Cat. According to legend, Sinh was the founding father of the Birman breed – the Sacred Cat of Burma. Sinh belonged to the High Priest, Mun-Ha and was with the old man when he died during an attack on his ancient Burmese temple. Placing his paws on the body of the dying man, Sinh absorbed the soul of the priest and, as he did so, his paws turned white. (For details see Birman Cat.)

Si-Rex

Domestic Breed. A recent form of Cornish Rex Cat, with a coat pattern showing Siamese points. For some years it was ignored as a distinct breed, but was eventually recognized by the CFA in America and given championship status in 1986. It was created by crossing Cornish Rex Cats with Siamese Cats.

The dramatically proportioned Si-Rex, a recently developed cross between Cornish Rex Cats and Siamese, now becoming established as a new breed in its own right.

S

Si-Sawat

Domestic Breed. The Thai name for the Korat Cat, a breed which appears in *The Cat Book Poems,* dating from before 1767. The meaning of the name is 'purple grey, the colour of the Sawat nut'. The word 'Sawat' also carries a meaning of 'good fortune' or 'prosperity', and the Si-Sawat Cat is known locally as a 'good luck cat'. (See entry for Korat Cat.)

Sizi

Pet Cat. Sizi belonged to the Nobel Prize-winning French Missionary Albert Schweitzer (1875–1965) and lived with him at his famous clinic in Africa. Visitors noted his deep affection for the cat and the way that he pandered to its needs.

Sleep

Feline Behaviour. Cats sleep twice as much as humans do. The average daily sleeping time for a cat is 16 hours, compared with the typical eight hours for the healthy human. This means that a nine-year-old cat, approaching the end of its life, has only been awake for a total of about three years.

This is the typical sleeping pattern of a predator with a highly efficient killing technique. Like the snake, the cat has time on its hands and uses it to sleep and to dream. Nothing falls asleep quite so easily as a cat.

Whereas the normal adult human sleeps in one long spell through the night, cats indulge in many, shorter periods of sleep during each 24 hours. There are three types of feline sleep: the brief nap (which has given us the word 'catnap'), the longer light sleep, and the deep sleep. The light sleep and the deep sleep alternate in characteristic bouts. When the animal settles down for more than a nap, it floats off into a phase of light sleep which lasts for about half an hour. Then the cat sinks further into slumber and, for six or seven minutes, experiences deep sleep. After this it returns to another bout of 30 minutes of light sleep, and so on until it eventually wakes up.

During the periods of deep sleep, the cat's body relaxes so much that it usually rolls over on to its side and this is the time when the animal appears to be dreaming, with frequent twitchings and quivering of ears, paws and tail. The mouth may make sucking movements and there are even occasional vocalizations, such a growls, purrs and general mutterings. There are also bursts of rapid eye movement, but throughout all this, the cat's trunk remains immobile and totally relaxed. At the start of life, the very young kitten experiences only this deep type of sleep which lasts for a total of about 12 hours out of every 24. After the first month, the kittens rapidly switch to the adult pattern.

Bibliography:

1966. Hoofdakker, R.H. *Behaviour and EEG of Drowsy and Sleeping Cats.* Holland.

Slippers

Pet Cat. Slippers was the much loved pet of American President Theodore Roosevelt (1858–1919). Anatomically, he was an unusual cat in having six-toed feet. A grey tabby with a self-confident, almost arrogant air, he deferred to nobody as he strolled around his White House domain. His main claim to fame was that, one evening in 1906, he forced an entire procession of important White House guests to make a detour around his recumbent form, as they moved from the State Dining Room to the East Room. He frequently wandered off for days on his own, but always returned to the Presidential residence after a while, to laud it again over the mere humans who lived there.

Small Spotted Cat

Wild Feline. An alternative name for the Black-footed Cat of Africa *(Felis nigripes)*. The name is preferred by some authors because the African Wild Cat *(Felis sylvestris lybica)* also has black feet. But the title of Small Spotted Cat is easy to confuse with the name of the diminutive South

American species *Felis tigrina*, which is sometimes called the Little Spotted Cat. So, for the sake of clarity, the traditional name of Black-footed Cat is preferred. (For details see separate entry for Black-footed Cat.)

SMOKE

COAT COLOUR. Smoke is a coat pattern that is similar to Chinchilla (see separate entry), but whereas each Chinchilla hair is pale along its length except for a dark tip, a Smoke hair is pale at the base and then gradually darkens towards the tip. In other words, a greater proportion of each Smoke hair is dark. The effect of this is to make the cat literally change colour as it becomes active. A Black Smoke Persian, for example, will appear jet black when lying down in a relaxed posture, but when it jumps up and starts to move, its coat will shift to reveal the pale under-coat.

Persian Cats with a Smoke coat pattern were originally ignored and were placed in the 'any other colour' category at the first cat shows, but by 1893 Smoke Persians had already been given their own separate class.

Today the following 24 smoke colour variants are recognized: (1) Black Smoke (= Ebony Smoke); (2) Blue Smoke; (3) Blue-Cream Smoke; (4) Cameo Smoke; (5) Dilute Cameo Smoke (= Cream Smoke); (6) Chestnut Smoke; (7) Chocolate Smoke; (8) Chocolate Tortoiseshell Smoke; (9) Cinnamon Smoke; (10) Cinnamon Tortoiseshell Smoke; (11) Cream Smoke; (12) Ebony Smoke (= Black Smoke); (13) Fawn Smoke (14) Fawn-Cream Smoke; (15) Lavender Smoke; (16) Lavender Cream Smoke; (17) Particolour Smoke; (18) Red (= Cameo) Smoke; (19) Smoke-and-White Smoke; (20) Tortoiseshell Smoke; (21) Van-Smoke-and-White Smoke; (22) Smoke and White; (23) Black Smoke and White; (24) Van Smoke and White.

These colours are distributed among the various breeds as follows (according to American CFA listings):

AMERICAN CURL: Black, Blue, Red, Chocolate, Lavender, Cream, Tortie, Chocolate Tortie, Blue-Cream.

AMERICAN SHORTHAIR: Black, Blue, Red, Tortie, Blue-Cream, Smoke-and-White.

AMERICAN WIREHAIR: Black, Blue, Cameo.

BRITISH SHORTHAIR: Black, Blue.

EXOTIC: Black, Blue, Red, Cream, Tortie, Blue-Cream, Smoke-and-White, Van-Smoke-and-White.

MAINE COON: Black, Blue, Red, Tortie, Blue-Cream, Smoke-and-White.

MANX: Black, Blue.

NORWEGIAN FOREST: Black, Blue, Red, Cream, Tortie, Blue-Cream.

ORIENTAL LONGHAIR: Black (Ebony), Blue, Red, Lavender, Cream, Fawn, Cinnamon, Particolour, Chestnut.

ORIENTAL SHORTHAIR: Black (Ebony), Blue, Red, Lavender, Cream, Fawn, Cinnamon, Particolour, Chestnut.

PERSIAN: Black, Blue, Red, Cream, Tortie, Blue-Cream, Smoke-and-White, Van-Smoke-and-White.

SCOTTISH FOLD: Black, Blue, Red.

TURKISH ANGORA: Black, Blue.

Specialist Club:

Smoke Cat Society. Address: 36 Alden Avenue, Morley, Leeds, England.

SMOKY

PET CAT. Smoky was an unusual gift for American President Calvin Coolidge (1872–1933). He was not a domestic cat, but a wild Bobcat caught for the President in Tennessee. Smoky was graciously accepted, but then quickly moved on to a zoo for safe-keeping. Other strange gifts he received included a female raccoon called Rebecca (which he did keep at the White House), a wallaby, a hippopotamus, a bear and a pair of lion cubs (which he did not).

S

THE SNOW CAT, or Alaskan Snow Cat, is a dramatic new breed being developed in the 1990s in the United States. It is a heavily built cat with a striking coat pattern achieved by crossings between Somalis and Silver Persians.

Snow Cat

Domestic Breed. Also known as the Alaskan Snow Cat. A new, experimental breed developed in the United States during the 1990s. Several breeders in Florida and Minnesota have been working towards producing a heavy-boned, thick-furred, silvery-coloured, round-headed cat, similar to the Siberian Forest Cat. This has been achieved by crossings between Somalis and Silver Persians. The early stages of this programme are still in progress at the time of writing.

Snow Leopard

Wild Feline. *(Panthera uncia)* Also referred to as the Ounce, Snow Panther, or Mountain Panther. In some regions it is known locally as the Bharal-Hay, or Bharal-Tiger. In Tibet it is called the Iker. It has been suggested that a better name for this species would be the Rock Leopard.

As an example of the amazingly complicated ways in which some animals acquire their scientific names, the derivation of the Snow Leopard's specific name of *uncia* takes some beating. Here is A.F. Gotch's explanation, from his 1995 publication *Latin Names Explained:* 'The Greeks were familiar with a moderate sized feline and called it *lynx*. The Romans borrowed the Greek word and it became the Tuscan *lonza*. Later the word passed into French as *lonce,* and the initial l being mistaken for the article [as in *l'once*] it was elided and the word became *once,* whence it passed into Spanish as *onca* and English as *ounce*. Finally, *onca* was Latinized into *uncia,* although this was Latin for a measure of weight and not an animal!' After all this, the only real meaning of the animal's scientific name *Panthera uncia* is 'a Big Cat of moderate size'.

The Snow Leopard is one of the five species of Pantherines, or Big Cat (the other four being the Lion, Tiger, Leopard and Jaguar). It inhabits remote, mountainous regions, living above the highest forests, up in the bleak, rocky landscapes where no other member of the cat family could survive. It is helped by its unusually thick coat of dense fur. As adaptations to the intense cold, it has a stocky body, short, thick legs with big paws, a heavily furred tail, a small head and short round ears. It has a characteristically wide forehead, with the ears set low and wide apart. There is an 'eye-spot' on the back of each ear. Its coat is a pale grey colour, with dark spots on the legs and dark rosettes on the trunk and upper tail. The tail tip is ringed and becomes darker near the extremity.

Little is known about its social life, except that it is a solitary hunter that breeds in the spring and rears its litter in a cave or rock cavity. It has been seen in pairs occasionally, but how long these stay together is not known. There are regular tracks that are followed week after week, and it is said that if two animals meet on one of these tracks they exchange a puffing greeting sound similar to that of the Tiger.

The Snow Leopard hunts anything that can live in the high altitudes, including marmots, wild sheep, deer, ibex, hares and birds. Despite its short legs, it is capable of an amazing leap when hunting. On one occasion it was observed to jump 16 metres (17½ yards) across a ditch when running uphill.

Some idea of how poorly known this species is in the wild can be gained from the wide variation in the different estimates given for its total population. One report stated that it was nearly extinct, with only 400 animals remaining alive. Another survey put the figure at between 3,000 and 10,000, while a third estimated the world population as high as 40,000. Bearing in mind the animal's remote Himalayan habitat, it is doubtful if we will ever be certain of the true figure.

In addition to the wild population, there are over 370 Snow Leopards in captivity in zoos around the world, where breeding successes are improving.

Size: Length of Head + Body: 100–130 cm (39½–51 in). Tail: 80–100 cm (31½–39½ in). Weight: 25–75 kg (55–165 lb).

Distribution: Restricted to the mountains of Central Asia, it is found in the following countries: Russia, Mongolia, Tibet, China, Nepal, Bhutan, India, Pakistan and Afghanistan.

Bibliography:

1978. Matthiessen, P. *The Snow Leopard*. Viking, New York.

1989. Fox, J.L. *A Review of the Status and Ecology of the Snow Leopard*. ISLT, Seattle.

The Snow Leopard *(Panthera uncia)* from the cold, mountainous regions of Central Asia. Its massive legs and heavy tail help to protect its extremities from the freezing temperatures.

The Snowshoe Cat is yet another recent American breed. First developed in the 1960s, it is based on crosses between Siamese and Bi-coloured American Shorthairs, giving it a Siamese pointed pattern, but with the addition of white feet.

Snowshoe Cat

Domestic Breed. A recent American short-haired breed with white 'snowshoe' feet, created by crossing a Siamese with a bi-coloured American Shorthair.

Appearance: The body of this cat is halfway between the long, lean and lanky Siamese and the short, stubby, stocky American Shorthair, presenting a well-balanced, elegant compromise. The key to its success, however, lies in the combination of the two contrasting colour patterns – the pointed pattern of the Siamese and the white spotting of the American Shorthair. In a well-marked individual this shows itself as a typical Siamese colouring with dark extremities, but with contrasting white patches on the face and feet. The ideal is for the white patches to lie symmetrically on the otherwise dark points. Breeder Pat Turner sums up the perfect Snowshoe markings as follows: 'The preferred pattern is that with white to the ankles in front, white to the hocks at the back and an inverted V on the face.'

History: As with a number of recent breeds, the Snowshoe began as an 'error'. White spotted individuals would turn up occasionally in Siamese breeding programmes and then be discarded. But in the 1960s an American breeder who specialized in Siamese, Dorothy Hinds-Daugherty of Philadelphia, decided to keep some of these strangely marked individuals and consider them as a new breed. There was strong opposition to this from the more traditional Siamese breeders, and for a while it looked as though the Snowshoe Cat would prove to be a non-starter. One breeder, Vikki Olander, persisted, however, and wrote the first breed standard for the Snowshoe. By 1977 she was almost alone in her support of the new breed and it was on the verge of dying out when she was contacted by another interested party, Jim Hoffman from Ohio. Together they began a serious campaign to support and develop the Snowshoe and by the mid-eighties had succeeded, with championship status attained at last.

The British breeder, Pat Turner, who encountered the Snowshoe when judging at an international cat show in New York in 1986, was later to form a British breed club to promote the breed in Europe. It is still comparatively rare, but its visual beauty and structural elegance will undoubtedly secure its future.

When it first appeared it was rumoured that the Snowshoe was merely a short-haired version of the Birman – the Sacred Cat of Burma – but this is not true. These two white-footed breeds have completely different, separate origins. Despite this, the Snowshoe has sometimes been incorrectly referred to as the 'Short-haired Birman'.

Another name that was given to the breed at one stage of its development was the 'Silver Lace Cat', but it is now universally known as the Snowshoe.

Personality: Terms used to describe this breed include: gentle, loving, affectionate, docile, inquisitive, adaptable, unflappable and happy-go-lucky. Described by owners as 'bomb-proof'.

Colour Forms: The white face and feet can be combined with any of the Siamese point patterns, although some organizations only recognize Seal and White Point and Blue and White Point. Because of the maximum contrast it affords, the Seal and White Point can be considered as the key pattern for combining with the white patches.

Bibliography:

1987. Turner, P. 'Snowshoe'. In: *Cat World*, July 1987, p.17-18.

1991. Swinyard, J.A. 'Snowshoes – a Rarity in the UK'. In: *Cat World*, December, 1991, p.8.

Breed Clubs:

The Snowshoes Cat Fanciers of America. A CFF-affiliated club.

The Snowshoe Breed Club. Address: P.O. Box 3201, Sidell, LA 70459, USA.

Snowshoes International (SSI). Formed in 1984. Address: 333 Hoyt Street, Buffalo, NY 14213, USA, or P.O. Box 121, Watkins, CO 80137, USA.

Snowshoe UK. Address: Tudor Cottage, 10 Lyncroft Gardens, Ewell, Epsom, Surrey, KT17 1UR, England.

SOCIABILITY

FELINE BEHAVIOUR. The cat is often characterized as a solitary, selfish animal, walking alone and coming together with other cats only to fight or mate. When cats are living wild, with plenty of space, it is true that they do fit this picture reasonably well, but they are quite capable of changing their ways when they become more crowded. Living in cities and towns, and in the homes of their human owners, cats show a remarkable and unexpected degree of sociability.

Anyone doubting this must remember that, to a pet cat, human beings are perceived as giant cats. The fact that domestic cats will share a home with a human family is, in itself, proof of their social flexibility. But this is only part of the story. There are many other ways in which cats demonstrate co-operation, mutual aid, and tolerance. This is particularly noticeable when a female is having kittens. Other females have been known to act as midwives, helping to chew through the umbilical cords and clean up the newborn offspring. Later, they may offer a baby-sitting service, bring food to the new mother, and occasionally feed young from other litters as well as their own. Even tom-cats sometimes show a little paternal feeling, cleaning the kittens and playing with them.

Where a large number of female cats are kept together in a cattery, observers have noticed that kittens which are born there are often shared out between the mothers. These group-living mothers show remarkable degrees of social tolerance and sometimes take up residence in large, communal nests, carrying all their kittens into the nest and piling them up in a huge squirming mass.

On one occasion no fewer than six females with 18 kittens established a communal nest of this type and each female allowed the other mothers to offer milk to any kittens whenever they felt like it. Normally, when there is a single mother cat, each kitten is the 'owner' of its own personal nipple and always returns to the same nipple every time it feeds. But in these nursery nests, the kittens took the first nipple they came across. This free-and-easy arrangement produced strong, healthy kittens that flourished because of the division of labour of the mother cats. The one drawback was that the weaker kittens tended to end up at the bottom of the pile and were occasionally suffocated. However, in other respects the group-maternity home worked efficiently enough.

These are not usual feline activities, but despite the fact that they are uncommon occurrences, they do reveal that the cat is capable, under special circumstances, of behaving in a less selfish way than might be expected on the basis of its usual reputation.

Even outside, in their territorial spaces, cats may show a considerable degree of restraint. There are often parts of the environment where, for some reason, they call a 'truce' and come together without too much fighting. This is common with feral city cats, especially where there is a communal feeding site.

Despite these observations, it cannot be said that cats are as sociable as dogs. The truth is that, as far as social life is concerned, cats are opportunists. They can take it or leave it. Dogs, on the other hand, can never leave it. They are, by nature, pack animals. A solitary dog is a wretched creature. A solitary cat is, if anything, relieved to be left in peace.

Socks

Pet Cat. The 'First Cat', officially belonging to Bill and Hilary Clinton, but in reality owned by their daughter, Chelsea. A black and white cat, he was called 'Socks' because of his four white feet. When she was 14, Chelsea was reputed to have written a 'rap' song which included the words: 'Socks sucks, I hate that cat. Socks sucks, worse than GATT.' It later emerged that this was the work of anarchic leftist journalist Tom Gargola, who published the words of the song as a satirical joke against the White House.

Because of his fame, Socks is reputed to receive 75,000 letters and parcels at the White House each week and 1993 saw the publication of his diary, called *Socks Goes to Washington*.

Socks, the black and white cat belonging to Bill Clinton's daughter, Chelsea.

Sokoke Forest Cat

Domestic Breed. Originating from the Sokoke district of eastern Kenya in East Africa, this is a new breed that is now being developed in Denmark. It has an unusual form of tabby coat pattern and there is still some disagreement as to how it acquired this. One theory suggests that it is a local, spontaneous mutation of an ordinary domestic cat. Another prefers to see it as a local subspecies of wild cat, while a third views it as a cross between a Kenyan domestic cat and a wild cat.

The Sokoke Forest cat is a rarity – a new domestic breed originating from tropical Africa. Its appeal lies in its modified tabby pattern, now described as 'African Tabby', which gives it a 'wood-grain' appearance.

Appearance: The Sokoke Forest Cat, or Sokoke Cat, has a tabby pattern that has been designated 'African Tabby' to distinguish it from the other types. It is similar to Blotched or Classic Tabby, but with a 'wood-grain' look. Pat Turner has accurately described the way in which it differs from the typical Blotched Tabby: 'The differences are really only in the shape of the "oysters" which can easily be accounted for by a modifying gene or genes extending the central spot. The remainder of the pattern is as found in other blotched breeds with bonnet strings, eye liner, necklaces (Alderman's chains), butterflies and black dots at the whisker roots.'

As might be expected with a tropical feral cat, the Sokoke Cat has an elegant, slender body and a long, pointed, tapering tail.

History: In 1977 a female cat with a litter of kittens was discovered in a hollow under a dead bush during land clearance at the edge of the forest. The owner of the land, wildlife artist Jeni Slater, inspected the family and realized that they all had unusual markings of a kind she had not seen before. She took a male and female kitten home with her, hand-reared them, and later started breeding from them.

The ease with which they became tame suggests that they were, in fact, domestic cats that had gone wild, rather than true wild cats. It is perhaps significant that no further 'wild' specimens have been seen since that first encounter in 1977. This points to the likelihood that the Sokoke cats were a very restricted phenomenon, probably resulting from a few escaped domestic cats (belonging to Europeans resident in Kenya) that began breeding and at some point developed the novel coat pattern through a mutation in the small local population.

When Danish cat enthusiast Gloria Moldrup visited Jeni Slater, she was given a pair of Sokoke kittens and took them home with her to Denmark. There they were exhibited at the JYYRAK Show at Odense, and became the foundation pair for the breed in Europe. Jeni Slater has refused to allow any Sokoke Cats to go to Great Britain because of the strict, six-month quarantine laws.

Bibliography:

1993. Turner, P. 'The Sokoke Forest Cat'. In: *Cat World Magazine,* February 1993, p.8-9.

Solid

Coat Pattern. An alternative name for self-coloured, meaning a cat whose coat is all of one, single colour, without any markings. (For further details see Self-coloured.)

Somali Cat

The official emblem of the Somali Cat Club.

Domestic Breed. The long-haired version of the Abyssinian Cat. The ticked coat is not only longer but also softer, silkier and with more colour-bands per hair. Apart from its coat, the breed is essentially the same as the Abyssinian.

Its name has no historical significance. It is doubtful whether any Somali Cat has ever trodden on Somali soil. It was given to the new breed simply because Somalia is close to Abyssinia (now Ethiopia) and the Somali cat is close to the Abyssinian Cat. It has been referred to as a 'soft orange cloud' and a 'striking red fox', or simply the 'fox cat'.

Appearance: As for the Abyssinian Cat except for the semi-long hair on its body, the ruff and the thickly plumed tail. Often described as a 'wild-looking cat'.

History: The Somali began as unwanted accidents in the 1950s and 1960s, with long-haired kittens turning up unexpectedly in short-haired Abyssinian litters. Initially, they were given away as pets and excluded from future pedigree breeding plans, but then it was decided that they had a special appeal of their own and were treated more seriously, leading eventually to the establishment of a new breed. Long-haired Abyssinians from the United States, Australia and New Zealand were exchanged to improve the quality of the foundation stock.

The moving force in developing the Somali was the American breeder Evelyn Mague, from Gillette, New Jersey. It was she who named the breed and whose male kitten, George, became its 'founding father'. He was born in 1967 and heralded a long-term breeding programme. It was successful and eventually, in 1972, a breed club was formed – The Somali Cat Club.

The Somali cat – the long-haired version of the Abyssinian, first seriously developed as a new breed in the late 1960s in the United States. It arrived in Continental Europe in the 1970s and in Britain in the 1980s.

In 1978, the new Somali Cat achieved championship status with the CFA in the United States. A year earlier, in 1977, Somalis had been exported to continental Europe, where breeding programmes were quickly instigated. Matters moved more slowly in Britain. British breeders have always been more resistant to novelties and were reluctant to accept the Somali. As early as 1971, two long-haired Abyssinians had been exhibited at a cat show in London, but they were badly received and were ignored as potential pedigree cats for the future. It was not until 1981, when the breed was already fully accepted elsewhere, that the first imported pair arrived in Britain and were given due attention. The breed was recognized by FIFe in 1982.

In Australia it is reported that the Somali has almost eclipsed its ancestor, the Abyssinian.

It should be noted that there has been considerable controversy over the true source of the original 'accidents' that led to this breed. Some have claimed that a long-haired breed must have been introduced into the Abyssinian stock at some early stage in the development of that breed (a Persian in 1900 is specifically mentioned), and that these elements then re-emerged years later. Others feel strongly that such a crossing played no part and that the recessive long-haired gene cropped up naturally, as a simple mutation in otherwise pure Abyssinian stock. The latter explanation seems to be more likely because, apart from its longer hair, the Somali does not show any non-Abyssinian features.

Personality: Terms used to describe this breed include: extrovert, active, alert, aware, athletic, shrewd, lively, friendly, good-tempered, affectionate, playful, intelligent, demonstrative and gentle. Requires considerable freedom.

Colour Forms: To simplify this list, the colours are grouped into convenient categories.

GCCF: Usual (= Ruddy); Sorrel; Chocolate; Blue; Lilac; Fawn; Red; Cream.

Tortie: Usual Tortie; Sorrel Tortie; Chocolate Tortie; Blue Tortie; Lilac Tortie; Fawn Tortie.

Silver: Usual Silver; Sorrel Silver; Chocolate Silver; Blue Silver; Lilac Silver; Fawn Silver; Red Silver; Cream Silver.

Tortie Silver: Usual Tortie Silver; Sorrel Tortie Silver; Chocolate Tortie Silver; Blue Tortie Silver; Lilac Tortie Silver; Fawn Tortie Silver.

CFA: Ruddy (= Usual); Red; Blue; Fawn.

Bibliography:

1994. Talbert, K. 'The Somali: That Foxy Cat!' In: *Cat Fancy*, June 1994. p.32-33.

Breed Clubs:

The Grand Somali Society. Address: 238, Church St., Poughkeepsie, NY 12601, USA.

International Somali Club. A CFA-affiliated club, formed in 1975. Address: 10 Western Blvd., Gillette, NJ 07933, USA.

Somali Cat Club (UK) Formed in 1981, it issues a twice-yearly *Journal*. Address: 21 Norman Road, Sutton, Surrey, SM1 2TB, England.

Somali Cat Club (USA). Formed in 1972. Address: 10 Western Blvd., Gillette, NJ 07933, USA.

Somali Cat Club of America, Inc. Address: 5027 Armstrong, Wickita, KS 67204, USA.

Sorrel

Coat Colour. Described as 'brownish orange to light brown', this colour term is used exclusively by British breeders of Abyssinian and Somali Cats. The agouti coat of the sorrel variants of these breeds is officially given as 'base colour – copper red; ticking colour – chocolate'. The Silver Sorrel variant is given as 'base colour – silver peach; ticking colour – chocolate'.

In America the name 'red' is used in place of sorrel, but the matter is complicated by the fact that genetically there are two types of 'red' Abyssinian and Somali Cats which are being developed at present, in attempts to obtain deeper shades.

South American Dwarf Cat

Domestic Breed. According to Frances Simpson, writing in 1903, a miniature breed of cat then existed. She called it the South American Dwarf Cat and commented: 'We have seen specimens of a very tiny domestic cat, full-grown individuals of which weigh only about three pounds. Those we saw came from South America.' Since the weight of a typical domestic cat is between 4.5 and 5.5 kg (10 and 12 lb), this would make her dwarf cats, astonishingly, only about a quarter the normal size.

In an earlier work by Richard Lydekker, in 1896, he too makes a reference to a midget cat from South America 'one-fourth the size of the ordinary domestic breed', which he refers to as the Paraguay Cat. It is amazing that, if such minute cats really did exist, they were not an immediate sensation and were kept and bred and treasured.

Unless additional information is unearthed concerning them, and confirming their existence beyond doubt, they must remain a mystery, bordering on a figment of the imagination (particularly in view of the wording of Charles Darwin's report on these cats – see Paraguay Cat). But if they are in fact fictional, there remains the intriguing question of what precisely Frances Simpson did see.

Spanish Blue Cat

Domestic Breed. An early name for the Russian Blue Cat (see entry), mentioned by Rush Huidekoper in 1895.

Spanish Cat

Domestic Breed. An early, alternative name for the Tortoiseshell Cat (see entry). Charles Ross, writing in 1868, uses this name and comments that this type of domestic cat is 'quite common in the South of Europe', which suggests that it originated in that region, perhaps explaining its Spanish connection.

Spanish Lynx

Wild Feline. *(Lynx pardinus)* Also known as the Pardel Lynx, the Pardine Lynx or the South European Lynx, this has been described as 'Europe's most endangered carnivore'.

S

The Spanish Lynx *(Lynx pardinus)*, a smaller and more heavily spotted relative of the Eurasian Northern Lynx. It is a seriously endangered species whose total number may now have fallen to no more than 400.

The Spanish Lynx is a medium-sized cat with long legs, a short tail, big, tufted ears and a conspicuous throat-ruff. It is a solitary, terrestrial, nocturnal hunter of rabbits and hares, also squirrels, small deer, ground birds, water-fowl, fish and large insects. It occupies extensive territories in wooded hill country and mountainous regions, and is also occasionally found among the sand dunes and scrubland of the lowlands.

This species differs from the Northern Lynx in both size and markings. It is smaller and more heavily spotted than the cold-country Lynx *(Lynx lynx)* that inhabits Scandinavia, northern Russia, and right across the Siberian wastelands.

Breeding takes place in the early part of the year, when females come onto heat and begin to wander through the homes ranges of the nearby males. When giving birth, the female retreats to a rock cavity, a dense thicket or a hollow tree. Breeding has been savagely curtailed in the past century, thanks to human sportsmen, fur-traders and agriculturists. It has been estimated that the present world population of Spanish Lynxes has fallen to no more than 1,000–1,500 individuals. One authority puts the figure as low as 400. It is now considered to be a seriously endangered species.

There has been much argument about whether the Spanish Lynx is really a separate species from the Northern Lynx. The problem lies in what happened in the middle European zone, between the frozen north and the sunny south, before mankind arrived and obliterated the natural habitats there. All the Lynxes from that intermediate area have long since been exterminated and there is now a huge geographical gap between the big Northern and small Spanish species. We will never know whether, when they met in the past, somewhere in the

middle, they graded gently from one form to the other, or whether they overlapped and never interbred. Without that information we can only guess. At least, by considering them as separate species, it is possible to put greater pressure on authorities to protect the rare Spanish form. If it is merely a race of the Northern species, then it is of far less interest in terms of 'endangered species'. And it needs all the help it can get, if it is to survive the twenty-first century.
Size: Length of Head + Body: 85–110 cm (33½–43 in). Tail: 12–13 cm (4½–5 in). Weight: 10–13 kg (22–28½ lb).
Distribution: Clinging on today in isolated groups in the more mountainous regions of Spain and Portugal, and occasionally in the lowlands. The main stronghold, if it can be called that, is in S.W. Spain and S.E. Portugal. The one definite lowland site, the Doñana National Park in southern Spain, where 15 pairs are said to be surviving, has recently been purchased from the Spanish government by the World Wildlife Fund.

(Writing in 1881, George Mivart was able to give its distribution then as also including Turkey, Greece, Sicily and Sardinia, but that was before various governments put a bounty on the animal's head, efficient firearms were introduced, and the human population had swollen to its present level.)

Spaying

Feline Reproduction. The neutering of a female cat, to prevent further breeding. Spaying has been carried out as a method of feline birth control since the end of the 19th century. Writing in 1903, Frances Simpson warns of the dangers of the operation at that time (when compared with the neutering of males): 'Female cats can also be rendered sexless, but in their case the operation is more likely to be attended with dangerous results.' Since then, the surgical procedure has been refined and today there is little physical risk, although there is always a danger of psychological trauma.

Technically, the operation is called *ovariohysterectomy* and consists of the removal of most of the female's internal reproductive system, including the ovaries, the fallopian tubes and the uterus. It not only prevents the cat from producing kittens, it also destroys her periods of heat.

For owners who prefer a less extreme approach that leaves the female cat with her normal sexual behaviour unaltered, there is the much less drastic operation of having her fallopian tubes tied or cut. This prevents the female from breeding, but without removing her sexual urges. It is not always easy, however, to persuade a veterinary surgeon to carry out this more delicate operation.

Sphynx Cat

Domestic Breed. The most controversial of all modern cat breeds, the nearly naked Sphynx Cat is a recent Canadian discovery. It has also been called the Canadian Hairless Cat and the Moon Cat, and has been nicknamed the Wrinkled Cat and the Birthday Suit Cat. In France it is known as the *Chat sans Poils*. It has been said that it is 'so ugly that it is beautiful'.
Appearance: A slender, elongated cat with suede-like, almost hairless skin, and a long, pointed tail. Its wedge-shaped head has very large ears and no whiskers. It is hot to the touch, and has sometimes been referred to as 'a suede hot-water bottle'. Its skin 'should look like velvet and feel like moss'. It has been likened in appearance to E.T., the extra-terrestrial in Steven Spielberg's 1982 film.
History: On 31st January 1966, a black and white pet cat called Elizabeth, belonging to a Mrs Micalwaith of Toronto, gave birth to a mutant hairless male kitten which was given the name of Prune. A young science student from the university heard of this strange new arrival. His mother, Mrs Yania Bawa, happened to be a breeder of Siamese Cats and together they acquired both the naked kitten and its mother.

The official emblem of the Sphynx Cat Club.

When the kitten became adult it was mated back to its mother to produce more hairless kittens. A serious breeding programme was planned, involving a complicated series of crosses with American Shorthair females and hairless males. It was decided to name the hairless

THE EXTRAORDINARY, naked Sphynx Cat from Canada. No domestic breed has caused more heated debate that this amazing-looking feline, which is either loved or hated but rarely ignored.

progeny as a new breed, the Sphinx, later changed to Sphynx, and to develop it further as a pedigree cat for show competition. Championship status was obtained by 1971 but concern about difficulties in rearing the kittens, especially the female ones, soon led to a decline in interest and, indeed, some strong opposition to it.

Its championship status was later revoked and the breed was in danger of dying out altogether, but a few specimens were exported to Europe, where the Sphynx found new supporters. Breeding programmes were begun in both Holland and France and the 'naked cat' eventually arrived in Britain. Even today it remains a rare breed, but its future survival now seems reasonably secure. In the early 1990s TICA granted it championship status.

An interesting feature of this cat is that the recessive gene which causes the hairlessness also appears to modify the body shape. The domestic cat that gave birth to the first hairless kitten was of 'average' shape, but the Sphynx Cat is exceptionally elongated and angular. In this respect it is reminiscent of the Rex breeds, where the sparse coat is again apparently linked to a lanky, angular body-shape.

Although this breed has the obvious disadvantage that it cannot stand a cold climate and must always be thought of as an 'indoor cat' needing special protection from its owners against the cold, it does have one particular advantage, namely that it does not cause allergic responses in those sensitive to cat fur. (However, it has now been reported that, in cases of extreme allergy, even this cat may cause problems because of the very fine 'peach-fuzz' of down hair which is present on its skin.)

Personality: As anyone who has encountered this cat in the flesh will testify, its sensitivity and loving nature more than compensate for its bizarre appearance. It is unusually sociable and affectionate. It has been described as 'part monkey, part dog, part child and part cat'.

Those who have only seen the cat in photographs sometimes take a less flattering view of it. It has also been described as 'the ugliest cat alive' and 'a creature with a hairless body, a snake's head, a rat's tail, and ears like bats' wings'.

Colour Forms: Any colours accepted.

Breed Clubs:

International Sphynx Breeders and Fanciers Association. Address: HC66, Box 70035, Pinetop, AZ 85935, USA.

Sphynx Cat Club. Address: 10 York Road, Waltham Cross, Herts., EN8 7HW, England.

Spooky

Cartoon Cat. Spooky, a black and white cat with a conspicuously bandaged tail, appeared in strip cartoons by artist Bill Holman, in the 1950s.

Spotted

Coat Pattern. The origin of the spotted coats seen in domestic cats is not clearly understood. It may have been developed by gradually modifying mackerel tabby streaks, making them more and more fragmented, into small blobs and finally into spots, by selective breeding. Or it may have been developed by utilizing a new, spotted mutation. Geneticists favour the first of these two explanations because, although the pedigree mackerel tabby is chosen for its long, unbroken streaks and stripes, stray non-pedigree mackerel tabbies frequently show much shorter and more broken streaks and stripes. By using such non-pedigree animals, those shorter marks could soon be rounded off into elegant, circular spots.

Spotted Cats (1)

Domestic Breeds. Because so many wild cat species have spotted coats, breeders of domestic cats have several times attempted to develop a spotted pet cat that looks like its natural relatives. At present there are six different, exclusively spotted domestic breeds (for details see individual entries for each breed):

1 Egyptian Mau (Natalie Troubetskoy, Egypt, 1953)
2 Oriental Spotted Tabby (Angela Sayer, 1960s)
3 Bengal (Jean Mill, USA, 1963)
4 Ocicat (Virginia Daly, USA, 1964)
5 California Spangled (Paul Casey, USA, 1971)
6 Spotted Mist (Australia, 1980)

In addition to the foregoing breeds, in which spotted individuals *only* are allowed, there is also a 'Spotted Tabby' variant in a number of other breeds, including the American Curl, the British Shorthair, the Norwegian Forest, the Devon Rex and the Scottish Fold. Spotted Tabby Cats were recorded as early as the 19th century. Gordon Stables, writing in 1874 about the classes recognized at the very first cat shows, includes the following category: 'CLASS VII. *Spotted Tabby*. Colour to be brown, blue, or light or dark grey, marked with black or white. At most cat-shows, a good deal of confusion exists, about what this cat ought really to be like, even among the best judges.' After some discussion he gives his ideal Spotted Tabby: 'The ground colour was dark grey; a broad black band ran along his back and down his fine tail; and diverging from this band came dark stripes of colour down the sides, converging round the thighs, and swirling round his chest in two Lord Mayor's chains; but the stripes had this peculiarity, they were all *broken up into spots.*'

The Spotted Tabby Cat as depicted by Harrison Weir in his feline classic, *Our Cats and All About Them,* in 1889.

A little later, writing in 1889 and 1895, Harrison Weir and Rush Huidekoper respectively also give the Spotted Tabby a separate category of its own and include illustrations of good examples.

By the start of the 20th century, however, Spotted Tabbies were becoming rare, and they almost vanished for the next 50 years, as the glamorous long-haired cats came to dominate the show scene.

They were revived in 1965, now called simply 'Spotted Cats'. Within a year or so they had become established as the Spotted British Shorthair Cat, with the nickname of 'Spottie'.

Spotted Cats (2)

Wild Felines. The spotted coat is the most common form of pattern found on wild species. Of the 36 species recognized today, 17 of them are spotted cats, four may be either spotted or plain, two are blotched, 11 are plain, and two are striped.

Spotted wild cat species: (1) Black-footed Cat; (2) Serval; (3) Leopard Cat; (4) Rusty-spotted Cat; (5) Fishing Cat; (6) Ocelot; (7) Tiger Cat; (8) Margay Cat; (9) Pampas Cat; (10) Geoffroy's Cat; (11) Kodkod; (12) Mountain Cat; (13) Spanish Lynx; (14) Snow Leopard; (15) Leopard; (16) Jaguar; (17) Cheetah.

Wild cat species that may be either spotted or plain: (1) African Golden Cat; (2) Bobcat; (3) Canadian Lynx; (4) Northern Lynx.

Blotched wild cat species (essentially spotted coats, but with the largest spots enlarged into cloud-like blotches): (1) Marbled Cat; (2) Clouded Leopard.

Plain wild cat species (but which may have minor markings on restricted areas of the coat): (1) Chinese Desert Cat; (2) Jungle Cat; (3) Sand Cat; (4) Caracal; (5) Pallas's Cat; (6) Flat-headed Cat; (7) Temminck's Cat; (8) Bay Cat; (9) Jaguarundi; (10) Puma; (11) Lion.

Striped wild cat species: (1) Wild Cat; (2) Tiger.

There are some minor variations in the above. Young lions and young pumas, for example, are spotted, but lose their spots when they mature. And in some of the usually plain species there may be a local race of spotted animals.

Spotted Lion

Mystery Cat. Since 1903, rumours of Spotted Cats have filtered through from tropical Africa. To the locals it is known as the *Marozi*. To science it is looked upon simply as a freak – an occasional oddity of no special interest. Young lions often show distinct spotting of the coat and these spots disappear as the animals become adult, so it would not be particularly surprising if, in one or two isolated cases, this juvenile spotting was late in disappearing.

In the early 1930s two adult Spotted Lions were shot near a farm in the Aberdares and their heavily spotted skins at last proved beyond any doubt that such animals really did exist. But it was still felt that they were merely isolated genetic freaks.

Despite the lack of scientific interest, and inspired by these skins, a young explorer called Kenneth Dower set off, later in the 1930s, to discover what he thought was an exciting new 'species'. Although he failed in his quest, he bravely wrote a whole book on the subject.

Supporters of the Spotted Lion have since suggested that it might perhaps be a rare forest race of Lions, adapted to the dappled light, where the spots would improve the animal's camouflage. This is reasonable enough in theory, but until hard evidence is available, the animal must continue to be looked upon as a local mutant rather than as a whole new subspecies.

Bibliography:

1937. Dower, K.C.G. *The Spotted Lion*. Heinemann, London.

1989. Shuker, K.P.N. *Mystery Cats of the World*. Robert Hale, London.

Spotted Mist Cat

Domestic Breed. An experimental breed from Australia developed in the late 1970s from crosses between Burmese and Abyssinian, with the addition of domestic tabby. The result is a cat with a short, fine, spotted coat. This is Australia's first important home-grown pedigree cat breed and has recently been included in a CD-ROM listing 'Australian Innovations'.

Appearance: The short coat is described as glossy, dense and resilient. The spots occur over the sides, flanks and belly, and are seen against a misty ground colour, which gives the breed its name. The legs and tail are marked with dark rings and the face shows a typical tabby pattern. The rounded head has large, green eyes.

History: In 1976 a Sydney ecologist, Dr Truda Straede, began a ten-year breeding programme to create a spotted Australian breed. In order to avoid a narrow gene pool, no fewer than 30 foundation cats were involved. Half of these were Burmese, a quarter were Abyssinian and a

The Spotted Mist is the first truly Australian breed of domestic cat. It was developed in Sydney, starting in the late 1970s with a carefully planned, ten-year breeding programme using 30 foundation cats, including Burmese, Abyssinian and domestic tabbies.

quarter were domestic tabbies. The Burmese were used to provide temperament, size, conformation and colour dilution; the Abyssinians provided intelligence, colours and ticking; and the domestic tabbies provided vigour, health and reproductive qualities. All three types contributed to the creation of the spotted coat.

The result is a well-balanced cat, lacking in extremes and with a friendly temperament. It is claimed that Spotted Mists suffer little distress at being kept indoors. This is a significant feature in a new breed that is being developed in a country where government rules often demand a 'feline curfew', in order to protect the native wildlife.

In 1986 the breed was accepted for registration by the Royal Agricultural Society Cat Control of New South Wales. 1988 saw the first Spotted Mist Champion, and 1989 the first Grand Champion.

Colour Forms: Already five colour forms are recognized: Brown (Seal brown markings on silvery fawn); Blue (bluish-grey markings on silvery cream); Chocolate (chocolate markings on creamy-fawn); Lilac (dove grey markings on pinkish-grey); Gold (old gold markings on rich cream); Peach (salmon pink markings on pinkish-cream).

Breed Club:

The Spotted Mist Breeder's Association. Address: P.O. Box 384, Epping, New South Wales 2121, Australia.

Spraying

Feline Behaviour. Tom-cats mark their territories by squirting a powerful jet of urine backwards on to vertical features of their environment. They aim at walls, bushes, tree-stumps, fence-posts or any landmark of a permanent kind. They are particularly attracted to places where they or other cats have sprayed in the past, adding their new odour to the traces of the old ones already clinging there.

The urine of tom-cats is notoriously strongly scented, so much so that even the inefficient human nostrils can detect it all too clearly. To the human nose it has a particularly unpleasant stench and many people are driven to having toms neutered in attempts to damp down this activity. Other cat odours are almost undetectable by humans. The glands on the head, for example, which are rubbed against objects to deposit another form of feline scent-mark, produce an odour that is of great significance to cats but goes completely unnoticed by the animals' human owners.

Some authorities have claimed that the squirted urine acts as a threat signal to rival cats. Hard evidence is lacking, however, and many hours of patient field-observation have never revealed any reactions to support this view. If the odour left on landmarks was truly threatening to other cats, it should intimidate them when they sniff it. They should recoil in panic and slink away. Their response is just the opposite. Instead of withdrawing, they are positively attracted to the scent-marks and sniff at them with great interest.

If they are not threatening, what do the territorial scent-marks signify? What signals do they carry? The answer is that they function rather as newspapers do for us. Each morning we read our papers and keep up-to-date with what is going on in the human world. Cats wander around their territories and, by sniffing at the scent-marks, can learn all the news about the coming and goings of the feline population. They can check how long it has been since their own last visit (by the degree of weakening of their own last scent-spray) and they can read the odour-signals of who else has passed by and sprayed, and how long ago. Each spray also carries with it considerable information about the emotional state and the individual identity of the sprayer. When a cat decides to have another spray itself, it is the feline equivalent of a letter to *The Times,* publishing a poem, and leaving a calling card, all rolled into one jet of urine.

It might be argued that the concept of scent-signalling is far-fetched and that urine-spraying by cats is simply their method of getting rid of waste products from the body and that it has no other significance whatever. If a cat has a full bladder it will spray; if it has an empty bladder it will not spray. The facts contradict this.

Careful observation shows that cats perform regular spraying actions in a set routine, regardless of the state of their bladder. If it happens to be full, then each squirt is large. If it is nearly empty, then the urine is rationed out. The *number* of squirts and the territorial areas which are scent-marked remain the same, no matter how much or how little liquid the cat has drunk. Indeed, if the cat has completely run out of urine, it can be seen continuing its scent-marking routine, laboriously visiting each scent-post, straining and quivering its tail, and then walking away. The act of spraying has its own separate motivation, which is a clear indication of its importance in feline social life.

Although it is not generally realized, females and neutered cats of both sexes do spray jets of urine, like tom-cats. The difference is that their actions are less frequent and their scent is far less pungent, so we barely notice it.

Stable Companions

Working Cats. It has often been said that in modern times cats have had only two functions – as pest-controllers and as pets. But there is a third, albeit much less common role that they can play. Thoroughbred racehorses are notoriously highly strung and some trainers have found that providing them with feline stable companions helps to calm them down.

Daunt, the famous winner of the 1945 Derby, was said to be inseparable from a tom-cat called Ginger.

George Stubbs, in his portrait of the famous stallion, the Godolphin Arabian, who died in 1753, includes his companion black cat in the picture (although for some reason he shows it as a tabby). When the horse died, the cat remained with its body, refusing to move. It continued to sit on the carcass until it was buried. It then crept reluctantly away and hid in the hayloft where it, too, was soon found dead.

In the 1930s, a champion horse called 'Fet', who won the Cesarewitch three times, insisted on having two stable companions – a goat and a black tom-cat. Unless both were present at the end of the day, he became agitated and refused to bed down for the night.

Another champion horse, called Foxhall, after he had been rubbed down in his stable, used to allow two young cats to sleep curled up on his back.

The importance of companion cats to racehorses was the basis of a story by P.G. Wodehouse in which Bertie Wooster and Jeeves must prevent the catnapping of a stable companion. If they fail, the favourite will become so distraught that he will be unable to win the race on the following day.

Stables, Gordon

Feline Authority. One of the earliest of cat authors, Gordon Stables (1840–1910), a Berkshire doctor and well-known judge at the early cat shows, was the only person to write more than one serious book about cats in the 19th century. His style may have been patronizing, but he must be given credit for having been one of the few serious voices raised in defence of the cat in Victorian times.

Bibliography:

1874. Stables, G. Cats. *Their Points and Characteristics*. Dean, London.

1876. Stables, G. *The Domestic Cat.* Routledge, London.

1877. Stables, G. *Friends in Fur. True Tales of Cat Life*. Dean, London.

1895. Stables, G. *Shireen and her Friends. Pages from the Life of a Persian Cat.* Jarrold, London.

1897. Stables, G. *Cats. Handbook to their classification and diseases.* Dean, London.

Staring

Feline Behaviour. For the cat, staring intently at another animal is an aggressive act. This is something that it is hard for human beings to remember when they encounter a cat, but it can easily have an unwanted impact. If a cat enters a room where several people are talking, it is very likely that the animal will make for the one person there who has an abnormal fear of felines. To that individual's horrified disbelief, the animal then proceeds to rub around his or her legs and may even jump up on the person's lap.

To some people, this is a confirmation of the old idea that there is something inherently wicked in the feline personality, and that the animal deliberately selects someone with a cat phobia and then sets out to cause embarrassment. But this kind of superstitious romanticizing is superfluous. There is a much simpler explanation of the animal's behaviour.

When the cat enters the room and looks around, it notices that several of the people there are staring at it. They are the cat-lovers, gazing at the cat because they like it. If they are strangers, then to the cat this means that they are hostile ones in the group and to be avoided. (The cat's owners comes into a different category since, being 'pseudo-mothers', they are allowed to stare at their 'kitten' out of concern for its welfare.) The only stranger who is *not* staring is the cat-hater, who is looking away and trying to keep still, so that the animal will not be attracted towards them.

Unfortunately, this behaviour has precisely the opposite effect to what is intended. The cat makes a bee-line for the one person who is appealingly immobile, is not making shrill remarks and, above all, is not staring. The cat is, in this way, showing its appreciation of non-intimidating body language.

The secret for any cat-phobic individuals who want to keep their distance from these animals is to lean towards a cat, stare fixedly at it with wide-open eyes and make agitated hand movements, asking the cat in strident tones to come and sit on their lap. This will have exactly the opposite effect and the persons will then be able to relax without appearing to have insulted their host's favourite pet.

A sleeping cat, by the French artist Théophile Steinlen.

Steinlen, Théophile

Cat Artist. The cats sketched by the French artist Théophile Steinlen (1859–1923) are not cartoon cats, although they are often presented in a series of images similar to those of a strip

THE FELINE DRAWINGS of Théophile Steinlen are clearly based on a great deal of accurate observation of cat behaviour.

cartoon. But the individual cats are true felines. Their adventures are those of cats, not caricatured humans. In a classic example, a cat sees a snowman standing outside the house. With the typical feline greeting gesture, the cat rubs up against the legs of the snowman. The heat of the cat's body melts the snowman's leg and it falls on top of the startled cat.

Bibliography:

1933. Steinlein, T. *Cats and other Animals.*

Steinlein, T. *Des Chats; Images sans paroles.* Flammarion, Paris. (Facsimile edition, Libro, 1981)

Steppe Cat

Wild Feline. An alternative name for Pallas's Cat *(Felis manul)*. This name was employed by earlier authors because this species is found in the steppe country of the high plains of Asia, but it is rarely used today. (For details see Pallas's Cat.)

Sterling Cat

Domestic Breed. This is a new name given to the long-established, silvery-coloured, Chinchilla Persian Cat, elevating it from a colour variant to a full breed. This move was proposed in the 1980s by the American breeder Jeannie Johnson and was recognized by TICA in 1994. The official show debut, using this name, was in New York in October 1995.

THE STERLING CAT is the new name given to the Chinchilla Persian to elevate it to the status of a distinct breed. The idea was put forward in the 1980s and first gained acceptance in 1994.

STRIPED

COAT PATTERN. A coat with dark lines. Among wild species, the fully striped pattern is far less common than the spotted, appearing only on the Wild Cat *(Felis sylvestris)* and the Tiger *(Panthera tigris)*. With several other species there are linear markings on the tail and legs, but as these are encircling lines, they are technically bands rather than stripes.

Among domestic cats the striped pattern appears only on the Mackerel Tabby coat. This is the ancient form of tabby pattern and was once common over the whole range of the domestic cat. However, in medieval Europe a new form of tabby pattern arose, now called the Blotched, Marbled or Classic Tabby. Its estimated first appearance was somewhere around the year 1200 and it then proceeded to spread and spread, dominating and displacing the Mackerel or Striped Tabby in more and more regions. Today the striped tabby pattern has become rare in Europe, but it is still encountered quite commonly among feral domestic cats further east.

It has been suggested that the striped tabby coat provides better camouflage in rural settings and that the blotched pattern blends in better in the urban environment, and that this may account for the modern differences in distribution of the two types. (See also Mackerel Tabby and Blotched Tabby.)

A FANCIFUL INTERPRETATION of a striped tabby cat from an 1890 edition of the magazine *Fur and Feather*.

STROKING

FELINE BEHAVIOUR. Cats like being stroked because they look upon humans as 'mother cats'. Kittens are repeatedly licked by their mothers during their earliest days and the action of human stroking has much the same feel on the fur as feline licking. To the kitten, the mother cat is 'the one who feeds, cleans and protects'. Because humans continue to do this for their pets long after their kitten days are behind them, the domesticated animals never fully grow up. They may become full-sized and sexually mature, but in their minds they remain kittens in relation to their human owners.

For this reason cats – even elderly cats – keep on begging for maternal attention from their owners, pushing up to them and gazing at them longingly, waiting for the pseudo-maternal hand to start acting like a giant tongue again, smoothing and tugging at their fur.

One very characteristic body action they perform when they are being stroked, as they greet their 'mothers', is the stiff erection of their tails. This is typical of young kittens receiving attention from their real mothers and it is an invitation to her to examine their anal regions.

STUD CAT

FELINE TERM. A male cat that is kept specifically for breeding purposes. The term is borrowed from the equine world where it originally meant a special place where horses 'stood' for mating. Over the centuries, 'stood' became 'stud'.

The term 'stud cat' was already in use by 1903, when Frances Simpson comments: *'Stud cat.* A male cat should not be allowed to mate under a year old, and if you wish to keep your stud in good condition do not allow more than two, or at most three, lady visitors a week.' She goes on to say that 'a really reliable stud cat is a very profitable possession . . . The usual fee for a visit to a stud cat is £1.1s.'

SUARÈS, JEAN-CLAUDE

CAT OWNER. The Egyptian-born New York graphic designer Jean-Claude Suarès has allowed his passion for cats to develop into wide-ranging studies of cats in art, literature and photography, providing us with a fascinating group of illustrated books. Surprisingly, he reports that, growing up in Egypt, the homeland of the domestic cat: 'I was never allowed to have cats and I was never allowed to drive, so when I finally came to the United States and moved into an apartment I got a cat and a Rolls-Royce. And then I started multiplying everything . . . so my record number of cats is thirteen and my record number of Rolls-Royces is nineteen.' Interviewed in 1978, he mentioned that one of his cats was called Maurice because it was the name of his (then) wife's lover, who was 'not allowed on the bed either'.

Bibliography:
1976. Suarès, J-C. and Chwast, S. *The Illustrated Cat*. Harmony Books, New York.
1977. Suarès, J-C. and Chwast, S. (Editors) *The Literary Cat*. Berkley Windhover Books, New York.
1981. Suarès, J-C. *Great Cats. The Who's Who of Famous Felines*. Bantam Books, New York.
1983. Suarès, J-C. *The Indispensable Cat*. Stewart, Tabori & Chang, New York. (British edition by Webb & Bower, Exeter, 1984).
1992. Suarès, J-C. (Editor) *Black and White Cats*. Collins, San Francisco.
1993. Suarès, J-C. (Editor) *Hollywood Cats*. Collins, San Francisco.
Also: *The Photographed Cat; The Preppy Cat;* and *The Cat Scrapbook*.

SUCKLING

FELINE BEHAVIOUR. As the kittens recover from the trauma of birth, they start rooting around, searching for a nipple. The first feed they enjoy is vitally important because it helps to immunize them against disease. Before she produces her full-bodied nutritional milk, the mother provides a thin first-milk called *colostrum*, which is rich in antibodies and gives the kittens an immediate advantage in the coming struggle to avoid the diseases of early infancy. It is also rich in proteins and minerals and its production lasts for several days, before the mother cat starts to produce the normal milk supply.

This naturally acquired immunity which the colostrum gives lasts for about eight to 12 weeks, after which many owners like to have their cats vaccinated to provide them with extra protection against disease.

The kittens each obtain between two and three millilitres (about half a teaspoon) of milk at each meal and they feed, on average, every three hours. By the age of two weeks they are taking between five and seven millilitres (1 to 1½ teaspoons) at each meal.

Each kitten develops a preference for a particular nipple and always returns to the same one, which it can identify by its odour. This was proved by simple tests. If the belly region of a mother cat is carefully washed by her human owner, so that it is cleansed of natural fragrance, the kittens fail to find their favourite nipples. Instead of peacefully taking up their usual stations, they become disorientated. Confusion reigns and squabbling occurs. It is clear from these experiments that the function of 'nipple identification' by kittens is to ensure an orderly sharing of the milk supply at feeding times.

The nipples towards the rear of the mother's body are the ones that provide most milk, so the kittens that have managed to establish ownership of those nipples will always be slightly ahead of their litter-mates in growth and development.

SUGAR

PET CAT. Sugar achieved the seemingly impossible feat of travelling 2,400 km (1,500 miles) to be reunited with his owners. When Mr and Mrs Woods, who owned Sugar, decided to move to Oklahoma in 1951, they left the cat behind with neighbours because he hated travelling in cars. After two weeks in the neighbours' house, the cat vanished and they never saw him again. Fourteen months later he jumped though a window and on to the shoulder of Mrs Woods in her Oklahoma farm. She could hardly believe it was the same cat, but close inspection revealed that it was.

Many claims for long treks made by pet cats are simply cases of a similar cat adopting a family when it moves into a new home. The family, missing their old cat, imagines that the stray that is now purring at their feet is their original pet. In this case, there was a way to be certain, because Sugar was unmistakable. He was a cream-coloured part-Persian with a deformed left hip. When Mrs Woods examined the new arrival at her farm, she found that it was not only a cream-coloured part-Persian, but that it, too, had a deformed hip. It could not be any other cat – it had to be Sugar. How the animal had managed to navigate its way over such a vast distance to a *new* home (rather than back to an old, well-known one) is not clear.

SUMATRAN CAT

WILD FELINE. Originally considered to be a separate species *(Felis sumatrana* or *Felis minuta)*, the Sumatran Cat is now looked upon as no more than a local Sumatran race of the widespread Leopard Cat *(Felis bengalensis)*.

SUPALAK

DOMESTIC BREED. An old name (sometimes spelt Sopalak) for 'The Copper' that appears in *The Book of Cat Poems* now housed in the Thai National Library in Bangkok, where it is also known as the 'Thong Daeng'. Although this was originally an early type of Siamese domestic feline, it is known today as the Burmese Cat, because that was the country of origin of the founder cat of the modern breed. (See entry for Burmese.)

SUPERFECUNDATION

FELINE REPRODUCTION. This occurs when a single litter of kittens has more than one father.

When a female cat comes into heat, her calling and her sexual fragrance attract tom-cats from all around. They gather near her and squabble among themselves with much caterwauling. Then one of them approaches her and mates. The act of copulation usually only takes about five seconds, ejaculation occurring as soon as the male has entered the female. After a rest of about 20 minutes, they copulate again and this process is repeated approximately seven times, by which time the male is usually satiated. Most female cats will allow one male after another to mount her until her whole circle of admirers has been accommodated. This means that her reproductive tract will contain a mixture of sperm from several sources and it becomes almost a matter of chance as to which particular male's sperm fertilizes each of her shed eggs.

The result of this is sometimes a multi-patterned litter of kittens, which some owners mistakenly consider to be the outcome of 'genetic variety' within the make-up of their female and an unknown 'husband'. But the wildly differing kittens may instead be the product of the sexual promiscuity of their female.

This is essentially a phenomenon of domestic cats because the territories of wild cats are so much bigger, and the chances of a whole group of wild toms gathering together in one spot when a wild female is on heat are more remote. Superfecundation is more likely to occur in town and city cats, where the individual territories have become so reduced in size that the odour of a sexually active female can easily be detected by a whole collection of different males.

SUPERFETATION

FELINE REPRODUCTION. Female cats are such powerful breeding machines that some of them (about 10 per cent) may even come into heat while they are pregnant. If this results in a second set of eggs being fertilized before the first litter has been born, the condition is said to be one of 'superfetation'.

It is one of the basic rules of reproductive behaviour that the condition of pregnancy suppresses a female's sexual physiology, but female cats frequently break this golden rule. Where there is a low level of pregnancy hormone in the system, there is another phase of sexual receptivity actually during the pregnancy cycle. Feline pregnancy lasts about nine weeks and the additional heats usually occur after three weeks or after six weeks. They are most common between the 21st and 24th day. If, as a result of these new periods of heat, the females are mated and fertilized again, they end up carrying two litters at two different stages of development.

In these cases, both sets of kittens continue to develop alongside one another, with the later group three or six weeks behind the earlier one. This creates two alternative problems for the mother-to-be. When she starts to give birth to the older litter, the upheaval of delivery may lead to the younger litter being ejected as well. If this happens they are so premature that they nearly always die. If, on the other hand, they manage to hang on inside the uterus, they may be born successfully at full term, three or six weeks later. This causes a second type of problem – an almost impossible demand for nipples and milk supply. But if the female is able to cope with all or part of this added maternal burden she can, of course, contribute even more spectacularly to the feline population explosion.

SUPERSTITIONS

FOLKLORE. There are more superstitions associated with cats than with any other animal, and the main ones are listed here. Apart from a few that are concerned with a cat's reactions to alterations in the weather, where there may sometimes be an element of truth based on the cat's sensitivity to climatic changes, it is fair to say that they are all completely nonsensical. Many flatly contradict one another. However, they have been collected together here to show how intense and widespread is the feeling that cats have some kind of supernatural influence.

LUCK:

Cats bring good luck.
Cats bring bad luck.
If a cat crosses the street it is a sign of bad luck.
If a black cat crosses your path, you will have good luck.
It is lucky to own a black cat, but unlucky to meet one.
Stroking a black cat brings good luck.
If a black cat is chased away it will take the luck of the house with it.
If a black cat pays you a brief visit it will bring you good luck.
If a black cat comes to stay it will bring you bad luck.
It is good luck to sleep with a cat.
Miners refuse to utter the word 'cat' when working down a mine.
Sailors refuse to say the word 'cat' at sea, although a ship's cat brings good luck.
If a sailor's wife keeps a cat it will ensure her husband's safe return.
At a theatre, a cat is good luck backstage.
If a theatre cat makes a mess backstage, the performance will be good.
Cats are bad luck on-stage.
For a cricketer it is lucky to see a black cat when going out to bat.
A tortoiseshell cat brings luck to its owner.
A stray tortoiseshell coming into your home is an omen of misfortune.
A blue cat brings luck to its owner.
If your cat cries when you leave for a journey, some disaster will befall you.

HEALTH:

It is bad for one's health to fondle cats.
If you kick a cat you will get rheumatism.
Cats suck the breath out of sleeping people.
Cats suffocate sleeping babies.
If your cat sneezes three times, everyone in the house will develop colds.
A wart can be cured by smearing three drops of cat's blood over it.
To get rid of warts, kill a cat and bury it in a black stocking.
Black cat broth cures consumption.
A stye on the eye can be cured by stroking it with a black cat's tail.
A dried cat's skin held to the face will cure toothache.
A cat's body boiled in olive oil makes a good dressing for wounds.
Water that has washed a sick person, if thrown over a cat, will cure that person if the cat is then driven from the house.

WEATHER:

Cats can foretell the weather.
When a cat washes its face it is a sign of good weather.

When a cat washes its face it is a sign of rain.
If a cat looks out of the window it is looking for rain.
When a cat's pupil broadens there will be rain.
If a cat sneezes once, rain is coming.
Bathing a cat will bring rain.
A restless cat means a storm is brewing.
When a cat licks its tail a storm is coming.
If you throw a cat overboard there will be a storm at sea.
If you throw a cat overboard, you will raise a favourable wind.
If a ship's cat is playful, there will be a gale of wind astern.
If a ship's cat meows on board ship, it will be a difficult voyage
When a cat puts its tail towards the fire, bad weather is coming.
If a cat sits with its back to the fire there will be a frost.
If a cat claws the carpet there will be high winds.
If a cat dashes around the house, there will be high winds.
If a cat scratches the leg of a table there will be a change in the weather.
You can tell the tides by the pupils of a cat's eyes.
A kitten born in May will grow up melancholy.

Fertility:
If the cat in your house is black, of lovers you will have no lack.
It is good luck to have the family cat at your wedding.

MANY FELINE superstitions developed because of the supposed link between witches and cats. In this detail of a 1647 woodcut, two seated witches name their familiars, including a cat called Pyewacket.

If a cat sneezes near a bride on her wedding-morning, her happiness is assured.
A cat rocked in a cradle a month after a wedding will make a couple fertile.
A cat buried in a field of grain will help the crops to grow.

Visitors:
When a cat washes its face company is coming.
If a cat washes itself in a doorway, a clergyman will visit the house.

Hunting:
A kitten born in May will never be a mouser.
If you pay money for a cat it will never catch mice for you.

Spirits:
The cat has psychic powers.
Cats can see ghosts.
A cat purrs when encountering a ghost.
If you take even one of the nine lives of a cat it will haunt you.
A black cat is the Devil.
If you drown a cat the Devil will get you.
If a black cat crosses your path, Satan has been taking notice of you.
Witches can change themselves into cats.
A black cat is a witch's familiar
When a holy man dies, his spirit will enter a cat; when the cat dies, his spirit is free.
A cat has nine lives.

Death:
Cats prey on corpses.
If a cat jumps over a corpse, that corpse will become a vampire.
If a cat leaves the house of an invalid and cannot be coaxed back, the invalid will die.
If a sick person dreams of cats he will die.
If a sick person sees two cats fighting he will die.
If there is a corpse indoors, a cat will desert the house.
A dying cat will attract Death to the house.

Suqutranese Cat

Domestic Breed. A dazzling white, unticked version of the Somali (the long-haired form of the Abyssinian), recently developed in Britain. It was first exhibited at a Cat Association show in England in 1990.

Susan

Fictional Cat. One of Beatrix Potter's feline characters, Susan is the white cat that appears in *The Tale of Little Pig Robinson* (1930).

Swimming Cat

Domestic Breed. When Turkish Van Cats first appeared in the West, in 1955, they became known to the public as 'Swimming Cats'. This was because of a report about the behaviour of the first pair brought back to England by Laura Lushington. Driving through Turkey in the intense summer heat, she stopped to cool off in a river and, without prompting, her two newly acquired kittens joined her in the water. Writing about the incident in 1962, she commented: 'To my astonishment, the Van kittens strolled into the water too and swam out of their depth – apparently thoroughly enjoying themselves. This, I suppose, is the reason they were dubbed "Swimming Cats" by the Press on my return to Britain.'

Sylvester

Cartoon Cat. MGM's immense success with their 'Tom and Jerry' animated cartoons for the cinema, which began in 1939, prompted Warner Brothers to create their own, rival feline. Sylvester first appeared on 24th March 1945 in *Life with Feathers*. A skinny, black and white cat with a red nose and a large white ruff of fur protruding from either side of his face, he was the creation of I. 'Friz' Freleng.

Just as Tom had a potential victim in the shape of the little mouse Jerry, so Sylvester had Tweety Pie, a tiny, baby-faced canary in a cage, on which to set his sights. As with Tom, the prey was never devoured, the hungry feline inevitably suffering considerably in his attempts to consummate his predatory urges.

Sylvester's voice was provided by actor Mel Blanc. The cat's catch phrase was 'Sufferin' Succotash!' The canary, who suffered from a speech impediment, was best known for 'I taut I taw a puddy tat'.

Sylvester first met the canary in a 1947 cartoon called *Tweety Pie*, for which Freleng won an Academy Award. He won another Oscar in 1957 for *Birds Anonymous*, in which Sylvester attended therapy sessions in an unsuccessful attempt to give up his bird-addiction.

Tabby (1)

Feline Term. The name is thought to be derived from 'Atabi', a type of silk manufactured in the Attabiah district of Baghdad. It was exported to England in large quantities and on one occasion its striped patterns were compared with the markings on what was originally called the Striped Cat or 'Tiger' Cat. As a result, the breed soon became known as the 'Tabbi', which was later modified to 'Tabby'.

Tabby (2)

Coat Pattern. The history of the tabby pattern is complicated. The modern domestic cat originally appears to have developed from the African Wild Cat *(Felis sylvestris lybica)* in ancient Egypt. When this early domesticated cat was brought to ancient Greece and Rome by Phoenician traders, it spread across the European continent and, in so doing, hybridized freely with the local European Wild Cat *(Felis sylvestris sylvestris).*

The coat pattern of both the African and the European races can best be described as suppressed, weak or washed-out tabby. The pattern is there, but not impressive. This is undoubtedly what the original domestic cats looked like and wall paintings confirm that three to four thousand years ago the Egyptian cats had light or broken stripes. But when this type of cat, transported abroad, began to hybridize with its European counterparts, the result was a full-tabby cat.

Tests have since shown that when the weak-tabby European and African Wild Cats are experimentally crossed with one another, the hybrid kittens develop coat patterns which are much closer to the full-tabby pattern of modern domestic cats than they are to the markings of either of their parents. This, it seems, is how the history of the tabby began.

The first cats of this type were what is called today the Mackerel Tabby, covered with thin, dark lines. Some of these lines break up into dashes or spots, but the overall effect is of a tigerish striping. To begin with, this was the only such pattern in existence, but then a new mutation arose. A Blotched Tabby arrived on the scene. On this animal the markings were much bolder and more complex; the narrow striping survived only in certain areas.

It is believed that these Blotched Tabbies arose first in Britain, in the Elizabethan era. It was a time of great British expansion and it is thought that, in the guise of ships' cats, they were scattered from the British Isles all over the globe in a comparatively short space of time. With the growth of the British Empire in the Victorian era, they spread still further.

For some reason that is not fully understood, the Blotched Tabby was a winner. Perhaps the gene for this pattern was linked to an unusual level of aggressiveness or assertiveness, with the result that these cats soon managed to oust most other colour forms whenever there was a dispute over territory or females. Perhaps they were simply more healthy or more fertile. Whatever the reason, this new pattern began to dominate. The earlier striped tabby went into a rapid decline. Today it has become quite rare, while the Blotched Tabby is the most common form of all. It would not be too far from the truth, as cat authority Roger Tabor put it, to christen this most successful of all domestic felines 'the British Imperial Cat'.

Looking at the great variation in cat coat colours today, the first impression is that tabbies are now only one small part of the general spectrum of available patterns and hues. Genetically, the truth is rather different, because in reality *all* domestic cats are tabbies. If they do not appear to be so, it is because the tabby pattern is masked by the other non-tabby colours. In the absence of these masking colours, the cat's coat is seen as a mixture of banded (agouti) hairs and black hairs. The black hairs are arranged in patches, and it is this arrangement that we call 'tabby'. In addition to the two types mentioned already, there are three others that can be seen today. The five types are as follows:

MACKEREL TABBY: The patches are mostly in narrow streaks. This is the ancient type of tabby pattern, close to that seen in the ancestral wild cat species.

BLOTCHED TABBY: The patches are in the form of large smudges. Among domestic cats this is the most common form of tabby marking and is therefore referred to as the 'Classic Tabby Pattern'. This name is somewhat inappropriate because, with the Mackerel Pattern being closer to the wild feline condition, it could be argued that the more ancient pattern should be given the name of 'Classic'.

SPOTTED TABBY: In a few breeds the dark patches are formed into small spots. For most people, such animals would simply be described as 'Spotted Cats' rather than 'Spotted Tabbies'. It is not known whether the spots develop from broken Mackerel Tabby streaks, or from a separate mutation.

TICKED TABBY: This is the Abyssinian form of tabby marking, with very faint markings on a generally ticked coat.

PATCHED TABBY: This is the two-toned tabby, or Tortoiseshell Tabby, sometimes called the Torbie. In the typical form, there are separate patches of brown tabby and red tabby on the same animal.

Pedigree cat breeders have been busy and today there are many colour variants of these basic tabby patterns, including the following (some of which are simply alternative names for the same variant): (1) Blue Tabby; (2) Blue Patched Tabby; (3) Blue Silver Patched Tabby; (4) Blue Silver Tabby; (5) Brown Tabby; (6) Brown Patched Tabby; (7) Cameo Tabby; (8) Dilute Cameo Tabby; (9) Chestnut Tabby; (10) Chestnut Silver Tabby; (11) Chocolate Silver Tabby; (12) Cinnamon Tabby; (13) Cinnamon Silver Tabby; (14) Cream Tabby; (15) Cream Silver Tabby; (16) Ebony Tabby; (17) Fawn Tabby; (18) Fawn Silver Tabby; (19) Lavender Tabby; (20) Lavender Silver Tabby; (21) Red Tabby; (22) Silver Tabby; (23) Silver Patched Tabby.

In some tabby cats, there are areas of pure white in addition to the tabby zones: (24) Tabby and White; (25) Patched Tabby and White (= Torbie and White = Brown Tabby/Red Tabby/White); (26) Dilute Patched Tabby and White (= Blue Tabby/Cream Tabby/White); (27) Blue Tabby and White; (28) Blue Patched Tabby and White (= Dilute Patched Tabby and White); (29) Blue Silver Tabby and White; (30) Brown Tabby and White; (31) Brown Patched

THE BLOTCHED or Classic Tabby pattern, as displayed by a European Shorthair Cat *(opposite)*.

Tabby and White; (32) Cameo Tabby and White; (33) Cream Tabby and White; (34) Red Tabby and White; (35) Silver Tabby and White; (36) Silver Patched Tabby and White.

In some tabby cats, the coloured portions are restricted to the extremities of an otherwise white cat. This is known as the 'Van Tabby Pattern': (37) Van Tabby; (38) Van Tabby and White; (39) Van Cream Tabby and White; (40) Van Parti-colour Tabby and White; (41) Van Red Tabby and White.

Tabby (3)

Pet Cat. During Abraham Lincoln's presidency, his son Tad's cat, 'Tabby', became America's 'First cat'. It is also reported that he himself adopted three orphaned cats that he found half-frozen in a tent when he was visiting General Grant's camp during the Civil War.

Tabitha Twitchit

Fictional Cat. A fretful mother cat in several of Beatrix Potter's books for children. Her kittens were Mittens, Moppet and Tom Kitten, who were smacked and sent to their rooms when they annoyed her.

Tabor, Roger

Cat Authority. His field studies of the behaviour of feral cats in a city environment resulted in one of the modern classics of feline literature. In addition to his research into urban ecology, he also began broadcasting in the early 1970s, covering a wide range of feline topics. In 1990 he travelled the world in search of new information about domestic cats, for his BBC TV series *The Rise of the Cat*. In 1995 he presented a further TV series for the BBC, *Understanding Cats*, dealing with feline behaviour.

Bibliography:

1983. Tabor, R. *The Wild Life of the Domestic Cat*. Arrow Books, London.
1991. Tabor, R. Cats: *The Rise of the Cat*. BBC Books, London.
1995. Tabor, R. *Understanding Cats*. David & Charles, Newton Abbot, Devon.

Taffy

Pet Cat. A thieving cat which is commemorated in Christopher Morley's 1929 poem *In Honour of Taffy Topaz*.

Tail

Feline Anatomy. In a typical cat, the long, flexible feline tail contains between 21 and 23 caudal vertebrae. In exceptional cases, a fully tailed cat may have as few as 18 or as many as 28 of these bones. In the three stump-tailed domestic breeds – the Manx, the Japanese Bobtail and the American Bobtail – and the five stump-tailed wild species – the Caracal, Bobcat, the Canadian Lynx, the Northern Lynx and the Spanish Lynx – the number of tail-bones is drastically reduced.

In a normal tail, the tail-bones decrease in size gradually to the last one. Towards the tip they become reduced to slender rods of bone, slightly enlarged at each end. The final one, at the very tip of the tail, has a small conical 'cap', a mere rudiment of the last vertebra that finishes off the spinal column. The tails of domestic cats vary slightly in length, according to breed, but are nearly always more than 20 cm (8 inches) and less than 30 cm (12 inches), with 25 cm (10 inches) being the average.

Because of the numerous tail-bones and the longer, more flexible spine, the cat has a greater total number of bones in its body than we do – usually 244, compared with only 204 in the human being.

When Siamese Cats first appeared in the West it was noticed that many of them had kinks in their tails. This has now been bred out of them, but in the Orient, where the gene for kinky tail is widespread, a large percentage of the local cats exhibit this feature. Surveys have revealed that, in Hong Kong, about one-third of the cats have tail kinks; in the more northerly Malay states this rises to two-thirds; and in Singapore, it is at its highest, with 69 per cent of the local cats showing it.

The kink itself is caused by a twisting and often a fusing of several of the tail-bones. Clearly it causes no serious disadvantage, or it would have disappeared from the Eastern populations, or at the very least become extremely rare. Whether it carries some hidden, associated advantage for the cats concerned is not yet known.

Tailless Cats

Domestic Cats. There are currently seven breeds of domestic cat with abbreviated tails: the Manx, the Cymric, the Japanese Bobtail, the Japanese Bobtail Longhair, the Karelian Bobtail, American Bobtail and the American Lynx.

The Manx Cat from the Isle of Man, which has been known for centuries, has been exhibited as a distinct breed since the 19th century. Its long-haired version, the Cymric, did not appear at cat shows until the 1960s.

The Japanese Bobtail, known in Japan since the sixth century, the Japanese Bobtail Longhair, identified as a breed since the 1950s, the American Bobtail, established in the 1960s, the American Lynx from the 1980s, and the little-known Karelian Bobtail from Russia are not strictly speaking tailless breeds. They have separate genetic origins and should be considered as 'short-tailed' rather than as tailless.

In addition to these six established breeds, individual cats born without tails have appeared in a number of locations. As early as 1809, tailless cats were reported from Edinburgh, where a female 'had many litters of kittens; and in every litter there was one or more that wanted the tail, either wholly or in part'.

In the same year 'the continuance of a breed of tailless cats' was observed at Pendarvis in Cornwall. A little later, in 1837, tailless cats are mentioned: 'of which a considerable number exist in Cornwall and in the Isle of Man . . . [also] in a little obscure village in Dorsetshire, where it is rather numerous, but all of them had sprung from the same stock'.

The Japanese Bobtail has a tail that is not merely shortened but also tightly twisted. Genetically, this is quite distinct from the tail-shortening of the Manx Cat.

The Cornish connection resurfaces again much later, in 1909, when an encyclopedia reports that tailless cats 'were called Cornwall Cats but later became known as the Manx'.

Other reports of tailless cats emanate from locations as diverse as Burma, China, Java, Malaya, Russia and Thailand. The only place where they are said to have been particularly common, outside the Isle of Man, is in the Crimea and it has been suggested that they may have journeyed from there, as ship's cats, through the Mediterranean, to the tin-mine districts of Cornwall and from there, eventually, to the Isle of Man. This appears to be no more than speculation, however, and it is just as likely that the tailless Manx mutation appeared spontaneously on the Isle of Man itself.

(For further details see separate entries for American Bobtail, American Lynx, Cymric, Japanese Bobtail, Japanese Bobtail Longhair, Karelian Bobtail, Malay Cat and Manx Cat.)

Tail Signals

Feline Behaviour. Because the cat's tail is a balancing organ its actions reflect its varying moods. Each tail movement or posture tells us (and other cats) something about the animal's emotional condition and it is possible to draw up a 'decoding key', as follows:

1 *Tail curves gently down and then up again at the tip:* This is the relaxed cat, at peace with the world.

2 *Tail raised slightly and softly curved:* The cat is becoming interested in something.

3 *Tail held erect but with the tip tilted over:* The cat is very interested and is in a friendly, greeting mood, but with slight reservations.

4 *Tail fully erect with the tip stiffly vertical:* An intense greeting display with no reservations. In adult cats this posture is 'borrowed' from the action of a kitten greeting its mother. The kitten's signal is an invitation to the mother cat to inspect its rear end, so there is an element of subordination in the display, as there is in most greeting ceremonies.

5 *Tail fully lowered and possibly even tucked between the hind legs:* This is the signal of a defeated or totally submissive cat that wishes to stress its lowly social status.

6 *Tail lowered and fluffed out:* The cat is indicating active fear.

7 *Tail wagged from side to side:* This familiar feline signal indicates that the cat is in a state of conflict. It wants to do two things at once but each impulse blocks the other. It does not, as some people think, always indicate anger. For example, if a cat is let out of the back door but finds it is pouring with rain, it may hesitate and wag its tail. Here, the tail-wagging indicates a conflict between wanting to go out and not wanting to get wet. On other occasions the conflict may be between the urge to attack and to flee.

8 *Tail swished violently from side to side:* This is the conflict signal of tail-wagging in its most intense form. If the tail swings very vigorously from side to side it usually means that the cat is about to attack, if it can summon up the last ounce of aggression.

9 *Tail held still, but with tip twitching:* This is the version of tail-wagging that indicates only mild irritation. But if the tip-twitching becomes more powerful, then it can act as a clue that a swipe from a bad-tempered paw is imminent.

10 *Tail held erect with its whole length quivering:* This gentle quivering action is often seen after a cat has been greeted by its owner. It is the same action that is observed when urine-spraying is taking place out of doors, but in this case there is no urine produced. Whether some slight, invisible scent is expelled is not clear, but the gesture appears to have the meaning of a friendly, 'personal identification' as if the cat is saying, 'Yes, this is *me* !'

11 *Tail held to one side:* This is the sexual invitation signal of the female cat on heat. When she is ready to be mounted by the male she conspicuously moves her tail over to one side. When he sees this, the tom-cat knows he can mount her without being attacked.

12 *Tail held straight and fully bristled:* This is the signal of an aggressive cat.

13 *Tail arched and bristled:* This is the signal of a defensive cat, but one that may attack if provoked further. The bristling of the fur makes the animal look bigger, a 'transformation display' that may deter the enemy if the defensive cat is lucky.

Tao

Fictional Cat. A male Siamese, who plays a central role in *The Incredible Journey* (1961) by Sheila Burnford. The cat and two dogs, Bodger (a Bull Terrier) and Luath (a Labrador), become separated from their owners and must make an arduous, 400 km (250 mile) journey to return home. The cat is depicted as resourceful, fearless and an excellent hunter. The book was made into a successful feature film by Walt Disney in 1963.

Tarawood Antigone

Pet Cat. A female brown Burmese Cat owned by Mrs Valerie Gane of Church Westcote, Kingham, Oxfordshire, England, which currently holds the record for producing the largest litter of kittens in recorded history: 19, consisting of one female, 14 males and four stillborn. They were born on 7th August 1970. The mother was four years old when the huge litter was delivered by Caesarean section. The father was a half-Siamese.

Taste

Feline Biology. The sense of taste is weak in cats, compared with humans. We have 9,000 taste buds, while they have only 473. But they make up for this with a much better sense of smell – 30 times better than ours. For this reason cats much prefer warm food to cold food, because when it is heated up, its aroma intensifies. It also means that a cat with a cold in the head is at an even greater disadvantage at mealtimes than a human being in a similar condition.

Like human beings, cats are responsive to four basic tastes: sour, bitter, salt and sweet. Being omnivores, we respond strongly to all four tastes, but cats, being strict carnivores, are weak when it comes to sweet tastes. They lack our 'sweet tooth', which evolved because fruits are part of our natural diet. It was important for us to respond positively to the ripening of fruits, but this had no meaning for the predatory cats.

Until recently many authorities stated categorically that cats, almost alone among mammals, were totally incapable of responding to sweet tastes. One said, without qualification, 'The cat shows no response to sweet tastes.' Another declared,'Sweet tastes cannot be discerned by the cat.' This traditional wisdom must now be discarded. New tests have proved conclusively that cats can appreciate the presence of sweet tastes, even if this is not a powerful reaction. If milk is diluted to one-quarter of its normal strength, and hungry cats are then offered a choice between this weak milk laced with sucrose against the same milk without any sweetening, they always prefer the sweetened dishes.

If this is the case, it is surprising that this ability has been denied in the past. The reason seems to have been that, in most tests, cats do ignore the sweetness factor when making their choices. It is of such insignificance to them that they 'override' it. If, for example, they are tested with full-strength or half-strength milk, they show no preference for the more or the less sweetened examples. Their reaction to the milk itself is too strong. Only when the milk factor is reduced by dilution does the sweetness factor begin to show. So although cats do enjoy this taste – presumably as a hang-over from their kittenhood, when like all young mammals they reacted strongly to their mother's sweet milk – they do so as adults to only a very mild degree. We keep our sweet tooth throughout life, but they largely lose theirs as they mature.

Their strongest reaction is to sour tastes; next come bitter, then salt and finally sweet tastes. As food touches the tongue it comes into contact with the sensory papillae there. In the middle of the tongue these papillae are strong, rough and backward-pointing. In this area, there is a specialization of the tongue's surface that has nothing to do with taste. Indeed, there are no taste buds in this central region. It is a zone concerned entirely with rasping meat from bones or with cleaning fur. The taste buds are confined to the tip, the sides and the back of the tongue only. Sour tastes can be detected in all these areas, but bitter is confined to the back part and salt to the front.

However, as mentioned above, the most powerful response of all to the food is to its smell, or fragrance. This is the really important information cats are receiving when they approach a meal. It is why many will sniff at it and then walk away without even attempting to taste it. Like a wine connoisseur who only has to sniff the vintage to know how good it is, a cat can learn all it wants to know without actually trying the food.

If the animal does take a mouthful, then the tongue also has a sensitive reaction to the food's temperature. The wild ancestors of our domestic cats liked to eat freshly killed prey – they were not scavengers. And the tame descendants have kept the same views on this matter. The ideal, preferred temperature for feline food is 30 degrees C (86 degrees F), which happens to be the same temperature as the cat's tongue. Food taken straight from the refrigerator is anathema to the cat – unless it is very hungry, in which case it will eat almost anything. Sadly, for most pet cats today, heated food is something of a luxury and, like many humans, they have learned to live with the 'fast food' mentality of modern times.

Tawny Cat

Wild Feline. An alternative name for the African Wild Cat *(Felis sylvestris libyca)*, the wild ancestor of the domestic cat.

Teeth

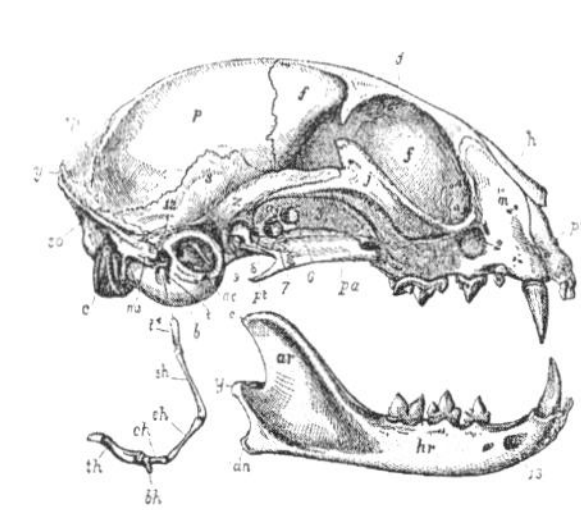

Feline Anatomy. The adult cat has 30 teeth: 12 incisors, four canines, ten premolars and four molars. It uses them to attack, to defend itself and to kill food. A tom-cat also uses his teeth to grasp the neck of the female when he is mating. And a mother cat will use them, with great care, to grasp the neck of her kittens when transporting them.

The large, curved, pointed canines (or should they be felines?) are important stabbing and clasping weapons. The premolars are shearing implements used to cut the prey into pieces that are small enough to swallow. Cats do not chew their food. They chop it up and swallow it. One of the problems they face when given nothing but prepared pet foods is that they never have to face the challenge of slicing up a large, tough food object. The soft food from the can or packet does not make them work hard enough and their teeth may suffer as a result.

Teeth-chattering

Feline Behaviour. When a cat sees a bird through a window it may stare intently at it and then perform a strange juddering action with its jaws that has been described variously as a 'teeth-chattering', a 'tooth-rattling stutter', a 'tetanic reaction', or the 'frustrated chatter of the cat's jaws in the mechanical staccato fashion'.

The explanation of this peculiar response is that the cat is performing an exaggerated version of its highly specialized killing-bite. It is behaving as if, in its mind, it already has the unfortunate bird in its jaws and is delivering the *coup de grâce*. It is rather like a man licking his lips in anticipation of a tasty meal.

Close observation of the way in which cats kill their prey has revealed that there is an unusual jaw movement employed to bring about an almost instantaneous death. This is important to a feline predator because even the most timid of prey may lash out when seized, and it is vital for the cat to reduce as much as possible any risk of injury to itself from the sharp beak of a bird or the powerful teeth of a rodent. So there is no time to lose. After the initial pounce, in which the prey is pinioned by the strong claws of the killer's front feet, the cat quickly crunches down with its long canine teeth, aiming at the nape of the neck. With a rapid juddering movement of the jaws it inserts these canines into the neck, slipping them down between the vertebrae to sever the spinal cord. This killing bite immediately incapacitates the prey and it is an enactment of this special movement that the frustrated, window-gazing cat is performing, unable to control itself at the tantalizing view of the juicy little bird outside.

Incidentally, the killing-bite is guided by the indentation of the body outline of the prey – the indentation which occurs where the body joins the head in both small birds and small rodents. Some prey have developed a defensive tactic in which they hunch up their bodies to conceal this indentation and in this way make the cat miss its aim. If the trick works, the cat may bite its victim in a part of the body which does not cause death, and on rare occasions the wounded prey may then be able to scrabble to safety if the cat relaxes for a moment, imagining that it has already dealt its lethal blow. (See also Voice.)

Temminck's Cat

Wild Feline. *(Felis temminckii)* Named after the Dutch naturalist Coenraad Jacob Temminck, who had discovered the other species of golden cat in Africa, Temminck's Cat is also known as the Golden Cat, the Asian Golden Cat, the Asiatic Golden Cat or Temminck's Golden Cat. In China it is called the Shilului, or Huang Poo, meaning Rock Cat or Yellow Leopard. In Burma it is sometimes given the name Kya Min, Fire Cat, or Fire Tiger. In Malaya it becomes the Kuching Tulap, or Harimau Anjing. Early authors also gave it the name of Bay Cat, because of its rich chestnut colour, but this has been abandoned because it leads to confusion with the much smaller species, the Bornean Bay Cat.

This medium-sized cat has a uniform, pale reddish-brown coat with markings only on the face and underside of the tail. On the face there is a pattern of white, grey and black stripes. On the underside of the tail there is a white patch that probably acts as a flag when the kittens are following their mother, and her tail is held erect.

Apparently it occupies a wide range of different kinds of habitat, from tropical rain forests to open country, but prefers rocky woodland. In the hotter, wetter parts of its range, melanistic individuals are not uncommon.

This is a ground-level hunter, taking small deer, sheep, goats, hares, larger birds and reptiles.

It is said to be closely related to the African Golden Cat, but their resemblance may simply be due to parallel development. The fact that there is a gap of over 6,400 km (4,000 miles) between their two ranges suggests that they may not, after all, be closely related at all.

Little is known about its social life in the wild. Captive specimens have proved to be unusually friendly and co-operative. One pet Temminck's Cat was so affectionate towards its owner, the famous naturalist E.P. Gee, that, even when nearly adult, it used to suck his earlobes while 'milk-treading' with its paws on his lap. In his book *The Wild Life of India* he describes

Temminck's Cat *(Felis temminckii)* is a medium-sized, Asiatic feline with a plain golden coat that is in striking contrast with its elaborately marked face.

the remarkably 'domesticated' behaviour of his animal: 'He was free to come and go as he pleased during the day time, and if I was not available for him to play with he would disappear for hours on end into the forest down the hillside. But he invariably came back when called. A cat of two worlds, docile and affectionate with me but potentially savage in the forest and nearby villages.'

Size: Length of Head + Body: 73–105 cm (29–41½ in). Tail: 43–56 cm (17–22 in). Weight: 12–16 kg (26½–35 lb).

Distribution: Tropical Asia, including: India, Nepal, Tibet, Bangladesh, Burma, China, Thailand, Laos, Cambodia, Vietnam, Malaysia and Sumatra.

Temperature

Feline Biology. The normal body temperature of a domestic cat is usually considered to be 38.6 degrees C (101.5 degrees F), slightly higher than that for humans.

Territory

Feline Behaviour. The wild counterpart of the domestic cat has a huge territory, with males patrolling up to 71 hectares (175 acres). Domestic cats which have gone wild and are living in remote areas where there is unlimited space also cover impressively large areas. Typical farm cats use nearly as much space, the males ranging over 61 hectares (150 acres). Female farm cats are more modest, using only about six hectares (15 acres) on average. In cities, towns and suburbs, the cat population becomes almost as overcrowded as that of the human citizens. The territories of urban cats shrink to a mere fraction of the home range enjoyed by their country cousins. It has been estimated that cats living rough in London, for example, enjoy only 810 square metres (about one-fifth of an acre) each. Pampered pet cats living in their owners' houses may be even more restricted, depending on the size of the gardens attached to the houses. The maximum density recorded is 81 square metres (one-fiftieth of an acre).

This degree of variation in the size of feline territories shows just how flexible the cat can be. Like people, it can adjust to a massive shrinkage of its home ground without undue suffering. From the above figures it is easy to calculate that 8,750 crowded pet cats could be fitted into the territory of one wild cat living in a remote part of the world. The fact that the social life of the crowded cats does not become chaotic and vicious is a testimony to the social tolerance of felines. In a way this is surprising, because people often speak of the sociability of dogs, but stress that cats are much more solitary and unsociable. They may indeed be less sociable by choice, but given the challenge of living whisker-by-tail with other cats, they manage remarkably well.

They achieve this high-density success in a number of ways. The most important factor is the provision of food by their owners. This removes the need for lengthy daily hunting trips. It may not remove the urge to set off on such trips – a well-fed cat remains a hunting cat – but it does reduce the determination born of an empty stomach. If they find themselves invading neighbouring territories, they can give up the hunt without starving. If restricting their hunting activities to their own cramped home ranges makes them inefficient prey-catchers, it might prove frustrating, but it does not lead to starvation and death. It has been demonstrated that the more food the cats are given by their owners, the smaller their urban territories become.

Another factor helping them is the way in which their human owners divide up their own territories – with fences and hedges and walls to demarcate their gardens. These provide natural boundary-lines that are easy to recognize and defend. In addition there is a permissible degree of overlapping in feline territories. Female cats often have special areas where several of their home ranges overlap and where they can meet on neutral ground. The males – whose territories are always about ten times the size of those of the females, regardless of how great or small the crowding – show much more overlap. Each male will roam about on an area that takes in several female territories, enabling him to keep a permanent check on which particular queen (female) is on heat at any particular moment.

The overlapping is permitted because the cats are usually able to avoid one another as they patrol the landmarks in their patch of land. If, by accident, two of them do happen to meet up unexpectedly, they may threaten one another or simply keep out of one another's way, watching each other's movements and waiting their turn to visit a particular zone of the territory.

The numbers of pet cats are, of course, controlled by their owners, with the neutering of adult cats, the destruction of unwanted litters and the selling or giving away of surplus kittens. But how does the territorial arrangement of feral cats survive the inevitable production of offspring? One detailed study of dockland cats at a large port revealed that in an area of 85 hectares (210 acres) there were 95 cats. Each year they produced about 400 kittens between them. This is a high figure of about ten per female, which must mean that on average each queen gave birth to two litters. In theory this would mean a fivefold increase in the population each year. In practice it was found that the population remained remarkably stable from one year to the next. The cats had established an appropriate territory size for the feral, dockland world in which they lived, and then kept to it. Closer investigation revealed that only one in eight of the kittens survived to become adults. These 50 additions to the population each year were balanced by 50 deaths among the older cats. The main cause of death here (as with most urban cat populations) was the fatal road accident.

Thai Cat

Domestic Breed. Breeders of Siamese Cats in Germany have been developing a new form that they are calling the 'Thai Cat' *(Thaikatze)*. To be more precise, they are re-creating the old-fashioned type of Siamese, with a rounder face and less elongated body. This completely reverses the competitive breeding trend that has been changing the Siamese form, year by year, until it has become a greatly exaggerated version of its earlier self.

There is a special reason for the reversal of this trend. The increasing angularity of Siamese Cats in pedigree cat shows has led to criticisms from the German authorities. Breeders there now fear that the more extreme forms of Siamese may eventually be banned, and they are trying to anticipate this by a voluntary return to the older type. Hence the re-introduction of the old-fashioned Thai Cat.

A similar breeding trend has been occurring in America, where the Thai Cat is referred to either as the Traditional Siamese or the Apple-head Siamese. (For further details see Apple-head Siamese.)

Note: There is a breed publication called *Thai Line*. Address: P.O. Box 1106, Placentia, CA 92670, USA.

Therapy

Feline History. Studies of the effects that pet cats have on their owners have revealed that sharing a home with these animals is significantly therapeutic. In short, cat-owning is good for your health. There are two reasons for this:

First, it is known that the friendly physical contact with cats actively reduces stress in their human companions. The relationship between human and cat is touching in both senses of the word. The cat rubs against its owner's body and the owner strokes and fondles the cat's fur. If such owners are wired up in the laboratory to test their physiological responses, it is found that their body systems become markedly calmer when they start stroking their cats. Their tension eases and their bodies relax. This form of feline therapy has been proved in practice in a number of acute cases where mental patients have improved amazingly after being allowed the company of pet cats.

Most cat-owners feel somehow released by the simple, honest relationship with their cat. This is the second reason for the cat's beneficial impact on humans. It is not merely a matter of touch, important as that may be. It is also a matter of psychological relationship which lacks the complexities, betrayals and contradictions of human relationships. We are all hurt by certain human relationships from time to time, some of us acutely, others more trivially. Those with

T

severe mental scars may find it hard to trust again. For them, a bond with a cat can provide rewards so great that it may even give them back their faith in human relations, destroy their cynicism and their suspicion and heal their hidden scars. And a special study in the United States has recently revealed that, for those whose stress has led to heart trouble, the owning of a cat may literally make the difference between life and death, reducing blood pressure and calming the overworked heart.

Actress Susan Hampshire with her co-star, the female ginger cat who played the title role in the 1963 film *The Three Lives of Thomasina.*

Thomasina

Fictional Cat. In Paul Gallico's *Thomasina: The Cat Who Thought She Was God* (1957), the central figure is a female ginger cat who belongs to a vet's daughter. Thinking that she is ill, he decides to put the cat to sleep. She does not, however, die from the anaesthetic and is saved by a stranger. Coming round from the anaesthetic, the cat is convinced that she has been reincarnated as an Egyptian cat goddess.

Believing that her beloved cat is dead, the vet's daughter becomes deeply depressed and even suicidal. When she lies dying, the cat, now fully recovered, struggles home through a terrible storm to save her life.

In 1963, the story was used as the basis for a feature film by Walt Disney called *The Three Lives of Thomasina*, starring Susan Hampshire and Patrick McGoohan.

Thong Daeng

Domestic Breed. This is the early name for 'The Copper', an ancient Siamese domestic feline that appears in the set of manuscript scrolls known as *The Cat Book Poems,* now housed in the Thai National Library in Bangkok. Also known as the Sopalak or Supalak, it is thought to be the ancestor of the modern Burmese Cat. (See Burmese Cat.)

Tib

Fictional Cat. A female farmyard tabby cat, Tib features in an otherwise excessively canine story, *The Hundred and One Dalmatians* (1956) by Dodie Smith. According to the plot, young puppies are being systematically stolen for their skins and Tib is active in helping to find the missing animals. In 1961 the story was made into a cartoon feature film by Walt Disney.

Tibert

Fictional Cat. Tibert the Cat was one of the victims of the wily fox in the 12th-century epic *Reynard the Fox.* Tibert is sent to bring Reynard before an angry king. The fox agrees to go with Tibert, but suggests that he might like a tasty meal of mice before setting off. The cat is directed to a barn to catch the mice, only to find himself caught in a snare that had been set to trap the chicken-thieving fox.

Tibert is badly beaten by the priest who owns the barn, who leaps out of bed when he hears the yowling of the cat, and runs naked to kill the intruder. As Tibert is being attacked, he retaliates by biting off one of the priest's testicles, much to Reynard's amusement.

The cat just manages to escape death and struggles back to the court to tell the king what has happened. The fox is condemned to death and the story ends with Tibert the Cat sitting on top of the gallows and holding the rope tight as Reynard is hanged.

Tibetan Temple Cat

Domestic Breed. Two American authors, John Hickey and Priscilla Beach, writing in 1946, identify this as a rare breed. 'The Tibetan Temple Cat', the 'Sacred Cat of Tibet', is seldom, if ever, seen in Western countries, owing to its exclusive and sacred nature. It is similar to the Siamese Cat, having dark markings on the face, legs, and tail, but it is larger in stature and slightly darker.

Its 'exclusivity' seems to have kept it well hidden because it is not heard of again until 1960, when an American breeder, Mrs G. Griswold, imported a pair of Tibetan Temple kittens. When they arrived in the United States it was soon realized that they were not 'large Siamese', but the same as the Birman Cats that were reputed to have originally come from a Burmese temple. In the history of the Birman there is a story that in 1916 the Burmese priests were driven out of their temple during a rebellion and took refuge, along with their sacred cats, in Tibet. Some authorities had doubted the validity of this story, but the discovery of the Tibetan Temple Cats – if they are genuine – strongly supports it.

Tibetan Tiger-cat

Wild Feline. Originally considered to be a separate species *(Felis scripta)*, the pale grey Tibetan Tiger-cat is now looked upon as no more than a northern race of the widespread Leopard Cat *(Felis bengalensis)*.

Ticked

Coat Pattern. An alternative name for the agouti coat, in which each hair is banded with black, brown and yellow. This is the typical coat pattern of the Abyssinian, the Somali, the Wild Abyssinian, the Singapura and the Ceylon, and of certain species of wild felines, such as the Jungle Cat *(Felis chaus)*.

Tiffanie Cat

Domestic Breed. Essentially, a long-haired Burmese. A recent British breed which is frequently confused with the superficially similar American breed called the Tiffany (see entry for Tiffany Cat). The Tiffanie was a long-haired by-product of the Burmilla breeding programme instigated in the 1980s. It is a member of the Asian group and was originally called the 'Asian Longhair'. It was renamed the Tiffanie when it was wrongly believed to be closely related to the American Tiffany Cat.

Appearance: A golden-eyed cat with a long, silky coat, a ruff and a full tail. Otherwise it has the body proportions of a Burmese. Typically, the coat is brown but may also be in a variety of other colours.

History: During the 1980s Asian Shorthair breeding programmes, producing variations on the Burmese theme, several breeders accidentally began to produce long-haired kittens. The first to do so was Jeanne Bryson of Droitwich in Worcestershire, England. The Longhairs were often neutered and sold as pets, but some were kept and formed the basis of the new breed.

Colour Forms: The Tiffanie can be in any colour or pattern found in the Asian group.

Tiffany Cat

Domestic Breed. Often mistakenly referred to as a 'Long-haired Burmese', this recent American breed has a different origin from the British cat called the Tiffanie (see separate entry), and should not be confused with it. Attempts to avoid this confusion have led some authorities to rename the Tiffany as the Chantilly.

Appearance: A medium-sized cat with golden eyes and a rich, lustrous brown coat which is long and silky. There is a pronounced neck ruff and a plumed tail.

History: The genetic origin of the American breed known as the Tiffany is something of a mystery. The founding cats were a pair of golden-eyed, chocolate-coloured, long-haired cats of unknown background. They were bought from an estate sale by American breeder Jennie Robinson of New York in 1967. The male, Thomas, was a little over a year old and the female, Shirley, was only about six months old. It is probable that they had the same parents, but they were clearly not litter-mates. Two years later, in May 1969, they produced their first litter. To the breeder's surprise, all six kittens had identical, rich chocolate-brown coats, and this prompted further breeding. In the early 1970s the cats from this programme were registered with the ACA under the name of Foreign Longhairs.

Several breeders guessed that these must be Long-haired Burmese, or that at the very least they must have had elements of Burmese in their ancestry. Close examination of the finer details

T

THERE HAS BEEN CONSIDERABLE confusion between the British Tiffanie and the American Tiffany. The Tiffanie is essentially a long-haired Burmese. The Tiffany is superficially similar but, contrary to widespread published statements, does not have Burmese origins. The type pictured here is the British Tiffanie.

of their coat-colouring and their paw-pads (which were pink instead of brown) revealed that 'none arose from nor were bred to Burmese'.

The history of the breed then took a misleading turn. Some of the Robinson kittens were bought by a Florida breeder, Sigyn Lund, who was well-known for her Burmese stock. She became the new champion of the Foreign Longhairs and it was she who devised the new name of Tiffany for them. They were given this name after a Los Angeles theatre and it was meant to suggest a classy elegance – much more appropriate than the colourless title of Foreign Longhair. Unfortunately, not knowing of their mysterious New York beginnings, many people naturally assumed that these delightful animals must be long-haired versions of the Lund Burmese stock. And so the myth of the 'Longhair Burmese' began.

Book after book repeated the error that the American Tiffany Cat was a Longhair Burmese. As recently as 1995, one stated bluntly: 'Tiffany – This new breed, the result of crossing a Burmese with a Persian, was developed in the United States.' Another describes it as resulting from 'a cross between a Burmese and a self longhair'.

Yet another comments: 'In the United States the Tiffany was developed from long-coated cats which appeared in litters of normal Burmese.'

Like a game of Chinese Whispers, the error was repeated and repeated until it became firmly entrenched. Only one recent book, the diminutive *Letts Pocket Guide to Cats,* by David Burn and Chris Bell, avoided this mistake. They correctly state: 'Documentation of the true origins of the US Tiffany seem to have been lost . . . Burmese brown is the most common Tiffany (US) colour but the gene that gives rise to it is independent of the Burmese type and there is now doubt as to whether the American breed of this name has any Burmese (breed) ancestry at all.' Quite so. As stated at the outset, the origin of this breed must remain a mystery, a mystery that began with two unidentified brown cats at a New York estate sale.

To confuse matters further, in the 1980s British breeders working on variations of the new Burmilla breed accidentally created a long-haired brown cat that really did have some Burmese blood in its veins (see previous entry). At first it was known as the Asian Longhair, but then, when it was wrongly assumed that the American Tiffany was also a long-haired Burmese, the British breeders decided to call their animals by the same name. By a lucky chance this was not possible because in Britain the word 'Tiffany' was already registered as a breeder's prefix and was therefore unavailable as the title of a new breed of cat. Wishing to keep the UK/USA link alive, it was then decided to call the British long-haired cats by the name of 'Tiffanie'.

Needless to say, this only added further confusion, with many authors talking about the 'American Tiffanie' and others referring to the 'British Tiffany', neither of which existed.

As if this were not enough, to make matters worse, a third plot had been quietly unfolding, this time in Canada. This story had a beginning as mysterious as the New York estate sale. In 1973, a pregnant, golden-eyed, long-haired, chocolate brown cat walked unannounced into the home of a Canadian land-owner and promptly presented him with a litter of identically coloured kittens. Canadian breeders eventually acquired some of the offspring of these cats and began to develop them. By the late 1980s, in co-operation with their American counterparts, they had managed to boost the fortunes of the Tiffany breed, which at one point had been in danger of disappearing. In the meantime, however, word had spread across the Atlantic about the British Tiffanie and, in order to avoid further confusion, it was decided to give the North American breed a new name. The one chosen was 'Chantilly'. However, in the world of pedigree cats, matters are never that simple. Some cat associations accepted the new name, others retained the original 'Tiffany' and still others went for a safe compromise with the clumsy title of 'Chantilly/Tiffany'. And that is how the situation stands at the present time.

Personality: Terms used to describe this breed include: loyal, affectionate, gentle, sociable, devoted, outgoing, inquisitive, friendly. The voice includes 'quiet chirps or trills'.

Colour Forms: Traditionally, the self-coloured Tiffany coat is a rich, dark brown colour, but already there are a number of dilutions and variations of this, including blue, cinnamon, lilac and fawn, in both solid and tabby patterns.

TIGER (1)

WILD FELINE. *(Panthera tigris)* The Tiger has a number of local names. For example: Hindi: *Bagh* or *Sher;* Bengali: *Sela-vagh* or *Go-vagh;* Tibetan: *Tagh;* Malay: *Harimau Belang.*

The tiger is the largest member of the cat family and, indeed, the largest hunter of any kind to stalk the earth today. Its immense power enables it to kill almost any kind of hoofed animal, from deer and pigs to large wild cattle. Unfortunately, it also preys upon domestic animals and occasionally even human beings, which has been its undoing.

Using its black-striped, orange coat as camouflage, the tiger approaches its prey from upwind, with great stealth, and then makes a last-minute dash in an attempt to deliver a massive blow with a front paw. Because its body is so heavy, this final dash must be comparatively short if it is to succeed – 30 metres (33 yards) is about the maximum it can manage at top speed. Once it has knocked the prey down, it grabs it with the sharp claws of its front feet. At the same time, it clamps its jaws on the throat of the prey and begins to suffocate it. This killing process is surprisingly quick, but the big cat will remain gripping the victim's neck for several minutes after it has ceased to struggle. Then, it will probably drag the carcass to a safe place to devour it. It is capable of pulling weights of up to 230 kg (507 lb).

Once in cover, it will set about gulping down as much as 30 kg (66 lb) of meat at a single sitting. When it is finished, it may remain with the partially devoured body until it is hungry again, and then continue its huge meal. Alternatively, it may scoop leaves and branches over the carcass, hiding it from view. Having stashed it cautiously away like this, it can then return later to finish it off. The tiger is a careful eater, leaving little for scavengers. One of the reasons for this is that it is not as efficient at hunting as most people imagine. Careful observations have revealed that, out of all its attempts to catch a prey animal, this giant cat only has a one-in-20 chance of succeeding. A female with cubs does better. Driven on by her urgent need to feed her growing offspring, she has a one-in-five chance. But clearly the tiger must make the most of its successes and leave as little surplus as possible.

Because of its large food demands, each wild tiger has a territory about as big as a modern city. Territorial ownership is marked out by spraying scented urine against trees or by scratching the bark with the sharp claws. Because fights between rivals would be so damaging – even to the winner – these heavyweights of the feline world do their best to avoid one another as they patrol their home ranges. Males avoid other males and females avoid other females. But when a male meets a female, even outside the breeding season, there is a small, friendly greeting. It consists of a soft *fuf-fuf-fuf* noise and the impact of this signal is so strong that even a human, crudely imitating the sound, can illicit a reply from a captive tiger.

A female produces a litter every two years. When she comes into heat, she starts wandering until she encounters a male. Sometimes the change in her scent will make this unnecessary, because it will attract males towards her own territory. Once the mating has occurred, the male departs and the female takes full responsibility for rearing the offspring. When they are very young, she leaves them snugly in her chosen den if she needs to set off on a hunt. Later, she will allow them to follow her and watch proceedings from a distance. On the back of each of her ears she has a vivid black and white 'eye-spot', which the young can use as a guide when following her through the bush. When she has made a kill, she may eat some of the flesh and then return to the cubs to regurgitate the half-digested meat for them, as an intermediate weaning process. Later she will encourage them to join her at the kill itself. Later still, when the cubs are about two years old, she will one day simply walk away and leave them. After that, they are on their own and must fend entirely for themselves. Of each litter of two or three cubs, only one cub is likely to survive this phase of the life cycle, and achieve adulthood successfully.

Unlike many other cats, the tiger solves its problems of over-heating (in the tropical parts of its geographical range) by cooling off in shallow water. On very hot days, it may spends several hours sprawled out in a small pool.

Size: Length of Head + Body: 160–290 cm (63–114 in). Tail: 80–100 cm (31½–39½ in). Weight: 190–320 kg (419–706 lb).

Distribution: Asia. From Russia, China and Korea in the north, through Nepal, Bhutan, India, Bangladesh, Burma, Thailand, Laos and Vietnam, to Malaysia and Sumatra in the south. During recent years it has been exterminated in Iran, Afghanistan, Pakistan, Java and Bali.

Population: It is estimated that, at the end of the 19th century, there were approximately 100,000 tigers living in Asia, from the cold wastelands of Siberia down to the steamy forests of Indonesia. Recently, this number had shrunk to a mere 8,000. Population surveys made in the 1970s and 1980s gave the following figures for the eight sub-species:

Tiger Population

SUBSPECIES	POPULATION
Caspian Tiger	A few still in 1970s; probably extinct by 1980s
Bengal Tiger	4,000 in India; 400 in Bangladesh; 300 in Burma; 230 in Nepal; 200 in Bhutan
Indochinese Tiger	2,000
Chinese Tiger	40–80 in the wild; 40 in captivity
Siberian Tiger	200–300 in the wild; 567 in captivity
Sumatran Tiger	500–600 in the wild; 157 in captivity
Javan Tiger	4–5 in 1970s; probably extinct by 1980s
Bali Tiger	Last seen in 1937; probably extinct by 1980s

There are four reasons why the tiger populations are falling:

1 The human population of Asia has more than doubled since 1950 and now stands at over 3,000 million. At the present rate of increase, this figure will have doubled again in another 30 years. Living space for the tigers is vanishing, year by year.

THE WORLD'S GREATEST CAT, the Tiger *(Panthera tigris),* was once common over vast regions of Asia, from the frozen wastes of Siberia in the north to the steamy jungles of Java and Bali in the south, but today its numbers have shrunk to only a few thousand.

2 Sport hunting still continues in certain regions, even where it is illegal. Bagging a tiger used to be one of the dreams of human hunters and for some the challenge remains irresistible. (In earlier days, one Maharajah was known to have announced with regret: 'My total bag of tigers is 1,150 only.')
3 The world demand for wood is insatiable and destruction of the ancient forests continues, robbing the tigers of their habitat.
4 Traditional Chinese medicine demands a regular supply of tiger items to satisfy its clients. In particular, ground-up tiger bone, tiger teeth, tiger claws, and tiger skin are greatly sought after to cure a variety of ailments. The tigers of Vietnam, Cambodia, Laos, Thailand, Burma (Myanmar) and Malaysia are all being hunted to extinction to satisfy this lucrative trade. Even the West is not immune to this craving for useless medicines. In 1995 a survey of Chinese chemist and craft shops in Britain revealed that half were selling products made from tiger bone.

Note: A charity now exists for the sole purpose of protecting the Tiger. Formed by Michael and Sophy Day, The Tiger Trust has its headquarters at Chevington, Bury St. Edmunds, Suffolk, IP29 5RG, England. According to their 1995 report *Fight for the Tiger,* the wild population has fallen drastically again, even in the space of only a few years, to an all-time low of about 5,000.

Bibliography:

1933. Burton, R.G. *The Book of the Tiger.* Hutchinson, London.
1964. Perry, R. *The World of the Tiger.* Cassell, London.
1967. Schaller, G. *The Deer and the Tiger.* University of Chicago Press, Chicago.
1971. Schaller, G. & Selsam, M.E. *The Tiger. Its Life in the Wild.* World's Work, London.
1973. Mountfort, G. *Tigers.* Crescent, New York.
1973. Singh, A. *Tiger Haven.* Macmillan, London.
1977. Sankhala, K. *Tiger! The Story of the Indian Tiger.* Simon & Schuster, New York.
1980. Courtney, N. *The Tiger, Symbol of Freedom.* Quartet Books, London.
1981. Mountfort, G. *Saving the Tiger.* Viking, New York.

Tiger (1)

This White Tiger is a mutant form in which the natural colouring is diluted. Dilutant genes of this kind have been the basis for much of the colour variation pursued so keenly by pedigree domestic cat breeders during the past century.

1981. Singh, A. *Tara. A Tigress*. London.
1984. Singh, A. *Tiger! Tiger!* Jonathan Cape, London.
1986. Thapar, V. *Tiger: Portrait of a Predator*. Collins, London.
1987. Tilson, R.L. & Seal, U.S. (Editors) *Tigers of the World*. Noyes, New Jersey.
1988. McNeely, J. & Wachtel, P. *Soul of the Tiger*. Doubleday, New York.
1989. Thapar, V. Tigers: *The Secret Life*. Rodale, Emmaus.
1990. Jackson, P. *Endangered Species: Tigers*. Chartwell, New Jersey.
1992. Thapar, V. *The Tiger's Destiny*. Kyle Cathie, London.
1992. Zwaenepoel, J-P. *Tigers*. Chron., San Francisco.
1993. Sankhala, K. *Return of the Tiger*. Lustre Press, New Delhi.
1993. Singh, A. *The Legend of the Maneater*. Ravi Dayal, New Delhi.
1994. Barnes, S. *Tiger!* Boxtree Books, London.
1995. Day, M. *Fight for the Tiger*. Headline, London.

Tiger (2)

Pet Cat. One of the heaviest domestic cats in the world, according to *The Guinness Book of Records*. Tiger was a long-haired cat, part Persian, who belonged to a Mrs Phyllis Dacey of Billericay, Essex, England. His great weight – 19.5 kg (43 lb) – was recorded when he was eight years old. This is four times the average weight of an adult domestic cat. Tiger died of kidney failure in 1980. His record was finally broken by Poppa, a male tabby who weighed 20 kg (44 lb) and another male tabby called Himmy who achieved an astonishing 21 kg (46 lb).

Tiger (3)

Pet Cat. Tiger was the much loved pet of the English novelist Charlotte Brontë. Homesick during a trip to Brussels in 1843, she wrote to her sister Emily that she longed to be home, in the kitchen with 'you standing by, watching that I save the best pieces of the leg of mutton for Tiger . . . [who] would be jumping about the dish and carving knife'.

Tiger (4)

Pet Cat. Tiger was the name given to a stray cat which appeared in the grounds of the White House in Washington in the 1920s, and stayed on to become the 'First Cat' of America. A grey-striped alley cat, he was adopted by President Calvin Coolidge, who used to walk around the Presidential residence with the animal draped about his neck. The President became so attached to him that, when Tiger went missing on one occasion, he instructed that a radio appeal be broadcast to recover him. He was eventually tracked down in the Navy Building.

Tiger (5)

Working Cat. Also known as 'The Terror of the Ritz', this Tiger was a huge tom-cat who was employed as a mouser at the Ritz Hotel in London. Unfortunately, he was given so many titbits and fed such a luxurious diet that he had to be sent away annually for a slimming course.

Tiger (6)

Domestic Cat. An informal name given to the Striped or Mackerel Tabby. Writing in 1940, Ida Mellen comments:

'The lined and striped tabbies, called tigers, have been bred in Europe for four hundred years, And the blotched tabby, called tabby, was noticed by Linnaeus in Sweden in 1746. In the tigers the ground colour is gray, the sides marked with narrow (lined) or wide (striped) vertical bands running from the shoulder to the tip of the tail, and a black stripe runs down the back from the head to the tip of the tail.'

Tiger Cat

Wild Feline. *(Felis tigrina)* Also known as the Little Spotted Cat or the Oncilla. Local names include Tigrillo Chico, Gato Tigre, Gato-do-Mato and Chivi. This is one of the smallest of the South American cats, with a delicate build. Its coat is covered in dark spots which may have pale centres. However, melanism is common and one in five is reported to have a black coat.

It is an extremely shy, forest-dwelling species and little is known of its natural history. It hunts

The small, slightly built Tiger Cat *(Felis tigrina)* of Central and South America is poorly named, since its coat is covered in spots rather than stripes. It is a shy, solitary forest-dweller that is becoming increasingly rare.

for small mammals and birds and is said to be an efficient climber. The litter size is small – only one or two kittens.

Because of the banning of other wild cat species, the Tiger Cat became the major source of wild skins for the fur trade in the 1980s, leading to an annual slaughter that reached a peak in 1987, with 84,500 animals killed. Because of the widespread hunting and the loss of habitat, this cat, like most other species of wild felines, is becoming increasingly less common.

Size: Length of Head + Body: 40–55 cm (16–21½ in). Tail: 20–30 cm (8–12 in). Weight: 2–3 kg (4½–6½ lb).

Distribution: The Tiger Cat is found from Costa Rica in Central America down as far south as northern Argentina.

Tiger Tim

Cartoon Cat. One of the very first of the cartoon cats, Tiger Tim was a playful tiger cub created by Julius Stafford Baker in 1904, making his debut in *Mrs Hippo's Kindergarten*. This was the first-ever strip cartoon in a British newspaper.

Tigger

Fictional Cat. The 'Large and Helpful Tigger' from A.A. Milne's classic children's tale *The House at Pooh Corner* (1928), Tigger was a tiger-like feline who was described as 'a very bouncy animal'. The other animals tried to unbounce him, but failed.

Tigon

Hybrid Cat. A cross between a male tiger and a female lion.

Tigrillo

Wild Feline. Local Spanish name for the Tiger Cat *(Felis tigrina)*.

Timothy

Pet Cat. A white cat belonging to author Dorothy L. Sayers. He appears in two of her poems, *For Timothy* and *War Cat*.

Tinker Toy

Pet Cat. A male Blue Point Himalayan, he holds the official record for the smallest known domestic cat, measuring only 7 cm (2¾ inches) tall and 19 cm (7½ inches) long. He is owned by Katrina and Scott Forbes of Taylorville, Illinois, USA.

Toddy Cat

Wild Viverrid. Despite its name, the Toddy Cat *(Paradoxurus hermaphroditus)* is not a true cat. It is the Common Palm Civet of southern Asia, a member of the Viverridae related to mongooses and genets. Its alternative popular name of 'Toddy Cat' is confusing and misleading.

Tom (1)

Feline Term. A male domestic cat. The term is derived from an 18th-century work of fiction. Before 1760 a male cat was known as a 'boar' or a 'ram' but in that year an anonymous story called *The Life and Adventures of a Cat* was published. The hero of the story was 'Tom the Cat'. The story enjoyed such popularity that before long anyone referring to a male cat, instead of calling it a 'boar' or a 'ram', used the word Tom, which has survived throughout the English-speaking world for over 200 years.

The identity of the author of the book remains a mystery, but Claire Necker in her feline bibliography lists it under the name Willoughby Mynors. She quotes a critic who describes it as a 'rambling fiction printed for W. Mynors and probably written by him, although his knowledge of continental prostitution seems inappropriate for a clergyman'.

Tom (2)

Cartoon Cat. In countless *Tom and Jerry* film cartoons, Tom (the cat) and Jerry (the mouse) have conducted a non-stop personal war for over half a century. The cat's repeated attempts to kill and eat the mouse are always foiled, usually with melodramatically violent retaliations by the triumphant mouse. The battling duo first appeared in an MGM animated cartoon called *Puss Gets the Boot* in 1939. They were the immensely successful creation of Fred Quimby, William Hanna and Joseph Barbera, who received no fewer than seven Oscars during the 18 years that followed. Tom and Jerry also appeared on the pages of comic books from 1942 to 1972.

Tom Kitten (1)

Fictional Cat. Created by children's fiction author Beatrix Potter in 1907 and introduced in *The Tale of Tom Kitten*: 'Once upon a time there were three little kittens and their names were Mittens, Tom Kitten and Moppet . . . '

Tom Kitten (2)

Pet Cat. The White House 'First Cat' during the Kennedy years. Tom Kitten, who was the pet of President Kennedy's daughter, Caroline, was sufficiently famous when he died in 1962 to receive obituary notices in the press.

Tom Quartz (1)

Fictional Cat. Tom Quartz played an important role in Mark Twain's story *Roughing It* (1872). After his owner, Dick Baker, switched from gold mining to quartz mining, the cat was accidentally blown up when the prospectors were dynamiting some rocks. As the rocks exploded upwards, 'right dead in the center of it was old Tom Quartz a goin' end over end'. When he fell back to earth two and a half minutes later, he glared at the men and then marched off home with great dignity, but 'very prejudiced against quartz mining'.

Tom Quartz (2)

Pet Cat. This Tom Quartz was a kitten belonging to President Theodore Roosevelt, who named him after Mark Twain's fictional cat (see above). It lived in the White House at the turn of the century, where it repeatedly tormented the little black terrier belonging to the President's youngest son, Quentin.

Tongue

Feline Anatomy. The long, flat, flexible tongue of the cat is smooth underneath and rough on top. On its upper surface there are four kinds of papillae: (1) *Conical* papillae are the most common form and are the large ones that point backwards, giving the cat's tongue its rasping quality. (2) *Flattened* papillae are found at the very root of the tongue. (3) *Fungiform* papillae are arranged along the sides of the tongue. (4) *Circumvallate* papillae, which are few in number, are found at the back of the tongue. (For details of the tongue's tasting ability, see the entry for Taste.)

The cat's tongue has many uses. Apart from (1) tasting food, it is also employed (2) to move food into the mouth; (3) to rasp clinging morsels of meat from the bones of its prey; (4) to greet the cat's companions with a licking 'kiss'; (5) to wash and clean the animal's fur; (6) to smooth the fur when ruffled; (7) to dry the fur when wet; (8) to pant when the cat is hot; (9) to lap up liquid when the cat is drinking (for details see Drinking); and (10) to cool the animal when it is seriously overheating, by covering its fur in wet saliva which will then evaporate and cool the cat in the process.

The French historian Hippolyte Taine sums up the nature of this powerfully muscular, endlessly busy organ, so essential to the cat, with the words: 'Poor little wash-rag, smaller than a finger./ His tongue is by turns a sponge, a brush, a comb./ He cleans himself, he smooths himself, he knows what is proper.'

T

Tonkinese Cat

Domestic Breed. A recent short-haired American hybrid created by crossing Siamese and Burmese. In its early days it was sometimes referred to as the Golden Siamese, and this name was used in print as recently as 1961. Its present name has sometimes been incorrectly spelled Tonkanese. It was christened the Tonkinese after the Gulf of Tonkin which, like the cat itself, is close to Burmese and Siamese territories, but does not belong to either of them. Among owners they have the nickname of 'Tonks'. In France it is called the *Tonkinois;* in Germany the *Tonkinesen;* and in Holland the *Tonkanees.*

Appearance: Intermediate between Siamese and Burmese, with dark Siamese points, but a body colour that has a richer hue than that of the typical Siamese. The body shape is also intermediate, lacking the exaggerated elongation of the Siamese.

History: In the 1950s the American feline expert Milan Greer began a breeding programme to create what he called the Golden Siamese. He did this initially by crossing a male Burmese with a female Chocolate-point Siamese. At his specialist cat centre called *Fabulous Felines* he continued to develop the breed through five generations. Then, when he was satisfied that the breed was secure, he passed the baton on to other breeders. Edith Lux was one of these and it was she who decided to change the name to Tonkinese.

Summing up the breed, Milan Greer commented: 'It has the better traits of both the Siamese and the Burmese. It is a perfect combination of brains and beauty . . . After developing this breed I discovered that I had created a prodigy in fur.'

Later, in the 1960s, Canadian breeders, especially Margaret Conroy, took a special interest in the breed and helped to gain recognition for it. In 1965 she was the first to register a Tonkinese with a cat club – the Canadian Cat Association. So great was her contribution that some authors incorrectly refer to the Tonkinese as a Canadian breed.

Most of the American societies soon accepted the breed. Before long there was a Tonkinese Breed Club of USA, Canada and Australia to promote this appealing cat, based in the United States at Gillette, New Jersey. By the 1990s it was accepted by all of the North American cat societies. In 1991 it was recognized by the GCCF in Britain.

The Tonkinese, first developed as a breed in the United States during the 1950s, was initially referred to as the Golden Siamese. It was created from crosses between Siamese and Burmese.

As regards the breeding of this cat, if a Burmese is crossed with a Siamese all the kittens are Tonkinese. If a Tonkinese is mated to another Tonkinese, then half the kittens are Tonkinese, a quarter are Burmese and a quarter are Siamese. It was for this reason that some feline authorities refused to accept it as a true breed.

Historically, it is interesting that the first Burmese Cat to arrive in America – a female called Wong Mau, who arrived in the United States in the early 1930s – was not, in fact, a pure-bred animal, being part Siamese. This means that the Burmese Cat who founded the modern Burmese breed was, in reality, what we would today call a Tonkinese, the very first one ever seen in North America. (For details see Burmese Cat.)

Personality: Terms used to describe this breed include: inquisitive, exceptionally intelligent, condescending, witty, wilful, clever, loyal, loving, mischievous, clownish, active, sociable, gregarious, outgoing, lively and affectionate.

Supporters of the breed claim that it has the good qualities of both parent breeds, but none of their bad qualities.

Colour Forms: It appears in a variety of colours. In America these colours have been given exotic names (see below).

GCCF: Brown; Blue; Chocolate; Lilac; Red; Cream; Brown Tortie; Blue Tortie; Chocolate Tortie; Lilac Tortie; Brown Tabby; Blue Tabby; Chocolate Tabby; Lilac Tabby; Red Tabby; Cream Tabby; Brown Tortie Tabby; Blue Tortie Tabby; Chocolate Tortie Tabby; Lilac Tortie Tabby.

CFA: Natural Mink (warm brown with dark brown points); Champagne Mink (beige or buff-cream with medium brown points); Blue Mink (soft, blue-grey with darker, slate-blue points); Platinum Mink (pale silvery-grey with darker grey points). An additional colour is sometimes recognized: Honey Mink (ruddy brown with darker brown points).

Bibliography:

1961. Greer, M. *Fabulous Feline.* The Dial Press, New York. (See p.23-25 for Golden Siamese.)

1988. Maggitti, P. 'The Tonkinese'. In: *Cats Magazine.* September 1988.

1989. Burns, B.S. 'The Tonkinese'. In: *Cat Companion.* Sept./Oct. 1989. p. 10-12.

Breed Clubs:

Tonkinese Breed Association. Address: 2462 Primrose Avenue, Vista, CA 92083, USA.

Tonkinese Breed Association UK. Address: 2 Rose Walk, Seaford, East Sussex, BN25 3DH, England.

Tonkinese Breed Club. This club issues a magazine, *Tonkinfo.* Address: Lansdale, 12 Robin Hood Lane, Winnersh, Wokingham, Berks, RG41 5LX, England.

Tonkinese Cat Club. This club issues a *Tonkinews* journal. Address: 2 Rose Walk, Seaford, East Sussex, BN25 3DH, England.

Note: There is also a breed publication called *Aqua Eye.* Address: P.O. Box 115, Sunland, CA 01041, USA.

Tonto

Film Cat. A large, 11-year-old, ginger tabby cat with eyes the colour of *marrons glacés,* Tonto was the star of the feature film *Harry and Tonto* (1974). The touching story was written by Josh Greenfield and Paul Mazursky. Harry, an elderly widower, evicted from his Manhattan apartment, sets off with his much loved feline companion on a long journey to California. When they finally reach there, Tonto falls sick and dies. Harry is played by Art Carney, who won an Oscar for his performance.

Top Cat

Cartoon Cat. An animated cartoon cat created by Hanna-Barbera for ABC TV in 1961. Top Cat (TC to his friends) is a fast-talking alley cat based on the Sergeant Bilko character. He lives in a garbage can in Manhattan with five other cats. A streetwise wheeler-dealer, he is constantly trying to improve their standard of living by various tricks and strategies.

Torbie

Coat Pattern. A commonly used abbreviation of tabby tortoiseshell. In this version of the tortoiseshell coat, the black areas are replaced by dark tabby patterning. Also known as a patched tabby.

Tortie

Coat Pattern. A commonly used abbreviation of tortoiseshell.

Tortoiseshell

Coat Pattern. Any domestic cat with a coat pattern that appears to be black, red and cream. On closer scrutiny, it becomes clear that the coat is, in reality, black plus orange tabby. The lighter, orange tabby areas, being two-toned, create the overall impression of a three-coloured cat. It is nearly always female; when male, it is sterile.

The chances of finding a male tortoiseshell cat have been calculated at about 200 to one. What makes the sex distribution of these cats so odd is that normally only a female kitten can display black patches inherited from one parent and red tabby patches inherited from the other. This is because the genes controlling these particular colour forms are both carried on the X chromosomes, the red gene on one and the non-red gene on the other. The catch is that only females have two X chromosomes, so only females can display the 'red plus non-red' tortoiseshell combination. Males have instead one X chromosome and one small Y chromosome, which means that on their single X they carry either the red *or* the non-red gene, but cannot have both. So they are either all-over red tabby or all-over black.

If this is the case, it is hard to see, at first glance, how male tortoiseshells can exist at all. The answer is that occasionally there is a minor genetic error and a male cat develops with the genetic combination XXY. The double X gives it a chance to be red and black, while the Y chromosome gives it male characteristics. It does, however, have a problem because its masculinity leaves a lot to be desired. To start with, it is sterile. Also its behaviour is extremely odd. It acts like a masculinized female rather than a true male.

One particular male tortoiseshell cat that was observed in a colony of cats revealed a strange personality. It was nonchalant in its dealings with other cats, disdainfully ignoring the usual status battles, which were nearly always between males or between females – there was little social fighting across the genders. Perhaps because the tortoiseshell male cat was neither fully male nor fully female, it did not feel the need to compete in these single-sex pecking-order disputes.

In other respects it was also peculiar. It did not start to spray urine at the age when any typical male would have done so. It did not court or attempt to mate with females on heat, even though it appeared to be anatomically well equipped to do so. It did, however, allow young tom-cats to mount and attempt to mate with it.

When it had grown older it did show a little interest in females and even deigned to mate with a few, though never with much enthusiasm. It also sprayed urine in a desultory fashion, but never behaved like a full-blooded tom at any stage. Once, it was experimentally isolated with a highly sexed female and was observed to mate several times, but the female failed to become pregnant, confirming the typical male tortoiseshell infertility.

So, although it is not true to say that *all* tortoiseshell cats are female, it is true to say that they are all feminine – even the rare males. And it is probably true to add that no tortoiseshell cat has ever fathered a litter of kittens.

There is one compensation, however, for the unfortunate tortoiseshell toms. Their great rarity has given them a special value in times past, so that they have often escaped the indifference and persecution that has befallen the commonplace moggies. In Celtic countries it was always considered a good omen if one of these cats decided to settle in the home. In England there was a belief that warts could be removed simply by rubbing them with the tail of a tortoiseshell tom during the month of May. And Japanese fishermen would pay huge sums for a tortoiseshell

tom, to keep as a ship's cat, for it was thought it would protect the crew from the ghosts of their ancestors and the vessel itself from storms.

So, although these cats may be doomed to a disappointing sex life, in other respects they have fared rather well.

There are many colour variants of this coat pattern, which occurs in both short and long-haired versions. These variants including the following: (1) Blue Tortoiseshell; (2) Chestnut Tortoiseshell; (3) Chinchilla Shaded Tortoiseshell (= Shell Tortoiseshell); (4) Chocolate Tortoiseshell; (5) Chocolate Tortoiseshell Point; (6) Chocolate Tortoiseshell Lynx Point; (7) Chocolate Tortoiseshell Shaded; (8) Chocolate Tortoiseshell Smoke; (9) Cinnamon Tortoiseshell; (10) Cinnamon Tortoiseshell Smoke; (11) Dilute Tortoiseshell; (12) Dilute Chinchilla Shaded Tortoiseshell (= Dilute Shell Tortoiseshell); (13) Dilute Shaded Tortoiseshell; (14) Ebony Tortoiseshell; (15) Lilac Tortoiseshell; (16) Seal Tortoiseshell; (17) Shaded Tortoiseshell; (18) Shell Tortoiseshell; (19) Smoke Tortoiseshell; (20) Tortoiseshell Point; (21) Tortoiseshell Lynx Point; (22) Tortoiseshell and White.

Folklore: According to the ancient Khmers of South-east Asia, the first tortoiseshell cat was created in a magical ritual performed by a wise old man. During the course of the ritual, the cat sprang from the menstrual blood of a young goddess born of a lotus flower.

Towser

Pet Cat. Towser (1963–1987) holds the record for the champion mouser of all time. A female tortoiseshell owned by Glenturret Distillery near Crieff, Tayside, Scotland, she is reported to have killed an average of three mice a day, every day of her adult life, giving an estimated lifetime total of 28,899.

Traditional Siamese Cat

Domestic Breed. This is an alternative name for the recently re-created, old-style Siamese Cat. Because this is a new development, no agreement has yet been reached concerning the official title of this cat. At present it is known by many names, including: Applehead Siamese, Applecat, Old-fashioned Siamese, Classic Siamese, Opal Cat and Thai Cat.

Appearance: A Siamese Cat with a well-balanced, solid form, lacking extreme elongation of the neck and body. The head is rounded instead of wedge-shaped and the ears only medium size.

History: The elongated angularity of the modern 'show' Siamese has become so extreme in the second half of the 20th century that many people have expressed a nostalgic longing for the old-fashioned, more moderate body-type of the breed, known from early photographs. Some American breeders have now set about reinstating this cat and it has become easier to obtain a 'Traditional' Siamese. This revived form of the breed is also becoming popular in Europe where it is known as the Thai Cat. It remains to be seen whether its popularity will increase to the point where it will eventually eclipse the exaggerated 'Modern Siamese', as some of its champions predict.

It is possible today to obtain two types of Traditional Siamese. The first is a 'reconstituted' cat, created by introducing stocky, short-haired cat elements into a strain of slender, modern Siamese, to modify the extreme angularity. The second type – the true classic Siamese – comes from purebred lines belonging to conservative breeders who have never succumbed to the extreme modernization of the breed and have kept their old lines unadulterated and pure. At first glance it is impossible to distinguish between these two types. Only an examination of breeders' records will give the answer. (For details see Applehead Siamese Cat and Thai Cat.)

Colour Forms: The traditional breed is accepted only in traditional colours: Seal Point, Blue Point, Chocolate Point and Lilac Point.

Breed Club:

The Traditional Cat Association (TCA). Address: 1000 Pegasus Farms Lane, Alpharetta, GA 30201, USA.

Traditional Siamese. Address: 8752 Woodsman Court, Washington, MI 48094, USA.

Tricolour

Coat Pattern. This term was first introduced by Leslie Williams in 1907 when she referred to the 'Tortoiseshell and White, or Tricolour Persians'. Since then the Tortie and White Cat has been given the modern name of Calico Cat, but the title of 'tricolour' has found a new use in connection with the Japanese Bobtail Cat, where the following versions have been recorded:

(1) Tricolour (= black, red and white – the traditional Mi-Ke version); (2) Dilute Tricolour (= blue, cream and white); (3) Patched Tabby and White (= brown tabby, red tabby and white); (4) Dilute Patched Tabby and White (= blue tabby, cream tabby and white).

Trixie

Pet Cat. Trixie was a black and white cat belonging to the third Earl of Southampton, in the reign of Elizabeth I. When the Earl was imprisoned in the Tower of London by the Queen, tradition has it that his devoted cat made its way across London and climbed down the chimney that led to his cell. Once there, it remained to keep him company until he was released, two years later. The Earl was so impressed with his cat's loyalty that he commissioned a portrait showing himself and his pet together in his cell.

When the Earl of Southampton was released from his cell in the Tower of London, he commissioned this portrait of himself and his faithful cat, Trixie, in honour of his pet, who had kept him company during his years of incarceration.

Although cats do have a remarkable homing instinct, it is not clear how Trixie would have known where to find her owner, and the heart-warming story may have been slightly embellished during the course of time. In her biography of the Earl, Charlotte Stopes puts forward the less impressive, but rather more convincing suggestion that Southampton's wife was involved and 'that it was her happy thought to take his favourite cat with her to help to comfort him'.

Despite this, it is clear that, however the cat did come to be in the Earl's cell, it certainly remained there to keep him company during the long dreary months of his imprisonment, because the portrait of the Earl with Trixie appears to have been painted towards the end of his period of incarceration, in 1603.

Turkish Angora Cat

Domestic Breed. The original Angora Cat from Turkey, so popular in Victorian times, was gradually overshadowed by the Persian Cat and had vanished from the West as a pure breed by the early part of the 20th century. It was rediscovered by Western enthusiasts in its Turkish homeland in 1962, where a breeding programme had been quietly operating over a period of 45 years at the Ankara Zoo. Some of the progeny were exported to the United States where they were once again introduced into the world of pedigree cats. In the 1970s they finally returned to Europe, where, a century earlier, they had been held in such high regard.

This return of the original Angoras created some confusion because, in the meantime, certain British breeders had worked hard to re-create an 'Angora type', using long-haired Oriental cats. By the 1960s, these artificially reconstituted cats had taken over the title of 'Angoras', with the result that the rediscovered *original* Angoras had to be given a more specific title. It was agreed that they should be called 'Turkish Angoras' to distinguish them from the 'British Angoras'. (For further details see Angora Cat.)

Turkish Cat

Domestic Breed. This was the official GCCF name for the cat known to everyone else as the 'Turkish Van Cat'. When the breed was first discovered in 1955 near Lake Van in Turkey, it was immediately christened the 'Van Cat'. Its discoverer, Laura Lushington, then unwisely used the name 'Van' as her registered cattery name, which automatically invalidated it as an official GCCF breed name. The problem was solved in Britain by dropping the word 'Van' from the title, and calling it simply the Turkish Cat. Outside the GCCF this name did not find favour because it was felt to be too vague and led to confusion with the related Turkish breed, the Turkish Angora. Also, the name 'Van' had already become so widely popular for the breed, that public opinion simply ignored officialdom and everywhere continued to refer to it as the 'Turkish Van Cat'. (For further details, see under that heading.) Eventually, when Laura Lushington retired from cat breeding, the GCCF was able to revert to the more suitable title of Turkish Van Cat.

Turkish Swimming Cat

Domestic Breed. An early name for the Turkish Van Cat. When the Van Cat first arrived in the West in 1955, it was shown on television enjoying a swim and immediately became labelled as the 'Swimming Cat'. In his 1965 feline dictionary, Frank Manolson included it under the title of 'Turkish Swimming Cat', commenting wryly, 'It's the answer for those people who dislike Labradors and are afraid of otters, but who simply must have a furry ornament to enhance the pool.' In reality, its interest in the water was primarily a response to the intense heat of the Turkish summers.

Turkish Van Cat

Domestic Breed. A native Turkish cat found in the region of Lake Van, in eastern Turkey near the border with Iran. Also known as the Van Cat, the Turkish Cat, the Swimming Cat, and the Turkish Swimming Cat. In Turkey it is called the *Van Kedi*.

Appearance: The Van Cat looks like a slightly larger version of the Angora, with the same long, silky fur. There is no undercoat, which gives the animal a sleek, elegant, long-bodied appearance. The coat is white except for the head and the plumed tail, which are auburn in colour. There are from five to eight faint ring-markings on the tail. (But see below for controversy concerning the auburn markings.) The eyes are unusual because they are often of different colours – one amber and one blue. This feature, combined with their glamorous coat and their unusual love of water, quickly made them favourites with the public.

Legendary History: The city of Van, in Eastern Turkey, is close to Mount Ararat, the legendary site of Noah's Ark. A local folk-tale tells of the day when, after the Ark came to rest on the mountain and the floods receded, the cats left its protection and made their way down the mountain slopes and into the ancient settlement of Van. As they left the Ark the cats were blessed by Allah and the patch of auburn hair at the front of their bodies is believed to be the place where he touched them.

Factual History: There is archaeological evidence to suggest that domestic cats have been present in Turkey for over 7,000 years. A recent excavation by the British Archaeological Institute in Ankara, at the Neolithic site of Hacilar, revealed small terracotta figurines thought to show women playing with cats.

Much later, during the Roman occupation of the Van region (then part of ancient Armenia) in the period AD 75 to 387, a large, pale, self-coloured cat with rings on its tail appears on battle-standards and armour. These relics, now housed in the Louvre, suggest an early presence for the Turkish Van Cat.

Whether this ancient evidence is accepted or not, we can be sure that these cats have been well known locally for centuries and were valued highly as pets. Despite this, they were not discovered by Western enthusiasts until the year 1955, when two British photographers, working for the Turkish Tourist Board, visited the Lake Van region. Laura Lushington and Sonia Halliday were given a male and female kitten which were named Van Attala and Van Güzelli Iskenderün respectively. Fascinated by these unusual cats, they took them back with them to Britain.

After the inevitable long period of quarantine, the two animals arrived at the Buckinghamshire home of Laura Lushington, where it soon became clear that they belonged to an exceptionally attractive breed which was new to the world of pedigree cats. In order to start a serious breeding programme with them, they collected five more examples on subsequent trips to eastern Turkey, again putting them through the lengthy British quarantine process.

Then began the even longer procedure of establishing them as an officially recognized new breed. This was not achieved for 14 years. Although their owners' photographs – especially those showing them swimming – had made them unusually familiar to the general public, they were not so popular with the conservative feline authorities. Delays were caused because of their owners' decision to use the name of 'Van' for both the cats and their registered cattery. This was not permitted by the GCCF rules and the name of the breed had to be changed from Van Cat, or Turkish Van Cat, simply to 'Turkish Cat'. The owners also had to agree to allow other breeders to acquire specimens, to create a competitive situation for showing purposes. Furthermore, because the original Turkish owners had never kept records of the ancestry of their cats, there had to be four generations of true-breeding before they could be accepted as pedigree animals. When all this had been done, the breed was at last given recognition in 1969.

The Turkish Van Cat was late appearing in America, the first specimens not arriving there until 1982, and the first official registrations not occurring until 1985.

There, the history of this attractive breed might have rested, but an unforeseen problem arose. A curious discovery about the true colouring of the Van Cat was made by feline expert Roger Tabor during location filming for his 1991 television series *The Rise of the Cat*. He visited Lake Van and discussed the breed with local people, only to find that they considered a true Van Cat to be an all-white animal, without any darker markings on the head or tail. There were some specimens with the auburn markings that are so well known in the West, but those were

A Turkish Van Cat at the water's edge of Lake Van, its traditional homeland in eastern Turkey. When it first arrived in the West, this breed became known as the 'Swimming Cat'.

considered to be inferior to the all-white ones. For these local people, the key difference between their Van Cats and the typical Angoras from further west in Turkey was to be found in their eyes. The Angora has blue eyes, whereas for them, the Van Cat ideally has one blue and one amber eye.

This came as no surprise to Turkish Van Cat breeder Lois Miles who, in 1989, had been given the same information when she had contacted the Turkish Cultural Attaché in Van to ascertain the true status of the breed in its city of origin. She had become concerned that all the 300 Van Cats registered at that time were descendants of the small, foundation group imported in the 1950s. The original cats, now known as 'the magnificent seven', had been able to provide only a small gene pool for the further development of the breed, and none of the seven had actually come from the city of Van itself.

What Lois Miles now wanted was a genuine Turkish Van Cat *from* Van, and it was clear to her that, despite the difficulties it might cause with Western show-judges, to be correct it would have to be an all-white, odd-eyed cat. In 1992 she persuaded two friends, John and Pamela Hulme, who already owned four Turkish Vans, and who visited Istanbul each year, to make the long trek eastwards across Turkey to Lake Van, to find new blood. The Hulmes agreed, but when they reached Van they initially encountered difficulties in locating pure stock. Then they had the good fortune to meet a local professor, Yusef Vanli, and discovered that the Yüzüncü Yil University in the lakeside city had recently established a Van Cat Research Centre. Careful surveys by this centre had revealed the surprising fact that in 1992 there were only 92 pure Turkish Van Cats surviving in the whole of Turkey. For this reason, the continued breeding of pure lines outside Turkey was clearly even more important, and the Hulmes managed to persuade the professor to introduce them to a family with four generations of the all-white, odd-eyed cats. They reserved one of the three small kittens that were present, but which was too young to travel and then, three months later, John returned with Lois Miles to collect it. It was a female, called Garip (meaning 'alone'), who was renamed Layla. She was flown to Heathrow and placed in quarantine, waiting for the day when she could inject new Van blood into the inbred Western population.

A TURKISH VAN CAT with her kittens. These auburn and white markings, essential for showing this breed in the West, are viewed as inferior in Turkey, where all-white cats are preferred.

Like Roger Tabor, Lois Miles found that the local Turks preferred the all-white Van Cat. She feels it was purely accidental that the original pair brought back to England in 1955 happened to have auburn markings on the head and tail. These markings became enshrined as the diagnostic feature of the breed and, in the world of pedigree show cats, are now considered essential. To the Turks themselves it is something of a joke that what they consider to be an inferior version of their breed should have become the only form that is officially recognized in the West.

With the advent of Layla, this situation should soon begin to change, as modern Western ways finally fall into line with ancient Eastern traditions. Since her arrival in the West she has already produced 16 kittens from three litters, and one of her first female offspring has also bred. Among her progeny there have been several of the 'Turkish Ideal' – the all-white, odd-eyed cats – so the future for the breed looks interesting if complicated. Lois Miles has already been refused permission to exhibit her true, all-white Turkish Van Cats as such, and it remains to be seen how long it will take for the irony of this situation to be recognized by the Western cat-show officialdom.

Personality: Terms used to describe this breed include: adaptable, affectionate, independent, tranquil, sociable, soft-voiced, friendly, intelligent and modestly playful. The earliest Van Cats taken to cat shows were notorious for being difficult to hold, but later examples have become more amenable. The inhabitants of Van themselves describe the cat as 'proud and brave as a lion', making 'lovable, affectionate pets with a remarkably long lifespan'.

Colour Forms: The officially accepted Van pattern, of white with dark patches on the head and a dark tail, is always the same, but there are variations in the head and tail colour. The typical form is white and auburn, but the auburn may be replaced by certain other colours.

GCCF: Blue-eyed Auburn Turkish Van; Odd-eyed Auburn Turkish Van; Blue-eyed Cream Turkish Van; Odd-eyed Cream Turkish Van.

CFA: White body with head and tail coloured: Red (= Auburn); Cream; Black; Blue; Red Tabby; Cream Tabby; Brown Tabby; Blue Tabby; Tortie; Dilute Tortie; Brown Patched Tabby; Blue Patched Tabby.

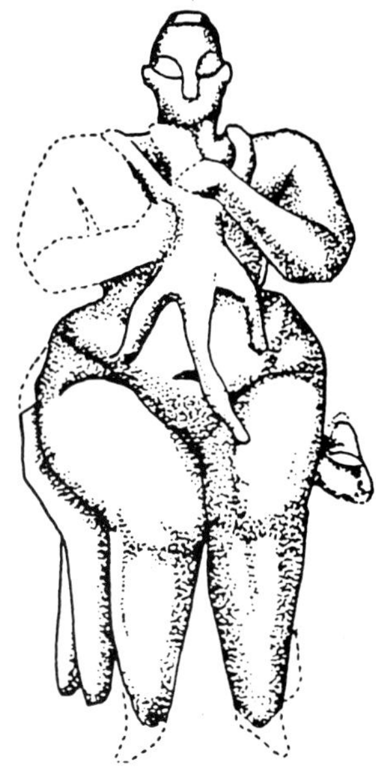

A sketch of an ancient model showing a woman playing with a cat, dating from more than 7,000 years ago. The figurine was found at Hacilar, a Neolithic site in Turkey, and is probably the oldest known representation of a pet cat in the world.

Bibliography:

1972. Ashford, A. and Pond, G. *Rex, Abyssinian and Turkish Cats*. Gifford, London.

1982. Gautschi, G. *Türkische Van-Katzen*. Rudolf Muller, Köln-Braunsfeld.

1986. Grice, J. et al. 'The Turkish Van'. In: *Cat World*, May 1986. p.9-12.

1990. Inan, M.S. *The General Characteristics and Biology of the Van Cat.* (Ph.D. Thesis)

1992. Erdinç, H. 'An Aristocrat among Cats . . . Van Kedisi'. *Skylife*, July 1992, Temmuz (Turkish Airlines Inflight Magazine.)

1992. Thomas, Y. 'This Van Could Run and Run'. In: *You Magazine*, 18th October 1992. p.62-65.

1993. Miles, L. *The Turkish Van Cat. History and Folklore*. Classic Turkish Van Cat Association.

1993. Tabor, R. 'The Cats of Van'. In: *Cat World*, November 1993. p.28-30.

Breed Clubs:

The Classic Turkish Van Cat Association. Publishes a twice-yearly magazine, *Vantasia*. Address: 2a Woronzow Road, St. Johns Wood, London, NW8 6QE, England.

Progressive Turkish Van Cat Association. Address: 4 Rockwood Close, Darton, Barnsley, South Yorkshire, S75 5LR, England.

The Turkish Van Cat Club. Formed in 1981. Address: The Cheratons, 129 Balgores Lane, Gidea Park, Romford, Essex, RM2 6JT, England.

Tuxedo Cat

Domestic Cat. The informal title of 'Tuxedo Cat' has been given to all those felines (regardless of breeding) which have predominantly black coats, but with patches of white on their lower legs and feet, their necks, and sometimes on their faces. The name 'tuxedo' was chosen 'because they appear to be dressed for a formal occasion'.

Essentially, these are black cats carrying the 'white spotting' gene that always favours the frontal and lower regions of the animal's body. This colour pattern is common among non-pedigree cats, but rare among pedigrees. It has been popular with cartoonists, both Felix and Sylvester being Tuxedos. In real life, Socks, the White House cat, is the most famous of recent Tuxedo Cats.

THE AMERICAN AUTHOR Mark Twain adored his cats, and one day made this sketch of them. The best that can be said of it is that what it lacks in skill it makes up for with vigour.

TWAIN, MARK

CAT OWNER. The American humorist and author, Samuel Langhorne Clemens (1835–1910), better known by his pen name of Mark Twain, was devoted to his cats and could not imagine life without them: 'A house without a cat, a well-fed, well-petted, and properly revered cat, may be a perfect house, perhaps, but how can it prove its title?' He gave them exotic names, such as Apollinaris, Zoroaster, Blatherskite and Sour Mash, and explained why: 'names given them, not in an unfriendly spirit, but merely to practise the children in large and difficult styles of pronunciation. It was a very happy idea – I mean, for the children.'

Ubasti

Legendary Cat. An alternative name for Bast, Bastet or Pasht, the ancient Egyptian goddess who was represented as either a seated cat or as a cat-headed woman. (See Bastet for details.)

Ultra

Domestic Breed. At British cat shows, Persian cats with very flattened faces are called 'Ultras', or Ultra-type Longhairs. The American Peke-faced Cat is forbidden on health grounds in Britain, but some British breeders have avoided this ban by selecting for flatter and flatter faces until their 'Longhairs' are as extreme as anything seen in the Peke-faced classes in America.

Urals Rex Cat

Domestic Breed. According to a recent report, a new example of the wavy-haired Rex gene was discovered in the Urals in Russia in 1991.

Usual

Coat Colour. The word 'Usual' has become a technical term in the world of pedigree cats, where it refers to the traditional coat colour of a particular breed – the one that was present with the original specimens when the breed began, before modern trends began to add all kind of variations. It is a term favoured for a few breeds by the GCCF in Britain, but which is rarely used elsewhere. For example, the rich golden-brown colour of the typical, original Abyssinian Cat is called 'Usual' by the GCCF, but 'Ruddy' by feline organizations in Europe and America.

Vampire Cat

Legendary Cat. In ancient Japanese folklore, the Vampire Cat of Nabéshima plays a role very similar to that of the Vampire Bat in Western mythology. The demon cat kills a beautiful maiden

In Japanese mythology, this monstrous Vampire Cat takes the role usually reserved for vampire bats in Western legends, biting the necks of its victims and then sucking their blood.

by biting her neck and sucking out her blood. It then buries her body and assumes her identity. In its new female form, it turns its attention to the maiden's lover, a handsome prince. By gradually extracting the prince's life force from his body, during nightly visits, the vampire weakens him almost to the point of death. The prince's aide, concerned about his master's condition, decides to stand guard over him throughout the night, and eventually forces the demonic cat to flee the palace. It escapes to the mountains where it is hunted down and killed.

As recently as 1929, a report in a London newspaper suggested that this dreaded Vampire Cat was once again active and was, according to local belief in Japan, setting out to ensnare the wives of descendants of the old Samurai warriors.

There is also a Spanish–Jewish folk-tale about a Vampire Cat. According to this legend, Lilith was the first wife of Adam, but left him and flew away as a vampire. She became immortal and took the shape of a huge black cat called 'El Broosha'. In this form, she descends in the night on innocent, sleeping babies and sucks the blood out of them. Author Mildred Kirk has suggested that this might be the origin of the false idea that pet cats should not be allowed in the same room as a sleeping baby, because they may sit on the child and suffocate it.

Van

Coat Pattern. The Van pattern, as seen on the Turkish Van Cat, consists of a white body with coloured areas confined to the head and tail. The original, typical colouring of the extremities was auburn, but in recent years other colour forms have been developed. (See Turkish Van Cat.)

Van Cat

Domestic Breed. Shortened name sometimes used for the Turkish Van Cat.

Van Kedi

Domestic Breed. The Turkish name for the Van Cat.

Veterinary Care

Feline Biology. The treatment of feline diseases and injuries is a specialized subject that is not included in this volume. There are, however, a number of useful books on the subject, written by veterinary surgeons. They include those listed in the following bibliography.

Bibliography:
1901. Hill, W. *Diseases of the Cat.* Balliere, Tindall & Cox, London
1925. Hamilton, K. *Diseases of the Cat.* Balliere, London.
1926. Kirk, H. *The Diseases of Cats.* Balliere, Tindall & Cox, London.
1953. Whitney, L.F. *The Complete Book of Cat Care.* Doubleday, New York.
1965. Joshua, J. *The Clinical Aspects of some Diseases of Cats.* Heinemann, London.
1966. Wilkinson, G.T. *Diseases of the Cat.* Oxford.
1969. McCoy, J.J. *The Complete Book of Cat Health and Care.* Herbert Jenkins, London.
1976. McGinnis, T. *The Well Cat Book.* Wildwood House, London.
1977. Catott, E.J. *Feline Medicine and Surgery.* American Veterinary Publications.
1979. Joshua, J. *Cat Owner's Encyclopedia of Veterinary Medicine.* TFH, New Jersey.
1980. Beaver, B. *Veterinary Aspects of Feline Behaviour.* Mosby, St. Louis.
1981. Bush, B. *The Cat Care Question and Answer Book.* Bloomsbury, London.
1985. Allan, E., Bonning, L. and Blogg, J.R. *Everycat: The Complete Guide to Cat Care, Behaviour and Health.* Peter Lowe, Australia.
1986. Viner, B. *The Cat Care Manual.* Stanley Paul, London.
1987. Holsworth, J. *Diseases of the Cat.* Saunders.
1989. Siegal, M. (Editor) *The Cornell Book of Cats: a Comprehensive Medical Reference for Every Cat and Kitten.* Villard Books, New York.
1989. Taylor, D. *British Veterinary Association Guide to Cat Care.* Dorling Kindersley, London.
1990. Chandler, E.A. *Feline Medicine and Therapeutics.* Oxford.
1991. August, J.R. *Feline Internal Medicine.*
1991. Boden, E. *Feline Practice.* London.
1993. Norsworthy, G. *Feline Practice.* Lippincott.
1993. Wills, J. and Wolf, A. *Feline Medicine.*
1994. Farrow, C.S. *Radiology of the Cat.* USA.
1994. Fogle, B. *100 Questions your Cat Would Ask its Vet.* Signet Press, London.
1994. Turner, T. (Editor) *Veterinary Notes for Cat Owners.* Stanley Paul, London.
1995. Fogle, B. *First Aid for Cats.* Pelham Books, London.

Vichien Mat

Domestic Breed. The old name for the cat now known as the Siamese, as it appears in the ancient *Cat Book Poems* written before 1767.

Victoria Rex Cat

Domestic Breed. In 1972 a kitten carrying the wavy-haired Rex gene was born to feral cats in the Victoria district of London. It was named Tuoh, and Peter Davis reported in the 1972 *Cats Annual* that hair samples from it showed incompatibility with Devon Rex. Nothing further is known about it.

Voice

Feline Behaviour. The repertoire of the domestic cat is large because it uses two vocabularies at once. In the wild it would have one set of sound signals for mother–offspring communication and another for contacts between adults. But the tame cat has a double personality – remaining a permanent kitten towards its human owners, while becoming a fully adult cat towards other felines. In this way it retains its juvenile sounds while acquiring its adult ones. This gives it twice as many calls as a typical wild animal.

Although there are many subtle variations in sound, there are only seven basic messages. They are as follows:

1 *I am angry.* When adult cats fight they become extremely noisy. The 'caterwauling' of felines in dispute with one another includes growling, snarling, gurgling, wailing and howling. This is

a good example of a single signal taking many different forms. Each of these forms, or intensities, can be given a different name, but they all carry the same message, namely 'Clear off, or I will attack you'. Because the vocalization is prolonged and because the mood of hostility rises and falls second by second, the strength of the sound increases and decreases as well. As it does so, instead of simply becoming louder or softer, it changes its whole quality. These sounds are most often heard when several males have gathered around a female on heat. On such occasions, their rivalry creates a symphony of aggressive vocalizing that may last for several hours.

2 *I am frightened.* When a terrified cat is cornered and cannot escape, it performs a strange, throaty yowling noise. The message is: 'I fear you, but do not push me too far or I will turn on you despite my fear.' Pressed further, it will lash out and will probably perform the 'spit and hiss' display. This often has a powerful impact on, say, an attacking dog, probably because it is reminiscent of the spitting and hissing of a poisonous snake. Many predators have a protective, instinctive reaction to snakes, and if the cat can imitate the serpent's threat sound, it can sometimes keep its tormentor at bay.

3 *I am in pain.* When a cat is in agony it screams in a way that is easy for a human being to understand. This is an adult version of the squeal of a distressed kitten.

4 *I want attention.* For cat owners this is the most common sound to emanate from their feline companions. The 'miaow' says many things in many contexts, but always has the same basic message, namely, 'I require your immediate attention.' It originates as a mewing sound in tiny kittens, letting their mother know that they need some kind of help. In wild cats it more or less disappears when they become adult, but in domestic cats it persists throughout life. They use it whenever they start to act like pseudo-kittens towards their human owners. In this context they build on it, developing it into a variety of subtly different miaows. They modify it to suit each occasion. There are begging miaows and demanding miaows, complaining miaows and anxious miaows. There are soft, flat miaows to be let out of the house and pitiful, drawn-out miaows to be let in again when it begins to rain. There are expectant miaows when tin-opener noises are detected and irritated miaows when some fixed routine has been disregarded. An alert owner will know each of these variants on the basic 'I want attention' signal and may become quite fluent in understanding the subtle variations of 'cat-ese' after a few years.

5 *Come with me.* When a mother cat wants her kittens to come near to her or to follow her, she gives a soft little chirruping noise. She may also use it as a greeting when she has been away from the kittens for a while. Adult domestic cats employ this same 'rising trill', as it has been called, when they greet their human owners. At such moments they are reversing the usual relationship and treating the humans as their kittens rather than as their mothers. Significantly, this greeting trill is generally done when they are on the move, usually when they have come in from outside and are about to move off towards the place where they expect food to be waiting. So, although it sounds like a greeting, it probably still has some of the 'come along, follow me' meaning in it.

6 *I am inoffensive.* This is the famous purring sound. Although many people think that the purr means 'I am content', a close study of the conditions under which it occurs tells a different story. Purring is heard under the following conditions: (1) When kittens are sucking at the nipple, letting the mother know all is well. (2) When the mother is lying with her kittens, reassuring them that all is well. (3) When the mother approaches the nest where the kittens are hiding, letting them know that there is nothing to fear by her approach. (4) When a young cat approaches an adult for play, letting it know that it is in a relaxed mood and accepts its subordinate social position. (5) When a dominant adult cat approaches a young cat in a friendly way, reassuring it of its non-hostile intentions. (6) When an inferior cat is approached by a dominant enemy, as an attempt to appease the more powerful one with its submissive, non-hostile signal. (7) When a sick or injured cat is approached by a dominant one, letting it know that it is in a weak, non-hostile mood.

The nearest human equivalent to purring is smiling. Just like purring, smiling can occur when we are being reassuring, submissive, non-hostile and appeasing, as well as when we are blissfully happy. As with the purr, the key message of the smile is 'I am not going to do you any harm'. As such it is vitally important for softening social relationships and for lowering the tension of moments of close proximity.

7 *I want to sink my teeth into you.* Although it is not strictly 'vocal', there is a strange little clicking noise made by cats that are on the prowl and have spotted a prey animal, which deserves to be included here. It appears to be made by striking the teeth together sharply. They use a variant of this, a kind of teeth-gnashing, when they see a bird through a window. It is no more that the act of forcefully and repeatedly bringing the teeth together as if sinking them into the neck of the prey, in the specialized killing-bite of the cat, but it has also become a sound signal that many observers have commented on. As small wild cats and domestic cats are all solitary hunters, the function of the noise is something of a mystery. The only possible explanation is that it is employed by mother cats when out with their nearly fully-grown kittens, to help focus their attention on potential prey, as part of a general hunt-training process. (See also Teeth-chattering.)

These are the seven most important sound messages made by domestic cats. With their many variants and subdivisions they provide a wonderfully expressive earful for the alert feline as it goes about its business.

Wild Species: Many of the vocalizations of the domestic cat are shared by the wild species, especially the smaller wild cats. The major vocal differences occur between these small wild cats and the big cats. The two main contrasts have to do with purring and roaring. Small cats have a two-way purr, while the big cats have a one-way purr. That is to say, small cats purr rhythmically with each inhalation and exhalation, while big cats purr only on exhaling. This one-way purr is particularly common in the tiger, which frequently makes a friendly greeting noise that sounds like *fuf-fuf-fuf.*

BIG CATS such as this can roar; Small Cats cannot. Small Cats have a two-way purr; Big Cats do not. Apart from their size, these are the most obvious differences between them.

Roaring, on the other hand, is something that small cats cannot do. They cannot even manage a high-pitched roar adapted to their size. The structure of their vocal apparatus differs from that of the big cats.

A recent study of the vocalizations of the larger cat species, by the German zoologist Gustav Peters, has led to some interesting suggestions concerning the relationships between the various species. For example, he contends that, on voice alone, the Lion, Leopard and Jaguar are close to one another, but the Tiger is rather separate from these three. He feels that the Tiger should not be in the same genus with them. He also comments that the Snow Leopard, the Clouded Leopard and the Puma are each rather on their own, without very close vocal affinities with the other species. However, when considering such suggestions it is important to recall that it is easy enough to produce hybrids between these animals – so they cannot be so very far apart, in the evolutionary scheme of things.

Bibliography:

1978. Peters, G. *Vergleichende Untersuchung zur Lautgebung einiger Feliden.* Spixiana, Supplement 1. Munich. (with a 21-page summary in English)

Wain, Louis

Cat Art. Louis Wain (1860–1939) was a prolific British illustrator whose anthropomorphic portrayals of cats made him the most easily recognized of all feline artists. His strict upbringing in a Victorian family (he was described as a sickly child with a hare-lip) resulted in a quiet, delayed rebellion that, in his adult life, took the form of a sentimental, infantile sense of humour. It was the intensity of this humour that gave his cloyingly sweet pictures their undeniable strength. It was as though, when he put pen to paper, he was able to unleash his own, hitherto suppressed childhood. His marriage was a disaster. His family disapproved of his wife and she became bedridden, dying after only three years. During her illness their only pleasure stemmed from a black and white kitten called Peter and it was this animal that Wain began to sketch. From these sketches he began to develop a personal style which, in 1886, led to his first illustrated book, *Madame Tabby's Establishment*. It was the start of four decades of high output of both book illustrations and postcards. In 1890 he was invited to become the second President of the National Cat Club, following the resignation of Harrison Weir. His popularity was enormous in the early 20th century. In 1925 H.G.Wells said of Wain in a radio broadcast: 'He has made the cat his own. He invented a cat style, a cat society, a whole cat world.'

His career ended tragically, his last 14 years being spent in asylums. In 1914 he had been thrown off the top of a horse-drawn bus and was badly concussed. The accident seemed to affect his brain and in the early 1920s he became paranoid and eventually violent, attacking his sisters without reason. In 1924 he was certified insane and admitted to a pauper ward in the Middlesex County Mental Asylum, suffering from schizophrenia. Thanks to the intervention of the Prime Minister, in 1925 he was moved to Bethlehem Royal Hospital. In 1930 he was moved again, this time to the mental hospital at Napsbury near St. Albans, and he remained there until his death in 1939. During his final years he continued to draw cats, but now, in his confused state, they were transformed into little more than fantastic patterns.

The official badge of the National Cat Club, designed by the British artist Louis Wain, who was also invited to become its second President. He went on to become the most famous feline illustrator of all time.

During his final, sad years in a lunatic asylum, Louis Wain continued to draw, but now his cats had become fantastic, imaginative patterns. To some eyes they are far superior to the infantile sentimentality of his earlier, more popular work.

Bibliography:
1917. Shaw, J.F. *In 'Louis Wain' Land.*
1968. Dale, R. *Louis Wain, the Man who Drew Cats.* William Kimber, London. (Enlarged edition in 1991)
1972. Reade, B. *Louis Wain.* Victoria & Albert Museum, London. (Exhibition catalogue)
1977. Dale, R. *Catland.* Duckworth, London.
1982. Silvester, J. and Mobbs, A. *The Cat Fancier.* Longman, London.
1983. Parkin, M. *Louis Wain's Edwardian Cats.* London.
1982. Latimer, H. *Louis Wain. King of the Cat Artists.* Papyrus, New York.
Note: Claire Necker also lists no fewer than 87 books illustrated by Wain.

Walks

Feline Behaviour. Owners who wish to take their cats for a walk on a collar and lead are doomed to disappointment. Dogs love going for long walks, cats do not. A glance at the wild ancestors of the domestic dog and the domestic cat explains this difference. Wolves, the ancestors of our pet dogs, are pack animals and have an inborn urge to explore, patrol and hunt in groups. Dogs have inherited this urge and, for them, it is one of the great joys of life to set off on a long trek with their owner (who is now the leader of their 'pack').

Wild cats do not patrol in groups or hunt in packs. As adults they are independent, rather solitary animals. Whenever they are on the move they are disturbed by the presence of companions and find it quite inexplicable that their owners should wish to indulge in communal walking. Pet cats therefore find it highly unnatural to be expected to go for long walks with their owners, and they usually resist all attempts to train them to do this. Cat-owners must walk alone.

And yet, despite this general rule, there are certain cat-owners who report that *their* cats, unlike the majority, do like to accompany them on short walks. At first sight, such cases are difficult to interpret in terms of normal feline behaviour, but closer examination gives the clue as to what is happening. It is nearly always the case that the 'walking cats' are not on collars and leads, but instead simply follow in their owner's footsteps. And these footsteps are nearly always progressing along a well-known garden path or country lane. The village cat-owner sets off from home and finds the pet cat tagging along. After a while, the animal gives up and returns to its familiar territory. This is nothing like a synchronized, long-distance, man-and-dog walk and should not be confused with it. It is based on a different kind of natural behaviour pattern.

The explanation is found in the behaviour of half-grown kittens. When they have arrived at the fully mobile stage of their development, but have not yet ventured off on their own, they may accompany their mother on short trips away from the 'nest'. She will slow her pace down for them and keep a close eye on them as they amble along beside her, but she will not let them get too far away from the home base.

When an adult cat follows its owner down a path it is reverting to this half-grown kitten stage. All through its adult life, as a domesticated pet, it will continue to look upon its human companions as 'mothers'. Inside its brain it will always remain a 'part-kitten', and it is this part that is occasionally able to enjoy a short 'social walk'. So it follows its pseudo-parents as they set off for the village shops until it feels itself getting too far from the 'nest', and then breaks off to return to safety.

Many aspects of adult cat behaviour can be explained in this way, as relics of kittenhood remaining with our pets until they are old and senile. (See also Milk-treading.)

Waracabra Tiger

Mystery Cat. The Waracabra Tiger is supposed to be a pack-hunting Jaguar whose terrifying, eerie howls are frequently heard echoing through the Guyanan forest in the dead of night. These howls sound like the cries of the Trumpeter Bird (known locally as the Waracabra Bird), hence the name of the 'Tiger'.

Unfortunately, although often heard, this mysterious beast is never seen. American zoologist Lee Crandall investigated the phenomenon and came to the conclusion that the pack-hunters in question were, in reality, South American Bush Dogs *(Speothos)*, but it has been pointed out that these animals, although they do, indeed, hunt in packs in the forest, do not have such loud, eerie cries.

For this reason, there are those who believe that the Waracabra Tiger is of considerable interest. What they overlook, of course, is that the packs of wild dogs could easily disturb sleeping Trumpeter Birds and set off their very loud alarm cries. This combination – of a pack of scurrying mammalian figures in the forest, accompanied by loud, echoing cries – could easily create a legend of a nightmarish, pack-hunting Jaguar.

WARFARE

FELINE HISTORY. Surprisingly, there are reports that cats have been used in warfare on a number of occasions. The first dates back 2,500 years to the time when the Persians were at war with the Egyptians. Knowing that the Egyptians revered the cat and considered it to be sacred, the Persians developed the idea of a 'feline armour'. When their advance guard was making a hazardous push to secure a new stronghold, the Persian warriors went forward carrying live cats in their arms. (One authority suggests that the live cats were not carried, but attached to their shields.) Seeing this, the Egyptian soldiers were unable to attack them in case they accidentally killed one of these sacred animals. For them, such an act of violence against one of their animal deities was unthinkable. Indeed, if any one of them had killed a cat, even in these special circumstances, he would have risked being put to death for it. So in this way the Persians were able to advance with ease and the Egyptians were helpless to retaliate.

The second example appears much later, being illustrated in Christopher of Hapsburg's book in the year 1535. He was an artillery officer and in his report to the Council of One and Twenty at Strasbourg he described the way in which 'poisoned vapours were shed abroad' by means of cats. The unfortunate animals apparently had poison bottles strapped to their backs, with the openings pointing towards their tails. They were then sent off towards the enemy, running panic-stricken, this way and that, and in the process spreading poisonous fumes. Christopher of Hapsburg was clearly a man of delicate sensibilities, for he added the comment: 'This process ought not to be directed against Christians.'

The third example dates from World War I, when the British government was fearful about the use of lethal gas by the Germans. They drafted 500 cats and sent them up to the front to be used in the trenches (in the same way that canaries had always been used down the mines) as chemical 'detectors'. Because the cats were much more sensitive to approaching gas than their human companions, they would act as an early warning system. If the cats suddenly collapsed and died, it acted as a signal that trouble was imminent for the troops. Whether any of these unfortunate cats ever saw England again is not on record.

The fourth example comes from World War II. During the terrible siege of Stalingrad in 1942, a cat called Mourka was used to carry messages about enemy gun emplacements. These dispatches had to be taken across a street that was alive with sniper fire. For a target as large as a human body, the short journey would have meant almost certain death. Mourka's tiny form stood a much better chance. And he had a good reason to make the trip – half-starved like everyone else in Stalingrad at the time, he knew that the company kitchens were situated inside the house to which the messages had to be taken. With this knowledge, he was never reluctant to make the perilous dash through the danger zone. Mourka rapidly became a hero, celebrated in the world's press. *The Times* of London paid him a special tribute in a leading article, ending with the words: 'he has shown himself worthy of Stalingrad, and whether for cat or man there can be no higher praise.'

During the blitz on Britain, pet cats seemed to develop an uncanny awareness of impending attacks. One animal, nicknamed 'Bomber', could always tell the difference between the sounds of RAF and German aircraft. When a Nazi bomber was approaching, the characteristic throbbing

EARLY CAT WARFARE, in which the terrified felines were despatched to run about in enemy lines, spreading poisonous fumes from containers strapped to their backs.

noise of its engines sent the cat scurrying for its personal shelter. Because of its sensitive hearing, it could be used as an early warning system for its human companions. This was not an isolated case, and there were several instances where the quick reactions of cats saved the lives of whole families. Seeing their cats dashing for cover, people would hurriedly follow suit, gaining the safety of shelters just before the bombs starting falling.

Naval cats were also prominent in World War II. On board the beleaguered warships they doubled up as rodent-destroyers and as lucky mascots. The most famous was a cat called Oscar who saw service with both the German and the British Navy. He started out as the much loved mascot of the famous German battleship *Bismarck*. When this vessel was sunk in 1941, he managed to escape and was seen swimming among the wreckage by a British sailor who rescued him and took him on board the Royal Navy destroyer HMS *Cossack*. Five months later, the *Cossack* itself was sunk. Again Oscar survived and was transferred to the aircraft-carrier *Ark Royal*. When *Ark Royal* was torpedoed by a U-boat, Oscar was rescued yet again. With three of his nine lives gone, it was decided to retire him to a sailor's home, where he quietly lived out his days in a less violent and much drier environment.

As sailor Charles Hodgson remarked, a ship's cat 'could create an oasis of peace and serenity, even amidst the noise and clamour of war'. Which makes one fear for the sanity of the inmates of the British Admiralty who, in 1975, dismayed sailors everywhere by banning all animals from HM ships.

Finally, in even more recent times, American military advisers suggested using the cat's excellent nocturnal vision to assist their troops as field-guides during jungle night-patrols in Vietnam. Training was begun and, in 1968, a platoon of military guide-cats was shipped out to the Orient to play their part in the Vietnam War. The cats could hardly believe their luck. The night-time jungle was alive with exotic rodents and as soon as the cats were released they set off in hot pursuit. The American soldiers did their best to keep up with them as they scattered in all directions, racing through the undergrowth. Those cats that were kept closer to hand satisfied themselves by stalking and attacking the dangling pack straps of the soldiers immediately in front of them. The only consolation to be gained from this bizarre experiment was that, when the Viet Cong heard of this new American secret weapon, several of them died laughing.

(Sadly, it has to be admitted that this last example of the use of cats in warfare was reported by a humorist called Brian McConnachie, who writes for the satirical magazine, *National Lampoon*, a fact that was overlooked by several gullible authors in recent feline publications.)

Bibliography:

1873. Duparcq, De La B. (Editor) *Les Chats de Guerre*. Paris. (Includes: Chats de guerre antiques; Chats de guerre modernes; Chats de pontonniers; Chats maritimes.)

Warhol, Andy

Cat Owner. The American pop artist Andy Warhol (1928–1987) was notorious for his outrageous lifestyle, but privately enjoyed quieter, more traditional moments than his public image would suggest. Among his private passions was his love of cats. This was not made public until the year after his death, when his two cat books were published by his estate. Originally created in the 1950s, these books were privately printed in limited editions (of only 190 numbered copies) exclusively as gifts for his friends. They were illustrated by Warhol with uncharacteristically sentimental sketches of his cats Hester and Sam.

Bibliography:

Early 1950s. Warhol, A. *Holy Cats by Andy Warhol's Mother*. Chatto & Windus, London.

c.1954. Warhol, A. *25 Cats Named Sam and One Blue Pussy*. Chatto & Windus, London.

Water Tiger

Mystery Cat. The local people in various regions of South America have sinister legends about a 'Tigre de Agua' or Water Tiger. It is said to be a savage beast capable of dragging a swimming horse down and disembowelling it, and is described as a huge cat with powerful claws and fangs – fangs that are sometimes described as so huge as to be 'tusks'.

The Water Tiger goes by many names in different places – the Yaguaro, the Yaguaruigh, the Iemisch, the Maipolina, or the 'Water Mother'. The romantic view is that, in some dark, remote forest river system, there still lurks a form of Sabre-toothed Tiger, a relic from prehistoric days. A more realistic view is that the sightings are a confused combination of Giant Otters, swimming Jaguars and even crocodiles.

WAVED CAT

FERAL CAT. A small Indian cat, the same size as a domestic cat, with a streaked coat pattern, that was first identified in 1863. It was originally thought to be a distinct wild species *(Felis torquata)*, but it is now considered to have been no more than a local domestic cat gone wild. Even the Victorian zoologists who listed it as a genuine wild cat species had their doubts. Blandford, writing in 1888, commented: 'it is far from improbable that specimens of the present form are merely descendants of tame cats that have run wild.'

WEANING

FELINE BEHAVIOUR. Domestic kittens are weaned between the ages of four and seven weeks. If the mother is a 'working cat' or a feral cat, she will bring freshly caught prey to her kittens and encourage them to join her in the feast. (For further details see Maternal Care.) If she is a pet cat, she will encourage her litter to join her at feeding time.

When they start to explore at four weeks of age, the kittens will soon discover the mother's milk bowl and her food dish and will begin to take sips of milk and tiny morsels of solid foods. The proportion of solids will increase gradually during the next few weeks until, by the age of about two months, the young are fully weaned.

During this delicate stage of their development, it is important that the kittens obtain their lapped milk and their solids at a warm temperature. Taking cold food or drink when this young can cause digestive problems.

WEBSTER

FICTIONAL CAT. An imposing, aristocratic feline, large and black (whose 'ancestors had conducted their decorous courtship beneath the shadow of cathedrals'), invented by P.G. Wodehouse, and described in delightful detail in *The Story of Webster*. The cat's bearing was so refined, and his poise so exquisite, that he made humans feel clumsy and uncomfortable in his dignified presence.

THE HAUGHTY WEBSTER, invented by P.G. Wodehouse, was a feline so refined that he made humans feel inferior.

WEIGHT

FELINE BIOLOGY. The typical domestic cat weighs from 3.6 to 6.8 kg (8 to 15 lb), usually between 4.5 and 5.5 kg (10 and 12 lb).

Some neutered animals become grossly overweight. The record figures for domestic cats, given by *The Guinness Book of Records*, are 21 kg (46 lb) for a neutered male tabby called Himmy, living in Queensland, Australia; 20 kg (44 lb) for a male tabby called Poppa, from Newport, Wales; and 19 kg (43 lb) for a long-haired part-Persian called Tiger, from Essex in England. Among the various breeds, the largest is the Maine Coon from America, which sometimes weighs as much as 13.6 kg (30 lb), and the smallest (authenticated) is the Singapura, or 'Drain Cat' from Singapore: these males on average weigh only 2.7 kg (6 lb) , and the females only 1.8 kg (4 lb).

Writing about small breeds in 1903, Frances Simpson refers to the existence of a mysterious dwarf cat: 'We have seen specimens of a very tiny domestic cat, full-grown individuals of which weigh only about three pounds. Those we saw came from South America.' Unfortunately there is no supporting evidence for this statement and no further record of such cats, so their validity must remain in doubt.

Among wild felines, the heaviest is the male Siberian Tiger *(Panthera tigris altaica),* weighing up to a massive 305 kg (673 lb), and the lightest is the little Asiatic species, the Rusty-spotted Cat *(Felis rubiginosa),* which only manages 1.25 kg (2¾ lb).

Weir, Harrison

Cat Authority. Journalist, author and artist, Harrison Weir (1824–1906) has justly been described as the 'father of the pedigree cat show'. The holding of the first major cat show – at Crystal Palace in 1871 – was entirely his idea. He also organized it and he and his brother were two of the three judges. There were 170 cats present, arranged in 25 classes, and the show proved so popular with the public that it started a whole new trend in competitive cat breeding, a trend that has grown and expanded to become a worldwide pursuit at the present time. Commenting on his motives, he said: 'I conceived the idea that it would be well to hold "cat shows", so that the different breeds, colours, markings, etc. might be more carefully attended to, and the domestic cat, sitting in front of the fire, would then possess a beauty and attractiveness to its owner unobserved because uncultivated heretofore.'

His 1889 book *Our Cats and all about them* is considered one of the early classics on the subject. In his *Who's Who* entry he listed as his recreation: 'no games of any sort at any time.'

Bibliography:

1889 Weir, Harrison. *Our Cats and all about them; their varieties, habits, and management.* Tunbridge Wells: Clements & Co., Mount Pleasant.

Western Cats

Domestic Cats. In the late 19th century, the term 'Western Cats' was used when contrasting the 'Ordinary, Short-haired, European Cats' with the 'Long-haired, Asiatic or Eastern Cats'. These were the two main categories employed to divide the domestic cats exhibited at the National Cat Show into two 'sub-orders'. Writing in 1895, Rush Huidekoper comments: 'The Short-haired Cat, otherwise known as the European or Western Cat, is the one derived from the European Wildcat, with an intermixture of the blood of the Egyptian Cat.'

Whiskers

Feline Anatomy. In addition to their obvious role as feelers sensitive to touch, the whiskers also operate as air-current detectors. As the cat moves along in the dark it needs to manoeuvre past solid objects without touching them. Each solid object it approaches causes slight eddies in the air (minute disturbances in the currents of air movement) and the cat's whiskers are so amazingly sensitive that they can read these air changes and respond to the presence of solid obstacles even without touching them.

The whiskers are especially important – indeed vital – when the cat hunts at night. We know this from the following observations: a cat with perfect whiskers can kill cleanly both in the light and in the dark. A cat with damaged whiskers can kill cleanly only in the light; in the dark it misjudges its killing-bite and plunges its teeth into the wrong part of the prey's body. This means that in the dark, where accurate vision is impeded, healthy whiskers are capable of acting as a highly sensitive guidance system. They have an astonishing, split-second ability to check the body outline of the victim and direct the cat's bite to the nape of the unfortunate animal's neck. Somehow the tips of the whiskers must read off the details of the shape of the prey, like a blind man reading Braille, and in an instant tell the cat how to react. Photographs of cats carrying mice in their jaws after catching them reveal that the whiskers are almost wrapped around the rodent's body, continuing to transmit information about the slightest movement, should the prey still be alive. Since the cat is by nature predominantly a nocturnal hunter, its whiskers are clearly crucial to its survival.

Anatomically the whiskers are greatly enlarged and stiffened hairs more than twice the thickness of ordinary hairs. Technically they are known as vibrissae. They are embedded in the tissue of the cat's upper lip to a depth three times greater than that of other hairs, and they are supplied with a mass of nerve-endings which transmit the information about any contact they make or any changes of air pressure.

On average, a cat has 24 whiskers, 12 on each side of the nose, arranged in four horizontal rows. They are capable of moving both forwards, when the cat is inquisitive, threatening, or testing something, and backwards, when it is defensive or deliberately avoiding touching something. The top two rows can be moved independently of the bottom two, and the strongest whiskers are in rows two and three. (See also entry for Hair.)

White

Coat Colour. The pure white cat has long been a favourite of the show bench, but, surprisingly, this colour was originally preferred for functional rather than aesthetic reasons. Writing in 1874, Gordon Stables comments: 'Millers often prefer them as hunters to black cats, thinking, perhaps with reason, that they are not so easily seen among the bags [of white flour].'

All-white cats usually have either golden or blue eyes, and it is well known that many of these animals, especially the blue-eyed ones, suffer from deafness. A survey carried out by two geneticists in 1971, revealed the following figures. Of 185 white cats examined, 25 per cent had golden eyes and normal hearing; 7 per cent had golden eyes and were deaf; 31 per cent had blue eyes and normal hearing; and 37 per cent had blue eyes and were deaf.

A white British Shorthair Cat with golden eyes. The golden-eyed is far less likely to suffer from deafness than the blue-eyed white.

Many cats are only partially white. This is the result of a 'white-spotting gene' that masks the cat's true colour. It usually appears in irregular patches, but generally favouring the lower regions of the body. There are special names given to the different degrees of white-masking:

1 A cat with white paws is said to be 'mitted'.
2 A cat with a white patch on its chest is said to have a 'locket'.
3 A cat with several small, white belly-patches is said to have 'buttons'.
4 A cat with roughly half its body surface white is said to be 'bi-colour'.
5 A cat with a predominantly white coat and a few colour-patches is a 'harlequin'.
6 A cat with a white coat except for colouring on the tail and head is a 'Van'.
7 A black cat with white legs, underside and chest is called a 'tuxedo cat'.
8 A black and white cat is sometimes called a 'jellicle cat'.

There are many pedigree colour forms that include areas of white: (1) Black and White (Bi-colour); (2) Black Smoke and White; (3) Black, Red and White (Tricolour); (4) Blue and White (Bi-colour); (5) Blue-Cream and White; (6) Blue Tabby and White; (7) Blue Patched Tabby and White; (8) Blue Silver Tabby and White; (9) Blue, Cream and White (Dilute Tricolour); (10) Brown Tabby and White; (11) Brown Patched Tabby and White; (12) Cameo and White; (13) Cream and White (Bi-colour); (14) Cream Tabby and White; (15) Patched Tabby and White (Torbie and White); (16) Red Tabby and White; (17) Silver Tabby and White; (18) Silver Patched Tabby and White; (19) Smoke and White; (20) Tabby and White; (21) Tortie and White; (22) Van Black and White; (23) Van Blue and White; (24) Van Blue-Cream and White; (25) Van Cream Tabby and White; (26) Van Parti-colour and White; (27) Van Red and White; (28) Van Red Tabby and White; (29) Van Smoke and White; (30) Van Tabby and White.

White Cat

Folk-tale. According to some authorities, the legend of the White Cat is based on an early fable that originated with Aesop. In this tale, Venus agrees to turn a beautiful White Cat into a princess, so that she can be united with the handsome young man she loves. The princess manages to hide her true identity from her beloved until she happens to see a rat scampering across the bedroom floor. At that moment she cannot resist the temptation to leap out of bed and chase after the rodent, thus giving the game away.

This tale is not, however, the traditional fairy-story that is usually associated with the legend of the White Cat. For that we must turn to France where, in 1682, the Comtesse D'Aulnoy wrote a fairy-tale, using that title, in which a young prince falls in love with a beautiful White Cat and wants to marry her. She tells him he must cut off her head and her tail and throw them in the fire, which, with great reluctance, he does. At this, she is freed from an ancient curse and is turned back into the beautiful princess she once was. The prince is overjoyed and they live happily ever after.

Although once immensely popular, this folk-tale has lost ground in the 20th century, being almost completely overshadowed by the stories of Dick Whittington and his Cat and Puss-in-Boots (see separate entries).

Bibliography:

1803. *The Renowned History of the White Cat.* Harris, London.
1847. *The White Cat.* Blackwood, Edinburgh.
1863. *The History of the White Cat.* Routledge, London.
1867. *The White Cat.* Nimmo, Edinburgh.
1870. *The White Cat.* McLoughlin, New York.
1873. *The White Cat.* Gall & Inglis, Edinburgh.
1893. *The White Cat.* Farqharson, London.
1905. *The White Cat.* Altemus, Philadelphia.
1906. *The White Cat.* Newnes, London.

1914. *The White Cat.* Arnold, London
1923. *The White Cat.* Blackie, London.
1925. *Tales of the Fairies; The White Cat.* Chelsea, London.
1955. *Columbine the White Cat.* Concora, New York.

WHITE HEATHER

PET CAT. A long-haired black and white cat that lived in luxury in Buckingham Palace. Owned by Queen Victoria in her old age, White Heather outlived the Queen but managed to maintain its royal status by staying on as the pet of her son, Edward VII.

WILBERFORCE

WORKING CAT. A large black and white cat called Wilberforce proved to have greater staying power than his distinguished owners. A resident mouser at No. 10 Downing Street in London, Wilberforce outlasted several Prime Ministers, carrying out his pest-control duties during the occupancies of Edward Heath, Harold Wilson, James Callaghan and Margaret Thatcher (who is rumoured to have purchased a tin of pilchards for him during her state visit to Russia). After he appeared on television with Mrs Thatcher he received more fan mail than his owner.

Wilberforce was acquired as a kitten from Hounslow RSPCA in 1973 and naming him became an immediate problem. Rival political factions insisted that he should be called Winston, Disraeli, Gladstone, Pitt or Walpole. Eventually, the caretaker of No. 10, irritated by the over-enthusiastic member of the Disraeli lobby, looked up at the bust of William Wilberforce, the man who had fought for 20 years to abolish the slave trade, and announced, 'The cat is called Wilberforce.'

When the cat became adult, he began a campaign of terror against the Downing Street mice which was so successful that they evacuated the premises and moved to the Home Office, where the custom of keeping a resident mouser had unwisely just been abandoned.

After 13 years of service on the staff of No. 10, Wilberforce was retired to the country where he turned his attention to dominating a large dog, interrupting this pursuit only occasionally for press calls at No. 10. Two years later, his death prompted glowing obituaries. *Cat World* reported: 'The best mouser in Britain died peacefully in his sleep on 19 May 1988.'

Bibliography:

1986. Sturgis, M. *The English Cat at Home.* Chatto & Windus, London.

WILD ABYSSINIAN CAT

DOMESTIC BREED. Despite its name, this is not a wild feline, but a recent attempt on the part of pedigree cat breeders to recreate the original version of the Abyssinian, as it was back in the 19th century.

Appearance: This short-haired breed is similar to the modern Abyssinian except for the following features: it has a larger body, dark ring-markings on the tail, dark bars on the legs, a dark, M-shaped 'frown' marking on the forehead and dark rings on the neck. It is also slightly larger than the Abyssinian. It gives the impression of being a cross between an Abyssinian Cat and a Tabby Cat.

History: In the 1980s cats of this type were found living wild in Singapore and some were taken to the United States where Tord Svenson of Massachusetts has been developing and promoting the breed.

Personality: This cat has been referred to as independent and friendly.

WILD CAT

WILD FELINE. *(Felis sylvestris)* In earlier records, the Wild Cat is sometimes referred to as the Wood Cat, or the British Tiger. In other countries: German: *Wilde Katze, Graue Katze, Baumritter;* French: *Chat Sauvage, Chat de Bois, Chat Haret;* Dutch: *Wilde Kat;* Spanish: *Gato Montés, Gato Romano;* Italian: *Gatto Silvatico;* Russian: *Stepnaja Koschka;* Polish: *Kot Dziki.*

THE 17TH CENTURY IMAGE of the Wild Cat. A woodcut from the *Natural History* of Aldrovandus (1645).

Wild Cat

Today, the Wild Cat is usually named according to the district from which it comes. People write of Scottish Wild Cats, because this is the last refuge of the British Wild Cat. They talk of the European Wild Cat, because it has a heavy body and thick coat, creating a typical race of the main species. Or they make special reference to the African Wild Cat, because it is generally accepted as the original ancestor of all our domestic breeds. But, in reality, these different forms are no more than subspecies of the Common Wild Cat. In the past, they have often been designated as different species (the African Wild Cat, for example, being named as *Felis lybica*), but that view is no longer held.

If earlier zoological works are consulted, it emerges that no fewer than 88 forms of this species have been recognized from time to time in the past, most of them often rashly considered as full species. Some authorities have whittled these down to three main geographical sub-species, called the European Wild Cat, the Asiatic Steppe Cat and the African Wild Cat. Elsewhere in this book, there are separate entries for each of these three forms, but it is also important briefly to consider them together, in order to understand the overall range of the species.

The Wild Cat in its natural habitat. It is increasingly difficult today to find pure specimens that are not the result of interbreeding with feral domestic cats.

The Wild Cat looks very much like a domestic tabby cat, but with less clearly defined markings. It is shy, secretive, solitary and strongly territorial in its natural woodland and scrub habitat and has rarely been observed directly in any detail. In many regions it has crossed freely with feral domesticated cats, so that pure Wild Cat stock is no longer easy to find for serious study.

It is primarily a rodent-eater (77 per cent of its diet), which makes its widespread persecution by many agricultural communities inexplicable. In this respect the ancient Egyptians were more advanced than many later cultures. It is a shaming thought that modern European farmers have behaved more stupidly than early Egyptian ones.

Size: Length of Head + Body: 47–75 cm (18½–29½ in). Tail: 21–35 cm (8½–14 in). Weight: 4–8 kg (9–17½ lb).

Distribution: The Wild Cat was once found over a much wider region that it is today, especially in the European part of its range, but it has been exterminated over huge areas as human farming and settlements have spread, destroying its woodland and scrub strongholds.

It survives today in the following regions: northern Scotland, Spain, Portugal, France, Italy, Sicily, Sardinia, Corsica, Majorca, Germany, Switzerland, Austria, Czech Republic, Slovakia, Poland, Hungary, Bosnia-Herzegovena, Croatia, Serbia, Romania, Bulgaria, Greece, Turkey, southern Russia, Saudi Arabia, Iraq, Iran, Israel, Syria, Afghanistan, N.W. India, Morocco, Algeria, Libya, Egypt, and the whole of Africa south of the Sahara, except for the rain forests of central West Africa.

Bibliography:

1896. Hamilton, E. *The Wild Cat of Europe.* Porter, London.
1951. Pocock, R.I. *Catalogue of the Genus Felis.* British Museum, London.
1965. Kurten, B. *The Evolution of the European Wildcat.* Helsinki University.
1974. Dudley, E. *Scrap the Gentle Wildcat.* Frederick Muller, London.
1975. Dudley, E. *Our Unknown Wildlife: The Wildcat.* Frederick Muller, London.
1975. Haltenorth, T. *Die Wildkatze.* Wittenberg Lutherstadt.
1978. Tomkies, M. *My Wilderness Wildcats.* Doubleday, New York.
1979. Tomkies, M. Liane, *A Cat from the Wild.* MacDonald & Jane's, London.
1987. Tomkies, M. *Wildcat Haven.* Jonathan Cape, London.
1993. Stahl, P. et al. *Seminar on the Biology and Conservation of the Wild Cat (Felis silvestris).* Council of Europe Press, Strasbourg.

WILD SPECIES

WILD FELINES. The relationships between the various wild members of the cat family have been much debated in recent years and there is still no final agreement. No two authorities present exactly the same classification. Future genetic studies will undoubtedly change some of the finer points but, for the time being, the best arrangement is as follows:

Family Felidae

Sub-family **Felinae**

Genus **FELIS**

	Sub-genus **Felis**	
1 *Felis silvestris*	WILD CAT	Europe, W. Asia, Africa
2 *Felis bieti*	CHINESE DESERT CAT	N. Asia
3 *Felis chaus*	JUNGLE CAT	Asia & N. Africa
4 *Felis margarita*	SAND CAT	S.W. Asia & N. Africa
5 *Felis nigripes*	BLACK-FOOTED CAT	S. Africa
	Sub-genus **Leptailurus**	
6 *Felis serval*	SERVAL	Africa
	Sub-genus **Profelis**	
7 *Felis aurata*	AFRICAN GOLDEN CAT	Africa
	Sub-genus **Caracal**	
8 *Felis caracal*	CARACAL	Africa & Mid. East
	Sub-genus **Ototcolobus**	
9 *Felis manul*	PALLAS'S CAT	Asia

	Sub-genus **Prionailurus**	
10 *Felis bengalensis*	Leopard Cat	S. Asia
11 *Felis planiceps*	Flat-headed Cat	S. Asia
12 *Felis rubiginosa*	Rusty-spotted Cat	S. Asia
13 *Felis viverrina*	Fishing Cat	S. Asia
	Sub-genus **Catopuma**	
14 *Felis temminckii*	Temminck's Cat	S. Asia
15 *Felis badia*	Bay Cat	Borneo
	Sub-genus **Pardofelis**	
16 *Felis marmorata*	Marbled Cat	S. Asia
	Sub-genus **Herpailurus**	
17 *Felis yaguarondi*	Jaguarundi	Cen. & S. America
	Sub-genus **Leopardus**	
18 *Felis pardalis*	Ocelot	Cen. & S. America
19 *Felis tigrina*	Tiger Cat	Cen. & S. America
20 *Felis wiedii*	Margay Cat	Cen. & S. America
	Sub-genus **Oncifelis**	
21 *Felis colocolo*	Pampas Cat	S. America
22 *Felis geoffroyi*	Geoffroy's Cat	S. America
23 *Felis guigna*	Kodkod	S. America
	Sub-genus **Oreailurus**	
24 *Felis jacobita*	Mountain Cat	S. America
	Sub-genus **Puma**	
25 *Felis concolor*	Puma	N. & S. America

Genus **LYNX**

26 *Lynx rufus*	Bobcat	N.America
27 *Lynx canadensis*	Canadian Lynx	N.America
28 *Lynx lynx*	Northern Lynx	Europe & N. Asia
29 *Lynx pardinus*	Spanish Lynx	Spain & Portugal

Genus **NEOFELIS**

30 *Neofelis nebulosa*	Clouded Leopard	S. Asia

Sub-family **Pantherinae**

Genus **PANTHERA**

	Sub-genus **Uncia**	
31 *Panthera uncia*	Snow Leopard	Asia

	Sub-genus **Panthera**	
32 *Panthera leo*	Lion	S. Asia & Africa
33 *Panthera tigris*	Tiger	Asia
34 *Panthera pardus*	Leopard	Asia & Africa
35 *Panthera onca*	Jaguar	Cen. & S. America

Sub-family **Acinonychinae**

Genus **ACINONYX**

36 *Acinonyx jubatus*	Cheetah	Africa & N. Iran

Bibliography:

General books dealing with the wild felines include the following:

1834. Jardine, W. *The Natural History of the Felinae.* Lizars, Edinburgh.
1883. Elliot, D.G. *A Monograph of the Felidae.* London.
1896. Lydekker, R. *A Handbook of the Carnivora. I. Cats, Civets and Mungooses.* Lloyd, London
1951. Pocock, R.I. *Catalogue of the Genus Felis.* British Museum, London.
1955. Stanek, V.J. *Introducing the Cat Family.* Spring Books, London.
1963. Blonk, H.L. *Wilde Katten.* Thieme & Cie, Zutphen.
1964. Denis, A. *Cats of the World.* Constable, London.
1968. Edey, M. *The Cats of Africa.* Time-Life, New York.
1969. Boorer, M. *Wild Cats.* Hamlyn, London.
1973. Eaton, R. (Editor) *The World's Cats, Vol. 1.* Carnivore Research Institute, Washington.
1975. Badino, G. *Big Cats of the World.* Orbis, London.
1975. Eaton, R. (Editor) *The World's Cats. Vols. 1 & 2.* World Wide Life Safari, Oregon.
1975. Guggisberg, C.A.W. *Wild Cats of the World.* David & Charles, Newton Abbot.
1976. Eaton, R. (Editor) *The World's Cats. Vol. 3.* Carnivore Research Institute, Washington.
1976. Graves, E. (Editor) *The Cats.* Time-Life, New York.
1979. Ricciuti, E.R. *The Wild Cats.* Windward, Leicester.
1986. Miller, S.D. & Everett, D.D. *Cats of the World.* National Wildlife Federation, Washington.
1991. Green, R. *Wild Cat Species of the World.* Basset Publications, Plymouth.
1991. Seidensticker, J. and Lumpkin, S. (Editors) *Great Cats.* Merehurst, London.
1991. Kitchener, A. *The Natural History of the Wild Cats.* A. & C. Black, London.
1991. Tomkies, M. *Wild Cats.* Whittet Books, London.
1993. Alderton, D. *Wild Cats of the World.* Blandford, London.
1993. Lumpkin, S. *Small Cats.* Facts on File, New York.
1993. Savage, C. *Wild Cats. Lynx – Bobcats – Mountain Lions.* Sierra Club, San Francisco.
1995. Cleave, A. *Big Cats.* Magna Books, Leicester.

Note: In addition, there is the publication *Wild Cat; The Journal of the Cat Survival Trust,* from The Cat Survival Trust, Marlind Centre, Codicote Road, Welwyn, Herts., England.

Wiley Catt

Cartoon Cat. A comic-strip cat created by Walt Kelly in 1948, Wiley Catt was a Commie-hating, reactionary, shotgun-toting bobcat who lived in the Okefenokee Swamp. He appeared in Kelly's strip *Pogo* from 1948 to 1975.

William (1)

Pet Cat. A white cat, William belonged to author Charles Dickens (1812–1870). When William produced a litter of kittens she was renamed Williamina. The litter was born in the kitchen, but

the mother cat insisted on carrying them, one by one, into the great man's study. Not wishing to be disturbed, he removed them, but she persisted, bringing them back and placing them at his feet. He was forced to give in and the family was reared nearby as he worked at his desk. When the kittens had grown he kept one of them, which was called The Master's Cat.

William (2)

Fictional Cat. William was an invention of American humorist James Thurber in his story *The Cat in the Lifeboat* (1956). A cat with a large ego, he imagined that he was the Will referred to in 'Last Will and Testament'. Taken on a round-the-world voyage, he encountered a terrible storm. As the ship was sinking he heard the cry 'William and children first' and immediately leapt into the lifeboat, only to be thrown out by an irate sailor. When he swam ashore on a remote island he was so shocked that he could not remember his name.

Windy

Pet Cat. Wing-Commander Guy Gibson, V.C., the famous dambuster of World War II, was often accompanied on his dangerous wartime missions by his pet cat Windy, 'an all-swimming and all-flying cat' who 'put in more flying hours than most cats'.

Winged Cat

Feline Mutation? In his study of *Animal Fakes and Frauds*, Peter Dance reports on a mysterious Winged Cat which was offered for sale in the early 1960s. Information on the amazing animal was distributed from an address in Bond Street, London. It was claimed that the wings had started to grow when the cat was very young. A circus owner exhibited it, but its original owner demanded its return and there was a lawsuit about legal ownership at some time in the 19th century. The original owner won his case and the cat was shipped back to him. It was dead on arrival and there were claims that its food for the journey had been deliberately poisoned. The animal was sent to a taxidermist, stuffed and placed in a mahogany and glass case. After many years it ended up gathering dust in an attic. It had now been rescued and was being offered for sale. However, offers by Peter Dance to buy it remained unanswered.

This is not the only report of a winged cat. Another dates from 1899. The animal in question, a tabby cat, lived in England at the village of Wivelscombe in Somerset and had two fur-covered flanges protruding from its back which flapped about when the cat ran. A photograph of it appeared in the November 1899 issue of *Strand* magazine and caused a minor sensation.

A third example is said to have been exhibited in the 1930s at the Oxford Zoo (which closed down in 1939). A fourth was exhibited at Blackpool museum. Further cases have been reported from the United States and Sweden. The Swedish winged cat was shot in 1949 and carefully examined. Its wing-span was said to be 58 cm (23 inches) and it weighed 9 kg (20 lb).

There are three possible explanations for these freak animals. Either (1) all of these 'winged' cats together represent a widespread deception – a faking tradition that keeps re-surfacing – or (2) they indicate the existence of a strange mutation that occurs spontaneously from time to time, or (3) they suggest some sort of recurrent congenital deformity. The most likely explanation of the phenomenon would seem to be a rare mutation, but without a specimen to examine scientifically, the case remains open.

Bibliography:

1976. Dance, P. *Animal Fakes and Frauds.* Sampson Low, Maidenhead.
1986. Brandreth, G. *Cats' Tales.* Robson Books, London.

A sad-looking Cat Familiar who lived at Windsor in Berkshire, England, until its witch companion was apprehended and executed on 26th February 1579 for committing 'hainous and horrible actes'.

Witchcraft

Feline History. Religious bigots have often employed the cunning device of converting other people's heroes into villains, to suit their own purposes. In this way, the ancient horned god that protected earlier cultures was transformed into the evil Devil of Christianity. And the revered sacred feline of ancient Egypt became the wicked, sorcerer's cat of medieval Europe.

In the same way, Freya, the Viking goddess of love, became a loathsome witch, and her faithful cats became the despised witch's familiars. Anything considered holy by a previous religious faith must automatically be damned by a new religion. In this way began the darkest chapter in the cat's long association with mankind. For centuries it was persecuted and the cruelties heaped upon it were given the full backing of the Church.

During this bleak phase of its history the cat became firmly linked in the popular mind with witchcraft and black magic. As late as 1658 Edward Topsel, in his serious work on natural history, followed detailed descriptions of the cat's anatomy and behaviour with the solemn comment that 'the familiars of Witches do most ordinary appear in the shape of Cats, which is an argument that this beast is dangerous to soul and body'. (The last execution of a cat for witchcraft in England was in the year 1712.)

The earliest record we have of this superstitious belief dates from the tenth century when, in the year 962 at the city of Metz (now in north-east France) the ceremony of 'Cat Wednesday' took place on the second Wednesday in Lent. This involved the burning alive of hundreds of local cats on the grounds that they were 'witches in disguise'. This was the start of a period of appalling feline persecution that was to last for eight centuries. There was, however, one period of respite following the Crusades. When the Crusaders returned to their European homelands they brought with them, in the holds of their ships, the dreaded Black Rat, and cats were suddenly in great demand to control this scourge. But the Christian persecutions were soon to resurface. In the 13th century, Papal might was brought to bear against supposed sorcery, and unspeakable atrocities were inflicted on innocent humans and felines alike.

Worse was to come. The reign of terror for witches and their cats was further intensified in the 15th century and did not decline until as late as the 18th. Records show that in the 16th and 17th centuries, 100,000 witches were legally executed in Germany, 75,000 in France and 30,000 in Britain. Wherever possible, cats were destroyed with them. The total slaughter of domestic cats must have run into the hundreds of thousands.

Because the cat was seen as evil, all kinds of frightening powers were attributed to it by the writers of the day. Its teeth were said to be venomous, its flesh poisonous, its hair lethal (causing suffocation if a few were accidentally swallowed), and its breath infectious, destroying human lungs and causing consumption. All this created something of a problem, since it was also recognized that cats were useful 'for the suppressing of small vermine'. Topsel's compromise

DURING THE SAVAGE witch-hunts of earlier centuries, it was assumed that any black cat was an evil spirit. To be more precise, it was not the cat that was at fault, but the fiend that occupied its body. For the unfortunate feline this subtle distinction made little difference.

was to suggest to his readers that 'with a wary and discreet eye we must avoid their harms, making more account of their use than of their persons'. In other words, exploit them, but do not get too close to them or show any affection.

This restrained attitude did, at least, enable farm cats and some town cats to live a tolerable life as unloved pest-controllers, but for certain village cats life was far more unpleasant. If they happened to attach themselves to an old woman who lived by herself, they were risking a savage death as a witch's familiar. The sad irony of this unhappy state of affairs was that these animals played a comforting role in the lives of such old women. Any elderly crone, who happened to be ugly or misshapen enough to have repelled all potential husbands, and who was therefore forced to live a solitary life with no children of her own, often as an outcast on the edge of the village, was desperately in need of companionship. Maltreated cats, finding themselves in a similar plight, often approached such women, who befriended them as substitutes for human companionship and love. Together, they brought one another many rewards, and the kindness of these old women towards their cats was excessive. Anyone teasing or hurting their beloved felines was cursed and threatened. All that was required then was for one of these tormentors to fall ill or suffer a sudden accident and the old 'witch' was to blame. Because the cats wandered about, often at night, they were thought to be either the supernatural servants of the witches, or else the witches themselves, transformed into cat-shape to aid their nocturnal travels when seeking revenge.

So it was the reaction against the cat's ancient 'holiness' in Egyptian religion, combined with the feline links with the goddess Freya, and the cat's connection with childless, elderly women, that made it the 'wicked' animal of the medieval period. Added to this was its haughtiness and its refusal to become completely subservient to human demands, unlike the dog, the horse, the sheep and other easily controlled domestic animals. Also, its nocturnal caterwauling during the breeding season gave rise to tales of orgies and secret feline ceremonies. The outcome was a savage persecution perpetrated against an animal whose only serious task was to rid human habitations of infestations of disease-carrying, food-spoiling rats and mice. It is a strange chapter in the history of Christian kindness. (See also Cat-haters and Freya's Cats.)

Wobo

Mystery Cat. According to the local people in remote parts of Ethiopia, when encountered by Victorian explorers, there existed in that country a huge cat, called a Wobo, which was bigger than a lion and which had dark stripes. It was also referred to as the Mendelit and, in neighbouring Sudan, as the Abu Sotan. There were specific claims that a pelt existed and had been seen by many people. The most likely explanation is that the pelt was of an imported tiger-skin and that vivid imaginations related this skin to nocturnal, dimly observed sightings of Lions or Striped Hyenas, to create in the mind a monstrous 'African Tiger'.

Wolsey, Cardinal Thomas

Cat Owner? It is frequently stated that Cardinal Wolsey (1471–1530), the chief minister of Henry VIII, was a cat lover who was so attached to his pets that he insisted on taking them with him on formal occasions. According to one report, he took them to state dinners and even to church services. According to another, he always had his favourite black cat beside him on his throne when he was administering justice as Lord Chancellor of England.

Carl van Vetchen in his classic work *The Tiger in the House* (1938) comments: 'holy men as well as devils found the cat the most attractive of animals. The profound wisdom, the concealed claws, the stealthy approach, and the final spring, all seem to typify the superior attorney. We should not be astonished, therefore, that Cardinal Wolsey placed his cat by his side while acting in his judicial capacity as Lord Chancellor.'

Unfortunately, no written or pictorial evidence or reference is ever given to support these claims and it looks as though the ever-present Wolsey 'cat' may have been an invention, perhaps concocted by his enemies to suggest that he had a sinister 'familiar'.

Woolly Cheetah

Wild Feline. In 1877 the London Zoo recorded the arrival of a new form of Cheetah from the Beaufort West region of South Africa. It had shorter legs, a heavier body and a thicker tail than the common Cheetah. Above all, it had a most unusual coat. Its fur was much more woolly than normal and instead of the usual black spots was covered with tawny-coloured blotches. Also, the characteristic black line between the eye and the mouth was absent. It was named the Woolly Cheetah *(Felis lanea,* at first, then *Cynaelurus laniger),* but was soon rejected as 'merely a variety' of the common Cheetah. It has never since been accepted as a separate species, despite the fact that it was clearly far more than a mere colour variant.

Wool-Sucking

Feline Behaviour. Some cat owners notice that their pets become wool-suckers at a certain age. A cat will find a woollen garment or soft furnishing in the house and then settle down on it in a contented fashion. Pressing its mouth to the cloth, it starts to suck or chew it rhythmically while treading alternately with the front feet. While doing this it appears to be lost in pleasure and increasingly unaware of the world around it. Clearly there is a huge reward for the animal in performing these seemingly useless actions and, were it not for the risk of ingesting wool fragments, there would be no harm in it.

The reason for the attraction of the wool is not hard to find. The actions directed towards the cloth are identical with those performed by a tiny kitten when feeding at its mother's nipple. The trampling movements are intended to stimulate her milk flow and when these are done by the wool-sucking cat they reveal that it is treating the piece of woollen material as a surrogate mother. In other words, wool-sucking is the act of feeding at a 'ghost-nipple' and is the feline equivalent of thumb-sucking in human infants, or pipe-sucking in elderly human males.

Wool-sucking seems to be most common among young cats that have been orphaned or have for some other reason been deprived of the maternal nipple too soon. It usually starts shortly after the animals have been weaned and in most instances it only persists for a few months. But for some cats – especially Siamese – it continues for a lifetime and is extremely difficulty to eradicate.

The special attraction of wool is that the presence of lanolin acts as a powerful unconscious reminder of the mother's belly. Sucking the wool and making it damp enhances the lanolin odour, and this keeps the cats contented and fully absorbed in their sucking and chewing.

If there is no wool available to them, cats with an urge to re-create the pleasures of sucking at the maternal nipple have been known to suck their own fur, sometimes their feet and sometimes the tips of their own tails; or they occasionally develop a fixation on their owner's hair and make repeated attempts to suck on that, if they are given half a chance.

Most of the suggested cures for this pattern of behaviour (diet-changes, punishments, noxious chemicals) fail to make any impact on a determined wool-sucker. Probably the only long-term solution is to change the cat's way of life so that it is less empty and more surprising and complex. If, somehow, the cat's mental state can be altered by ridding it of the monotony or stress that drives it to perform these 'pseudo-infantile' actions, it should be possible to reduce this stereotyped behaviour.

Yellow

Coat Colour. An early name for 'orange', which is the geneticist's name for the colour of a ginger cat. To cat-breeders this colour is now known as red. To storytellers it is usually 'marmalade'. See also Ginger (1).

York Chocolate Cat

Domestic Breed. The York Chocolate Cat is a new American cat that takes the first part of its name from New York State, where it originated, and the second part from the rich chocolate brown colour of its coat.

Appearance: The body proportions are similar to those of the Siamese, but it is bigger. The long coat comes in a variety of chocolate colours and patterns.

History: This recent breed arose in 1983 on a farm belonging to Janet Chiefari. The foundation stock consisted of a pair of house cats of uncertain ancestry. The male was long-haired and black; the female was long-haired and black and white. Somewhere in their past lurked a trace of Siamese.

Because of the confused genetic background of this breed, it is generally frowned upon by the official feline organizations. As a result it remains a rare breed, and as recently as the 1990s there were no more than 100 specimens in existence.

Personality: Terms used to describe this breed include: energetic, lively, playful, enthusiastic, agile and cheerful.

Zapaquilda

Fictional Cat. In Lope de Vega's epic poem *The Battle of the Cats* (Gatomaquaia, 1634), Zapaquilda is the feline heroine who is abducted on her wedding day and taken to the villain's castle. The poem is a feline satire on the theme of the literary epic.

Another new American breed, the York Chocolate *(opposite)*, dates from 1983. It appears in many patterns, the dark areas being a rich, dark chocolate brown. Some are predominantly brown; others, like this one, show large areas of white.

Z

ZIBELINE CAT

ZIBELINE CAT

DOMESTIC BREED. This name, meaning 'like the sable' (that is, very dark brown), was suggested as an alternative to 'Burmese', but was never widely accepted. Dechambre, writing in 1957, proposed that the modern, pedigree Burmese Cats should be called 'Zibelines or Sables, because of their coat, and to distinguish them from the true Burmese'.

INDEX

Dessins sans paroles

des Chats

par

Steinlen

PARIS
ERNEST FLAMMARION
EDITEUR
26 RUE RACINE
PRÈS L'ODÉON

ACKNOWLEDGEMENTS

The publisher thanks the photographers and organisations for their kind permission to reproduce the following photographs in this book:

page 2 Adriano Bacchella; 6 Desmond Morris; 8 Bob Schwartz; 11 Chanan; 14 Frank Lane Picture Agency /T Whittaker; 15 (left) Frank Lane Picture Agency /E & D Hosking; 17 Collection Viollet; 18 Mary Evans Picture Library; 19 The Royal Collection © Her Majesty, Queen Elizabeth II; 23 Bruce Coleman /Jane Burton; 25 Bob Schwartz; 26 Jacana /Axel; 27 Zoological Society of London /Michael Lister; 29 Jacana /Axel; 30 Chanan; 32 Desmond Morris; 33 (left) Chanan; 35 Desmond Morris; 36 The Hulton Deutsch Collection; 38 NHPA /Mandal Ranjit; 40 Mary Evans Picture Library /reproduced by permission of Elizabeth Banks; 42 Animals Unlimited; 45 (left and right) Sotheby's London; 46 from *Cats of the World* by Armand Denis, published in 1964 by Constable & Co Ltd; 47 Bob Schwartz; 49 Mary Evans Picture Library; 50 Chanan; 52 Animals Unlimited; 55 Marc Henrie; 57 (below) Images Colour Library; 59 NHPA /Kevin Schafer; 60 Courtesy of the San Diego Zoo/Ron Garrison; 61 Oxford Scientific Films /Nick Gordon/Survival; 63 NHPA /Kevin Schafer; 64–68 Marc Henrie; 71 Ardea London /John Daniels; 75 Adriano Bacchella; 76 Chanan; 78–81 Marc Henrie; 83 Animals Animals /Joe McDonald; 84 Bruce Coleman /Steven C Kaufman; 85 Bruce Coleman /Rod Williams; 89 Bridgeman Art Library /Private Collection; 100 Adriano Bacchella; 103 ET Archive; 105 Images Colour Library; 110 (right) Bob Schwartz; 121 Sotheby's London; 124 NHPA /Gerard Lacz; 127 Ardea London/Ferrero-Labat; 130 Prenzel-Anthony; 131 Desmond Morris; 132 Peter Jackson; 136 Oxford Scientific Films /Alan & Sandy Carey; 138 Collection Viollet; 140 Marc Henrie; 142 Chanan; 145 Marc Henrie; 146 NHPA /Henry Ausloos; 148 The Kobal Collection /MGM; 149 (below) Marc Henrie; 155 Chanan; 156 NHPA /Gerard Lacz; 169 Ardea London /Yann Arthus-Bertrand; 171 The Kobal Collection; 174 Marc Henrie; 176 (above) Jacana /Manfred Danegger; 177–8 Adriano Bacchella; 180 Desmond Morris; 191–193 The Kobal Collection; 195 Frank Lane Picture Agency /Terry Whittaker; 196 Jacana /Jean-Philippe Varin; 199 Chanan; 202 The Kobal Collection; 204 Bruce Coleman /Rod Williams; 206 Bruce Coleman /Hans Reinhard; 214 The Algonquin Hotel, New York; 217 Marc Henrie; 221 Chanan; 225 Press Association/Louisa Buller; 226 (above) Mary Evans Picture Library; 227 ET Archive /Victoria and Albert Museum, London; 228 By Courtesy of the Board of Trustees of the Victoria and Albert Museum; 232 Nature Production /Tadaaki Imaizumi; 234 BBC Natural History Unit /Gerry Ellis; 235 Bruce Coleman /Erwin and Peggy Bauer; 236 Frank Lane Picture Agency /Terry Whittaker; 238 (above) Marc Henrie; 239 Bob Schwartz; 240 Marc Henrie; 242 Oxford Scientific Films /Eyal Bartov; 245 Desmond Morris; 247 Collection Harlingue-Viollet; 248 NHPA /Anthony Bannister; 249 NHPA /Yves Lanceau; 250 Norton Simon Museum, Pasadena, California – The Blue Four Galka Scheyer Collection/© DACS 1996; 251 (left) courtesy of the Munich Zoo/D Halteworth; 251 (right) Focus Stock Fotografico; 253 Marc Henrie; 256 Tetsu Yamazaki; 258 Jacana /Fritz Polking; 259 Courtesy of the Zoological Society of London/ Michael Lyster; 260 Animals Animals /Michael Dick; 265 BBC Natural History Unit /Gerry Ellis; 266 NHPA /Nigel J Dennis; 268 Bob Schwartz; 273 Chanan; 275 Marc Henrie; 279 Adriano Bacchella; 280 Royal Mint; 281 NHPA /Gerard Lacz; 282 Bruce Coleman /Rod Williams; 284 Oxford Scientific Films /Partidge Films Ltd; 285 BBC Natural History Unit /Miles Barton; 287 Desmond Morris; 288 Desmond Morris; 298 Bruce Coleman /Gunter Ziesler; 300 Bridgeman Art Library /Louvre, Paris; 301 Chanan; 306 Daily News, New York; 309 Jacana /Herbert Schwind; 310 Adriano Bacchella; 314 Animals Animals /Ken Cole; 315 Marc Henrie; 317 Chanan; 320 Jacana /Axel; 322 Animals Unlimited; 324 Animals Animals /Zig Leszczynski; 325 (below) Peter Arnold Inc /Martin Wendler; 330 Larry Johnson; 331 Marc Henrie; 333 Adriano Bacchella; 334 NHPA /Gerard Lacz; 337 Reunion des Musées Nationaux/© Succession Picasso/DACS 1996; 342 Wolfgang Lohs; 345 Mary Anne Fackelman-Miner /The White House (Courtesy The Ronald Reagan Library); 348 Animals Animals /Joe McDonald; 349 Animals

Animals /Breck P Kent; 351 ET Archive; 354 Verle & Sue Castle; 355–356 Marc Henrie; 361 Chanan; 363 David Brinicombe; 367 Marc Henrie; 369 Frank Lane Picture Agency /Terry Whittaker; 372 Jacana /Francis Petter; 375 Bruce Coleman/Werner Layer; 378 Chanan; 380 Frank Lane Picture Agency /Fritz Polking; 381 Alan Robinson; 383 Bob Schwartz; 385 Animals Unlimited; 389 Spectrum Colour Library; 392 Marc Henrie; 395 Animals Unlimited; 396 Bob Schwartz; 398 Chanan; 401 Larry Johnson; 402 Animals Animals /Zig Leszczynski; 403 Marc Henrie; 405 (above) The White House; 405 (below) Bob Schwartz; 407 Chanan; 409 Bruce Coleman /Rodney Dawson Trust; 411 NHPA /Gerard Lacz; 414 Dr Truda Straede; 417 (below) Larry Johnson; 427 Adriano Bacchella; 429 Animals Unlimited; 433 Jacana /Jean-Philippe Varin; 436 The Kobal Collection; 438 Animals Unlimited; 441 Animals Animals /Zig Leszczynski; 442 Myra-Naturfoto /Jorgen Larsson; 443 Peter Arnold Inc /Luiz C Marigo; 446 Chanan; 450 Robert Harding Picture Library; 453 Bruce Coleman /Kim Taylor; 454 Ardea London /Yann Arthus-Bertrand; 461 Adriano Bacchella; 469 Jacana /Axel; 472 BBC Natural History Unit /Rico & Ruiz; 477 Mary Evans Picture Library; 480 Chanan; 484 BBC Natural History Unit /Gerry Ellis: 494 Jean-Loup Charmet.

Photography of out-of-copyright books by John Stewart